Handbook of
Social Movements Across Disciplines

Handbooks of Sociology and Social Research

Series Editor:
Howard B. Kaplan, *Texas A&M University, College Station, Texas*

Handbook of
Social Movements Across Disciplines

Edited by

Bert Klandermans

Free University
Department of Social Sciences
Amsterdam, The Netherlands

Conny Roggeband

Free University
Department of Social Sciences
Amsterdam, The Netherlands

 Springer

Bert Klandermans
Faculty of Social Sciences
Vrije Universiteit,
De Boelelaan 1081c
1081 HV Amsterdam, the Netherlands

Conny Roggeband
Faculty of Social Sciences
Vrije Universiteit,
De Boelelaan 1081c
1081 HV Amsterdam, the Netherlands

ISBN-13: 978-0-387-70959-8   e-ISBN-13: 978-0-387-70960-4

Library of Congress Control Number: 2007929232

Printed on acid-free paper.

9 8 7 6 5 4 3 2 1

springer.com

Contributors

Ronald Aminzade, Department of Sociology, University of Minnesota, Minneapolis, MN

Willem Assies, Van Vollenhoven Institute, University of Leiden, Leiden, the Netherlands

Brian Dill, Department of Sociology, University of Minnesota, Minneapolis, MN

Tina Fetner, Department of Sociology, McMaster University, Hamilton, Ontario, Canada

James M. Jasper, Independent Scholar, New York, NY

Bert Klandermans, Faculty of Social Sciences, Vrije Universiteit, Amsterdam, The Netherlands

Lindsey Lupo, Department of Political Science, University of California Irvine, Irvine, CA

David S. Meyer, University of California Irvine, Irvine, CA

Conny Roggeband, Faculty of Social Sciences, Vrije Universiteit, Amsterdam, The Netherlands

Ton Salman, Department of Cultural Anthropology, Vrije Universiteit, Amsterdam, the Netherlands

Jackie Smith, Department of Sociology, State University of New York at Stony Brook, Stony Brook, NY

Jacquelien van Stekelenburg, Department of Sociology, Vrije Universiteit, Amsterdam, the Netherlands

Table of Contents

CHAPTER 1

Introduction

CONNY ROGGEBAND AND BERT KLANDERMANS

Students from divergent academic disciplines share an interest in the phenomena of social movements and collective action. Through a variety of disciplinary approaches and techniques, researchers seek to understand the emergence and development of social movements, protest, and contentious politics. Their different perspectives have contributed to development of research and theory in the field of social movements. The last few decades social movement studies have proliferated enormously, covering a wide array of movements, issues and places, as evidenced by the rapid growth of the number of journal articles on social movements published since the 1980s (see Fig. 1.1).

The growing interest and importance of the study of social movements as an area of the social sciences appears to be closely related to how its object of study developed in the course of time. Over the last decades, social movements as a social phenomenon grew rapidly. In the early 1960s, many sociologists believed society had reached a stage of development in which pluralist, pragmatic consensus, instead of protest, would resolve social conflict. Their expectations proved wrong and the 1960s became a decade of activism, riots, demonstrations, sit-ins, strikes, and many other forms of collective action. Over the last decades, social movements emerged as a common and central feature of the political landscape across the globe. Diverse and multifaceted forms of mobilization materialized; "left-libertarian" movements such as the student, women's, peace, and ecology movements and right-wing organizations such as the pro-life movement, fundamentalist religious movements, and the extreme right movement alike. In the 1970s, for instance, Islamic fundamentalist and Marxist movements mobilized in Iran, in Nicaragua the Sandinistas organized, and in Germany and Italy a number of radical leftist terrorist groups were formed. These instances of protest gained international visibility and in some cases sparked new mobilizations and counter-movements. Over the past two decades, we have witnessed further expansion of the movement sector, but also new forms of mobilization such as the rise of transnational protest, ethnic mobilizations, Internet protest, and Islamic movements. The myriad of movements, issues, action forms, and strategies has clearly fueled the proliferation of social movement studies.

The increasing interdisciplinary cooperation of the field has resulted in a crossing of the various boundaries—disciplinary, thematic, historical, and geographic. Owing to the efforts of social historians, political scientists, sociologists, social psychologists, and anthropologists from all parts of the world, our knowledge of the dynamics of collective action in past episodes has extended tremendously. Geographically, social movement studies are no longer

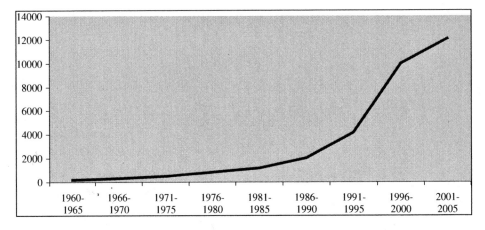

FIGURE 1.1. Number of journal articles on social movements in English language journal (1960–2005).
Source: Google scholar

mainly the domain of European and North American scholars. The expansion of the field has also been the result of an important internationalization of social movement studies. Cross-national collaborations and networking have been important goals for social movement scholars who since the 1980s have tried to bridge theoretical gaps and divides (Klandermans, Kriesi, and Tarrow 1988). All this offers us the potential of making systematic comparisons across time and also across space. Institutional infrastructures such as the International Sociological Association (ISA), the International Political Science Association, and the International Society of Political Psychology have enabled independent interaction and networking of scholars across national borders. Internationalization has offered the opportunity to learn about new cases, to test theoretical insights in different settings, and to study cross-national similarities and differences. Such knowledge of cases across the globe helped to determine what general variables apply across boundaries and what variables must be specified and particularized with respect to different national–cultural settings and different historical periods.

As a result of all these efforts, central concepts and frameworks have been developed across disciplines and one could argue that social movement studies in itself contain what Smelser (2002) calls a "hybrid subfield" with shared concept and approaches.

The proliferation of the field has led to increased theoretical debate and attempts to synthesize the different theoretical perspectives (Goodwin and Jasper 2003; McAdam, McCarthy, and Zald 1996; McAdam, Tarrow, and Tilly 2001; Tarrow 1998). Nonetheless, McAdam, Tarrow, and Tilly (2007) recently complained that "with expertise divided across a confusing patchwork of disciplinary boundaries, geographic areas, historical era, and nominal different types of contention" the field of social movement studies has become very much fragmented.

Perhaps such a state of affairs is given with the object of study. Social movements are phenomena that are not concerned about disciplinary boundaries. The study of social movements is by definition interdisciplinary, as many scholars of social movements never tire of asserting. At the same time, real interdisciplinary research on social movements is rare, because the awareness of what is available in the neighboring discipline is limited. Social movement students from different disciplines often speak little beyond their discipline and fail to connect their theories and concepts to that of neighboring disciplines. As a consequence, wheels are invented for the umpteenth time and cross-disciplinary collaboration can easily lead to mis-understandings, because researchers use an identical vocabulary with different meanings and operationalizations.[1] Moreover, different disciplines have different subcultures, which may be overlooked by focusing on similarities and adopting common conceptual frameworks.

Instead of a new attempt to integrate theoretical perspectives, this volume aims to revisit the disciplinary roots of social movement studies. The focus is on sociology, political science, anthropology, social psychology, and history, which we consider the central disciplines studying social movements, although admittedly the field is much broader and still growing.[2] The various disciplines involved in the study of social movements raise their own specific questions and approach social movements from a variety of angles or perspectives. Moreover, each discipline has distinctive working arrangements, vocabularies, and "standards of explanation" to which students are exposed during their professional socialization, and which are enforced by a variety of disciplinary gatekeepers, from journal editors to grant reviewers. Let us give a few examples of questions characteristic to disciplines. While social psychologists focus on the individual level and look at attitudes, motives, and identities of activists, they pay little attention to the political or cultural context of mobilization or the impact of protest. Nor do they provide explanations for the rise and decline of social movements or the role of globalization. Political opportunities and the impact of protest are obviously topics political scientists are exploring, while such topics as the rise and decline of social movements are food for sociologists and historians. The role of culture in shaping protest and the cultural consequences of social movements are central topics for anthropologist and sociologists.

We hold that knowing the specific questions and approaches of the various disciplines will help us in our interactions with colleagues from disciplines other than our own. Therefore, we invited scholars from what we defined as central disciplines of social movement studies to elaborate on how their own disciplines approach and conceptualize the dynamics of social movements. It is our conviction that genuine interdisciplinary research requires scholars who are firmly rooted in a disciplinary tradition, but at the same time well aware of what other social science disciplines have to offer. Despite the wealth of written material on social movements, we are not aware of a comprehensive publication that takes the major disciplines that are involved in the study of social movements as its point of departure. Most anthologies instead provide synthetic examinations of a comprehensive set of movement-related issues or focus on central theoretical perspectives on social movements such as resource mobilization, political process approach, or framing (Buechler 2000; della Porta and Diani 1999; Snow, Soule, and Kriesi 2004; Tarrow 1998).

---

[1] The concept of political opportunity structure is a case in point. McAdam (1996) demonstrated that this concept is understood in multiple ways. Also, in many cases the concept is either narrowed or stretched, which leads respectively to very limited or tautological explanations (Koopmans 1999). This volume makes clear that concepts such as culture and identity are also interpreted and used very differently across disciplines.

[2] Recently social movement and collective action have become the object of study in other disciplines like social geography (Miller 2000), organizational studies (Davis et al. 2005), and communication studies (Downing 2000). Also, social movement literature and theory are applied to areas of research as diverse as education policy, civil wars, terrorism, health care, and international relations.

DISCIPLINARY APPROACHES

Distinctive disciplines have different approaches to the study of social movements. Guided by our authors, we venture a first characterization of the approaches taken by the five disciplines encompassed in this volume. We begin with sociology; after all, sociologists managed to turn research on social movements into "one of the most vigorous areas of sociology" (Klandermans and Staggenborg 2002; Marx and Wood 1975). Sociological definitions of movements stress qualities such as collective and innovative behavior, extra-institutionality, their network character and multi-centeredness, the shifting and fluid boundaries of movement membership, and the willingness of members to disrupt order (Gerlach and Hine 1970). A strong emphasis has been on how social institutions influence people's choices about how they live and how people's decisions and collective actions in turn bring about social change. During the last decade, however, a growing divide developed between more structural and cultural approaches of social movements (Eyerman and Jamison 1998; Goodwin, Jasper, and Polletta 2001; Johnston and Klandermans 1995). Whereas the more structural approach emphasizes the importance of mobilizing structures, the distribution of material resources, and political opportunities for the emergence of social movements, the cultural approach instead concentrates on questions about how individuals and groups perceive and interpret these material conditions and focuses on the role of cognitive, affective, and ideational roots of contention. We have chosen to have two separate chapters on the structural and cultural approaches in sociology, respectively.

The authors of the chapter on *structural approaches*, Jackie Smith and Tina Fetner, argue that many structural analysts have considered the national state as the primary target or arena against or within which modern social movements operate, which resulted in the development of two central concepts: political contexts and mobilizing structures. Global structural changes, however, have affected both the political contexts and mobilizing structures, which makes it necessary to re-elaborate these concepts and examine how global integration is affecting the character of the nation-state, as well as social movements' attempts to influence it. Smith and Fetner contend that the national state can exist only in a global context that recognizes national sovereignty and certifies national governments as legitimate actors on the world stage. The nature of the state, moreover, is changing owing to the emergence of new actors in the global arena and shifting power constellations among actors.

The strong focus on political contexts and mobilizing structures in social movement studies led to a neglect of processes of meaning construction and the role of culture in mobilizations. The *cultural approach* developed in reaction to this neglect. According to Jim Jasper (Chapter 3), a cultural approach focuses on "the shared mental worlds and their perceived embodiments." In his chapter, he discusses a number of specific embodiments such as words, artifacts, artworks, rituals, events, individuals, and any other action or creation that carries symbolic meanings. Culture, according to Jasper, also includes cognitive understandings of how the world is, moral principles and intuitions about how the world should be, and emotions. Analyzing the role of culture in social movements, Jasper argues, requires a fundamental rethinking of structural concepts such as resources, rules, and opportunity structures.

Despite the different focus of the two approaches, there is a growing convergence between them. Many "structuralist" analysts have integrated culture into their approaches. McAdam, Tarrow, and Tilly (2001), who claim to come from a structural tradition, discovered "the necessity to take strategic interaction, consciousness and historically accumulated culture into account" (p. 22). Jasper (this volume) contends that both approaches, with some adjustments, can be made compatible with one another.

The emphasis on the importance of the political context of mobilization has enlarged the contribution of political scientists to the field. *Political science* examines the role of social movements as players in the political arena and how political opportunities may shape collective action. While the state often plays a critical role in political science social movement literature, David Meyer and Linda Lupo (Chapter 4), argue that "state–movement interaction is not always the focus of the [political science] literature" and that social movement studies have not been developed as a specific area within political science. As a result, no specific social movement framework has been developed. Instead, as Meyer and Lupo claim, the discipline offers a number of important insights in relation to social capital, political institutions, political strategy, and the impact of collective action on public policy.

From a *social psychological perspective* the emphasis is on the individual's role in social movements and processes of construction and reconstruction of collective beliefs, the transformation of discontent into collective action, and sustained participation and disengagement. The authors of Chapter 5, Jacquelien van Stekelenburg and Bert Klandermans, highlight four fundamental social psychological processes as they are employed in the context of social movement participation: social identity, social cognition, emotions, and motivation that link collective identity and collective action. These interacting mechanisms result in a specific motivational constellation for participation in collective action. Van Stekelenburg and Klandermans continue to discuss the phenomenon of social movement participation and examine processes such as short-term versus sustained participation and the dynamics of disengagement.

Like the cultural approach within sociology, *anthropology* traditionally focuses on the role of culture for social movements. According to the authors of Chapter 6, Ton Salman and Willem Assies, anthropology aims to examine systematically the role of meaning and identity in protest. In this effort, the cultural aspects of social movements and the "cultured dispositions" of the various agents involved are central. The connection between social movements and culture involves a range of themes such as the "cultural" characteristics of societies at large, influencing both protesters and authorities, and the cultural narratives and symbols (re)produced by social movements to justify their case and recruit supporters. Another distinctive characteristic of anthropology is its emic and holistic approach to social movements. An emic perspective, according to Salman and Assies, implies a "[focus] on the intrinsic cultural distinctions that are meaningful within a society," which are derived from the perceptions of the individuals and groups that are involved in contention.

Historians principally study social movements as historical phenomena and look into long-term developments such as changing action repertoires. According to Brian Dill and Ronald Aminzade (Chapter 7), historians, in contrast to sociologists, do not provide explanations in terms of general patterns or laws. Instead, their aim is to give a credible account of a sequence of events leading up to collective action or the motives that impelled it. The explanations offered are relevant only to a particular time and place. Dill and Aminzade suggest that, as a result of this context-dependent approach, historians who study social movements have only marginally engaged in relevant theoretical debates and made conceptual and/or theoretical contributions. Historians, however, offer a crucial contribution to social movement studies by their rich and detailed analyses of the origins, dynamics, and outcomes of a wide range of mobilizations. They have examined not only some of the large-scale social movements operating in the context of modern nation-states, but also a wide range small, isolated mobilizations across the globe during different time periods.

So far, our authors are focusing on their respective disciplines. Framing the scholarly approaches to a field along disciplinary boundaries raises, of course, the question of how these disciplines communicate. Obviously, scholars from the various disciplines are aware of each other and do exchange views and insights, if only because some "fellow-travelers" chose to cross the disciplinary borders. The dynamics of exchange between disciplines is a topic that is interesting in itself. In an attempt to describe these dynamics, we have employed a network model of reciprocal influence.

DYNAMICS OF INTERDISCIPLINARY EXCHANGE

The relationships between the different disciplines studying social movements can be characterized as a network model of reciprocal influence. Within this network, sociology functions as the core discipline—numerically and theoretically. The former is the case because most studies and students of social movements take a sociological perspective. The study of social movements has grown to become one of the larger subfields of sociology, as the membership of the sections on social movements and collective behavior within the American Sociological Association (ASA) and ISA demonstrate. Other national and international disciplinary associations such as the International Political Science Association, the American Psychological Association, the World Council of Anthropological Associations, and the International Historians Association (and regional counterparts) do not have similar, separate sections dedicated to collective behavior or social movements.

As a result, sociology outnumbered any other discipline and became the largest and most important discipline studying social movements. The centrality of sociology and, for that matter the marginal position of the other disciplines, also has important theoretical implications. Sociology became the theoretical "home front" of social movement studies. Theoretical innovations imported from the disciplinary "outskirts" are filtered, reformulated, and built into sociological theories of social movements. Reconstructed in such a manner theory was exported again to the neighboring disciplines including the discipline of origin. The dynamics between the different disciplines that study social movements can be pictured as a network, where sociology functions as the central node (Fig. 1.2).

As examples of such theoretical trading, Meyer and Lupo (Chapter 4)point to the fact that "[some of the] key concepts for the analysis of social movements originated in political science, but were far more fully developed in sociology. Michael Lipsky (1968) coined the term 'resource mobilization,' but McCarthy and Zald (1973, 1977) developed the concept into a broad theoretical framework that animated a great deal of additional research. Peter Eisinger (1973) coined the phrase 'political opportunity structure,' and it has been employed across disciplines, but far more extensively in sociology." Another example provides the conference organized at the University of Michigan by Aldon Morris and Carol Mueller in 1988. The conference aimed "to explore social psychology in order to complement 'the structural-political framework' of the Resource Mobilization approach" (Morris and Mueller 1992:ix). Among the concepts that were discussed intensively were the notions of "collective action frame" and "identity." Gamson argued, for example, that social psychology was the discipline best equipped to elaborate the concept of collective action frame, while Klandermans employed his background in social psychology to elaborate the concepts of consensus formation and consensus mobilization in the context of multiorganizational fields.

Since sociology has become the main producer in social movement studies and theory, other disciplines follow developments in sociology, including sociological journals and conferences, to trace new issues and developments in the field. Individual authors concerned with social movements in other disciplines tend to borrow frameworks and paradigms from sociology, and adapt

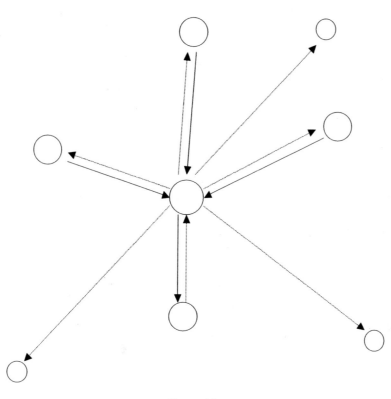

FIGURE 1.2.

them again to fit their own discipline. This results in diffusion dynamics between "the core" and the more "peripheral" disciplines, resembling a boomerang or perhaps even a Ping Pong game. Sociologists who study social movements often use and adapt concepts and frameworks from neighboring disciplines, which once further developed and established within sociology, are then "back-imported" and adapted by the other disciplines.

It is important to note that no or few direct cross borrowing takes place between the "peripheral" disciplines. If any exchange exists, it occurs via the core discipline of sociology. As a consequence, concepts from the one "peripheral" discipline make it to the other in the sociological reconstruction rather than in its original form.

Sociology, thus, appears to be the only discipline that has generated a critical mass that managed to achieve standing and establish itself as a central field within the discipline, thereby attracting and generating more resources such as students, funding. and voice. As a result, sociology has been the domain that has made the most important contributions, at least numerically, to social movement theory and research.

CROSS CUTTING AND DISTINCTIVE
ISSUES AND THEMES

A comparison of the central issues and themes of the different disciplinary approaches reveals that, although there are important overlaps, the differences stand out as well. A scrutiny of the central concepts that are employed in the different chapters makes clear which issues dominate the agenda of social movement studies in the different disciplinary approaches. The list includes culture, emotions, globalization, grievances, identity, meaning construction, networks, resources, and strategy. Remarkably, the themes that dominated the social movement studies in the 1980s and 1990s, the triad of collective action frames, mobilizing structures, and political opportunities (labeled the "classic agenda" by McAdam, Tarrow, and Tilly 2001:14) now appear to occupy a less central position. The "classic agenda" seems to have lost its centrality or is at least questioned and re-elaborated from various angles. Within structural sociology, the increasing attention to processes of globalization and transnationalization resulted in a critical examination of the usefulness of the concepts of mobilizing structures and political opportunities. Cultural approaches have sought to rethink these concepts from a cultural point of view, demonstrating their meaningful character. Structures and opportunities depend on perceptions and interpretations of the actors involved. Surprisingly, the third concept of the classic triad, collective action frames or framing, appears to have almost completely dropped off the agenda, or perhaps has been substituted by the related concepts of identity, cognition, and culture.

The decline of the "classic agenda" resulted in greater diversity, but also fragmentation of the field of social movement studies. New dominant themes—such as globalization, culture, identity, and emotions—have emerged, but their importance is highly dispersed across disciplines. While processes of *globalization* are important study topics in the structural sociological approach, in anthropology and, to a lesser extent, in political science, virtually no attention is paid to these processes in the cultural sociological approaches, history, and social psychology. The recent character of these phenomena may explain the lack of attention to globalization processes in history. The lack of attention to contextual factors and processes in social psychology may explain the neglect of globalization by that discipline. Most remarkable, however, is its marginal presence in the cultural sociological approach, since globalization clearly affects culture.

How processes of globalization affect *culture* is an important issue in both anthropology and structural sociology. In anthropology, much attention is directed to the local effects of globalization processes and reactions to this. Globalization processes have triggered initiatives to protect, secure, or purify local cultural heritages. In addition, new forms of organizing transnational mobilization have emerged from small local communities that connect local leaders, activists, and intellectuals to transnational networks. In anthropology such local initiatives are documented and analyzed. Structural sociology also studies how global integration affects cultures and collective identities of communities, but the focus here is stronger on mapping these structural changes and the processes involved, such as the extensive flow of information and resources. Also, the consequences of these processes, such as feelings of relative deprivation and defensive responses, or, more positively, transnational dialogue, communication, and mobilization, are studied.

Next to globalization, *identity* is a second shared central theme, important in social psychology, anthropology, and cultural sociology. While social psychologists carefully distinguish collective identity, as a group characteristic from the identity of individual participants, this distinction is absent in anthropology and cultural sociology. In cultural sociology, the concept of identity concerns mainly collective identity and the focus is on the construction and negotiation of collective identity. Even though social psychology is concerned with the relationship between collective identity and individual identity, the emphasis is mainly on how individuals identify with the collective. The construction of identities, at both the group and individual level, receives less attention. Nor does social psychology examine the content of these identities. Cultural approaches in sociology and anthropology, instead, aim to reconstruct the ideas, symbols, rituals, and emotions that are shared by a collective and are less concerned with the individual and the extent to which (s)he identifies with the collective.

Both social psychology and cultural sociology link identity and *emotions*. So far, within social movement research little is known about the role of emotions in movement participation. Emotions are important in motivating people to participate in collective action. A difference between the social psychological and cultural sociological approach is that cultural sociology sees emotions as an important constitutive element of identity. According to Jasper, emotions are central in identity construction and negotiations. He also stresses that in the interaction between political players, characteristic emotions may arise that either advance or hinder collective identities. From a social psychological point of view, identity precedes emotions. The idea is that the stronger the group identification, the more people experience group-based emotions. Social psychologists have a long history of studying emotions. They have developed instruments to measure emotions and models to explain how emotions influence cognition and behavior. We hold that importing social psychological expertise on emotions into the sociology of social movements may further our understanding of the role of emotions in protest behavior.

Culture and identity are concepts that are linked in the realm of anthropology and cultural sociology. Each discipline conceives of culture and identity as intertwined concepts. This is evidenced by the fact that identity is seen as a "carrier" of culture and as "culturally constructed" by both disciplines, and that for both collective identities of social movements supposedly reflect the culture surrounding the movement and react against the dominant culture. Finally, both see the new identities that are constructed in the context of social movements as contributing to cultural change. The two approaches differ as well; while current anthropological research focuses mainly on how processes of globalization affect and mobilize local identities, cultural sociology views collective identity mainly as a possible carrier of culture among many others.

The (sometimes loose) connections that are constructed between these concepts suggest that two prevalent lines are currently developing in the study of social movements. One is a more macrostructural approach that focuses on the impact of globalization on economic and political contexts and social movement organizations and networks, and the other emphasizes the micro and meso levels and examines the relationship between cultural change and processes of identity and meaning construction. The different disciplinary contributions in this book do not suggest that clear theoretical frameworks have been developed that could replace the "classic" approach.

Also apparent is a new focus on actor-oriented analyses that draw our attention to the individual participants in movements. This focus is most clearly voiced in Chapter 6. According to Salman and Assies "the actors that make the movements need to be studied much more intensively. Insights in the doubts, aspirations, motivations, and even 'improper' considerations of these participants will help us to understand the movements as a polyvalent, multilayered phenomenon, and will contribute to our insights in their successes and failures." The use of narratives as a central source of information in history and cultural sociology also turns our attention to individual activists and leaders and may help to unravel the puzzle of human agency. From a sociological perspective, Passy and Giugni (2000) have called for more attention to the individual level in order to better understand the dynamics of sustained participation and disengagement. Their perspective draws from social phenomenology and symbolic interactionism, which both highlight the symbolic (subjective) dimensions of participation and the structural positions of actors. This focus on the individual activist calls for new cross-disciplinary partnerships and cooperation. Sociologists and political scientists interested in individual social movement actors may draw from the insights of social psychologists and anthropologists.

The authors of the different chapters also point to a number of unanswered questions and emerging issues that may guide future (interdisciplinary) research. One first central issue has to do with the changing context of mobilization. Scholars from different disciplines are analyzing the processes and mechanisms of change that globalization involves. To understand better not only the changes, but also the continuities that social movements face, the authors of different chapters make an appeal for more spatial and temporal comparison. Such comparison may help us to avoid treating a social movement as the only possible political formation without inquiring into its form elsewhere or into its historical transformation (Tilly 2003:9–10). Dill and Aminzade (Chapter 7) assert that such knowledge would enable social scientists to understand better the scope conditions of various theories. Other authors in this volume stress the importance of investigating the activist perceptions of globalization processes, what changes they perceive, and whether these are framed as threats or as opportunities for mobilization. Van Stekelenburg and Klandermans (Chapter 5) allude to the importance of identifying the conditions that are important in affecting peoples' subjective interpretations of their collective disadvantages in terms of identities, opportunities, or constraints and injustice.

A second theme, related to globalization, is diffusion. Increasing transnational ties and information flows may result in more cross-national learning processes. One of the questions raised is to what extent identities, ideologies, strategies, or mobilizing structures can be transferred to other contexts. We also need to explore the cultural dimensions of how new tactics spread. What learning and discursive processes are involved? The authors of Chapter 6, Salman and Assies, argue that we need to examine not only external influences on local narratives and traditions, but also why such influence is denied. Local movements often claim that their identities and strategies are rooted in local historical traditions. Anthropology might be able to help decipher these reification mechanisms.

A third important theme for further investigation is the issue of identity. As different authors note, despite the considerable attention given to this subject over the last years, many unresolved questions remain. In the context of globalization, collective identities become more local and transnational at the same time. We need to explore the relationships between economic and political structures and processes of identity formation. What conditions make transnational identity formation more likely and when do people recur to local identities? Also, we need more research into the relation between collective identities, on the one hand, and the appropriations and adjustments of made of these identities by individual participants, on the other. How do people deal with inconsistencies and tensions between their self-perception and identity and that of their group?

Finally, group dynamics in organizations; processes of negotiation; and deliberation over strategic choices, identities, and organizational forms and struggles over leadership are important issues for future research. Also, we need to explore the new ways of organizing that are developing owing to the global availability of information technologies. We have witnessed a number of innovative action forms and can expect new "virtual" ways of organizing. How do different communication strategies impact on the organizational processes and negotiations in looser networks and what new ties and loyalties are developing?

OUTLINE OF THE CHAPTERS IN THIS BOOK

Although the chapters on the various disciplines each have their own, unique appearance, they all address the same set of issues. We asked the authors of the different chapters to describe the core or focus of the discipline, to address the question of what is specific about the discipline's approach to social movements, and what central issues and questions are dealt with. In addition, we asked for a short overview of the development of the field in order to understand why some issues have become core, while others remained marginal. Furthermore, we asked them to present exemplary studies as an illustration of how social movements are typically studied within that discipline. The authors were also asked to address the overlaps with other disciplines and the gaps and unanswered questions. Most chapters conclude with a selection of suggested readings.

CODA: A PRIMER ON INTERDISCIPLINARY COLLABORATION

The reason why we put together a collection of essays on disciplinary approaches to social movements is to stimulate interdisciplinary collaboration. We contend that knowledge about the basic assumptions and methodologies in each discipline is a necessary requisite for building bridges between disciplinary approaches. State-of-the-art reviews of the advances and challenges within the social science disciplines hopefully stimulate debate and cooperation. This handbook may be an important tool in advancing cross-disciplinary theoretical debates. It is our firm belief that interdisciplinary collaboration produces innovation.

But as Smelser (2002) notes, interdisciplinarity has many different meanings and connotations. It can refer to institutional embodiments; to cooperation of people from different (social) sciences; to the use of the same concept, assumption, or framework in more than one discipline; to the development of hybrid subfields; and to theoretical efforts such as seeking conceptual analogies, cross-disciplinary generalizations, or principles (p. 645). Each of these aspects applies to the study of social movements. Interdisciplinary collaboration is a complicated matter. It is our hope that this handbook will be instrumental in encouraging genuine interdisciplinary research on social movements.

REFERENCES

Buechler, Steven M. 2000. *Social Movements in Advanced Capitalism: The Political Economy and Cultural Construction of Social Activism*. New York: Oxford University Press.

Miller Byron, 2000. Geography and Social Movements: Comparing Antinuclear Activism in the Boston Area. Minnesota: University of Minnesota Press.

Davis, Gerald F., Doug McAdam, W. Richard Scott, and Mayer Zald, eds. 2005. *Social Movements and Organizational Theory*. New York: Cambridge University Press.

della Porta, Donatella and Mario Diani. 1999. *Social Movements: An Introduction*. Oxford, Basel: Blackwell.

Downing, John D. H. 2000. *Radical Media: Rebellious Communication and Social Movements*. London: Sage.

Eisinger, Peter K. 1973. "The Conditions of Protest Behavior in American Cities." *The American Political Science Review* 67(1)/:11–28

Eyerman, Ron and Andrew Jamison. 1998. *Music and Social Movements*. New York: Cambridge University Press.

Gerlach, Luther P. and Virginia H. Hine. 1970. *People, Power, Change: Movements of Social Transformation*. Indianapolis, IN: Bobbs-Merrill.

Goodwin, Jeff and James M. Jasper, eds. 2003. *Rethinking Social Movements: Structure, Meaning, and Emotion*. Lanham, MD: Rowman & Littlefield.

Goodwin, Jeff, James M. Jasper, and Francesca Polletta, eds. 2001. *Passionate Politics*. Chicago: University of Chicago Press.

Johnston, Hank and Bert Klandermans, eds. 1995. *Social Movements and Culture*. Minneapolis, MN: University of Minnesota Press.

Klandermans, Bert, Hanspeter Kriesi, and Sidney Tarrow, eds. 1988. *From Structure to Action: Comparing Social Movements Across Cultures*, International Social Movement Research I. Greenwich: JAI.

Klandermans, Bert and Susanne Staggenborg, eds. 2002. *Methods of Social Movement Research*. Minneapolis, MN: University of Minnesota Press.

Koopmans, Ruud 1999. "Political Opportunity Structure. Some Splitting to Balance the Lumping." *Sociological Forum* 14(1):97–110.

Lipsky, Michael. 1968. "Protest as a Political Resource." *American Political Science Review* 62:1144–1158.

Marx, Gary T. and James L. Wood. 1975. "Strands of Theory and Research in Collective Behavior." *Annual Review of Sociology* 1:363–428.

McAdam, Doug. 1996. "Political Opportunities: Conceptual Origins, Current Problems, Future Directions." Pp. 23–40 in *Comparative Perspectives on Social Movements: Political Opportunities, Mobilizing Structures, and Cultural Framings*, edited by Doug McAdam, John McCarthy, and Mayer Zald. New York: Cambridge University Press.

McAdam, Doug, John McCarthy, and Mayer Zald, eds. 1996. *Comparative Perspectives on Social Movements: Political Opportunities, Mobilizing Structures, and Cultural Framings*. New York: Cambridge University Press.

McAdam, Doug, Sidney Tarrow, and Charles Tilly. 2001. *Dynamics of Contention*. New York: Cambridge University Press.

——. 2007. "Comparative Perspectives on Contentious Politics." in *Comparative Politics: Rationality, Culture, and Structure: Advancing Theory in Comparative Politics*, edited by Mark I. Lichbach and Alan Zuckerman. New York: Cambridge University Press.

McCarrthy, John D. and Mayer N. Zald. 1973. *The Trend of Social Movements in America: Professionalization and Resource Mobilization*. Morristown, NJ: General Learinig Press.

——. 1977. "Resource Mobilization and Social Movements: A Partial Theory." *American Journal of Sociology* 82:1212–1241

Morris, Aldon D. and Carol M. Mueller, eds. 1992. *Frontiers of Social Movement Theory*. New Haven: Yale University Press.

Passy, Florence and Giugni, Marco 2000. "Life-Spheres, Networks, and Sustained Participation in Social Movements: A Phenomenological Approach to Political Commitment." *Sociological Forum* 15(1):115–144.

S! Smelser N.J., 2003. On Comparative Analysis, Interdisciplinarity and Inernationalization in Sociology. *International Sociology*. 18 (4): 643–657.

Snow, David A., Sarah A. Soule, and Hanspeter Kriesi, eds. 2004. *Blackwell Companion to Social Movements*. Oxford and Malden, MA: Blackwell Publishing.

Tarrow, Sidney. 1998. *Power in Movement: Social Movements, Collective Action and Politics*, 2nd edition. New York: Cambridge University Press.

Tilly, Charles. 2003. *Contention and Democracy in Europe, 1650–2000*. New York: Cambridge University, Press.

CHAPTER 2

Structural Approaches in the Sociology of Social Movements

Jackie Smith and Tina Fetner

Sociological research emphasizes how social institutions, such as the family, religion, corporations, and governments, influence people's choices about how they live. While acknowledging that individuals have some freedom to pursue different paths, sociologists argue that this freedom is limited in important ways by forces outside the control of individuals. Sociology, therefore, asks how these broader forces operate to affect the actions and beliefs of individuals and groups. As the editors have noted, sociological research on social movements can be classified as adopting either a structural or cultural emphasis. While the former focuses on the distribution of material resources and the organizations and institutions that govern such distribution, the latter approach emphasizes questions about how individuals and groups perceive and interpret these material conditions.

In practice, distinguishing between actual material conditions and popular understandings of these can be difficult. For instance, categories such as gender, class, or ethnicity that classify individuals are structurally defined, but their sociological relevance grows not simply from their existence bur rather from the cultural work of individuals who help define group identities according to these structural categories. As Buechler observed, "[c]ollective identity and political consciousness are thus decisive factors mediating structures of power and collective action" (2000:123). In other words, a group must somehow come to perceive itself as both distinct and subject to unjust material or social conditions. Such "collective identities" are far from automatic, because the "interlocking systems of domination" embedded in broader political and economic structures affect possibilities for social groups to articulate and mobilize around social movement identities. Thus, any attempt to understand social change requires attention to questions about how the resources and power needed to define and defend group interests are distributed within a society. Structural approaches recognize that inequalities are closely linked to macro-level factors such as a country's position in the world economy or to meso-level ones, such as class, race, and gender. Thus, any attempt to reduce inequalities in society must include a consideration of how these broad structures are shaping broader power relationships.

A key starting point for much sociological work is the observation that virtually all societies experience inequality. The benefits and risks of society are nowhere near equally distributed, and therefore we would expect that particular clusters of people would be more likely candidates for participation in social movements. In particular, more aggrieved groups might be expected to be engaged in protests against the status quo. Important debates have taken place among social movement scholars regarding the role of grievances in the generation of social movements. Early research in social movements saw political protest as emerging from groups that were relatively disadvantaged by the status quo. Structural inequalities generated strains that led individuals to protest their conditions (e.g., Davies 1962; Gurr 1970; Rose 1982; for a review, see Gurney and Tierney 1982). But while it made intuitive sense to argue that relative or absolute deprivation is a *sine qua non* of movement emergence, in reality very few of the most deprived groups actually engaged in protest. And while social scientists did quite well at mapping the causes and dimensions of deprivation, they were less successful at predicting when and where resistance to structural inequalities would emerge.

Other analysts criticized deprivation theories for failing to consider how individuals experiencing deprivation are embedded within broader social structures. Society's weakest and most marginalized people are typically not well placed to engage in what can be highly risky political actions. Lacking secure economic opportunities and savings, they cannot afford to take many risks. Facing discrimination from a more powerful majority, they may seek to remain invisible or to engage in symbolic forms of resistance as they go about their efforts to survive (e.g., Scott 1985). These people also tend to lack the time and political skills required to work for social change, and their community organizations are more likely to lack the money needed to engage in extensive political work. Thus, not only are certain groups materially deprived, but they are also denied equal capacity to influence the political processes that help determine how society's resources are used and distributed (King, Cornwall, and Dahlin 2005; McCarthy and Zald 1977).

While debates about the role of deprivation in social movement mobilization developed largely among political scientists, sociologists were beginning to articulate a model of social movement mobilization that focused on the *capacities* of challengers to resist injustice rather than on the conditions of inequality themselves. An important contribution in this regard is Charles Tilly's *From Mobilization to Revolution* (1978), which explored how the war-making and tax-collecting activities of eighteenth century political elitists contributed to the institutional elaboration of the modern national state. Tilly found that, as national states took shape, popular groups adopted new forms of resistance that resembled their new, national targets more than they resembled earlier protest forms. Thus, bread riots gave way to the emergence of more structured associations for popular resistance. It is to the earliest days of the modern state that Tilly traces common tactics in modern protest repertoires—including petitions, rallies, blockades, and protest marches. In short, localized direct action against an immediate target gave way to more symbolic forms of protest designed to communicate with other political actors and generate wider sympathy and support for challengers' claims. Challengers had to focus their efforts on the emerging states, which increasingly controlled key decisions about the distribution of resources and power. In the course of this shift, they had to mobilize larger numbers of people and resources than were needed for earlier types of challenges. Challengers thus needed to expand their organizational capacities accordingly to compete effectively in the emerging national polity.

Social and material inequalities have often formed the bases on which the largest social movements have emerged. In the West, for example, we see a history of robust social movements organized around labor, gender, and race. Each of these categories represents not only a group of people wishing to improve their lot, but also a systemic social division in which one group is allocated less than another. The structural approach to social movements brings to the forefront of analysis the institutionalized injustices and inequalities over which contested politics are fought. These include social barriers to material success, state policies that treat groups unequally, or bureaucratic rules that favor one group (e.g., corporations) over another (workers). Social movement actors form organizations to influence states and institutions. These structural elements of activism are of primary interest to structural approaches to the study of social movements. Inequalities of political access have motivated some of the largest and most successful social movements in the United States. For example, the women's suffrage movement was born out of the political exclusion of women. Although women's suffrage activists were disadvantaged by their gender, they were able to leverage the class privileges of some key activists (Banaszak 1996; King, Cornwall, and Dahlin 1996). Significantly, they also took advantage of skills, ideologies, and networks that emerged in the course of abolitionist struggles.

Structural approaches to social movements, in short, can be seen to cover an enormous terrain that takes us from questions about the nature and causes of inequality to the creation of social groupings to the causes of institutional change. The centrality of the modern state to shaping the distribution of resources and capacities has led many structural analysts to consider the national state as the primary target or arena against or within which modern social movements operate. The national state not only defines the possibilities for groups to affect social change, but it also structures the possibilities for different groups to articulate grievances and organize in support of social change goals. Thus, we focus much of this chapter on how understandings of the national state impact analyses of social change.

Two concepts that have emerged from what is largely a state-centric body social movements research—political contexts and mobilizing structures—provide useful analytical tools for helping scholars analyze the ways states and other actors and structures shape social movement dynamics. The concepts' usefulness grows in part from their effectiveness at helping analysts assess the relative distribution of power across groups in a given society and the possibilities for altering power relations. We therefore focus much of our discussion on these concepts, identifying both how they have contributed to our knowledge of social movements and how they have changed over time. We pay particular attention to the ways global structural changes have affected both the political contexts and mobilizing structures. Finally, we identify some remaining questions and demonstrate how structural approaches can complement and contribute to cultural ones to enhance our overall understanding of social movements.

We emphasize a global perspective in our discussion of the structural approaches to social movements, because we find it increasingly difficult to ignore the ways that national states are embedded within broader sets of relationships to other states and to global institutions. If the modern state was key to the emergence of what we know as social movements, then we must consider how global integration is affecting the character of the national state, as well as social movements' attempts to influence it. Our perspective, which views states as interdependent actors embedded within a complex system of global relationships rather than as free-standing, autonomous social entities, has important implications for how we think about the state as actor and as movement target.

POLITICAL CONTEXTS

Structuralist accounts in sociology build on the work of Karl Marx, who saw basic material or economic relationships as the key factor shaping the evolution of society. As Marx stated, "Men [*sic*] make their own history, but they do not make it just as they please." For social movement analysts, this basic premise has led to research exploring how social structures affect the possibilities for collective attempts to make history. The idea of political opportunities or alternately, *political contexts,*[1] refers to the ways formal political institutions and more informal alignments of relevant actors condition the prospects for relatively powerless groups to effectively challenge the existing order. Factors such as the extent to which the political system is open to public participation, the presence or absence of influential allies, state capacities to repress or respond to movement demands, and divisions among elitists all shape the political opportunities and limitations of movements. While some factors—such as state capacities and the degree of openness of the polity—change little over time, others—such as constellations of potential and actual allies and opponents—can shift more quickly to favor or hinder political activism. Political contexts affect both how people can try to influence political outcomes as well as how they can come together as a group.

A key insight of research on political contexts is that we must look beyond movements themselves if we are to understand how movements arise and under what conditions they succeed or fail. People such as Mohandas Gandhi or Martin Luther King Jr. may indeed have been highly exceptional political leaders and strategists, but if they had lived at different historical moments, we would not be recalling them today. Similarly, other Gandhis and Kings have existed throughout history, but unless they were born into an era where political conditions favored movement activism, they remain outside of our understanding of history (e.g., Wuthnow 1989).

Political Opportunities

Early formulations of the external dynamics relevant to social movements consider the varying levels of "openness" of a particular political context to a social movement. Charles Tilly (1978) argues that social movements are likely to emerge when windows of opportunity for access to the polity open. Thus, several early studies in political opportunities gauge the relative "openness" of political structures. Kitschelt's comparison (1986) of antinuclear movements in four democracies is a key example. Eisinger (1973), analyzing U.S. cities, argued that the relationship between social movement emergence and political openness is an "inverted-U" shaped curve. If a city is extremely open to input from political outsiders, this will suppress social movements by rendering them unnecessary. At the other extreme, a very closed system will also suppress social movement activity. Social movements, he argued, would be most likely in states that fall between these two extremes. While later social movement scholarship has supported these propositions, many scholars have sought to develop a more multifaceted conceptualization of political opportunity (e.g., Gamson and Meyer 1996; Kriesi et al. 1995; Tarrow 1996; for a review, see Meyer and Minkoff 2004).

Doug McAdam's political process model of social movement emergence and decline is a key work in developing this perspective (1982). He argued that shifts in the structure of political opportunities promote the expansion of social protest and the emergence of social movements (see also Tarrow 1998b; Tilly, Tilly, and Tilly 1975). His conceptualization of relationships between large-scale structural forces, such as transformations of regional and national economies, migration patterns, and institutional configurations, has been central to

---

[1] Many analysts adopt the term "political opportunities" to discuss these, but since broader institutions and political alignments define obstacles as well as constraints, we adopt the more inclusive notion of political contexts (see Amenta et al. 2002).

encouraging a proliferation of new research on political contexts. By making explicit the connections between broad structural change and mobilization processes, McAdam's work contributed to the emergence of discussions about "social movement society" in the late twentieth century. This concept helped analysts think about social movements not as aberrations, but rather as constituent elements of routine politics. We discuss this concept further in relation to globalization later in this chapter.

Some have found it helpful to distinguish between more static, structural opportunities and dynamic opportunities. Structural opportunities refer to the more stable features of political institutions, such as bureaucratic agencies, formal mechanisms regulating access to political authorities, and the capacity of state agents to implement changes. These opportunities are relatively consistent across time, though not impervious to change. Dynamic opportunities are more volatile and particularistic. Important examples of dynamic opportunities that have been linked to social movement success are divisions among elitists, social control strategies by state actors, and momentary crises and events (Gamson and Meyer 1996). The latter are significant only if social movement actors recognize them as opportunities and act on them. Another possibility, however, is that movement actors fail to perceive opportunities or openings in the system, and therefore fail to take advantage of these. Thus, many analysts point to the problem of distinguishing between "objective" conditions and activists' perceptions of those conditions, and some have addressed this with the notion that "signaling" processes help link structure and action (more on signaling later).

Some contend that the opposite of an opportunity is a threat. Nonetheless, threats, too, have been shown to contribute to efforts for social movement mobilization (Francisco 1996; Rasler 1996; Staggenborg 1986; Van Dyke 2003). Movements, it is claimed, are sometimes more focused on preventing bad ends than for securing good ones. Tilly (1978) argued that groups may be more responsive to threats because they require less mobilization than opportunities. He argued that social movements can respond to threats using networks and practices already in place, whereas opportunities require new forms of mobilization.

Some social movement scholars have raised concerns with political opportunities as an analytic category. For example, Goodwin and Jasper (1999) argued that the concept of political opportunity was so vague and pliable as to apply to anything at all external to a social movement organization. They also argued that, as applied to studies of social movements, political opportunity theory tends toward a tautology: any source that produces social movement activity is *post hoc* identified as an opportunity (Gamson and Meyer 1996). They also were concerned that cultural factors are either subsumed under this concept or ignored altogether.

Some scholars responded to this criticism by further specifying their usage of the concept political opportunities. For example, McAdam, Tarrow, and Tilly (2001) articulate two key concepts: state capacity (the impact of the state on activities and resources) and democratization. With this model, states themselves are the unit of analysis, as well as a number of clearly articulated dimensions along which states may vary. This framework can be used to compare social movements in different state contexts. However, this framework is limited in its ability to explain variation in patterns of mobilization among states that are similar in terms of their capacities and levels of democratization.

Meyer and Minkoff (2004) also argued for retaining the political opportunity concept. While they agreed that there are discrepancies in how different scholars operationalized political opportunities, they argued for more conceptual clarity, as well as a clear explanation of causal mechanisms, rather than a new framework. In particular, they argue that *structural* political opportunities influence most strongly the policy-related outcomes of social movement efforts. Other political opportunities serve to structure the cultural dimensions of social move-ments' work by signaling to activists and the public at large which issues and frames might be successful at a given point in time (Tarrow 1996). These are most influential in the founding of social movement organizations and in the formation of coalitions. For instance, Wuthnow (1989) analyzed how the emergence of significant "communities of discourse" is shaped by environmental conditions, institutional contexts, and sequences of actions. Koopmans's analy-sis (2005) of the "discursive frames" that affected right-wing mobilization in Germany, Steinberg's analysis (1995) of labor mobilizations in the nineteenth century, and Maney, Woehrle, and Coy's analyses (2005) of peace movement frames illustrate how political contexts shape ideological work in social movements. Meyer and Minkoff (2004) called for scholars to keep in mind the questions, "political opportunity for whom?" and "political oppor-tunity for what?" as a method to avoid conceptual cloudiness.

From Political Opportunities to Political Contexts

Another approach has been to move away from the concept "opportunity" and instead focus on political contexts (Kriesi 1996; Rucht 1996). This shift has allowed scholars to avoid the limiting metaphor of the opening and closing "window" of opportunity and instead identify both durable and variable aspects of the state relevant to a given movement at a particular point in time. This approach centers on questions of how major political institutions structure the contexts for political action by both challengers and authorities.

Kriesi and colleagues (1995), and later Amenta and colleagues (2002) argued that the structure of the polity, ranging from highly centralized to highly dispersed, affects both social movement forms and outcomes by creating more or fewer points of access to (as well as "veto points" within) the polity (Skocpol 1992). Measures of democratization, such as suffrage, the number of political parties, and "direct democracy" legislative processes (e.g., ballot initia-tives) will also impact the number of social movements and their forms (Amenta et al. 2002). State policies are also a critical component of the political context. They have the capacity to shape the grievances of social movements as well as channel their actions (Burstein, Einwohner, and Hollander 1995; Clemens 1998; Feree 1987; Giugni, McAdam, and Tilly 1999; McCarthy, Britt, and Wolfson 1991; Piven and Cloward 1979; Quadagno 1992; Valocchi 1990; Western 1993). A final component of political contexts is state bureaucracies and repressive capacities. Kriesi and colleagues (1995), studying "new" social movements in Western Europe, argue that high levels of repression may effectively prevent protest, but the impact of low levels of repression is unclear. Della Porta (1998) argued that a state's failure to invoke repressive action increases the likelihood that social movements will use peaceful protest tactics. On the other hand, strong bureaucracies are likely to increase social movement mobilization in that they increase the state's capacity to implement social change (Amenta et al. 2002). To the extent that bureaucrats support social movement goals, they may aid chal-lengers directly (Orloff and Skocpol 1984).

Research on the ways states have worked to police public protests has shown that during the 1960s and 1970s a system of "public order management" evolved as authorities worked to balance their competing mandates to maintain public order while also protecting citizens' rights to speech and assembly (della Porta and Reiter 1998; McCarthy, McPhail, and Crist 1999). This institutionalization of protest and state responses to it, however, is just one aspect of the ways states have sought to neutralize threats from social movement challengers. For instance, researchers have detailed the covert actions of the U.S. government to repress movements of both the left and right during the 1960s (Cunningham 2005), and contemporary news accounts suggests that such practices may be expanding today. Davenport and his collaborators (2005) call for a wider interpretation of state repression to account for the varieties of tools available for modern states to channel and subvert challenges to their authority. One study in that volume calls for an extension of the historical emphasis of McAdam's political process approach to the study of movements to address the decline phase of movements. Zwerman and Steinhoff (2005) analyzed the effects of state repression on activism in the United States and Japan, and they found that repression in both cases generated enduring and robust forms of militancy. They concluded, "repression may have serious long-term costs not just for the activists it represses but for the state that imposes it [. . .]" (p. 102). These insights from research on state repression and other forms of protest control demonstrate the need for structural analyses to account for the ways interactions between challengers, authorities, and other actors shape the evolving contexts for protest (Earl 2006; Jenkins and Klandermans 1995).

Further demonstrating the importance of adopting an interactive and dynamic approach to understanding political contexts, newer analyses have shown that the system of "negotiated protest management" observed over recent years has broken down in recent years, and this is partly due to the expansion of the global neoliberal agenda and a related reduction in officially sanctioned spaces of protest, known as the public forum (McCarthy and McPhail 2006). As a result, more overtly repressive police tactics have been seen in many Western countries, reversing the earlier trend toward more nonviolent policing strategies (della Porta, Peterson, and Reiter 2007). Together this work illustrates the importance of understanding the ways states are organized to both manage and resist challenges from social change advocates, affecting the relevant political contexts.

Some critics wonder whether, if political contexts are so important to social change, social movements might themselves be irrelevant to the process of social change (e.g., Goodwin and Jasper 1999). However, several studies have shown that the movements themselves do matter to the process of social change (Burstein Einwohner, and Hollander 1995; Giugni 1998; Giugni et al. 1999; Piven and Cloward 1979). One study on the emergence of Old Age Assistance in the United States tests this question directly by using time-series and cross-sectional data (Amenta, Caren, and Olasky 2005). They find that the pension movement did influence social policy by acting as an important mediator between the favorable political conditions and the legislative process.

Not all movements are oriented to changing state policies or reforming state bureaucracies. Some movements, for example, target the policies or practices of private corporations. Nicole C. Raeburn's (2004) study of lesbian and gay employee associations' attempts to secure domestic partner benefits is an excellent example of one such movement. This analysis tracks the successes and failures of activists who are participating in a larger project of bringing benefits to lesbian and gay families; however, each employee association is bounded by the institution in which it operates. Even in this case, however Raeburn finds that contexts are very important to securing these benefits, both the political and labor market contexts in which the organization is embedded and the institutional context of the organization itself.

It is well established that political contexts affect mobilization, and research on political contexts has contributed to a more nuanced understanding of the ways broad structures as well as institutional practices affect the prospects for social change efforts to emerge. In particular, the concept of political context highlights the role of the state's more routine policies in channeling the activism of social movement organizations. For example, McCarthy and colleagues (1991) examined the role of federal tax law and postal service regulations in the United States. They found that the laws requiring non-profit organizations to be "nonpartisan" have a major impact on the day-to-day organization of activities, as well as the framing of social movement claims.

In subsequent work, McCarthy and his colleagues showed how relationships between protest groups and police have also served to channel forms of political protest. They found that government restrictions on people's rights to public assembly have evolved through a process of give-and-take between authorities and challengers, whereby authorities have sought to limit the time, place, and manner of public protests, while challengers have used the courts and other institutional mechanisms to press for more expansive rights to assembly and speech. This work highlights the ways states and other institutional actors "channel" social movement activities through often subtle and indirect means (e.g., McCarthy et al. 1999). Neoliberal economic trends over recent years have transformed public space even further, as shopping malls have replaced town commons as the primary public gathering spaces. The investment of public resources in the development of privately controlled consumer spaces, and the expansion of private housing communities further constrains the public forum (McCarthy and McPhail 2006).

In today's era of enhanced global interdependence, we find analysts rethinking their understanding of states and state power. The concept of political contexts can help us extend our analytical lens from conflicts that are usefully viewed in more localized terms to more global contexts. In particular, the notion that social movements are shaped by broad structural forces that affect distributions of economic resources and political power and that institutions play important roles to encourage, channel, and/or repress social change activism can be readily applied to a polity that is viewed in global, rather than national, terms. As we argue below, structural accounts of transnational, national, and local protest are critical to understand the relative strength of states, the utility of transnational activism, and the multiple access points for activists in this era of increasing globalization.

GLOBALIZATION AND ITS IMPLICATIONS
FOR THINKING ABOUT POLITICAL CONTEXTS

Globalization is not a new phenomenon, and in reality it is simply a new label for long-enduring social and economic processes (Arrighi and Drangel 1986; Chase-Dunn 1998; Chirot and Hall 1982; Robinson 2004; Wallerstein 1976, 1980). Sociologists have devoted extensive attention to the ways increasing interactions among national societies have affected social life on many levels, through processes such as modernization, urbanization, and secularization. The fact that we find similar patterns of behavior across many very diverse societies suggests that these processes have common structural roots, and that these roots extend beyond the national state context. For instance, Markoff's historical analysis (1996) showed that both social movements and democracy emerged through extensive transnational (and even pre-national) interactions that helped spread new ideas about politics and forms of collective action. Emerging pro-democracy forces learned from their counterparts around Europe, and practices diffused readily across national boundaries.

Popular politics has long spilled over national political boundaries, but the much more rapid speed and more extensive volume of these interactions—now commonly referred to as "globalization" have intensified transnational political activity. Some of the earliest organized social movements brought together people from a variety of cultural backgrounds around shared aims of, for instance, promoting an end to slavery, advancing equal political rights for women, and limiting the barbarism of warfare (Finnemore 1996a; Wittner 1993, 1997).

Nineteenth century transnational activism was similar to that of today in that it benefited from technological advances (Hanagan 2002) while also advocating notions of humanity that transcended geographically defined boundaries (Keck and Sikkink 1998; Rupp 1997). Today, we find thousands of civil society organizations that cross national borders, and more frequent and dramatic instances of transnational collective action. What forces are helping to push popular politics outside their traditional, nationally defined boundaries?

Structural accounts of social movements have highlighted the need for contemporary studies of social movements to consider states as actors within a broader system of players that make up what is an increasingly coherent and institutionalized global political arena. Most analyses portray national governments as embedded in networks of relationships with other states and international institutions. The ideas governments have about what their interests are and how they will pursue those interests are strongly influenced by these networks of relations (Boli and Thomas 1999; Finnemore 1996b; Frank et al. 2000; Meyer et al. 1997). The very basis of states' identity—the legal concept of sovereignty—is meaningful only in the international context where states themselves grant each other recognition. Analyses that do not account for this global system will fail to identify how global factors influence the articulation and negotiation of what might otherwise appear to be nationally rooted conflicts. And without considering how states are embedded within a broader system of relationships, we will underestimate how variations in state power may affect their responses to challengers. The next section summarizes the main elements of "globalization" and identifies how these processes are relevant for our understanding of the contemporary global political arena.

Economic Globalization

Many popular discussions of "globalization" refer implicitly to the idea that national economies are gradually becoming integrated into a single, global economy. While economic factors reflect just one aspect of globalization, any attempt to understand global political change must consider these underlying economic foundations. Analysts working in the World-Systems tradition have argued that the system of states is highly unequal, and that the global economic hierarchy is, for a variety of reasons, likely to persist, barring a major transformation of economic relations. "Core" or early-industrializing states have enjoyed the most benefits from the global expansion of capitalism, beginning with direct economic imperialism and colonial occupation. The "periphery" states have been—through colonization or some other form of unequal economic relations—relegated to a subordinate role in the world economic system. Economic globalization institutionalizes and reinforces this inequality (e.g., Bello 2000; Korzeniewicz and Moran 1997, 2006). "Semiperipheral" states lie somewhere in the middle, as they have substantial enough resources to influence world market relations but they lack enough influence to play a leadership role in this system.

The organization of economic relationships in the core and periphery has meant that these exploitative core-periphery relationships have persisted, even as periphery states formally obtained their "independence." As states in the core depend upon southern markets and resources for their economic development, they have used their power to institutionalize their dominant position in the global economic order. For instance, McMichael (2003) showed how the post-WWII settlement shaped a "national development project" that gradually evolved into a global market-oriented "globalization project," serving to perpetuate and even expand inequities between core and periphery states.

World-system scholarship has informed more recent attempts to articulate class-based analyses of global political and economic relations. Leslie Sklair (2001) analyzed the discourses and structures of the world's leading transnational corporations to assess whether we can speak of an emergent "transnational capitalist class." He argued that transnational corporate structures and the practices involved in reproducing and advancing a vision of globalized capitalism has indeed generated a social grouping that may be called a transnational capitalist class. Sklair showed how agents operating as part of this class have systematically advanced the interest of globalized capital over other interests and agendas. Similarly, Robinson (2004) made the case that a collection of corporate actors and their political allies have systematically altered relationships between states and citizens while shaping global institutional configurations. Opposing the transnational capitalist class is a structurally disadvantaged labor movement, which has been limited in its influence by the compromise strategy of business unionism used by organized labor in the global north, or the core countries (O'Brien 2000). This approach may have suited the short-term interests of some workers, but it has contributed to nationalist divisions in the labor movement that have contributed to labor's decline in the latter part of the twentieth century.[2]

An important conclusion from research on global economic relationships is that a state's position in the global economic hierarchy affects both its vulnerability to international pressure as well as the domestic political context. Core states in the world economic system depend on cheap labor and other resources from the periphery in order to support both high levels of consumption among their citizens as well as the maintenance of their predominant position in the world economy (Chase-Dunn 1998:42–3). Labor protests helped establish workers' rights in those countries, and protest mobilization throughout the nineteenth and twentieth centuries helped expand democratic rights and protections (Tilly 1995). Thus, citizens in core states have comparatively more opportunities and resources for participating in social movements, and—perhaps more importantly their governments have greater capacities for responding to citizens' demands (Arrighi 1999; Markoff 1999).

In contrast, citizens in periphery countries are far more likely to face violent repression (Jenkins and Schock 1992; Podobnik 2004; Walton and Seddon 1994). Because core states depend on cheap access to goods and labor from the periphery, they have an interest in maintaining political conditions in those countries that suit their economic interests. This further limits opportunities for political mobilization in the periphery. Not only are opportunities for political participation more limited in the periphery, but because their governments are so dependent on international finance and aid, their experiences are more strongly determined by global-level processes than are the domestic opportunities of activists in core states. So the policies of the World Bank and International Monetary Fund have more immediate consequences for people in countries that borrow money from these institutions—the global South—and yet the decisions taken in these organizations are determined by just a handful of core states. This leaves periphery citizens dually disenfranchised, since they have limited ability to influence their own governments that, in turn, have little capacity to influence the global policies that most affect them. As formal democracy has spread to periphery regions, some

---

[2] Recent years have witnessed a renewal of transnational labor organizing, and Ronaldo Munck (2002) has argued that we may be seeing a new "great transformation," similar to labor's success in reigning in the most destructive elements of early industrializing capital (see also Moody 1997; O'Brien forthcoming).

analysts have used the term "democratizing disempowerment" to describe the paradoxical position of the people of the global South (Hippler 1995).[3]

Despite the relative powerlessness of the global South, it is here that some analysts see the most promising developments in social movements. For instance, some analysts have identified new forms of political organizing in global South countries that may reinvigorate institutionalized politics in those countries while also providing models for parties elsewhere (Baiocchi 2004; Markoff 2003).[4] Semiperiphery countries such as Brazil, South Korea, and South Africa are also sites of labor movement revitalization, and transnational ties among labor groups as well as between labor and other movement sectors are seen as one of the most promising developments in contemporary global justice activism (Baiocchi 2004; Keck and Sikkink 1998; Levering 1997; Moody 1997; Munck 2002; O'Brien forthcoming; Waterman and Timms 2004).

Political Globalization

Alongside global economic integration, we see the formation and strengthening of international institutions designed to help states manage their external as well as internal insecurities. These insecurities are not only military, but also involve environmental, economic, and public health concerns, among others. Some speak of this process as "internationalization," in contrast to economic "globalization" (Daly 2002; Tarrow 2001). Internationalization refers to the development of formal cooperative relationships among states, usually through formal treaties and the establishment of international organizations.

The expansion of intergovernmental agencies that address substantive issues creates both challenges and opportunities for social movement actors. On the one hand, when governments relinquish part of their authority to global institutions, they undermine the traditional channels of political accountability. This leads to what is called the "democratic deficit" of international institutions, which are typically staffed by appointed rather than elected officials who have few if any ties to local or national constituencies (Evans 1997; Markoff 1999; Tilly 1995). In some instances, particularly within the global financial institutions, international officials are selected for their technical expertise alone, and institutional cultures either ignore or disdain democratic values (Markoff and Montecinos 1993; Montecinos 2001; Stiglitz 2003). In fact, the World Trade Organization (WTO) even posted on its Web site a "top ten list" of the main benefits of the WTO, which included the supposed "benefit" of "protecting governments from the influences of special interests" within their borders. Why is it that proponents of international trade oppose more input and oversight from groups that are affected by policies?

While international institutions can undermine democracy, they can also be used to strengthen democracy by enhancing transparency and providing opportunities and

---

[3] The end of the Cold War has also reduced the ability of states in the global South to impact global policy. During the era of competition between the U.S. and Soviet Union, these two countries courted Third World allies as a way to advance their own ideological positions and influence in the global system. With the demise of the USSR, there is no counterweight to the pro-capitalist initiatives of the U.S., and the lone superpower status of the U.S. means that it no longer needs to cultivate allies from among the world's poorer regions. Thus, we see declining flows of international aid between the global North and South, as well as a reduced political influence of global South countries in the inter-state system that has contributed to the strengthening of the Bretton Woods Institutions relative to the United Nations.

[4] There is also evidence that political parties in Western contexts are responding to pressures from contemporary global protests (see, e.g., della Porta, Donatella et al. 2006).

resources for social movements to strengthen their position vis-à-vis other more powerful actors (Hafner-Burton and Tsutsui 2005; Keck and Sikkink 1998; Korzeniewicz and Smith 2000; Risse, Ropp, and Sikkink 1999; Sassen 1998; Smith et al. 1997; Tarrow 2001). The fact that international institutions are charged with addressing global problems relating to peace, the environment, and human rights means that within these organizations, social movements can find powerful allies as well as material and symbolic resources. In fact, because international agencies lack the "natural" constituencies that support local and national elected officials, international officials see a need to build direct links between their agencies and popular groups. The fact that governments have signed international declarations and treaties indicating their support for the values movements advance provides both international and legal legitimacy for activists' claims as well as political leverage against states that would prefer to maintain reputations of good global citizenship. Although governments may sign treaties with no intention of actually implementing them, no government welcomes—and most actively resist—attempts to bring international attention to their violations of these treaties.[5]

The pattern of increased formalization and bureaucratization of interstate structures parallels the evolution of the modern state. Just as we saw with the rise of the modern national state, we see that social movements have had a similar relationship to global institutions as they do to national ones. They have pressed for the expansion of global institutions to establish citizens' rights and to promote and protect social welfare, and they have reinforced these institutions by making appeals to international authorities and norms (see, e.g. Smith 1995). This process parallels the strategy of U.S. civil rights activists, who appealed to federal authorities and the U.S. Constitution against repressive state and local officials. And as states move political decisions into transnational political arenas, we find more and more evidence that social movements are adapting their strategies to respond to—if not to affect—these shifts in the locus of authority.

Scholars who have examined the ways social movements make use of international political arenas in their struggles have used a variety of concepts to describe how internationalization affects movements' mobilizing prospects. Marks and McAdam, for instance, describe it as a system of "multilevel governance" arguing that,

> Whereas the classic nation-state tended to define the 'structure of political opportunities' for *all* challenging groups, the emergence of a multi-level polity means that movements are increasingly likely to confront highly idiosyncratic opportunity structures defined by that unique combination of governmental bodies (at all levels) which share decision making authority over the issues of interest to the movement. So instead of the rise of a single new social movement form, we are more apt to see the development and proliferation of multiple movement forms keyed to inherited structures and the demands of mobilization in particular policy areas. (1996:119)

Rothman and Oliver (1999) used the notion of "nested political opportunity structures," where "[l]ocal political opportunity structures are embedded in national political opportunity structures, which are in turn embedded in international political opportunity structures" (p. 43; see also Boyer and Hollingsworth 1997:470), creating possibilities for complex patterns of relations among actors seeking political influence. Tarrow (2001) sees a "composite polity," whereby international agreements add another overlapping layer to an

---

[5] Here we find an important link between structural and cultural accounts of social movements, as global institutions are seen as spaces where social movements and other actors compete to define global norms as well as to promote their implementation (Clark 2003; Risse et al. 1999; Sikkink 2005).

already existing national polity, creating "opportunities for coalitions of actors and states to formulate common positions and overcome their diversity and dispersion to exploit its political opportunities" (pp. 243–244).

The key point here is that as decisions of national governments become increasingly subject to political processes beyond national borders, existing structures designed to provide for public input and accountability can no longer ensure democratic governance. We must therefore understand the global political system as a set of interconnected and interdependent national polities linked by a growing array of international institutions. As the international political system expands and exerts more influence on people's everyday experiences, we see intensified demands for enhanced democracy in global institutions. Social movements have increasingly cultivated transnational alliances to enhance their influence in shaping the structures of global regulation and accountability (e.g., Clark 2003; Foster and Anand 1999; Fox and Brown 1998; Khagram, Riker, and Sikkink 2002; Smith, Chatfield, and Pagnucco 1997).

Social movements have long been involved in struggles to define the global political context and to support and expand international law. Throughout history, social movement actors have pressed governments to adopt new and different approaches to the world outside their borders. We now take for granted the idea that slavery is something that no society should allow, that governments engaged in warfare must adhere to some minimal standards of human decency, and that the world's sea beds are the common inheritance of all people. Without the tireless efforts of a relatively small number of dedicated citizen advocates, governments are unlikely to have agreed to these formal rules that limit their sovereignty (e.g., Chatfield 1997; Keck and Sikkink 1998; Levering 1997). More recently, social movement pressures have led to the adoption of important new treaties such as the International Convention to Ban Land Mines and the International Criminal Court (e.g., Glasius 2002; Price 1998; J. Smith forthcoming). Few analysts would disagree that without the concerted efforts of citizens' groups around the world, neither of these treaties would have been adopted. And despite continued opposition from the United States, both treaties were among the fastest to enter into force, setting new speed records in the evolution of international law. Transnational social movements have proved an important antidote to the glacial pace of many intergovernmental negotiations.

In addition to pressing for new laws that might limit and constrain state action, social movements play key roles to bring pressure on governments to comply with international norms and standards. Keck and Sikkink (1998) refer to this as the "boomerang effect," whereby citizens finding their governments unresponsive to domestic pressures appeal to international allies and institutions to bring international pressure onto their governments. Without such citizen efforts to engage "boomerangs" in many places around the world, the correspondence of national practice with international human rights and other norms would be very weak indeed. Key international human rights bodies rely on civil society groups to "name and shame" governments into complying with human rights norms. The boomerang process contributes to the "domestication" of international law (J. Smith forthcoming; Tarrow 2005). We should note, however, that these global-local pressures can also work in the other direction. For example, Stewart's analysis (2004) of an indigenous Guatemalan movement for the proper burial of victims of a political massacre indicate that local transnational activism can bring pressure to bear on global institutions, such as the World Bank, in addition to local governments.

Cultural Globalization

Global integration has important influences on the cultures and collective identities of communities everywhere. For instance, the extensive flow of information about diverse cultures helps encourage an appreciation for the diversity and richness of different peoples' histories and traditions. It can also foster perceptions of relative deprivation and rising expectations as global marketing promotes images of consumption pattern that eludes vast portions of the world's population. This helps fuel defensive responses from groups that perceive such information as threatening to their own cultural practices and identities (Barber 1995).

At the same time as it poses very real threats to many cultural traditions, the expansion of what might be called a global culture or at least a global media market also facilitates transnational dialogue and communication of all sorts. It helps create common grievances and reference points and shared sets of ideas upon which social movements and other groups can build. To unite individuals from very diverse political and cultural backgrounds, social movements must cultivate some shared ideologies and identities that help define a joint purpose and form a basis for trust and solidarity. Transnational associations cultivate group identities that transcend the geographic ones defined by national states. They encourage people, for instance, to emphasize their identity with their profession (i.e, the International Sociological Association), their hobby (i.e., the International Chess Club), or their political views (i.e., People's Global Action) over political nationalities. And important mobilizations have taken place in recent decades among diverse indigenous peoples around the world (Brysk 2000; Passy 1999). Indeed, many participants in these groups find that they have far more in common with the other members of the group than they do with many compatriots (Minkoff 1997a; J. Smith 1998).

Cultural globalization is therefore reinforced by both economic and political processes, and it helps provide a foundation upon which both of those processes build. While this chapter emphasizes the more structural aspects of globalization, it must be said that the cultural materials—the ideas, traditions, practices, and identities—that constitute culture have important influences on the processes we examine here. And indeed these cultural artifacts are shaped by the broader institutions and structures discussed throughout the chapter (Boli and Thomas 1999; Inglehart and Baker 2000; Meyer 2003). Of particular importance is the notion that transnational processes and interactions are helping to generate new ideas of citizenship and loyalty that are challenging traditional, nationally bounded identities. These provide important cultural foundations for transnational social movement mobilization.

Contextualizing the State

It is increasingly clear that the political contexts within particular states cannot be understood independently of that state's relations to other actors in the global system. There has been fairly extensive debate about the relative importance of global, as opposed to national, structures and institutions on the trajectories of social movements (e.g., Imig and Tarrow 2001; Koopmans and Statham 1999a; Laxer and Halperin 2003). Numerous analysts caution against arguments suggesting that a growth in global level institutions and policies signals the demise of the national state (e.g., Tarrow, 1998a). Some also show that earlier eras of global integration represented comparable or even greater levels of international trade and investment, questioning whether today's globalization is fundamentally new or different (Hanagan 2002; Laxer and Halperin 2003).

Without denying the continued importance of states, we emphasize the idea that the complex web of global relations has significant impacts on state structures and capacities, and this, in turn, influences the possibilities for movement mobilization and impact. Global institutions, structures, and processes are simultaneously shaping both states and other political actors, including social movements (and vice versa). Global institutions affect not only the political and legal contexts that define opportunities and constraints for states and all other actors, but they also influence the collective identities of those actors. Thus, the practices of states vis-à-vis their own citizens are increasingly defined in global terms (e.g., Reimann 2002; Sassen 1998). Moreover, the notion of a state itself is irrelevant without an interstate context of other states able to recognize the rights and legitimacy of a given national authority. Collectivities define themselves in terms of broader sets of relationships, and an interstate system provides the context that encourages and facilitates the elaboration of both national and transnational identities (Boli and Thomas 1999). As Buss and Hermann conclude,

> To dismiss transnational activism as relevant only in terms of domestic politics overlooks the extent to which international law and policy are important realms in their own right. The 'international' is more than just the space 'outside' of the domestic. It has taken on a significance as, among other things, a site of struggle over the shape and meaning of social relations in the context of global change. (2003:134)

Gay Seidman's analysis of anti-apartheid and labor activism leads her to conclude that activists are capable of articulating multiple identities in the course of their struggles, or "shifting the ground" on which they work, moving quite easily across national borders. The fact that many conflicts are oriented around national political structures is merely an artifact of the institutional arrangements in which people are embedded:

> [...] the institutional fact that international bodies are generally composed of national representatives forces potentially global identities into national frames. But it need not blind us to the possibility that activists might under other circumstances frame their concerns more globally. (2000:347)

While recognizing how global relations have transformed the nature of the state over time, we must also avoid another conceptual pitfall of thinking that global politics *must* take place in transnational contexts. Looking at women's activism in India, Subranamiam and her colleagues found that analyses of the global downplay the extent to which globally relevant politics occur in local settings:

> [Although] global processes are often viewed as taking place in a world context, above nation states, networks can be anchored between and across all borders (villages, districts, states, and nations) involving actors and groups at the grassroots. (Subramaniam, Gupte, and Mitra 2003:335)

These observations[6] suggest that we must relax our traditional notions of borders and instead see states as just a bundle of comparatively dense networks of relations that has a variety of diverse, and expanding, ties to similar national networks and to other transnational actors around the world. This networked, multilayered political structure provides the context in which social movements, states, and other political actors contend. As Tilly (1984, 1990)

---

[6] Is it just a coincidence that they are all made by women?!

found in his research on the rise of the modern state, it is these contentious interactions that are constantly shaping and reshaping social institutions at the local, national, and global levels. Thus, through their interactions with states and other global actors, social movements are helping to shape the course of globalization—even if the results aren't completely consistent with movement aims.

FROM ORGANIZATIONS
TO MOBILIZING STRUCTURES

Another key concept in structural approaches to social movements is the notion of *mobilizing structures*. This refers to the formal and informal organizations and networks that facilitate routine communication and coordination among groups of people. Early research in this tradition emphasized the importance of formal organizations—or social movement organizations or SMOs—to the development of social movements (McCarthy and Zald 1973, 1977). Though important debates have been waged in the literature on the tensions between the demands of building organizations and challenging predominant power relations,[7] most analysts accept that without some effort to organize, no movement can mobilize a sustained flow of resources and energy toward social change efforts.

Research in this area shows that SMOs have become routine and enduring features of the modern political landscape, contributing to what scholars have referred to as a "movement society." As we discuss in more detail later, the movement society refers to the increased prevalence in modern societies of formal and professionally staffed organizations advocating for social and political change (Meyer and Tarrow 1998; Tarrow 1998b). While social movement organizations have become more prevalent and professional, they still vary tremendously along a number of important dimensions. This variation affects both the audiences an SMO can reach as well as the likelihood that a given organization or movement will be successful in realizing its goals. For instance, organizations adopt more or less formal structures, work at different levels (e.g., local, national), depend on more or less volunteer labor, and have differing access to the resources they need for their work (Edwards and McCarthy 2004; Edwards and Marullo 1995, 2003; McCarthy and Wolfson 1996).

In addition, different movements and organizations vary in their strategic approaches to policy processes. While some engage formal political institutions by mobilizing voters or lobbying policymakers, others engage in "outsider" strategies such as public demonstrations or civil disobedience, and many groups use some combination of conventional and protest forms of political action. Cross-nationally, we find even more variation in how movements are organized, and this variation is shaped in part by the formal political institutions that define the possibilities for political mobilization as well as by historical and cultural traditions. For example, in authoritarian settings such as Kenya and China we find pro-democracy advocacy emerging through organizations and activities framed in environmental terms (Economy 2004; Michaelson 1994), whereas movements in core countries tend to form professional social movement organizations specifically devoted to their social change aims. Another important organizational difference seems to parallel class rather than national variation, as social movements for the poor may tend to be larger and more formal and hierarchical in structure than those of middle class activists (e.g., Lichterman 1996; Polletta 2002; Wood 2005).

---

[7] See, e.g., Piven and Cloward (1979); Gamson and Schmeidler (1984).

The concept of mobilizing structures takes the focus away from organizations specifically devoted to promoting social change (SMOs) to emphasize the roles that groups such as churches, unions, and others not explicitly focused on political advocacy play in most social movements. It has also sensitized scholars to the ways particular organizations or clusters of organizations (known as "populations") relate to each other and to their environments as they struggle to maintain their organization and promote social change (Hannan and Freeman 1977; McPherson and Rotolo 1996; Minkoff 1995, 1997b). This has led many analysts to include in their analyses a range of other types of less formal groupings as well as formal organizations that are not explicitly devoted to the aims of a movement. Especially in repressive contexts, the key organizational structures and networks that are engaged to challenge authorities are unlikely to be explicit in their oppositional stance. So, for instance, opposition to authoritarian regimes in Eastern Europe, Latin America, and South Africa emerged from religious institutions (Borer 1998; Chilton 1995; Mueller 1999; C. Smith 1996; Thomas 2001).

Successful movements are not necessarily those that generate their own organizations but rather they are ones that compete successfully for adherents within multi-organizational fields (Campbell 2005). By mobilizing constellations of diverse organizations and networks in society, social movements help to amplify the voices of less powerful groups by aligning their interests and issues with a broader public agenda (e.g., McCarthy, Smith, and Zald 1996). Successful movements are thus those that find their way into what we might call the structures of everyday life (Wuthnow 1998).

A variety of conditions—ranging from overt political repression to far more subtle developments such as shifting party structures or living and working patterns—reduce the time and space most citizens have to join political organizations. Thus, movements must work against the tide to convince people that particular problems are both urgent and subject to change. To convey such notions, movements must reach people within their daily routines of earning a living and raising families. By cultivating connections to groups such as labor unions, parent-teacher associations, churches, and other civic associations, SMOs can reach a much broader audience than they otherwise could. Increasingly, both activists and analysts use the term "networks" to characterize the broad and dense relationships among diverse types of organizations coming together around particular goals (della Porta 2005; Diani 1995, 2003; Escobar 2003; Escobar and Alvarez 1992; Rucht 2004). The notions of fluidity and contingency that networks imply shift the focus of research away from questions about whether or not organizations help or hinder movements to questions about how particular sets of relationships affect possibilities for social change.

Early Scholarship in Social Movement Organizations

The earliest scholars of collective action focused on the collective psychology and irrational actions of crowd behavior at political protest rallies. This scholarship was seen as critical of the activists, painting a portrait of irrational actors led by their emotions alone. In the 1970s, a handful of scholars set about to correct this partial portrait of collective behavior by documenting the rational, even bureaucratic, aspects of social movement activity. For example, Turner and Killian (1957) documented various types of social movements, and Killian (1964) argued that successful social movements become institutionalized in some way.

RESOURCE MOBILIZATION. Against this backdrop of debate about the emotionality of social movements, McCarthy and Zald (1973) borrowed from rational choice theory in their seminal work that outlines resource mobilization theory. Resource mobilization argues that social movements in the contemporary period have become professionalized. They see social movements as part of the flow of normal politics, with cycles of protest and quiescence. They demonstrate that much of the work of social movements is done by paid professionals in formal organizations, whose jobs include collecting, channeling and managing money, resources, and time. Their emphasis on social movement organizations meant that, rather than considering social action from the perspective of the individual participant, we can understand social movements to be the result of "social movement entrepreneurs" mobilizing individual participation by fostering discontent and channeling it into formal social movement organizations.

Resource mobilization theory focuses on the material resources, organizational capacities (including skills and networks), and tactics that enable organizations to mobilize support to address these grievances. They develop a framework for understanding movement success as a function of the resources available to social movement actors. Access to external resources—money, media attention, institutional ties, is considered at least as important to movement emergence or social movement outcomes as any individual processes. Gamson (1990 [1975]) provided an important test of these propositions by analyzing the outcomes of various social movements. He examined 53 "challenging groups" in the United States, and found that success entailed groups with reformist objectives that make use of available channels of political participation, such as the electoral system and political lobbying, were more successful than those who took to the streets. Lipsky (1968) posited that while powerful groups can engage in direct confrontation, relatively powerless groups used protest as a leverage to increase their bargaining ability. Protest groups were successful to the extent that they could gain the support of "reference publics" who would join the conflict in ways favorable to their protest goals.

Oberschall (1973) similarly emphasized the role of material and organizational resources in mobilizing people and channeling their action. In his analysis of the United States civil rights movement, he demonstrated that sympathetic third parties, such as northern whites and political insiders, were important to the effectiveness of civil disobedience as a protest tactic. Jenkins and Perrow's study (1977) of three farm worker union movements showed that support from third parties, such as labor unions and liberal interest groups were integral to movement success.

MOBILIZING STRUCTURES. Resource mobilization's focus on the institutionalization of social movement activity has led researchers to consider the role of social movement organizations in fostering mobilization, facilitating activism, and producing social change. Debates in this area, however, have stressed the inherent tensions between movements' need for flexibility and the demands of organizational maintenance (e.g., Oliver 1989). Scholars have also pointed to the wide variety of organizational forms that movement actors have used to build their struggles, noting how these differ from conventional assumptions about formal organizations (Ferree and Mueller 2004; Marwell and Oliver 1993; Staggenborg and Taylor 2005). Also important is the central importance of alliance-building to social movements' work, which contributes to their relatively amorphous and variable structures. Thus, the concept of mobilizing structures has been applied to help sensitize analysts to the importance of both formal and informal organizations or networks to most social movements. The mobilizing structures concept emphasizes the fact that most social movements combine diverse sets of actors—some of which are explicitly organized around movement goals and others that are organized for other social purposes (McCarthy 1996). How these diverse forms combine to form particular movements, moreover, is largely affected by the broader political context (Kriesi 1996). This concept was particularly useful in helping scholars explore relationships between the professional social movement organizations that had become increasingly dominant in the United States context and other organized and informal elements of movements. Professional SMOs are formal organizations that tend to have paid staff members to help organize fundraising, lobbying, and protest actions such as letter-writing campaigns (McCarthy and Zald 1973). Such organizations themselves can be key agents of social change, even when they have only limited participation by grassroots supporters. They can help sustain movement foundations and develop movement critiques even in times of movement abeyance (Rupp and Taylor 1987).

Such professional organizations are by no means the only example of mobilizing structures. Other classic accounts of mobilizing structures in social movements include Sara Evans' analysis (1980) of the informal friendship networks among women in the civil rights and New Left movements that gave rise to the women's liberation movement, and numerous examples of the role that black churches played in fostering the civil rights movement (McAdam 1982; Morris 1984). As we discuss later, global justice activists are inventing new, networked structures to support diverse forms of activism and movement goals. It is widely agreed that the organizational capacities of these various mobilizing structures deserve the attention of social movements scholars.

Ironically, despite resource mobilization's explicit emphasis on the organizational dynamics of social movement activity, social movements scholars have paid relatively little attention to the systematic study of organizations themselves (McCarthy and Zald 2002). And most work tends to be case studies of particular movement groups. What literature exists tends to focus on the level of formal organizational structure in social movements, as well as changes in organizational forms over time (e.g. Rucht 1999; Staggenborg 1988; Voss and Sherman 2000). This scholarship has found that, while many social movements do become "professionalized," meaning that they move from informal, grassroots organizations to centralized, bureaucratized organizations over time, there are numerous examples to the contrary (Edwards and Foley 2003; Edwards and McCarthy 2004; Kriesi 1996). Further, professionalization is not a singular process, and the degree of formality and centralization can vary. There is often a difference, for example, between the level of bureaucratization at higher organizational levels, such as a national office, than at local levels (Edwards and Foley 2003; Oliver and Furman 1989).

Organizations in Recent Scholarship

More recent work has sought to bridge the fields of social movement studies with the sociology of organizations. A small number of scholars have shown how analyses of organizational populations can contribute to our understanding of various dimensions of social movement organizational dynamics (McCarthy et al. 1988; Minkoff 1993). The emergence, growth and decline of social movement organizations have been important topics of study for social movement scholars (e.g., Zald and Garner 1994). Another important area of inquiry has been the relationship between social movement organizations and social movements. Studies of social movements over time often show that even when organizations are small or absent, the larger movement can carry on (e.g., Taylor 1989). Nonetheless, most scholars agree that social movement organizations are important centers for social movement activity.

Some scholarship has moved beyond studies of organizational populations to draw attention to the embeddedness of social movement organizations in various social, political, and institutional contexts. A recent collection explores various connections between the fields of social movements and organizational studies (Davis et al. 2005). This work emphasizes the need to account for broader organizational "fields," in which numerous organizations operate, cooperate, and compete in order to understand social movement dynamics. By examining social movements as players within these organizational fields, scholars can recognize the diversity of organizational forms within social movements, the response of social movement organizations to shifts in political contexts, and the relationships among social movement organizations.

For example, examining the case of the environmental movement in North Carolina, Andrews and Edwards (2005) looked at the relationship between an organization's position in the field and a number of aspects of their activism, such as the tactics they choose and whether they participate in coalitions with other organizations. They consider local organizations' affiliations with national groups, and their willingness to form coalitions with other local groups. They find that local organizations are more likely to be affiliated with a national organization than a state or regional organizations, but that they are less likely to ally themselves with organizationally distinct groups that share similar interests than state and regional groups are. This finding suggests that the field of environmental organizations is structured in such a way that inhibits coalitions between local groups, but facilitates cooperation between mid-level state and regional groups.

A number of social movement case studies analyze the fields of activism as well. One recent example is Elizabeth Armstrong's (2002) analysis of the lesbian and gay movement in San Francisco. Armstrong demonstrates that the emergence of a number of identity-based organizations in the 1970s was reflective of a new social movement field crystallizing around the concept of gay and lesbian identity, as opposed to the more radical New Left ideologies that previous organizations held. Similarly, Raka Ray's (1999) analysis of women's movement groups in India surveys the fields of activism in which movement organizations are positioned. This work shows the utility of the concept of organizational fields for understanding how organizational identities and tactics develop over time, through interactions with movement allies and opponents. The field-level analysis highlights a promising if underexplored approach to understanding the inter-organizational dynamics that influence movement activities. It also points to important relationships between structural and cultural approaches to the study of social movements.

Other scholars also consider the increasing importance of coalition building among organizations, including the factors that foster coalitions among movement organizations. In her analysis of six decades of student activism on college campuses, Nella Van Dyke (2003) found that movement organizations are more likely to work across social movement boundaries in the presence of a threat that affects multiple movements, while they are more likely to work together within movements in the presence of local threats. Gillian Murphy's analysis (2005) of the interdependencies of movement organizations suggested that there are unintended consequences to coalitions, however. She argues that increased coalition activity suppresses the emergence of new organizations, even as it optimizes the distribution of resources among coalitions. Coalitions are a particularly important aspect of transnational activism, which we discuss later.

GLOBALIZATION
AND MOBILIZING STRUCTURES

Studies of social movements in different parts of the world have generated important new questions and insights into the factors shaping social movements. For instance, why do movements in distant places tend to adopt similar forms, tactics, and ideologies? And why do we see an increasing tendency of activists from different countries to come together around common struggles? Marco Giugni (2002) summarizes three explanations for this. The first is that changes at the global level—such as international economic and political integration—generate common sets of complaints (e.g., loss of jobs due to trade competition) and targets (e.g., transnational corporations or international institutions) around which movements mobilize. Second, global political coordination has produced similar government structures within states (Meyer et al. 1997), something analysts call "structural affinity." Because the organization of governments is more similar across different national contexts, activists can more readily share useful knowledge and experiences across national borders. Third, the proliferation of international exchanges of all sorts—including international travel, communication, and expanding use of the Internet—greatly enhances opportunities for citizens in all countries to communicate with others around the world and to share ideas and experiences about political participation, among other activities. Global interconnectedness also increases the vulnerability of governments to international pressures.

Global integration thus affects both the ways people engage in political participation and state responses to popular pressures. Increasing flows of information and ideas as well as growing numbers of ties between people and organizations from diverse nations affect the character of societies and governments everywhere. First, they have helped produce a global emergence of what analysts have called a "movement society."[8] Once thought to be sporadic and short-term forms of political involvement, social movements are proving to be more permanent fixtures in all democratic political systems. A movement society perspective understands social movements as central to politics and to the evolution of social and political institutions at national and global levels.

Second, as we discussed earlier, increasing volumes of social, political, and economic interactions that cross national boundaries challenges the abilities of governments to affect conditions within their borders while making it increasingly difficult to separate national from global policy processes. As each nation's activities have more obvious impacts beyond their national borders, more decisions that once were the sole domain of national governments are now subject to international pressures and regulations. Social movements both contribute to and respond to these two interrelated developments.

A Global Movement Society?

According to Mayer Zald, key characteristics of today's movement society include "the growth of a relatively continuous social movement sector, the development of [social movement organizations] as enduring features of the society, the professionalization of movement

---

[8] See, e.g., Tarrow (1998b; Zald and McCarthy 1987; Rochon 1998). Tarrow is most explicit in his discussion of the parallel processes of globalization and the rise of a social movement society.

Box 2.1.   Transnational Social Movement Strategies in Multilevel Politics

This section discusses how political decisions are increasingly shaped by global policy arenas. This has altered the way many activists organize their political strategies. In particular, it often requires that activists operate at multiple levels simultaneously, or at least that they understand how politics at the global level impact the possibilities for local activism. We can identify several distinct, "multilevel" strategies in contemporary transnational campaigns. The first is the classic "boomerang" model discussed by Keck and Sikkink (1998), whereby activists look outside the state to international institutions to bring outside pressure on national governments. Such a strategy is evident in many human rights campaigns, when human rights advocates bring their grievances to international organizations or other international audiences in the hopes that other governments and international agencies will raise the costs of continued rights violations within their countries (e.g., Risse et al. 1999; Sikkink 1993). Such transnational coalitions activists' interpretations of how global forces affect local conditions, and several authors remind us of the mutual directions of influence between local human rights groups and their transnational allies (e.g., Rothman and Oliver 2002; Stewart 2004; Hertel 2006). In addition to seeking greater government adherence to international norms, activists work to shape the international normative context itself. By proposing and lobbying for new international agreements, and they help institutionalize new norms as well as mechanisms for their enforcement. For instance, citizens' groups were at the forefront of new treaties to ban landmines and to form the International Criminal Court (Glasius 2002; Price 1998). And indigenous communities have been very active internationally to press for their rights to self-determination within the international legal order (Brysk 2000; Passy 1999). Campaigns like that working to ban international trade in toxic wastes work at both levels to help define international norms while also pressing national governments to act (J. Smith 1999). And more recently we see more examples of "defensive transnationalization" by groups aiming to defend existing rights of democratic participation against encroachments by global institutions (Sikkink 2005).

leadership, and the transition from a search for [social movement] membership in the polity, to the search for specific policy outcomes" (1987:321). In other words, we see an ongoing and fairly stable mobilization of people and resources away from more conventional modes of political participation and toward more protest-oriented forms (Norris 2002). At the same time, movements are taking on a more formally structured character, adapting themselves to become more stable features of the institutional environments in which they operate (Soule and Earl 2005).

A movement society perspective thus anticipates that protest or movement politics will only become more central to the operation of our political institutions. Long-term shifts in the structure of our economies and political systems—such as urbanization, expansion of the scope and scale of government, increases in professionalization and in the centrality of information to economic and political life—make it easier for potential challengers to mobilize resources and people to promote social change (McCarthy and Zald 1987). At the same time, however, they also enhance the capacities of governments and corporate actors to resist changes that threaten their economic and political interests (McMichael 2003).

Because states are embedded within an increasingly dense web of relationships to other states, they have adopted—not always voluntarily—similar ways of organizing social relations and state functions (Meyer et al. 1997). This "structural affinity" has allowed for the development of a globalized movement society, since social change advocates everywhere find that they face similar conditions within their national contexts, or that the targets of localized grievances are interstate institutions (Giugni 2002; Walton and Seddon 1994). The need to develop strategies and organizational resources in order to confront modern states helps generate modularity among social movement forms that defies national and cultural differences (e.g., Tarrow 2005; Traugott 1995). And as the world capitalist economy unifies the world labor market through processes such as proletarianization, urbanization, industrialization, professionalization, and casualization, it structures both the capacities of diverse groups to resist exploitation as well as the specific conditions they are likely to protest (Boswell and Chase-Dunn 2000). In the text that follows we explore in more detail how large-scale changes in inter-state social institutions and processes have helped shape a global, movement society.

SOCIAL MOVEMENTS AND ECONOMIC CHANGE. In the preceding text we discussed above how military competition among states contributed to the expansion of state bureaucracies that could generate revenues through taxation and provide a growing range of services for citizens. States' need for revenues made them dependent on favorable ties to economic elitists, and most analyses of state formation treat the character of relations between state authorities and capitalists as central to the emergence and stability of democracy (e.g., Markoff 1996; Moore 1966; Tilly 1978; Wolf 1982; cf. Centeno 2002).[9]

Today it is largely taken for granted that the state should be involved in promoting the national economy, and today this often means that governments should help increase the global competitiveness of their "national" corporations (McMichael 2003; Moody 1997; Robinson 2004; Sklair 2001). But this assumption has not always existed, and it arose out of competitive interactions among globalizing states, international organizations and their officers, advocates of neoliberal globalization, and other organized social interests such as labor and other groups. Social movement challengers have long been involved in struggles to define the role of government and the character of local and national economies, and we have noted how they are increasingly mobilizing across national boundaries to transform global economic relations. At the same time, the policies designed to encourage economic development and to aid in the development of national states have also affected possibilities for social movements. In particular, both national states and the economies they fostered depended on mass media and education for their success. And these same institutions play central roles in our attempts to understand social movement development as well.

Mass Media. Benedict Anderson's work (1991) highlights the centrality of the promotion of a mass print media to the development of the modern nation state. He argues that the introduction of the printing press enabled emerging state authorities to cultivate national "imagined communities," such as France, where only locally defined communities had previously existed. For people to feel some connection with remote others, they needed some common

---

[9] Note: Latin American and other periphery and semi-periphery states are characterized by important differences in the relationship of states to capital and citizens. For instance, many Latin American countries supported their militaries through taxes on imports and exports, thereby eliminating the need for a democratizing bargain with citizen-taxpayers (Centeno 2002). We are grateful to John Markoff for this observation.

bond, and print media helped nurture such bonds. Together with systems of roadways that made direct contact more likely across groups within a given set of territorial boundaries, the print media helped expand people's sense of community to a wider, national level.[10]

Sidney Tarrow builds further on this notion of imagined communities to demonstrate how the print media also shaped the development of social movements. He argues that newspapers and journals allowed citizens with no direct contact to cultivate a sense of solidarity and shared experiences that made collective action more likely across very loosely connected networks. Moreover, print media contributed to a political leveling of society. It fostered greater scrutiny of political leaders who were once seen as "divine" rulers, and it expanded popular access to knowledge. In a sense, just as states were encouraging people to think of themselves as part of imagined national communities, social movement leaders were articulating other imagined identities around the shared experiences of exploitation and resistance (Tarrow 1998b).

The mass media represent an important site of struggle between those who benefit from the existing order and those who seek its transformation. To the extent that global processes are fostering the emergence of a global economy and political institutions, we would expect the mass media to be playing a similar role in cultivating shared assumptions and values as a way of fostering global markets and commitment to global institutions such as the European Union. We find what Leslie Sklair (2001) identifies as "consumerist elites," including merchants and mass media, to be an essential element of a "transnational capitalist class" that promotes a global capitalist order. Movements also recognize the importance of the mass media, even if they don't have equal access to its most visible forms.

Today, the Internet has amplified the traditional media forms and has become an important tool in this same process of disseminating information and fostering communication that both promotes the aims of governments while giving rise to various challenges to them. At the same time, the increasing privatization of the mass media reduces the space for programming that serves noncommercial, public purposes. Public concerns that directly threaten commercial interests, such as global warming and public health, receive limited and biased coverage in corporate-owned media.[11] Although the internet has helped create many new openings for public dialogue and communication, access to this technology varies widely cross-nationally and within countries. While the internet has facilitated access to information by people in poor countries and communities, the same groups have relatively less access to the technology and high-speed connections needed to make effective use of this medium (Bissio 1999). And increasing amounts of online material is now available only to paid subscribers, further exacerbating rich–poor inequalities in information access. Moreover, legislation like the U.S. Telecommunications Act of 1996 has helped centralize broadcast media in that country and constrained the diversity of and popular access to mainstream media sources (Herman 1995; Herman and Chomsky 1988; Kimball 1994; McChesney 1999). More broadly, international trade agreements on services threaten national governments' ability to influence media content and accessibility.

---

[10] We must remember, too, that, as they built systems of roadways and communications to cultivate national societies, nation-builders destroyed local communities and cultures. National languages displaced local and regional ones, and the process of national integration was often violent.

[11] Numerous scholars and policy analysts have engaged this question of whether and how corporate ownership affects the operation of the mass media. For instance, Project Censored offers an annual review of the top stories of the year that were un- or under- reported in the mass commercial media, based upon systematic reviews of the U.S. mainstream and alternative media by researchers (wee, e.g., Bennett and Entman 2001; Herman 1995; Herman and Chomsky 1988).

Education and Professionalization in the "Information Society." As governments have become involved in an increasing array of complex issues, and as global integration increases the complexity of economic and political life, the demand for expertise increases. Thus, states are increasingly faced with the challenge of educating their populations to build a skilled and globally competitive workforce. The professionalization and information-driven needs of government can undermine democracy and the prospects for popular mobilization by turning policy decisions into technical matters in which only experts can be involved. But most proponents of democracy would argue that many questions in which technical complexity is used as an excuse to limit public involvement in policy decisions are in fact political rather than technical ones. Experts can provide information relevant to policy debates—such as evaluations of evidence about global warming or of the effects of global trade on employment patterns—but they do not deserve a stronger voice than other citizens in the fundamentally political questions about how the benefits or risks associated with different policy choices should be distributed (e.g., Coleman and Porter 2000; Markoff and Montecinos 1993).

While the information needs of modern states can serve to exclude popular groups from policy arenas, an important consequence of education and professionalization within contemporary societies is the emergence of professionally-oriented associations that cultivate new, post-material identities and alliances that don't privilege national boundaries (Inglehart and Baker 2000; Melucci 1989). The expertise and professional credentials of such groups can counter the legitimacy and authority of governments (Moore 1996). Some analysts discuss the growing role of "epistemic communities"—or "networks of knowledge-based experts" in global policy decisions (Haas 1992).

A highly educated workforce is likely to be more independent and less deferential to state authorities than a less educated one. Educated citizens are better able to independently collect and analyze information and are less easily swayed by appeals to traditional charismatic authority. The availability of information and skills for analysis also makes governance more transparent, even in authoritarian settings. Thus, in contemporary society especially, political influence depends upon the effective mobilization of information (Florini 2003; Sikkink 2002).

The implications of these changes for social movements are numerous. First, the demand in government and the economy for highly skilled workers means that skills related to the mobilization and dissemination of information will be widely available in the population. Thus, movements mobilizing around highly technical problems can depend upon a certain level of knowledge within the population they seek to influence, and they also can hope to recruit activists with expertise related to the problems around which they are organizing. As Zald notes,

> The skills of networking, of meeting notification, of developing newsletters, have spread quite remarkably in the society. Networking, fund raising, and organizational techniques for utilizing the media are all transformed from techniques learned on the job to formally transmitted skills. (1987:329)

Sidney Verba and his colleagues also found a relationship between the skills people learned in the course of their everyday work routines and their participation in democratic politics (Verba, Schlozman, and Brady 1995).

Of course, as many have observed, the distribution of professional skills is by no means equitable, and we can expect to find higher concentrations of these capabilities among more privileged classes and groups. Moreover, given the stratification in the global labor market, we can also expect a higher concentration of such skills among populations in the richer countries of the global North. But Verba and his colleagues also found that, outside the workplace, participation in public associations such as churches and unions helped enhance people's skills for political participation. A wide range of studies show that people who are active in any form of association are also more involved in politics (e.g., Schofer and Fourcade-Gournchas 2001). This is due in part to the impacts these groups have not only on people's understandings of issues and access to information, but also on the skills they have in, for instance, public speaking, computing, policy analysis, coalition-building, etc. (Baiocchi 2003; Norris 2002; Verba et al. 1995).

In sum, the activities of governments aimed at promoting economic development expands the role of scientific professionals in government while also enhancing the pool of resources available to potential challengers. Today's economies depend on the rapid flow of information across national boundaries, and they demand a highly educated workforce. Structures that facilitate rapid communication and the development of technical skills also provide a foundation that citizens can use to mobilize interests that may counter those of economic and political elitists. And in the course of employing these resources in political contexts, challengers help transform political processes and institutions.

SOCIAL MOVEMENTS AND CIVIL SOCIETY.   While social movements are shaped by global political and economic changes, they also help transform the social contexts in which they operate (Rochon 1998). Political activism, according to Pippa Norris, is being reinvented around the world through the creation of new forms of association, new repertoires, and new targets for political action (Norris, 2002). Urbanization, education, communication, and other changes described above have contributed to the emergence of new values that are impacting political participation around the world (Curtis, Baer, and Grabb 2001; Inglehart and Baker 2000). Because these processes are global, they are producing parallel, although not identical, developments in different countries (Giugni 2002). To the extent that social movements help articulate and spread identities that challenge traditional loyalties (such as to national states or traditional political parties) and to the extent that they are active in promoting new forms of organizing and action, they are important catalysts in this "reinvention" of political action. Indeed, research on social movements shows that some protest tactics and movement actors become institutionalized (Meyer and Tarrow 1998), that is, they become part of the "normal" political process. Thus, the interactions between movements and more influential players in the policy process generate new ideas and forms of political action that shape subsequent action, organization, and policy (Kriesi 2004). So while movements might achieve relatively little in terms of their specific policy goals, they have, over time, exerted enormous influence over how we do politics today (e.g., Clemens 1996).

It is also important to remember that many different groups are seeking to mobilize popular support for their causes at any given time. While perhaps a majority of social movement actors work either directly or indirectly to advance democratic aims, we must keep in mind that anti-democratic movements adopt similar strategies and forms (Koopmans and Stratham 1999b). Indeed, the idea of a "movement society" anticipates that practices that evolve within the context of social movements will become institutionalized. As they do, a wider range of political actors will employ them in attempts at political gain. Moreover, those that democratic movements challenge—including corporations, governments, and other social groups—often appropriate ideas and action forms from progressive movements. Thus, we see corporate lobbyists engaging in efforts to demonstrate broad-based, "grassroots" support for policies they support by generating masses of public letters through "grass-tops" or "astroturf" campaigns (Faucheux 1995). And Nike has attempted (unsuccessfully) to appropriate its critics' approach by building its own Web site to criticize the company for allegedly producing such a superior product (Greenberg and Knight 2004). Corporate opponents of global agreements to reduce greenhouse gas emissions have employed similar strategies in order to prevent public mobilizations on environmental protection (McCright and Dunlap 2003). Thus, recent movement scholarship stresses the need to focus more attention on *interactions* between social movements and their opponents than has been the case in much research.

A movement society perspective, in short, seeks to link broader social changes with everyday practices throughout society. It sensitizes analysts to how issues and actors are defined through their interactions with other actors. It helps us understand politics as an ever-changing process involving the articulation of conflicts and struggles to win favorable policy outcomes. It also embeds social conflicts within a context of a globally integrated economy, recognizing that global-level actors and forces have helped create similarities in organizational forms across national societies. Also, a global economy implies a globalized labor market, whereby more and more people around the world are increasingly subjected to similar opportunities and pressures. Indeed, thousands of workers from scores of countries may be linked through a single complex commodity chain controlled by one transnational corporation (Silver 2003).

A key argument we are making here is that the processes that have shaped the development of a "movement society" are not confined to individual nations, and we can identify global trends that support the development of an interconnected, global movement society. This society shapes the evolution of national and international political institutions. National polities are nested within a much broader system of institutional relations, and analysts and citizens must consider how this influences any given political conflict by providing potential for alliances, symbolic or material resources, and/or political leverage for both challengers and authorities. Thus, we must view states as embedded within a broader network of transnational relationships to other states, international institutions, and other global actors. These complex relationships shape possibilities for movement emergence and impact, and we can also argue that the movement society itself is a global phenomenon.

Networks and Globalization

Another way we see globalization impacting social movements is in the increased recognition of—if not the reliance upon—networks as a form of social organization. While networks are certainly not new, globalization may be enhancing their prevalence and making actors more self-conscious of this form of social relationships. In the preceding section we discussed relations between globalization and the development of the social movement society because global processes have shaped fundamentally the ways people work, consume, socialize, and engage in political action. By linking production and consumption processes across geographic boundaries, global economic forces have led what were once highly varied communities to adopt similar forms of association and action. And the network form has thus been uniquely associated with globalization, since it adapts the modern formal bureaucratic organization to the demands placed on it by complex, rapidly changing, and highly uncertain environments (Castells 1996; Knoke 1990; Riles 2001). Thus, when scholars consider the mobilizing structures from which social change efforts are likely to emerge, they increasingly find themselves speaking in terms of "networks" of associations (Diani and McAdam 2003; Keck and Sikkink 1998; Khagram et al. 2002).

It is no coincidence that the concept of networks has gained prominence in the social sciences at the same time as we've seen a growing awareness of enhanced global interdependence and inter-connectedness. The evolution of modern political and social institutions has generated new forms of organization that resist the rigid structures and formalities of traditional bureaucratic institutions. As Wuthnow (1998) argues, changes in the demands on people's time, on the built environments in which people live, and in the character of our social and political institutions have generated a greater reliance on "loose connections," that foster communication and trust. Uncertain and changing environments require organizational flexibility and innovation, and so organizations must maintain ties to other actors in order to maximize their access to relevant information (Campbell and Pedersen 2001; Powell 1990). Thus, organizational analyses must increasingly address the reality that contemporary organizations are likely to have more porous and flexible organizational boundaries.

Much social movement scholarship focuses on contentious interactions between social movements and authorities, often neglecting the importance of movement links to affinity groups, public bystanders, and third-party mediators for explaining conflict dynamics. As Rucht argues, "[t]hese linkages . . .should become part and parcel of social movement studies. It is time to abandon the simplified image of a two-party struggle between a (unified) movement and its (unified) opponent acting in some kind of a social vacuum" (2004:212–213). Mediators operate both within and across conflicting groups, frequently intervening to de-escalate conflicts, add new resources, or to broker relations between adversaries (Rucht 2004). Others (e.g., Burstein et al. 1995; della Porta and Rucht 1995; Kriesi 2004; Kriesi et al. 1995; Rucht 1996) also argue for greater attention to the interplay between movements' "alliance" and "conflict" systems. Indeed, for most movements, cultivating allies that can help counteract the power of adversaries constitute the bulk of social change efforts (e.g., Diani 1995, 2004; Maney 2001; Mueller 1994; Osa 2003; Polletta 2002; Rochon 1998; J. Smith forthcoming; Winston 2004; Wood 2004). We have comparatively little systematic evidence about changing relationships among actors in these broad social movement alliance and conflict systems.

As some of our earlier discussion suggests, recent research on social movements seems to be moving in the direction that Rucht prescribes, and we find greater attention to how informal networks of actors contribute to social conflict processes. Much of this work points to the need to understand more about how networks of organizations and individuals develop durable cooperative relationships (e.g., Anheier and Katz 2005; Bandy and Smith 2005; Diani and McAdam 2003; Gamson 2004; Katz and Anheier 2006). Demonstrating the need for more nuanced understandings of movement actors, Ferree and Mueller argued that "organizational repertoires may be broader, more strategic and more interconnected than dominant ways of conceptualizing social movements suggests" (2004:595). Staggenborg and Taylor (2005) show how conventional approaches to social movement analysis produced inaccurate claims about the women's movement.

Some researchers have focused explicitly on the importance of *networks* of individuals and organizations to social movement outcomes (e.g., Bennett 2004; Davis et al. 2005; Diani and McAdam 2003; Marwell and Oliver 1993; Passy 2003). For instance, Caniglia (2001) found that transnational environmental organizations with informal ties to international agencies played more central roles in transnational social movement networks by helping channel information and pressure among disconnected social actors. Demonstrating the particular importance of networking for transnational alliances, Stark and his colleagues found in a study of civil society groups in Hungary that those with international links were comparatively more densely networked with local and national groups, suggesting that transnational associations may serve as brokers between international and more geographically proximate political arenas (Stark, Vedres, and Bruszt 2006). This finding resonates with one from a study of movement networks in Vancouver by Carroll and Ratner (1996), which found that groups working with a political economy and justice frame were more outward-oriented and connected to extra-local groups. Groups adopting other frames tended to remain more concentrated within their local geographic space. This may help explain why the global justice movement is undoubtedly the most widely visible and populous of transnational social movements. It also suggests that we should expect to find extensive networking going on within this movement, and even a cursory look at the literature confirms this (e.g., Adamovsky 2005; Bennett 2005; della Porta et al. 2006; Moghadam 2005).

Riles' study (2001) of transnational women's organizing at the 1995 United Nations Conference on Women highlights the centrality of the network as the recognized and legitimate form for transnational political work. She demonstrates how delegates at the UN Conference learned new skills through their ties to other participants in the Conference as well as how they brought new ideas and strategic proposals to local groups when they returned from the conference. The network form, Riles and others argue, is preferred for its ability to help people navigate across different levels of political engagement while affording them greater informational, material, and political resources than they could have as isolated individuals or groups.

The emergence of the network form of mobilization is, in short, closely linked with changes in the operation of governance institutions. As states shift their authority to supranational institutions, devolve some authority to local governments, and privatize government functions, they fundamentally redefine the character of the state as well as the meaning of citizenship (Brysk and Shafir 2004; Markoff 2004). Thus, citizens active in social movements have worked to forge new types of relationships with government officials as they have sought to remedy grievances and improve social conditions for their constituents (Coleman and Wayland 2004; Korzeniewicz and Smith 2003). Advocates of social change have found that they must adapt the mobilizing structures they employ as globalization processes have fundamentally altered the allocation of political authority.

Research on transnational organizing in particular has shown that social change advocates often benefit from connections to international institutions and their agents. For instance, Jackie Smith's analysis (2005) of networking among transnational social movement organizations finds that the shape of networks is largely determined by institutional contexts defined at both regional and global levels. While there was some variation across different issue areas, for the most part, groups within particular world regions adopted network structures that maximized the institutional openings for their particular region. Lending further support to the claim that network structures among transnational social movement groups reflects broader institutional contexts is Wiest and Smith's finding (2006) that regional network ties were more likely in regions with larger numbers of regional intergovernmental organizations and treaties.

The emergence of routinized and fairly cooperative relationships between social movement actors and agents of governments may seem puzzling to some, although social movement scholars have long recognized that movement–government cooperation is often essential to their efforts to affect policy (McCarthy and Wolfson 1992). Some analysts speak of the need for "networked governance" as an approach to managing the complex array of problems and actors under the jurisdiction of global institutions (United Nations 2004; World Commission on the Social Dimensions of Globalization 2004). And analyzing civil society networks in Latin America, Korzeniewicz and Smith (2000, 2001, 2003) argue for a more self-conscious cultivation of "polycentric governance coalitions" to address the inequalities that have hampered development efforts in that region and elsewhere.

Many United Nations agencies—especially those working on the environment, development, disarmament, and public health—share the values and objectives of social movements, and many analysts see movement pressure as key to strengthening international norms and institutions by pressing states to adopt multilateral over unilateral approaches to foreign policy (Clark 2003; Keck and Sikkink 1998; Passy, 1999; Risse et al. 1999; Smith et al. 1997). Moreover, underlying the entire UN system is a commitment to values of equity, fairness, and participation—principles that motivate and lend legitimacy to a considerable amount of social movement activity. Although links with authorities always introduce risks that movements will be co-opted, such links can fundamentally alter unequal power relations by expanding the political access of relatively powerless groups. Thus, understanding transnational social movement dynamics requires attention to the extensive links between transnational social change groups and international institutions as well as the transnational networks of social movement and other civil society actors.

Our approach to this discussion of structural approaches to the study of social movements has emphasized the centrality of the national state to our efforts to understand the causes and consequences of social movement emergence and impact. As a target of social movement pressure and an institution that shapes the distribution of resources and power in society, states are central to any social movement analysis. As global forces have altered the authority and structure of the national state, they have forced social movement actors to adapt their own organizing strategies accordingly. Thus, alongside the expansion of international institutions, we find an increasing reliance on networks by all groups seeking to operate transnationally. The network itself comprises the mobilizing structures from which social movements emerge. But networking as an activity becomes a form of agency whereby social change advocates might seek to enhance their political power by forging new alliances and other strategic ties.

UNANSWERED QUESTIONS

We chose to emphasize in this review our concern with how different conceptualizations of the state have shaped structural accounts of social movements. This emphasis grows from our recognition that our very notion of social movement is conceptually inseparable from the modern national state. National states both affect the distribution of power and resources in society and define possibilities for challenges from social movements. Therefore, social movement analysts should take into account the historical and geographic contexts in which relevant state actors are situated.

Despite the historical grounding of modern social movements in the era of the modern state, what is largely missing from much scholarship in social movements is attention to the possibility that the national state itself may be changing in fundamental ways, just as did the pre-national, competitive systems of warlords and localized sovereignties that were displaced by the national state during the eighteenth century.[12] Social movement research is, by and large, state-centric (McMichael 2005). Much existing work assumes that social conflicts are contained within the boundaries of the national state. But if states, and social movements, were not always around in their current forms, why should we expect the forms we observe

---

[12] Even this understanding of the state is challenged as European-centric. Looking at the Latin American experience, for instance, Centeno argues that the European experience was the exception rather than the rule in regard to the processes characterizing modern state formation Centeno, Miguel Angel. 2002. *Blood and Debt: War and the Nation-State in Latin America*. University Park, PA: Pennsylvania State University Press.

today to endure over the long-term? Structural analyses typically presume that change comes slowly and large structures have long-term impacts on social relations. But no one would argue that structures never change. Nevertheless, a considerable amount of debate has been generated over the rather simplistic question of whether an increase in global influences necessarily reduces the importance of the national state.

The implication in this dualism between globalism and the state is that the modern state is some unchanging entity that is in constant tension with forces of global integration. In reality, the national state can exist only in a global context that recognizes national sovereignty and certifies national governments as legitimate actors on the world stage. If national states only exist in relation with other states, then their structures have evolved in the course of interactions among states and other global actors. Thus, global embeddedness is not necessarily inversely related to the strength or viability of the national state. Further, the nature of the state will continue to change as new actors emerge in the global arena and as power constellations among actors shift. Our discussion has sought to draw attention to possible conceptual limitations that might prevent us from seeing fundamental changes in how social movements relate to states and other forces in an increasingly interconnected global environment.

Given this analytical starting point, we offer some thoughts about questions that deserve greater attention from researchers working in the field of social movements and social change.

Political Contexts

- To understand the ways political contexts shape social movement dynamics, it is imperative that analysts try to account for the transnational influences that may be impinging on a given social conflict. National borders are in many ways arbitrary boundaries that reside more in our conceptual maps than in the real world where political actors operate. This is not to say that national policies and institutions don't matter, but rather that these are often shaped by transnational or global forces. By ignoring global influences on national political contexts we fail to appreciate fully the range of constraints and opportunities that define the political contexts in which social movements operate. Analysts should seek a more complete understanding of the important relationships between national and global level economic, cultural, and political processes. For instance, how does the embeddedness of the state within a broader system of global political and economic relationships affect social movement mobilization and policy impact? How does the position of a given state in the broader world system define alliance opportunities for social movements within that state?
- By taking a global perspective, we quickly notice that recent years have witnessed a growing and widespread sense of disillusion with democratic institutions and the prospects for democratization in the global south. There are expanding discussions of a "legitimacy crisis" in global institutions, as states transfer authority and capacity to international organizations without developing a corresponding structure to allow democratic input and accountability (Bello 2003; Markoff 1999; McMichael 2003). At the same time, national democratic institutions are also losing the confidence of citizens (Norris 1999). This signals a vulnerability of global institutions that could either generate new nationalist mobilizations or contribute to expanded calls for global democratization (cf. Barber 1995). We can readily point to evidence that both nationalist and pro-democracy mobilizations are happening in different parts of the world,

and we need to better understand what shapes each one as well as how each affects the broader political context.

- Political contexts at national levels are increasingly influenced by inter-state institutional factors. But we need more research to assess how transnational political contexts impact social movement dynamics within and across states. For instance, in recent years, we have seen a turn toward more confrontational relationships between social movements and global institutions. Why has this change has happened, and does it signal changes in the configurations of opportunities at the global level, or does it result more from changing activist perceptions of these?

- As scholars puzzle over the structural aspects of social movements under increasing globalization, one of the questions that movements pose is the extent to which mobilizing structures can be transferred to other political contexts. As activists themselves endeavor to extend the reach of their movements beyond national borders, it is worth considering which institutional resources can be moved from one country to another, and which mobilizing structures can be replicated or approximated in other locations. Scholars have only begun asking questions about the relative transferability of structural aspects of social movements at this point, and it is sure to be an important ongoing pursuit among scholars and activists alike.

- Finally, in the post-9/11 era, it is crucial that social movement scholars consider the long-term impacts of the "war on terror" (or as it is now called the "long war") on both domestic and transnational social movements. Will the emphasis on counter-terrorism generate a strengthening of coercive state apparatus and a reversal of the international human rights regime? Will it help slow and reverse the globalization project that has been the predominant influence on the world political economy in recent decades? Will it alter our assumptions about the social movement society as it has been experienced in the West?

Mobilizing Structures

As our discussion in the preceding suggests, global integration has important implications for how people organize politically, in large part because it is driven largely by the expansion of capitalist modes of production and labor organization. As more people's lives are governed by production and distribution processes that are globally organized, we must account for how the global organization of work impacts the very local mobilizing contexts in which individuals are embedded. Also, global integration involves the emergence of new types of organizational structures that impact social movements as well as other parts of society.

- Social movement scholars have focused increasingly on questions of collective identity, and this is a promising development in the literature. Nevertheless, we see room for even more work to explore the relationships between economic and political structures and transnational identity formation in particular. One area that deserves more attention from social movement scholars is the labor movement. The U.S. labor movement's emphasis on business unionism as well as the conservative, anti-communist emphasis in much international labor organizing (e.g., O'Brien 2000) led many social movement researchers to neglect the labor movement as a topic of inquiry. But even though it is now clear that people are motivated to act politically around a range of different issues and identities, labor remains a crucial area of potential political engagement. Indeed, segments of labor movements from different parts of the world are playing leadership roles in contemporary transnational mobilizations. We need to know more about the possibilities for making connections between labor and other collective identities within and between nations. For instance, what are possibilities for transnational labor movement, given the changes brought about by global economic integration? Will the movement be mobilized as labor, or as a coalition of civil society actors/interests (cf. Clawson 2003; Turner, 2003; Waterman and Timms 2004).

- Another important feature of globalization's impact on the organization of labor is seen in patterns of migration and conflicts over definitions of citizenship (Brysk and Shafir 2004; Fox 2005; Sassen 2000). The contemporary immigrant rights mobilizations dramatize the importance of this theme, and social movements researchers can contribute to our understandings of these mobilizations and their impact by exploring questions such as: what shapes effective coalition-building between immigrant and non-immigrant sectors of particular societies? What sorts of claims-making are being articulated by different groups of immigrant activists, and are claims anchored in international human rights language or some other language? What variation exists in terms of national responses to immigrants' claims, and what explains this variation?

- As technologies enable new forms of political and social organization, we should expect changes in how social movements are organized. People around the world are increasingly likely to be involved somehow in globally organized commodity production and distribution chains, and therefore they are exposed to ways of thinking and acting that are consistent with globalized organizational structures. Forms of organization once unfamiliar are now well understood by people around the globe. This expands organizing possibilities, and may increase the extent of isomorphism between corporate and civil society organizational forms. For instance, we noted that social movements researchers speak increasingly of networks or multiorganizational fields of interconnected actors. But despite the importance of the network concept to our understanding of social movements, most existing networks research is based on case studies of single movements. We lack systematic data that will allow us to compare networks across issues or time (cf. Lauman and Knoke 1987). Future research should seek to develop more comparative analyses of networks across time, issue, and place. Also, more work needs to be done to examine networks of ties between social movement actors and governments, parties, and international organizations (e.g., della Porta et al. 2006). Analyses of global political institutions, for instance, suggest that network ties between social movements and the United Nations will differ in important ways from those between movements and global financial institutions.

BRIDGES AND OVERLAPS WITH OTHER DISCIPLINES AND REVIEW OF INTERDISCIPLINARY ADVANCES

Although we have focused here on structural approaches to the study of social movements, we do not claim that this lens is the only one through which social movements should be viewed. Rather, we consider this perspective is best utilized when taken as an orienting concept, keeping social movements theorists attuned to the structural, institutional, and contextual factors that order social movement activity. We therefore see many opportunities for structural perspectives to bridge with other approaches to the study of social movements. We see structural approaches in dialogue with, for example, cultural aspects of social movements. For instance:

- Constructivism in international relations research has focused on the ways nongovernmental actors, including social movements, interact with other global actors, shaping global institutions and norms.
- The world polity approach in sociology has expanded attention to institutional processes and cultural influences that affect the organizational forms, agendas, and systems of meanings across diverse national states.
- Organizational and institutional analyses can contribute to our understandings of social movement processes (Davis et al. 2005).

Social movement scholars will also find much in common with political scientists working on themes of democracy and democratization. While many scholars do read across these literatures, there is much room for expanding a dialogue here. Indeed, social movement scholars might be more explicit in their attention to questions of how movement mobilizations relate to broader processes of democratization and repression.

Understanding social change processes that take place within a context of multiple and inter-connected political arenas operating at local, national, and global levels requires that we re-think our methods and concepts. We have argued here, for instance, that globalization processes are fundamentally altering the structure and operations of national states. But much research continues to assume fairly constant state structures and meaningful boundaries between states. The expansion of global research highlights some of the historical, geographic, and disciplinary blinders that may be inhibiting our efforts to understand the processes of social change. Anheier and Katz (and others) warn against "methodological nationalism," or the "tendency of the social sciences to remain in the statistical and conceptual categories of the nation state" (2005:206). Overcoming methodological nationalism requires both intellectual openness and innovativeness on the part of researchers.

In particular, it is clear that understanding relationships between social structure, human agency, and social change requires a multiplicity of disciplinary approaches and research methods ranging from detailed qualitative studies to large-scale quantitative and historical work. This is required because many of the relationships between local contexts or experiences and global structures and processes remain to be uncovered. We need rich descriptive accounts of the global–local links in the specific places where relevant policies are enacted, decided, and invented in order to put the global puzzle together. And we also need "big picture," macro-level accounts that can help us understand how particular practices, beliefs, and structures have differed or changed across time and place.

Another methodological challenge is that the spaces in which global politics take place may not resemble those social spaces for which conventional research methodologies have been designed. For instance, the global conference is a unique site of social experience that differs fundamentally from the ethnographic field sites in which the architects of ethnographic methodologies worked. While we can draw from that foundation, attempts to adapt these research tools to somewhat novel social spaces can be fruitful. For instance, research on activist discourses and actions at the World Social Forums and other global meetings requires the short-term deployment of trained observers to meetings lasting several days, rather than the long-term embedding of a single observer within a single organization or community.

Greater efforts at collaborative research are needed to study effectively important events such as the World Social Forums and their counterparts at regional, national, and local levels.

While states are embedded within an increasingly global institutional arena, they still have distinct histories and social contexts, and therefore we need to enhance our access to data that can allow us to make comparisons across different national contexts. This is quite difficult for those studying social movements in particular, as it is often difficult to find valid records of civil society organizations and events in particular countries. Much more difficult is finding data sources that can be reliably compared across nations. But how useful it would be to have a measure, for instance, of the comparative strength of civil societies across nations and even time!

SUGGESTED READINGS

Buechler, Stephen M. 2000. *Social Movements in Advanced Capitalism: The Political Economy and Cultural Construction of Social Activism*. New York: Oxford University Press.

Clemens, Elizabeth S. and Debra Minkoff. "Beyond the Iron Law: Rethinking the Place of Organizations in Social Movement Research." Pp. 155–170 in *The Blackwell Companion to Social Movements*, edited by D. A. Snow, S. A. Soule, and H. Kriesi. Oxford: Blackwell.

Diani, Mario and Doug McAdam (eds). 2003. *Social Movements and Networks*. Oxford: Oxford University Press.

della Porta, Donatella, Hanspeter Kriesi, and Dieter Rucht, Eds. 1999. *Social Movements in a Globalizing World*. New York: St. Martin's Press.

Edwards, Bob and John D. McCarthy. 2004. "Resources and Social Movement Mobilization." Pp. 116151 in *Blackwell Companion to Social Movements*, edited by D. A. Snow, S. A. Soule, and H. Kriesi. New York: Blackwell.

Jenkins, J. Craig and Bert Klandermans. 1995. *The Politics of Social Protest: Comparative Perspectives on States and Social Movements*. Minneapolis: University of Minnesota Press.

Kriesi, Hanspeter, Ruud Koopmans, Jan Willem Duyvendak, and Marco Giugni. 1995. *New Social Movements in Western Europe: A Comparative Analysis*. Minneapolis, MN: University of Minnesota Press.

McAdam, Doug, John D. McCarthy, and Mayer Zald (eds). 1996. *Comparative Perspectives on Social Movements: Political Opportunities, Mobilizing Structures and Cultural Framings*. New York: Cambridge University Press.

McCarthy, John D. and Mayer N. Zald (eds). 1987. *Social Movements in an Organizational Society*. New Brunswick, NJ: Transaction.

Mueller, Carol. 1994. "Conflict Networks and the Origins of Women's Liberation." Pp. 234–263 in *New Social Movements: From Ideology to Identity*, edited by E. Larana, H. Johnston, and J. R. Gusfield. Philadelphia: Temple University Press.

Quadagno, Jill. 1992. "Social Movements and State Transformation: Labor Unions and Racial Conflict in the War on Poverty." *American Sociological Review* 57:616–634.

Ray, Raka. 1999. *Fields of Protest: Women's Movements in India*. Minneapolis, MN: University of Minnesota Press.

Tarrow, Sidney. 1998. *Power in Movement: Social Movements, Collective Action and Politics*, 2nd edition. New York: Cambridge University Press.

Tilly, Charles. 1978. *From Mobilization to Revolution*. Reading, MA: Addison Wesley.

REFERENCES

Adamovsky, Ezequiel. 2005. "Beyond the World Social Forum: The Need for New Institutions," vol. 2005: Opendemocracy.net.

Amenta, Edwin, Neal Caren, and Sheera J. Olasky. 2005. "Age for Leisure? Political Mediation and the Impact of the Pension Movement on U.S. Old-Age Policy." *American Sociological Review* 70:516–538.

Amenta, Edwin, Neal Caren, Tina Fetner, and Michael P. Young. 2002. "Challengers and States: Toward a Political Sociology of Social Movements." *Research in Political Sociology* 10:47–83.

Anderson, Benedict. 1991. *Imagined Communities: Reflections on the Origin and Spread of Nationalism*. London: Verso.

Andrews, Kenneth T. and Bob Edwards. 2005. "The Organizational Structure of Local Environmentalism." *Mobilization: An International Quarterly* 10(2):213–234.

Anheier, Helmut and Hagai Katz. 2005. "Network Approaches to Global Civil Society." Pp. 206–221 in *Global Civil Society 2004/5*, edited by H. Anheier, M. Glasius, and M. Kaldor. London: Sage Publications.

Armstrong, Elizabeth A. 2002. *Forging Gay Identities: Organizing Sexuality in San Francisco, 1950–1994*. Chicago: University of Chicago Press.

Arrighi, Giovanni. 1999. "Globalization and Historical Macrosociology." Pp. 117–133 in *Sociology for the Twenty-First Century*, edited by J. L. Abu-Lughod. Chicago: University of Chicago Press.

Arrighi, Giovanni and Jessica Drangel. 1986. "The Stratification of the World-Economy: An Exploration of the Semiperipheral Zone." *Review* 10:9–74.

Baiocchi, Gianpaolo. 2004. "The Party and the Multitudes: Brazil's Worker's Party (PT) and the Challenges of Building a Just Social Order in the Globalizing Context." *Journal of World Systems Research* 10:199–215. Available at: http://jwsr.ucr.edu.

Banaszak, Lee Ann. 1996. *Why Movements Succeed or Fail* Princeton, NJ: : Princeton University Press.

Bandy, Joe and Jackie Smith, eds. 2005. *Coalitions Across Borders: Transnational Protest and the Neoliberal Order*. Lanham, MD: Rowman & Littlefield.

Barber, Benjamin. 1995. *Jihad Vs. McWorld*. New York: Random House.

Bello, Walden. 2003. *Deglobalization: Ideas for a New World Economy*. London and New York: Zed Books.

Bello, Walden. 2000. "Building an Iron Cage: Bretton Woods Institutions, the WTO, and the South." Pp. 54–90 in *Views from the South: The Effects of Globalization and the WTO on Third World Countries*, edited by S. Anderson. Chicago: Food First Books.

Bennett, W. Lance. 2004. "Branded Political Communication: Lifestyle Politics, Logo Campaigns, and the Rise of Global Citizenship." Pp. 101–125 in *Politics, Products, and Markets: Exploring Political Consumerism Past and Present*, edited by M. Micheletti, A. Follesdal, and D. Stolle. New Brunswick, NJ: Transaction Books.

Bennett, W. Lance. 2005. "Social Movements Beyond Borders: Understanding Two Eras of Transnational Activism." Pp. 203–226 in *Transnational Protest and Global Activism*, edited by D. della Porta and S. Tarrow. Lanham, MD: Rowman & Littlefield.

Bissio, Roberto. 1999. "Occupying New Places for Public Life: Politics and People in a Network Society." Pp. 429–459 in *Whose World Is It Anyway? Civil Society, the United Nations, and the Multilateral Future*, edited by J. W. Foster and A. Anand. Ottawa: United Nations Association of Canada.

Boli, John and George M. Thomas, eds. 1999. *Constructing World Culture: International Nongovernmental Organizations Since 1875*. Stanford: Stanford University Press.

Borer, Tristan. 1998. *Challenging the State: Churches as Political Actors in South Africa, 1980–1994*. Notre Dame, IN: University of Notre Dame Press.

Boswell, Terry and Christopher Chase-Dunn. 2000. *The Spiral of Capitalism and Socialism*. Boulder, CO: Lynne Rienner Publishers.

Boyer, Robert and J. Rogers Hollingsworth. 1997. "From National Embeddedness to Spatial and Institutional Nestedness." Pp. 433–484 in *Contemporary Capitalism: The Embeddedness of Institutions*, edited by J. R. Hollingsworth and R. Boyer. New York: Cambridge University Press.

Brysk, Alison. 2000. *From Tribal Village to Global Village: Indigenous Peoples Struggles in Latin America*. Stanford: Stanford University Press.

Brysk, Alison and Gershon Shafir. 2004. *People Out of Place: Globalization, Human Rights, and the Citizenship Gap*. New York: Routledge.

Buechler, Stephen M. 2000. *Social Movements in Advanced Capitalism: The Political Economy and Cultural Construction of Social Activism*. New York: Oxford University Press.

Burstein, Paul, Rachel Einwohner, and Jocelyn Hollander. 1995. "The Success of Political Movements: A Bargaining Perspective." Pp. 275–295 in *The Politics of Social Protest: Comparative Perspectives on States and Social Movements*, edited by J. C. Jenkins and B. Klandermans. Minneapolis, MN: University of Minnesota Press.

Buss, Doris and Didi Herman. 2003. *Globalizing Family Values: The Christian Right in International Politics*. Minneapolis, MN: University of Minnesota Press.

Campbell, John L. 2005. "Where Do We Stand? Common Mechanisms in Organizations and Social Movements Research." In *Social Movements and Organization Theory*, edited by G.F. Davis, D. McAdam, W.R. Scott, and M.N. Zald. New York: Cambridge University Press.

Campbell, John L. and Ove K. Pedersen, eds. 2001. *The Rise of Neoliberalism and Institutional Analysis*. Princeton, NJ: Princeton University Press.

Caniglia, Beth Schaefer. 2001. "Informal Alliances Vs. Institutional Ties: The Effects of Elite Alliances on Environmental TSMO Networks." *Mobilization: An International Journal* 6:37–54.

Carroll, William K. and Robert S. Ratner. 1996. "Master Framing and Cross-Movement Networking in Contemporary Social Movements." *Sociological Quarterly* 37:601–625.

Castells, Manuel. 1996. *The Rise of the Network Society*. Oxford and Malden, MA: Blackwell Publishing.

Centeno, Miguel A. 2002. *Blood and Debt: War and the Nation-State in Latin America*. University Park, PA: Pennsylvania State University Press.

Chase-Dunn, Christopher. 1998. *Global Formation,* updated edition. Boulder, CO: Rowman & Littlefield.

Chatfield, Charles. 1997. "Intergovernmental and Nongovernmental Associations to 1945." Pp. 19–41 in *Transnational Social Movements and World Politics: Solidarity Beyond the State*, edited by J. Smith, C. Chatfield, and R. Pagnucco. Syracuse, NY: Syracuse University Press.

Chilton, Patricia. 1995. "Mechanics of Change: Social Movements, Transnational Coalitions, and the Transformation Process in Eastern Europe." In *Bringing Transnational Relations Back In*, edited by T. Risse-Kappen. New York: Cambridge University Press.

Chirot, Daniel and Thomas D. Hall. 1982. "World System Theory." *American Review of Sociology* 8:81–106.

Clark, Ann Marie. 2003. *Diplomacy of Conscience: Amnesty International and Changing Human Rights Norms*. Princeton, NJ: Princeton University Press.

Clawson, Dan. 2003. *The Next Upsurge: Labor and the New Social Movements*. Ithaca, NY: Cornell University Press.

Clemens, Elisabeth. 1996. *The People's Lobby*. Chicago: University of Chicago Press.

——. 1998. "To Move Mountains: Collective Action and the Possibility of Institutional Change." Pp. 109–123 in *From Contention to Democracy*, edited by M. G. Giugni, D. McAdam, and C. Tilly. Boulder, CO: Rowman & Littlefield.

Coleman, William D. and Tony Porter. 2000. "International Institutions, Globalization and Democracy: Assessing the Challenges." *Global Society* 14:377–398.

Coleman, William D. and Sarah Wayland. 2004. "The Origins of Global Civil Society and Non-Territorial Governance: Some Empirical Reflections." *Globalization and Autonomy Online Compendium*. Accessed November 7, 2006 at http://www.globalautonomy.ca/global1/article.jsp?index = RA_Coleman_Origins.xml.

Cunningham, David. 2005. "State versus Social Movement: FBI Counterintelligence Against the New Left." Pp. 45–77 in *States, Parties, and Social Movements*, edited by J. A. Goldstone. New York: Cambridge University Press.

Curtis, James E., Douglas E. Baer, and Edward G. Grabb. 2001. "Nations of Joiners: Explaining Voluntary Association Membership in Democratic Societies." *American Sociological Review* 66:783–805.

Daly, Herman. 2002. "Globalization versus Internationalization, and Four Economic Arguments for Why Internationalization is a Better Model for World Community." Accessed 13 November 2006 at www.bsos.umd.edu/socy/conference/newpapers/daly.rtf

Davenport, Christian, Hank Johnston, and Carol Mueller, Ed(s). 2005. *Repression and Mobilization*. Minneapolis: University of Minnesota Press.

Davies, John C. 1962. "Towards a Theory of Revolution." *American Sociological Review* 27:5–19.

Davis, Gerald, Doug McAdam, W. Richard Scott, and Mayer Zald, eds. 2005. *Social Movements and Organizational Theory*. New York: Cambridge University Press.

della Porta, Donatella. 2005. "Making the Polis: Social Forums and Democracy in the Global Justice Movement." *Mobilization: An International Journal* 10:73–94.

della Porta, Donatella, Massimiliano Andretta, Lorenzo Mosca, and Herbert Reiter. 2006. *Globalization From Below: Transnational Activists and Protest Networks*. Minneapolis, MN: University of Minnesota Press.

della Porta, Donatella, Abby Peterson, and Herbert Reiter, eds. 2007. *The Policing of Transnational Protest*. London: Ashgate.

della Porta, Donatella and Herbert Reiter, eds. 1998. *Policing Protest: The Control of Mass Demonstrations in Western Democracies*. Minneapolis, MN: University of Minnesota Press.

della Porta, Donatella and Dieter Rucht. 1995. "Left-Libertarian Movements in Context: A Comparison of Italy and West Germany, 1965–1990." Pp. 229–272 in *The Politics of Social Protest: Comparative Perspectives on States and Social Movements*, edited by B. Klandermans and C. Jenkins. Minneapolis, MN: University of Minnesota Press.

Diani, Mario. 1995. *Green Networks: A Structural Analysis of the Italian Environmental Movement*. Edinburgh: Edinburgh University Press.

——. 2003. "Networks and Social Movements: A Research Program." Pp. 299–319 in *Social Movements and Networks*, edited by M. Diani and D. McAdam. Oxford: Oxford University Press.

——. 2004. "Networks and Participation." Pp. 339–358 in *Blackwell Companion to Social Movements*, edited by D. A. Snow, S. A. Soule, and H. Kriesi. Oxford and Malden, MA: Blackwell Publishing.

Diani, Mario and Doug McAdam, eds. 2003. *Social Movements and Networks*. Oxford: Oxford University Press.

Earl, Jennifer (guest editor). 2006. *Special Focus Issue of Mobilization on Repression and the Social Control of Protest. Mobilization: An International Journal* 11(2):129–280.

Economy, Elizabeth C. 2004. *The River Runs Black: The Environmental Challenge to China's Future.* Ithaca, NY: Cornell University Press.

Edwards, Bob and Sam Marullo. 1995. "Organizational Mortality in a Declining Movement: The Demise of Peace Movement Organizations in the End of the Cold War Era." *American Sociological Review* 60:805–825.

Edwards, Bob and Sam Marullo. 2003. "Social Movement Organizations Beyond the Beltway: Understanding the Diversity of One Social Movement Industry." *Mobilization* 8:87–107.

Edwards, Bob and Michael Foley. 2003. "Social Movement Organizations Beyond the Beltway: Understanding the Diversity of One Social Movement Industry." *Mobilization: An International Journal* 8:87–107.

Edwards, Bob and John D. McCarthy. 2004. "Resources and Social Movement Mobilization." Pp. 116–151 in *Blackwell Companion to Social Movements*, edited by D. A. Snow, S. A. Soule, and H. Kriesi. Oxford and Malden, MA: Blackwell Publishing.

Eisinger, Peter. 1973. "Conditions of Protest Behavior in American Cities." *American Political Science Review* 67:11–28.

Escobar, Arturo. 2003. "Other Worlds Are (already) Possible: Self-Organisation, Complexity, and Post-Capitalist Cultures." Pp. 349–358 in *Challenging Empires: the World Social Forum*, edited by J. Sen, A. Anand, A. Escobar, and P. Waterman. Third World Institute: Available in Pdf format at www.choike.org.

Escobar, Arturo and Sonia E. Alvarez. 1992. "The Making of Social Movements in Latin America: Identity, Strategy, and Democracy." Boulder, CO: Westview Press.

Evans, Peter B. 1997. "The Eclipse of the State? Reflections on Stateness in an Era of Globalization." *World Politics* 50:62–87.

Evans, Sara. 1980. *Personal Politics: The Roots of Women's Liberation in the Civil Rights Movement and the New Left.* New York: Vintage Books.

Faucheux, Ron. 1995. "The Grassroots Explosion." *Campaigns and Elections*

Ferree, Myra Marx. 1987. "Equality and Autonomy: Feminist Politics in the U.S. and the Federal Republic of Germany." Pp. 172–195 in *The Women's Movements of the United States and Western Europe*, edited by M. F. Katzenstein and C. M. Mueller. Philadelphia: Temple University Press.

Ferree, Myra Marx and Carol Mueller. 2004. "Feminism and the Women's Movement: A Global Perspective." Pp. 576–607 in *The Blackwell Companion to Social Movements*, edited by D. A. Snow, S. A. Soule, and H. Kriesi. Oxford and Malden, MA: Blackwell Publishing.

Finnemore, Martha. 1996a. *National Interests in International Society.* Ithaca, NY: Cornell University Press.

——. 1996b. "Sociology's Institutionalism." *International Organization* 50:325–47.

Florini, Ann. 2003. *The Coming Democracy: New Rules for Running a New World.* Washington, D.C.: Island Press.

Foster, John and Anita Anand, eds. 1999. *Whose World Is It Anyway? Civil Society, the United Nations, and the Multilateral Future.* Ottawa: United Nations Association of Canada.

Fox, Jonathan. 2005. "Unpacking 'Transnational Citizenship'." *Annual Review of Political Science* 8:171–201.

Fox, Jonathan and L. David Brown, eds. 1998. *The Struggle for Accountability: The World Bank, NGOs, and Grassroots Movements.* Cambridge, MA: MIT Press.

Francisco, Ronald. 1996. "The Relationship between Coercion and Protest." *Journal of Conflict Resolution* 39:263–282.

Frank, David John, Ann Hironaka, and Evan Schofer. 2000. "The Nation-State and the Natural Environment over the Twentieth Century." *American Sociological Review* 65:96–116.

Gamson, William. 1990. *Strategy of Social Protest*, 2nd ed. Belmont, CA: Wadsworth.

Gamson, William A. 2004. "Bystanders, Public Opinion, and the Media." Pp. 242–261 in *The Blackwell Companion to Social Movements*, edited by D. A. Snow, S. A. Soule, and H. Kriesi. Oxford and Malden, MA: Blackwell Publishing.

Gamson, William and David Meyer. 1996. "The Framing of Political Opportunity." In *Political Opportunities, Mobilizing Structures and Framing: Social Movement Dynamics in Cross-National Perspective*, edited by D. McAdam, J. McCarthy, and M. Zald. New York: Cambridge University Press.

Giugni, Marco. 1998. "Was It Worth the Effort? The Outcomes and Consequences of Social Movements." *Annual Review of Sociology* 24:371–393.

——. 2002. "The Other Side of the Coin: Explaining Crossnational Similarities Between Social Movements." Pp. 11–24 in *Globalization and Resistance: Transnational Dimensions of Social Movements*, edited by J. Smith and H. Johnston. Lanham, MD: Rowman & Littlefield.

Giugni, Marco, Doug McAdam, and Charles Tilly. 1999. *How Social Movements Matter.* Minneapolis, MN: University of Minnesota Press.

Glasius, Marlies. 2002. "Expertise in the Cause of Justice: Global Civil Society Influence on the Statute for an International Criminal Court." Pp. 137–169 in *Global Civil Society Yearbook, 2002*, edited by M. Glasius, M. Kaldor, and H. Anheier. Oxford: Oxford University Press.

Goodwin, Jeffrey and James Jasper. 1999. "Caught in a Winding, Snarling Vine: The Structural Bias of Political Process Theory." *Sociological Forum* 14:27–54.

Greenberg, Josh and Graham Knight. 2004. "Framing Sweatshops: Nike, Global Production, and the American News Media." *Communication and Critical/Cultural Studies* 1:151–175.

Gurney, Joan Neff and Kathleen J. Tierney. 1982. "Relative Deprivation and Social Movements: A Critical Look at Twenty Years of Theory and Research." *The Sociological Quarterly* 23:33–47.

Gurr, Ted Robert. 1970. *Why Men Rebel*. Princeton, NJ: Princeton University Press.

Haas, Peter. 1992. "Epistemic Communities and International Policy Coordination." *International Organization* 46:1–35.

Hafner-Burton, Emilie M. and Kiyotero Tsutsui. 2005. "Human Rights in a Globalizing World: The Paradox of Empty Promises." *American Journal of Sociology* 110:1373–1411.

Hanagan, Michael. 2002. "Irish Transnational Social Movements, Migrants, and the State System." Pp. 53–74 in *Globalization and Resistance: Transnational Dimensions of Social Movements*, edited by J. Smith and H. Johnston. Boulder, CO: Rowman & Littlefield.

Hannan, Michael T. and John Freeman. 1977. "The Population Ecology of Organizations." *American Journal of Sociology* 82:929–964.

Herman, Edward. 1995. *Triumph of the Market: Essays on Economics, Politics, and the Media*. Boston: South End Press.

Herman, Edward and Noam Chomsky. 1988. *Manufacturing Consent*. New York: Pantheon Books.

Hertel, Shareen. 2006. *Unexpected Power: Conflict and Change Among Transnational Activists*. Ithaca, NY: Cornell University Press.

Hippler, Jochen, ed. 1995. *The Democratisation of Disempowerment: The Problem of Democracy in the Third World*. East Haven, CT: Pluto Press with Transnational Institute.

Huntington, Samuel. 1968. *Political Order in Changing Societies*. New Haven, CT: Yale University Press.

Imig, Doug and Sidney Tarrow. 2001. *Contentious Europeans: Protest and Politics in an Integrating Europe*. Lanham, MD: Rowman and Littlefield.

Inglehart, Ronald and Wayne E. Baker. 2000. "Modernization, Cultural Change, and the Persistence of Traditional Values." *American Sociological Review* 65:19–51.

Jenkins, J. Craig and Charles Perrow. 1977. "Insurgency of the Powerless: Farm Worker Movements." *American Sociological Review* 42:249–268.

Jenkins, J. Craig and Bert Klandermans. 1995. *The Politics of Social Protest: Comparative Perspectives on States and Social Movements*. Minneapolis: University of Minnesota Press.

Jenkins, J. Craig and Kurt Schock. 1992. "Global Structures and Political Processes in the Study of Domestic Political Conflict." *Annual Review of Sociology* 18:161–185.

Katz, Hagai and Helmut Anheier. 2006. "Global Connectedness: The Structure of Transnational NGO Networks." Pp. 240–265 in *Global Civil Society 2005/6*, edited by M. Glasius, M. Kaldor, and H. Anheier. London: Sage Publications.

Keck, Margaret and Kathryn Sikkink. 1998. *Activists Beyond Borders*. Ithaca, NY: Cornell University Press.

Khagram, Sanjeev, James V. Riker, and Kathryn Sikkink. 2002. *Restructuring World Politics: Transnational Social Movements, Networks, and Norms*. Minneapolis, MN: University of Minnesota Press.

Killian, Lewis M. 1964. "Social Movements." Pp. 426–455 in *Handbook of Modern Sociology*, edited by Robert E. L. Faris. Chicago: Rand McNally.

Kimball, Penn. 1994. *Downsizing the News: Network Cutbacks in the Nation's Capital*. Washington, DC and Baltimore: The Woodrow Wilson Center Press.

King, Brayden G., Marie Cornwall, and Eric C. Dahlin. 2005. "Winning Woman Suffrage One Step at a Time: Social Movements and the Logic of the Legislative Process." *Social Forces* 83(3):1211–1234.

King, Brayden G., Marie Cornwall, and Eric C. Dahlin. 2005. "Winning Woman Suffrage One Step at a Time: Social Movements and the Logic of the Legislative Process." *Social Forces* 83(3):1211–1234.

Kitschelt, Herbert P. 1986. "Political Opportunity Structures and Political Protest: Anti-Nuclear Movements in Four Democracies." *British Journal of Political Science* 16:57–85.

Knoke, David. 1990. *Political Networks: The Structural Perspective*. New York: Cambridge University Press.

Koopmans, Ruud. 2005. "Repression and the Public Sphere: Discursive Opportunities for Repression against the Extreme Right in Germany in the 1990s." Pp. 159–188 in *Mobilization and Repression*, edited by C. Davenport, H. Johnston, and C. Mueller. Minneapolis, MN: University of Minnesota Press.

Koopmans, Ruud and Paul Statham. 1999a. "Challenging the Liberal Nation-State? Postnationalism, Multiculturalism, and the Collective Claims Making of Migrants and Ethnic Minorities in Britain and Germany." *American Journal of Sociology* 105:652–696.

——. 1999b. "Ethnic and Civic Conceptions of Nationhood and the Differential Success of the Extreme Right in Germany." Pp. 225–252 in *How Social Movements Matter*, edited by M. Giugni, D. McAdam, and C. Tilly. Minneapolis, MN: University of Minnesota Press.

Korzeniewicz, Roberto P. and Timothy P. Moran. 1997. "World Economic Trends in the Distribution of Income, 1965–1992." *American Journal of Sociology* 102:1000–1039.

——. 2006. "World Inequality in the Twenty-First Century: Patterns and Tendencies." in *The Blackwell Companion to Globalization*, edited by G. Ritzer. Oxford and Malden, MA: Blackwell Publishing.

Korzeniewicz, Roberto P. and William C. Smith. 2000. "Poverty, Inequality, and Growth in Latin America: Searching for the High Road to Globalization." *Latin American Research Review* 35:7–54.

——. 2001. "Protest and Collaboration: Transnational Civil Society Networks and the Politics of Summitry and Free Trade in the Americas." North-South Center, University of Miami, FL.

——. 2003. "Mapping Regional Civil Society Networks in Latin America." Ford Foundation.

Kriesi, Hanspeter. 1996. "The Organizational Structure of New Social Movements in a Political Context." Pp. 152–184 in *Comparative Perspectives on Social Movements: Political Opportunities, Mobilizing Structures, and Cultural Framings*, edited by D. McAdam, J. D. McCarthy, and M. N. Zald. New York: Cambridge University Press.

——. 2004. "Political Context and Opportunity." Pp. 67–90 in *The Blackwell Companion to Social Movements*, edited by D. A. Snow, S. A. Soule, and H. Kriesi. Oxford and Malden, MA: Blackwell Publishing.

Kriesi, Hanspeter, Ruud Koopmans, Jan W. Duyvendak, and Marco G. Giugni. 1995. *New Social Movements in Western Europe: A Comparative Analysis*. Minneapolis, MN: University of Minnesota Press.

Lauman, Edward O. and David Knoke. 1987. *The Organizational State: Social Choice in National Policy Domains*. Madison, WI: University of Wisconsin Press.

Laxer, Gordon and Sandra Halperin. 2003. *Global Civil Society and its Limits*. New York: Palgrave Macmillan.

Levering, Ralph A. 1997. "Brokering the Law of the Sea Treaty: The Neptune Group." In *Transnational Social Movements and Global Politics: Solidarity Beyond the State*, edited by J. Smith, C. Chatfield, and R. Pagnucco. Syracuse, NY: Syracuse University Press.

Lichterman, Paul. 1996. *The Search for Political Community: American Activists Reinventing Commitment*. New York: Cambridge University Press.

Lipsky, Michael. 1968. "Protest as a Political Resource." *American Political Science Review* 62:1144–1158.

Maney, Gregory M. 2001. "Rival Transnational Networks and Indigenous Rights: The San Blas Kuna in Panama and the Yanomami in Brazil." *Research in Social Movements, Conflicts and Change* 23:103–144.

Maney, Gregory M., Lynne M. Woehrle, and Patrick G. Coy. 2005. "Harnessing and Challenging Hegemony: The U.S. Peace Movement after 9/11." *Sociological Perspectives* 48:357–381.

Markoff, John. 1996. *Waves of Democracy: Social Movements and Political Change*. Thousand Oaks: Pine Forge Press.

——. 1999. "Globalization and the Future of Democracy." Journal of World-Systems Research http://csf.colorado.edu/wsystems/jwsr.html 5:242–262.

——. 2003. "Margins, Centers, and Democracy: The Paradigmatic History of Women's Suffrage." *Signs: Journal of Women in Culture and Society* 29:85–116.

——. 2004. "Who Will Construct the Global Order?" in *Transnational Democracy*, edited by B. Williamson. London: Ashgate.

Markoff, John and Veronica Montecinos. 1993. "The Ubiquitous Rise of Economists." *Journal of Public Policy* 13:37–68.

Marks, Gary and Doug McAdam. 1996. "Social Movements and the Changing Structure of Political Opportunity in the European Community." Pp. 95–120 in *Governance in the European Union*, edited by G. Marks, F. W. Scharpf, P. C. Schmitter, and W. Streeck. Thousand Oaks, CA: Sage.

Marwell, Gerald and Pamela Oliver. 1993. *The Critical Mass in Collective Action*. Cambridge, UK: Cambridge University Press.

McAdam, Doug. 1982. *Political Process and the Development of Black Insurgency, 1930–1970*. Chicago and London: University of Chicago Press.

McAdam, Doug, John D. McCarthy, and Mayer Zald (eds). 1996. *Comparative dPerspectives on Social Movements: Political Opportunities, Mobilizing Structures and Cultural Framings*. New York: Cambridge University Press.

McAdam, Doug, Sidney Tarrow, and Charles Tilly. 2001. *Dynamics of Contention*. New York: Cambridge University Press.

McCarthy, John D. 1996. "Mobilizing Structures: Constraints and Opportunities in Adopting, Adapting and Inventing." Pp. 141–151 in *Comparative Perspectives on Social Movements: Political Opportunities, Mobilizing Structures and Cultural Framings*, edited by D. McAdam, J. McCarthy, and M. Zald. New York: Cambridge University Press.

McCarthy, John D. and Mayer Zald. 1977. "Resource Mobilization in Social Movements: A Partial Theory." *American Journal of Sociology* 82:1212–1241.

McCarthy, John D., David Britt, and Mark Wolfson. 1991. "The Institutional Channeling of Social Movements in the Modern State." Pp. 45–76 in *Research in Social Movements, Conflict and Change*, vol. 13. Greenwich, CT: JAI Press.

McCarthy, John D. and Clark McPhail. 2006. "Places of Protest: The Public Forum in Principle and Practice." *Mobilization* 11:229–248.

McCarthy, John D., Clark McPhail, and John Crist. 1999. "The Diffusion and Adoption of Public Order Management Systems." Pp. 71–95 in *Social Movements in a Globalizing World*, edited by D. della Porta, H. Kriesi, and D. Rucht. New York: St. Martin's Press.

McCarthy, John D., Jackie Smith, and Mayer Zald. 1996. "Accessing Media, Electoral and Government Agendas." Pp. 291–311 in *Comparative Perspectives on Social Movements: Political Opportunities, Mobilizing Structures and Cultural Framings*, edited by D. McAdam, J. McCarthy, and M. Zald. New York: Cambridge University Press.

McCarthy, John D. and Mark Wolfson. 1992. "Consensus Movements, Conflict Movements, and the Cooptation of Civic and State Infrastructures." Pp. 273–300 in *Frontiers in Social Movement Theory*, edited by A. Morris and C. M. Mueller. New Haven, CT: Yale University Press.

——. 1996. "Resource Mobilization by Local Social Movement Organizations: Agency, Strategy, and Organization in the Movement against Drinking and Driving." *American Sociological Review* 61:1070–1088.

McCarthy, John D., Mark Wolfson, David P. Baker, and Elaine Mosakowski. 1988. "The Founding of Social Movement Organizations: Local Citizens Groups Opposing Drunk Driving." Pp. 71–84 in *Ecological Models of Organizations*, edited by G. R. Carroll. Cambridge, MA: Ballinger.

McCarthy, John D. and Mayer N. Zald. 1973. *The Trend of Social Movements in America: Professionalization and Resource Mobilization*. Morristown, NJ: General Learning Press.

——. 1987. "The Trend of Social Movements in America: Professionalization and Resource Mobilization." Pp. 393–420 in *Social Movements in an Organizational Society*, edited by M. Zald and J. D. McCarthy. New Brunswick, NJ: Transaction.

——. 2002. "The Enduring Vitality of the Resource Mobilization Theory of Social Movements." In *Handbook of Sociological Theory*, edited by J. H. Turner. New York: Kluwer Academic/Plenum Press.

McChesney, Robert W. 1999. *Rich Media, Poor Democracy: Communication Politics in Dubious Times*. Champaign-Urbana, IL: University of Illinois Press.

McCright, Aaron and Riley Dunlap. 2003. "Defeating Kyoto: The Conservative Movement's Impact on U.S. Climate Change Policy." *Social Problems* 50:348–373.

McMichael, Philip. 2003. *Development and Social Change: A Global Perspective,* 3rd edition. Thousand Oaks, CA: Pine Forge Press.

——. 2005. "Review of *Coalitions Across Borders: Transnational Protest and the Neoliberal Order.*" *American Journal of Sociology* 111:954–956.

McPherson, Miller and Thomas Rotolo. 1996. "Testing a Dynamic Model of Social Composition: Diversity and Change in Voluntary Groups." *American Sociological Review* 61:179–202.

Melucci, Alberto. 1989. *Nomads of the Present*. Philadelphia, PA: Temple University Press.

Meyer, David S. and Debra C. Minkoff. 2004. "Conceptualizing Political Opportunity." *Social Forces* 82:1457–1492.

Meyer, David S. and Sidney Tarrow, Editors. 1998. *The Social Movement Society: Contentious Politics for a New Century*. Lanham, MD: Rowman & Littlefield.

Meyer, John. 2003. "Globalization, National Culture, and the Future of the World Polity." *Wei Lun Lecture- Chinese University of Hong Kong (Nov. 2001)*.

Meyer, John W., John Boli, George M. Thomas, and Francisco O. Ramirez. 1997. "World Society and the Nation-State." *American Journal of Sociology* 103:144–181.

Michaelson, Marc. 1994. "Wangari Maathai and Kenya's Green Belt Movement: Exploring the Evolution and Potentialities of Consensus Movement Mobilization." *Social Problems* 41:540–561.

Minkoff, Deborah. 1993. "The Organization of Survival." Social Forces 71(4):887–908.

——. 1995. *Organizing for Equality: the Evolution of Women's and Racial Ethnic Organizations in America, 1955–1985*. New Brunswick, NJ: Rutgers University Press.

Minkoff, Deborah. 1997a. "Producing Social Capital: National Social Movements and Civil Society." *American Behavioral Scientist* 40:606–619.

———. 1997b. "The Sequencing of Social Movements." *American Sociological Review* 62:779–799.

Moghadam, Valentine. 2005. *Globalizing Women: Transnational Feminist Networks.* Baltimore, MD: Johns Hopkins University Press.

Montecinos, Veronica. 2001. "Feminists and Technocrats in the Democratization of Latin America: A Prolegomenon." *International Journal of Politics, Culture and Society* 15:175–199.

Moody, Kim. 1997. Workers in a Lean World: Unions in the International Economy. New York: Verso Books.

Moore, Barrington. 1966. *Social Origins of Dictatorship and Democracy: Lord and Peasant in the Making of the Modern World.* Boston: Beacon Press.

Moore, Kelly. 1996. "Organizing Integrity: American Science and the Creation of Public Interest Organizations, 1955–1975." *American Journal of Sociology* 101:1592–1627.

Morris, Aldon. 1984. *The Origins of the Civil Rights Movement.* New York: The Free Press.

Mueller, Carol. 1994. "Conflict Networks and the Origins of Women's Liberation." Pp. 234–263 in *New Social Movements: From Ideology to Identity*, edited by E. Larana, H. Johnston, and J. R. Gusfield. Philadelphia, PA: Temple University Press.

Mueller, Carol. 1999. "Escape from the GDR, 1961–1989: Hybrid Exit Repertoires in a Disintegrating Leninist Regime." *American Journal of Sociology* 105:697–735.

Murphy, Gillian. 2005. "Coalitions and the Development of the Global Environmental Movement: A Double-Edged Sword." *Mobilization: An International Quarterly* 10:235–250.

Munck, Ronaldo. 2002. *Globalization and Labour: The New Great Transformation.* London: Zed Books.

Norberg-Hodge, Helena. 1996. "The Pressure to Modernize and Globalize." Pp. 33–46 in *The Case Against the Global Economy and for a Turn to the Local*, edited by J. Mander and E. Goldsmith. San Francisco: Sierra Club Books.

Norris, Pippa. 1999. *Critical Citizens: Global Support for Democratic Governance.* New York: Oxford University Press.

———. 2002. *Democratic Phoenix: Reinventing Political Activism.* New York: Cambridge University Press.

O'Brien, Robert. 2000. "Workers and World Order: the Tentative Transformation of the International Union Movement." *Review of International Studies* 26:533–555.

———. Forthcoming. *The Global Labour Movement.*

Oliver, Pamela. 1989. "Bringing the Crowd Back In: The Nonorganizational Elements of Social Movements." *Research in Social Movements, Conflict and Change* 5:133–170.

Oliver, Pamela and Mark Furman. 1989. "Contradictions Between National and Local Organizational Strength: The Case of the John Birch Society." Pp. 155–177 in *International Social Movement Research.* Greenwich, CT: JAI Press.

Orloff, Ann S. and Theda Skocpol. 1984. "Why Not Equal Protection? Explaining the Politics of Public Social Welfare in Britain and the United States, 1880s–1920s." *American Sociological Review* 49:726–50.

Osa, Maryjane. 2003. "Networks in Opposition: Linking Organizations Through Activists in the Polish People's Republic." Pp. 77–104 in *Social Movements and Networks*, edited by M. Diani and D. McAdam. Oxford: Oxford University Press.

Passy, Florence. 1999. "Supranational Political Opportunities As a Channel of Globalization of Political Conflicts. The Case of the Conflict Around the Rights of Indigenous Peoples." Pp. 148–169 in *Social Movements in a Globalizing World*, edited by D. d. Porta, H. Kriesi, and D. Rucht. New York: St. Martin's Press.

———. 2003. "Social Networks Matter. But How?" Pp. 21–48 in *Social Movements and Networks*, edited by M. Diani and D. McAdam. Oxford: Oxford University Press.

Piven, Francis Fox and Richard Cloward. 1979. *Poor People's Movements: Why They Succeed, How They Fail.* New York: Vintage Books.

Podobnik, Bruce. 2004. "Resistance to Globalization: Cycles and Evolutions in the Globalization Protest Movement." Presented at the American Sociological Association Annual Meeting. San Francisco.

Polletta, Francesca. 2002. *Freedom is an Endless Meeting.* Chicago: University of Chicago Press.

Powell, Walter W. 1990. "Neither Markets nor Hierarchy: Network forms of Organization." *Research in Organizational Behavior* 12:295–336.

Price, Richard. 1998. "Reversing the Gun Sights: Transnational Civil Society Targets Land Mines." *International Organization* 52:613–644.

Quadagno, Jill. 1992. "Social Movements and State Transformation: Labor Unions and Racial Conflict in the War on Poverty." *American Sociological Review* 57:616–634.

Rasler, Karen. 1996. "Concessions, Repression, and Political Protest in the Iranian Revolution." *American Sociological Review* 61:132–152.

Ray, Raka. 1999. *Fields of Protest: Women's Movements in India*. Minneapolis, MN: University of Minnesota Press.

Reimann, Kim D. 2002. "Building Networks from the Outside In: International Movements, Japanese NGOs, and the Kyoto Climate Change Conference." Pp. 173–189 in *Globalization and Resistance: Transnational Dimensions of Social Movements*, vol. 6, edited by J. Smith and H. Johnston. Lanham, MD: Rowman & Littlefield.

Riles, Annelise. 2001. *The Network Inside Out*. Ann Arbor, MI: University of Michigan Press.

Risse, Thomas, Stephen C. Ropp, and Kathryn Sikkink, eds. 1999. *The Power of Human Rights: International Norms and Domestic Change*. New York: Cambridge University Press.

Robinson, William. 2004. *A Theory of Global Capitalism*. Baltimore, MD: Johns Hopkins University Press.

Rochon, Thomas. 1998. *Culture Moves: Ideas, Activism, and Changing Values*. Princeton, NJ: Princeton University Press.

Rose, Jerry D. 1982. *Outbreaks, the Sociology of Collective Behavior*. New York: The Free Press.

Rothman, Franklin Daniel and Pamela E. Oliver. 2002. "From Local to Global: The Anti-Dam Movement in Southern Brazil 1979–1992." Pp. 115–131 in *Globalization and Resistance: Transnational Dimensions of Social Movements*, edited by J. Smith and H. Johnston. Lanham, MD: Rowman & Littlefield.

Rucht, Dieter. 1996. "The Impact of National Contexts on Social Movement Structures: A Cross-Movement and Cross-National Comparison." Pp. 185–224 in *Comparative Perspectives on Social Movements: Political Opportunities, Mobilizing Structures, and Cultural Framings*, edited by D. McAdam, J. D. McCarthy, and M. N. Zald. New York: Cambridge University Press.

——. 2004. "Movements, Allies, Adversaries, and Third Parties." Pp. 197–216 in *The Blackwell Companion to Social Movements*, edited by D. A. Snow, S. A. Soule, and H. Kriesi. Oxford and Malden, MA: Blackwell Publishing.

Rupp, Leila J. 1997. *Worlds of Women: The Making of an International Women's Movement*. Princeton, NJ: Princeton University Press.

Rupp, Leila J. and Verta Taylor. 1987. *Survival in the Doldrums: The American Women's Rights Movement*. New York: Oxford University Press.

Sassen, Saskia. 1998. *Globalization and Its Discontents*. New York: The New Press.

——. 2000. *Guests and Aliens*. New York: The New Press.

Schofer, Evan and Marion Fourcade-Gournchas. 2001. "The Structural Contexts of Civic Engagement: Voluntary Association Membership in Comparative Perspective." *American Sociological Review* 66:806–828.

Scott, James C. 1985. *Weapons of the Weak: Everyday Forms of Peasant Resistance*. New Haven, CT: Yale University Press.

Seidman, Gay W. 2000. "Adjusting the Lens: What Do Globalizations, Transnationalism, and the Anti-apartheid Movement Mean for Social Movement Theory?" Pp. 339–358 in *Globalizations and Social Movements: Culture, Power, and the Transnational Public Sphere*, edited by J. A. Guidry, M. D. Kennedy, and M. N. Zald. Ann Arbor, MI: University of Michigan Press.

Sikkink, Kathryn. 1993. "Human Rights, Principled Issue-Networks, and Sovereignty in Latin America." *International Organization* 47:411–441.

——. 2002. "Restructuring World Politics: The Limits and Asymmetries of Soft Power." Pp. 301–317 in *Restructuring World Politics: Transnational Social Movements, Networks, and Norms*, edited by S. Khagram, J. V. Riker, and K. Sikkink. Minneapolis, MN: University of Minnesota Press.

——. 2005. "Patterns of Dynamic Multilevel Governance and the Insider-Outsider Coalition." Pp. 151–173 in *Transnational Protest and Global Activism*, edited by D. della Porta and S. Tarrow. Lanham, MD: Rowman & Littlefield.

Silver, Beverly J. 2003. *Forces of Labor: Workers' Movements and Globalization Since 1870*. New York: Cambridge University Press.

Sklair, Leslie. 2001. *The Transnational Capitalist Class*. Oxford and Malden, MA: Blackwell Publishing.

Skocpol, Theda. 1992. *Protecting Soldiers and Mothers: The Political Origins of Social Policy in the United States*. Cambridge, MA: Harvard University Press.

Smith, Christian, ed. 1996. *Disruptive Religion: The Force of Faith in Social Movement Activism*. New York: Routledge.

Smith, Jackie. 1995. "Transnational Political Processes and the Human Rights Movement." Pp. 185–220 in *Research in Social Movements, Conflict and Change*, vol. 18, edited by L. Kriesberg, M. Dobkowski, and I. Walliman. Greenwich, CT: JAI Press.

——. "Global Civil Society? Transnational Social Movement Organizations and Social Capital." *American Behavioral Scientist* 42:93–107.

——. 1999. "Global Politics and Transnational Social Movements Strategies: The Transnational Campaign against International Trade in Toxic Wastes." Pp. 170–188 in *Social Movements in a Globalizing World* edited by D. d. Porta, H. Kriesi, and D. Rucht. New York: St. Martin's Press.

——. 2005. "Building Bridges or Building Walls? Explaining Regionalization among Transnational Social Movement Organizations." *Mobilization: An International Journal* 10:251–270.

——. Forthcoming. *Global Visions/Rival Networks: Social Movements for Global Democracy.* Baltimore, MD: Johns Hopkins University Press.

Smith, Jackie, Charles Chatfield, and Ron Pagnucco. 1997. *Transnational Social Movements and Global Politics: Solidarity Beyond the State.* Syracuse, NY: Syracuse University Press.

Soule, Sarah A. and Jennifer Earl. 2005. "A Movement Society Evaluated: Collective Protest in the United States, 1960–1986." *Mobilization: An International Journal* 10:345–364.

Staggenborg, Suzanne. 1986. "Coalition Work in the Pro-Choice Movement: Organizational and Environmental Opportunities and Obstacles." *Social Problems* 33:374–389.

Staggenborg, Suzanne. 1988. "The Consequences of Professionalization and Formalization in the Pro-Choice Movement." *American Sociological Review* 53:585–605.

Staggenborg, Suzanne and Verta Taylor. 2005. "Whatever Happened to the Women's Movement." *Mobilization: An International Journal* 10:37–52.

Stark, David, Balazs Vedres, and Laszlo Bruszt. 2006. "Rooted Transnational Publics: Integrating Foreign Ties and Civic Activism." *Theory and Society* 35:323–349.

Steinberg, Marc W. 1995. "The Roar of the Crowd: Repertoires of Discourse and Collective Action among the Spitalfields Silk Weavers in Nineteenth-Century London." Pp. 57–88 in *Repertoires and Cycles of Collective Action*, edited by M. Traugott. Durham, NC: Duke University Press.

Stewart, Julie. 2004. "When Local Troubles Become Transnational: The Transformation of a Guatemalan Indigenous Rights Movement." *Mobilization: An International Journal* 9(3):259–278.

Stiglitz, Joseph. 2003. *Globalization and its Discontents.* New York: W.W. Norton and Company.

Subramaniam, Mangala, Manjusha Gupte, and Debarashmi Mitra. 2003. "Local to Global: Transnational Networks and Indian Women's Grassroots Organizing." *Mobilization: An International Journal* 8:335–352.

Tarrow, Sidney. 1996. "States and Opportunities: The Political Structuring of Social Movements in Democratic States." Pp. 41–61 in *Political Opportunities, Mobilizing Structures and Framing: Social Movement Dynamics in Cross-National Perspective*, edited by D. McAdam, J. McCarthy, and M. Zald. New York: Cambridge University Press.

——. 1998a. "Fishnets, Internets and Catnets: Globalization and Transnational Collective Action." Pp. 228–244 in *Challenging Authority: The Historical Study of Contentious Politics*, edited by M. Hanagan, L. P. Moch, and W. T. Brake. Minneapolis, MN: University of Minnesota Press.

——. 1998b. *Power in Movement: Social Movements, Collective Action and Politics,* 2nd edition. New York: Cambridge University Press.

——. 2001. "Transnational Politics: Contention and Institutions in International Politics." *Annual Review of Political Science* 4:1–20.

——. 2005. *The New Transnational Activism.* New York: Cambridge University Press.

Taylor, Verta. 1989. "Social Movement Continuity: The Women's Movement in Abeyance." *American Sociological Review* 54:761–775.

Thomas, Daniel. 2001. *The Helsinki Effect: International Norms, Human Rights, and the Demise of Communism.* Princeton, NJ: Princeton University Press.

Tilly, Charles. 1978. *From Mobilization to Revolution.* Reading, MA: Addison Wesley.

——. 1995. "Globalization Threatens Labor Rights." *International Labor and Working Class History* 47:1–23.

Tilly, Charles. 1984. "Social Movements and National Politics." Pp. 297–317 in *Statemaking and Social Movements: Essays in History and Theory*, edited by C. Bright and S. Harding. Ann Arbor: University of Michigan Press.

Tilly, Charles, Louise Tilly, and Richard Tilly. 1975. *The Rebellious Century, 1830–1930.* Cambridge, MA: Harvard University Press.

Traugott, Mark. 1995. "Repertoires and Cycles of Collective Action." Durham, NC: Duke University Press.

Turner, Lowell. 2003. "Reviving the Labor Movement." Pp. 23–57 in *Research in the Sociology of Work*, edited by D. Cornfield and H. McCammon. Greenwich, CT: JAI Press.

United Nations. 2004. "We the Peoples: Civil Society, the United Nations and Global Governance: Report of the Panel of Eminent Persons on United Nations-Civil Society Relations." United Nations Secretary General, New York.

Valocchi, Steve. 1990. "The Unemployed Workers' Movement: A Re-examination of the Piven and Cloward Thesis." *Social Problems* 37:191–205.

Van Dyke, Nella. 2003. "Protest Cycles and Party Politics." Pp. 226–245 in *States, Parties, and Social Movements*, edited by J. Goldstone. New York: Cambridge University Press.

Verba, Sidney, Kay Schlozman, and Henry Brady. 1995. *Voice and Equality: Civic Volunteerism in American Politics.* Cambridge, MA: Harvard University Press.

Voss, Kim and Rachel Sherman. 2000. "Breaking the Iron Law of Oligarchy: Union Revitalization in the American Labor Movement." *American Journal of Sociology* 106:303–349.

Wallerstein, Immanuel. 1976. *The Modern World System*. New York: Academic Press.

——. 1980. *The Modern World System II: Mercantilism and the Consolidation of the European World Economy*. New York: Academic Press.

Walton, John and David Seddon. 1994. *Free Markets and Food Riots: The Politics of Global Adjustment*. Oxford and Malden, MA: Blackwell Publishing.

Waterman, Peter and Jill Timms. 2004. "Trade Union Internationalism and a Global Civil Society in the Making." Pp. 175–202 in *Global Civil Society 2004/5*. London: Sage Publications.

Western, Bruce. 1993. "Postwar Unionization in Eighteen Advanced Capitalist Countries." *American Sociological Review* 58:266–282.

Wiest, Dawn and Jackie Smith. 2007. "Globalization, Regionalism, and the Organization of Transnational Collective Action within World Regions, 1980–2000." *International Journal of Comparative Sociology* 48(1–2):Forthcoming.

Winston, Fletcher. 2004. "Networks, Norms, and Tactics in Long Island Environmental Organizations." Sociology, SUNY—Stony Brook, Stony Brook, NY.

Wittner, Lawrence. 1993. *One World or None: A History of the Nuclear Disarmament Movement Through 1953*, vol. 1. Stanford, CA: Stanford University Press.

——. 1997. *Resisting the Bomb: A History of the World Nuclear Disarmament Movement, 1954–1970*, vol. 2. Stanford, CA: Stanford University Press.

Wolf, Eric. 1982. *Europe and the People without History*. Berkeley, CA: University of California Press.

Wood, Lesley Julia. 2004. "The Diffusion of Direct Action Tactics: From Seattle to Toronto and New York." Sociology, Columbia University, New York.

Wood, Leslie. 2005. "Bridging the Chasms: The Case of People's Global Action." Pp. 95–119 in *Coalitions Across Borders: Transnational Protest and the Neoliberal Order*, edited by J. Bandy and J. Smith. Lanham, MD: Rowman & Littlefield.

World Commission on the Social Dimensions of Globalization. 2004. "A Fair Globalization: Creating Opportunities for All."

Wuthnow, Robert. 1989. *Communities of Discourse: Ideology and Social Structure in the Reformation, the Enlightenment, and European Socialism*. Cambridge, MA: Harvard University Press.

——. 1998. *Loose Connections: Joining Together in America's Fragmented Communities*. Cambridge, MA: Harvard University Press.

Zald, Mayer N. 1987. "The Future of Social Movements." Pp. 319–336 in *Social Movements in an Organizational Society*, edited by M. N. Zald and J. D. McCarthy. New Brunswick, NJ: Transaction.

Zald, Mayer N. and Roberta Ash Garner. 1994. "Social Movement Organizations: Growth, Decay and Change." Pp. 121–142 in *Social Movements in an Organizational Society* edited by Mayer N. Zald and John D. McCarthy. London and New Brunswick, NJ: Transaction Publishers.

Zald, Mayer N. and John D. McCarthy, Eds. 1987. *Social Movements in an Organizational Society*. New Brunswick: Transaction.

Zwerman, Gilda and Patricia Steinhoff. 2005. "When Activists Ask for Trouble: State-Dissident Interactions and the New Left Cycle of Resistance in the United States and Japan." Pp. 85–107 in *Repression and Mobilization*, edited by C. Davenport, H. Johnston, and C. Mueller.

CHAPTER 3

Cultural Approaches in the Sociology of Social Movements

James M. Jasper

In the late twentieth century, the social sciences underwent a broad cultural turn, building on an earlier linguistic turn (Lafont 1993) but finding human meanings in a variety of activities and artifacts not previously interpreted as cultural. Cognitive psychology played the vanguard role in this shift, but practitioners in all disciplines were soon able to find indigenous traditions and tools that helped them craft their own repertoires for understanding meaning (e.g., Crane 1994; Hunt 1989; Kuper 1999). Beginning in the 1970s, increasing numbers of social scientists began to pay attention to how humans understand the world, and not simply their (supposedly) objective behaviors and outcomes within it.

The cultural turn left its mark on the study of politics and social movements. Interestingly, it was more often those who studied culture who were able to see the politics behind it (Crane 1994); students of politics were slower to see the culture inside it (Jasper 2005). French post-structuralists such as Derrida and Foucault saw politics in all institutions and cultural artifacts (Dosse 1997) long before mainstream political scientists and sociologists recognized the meanings that permeate political institutions and actions.

The gap between more structural and more cultural approaches to mobilization often depended on how scholars who had been politically active in and around 1968 interpreted the barriers they had faced, especially whether they felt their intended revolutionary subjects had had the correct consciousness or not. Culturalists tended to try to explain why the working class had false consciousness, while structuralists concentrated on the defeat of those (such as radical students like themselves) who had had the correct consciousness. Accordingly, cultural and structural theories both flourished after the 1970s, with little interaction between them. One focused on the understandings that encouraged or discouraged collective action; the other on the resources, laws, and state actions that permitted or prevented it.

A central banner of the cultural shift is "social constructionism," a tradition that showed how aspects of the world that we take for granted as unchangeable or biological have instead been created by those in power as a means to retain their positions (gender being the most studied example). A dizzying number of institutions, expectations, and categories have been deconstructed to reveal the extensive work behind them (Hacking [1999] is a good survey). This tradition has enormous power when scholars remain true to the metaphor and show the concrete political, cultural, and economic work that strategic players put into establishing and maintaining favored meanings. Like all cultural analysis, however, it frequently lapses into interpreting hidden meanings without linking them to strategic players, projects, audiences, and arenas.

An appreciation of culture was slow to come to the study of social movements in the United States, in part because structural models had arrived at their full fruition only in the 1970s and early 1980s and still attracted the bulk of analytic attention. The cultural gaps in many of these models were filled only in the late 1980s and 1990s, relatively late in the broader cultural revolution. Scholars in other nations tended to be quicker to appreciate cultural aspects of politics. Ironically, voluntarist traditions in American politics meant that structural insights remained exciting and fruitful for a long time, while under British traditions of class awareness and under French statism the importance of cultural meaning and identity proved the important theoretical breakthrough (Jasper 2005). Other national traditions tended to fall between these extremes.

Culture, as I shall use the term, consists of shared mental worlds and their perceived embodiments. The latter may include words, artifacts, artworks, rituals, events, individuals, and any other action or creation that carries symbolic meanings. Solipsistic understandings are mere hallucinations unless or until they are shared with others. Yet culture is located both within individuals and outside them, and the most robust methodologies usually examine both sources. Cultural meanings need not be embodied: a group can think and feel the same way without articulating it (although there are obvious methodological challenges to establishing this). Finally, culture comprises cognitive understandings of how the world is, moral principles and intuitions about how the world should be, and emotions concerning both of these (and, often, the gap between them). Most cultural artifacts arouse cognition, morality, and emotion at the same time. (For more on this connection, see pages 80–89 below.)

In some cases, and in some models, culture comes in discrete units, which can simply be added to existing, noncultural models. Frames are necessary alongside resources, which help disseminate them; at a certain moment collective identities contribute to mobilization in parallel to interests. In other cases or other models, cultural meanings permeate apparently non-cultural factors, so that appreciation of culture requires a fundamental rethinking of these other concepts. In this more thoroughgoing cultural vision, culture is everywhere. But that does not mean it is everything.

Analytically, we can distinguish culture from physical resources, the logic of strategic interaction, and individual idiosyncrasies, each of which can have an impact distinct from that of shared meanings. But culture permeates the other factors: we use resources according to how we understand them, we engage in strategic projects with means and ends that are culturally shaped, and our biographies result from our cultural surroundings. Nonetheless, these other dimensions have their own logics not always reducible to culture (Jasper 1997).

Cultural insights can be sprinkled atop structural approaches, then, but they can also be used to fundamentally rethink the basic entities of structural approaches. Once rules, arenas, resources, and other traditionally structural variables are seen as partly cultural, we have a cultural approach alongside the structural. Yet at the same time, the two are, with some adjustments, made compatible with one another. Few cultural researchers wish to abandon the many insights developed over the years by structuralists—most of whom claim to have adopted cultural insights and to no longer be structuralists (Kurzman 2003; McAdam 2003; McAdam et al. 2001; Tarrow 2003).

The first section of this chapter briefly examines the history of the cultural turn, beginning with several early efforts to understand culture in politics that came to be ignored or dismissed in the 1960s and 1970s. Each intellectual fashion inspires a backlash, in what looks like a repetitive cycle but is more of a spiral: we never quite return to the same place. I then turn in part II to a number of the concrete forms that carry culture, arguing that they have not been adequately linked to strategic players and audiences. I also look at more metaphorical terms that have been applied to cultural meanings, often derived from physical artifacts. The third section addresses the emotions of social movements, giving them somewhat more attention only because they have been especially overlooked, even by proponents of the cultural turn. In the fourth section, I examine morality as a distinct aspect of culture, crucial to protest mobilization. Next, hoping to show that their causal impact derives partly from cognitive and emotional dimensions that other traditions deny, in the fifth section I reinterpret some basic noncultural metaphors and concepts from a cultural point of view. The sixth section addresses some of the methods used to get at cultural meanings. Finally, I conclude with some salient unanswered questions rem: cultural shift. Throughout, I cite exemplary studies and suggest further readings.

Cultural meanings and feelings do not exist in a vacuum. We always need their strategic contexts: who hopes to have rhetorical effects on others, in what what goals in mind, and how are audiences affected by the messages they receiv and morals they hold, the emotions they feel? Culture and strategy are insepar offer microlevel mechanisms that help us avoid the gross metaphors—states, st works, even movements—that have guided political analysis too often in the pa: than culture, strategy promises conceptual tools to overcome the deterministic r have hindered intellectual progress. Combined, culture and strategy offer u toolkit for explaining political action.

THE VICISSITUDES OF CULTURE

The Romance of Community

The ancient Greeks and Romans paid considerable attention to the intersection of politics and culture through the study of rhetoric, the processes by which speakers have effects on their audiences (and vice versa). Here was the first social-constructionist vision of the world, launching the oldest tradition of cultural analysis, which is still around today. It is a strategic, purposive vision that continues to provide lessons.

This venerable tradition lost status first with Christian metaphysics and then in the modern scientific revolution, both of which drew on Plato's belief that we could get at deeper truths beneath the give and take of rhetoric (from the start, rhetoric had critics who believed in Truth rather than constructionism). The convoluted debates over truth that tortured medieval Christian theologians found secular versions in the modern age (Blumenberg 1983).

In the Romantic backlash against the Enlightenment, culture returned to the fore as a way to explain politics, but in a very different form. Culture and community were celebrated as deep, often organic sources of spiritual values and purpose, more important than the material advancement promised by the scientific revolution. Until the middle of the twentieth century, concern with culture usually accompanied a conservative politics of community in opposition to the liberal and Utilitarian embrace of markets and individual rights (for more on this long development see Jasper [2005] and of course Williams [1958], who tried to recover its socialist potential).

By embracing traditional tropes of nation, culture, and community, yet giving them a savage reading, the fascists discredited them in the middle of the twentieth century. For

20 years after the fall of fascism, such terms remained taboo, allowing a generation to grow up in the United States and Europe who could rediscover culture and community in the 1960s without the conservative connotations. Now these tropes were more likely to have a left-leaning flavor (thanks in part to Williams and E. P. Thompson), a defense of community against the now-triumphant liberal individualism of the marketplace. The fruitful vocabulary of nature and the environment, once embedded in conservative or even fascist ideologies, could be transplanted into leftist fields (Bramwell 1989). Community was now something to be defended from the thuggish Cold War policies (and later, neoliberal policies) of the United States. The stage was set for the emergence of identity politics as a thread in the cultural revolution. But first, we need to examine an earlier (and liberal, in the sense of individualistic) tradition that had emerged in opposition to the Romantic embrace of community.

Emergence and Enthusiasm in Crowd Traditions

In contrast to the Romantic embrace of the *folk*, other urban intellectuals developed an image of crowds as folk devils: passionate, irrational, and dangerous. The people were fine as pictur-esque but inert peasants in the countryside, not as mobs of angry urban workers. The great revolts of nineteenth-century cities, and the specter of their periodic repetition, persuaded middle-class intellectuals that individuals in crowds were touched by insanity. In this version of liberalism, individuals were supposed to vote—if that—to express their political views, not riot. Along with several contemporaries across Europe, Gustave Le Bon (1960/1895) gave the crowd trope its classic form (van Ginneken 1992). "A commencement of antipathy or disap-probation, which in the case of an isolated individual would not gain strength, becomes at once furious hatred in the case of an individual in a crowd" (p. 50). Crowds generate "exces-sive" emotions and ideas: "To exaggerate, to affirm, to resort to repetitions, and never to attempt to prove anything by reasoning are methods of argument well known to speakers at public meetings" (p. 51). In most formulations, as in Le Bon's, anyone could prove suscepti-ble to crowd pressures.

In other visions, certain kinds of people were particularly open to the strong emotions of crowds and movements. Eric Hoffer (1951) formulated a popular version of this view, por-traying a desperate fanatic who needed to believe in something, no matter what it was (on Hoffer, who was something of a social isolate, see Trillin [1968]). These "true believers" went from movement to movement, driven by inner compulsions to belong. Their lack of stable personal identities or the frustrations of "barren and insecure" lives led them to lose them-selves in some big cause. The self-sacrifice of collective action, according to Hoffer (1951:25), is patently irrational, attracting "the poor, misfits, outcasts, minorities, adolescent youth, the ambitious, those in the grip of some vice or obsession, the impotent (in body or mind), the inordinately selfish, the bored, the sinners." Fascist mobs and communist sects cast a long shadow on intellectual formulations of the time, arousing in observers like Hoffer the same kind of exaggerated images and passions that he attributed to social movements them-selves. Ideology precluded careful observation.

Even the more sophisticated theories of the late 1950s and early 1960s, which focused on fragmented social structures rather than pathological individuals, built upon crowd imagery. William Kornhauser (1959) crafted the most precise model of "mass society" in which anomic individuals are cut loose from the social bonds of formal ("intermediary") organiza-tions. This atomization leaves them open to charismatic demagogues like Hitler, who can manipulate them directly through mass media such as radio and later television. Reflecting the broader crowd tradition's sharp distinction between normal institutional activities and abnormal noninstitutional ones, Kornhauser admired formal organizations but feared informal social networks, solidary communities such as mining towns, and other collective identities as dangerous. Even emotions such as affective solidarities with a collective were pathological.

Neil Smelser (1962) applied Talcott Parsons' systems approach to collective action, which he saw as deviant—something was wrong after all, or people would not protest—but that he attributed to strains in the social system that made it impossible for some to follow their prescribed roles. Like Parsons, Smelser left an important logical place for culture at the heart of his typologies and yet had surprisingly little to say about it. What he did say was often mildly pejorative—although he never used the term irrational. "Generalized beliefs," such as hysteria, wish fulfillment, and hostility, consisted of a "short-circuited" form of thought, in that they made symbolic leaps from one level of reality to another. But Smelser never admitted that these were emotional symbols, instead dismissing them as mistaken forms of reasoning which lacked sufficient evidence. Before the cultural revolution in social science, scholars who cared about cultural meanings and feelings were drawn to psychoanalysis, the most elaborated framework then available for serious symbolic interpretation (as I argue in Jasper [2004b]).

Strip away the unnecessarily pejorative labels, and most of Smelser's description of generalized beliefs deals usefully with how humans use culture. Today, we recognize the ubiquity of metaphors, which transfer meaning from one place to another in a short-circuiting kind of leap. Metonymy is very much a kind of short-circuiting, as a trait or object "stands in for" a person or group. These leaps are often based on emotional connections, which remain invisible if we treat beliefs only as truth statements as in science. Our webs of meanings and of feelings may be accurate or they may be inaccurate, but cognition and emotion operate the same way in either case. Cultural meanings are not as explicit as science (although even science operates partly through metaphors and other interpretive leaps).

Unfortunately, Smelser later elaborated (1968) on the questionable psychoanalytic concepts frequently applied to collective behavior, as he himself went through analysis in the years after his book had been published (as did so many serious intellectuals of the time, in an effort to understand meaning). Even as cognitive psychology was elsewhere gaining speed in ways that would help trigger the broader cultural turn (e.g., Bruner 1962), Smelser argued that protestors were working out oedipal impulses. "On the one hand there is the unqualified love, worship, and submission to the leader of the movement, who articulates and symbolizes 'the cause.' On the other hand there is the unqualified suspicion, denigration, and desire to destroy the agent felt responsible for the moral decay of social life and standing in the way of reform, whether he be a vested interest or a political authority" (1968:119–120). The cause is the beloved mother, authorities the despised father. Here psychoanalytic tools, oddly deployed outside any ongoing therapeutic context or even depth interviews, made emotions appear pathological and misguided, just as the earlier psychoanalytic application had made metaphorical thought seem a mistake (for an exception, based on actual depth interviews with activists, see Keniston [1968]). Such efforts hid the fact that emotions and cultural interpretation permeate all our actions and institutions.

Drawing on a microlevel tradition of American interactionism, Ralph Turner and Lewis Killian (1957) were able to appreciate some of the local dynamics of crowds, especially their ability to create new norms and meanings (although these were thought to "emerge" rather than to be consciously created, as a later generation of researchers might instead see it). Still operating within a "deviance" paradigm, they argued (1957:143) that "Crowd behavior consists, in essence, of deviations from the traditional norms of society." This deviation might be creative and fruitful, but it might also devolve into the crowd dynamics Le Bon had posited.

There was still no sense that protestors drew from all sorts of cultural expressions and references in their society, often very conservative ones. Most crowd traditions, like structural–functional theory of the time, posited "a culture" that dominated society. If protestors stepped outside this culture, they had to set up their own alternative culture, different in a full range of emotional and cognitive displays and positions. (Other crowd traditions addressed deviant individuals rather than universal crowd dynamics; psychoanalytic work did both.)

During these years, Joseph Gusfield (1963) managed to forge a cultural approach to protestors without pejorative psychoanalytic notions. He portrayed a century of U.S. conflict over alcohol consumption and prohibition as an ever-evolving dispute over moral visions: that of the new, urban industrial society on the one hand versus more rural and small-town ethics on the other. "Consensus about fundamentals of governmental form, free enterprise economy, and church power," he argued, "has left a political vacuum which moral issues have partially filled" (1963:2). In the end, Gusfield did not go far enough in his moral–cultural approach. He contrasted issues of structure and power with those of morality (which only filled a "vacuum"), as though these were not always entwined. In this view, some movements were expressive whereas most were instrumental. He also saw morality as a self-interested concern with personal status, certainly an important motivation (when combined with anxiety over status loss), but not the only moral motivation.

For nearly 100 years, crowd-inspired scholarship discouraged careful attention to the motivations, cognitive meanings, and emotions of protestors. These were present, but located either in individual pathologies or in the very local settings of crowds. Missing was a sense of culture as a social, collective product, as a set of understandings that could be carried from one situation to the next as well as being reshaped by those settings. Missing also was a view of emotions as displays for other people, according to implicit rules, in other words as a means by which people interact rather than as some kind of short-circuiting of interaction. This long tradition recognized that cognition and emotions are important to collective action, but they denied that they are normal —ubiquitous—aspects of all social life. Far from pathology, however, they are the stuff of political life.

Civic Culture

The flip side of "bad" mob participation was "good" civic participation (Almond and Verba 1963). In the American atmosphere of the 1950s, this meant avoiding fascist or communist movements, considered "mass." Voting for established political parties, joining safe groups such as parent associations, and supporting the ideas of formal democracy—in other words, playing by the rules—were admired as forming a stable civic culture. Scholars in this tradition expected these pluralist institutions and attitudes supporting them to spread gradually around the world, accompanying economic modernization (Gilman 2003; Rostow 1960).

A certain personality type, oriented toward achievement and merit, was expected to accompany these transformations (Inkeles and Smith 1974). Some versions of civic culture theory retained a psychoanalytic flavor, especially trying to explain childrearing patterns that led to "authoritarian personalities" (Adorno et al. 1950). This early work assumed a link between individual personality traits and a broader "national culture," an approach discredited when Stanley Milgram (1974) found—to his surprise—that Americans were as willing as Germans to follow the orders of authorities even when this involved giving nasty electrical shocks to others. The idea of "a culture," corresponding to a "society" and a "state," would not last long once the cultural revolution arrived and meaning was no longer thought to cohere at a national level, much less to be associated with national personality traits. As a result studies of "national character" (e.g., Hartz 1955; Potter 1954) would nearly disappear.

A more robust strain of this tradition produced research into the "postmaterial" values that were thought to grip the generation of the 1960s, the first cohort in history with a large proportion coming of age relatively free from material deprivation and the insecurity of war that had plagued humans throughout history. Ronald Inglehart (1977, 1990, 1997) documented the shift in values as well as in political behavior. Not only were party affiliations thought to be weakening and traditional left–right ideologies losing their grip (Dalton, Flanagan, and Beck 1984), but the new values were thought to encourage "new social movements" for peace, ecology, and cultural freedoms (e.g., Cotgrove 1982; Milbrath 1984).

Early civic-culture research primarily analyzed survey attitudes and voting behavior, and it is not always clear how its findings extend to more active forms of political participation such as social movements. A newer strain examines people engaged in collective action, following Tocqueville in arguing that participation in voluntary associations revitalizes community and strengthens democracy (Barber 1984; Putnam 1993, 1995, 2000; Wuthnow 1998). These researchers, although more sophisticated than earlier generations, favor the same kinds of "intermediary organizations" that pluralists and mass-society theorists preferred: bowling leagues, clubs, churches, unions, and so on. Many researchers who complain about a lack of community spirit (e.g., Bellah et al. 1985) may again be looking in the wrong places or with the wrong tools (Perrin 2006).

Because this approach typically encompasses—or conflates—individual and national levels, it has difficulties recognizing structures of power and advantage (Crenson and Ginsberg 2002; Szreter 2002). Certain groups are likely to organize to pursue basic structural changes, while others merely want to go bowling. Groups vary in their ability to organize to pursue their own interests, as Mancur Olson (1965) famously showed in his devastating critique of pluralist theory. Other critics have pointed out the negative side of intermediary groups, especially their tendency to exclude outsiders (Kaufman 2002; Portes 1998). Contemporary forms of civic associations may discourage cross-class contacts—a problem hidden by the survey method, which does not address structural changes as well as it does individual ones (Skocpol 2003).

Despite the tradition's flaws, efforts to show how individuals gain political and organizational confidence and skills through minor forms of participation contributes to our understanding of social movements. A sense of mastery may encourage participation in a range of arenas and organizations, as Putnam and others argue. Confidence is crucial to strategic action (Jasper 2006b). But meanings and skills, surveyed through individuals, must be put into their strategic contexts, the institutional arenas in which they become part of a stream of interaction. Instead of leaping from the individual to the institutional (a flaw civic culture and crowd theories share), we need to build from one to the other in concrete steps.

Ideology and Science in Marxism

Karl Marx and most of his long and influential line of followers sharply distinguished the false beliefs of class ideology from the more objective truths of science, the latter of course being what they were engaged in. There were nuances, to be sure, beginning with Marx's claim that all ideas are influenced by the social setting in which they emerge—presumably including science (or, in some formulations, all sciences except Marxism). It proved an especially useful distinction for Marxist parties that managed to seize power, allowing them to suppress democracy.

This contrast between science and ideology was, perhaps ironically, shared by Smelser and others writing in the United States in the shadow of the triumph over fascism. (World War II had a buoyant effect on American culture, despite doubts about the Bomb, in contrast to the devastation and gloom reflected in European thought.) Smelser, Kornhauser, and Almond and Verba wrote around the same time Daniel Bell published *The End of Ideology* with a somewhat similar faith in scientific understandings. "Normal" politics was based on objective knowledge, "mass" politics on ideology that analysts had to pick apart as pathology. Before the cultural revolution, liberals and Marxists both viewed consciousness as either false or true—with different models for understanding each kind.

In Britain in the late 1950s, a network of Marxist scholars reacted against the science–ideology contrast, planting what would eventually blossom into a main source of the cultural revolution (Lee [2003] is an interesting history from a world systems perspective). Rooted in working class culture and often teaching in its adult education programs, the scholars who became the New Left reacted against Labor's support for imperialist intervention in the Suez Canal, and against the Soviet invasion of Hungary and Kruschev's speech to the Twentieth Congress in 1956—both of which (in different ways) unmasked Stalinism. They concluded that a "new" left was necessary, more radical than the social democrats and labor but less authoritarian than communism. The dominant figures, Raymond Williams, E. P. Thompson, and Stuart Hall, also rejected Stalinism for its anti-intellectualism. All three worked to save culture from crude base-superstructure formulations (Williams 1977).

In *Culture and Society* (1958) Williams doggedly uncovered radical, socialist themes in the Romantic and largely conservative tradition in British culture, finding at both ends of the political spectrum a rejection of liberal individualism and an embrace of community. He saw himself as saving this tradition from conservative formulations such as T. S. Eliot's *Notes towards the Definition of Culture* (1948). More broadly, Williams, especially in *Marxism and Literature*, found ways to take culture seriously enough that it could not be reduced to a reflection of economic structures and processes. And yet he proved unwilling to give up Marxism's approach to class and historical change, seeing in "residual," "dominant," and "emergent" elements of culture (each connected to a social class) a pattern of social change from feudalism to capitalism to proletarian socialism.

Thompson's work culminated in *The Making of the English Working Class* (1963). It was about the self-making of the working class, a thorough study of the community and religious ideas which allowed a working class culture and collective player to emerge that would eventually be the carrier of social change and eventually socialism. Like Williams, Thompson rejected more economistic and structural aspects of Marxism, but not its theory of history as stages accomplished by a succession of triumphant classes. Craig Calhoun (1982) would later cast doubt on Thompson's assumption that this "working class" was a unitary culture and collective player that persisted over time.

Stuart Hall, joining the University of Birmingham's Centre for Contemporary Cultural Studies in 1964 and becoming its director several years later, imported French cultural analyses such as Althusser's structuralism and Barthes' semiotics (e.g., CCCS, 1978; 1980; Hall and Jefferson 1976). The Birmingham group examined semiotic codes, but linked them to more sociological issues of the creators and audiences for the codes (replicating Aristotle's analytic division of rhetoric into orator, audience, and speech: Hall 1980). Structural linguistics seemed to offer the hard edge of science, which the Birmingham school could apply to political conflict. Thus, for instance, Dick Hebdige (1979) found resistance in the clothing styles of punks, and Paul Willis (1977) examined the unintended consequences of working class youths' rebellion against their schools.

The British New Left, thoroughly steeped in the culture of working-class resistance, framed cultural struggles largely as hegemony, Antonio Gramsci's famous term for the cultural work that elites do (and must do, given the resistance of the oppressed) to maintain their privileged positions. Elites have the resources, material as well as cultural, to win most of the time—but not always. Imprisoned by the fascists from 1926 until his death in 1937, Gramsci could see the central, active role of the state in modern society, rejecting the economism of other Marxists at the time. He was also able to see the political and ideological work necessary for elites to maintain their privileges. Published in small bits beginning after 1945, Gramsci's letters and *Prison Notebooks* would have a greater and greater impact on culturally inclined analysts throughout the world.

In Paris, meanwhile, Louis Althusser (1969, 1971; Althusser and Balibar 1970) combined Marxism and structuralism in a way that highlighted culture—purveyed through schools, churches, and other "ideological state apparatuses"—but still didn't quite free it from economic determination "in the last instance." On the one hand, Althusser seemed to open the possibility of ideological struggle within any number of institutions (including academic ones, thus flattering scholars), on the other hand it was not clear how any of these battles could be won. At the least, it would involve smashing all these institutions rather than recalibrating them for progressive uses. In a model of ultimate determination, ideological struggle seemed doomed. (A pessimistic conclusion that felt too gloomy at the time but which in retrospect may be all too realistic.)

In the end, a pair of French scholars, Ernesto Laclau and Chantal Mouffe (1985), nailed shut the coffin of Marxist cultural analysis by using Gramsci against Althusser. Drawing on Derrida (e.g., 1978), they reconceptualized the economy as a discursive realm, among many others, in which are articulated claims about authority, efficiency, technique, money, and so on. Discourses, which allow an infinite play of meaning through differences, entail constant negotiation and construction of meanings. These include the construction of strategic players themselves: these cannot be taken for granted, but are generated through discursive claims and other tactics. There is no way to predict in advance exactly where "social antagonisms" will arise, or where they will lead. Laclau and Mouffe definitively discredited theories that proclaimed to know the direction in which history is moving and the collective players behind that movement. Cultural and political analysis were freed from the weight of historical metanarratives. The extensive toolkit of cultural concepts that British and French Marxists had developed could be freed from the distorting assumption that only classes had cultures or politics.

Gender as Culture

During the 1970s and 1980s, gender proved an especially useful laboratory for thinking about the cultural dimensions of politics, so that feminists studying the women's movement were often at the cutting edge of cultural research. If nothing else, gender was not the same as class, which had helped to impose a paradigm of material interest on theory and research for so long. For gender oppression to operate, women must to some extent absorb images and ideas that endorse their inferiority. They are not a community apart, with distinct boundaries, so that their oppression happens every day in subtle ways. There is violence, to be sure, but this is not the main mechanism by which gender inequality is reproduced. Instead, the very concept of gender is a pillar of women's oppression. Here more than anywhere else, it was recognized that knowledge is power. Scholarship meant to trace and undermine the "social construction of gender" exploded, providing the paradigm for deconstructing other oppressive ideologies (Butler 1990; de Beauvoir 1949; Leacock 1981; Martin 1987; Wittig 1992). The women's movement proved good to think about culture with (Elshtain 1981; Friedan 1963; Naples 1998; Young 1997). As T.V. Reed (2005:79) would later phrase it, changing consciousness was especially important "in shaping behavioral change in those 'personal' realms that feminist consciousness-raising redefined as 'political,' such as family life; male-female interactions in the kitchen, the bedroom, and the living room; female-female solidarity; female bodily self-image; and the right to reproductive decision-making."

In several nations, the internal battles of women's movements in the 1980s raised more troubling questions about what it was to be a woman, and about how to craft an identity around such a general concept. Could you be a feminist if you tolerated or even enjoyed pornography? Did lesbians have the same goals as other women? What about racial and ethnic minorities? Working-class women? Nowhere was the fragile, fictional nature of collective identities, nonetheless crucial to social movements, articulated so clearly—and painfully (Nicholson 1990). Journals such as *m/f* in Britain did a great deal to question "woman" as a category. Partly as a result of these debates, feminist scholars such as Leila Rupp, Verta Taylor, and Nancy Whittier helped promulgate the concept of collective identity in movement research (Taylor and Whittier 1992; Whittier 1995), especially by drawing on the work of Melucci (1985, 1988).

Other researchers examined the internal cultures of movements that assigned women inferior roles. Mary Katzenstein (1998) traced feminist mobilization within conservative organizations such as the military and the Catholic church. Belinda Robnett (1991) showed that women in the U.S. civil rights movement were different kinds of leaders than men, more oriented toward building bridges within the movement and less oriented toward gaining publicity with external audiences. Kathleen Blee (1991, 2002) was able to describe a special role that women played in two right-wing movements, bridging gendered expectations of passivity with aggressive activism. Historians found similar tensions between women's idealized passivity and political activism as early as the nineteenth century (Epstein 1981; Ginzberg 1990; Ryan 1990).

Attention to internal organizational cultures led a number of feminist scholars to examine emotions, especially as emotional expression in most societies is closely linked to gender. For instance, Sherryl Kleinman (1996) found that men and women in an alternative health organization achieved rhetorical effects through different kinds of emotional displays. Men were praised for being sensitive, against traditional expectations, whereas women were not. In the animal rights movement, according to Julian Groves (1997, 2001), activists carefully crafted appeals that relied on science rather than gut feelings, enlisting men to convey "hard" messages even though most activists were women. Both men and women in the movement anticipated that audiences would dismiss emotional arguments presented by women.

Emotion norms have often been used to women's disadvantage, as when women are discouraged from expressing anger (Hercus 1999; Hochschild 1975) or when their anger is dismissed as bitterness (Campbell 1994). Just as feminists had to make anger acceptable, so they addressed the norms of motherhood that made postpartum depression simply unthinkable: how could a woman be upset after such a blessed event (Taylor 1996)? Scholars of the women's movement have also shown how affective bonds can maintain the networks of movements that have fallen out of the public eye (Rupp and Taylor 1987; Taylor 1989). It is perhaps ironic that some feminists criticized the cultural association of women with emotions (and of men with rationality) at the same time that other feminists were cogently tracing so many emotional dynamics by studying women's actions and understandings (for more leads on gender and emotions in social movements, see Goodwin and Jasper 2006).

As issues of collective identity spread to the gay and lesbian rights movements, they spurred another wave of theorizing in the early 1990s (Gamson 1995; Seidman 1994; Warner 1993). One reason was an associated academic endeavor, "queer theory," much as there had been a large body of feminist theory that could point to the dilemmas and paradoxes of identity without being accountable to the movement itself. Scholars could explicitly identify tradeoffs that might paralyze collective action, such as the choice of whether to emphasize, in presenting gay collective identity, similarities to or differences from straight culture (Bernstein 1997). Gamson (1997) showed how gay activists policed their external image by expelling certain "kinds" of gays. In a few cases, identity again led to discussion of emotions: for instance, Gould (2001) traced the effects of shame on collective action; far from having the same effect in all circumstances, she argued, it can sometimes encourage quiescence and at other times militancy.

In the field of social movements as in so many others, feminist scholarship's great contribution has been to show the subtle webs that bind people to one another. Humans are not autonomous or selfish individuals who approach others to satisfy pre-existing goals. Often using the exemplar of a family rather than a marketplace, feminists have uncovered shared understandings and identities, affective loyalties, mutual recognitions, communication processes, and other ways in which people help shape one another. These are the heart of a cultural approach.

The Programmed Society

If there was one place where culture had a prominent role in research on social movements, it was CADIS in Paris, founded by Alain Touraine, whose theory of postindustrial trends highlighted conflict over cultural understandings. After 1968, having formulated the concept of the programmed society in which humans control their destinies (or "historicity"—the pace and direction of change) to an unprecedented degree (1969, 1973), Touraine began investigating a series of social movements through "sociological interventions." He and his team would invite a number of participants to a series of meetings aimed at defining the movement's goals, identity, opponents, and factions. In some cases, opponents of the movement would be invited to confront the members. In an astounding burst of research, Touraine recreated in a kind of laboratory setting the dilemmas that a series of movements and their leaders faced or had recently faced (Touraine 1978; Touraine et al. 1980, 1982, 1984).

The climax of each intervention came when Touraine presented the group with his own hypothesis about their historical significance: that their "real" purpose was a broad-based effort to oppose the corporate and government technocrats who initiated and directed most social change. The antinuclear, feminist, student, and other movements were different facets of one underlying antitechnocratic movement, struggling to emerge, which would assume a role in postindustrial society that the labor movement had occupied in industrial society. Cultural values and understandings were the main stakes in this conflict, in contrast to the distribution of material products that had (supposedly) been at stake in industrial conflicts. There was one problem: Touraine was unable to convince his movement representatives of their real significance. They insisted on their own purposes. Like Marxists before him, Touraine often seemed to think he knew participants' goals better than they did. In retrospect, this stance seems to have been a hopeful search for a universal player that might replace the "universal class" of Marxism.

Partly as a result of these rejections, Touraine mostly abandoned the project of discerning *the* social movement that would carry on the fight for social justice in postindustrial society. His mood today is more pessimistic, as the movements he studied lost their struggles to control social change, especially to giant corporations (Touraine 1997). After the election of Margaret Thatcher and of Ronald Reagan, history took a new direction. "During the last twenty years, the idea of a postindustrial society has disappeared because the most important change turned out to be not a structural transformation but the victory of a new kind of capitalism" (Touraine 1998b:207). In a process of "demodernization," society—as a unified system—has unraveled. Sociology, which traditionally looked for that underlying unity and order, must in turn change to study the constructions of identities and strategic projects (Touraine 1998a). His cultural vantage point helped Touraine (like Laclau and Mouffe) to recognize that collective players form new goals; these are never given by social structure or laws of historical change.

To express Touraine's ideas about programmed societies, Alberto Melucci helped to promulgate the term "new social movements" (1985, 1994). He later had some regrets about this, given the misunderstandings and misguided debates the phrase inspired. European and American movements of the 1970s and 1980s were certainly not entirely new, especially in their tactics, nor were they necessarily more oriented toward cultural meanings than the labor movement had been, especially in its early stages. Debates over what was new and what was old, if nothing else, had the salutary effect of inspiring research into the cultural dimensions of earlier movements as well as the new ones (such as Calhoun 1993; see also Pichardo 1997).

Melucci's main intent was to promote a cultural view of social movements, and concepts with which we might get inside them, to appreciate the point of view of participants. Identity was the central rhetorical device of his magisterial *Challenging Codes* (1996a). For instance, it defines an "us" and a "them," which Melucci (1996a:83) calls "a strong and preliminary condition for collective action, as it continuously reduces ambivalence and fuels action with positive energies." (This does the same work as Smelser's unresolved Oedipal conflict, but in a more concrete and realistic way.) Collective identities also define a player's relationship to the past and the future. Melucci (1996a:86) recognized the core dilemma of identity here (although he instead refers to it as a problem, a tension, and a paradox): "On the one hand, the actor must maintain a permanence which, on the other, must be produced continuously." Ambitiously, Melucci (1996a:69) thought collective identity can "bridge the gap between behavior and meaning, between 'objective' conditions and 'subjective' motives and orientations, between 'structure' and 'agency'."

But something is still missing at the psychological level. This is apparent in Melucci's discussions of the relationship between movement leaders and followers, where he lapsed into the language of exchange, of costs and benefits. He did not say enough to indicate whether he meant this at a vague, tautological level or at the measurable level of material trades—because he did not really fill in the complex psychology of leadership. This would perhaps lead to charisma, a concept currently out of fashion, as well as to a range of emotions, then also out of fashion. Even Melucci, more attuned to psychological and social-psychological dynamics than most (e.g., Melucci 1996b), had thin cultural foundations. To me, this shows that Touraine's approach, while it had a central logical place for culture and identity (J. L. Cohen 1985), still operated at a macrosocial level, with a theory of history that discouraged serious examination of cultural mechanisms—much like structural approaches.

The Cultural Synthesis

Having developed quietly for a decade or two, cultural analysis exploded throughout the social sciences in the late 1970s and 1980s. In addition to cognitive psychology and the British New Left, sources included French structuralism and poststructuralism, the history and philosophy of science, a resurgent Frankfurt School, and social theorists—such as Giddens, Habermas, Bourdieu, and Touraine—concerned with inserting agency (and the actor's point of view) into models dominated by structures and functions. History and anthropology, with their own longstanding cultural traditions, also provided a number of new tools for analyzing meaning (for more, see Jasper 2005).

For 100 years, French structuralism has concerned itself with meanings, first in Saussure's linguistics and later in Levi-Strauss's anthropology, especially his work on myth. The generation that came to dominate Parisian intellectual life in the 1960s dropped the objectivist scientific pretensions of this tradition, grounding it instead in social constructionism. Michel Foucault (1961, 1963, 1966, 1975, 1976), in particular, glamorized cultural approaches by "socializing" linguistic structuralism in a new kind of institutional analysis (on the French tradition see Dosse 1997). Jacques Derrida (1967) had a parallel influence by "deconstructing" our language and concepts to reveal the mechanisms of power and hierarchy beneath them. The work of these two charismatic figures did much to promote cultural analysis.

The new research and theory tend to differ from older cultural work in several ways. A broad social constructionism, which views all knowledge and institutions as shaped by our cognitive frameworks, implies that no crisp distinction between true and false political claims can be sustained. Both can be "deconstructed" by being linked to the social context and position of those making them. Culture can then be seen as an element of strategy and power, a site of contestation as much as a source for social unity (and when it is a source of unity, this is because elites deploy it toward that end). There is also a tendency to reject the idea of "a culture," corresponding to "a society," as older visions often had it. Cultural meanings rarely form a unified whole. On the other hand, they are not collapsed into the subjective beliefs of individuals, but have a distinct structure and persistence, an "objective" existence. This is not necessarily a "shared" culture, into which individuals are "socialized," but more a set of tools that individuals use (Turner 1994, 2002).

Emotions played little part in this great cultural revolution, but there was a simultaneous rediscovery of their role in social life. Just as cognition had long been an object of psychological research, only to spread belatedly to other social sciences, so emotions emerged in the late 1970s and early 1980s to form a new sociology of emotions (Hochschild 1983; Kemper 1978). Even today, feelings have not attained equal status to meanings in the study of social life generally or in the study of social movements specifically. But plenty of raw materials are there.

The cultural turn entered (especially American) scholarship on social movements modestly, foremost through the concept of frame alignment, the processes (bridging, amplification, extension, and transformation) by which organizers and recruits come (or do not come) to synchronize their ways of viewing a social problem and what should be done about it (Snow and Benford 1988, 1992; Snow et al. 1986). Structural paradigms could incorporate frames easily, as long as they were seen as a factor added on to the underlying structural story, a kind of "resource" that recruiters had to get right in order to succeed. As late as 1996, McAdam, McCarthy, and Zald (1996) embraced political opportunities, mobilizing structures, and cultural framings as the building blocks of a new synthesis that could answer the basic questions about social movements. A more serious rethinking of structures from a cultural perspective would appear only in the late 1990s (Goodwin and Jasper 2003; Jasper 1997; Melucci 1996a).

The next popular concept, which required more rethinking of structural approaches, was that of collective identities. Arising out of debates within a number of movements over "identity politics" in the 1980s (see pages 67–69 above), collective identity came to represent the subjective meanings that movements carried with them. Considerable initial work tried to discern the relationship between structural positions and the identities that might or might not emerge from them (e.g., Pizzorno 1978; Taylor and Whittier 1992). The influence of Touraine and Melucci increased even more thanks to their focus on identities—especially Touraine's (1978) I – O – T: movements need a sense of their own identity (I), their opponent's identity (O), and the stakes of the conflict ("totality" in Touraine's language).

In the late 1980s and early 1990s, dissatisfaction with existing models often surfaced in conferences where papers criticized rational choice and structural approaches without yet building systematic cultural alternatives (Morris and Mueller 1992), or ungainly concepts such as "new social movements" were used to discuss cultural mechanisms (Laraña, Johnston, and Gusfield 1994). By the mid-1990s scholars were developing broader approaches that reflected the insights of the cultural revolution without reducing them to one or two simple concepts (Johnston and Klandermans 1995). Melucci (1996a) staked his approach on identity, to be sure, but pushed it into new areas. Jasper (1997) distinguished a number of cultural mechanisms at work at both individual and group levels, including emotional as well as cognitive processes. In 1999, Goodwin and Jasper (2003) broadly challenged the structural tradition for its inability to take culture seriously, a point that prominent structuralists quickly conceded (McAdam 2003; McAdam, Tarrow, and Tilly 2001).

By the turn of the century, the new cultural synthesis had transformed social movement theory, providing ways to talk about meaning and feeling that were not only richer and more systematic but also less pejorative than earlier efforts. The cultural toolkit was now as rich as the structural one. No scholar of movements should ever plead ignorance about these processes or be able to ignore them in good faith. And yet the very extent of the cultural tool kit encourages scholars to focus on one medium or process rather than comparisons among them. Most analysts prefer a loose interpretation, in the style of literary criticism, to the rigors of research into institutional conditions. What actually does the work of carrying cultural meanings, and to what audiences? We still know too little about the strategic contexts in which meanings are deployed—a path of research that might lead cultural analysis to connect with more structural traditions. Cultural dynamics never stand alone. We need to see the carriers of culture in action.

CARRIERS OF MEANING

Physical Artifacts

Almost any object or action can convey messages to audiences. Yet this diversity of media rarely has been taken as an opportunity to make useful comparisons (even when several media are discussed, as in Reed 2005). Frequently one medium is implicitly used as the exemplar for all, with the result that culture's operations are either distorted or vague and ubiquitous. After I list some of these concrete embodiments, we can move on to more figurative concepts for getting at the shapes that meanings take.

Jokes, gossip, rumors, and other comments affect the reputations of players in strategic engagement and thus their ability to act. In face-to-face settings, these can be useful weapons of those with few other capacities (Scott 1985, 1990), depending heavily on shared understandings that allow a great deal of meaning to remain implicit. But the same materials can also be broadcast to more anonymous audiences, not only through broadcast media but also via graffiti, cartoons, and so on. They are rarely full programs for action, but they have an epideictic impact on the moral sensibilities of audiences. They shape common sense about the world and the players operating in it. Even obscenities can play a role like this (Rothwell 1971).

Speeches, the great exemplar for rhetoric, also consist of fleeting words, but conveyed in more formal settings to larger numbers of people. This immediacy is an advantage when a speaker hopes to inspire action and decisions here and now. This is the source of some uneasiness over rhetoric: groups can be rushed to decisions they might not make if they devoted more time to deliberation. Although they are the most obvious carrier of political messages to assembled audiences, speeches are rarely analyzed today in cultural analysis of social movements.

Clothing styles and other *lifestyle choices* use materials other than words to convey statements about the world, in this case more about the solidarity of a group than about the capacities of players. One of the most fruitful products of the Birmingham School was the notion of resistance in everyday life, through choices about how to dress, what to ride, and so on. Just as these help identify the members of a collective to one another, as with punk culture (Hebdige 1979), they can occasion attacks from others. Moral panics frequently target apparently innocuous lifestyle choices, demonizing those who ride motorbikes, listen to rock music, and so on (S. Cohen 1972). Both insiders and outsiders use aspects of lifestyles metonymically to "stand in" for a group—contributing in the process to its collective identity (for an extended discussion of metonymy in social movements, see Polletta 2006:chap. 3). (The *production* of clothing and other items is also an opportunity for political expression: Adams 2000.)

Lifestyle choices are a frequent occasion for a common form of protest, a simple refusal to do something. An individual's choice not to eat meat or drink alcohol, while not necessarily accompanied by a collective vow or collective action, is nonetheless a form of protest. It is also not necessarily mute, as it arouses curiosity and provides a rhetorical opportunity for explaining and defending one's choices. As Mullaney (2006:61) puts it, "When individuals abstain, others want to know why." Consumer choices, especially through boycotts but also through politically correct buying, have been central to many recent social movements (Kimeldorf et al. 2006). One reason is the global spread of information, making it possible for consumers to learn about the origins of the products they buy. In this case, our statements endow (absent) objects with political meaning.

Music, dance, and related *performing arts* also convey messages about politics and change, as well as being crucial components of rituals that build emotions. Music is an especially powerful combination of words—with an explicit ideological message—and concerted action of the kind that creates collective effervescence (Futrell et al. 2006). Although it is inevitably accompanied by music and often by song, dance has its distinct vocabulary as well. Songs are easily transferred and adapted across movements. Morris (1984) emphasized the African American church music that was easily given a civil-rights twist, and Eyerman and Jamison (1998) show that songs are a concrete legacy that defunct movements leave for successors to discover and adapt. In a study of textile strikes in the U.S. south, Roscigno and Danaher (2004) show how songs, often on the radio, articulated grievances and expressed collective identity and opposition. As Reed (2005:29) puts it in describing the civil rights movements, "Singing (along with prayer) became a perfect way both to keep a mass from becoming a mob, and to convey to opponents that one was witnessing an organized event, not a mob action." Music affected both internal and external audiences, in both individual listening and collective gatherings.

Theater is another performing art, but one that (unlike music and dance) almost always requires an audience distinct from the performers (Goldfarb 1980). Otherwise, it becomes more like a ritual. Even the "street theater" (or theatrics) of the Yippies was intended to attract attention, especially from the media. "Every man would be an artist," according to Abbie Hoffman, but artists need audiences. *Film*, even more, is a costly form in which the production of the artifact is unusually separated from its consumption. With theater, the production and consumption occur face to face, with immediate feedback possibilities; in film these are separated by both time and space. There is a tradeoff between broader dissemination and immediate interaction between audience and performers.

Rituals are complex embodied meanings that can combine music, dance, collective locomotion, theater, and spoken words (Kertzer 1988). They focus a group's attention, at salient times and places, with the possible effect of arousing emotions and reinforcing our solidarities and beliefs (and sometimes creating new ones). Because several carriers of meaning line up at once, rituals provide especially powerful messages, as Durkheim saw. They can be aimed at external audiences, as proclamations of intent or identity, as well as at participants. Coordinated actions are deeply satisfying; even mere shouting feels good in the right circumstances, enhancing solidarity. According to Randall Collins (2001, 2004), rituals generate an emotional energy and mutual attention that individuals crave. But this satisfaction, while an end in itself, also provides the confidence and energy for further action and participation, partly independently of the craving for more attention. By examining chains of interactions, Collins sees the microfoundations for broader structures.

People and events can carry symbolic meanings even though they are not created for that purpose. Other entities can also become symbols—parts of the landscape for instance— but groups, individuals, and events are especially easy to craft into symbols. Examples of important events—often called "precipitating events"—include institutional foundings and strategic victories or turning points. Again and again, acts of government repression inspire mass mobilization. Individuals, too, are important symbols: the leader of a group or a government is not only important for the decisions she makes, but also for the ways in which she represents her organization to insiders and to outsiders.

Perhaps the most important carriers of cultural messages consist of written words, *texts*: poetry, books, pamphlets, articles, posters, graffiti, and so on. Because messages are conveyed here in relatively permanent media, there is less control over audiences' interpretations, but at the same time meanings can be conveyed more broadly (an unavoidable tradeoff for all cultural artifacts). At one extreme texts are mere slogans which, like epithets, reinforce existing feelings about the world; at the other they are elaborate statements of goals and tactics, of moral positions, of carefully documented grievances.

Not all printed materials consist of words; some are *visual symbols* such as caricatures and other cartoons; abstract images such as peace signs or swastikas; photographs of real-life events, people, places; or highly schematized representations such as maps. Much has been written about the rhetorical power of all these, but let me just mention maps as a more unusual form. Elisabeth Wood (2003) asked peasant revolutionaries in El Salvador to draw elaborate maps of their holdings and towns, demonstrating changes in their thoughts and feelings about the land, such as the emotional memories of what had happened in different places during the civil war (especially where people had been killed). In struggles over land, certainly, maps will be key cognitive representations.

Also at the more permanent end of the spectrum of cultural artifacts, *buildings, memorials,* and other human constructions are intended to carry meanings to audiences and frequently to future generations. Social movements rarely have the permanence or control of public space for these creations, which are usually the tool of the powerful (and no less important for that). Louis XIV wanted the Versailles gardens to express his control over well-defined territory (Mukerji 1997). Corporations construct headquarters that send messages of permanence, power, or good will. States remind domestic and foreign observers of their own dignity, power, and venerable age through their military installations and other functioning buildings. Movements shape collective memories in ways that have similar cultural impacts, and they frequently use existing built spaces to make symbolic statements. Even if they do not build monuments, they use them as stages for their own events, transforming their meanings in the process.

Carriers of meaning vary along several rhetorical dimensions. These include whether creators and audiences are present at the same time, the relative durability of the cultural artifact after its creation, the scope with which the artifact can be reproduced or promulgated, and the relative control that one player may have over the production and consumption of the artifacts. Obviously, face to face settings offer more control over the reception of those meanings than more mediated ones, because of the possibility for constant monitoring and adjustment. And *any* object or idea can be interpreted as conveying symbolic messages, such as a rock formation, although some are designed precisely for that purpose (I have concentrated on these in this section).

These differences generate a number of different strategic choices for those who would create and deploy cultural messages, of which I'll name just a few (from Jasper 2006b). In the *Audience Segregation Dilemma,* you would like to convey different messages to different players, but you run the risk of appearing duplicitous if a message goes to the wrong audience. You must choose, for instance, between more local appeals and more global ones, which resonate with different audiences (Gordon and Jasper 1996). Attracting attention through the media publicizes your cause, but in the process your message and identity may be distorted (Gitlin 1980). In the *Articulation Dilemma,* being explicit about your goals may help arouse support for them, but it makes it harder for you to adjust them realistically in the face of new opportunities and constraints. Audiences, institutional settings, and media interact.

Exemplary research into audience dilemmas comes from a work that is not explicitly cultural in its orientation, Clifford Bob's *The Marketing of Rebellion* (2005). Bob examines the remarkable success of the Ogoni in Nigeria and the Zapatistas in Chiapas, both of whom managed to capture the imagination of broad audiences and nongovernmental organizations around the world. Using a "marketing" metaphor in which human rights groups must sell themselves to potential funders, Bob demonstrates the crucial importance of a leader (Ken Saro-Wiwa among the Ogoni and subcomandante Marcos for the Zapatistas) who embodies the group's moral aspirations and can speak the (literal and figurative) languages of the audiences the group wants to reach. Both were prolific writers, and both were articulate not only in the language of their followers but also in the English so useful in attracting international audiences. They succeeded in reaching out to external audiences, and Bob recounts how they had to make adjustments in order to do this. Insurgents rethink their identities and images, just as nongovernmental organizations think hard about the potential risks and benefits of supporting various groups. Both sets of players face innumerable dilemmas in trying to please more than one audience.

Metaphors of Meaning

In addition to the many physical carriers of meaning and feeling, there are a variety of metaphors through which scholars have tried to understand the cultural dimensions of social movements. Some of these are concrete carriers that have been used to stand in for broader processes of understanding, such as texts or narratives. Others are more clearly figurative concepts, such as frames or movement cultures. Most of these latter have variants along a continuum from a more structured, formal image to a more action-oriented, open-ended one.

One of the most popular terms is *movement culture* (or Fine's [1995] similar idea idioculture), meant to capture a hodgepodge of sensibilities, ways of operating, tastes in tactics, frames, ideologies, and other packages of meaning. The idea presumably contrasts the meanings and processes internal to a movement with those of the broader cultural context, even though the two interpenetrate at a number of points (Williams 2004). Although it recognizes that culture matters, I find that the term covers too much. If the trend is away from talking about "a culture" at the level of society, linking it to another vague entity, a "social movement" (as opposed to the organizations that ally to form a movement) helps little. At best, it becomes a catalogue of what participants share (Lofland 1995). We need to speak of the more concrete elements which make up that supposed "culture."

Frames were the main way analysts inserted cultural meanings into models in the late 1980s. In the process, they lost frames' specific context of efforts at recruitment, in which activists crafted messages for audiences of potential recruits. (Snow et al. [1986] had originally used active terms such as frame alignment, bridging, and so on—suggesting players constructing messages.) Instead, frames became something like worldviews, packages of meaning that—uncovered through content analysis of movement literature—were assumed to represent the motivations and visions of participants (as Benford 1997, complains). Specific artifacts metastasized into overly broad metaphors of meaning. At the same time, the active process of framing was transformed into static packages of meanings, and the latter's strategic purposes were lost.

Collective identity played a similarly spongelike role in the 1990s, after it was recognized that frames do not exhaust meanings (Snow 2001). Despite efforts in structural and rational-choice traditions to define strategic players on the basis of objective interests, collective players are as much an accomplishment as a given. Organizers must work hard to promulgate a collective identity that can attract potential participants and retain existing ones (there is often a tradeoff between these two tasks). Considerable research has shown how collective labels are necessary for action, even though they are largely fictional (Gamson 1995; Polletta and Jasper 2001). In some cases, both the means and the ends of collective action seemed to be the construction of collective identities for participants, in another overextension of a perfectly good concept (Cohen 1985; Melucci 1996a).

Shared structural positions—economic activity, legal and political status, strong cultural expectations—make it more likely that a group will develop a shared collective identity. Potential members of the group will have had the same experiences, and through consciousness raising of some sort will come to realize this. But structural similarities are neither necessary nor sufficient for identity. Rarely made explicit are the shared emotions that arise from those positions and experiences that make the identity possible and motivating. Sociological research shows that characteristic emotions arise from dominant or subordinate positions in hierarchies, and from changes in those positions and the power and status that accompany them (Hochschild 1983; Kemper 1978; Morgan and Heise 1988). For instance, we are contemptuous of those who claim more status than we think they deserve, and angry at those who don't grant us the status we think we deserve (Kemper 2001). When political players interact in the context of ongoing hierarchies, characteristic emotions will arise that may advance or hinder collective identities and the accompanying programs and actions.

In the same way that collective identities depend on the imagination as much as on actual interactions among people, *symbolic allies* and *symbolic enemies* can be constructed. I call them symbolic to the extent they are not allies in the sense of coordinating, opposing, or interacting in any way with us. Protestors like to think that others are engaged in the same fight as they are, share their moral vision, and are part of the same movement. Indeed, a social movement is less a coordinated effort by allied groups than a *sense* of a coordinated effort. It is an accomplishment of the imagination. Likewise, we can construct bad guys who we believe threaten us, even if they do not really interact strategically with us in any way, and perhaps do not know who we are. Symbolic allies and enemies are particular easy to construct from players who are in different places, especially different countries, from us—and with whom communication is difficult. Roggeband (2004), for instance, describes how European feminists were inspired by feminists in other nations even though they received little information from them and about them, and formed no strategic alliance.

Characters are one aspect of collective identity that receives little attention: collective players try to create these for themselves and others (part of the content of those identities). By this I mean the work of characterizing, often relying on traditional literary character types of hero, villain, victim, and (to fill in the 2 by 2 table formed along the dimensions of strong versus weak and good versus bad) sidekick or clown. To initiate political action, it is often useful to present yourself as a victim who is becoming a hero, to triumph over a villain and his minions. This mini-narrative encourages audiences to take sides emotionally, expressing sympathy for the victim, admiration for the hero, and hatred for the villain and his sidekicks. Other potential plots include the conversion of villain into hero (whistleblowers, for instance) and the martyrdom of a hero who sacrifices herself. Characters like these almost demand certain feelings toward them (although it is possible to play against type, for instance there are lovable villains and feared heroes). Even though "flat" (i.e., stereotyped) characters such as these have fallen out of favor in serious fiction, as a form of epideictic rhetoric they live on in political propaganda as efforts to shape our understandings of and feelings about the world.

Narrative is another metaphor of meaning that has recently become popular as a label to acknowledge that cultural meanings often come packaged as stories with beginnings and ends, recounted in a variety of social contexts (Hall 1995; Polletta 2006; Somers 1995). Some analysis—drawing on literary criticism—treats narratives as structured, predictable combinations of characters and events, forming a finite number of familiar plots. Other narrative analysis tends to place stories in the social contexts in which they are told, encouraging more attention to the interactions between the creators of stories and their audiences (Davis 2002). The latter loses the formal constraints featured in traditional narrative analysis but gains a more purposive, rhetorical dimension. Oddly, narrative research has paid little attention to characters (cf. Polletta 2006:chap. 5).

Francesca Polletta's *It Was Like a Fever* (2006) demonstrates the strengths of a narrative lens. Each chapter is a case study. One explains why black college students who began sit-ins at segregated stores in 1960 were so insistent that their actions were spontaneous rather than organized and planned. This story emphasized a break with more established civil rights organizations, dramatized the moral urgency of the student's actions, and helped to create a new collective political player. The following chapter revisits the group that formed out of these sit-ins several years later, SNCC, as debates over group structure led to the expulsion of whites. Polletta focuses here on metonymy, especially how particular strategies came to "stand in" for white or for black members of the group. Another chapter examines the rhetorical uses of stories in online debate over what kind of memorial to build on the World Trade Center site. Another discusses the dilemma that battered women and their advocates face between presenting themselves as victims or as competent, even heroic actors—one of the rare works on narrative that addresses characters. Victimhood gains sympathy but undermines images of power and rationality. Another chapter details the ways that African American congressional speakers refer to Martin Luther King Jr. in a manner that hides his radical activism. All these chapters are rich studies in how meanings are made (going far beyond the narrative metaphor in doing so).

Inspired by French poststructuralist thought, scholars have also treated cultural meanings as *texts*, using one artifact of meaning as exemplary of meaning more generally (Shapiro 1992). In addition to, in most cases, preferring literal texts—such as constitutions, novels, and other documents—as clues to worldviews, poststructuralists read all social life as though it were a text. Sensibilities, wars, cities, landscapes, and so on can all be interpreted in this fashion. This approach reminds us of the social construction behind so many events and processes that we might otherwise take for granted, but the approach frequently focuses on the text itself so that the activities of the creator disappear. The textual metaphor seems especially suited to more structured analysis, and less so to more dynamic analysis. If nothing else, it reminds us the world demands to be interpreted.

In a closely related development, *discourse* has, also following French poststructuralists, become a popular term for the deployment of cultural meanings (Snow 2004; Steinberg 1998, 1999). If textual approaches emphasize the structured (and usually static) nature of meanings, discourse instead focuses on human participants who interactively sustain or redirect meanings (in Saussurian terms discourse is about *parole* not *langue*). An infinite play of meanings allows constant negotiation over meanings. A variety of discursive practices "mediate the relationship between texts on the one hand and (nontextual parts of) society and culture on the other" (Fairclough 1995:10). Although they acknowledge more strategy and creativity than textual models, because discourse approaches see meaning in all actions, they can expand to cover any human actions. Even the physical world, to the extent it is meaningful to us, becomes part of a discursive practice (Laclau and Mouffe 1985; Torfing 1999). Sometimes this is a creative move, at others merely a confusing one.

Rhetoric

Is there any useful way to reconcile these many terms and ideas? And to recognize both their structured aspects and their more active, strategic ones? I find *rhetoric*, the world's oldest tradition of cultural analysis, especially suited to understanding the cultural dimensions of politics. Aristotle usefully stressed three major components to rhetorical settings: the creators of messages, the messages themselves, and the audiences. The orator's intended purpose was to have effects of various kinds—beliefs, emotions, and actions—on his audiences. Although rhetoric is less clear about structured or unconscious meanings, it is quite explicit about intended ones, placing meanings in the context of strategic action. We could usefully rethink the artifacts and the metaphors of meaning from a rhetorical perspective, setting them in their proper social contexts.

Rhetorical analysis forces clarity about several issues, especially the nature of the audience and the arena. Because speeches were such formal events in ancient Greece and Rome, they were distinguished according to the setting: orations in law courts were designed to establish what had happened in the past; in political assemblies to decide what course of action to adopt in the future; and in less formal settings such as funerals and festivals to establish more general moral understandings. Although not all political stakes are as clear as that in a law court, rhetoric encourages the cultural analyst to be precise about what purposes and outcomes the players seek.

The cultural analyst must also specify who the players are, who exactly is constructing, spreading, and interpreting cultural messages. Culture is still often spoken of in a vague way, as though it were like the air we breathe, surrounding us all beneath our awareness. But most important political messages are carefully, intentionally crafted. One message is purveyed to one audience, a slightly different one to another. And political players frequently take pains to segregate audiences in order to maximize their effects on each (although audience segregation carries risks: Jasper 2006b:132).

Although I am not devoting attention in this essay to the role of the media (for a summary see Gamson 2004), they become central (and integrated with other elements) in a rhetorical vision. In addition to players, arenas usually also contain audiences, who may or may not be able to become players themselves. With today's mass media, the size of the audience in most arenas is enormous, although not necessarily capable of being organized into active players. Audiences and media pose a series of dilemmas for players. Should activists rely on the media to purvey their message, knowing that the media have their own goals that are not those of the movement (Gitlin 1980)? Should they strive to create impressions of their power, since potential supporters will be less frightened to support them but may feel that the movement does not need the support? And should they strive for extensive coverage, which spreads the message but may arouse a counterattack from opponents (Jasper and Poulsen 1993)? The media have their own goals and means alongside other strategic players.

The carriers of meaning we have already examined can be placed in a rhetorical framework. Who writes and who sings the songs? Who listens to them, with what understandings and effects? How do the rhetorical settings differ for jokes, songs, logical arguments, films, memorials, and so on? The metaphors of meaning can also be clarified rhetorically. Who tells a story to whom? Who's our audience when we claim an identity? When we frame a social problem and suggest a solution? It should be no surprise that much existing work fits comfortably within rhetoric, as much of it emerged from rhetoric early in its history (the dialogical approach of Vygotsky, Bakhtin, and Volosinov, for example, is based on the idea of the "utterance," which has Aristotle's three elements of rhetoric, the speaker, the topic, and the listener).

The drawback of rhetorical approaches is that they tend to exaggerate the degree to which speakers' intentions determine or explain what happens, or "the extent to which actions are under the conscious control of subjects" (Fairclough 1995:45). In this, they are at the opposite end of the spectrum from textual approaches. Yet rhetoric has a place for preexisting meanings, in that successful orators must be sensitive to audiences' understandings, even of the most unconscious sort. The ability to tap into these is what distinguishes the great orator from the mediocre. The orator's awareness need not even be explicit, although 2400 years of rhetorical treatises have tried to formulate such knowledge.

Perhaps the closest to a rhetorical approach is the "cultural pragmatics" developed by social theorist Jeffrey Alexander (Alexander, Giesen, and Mast 2006), which focuses on "social performance" as the embodiment of cultural meanings. Alexander (2006:45–51) sees ancient Greece as the origin of this kind of self-aware performance as opposed to ritual situations in which meanings were more fused with social structure. Not coincidentally, this is the same social setting out of which rhetoric developed, in much the same way. As part of Alexander's group, Ron Eyerman (2006:198) recommends performance theory for "calling attention to the role of meaning and emotion." As in theatrical performances, he points out (2006:199), "Movement actors perform and convey; they also dramatize, adding powerful emotions to their actions which re-present known narratives through the use of symbols." Today, I am not sure we need performance theory to call attention to meaning and emotion, but it does pull together several of the carriers of meanings we have examined. Like rhetoric, performance could take its place alongside the other metaphors of meaning, at the same time it helps us understand their relationships.

In my opinion, all the conceptual tools examined in this section have their uses; all help explain how meanings operate. The danger is to embrace any one of them too enthusiastically, to the exclusion of the others. Not all meanings come packaged as narratives; not all convey messages about player identities. The more tools we have at our disposal the finer the cultural analysis we can craft with them. Rhetoric does not make any of them superfluous, it merely forces us to specify their contexts more clearly. Rhetoric is a lens for viewing culture that parallels strategy as a way of viewing political action.

EMOTIONS

What Are Emotions?

Emotions are our stances and reactions to the world that express how it matters for us. To some extent, they are cognitive evaluations, but typically with physiological components precisely because something makes a difference to our satisfaction and flourishing. The deep cultural grounding of emotions and their expression in no way denies their physiological components, any more than a cultural understanding of cognition denies the neurological pathways in the brain that underpin it. Vituperative debates between those who espouse cultural approaches to emotions and those of a biological or social–structural bent are fortunately a thing of the past.

The traditional image of emotions has generally contrasted them with rationality. "Passions" are a deviation from normal or rational action, as they "grip" us against our will. Most of the time, in fact, emotions are an essential part of our projects, shaping both ends and means. In the few cases when they disrupt our projects, I still prefer to view them either as extreme privileging of the short run over the longer run, or as mistakes later recognized as such. Lust may lead us to sleep with someone we know we should not, but the subsequent costs of doing so may range from nonexistent to enormous. The greater the resulting costs, the more we are tempted to call it an irrational act, but there is no clear cutoff point. For me, irrationality lies in an inability to learn from our mistakes—perhaps for psychoanalytic reasons such that we are trapped in reactions that do not change as our environment changes. Emotions are a fundamental part of rational action, not a diversion from it. Emotional mistakes are no more common—and probably less common—than cognitive mistakes such as incorrect information.

The study of emotions has emerged in the last decade as a hot area of research into social movements, no doubt because their recognition was repressed for so long under structural models (Goodwin et al. 2000; Gould 2003). I place them under the rubric of culture for a number of reasons. Cognition, emotion, and morality are inseparable components of culture, distinguishable only analytically. Most emotions involve cognitive appraisals of the world: how things are going for us (Nussbaum 2001). Thus our anger subsides when we learn it was based on mistaken information; transforming shock into outrage (a process central to protest) involves cognitive reframing. But the slow speed with which our anger may subside demonstrates that emotions have a reality partly independent of the cognitive component. (See Chapter 5, this volume, for more on the history of this appraisal approach to emotions, especially the influence of our identification with groups.)

Cognition, emotion, and morality also share a number of research challenges. All three components of culture have both public displays and interior, personal forms. As a result, individuals often deviate from "accepted" feelings and beliefs in ways that bedevil our research techniques, often requiring us to examine both private and public versions and the relationship between the two. Finally, the components are all capable of enormous complexity and combinations that are hard to pinpoint methodologically but which make them important and interesting. Viewing emotions as part of culture "normalizes" them, so that they no longer appear irrational or mistaken.

The carriers of culture we have already examined are as important for the feelings they arouse as for the cognitive meanings they convey. Characters such as heroes stimulate admiration and love, villains disgust and hatred. Collective identity, we saw, is an emotional solidarity as much as a cognitive boundary. Frames and rhetoric exert their influence through the emotions that cause audience members to pay attention because something matters to them.

In this part, after distinguishing several types of emotions, I describe some ways that emotions operate on or as ends of action and on or as means of action, accepting these as basic components of purposive action (also see Jasper 2006a, 2006c, on which this section draws). And although I do not address them here, emotions of solidarity help to form and maintain the collective political players who are capable of having ends and means in the first place.

Types of Emotions

A major obstacle to understanding emotions in politics is that our natural languages class numerous phenomena under the same term. Depending on what emotions we take as exemplars, we arrive at different visions of emotional processes. Crowd traditions favor eruptions of anger as the model for all emotions. Psychoanalysis adds anxieties and other behavioral neuroses. Cultural constructionism prefers complex moral emotions such as compassion or jealousy. As a way out of this seeming morass, I have found it useful to distinguish several types of emotion, which may operate via different neurological and chemical pathways (Goodwin et al. 2004; Griffiths 1997; Jasper 2006a, 2006c). They run, roughly, from the more physiological end of a continuum to the more cultural end. I have been unable to find a theory of emotions that deals equally well with each type.

Urges are physical impulses that demand our attention and crowd out other goals until they are satisfied. Jon Elster (1992b), who calls them "strong feelings," includes addiction, lust, fatigue, hunger and thirst, and the need to urinate or defecate. The role of culture in such urges is modest, although it may affect just what we lust after, and it certainly affects the means we use to satisfy our urges. Urges such as these help explain how political projects are sometimes derailed, for instance under conditions of extreme deprivation (or when key players get drunk!), but otherwise they have relatively little relevance to politics. Most accounts do not even classify them as emotions.

A second category near the physiological end of the continuum are *reflex emotions*, quick to appear and to subside. Inspired by Darwin, Paul Ekman (1972) has described these as universal and hardwired into us, sending quick signals through the hypothalamus and amygdala to set off automatic programs of action—facial expressions, bodily movements, vocal changes, hormonal charges such as adrenalin. His list includes anger, fear, joy, sadness, disgust, surprise, and contempt. Although reflex emotions sometimes lead to actions we later regret, Frank (1988) has argued that they may send important signals about our character. Being prone to anger may encourage compliance from others; disgust and contempt may encourage humans to keep their commitments.

Affects last longer and are normally more tied to elaborate cognitions than urges or reflexes are. They are positive and negative clusters of feelings, forms of attraction or repulsion. Examples include love and hate as well as respect, trust, resentment, suspicion, and perhaps dread. They are felt orientations to the world that we go to great lengths to maintain (Heise 1979). Affects include the solidarities behind collective identities, as well as the negative emotions toward outsiders that are often equally important (Alford 2006; Polletta and Jasper 2001).

Moods typically last longer than reflex emotions but not as long as affects, differing from both of them in not having a definite source or object (Clore, Schwartz, and Conway 1994). We frequently carry them from one setting to the next—although in some cases they are relatively permanent aspects of temperament or personality. They have a distinct biochemical basis, one reason that drugs affect them so directly. In my view, moods operate primarily as *filters* for perception, decision, and action—especially by giving us more confidence or less.

My final category consists of complex *moral emotions* such as compassion, outrage, and many forms of disgust, fear, and anger. These latter three, although they have their counterparts in reflex emotions, appear again here in more cognitively processed forms: the fear we feel about an automobile suddenly veering toward us is more automatic than the fear we feel about a hazardous waste dump down the road. Shame, pride, and jealousy are also complex results of our moral visions of the world (although evidence of something like shame in primates suggests that it too may have a counterpart in reflex emotions, upon which the more complex forms build).

Not all emotions fit neatly into these categories, not only because we frequently use the same term to connote very different feelings, but because any feeling that persists well beyond its initial stimulant can have the effects of a mood, especially pride. Nonetheless, I think a typology of this sort offers some analytic advantages, in that we no longer need to lump so many different processes together simply as "emotions." No single theory will explain them all.

Emotions and Ends

Occasionally, emotions are ends that we seek for their own sake. More often, they suggest other ends that would be emotionally satisfying, such as punishing those we hate.

Urges are immediate-term goals of action, not usually interesting for politics. Except that their urgency suggests conditions under which humans are distracted from political goals. We are near the bottom of Maslow's famous hierarchy of needs, and urges prevent us from moving up to others until the basic urges are satisfied (Inglehart 1977). Those suffering famine or other deprivation will not devote time and resources to political organizing. Nonetheless, we make elaborate plans, often over a long period, to satisfy our lusts—certainly one of the reasons people join social movements (Gitlin 1987).

Reflex emotions affect our means more than our ends, with one important exception. Sudden anger is capable of derailing political projects, and for this very reason our opponents are forever trying to goad us into losing our tempers. But someone who lashes out, either physically or verbally, can be viewed as satisfying an immediate-term goal at the expense of longer term goals. She is also pursuing her own personal satisfaction at the expense of her broader team. From their point of view, she has made a mistake. From hers, she has gained one satisfaction at the expense of others. (I assume here that the anger discredits her, but in many cases angry intimidation is effective in the short and the long term, with no adverse consequences and many positive ones.)

Affects shape some of our most basic goals. Melanie Klein believed that love and hate are the basic categories of human existence, a position compatible with Carl Schmitt's analysis of politics as dividing the world into friends and foes (Alford 1989; Schmitt 1976/1932). To the extent we love other humans (or places, organizations, other species, and so on), their well-being becomes one of our goals alongside our own well-being. And we take satisfaction in harming those we hate. As the well known fable of the prisoner's dilemma shows, it may be impossible to compare or rank-order personal and group goals. Certainly, there are times when the group goals are so important that individuals are willing to sacrifice their lives for them. We cannot understand zealots and martyrs unless we can grasp love and hatred for groups.

Hatred for others should never be underestimated as a human motive. *The power of negative thinking*, as I have called it (Jasper 1997:362), captures our attention more urgently than positive attractions, most of the time. Blame is at the center of much protest, requiring that protestors identify the humans who have made choices that harmed others. In any political engagement, it is possible for players to concentrate on harming opponents rather than on the original stakes available in the arena. Mutually destructive polarization then occurs, in which each side is willing to bear enormous costs to harm the other. Disgust, normally a reflex gagging, reappears as part of the bundle of negative images and affects humans can develop toward others, usually highly stereotyped categories of others.

Basic affects can cause individuals to defect from group projects by providing alternative goals, such as rebels who go home to protect their families or couples who fall in love and retreat into their own world. Goodwin (1997) has detailed this issue in the revolutionary Huk movement in the Philippines, whose leaders denounced (and often executed) participants who withdrew to be with their spouses and children. This is a recurrent dilemma for any collective effort: affective ties to the group aid cooperation and persistence, but those loyalties can attach instead to a small part of the broader whole. I call this the *band of brothers dilemma*, which applies not only to couples who fall in love but to soldiers who care more about their immediate comrades than the broader war effort, and to any movement with small cells or affinity groups (Jasper 2004a:13). Affective loyalties can attach themselves to subunits rather than to an organization or movement.

Like reflex emotions, *moods* more importantly affect means than ends. But there are some moods we seek out as directly pleasurable. We feel a surge of self-confidence and power when we are on a winning team, for instance. Or a kind of joy when we lose ourselves in crowds and other coordinated, collective activities such as singing, dancing, and marching (Lofland 1982; McNeill 1995). A great deal of political mobilization is aimed at transforming debilitating moods into assertive ones. Nationalism, which combines affects and moods, developed in large part when political elites wished to mobilize populations for war without sharing decision-making with them: a belligerent mood of pride, combined with hatred for others, was their rhetorical solution. But as this example shows, moods that we first seek out as ends then affect other emotions.

Finally, the special satisfactions of *moral emotions* make many of them important goals, especially when they are feelings about ourselves rather than about others. Foremost, we feel deontological (or moral) pride in doing the right thing, and in being the kind of person who does the right thing. In part, this is an elated mood similar to the joys of crowd activity—which itself is satisfying in part because we are giving voice to deep moral commitments. Thomas Scheff (1990, 1994, 1997) views pride and shame as the basic drives of human action, especially in that they (respectively) attach us to or detach us from human relationships.

Other moral emotions include pity and compassion, the emotions that victims are supposed to arouse. These are a kind of empathy, in that we feel pain at the plight of others. This displeasure moves us to try to remove the sources of pain. Photographs have proven an especially good means for arousing gut-level empathy, especially for suffering children or animals that are easily characterized as victims. As philosopher Richard Rorty (1993:118) put it, "The emergence of the human rights culture seems to owe nothing to increased moral knowledge and everything to hearing sad and sentimental stories." Social-movement organizers frequently aim to expand public compassion, building a case for pain, victimhood, and blame. At first, it seems that compassion is a means, leading us into actions, but I see it as adding a goal to our repertory. Like affective bonds, we care directly what happens to others; their suffering makes us suffer. Empathy for strangers is a recent triumph that it took humans a long time to accomplish—and which remains all too fragile.

Emotions and Means

Emotions permeate our political tactics as thoroughly as our political goals. Frequently, what is an emotional end for a grassroots participant is a means for the organizer who tries to arouse that emotion in her. It was in this rhetorical context—in which a creator of meanings aims at effects on audiences—that Aristotle discussed emotions and what causes them more than 2300 years ago.

Urges are rarely used as means in democratic politics, but they are regularly used in torture and other coercive acts. (Note that my urges are my tormentors' means, not my own.)

Reflex emotions on the other hand are frequently open to manipulation. The classic example is to goad opponents into anger so that they make mistakes. Protestors and forces of order frequently taunt each other in this way, hoping the other will discredit themselves through hasty actions, later regretted. Or we may try to startle or frighten them in order to paralyze them. Who- or whatever causes the reflex emotion, once in motion it certainly affects our ability to act. Evolutionary theorists believe that these deeply programmed emotions developed precisely to launch us into actions that we needed to undertake immediately, without thinking, typically because they moved us out of harm's way. In other words, they are pure means, packaged in an automatic, pre-programmed sequence unavailable to conscious thought. For instance, the adrenaline that accompanies reflex emotions may propel us into action quickly and forcefully. But the accompanying actions may be relatively short-term and not typical of political action.

Anger, like most emotions, can be a carefully cultivated performance as well as a direct reflex. Mediators "lose" their temper to gain compliance from recalcitrant parties, and protestors use anger to indicate urgency, frustration, and the threat that they may not be able to control themselves (or their radical wing) if they do not get what they want. It is not that the people in these examples do not feel anger, it is that they have considerable control over how to express it, following cultural scripts that yield advantages (just as Japanese cultural scripts regularly dampen the expression of anger). In such cases, emotions and their displays actually *are* means.

Most *affects* primarily affect ends, but some also affect means. Love and hate are basic loyalties that are hard to see as mere means (again, organizers arouse these in followers as means, but for the followers they become ends). But trust and respect for others are means that allow collective action to be fulfilled at lower costs (Putnam 2000). Perhaps the clearest case of affects informing means lies in followers' feelings toward their leaders. Love, trust, and respect for leaders ease a great number of activities carried out for the larger group. Attention to emotional dynamics may allow us to revive the concept of charisma, as a way of understanding the psychological benefits that leaders offer their followers (Madsen and Snow 1991). More generally, organizations devote considerable resources to making others trust them, through a number of symbolic activities and promotion (Meyer and Rowan 1977).

Moods clearly affect our means for carrying out political ends. Self-confidence aids any player, from the protestor facing the police to the prime minister making a speech. Moods of resignation or cynicism, on the other hand, can cripple anyone's willingness and ability to pursue her goals. The extreme is depression, which robs us of both goals and means for action. Some medium-term types of fear operate as moods, which can be manipulated to inspire or to freeze action—much like anxiety. In many cases, shame must be reworked into pride in order for action to occur or be sustained (Gould 2001).

The effects of moods can be complex. Hope, for instance, like other forms of confidence, stimulates action because we think it can be successful. But too much hope may undermine realistic assessments of a situation and discourage information gathering (Lazarus 1999). Similarly, a sense of threat can spur action, but if that threat is seen as overwhelming it can discourage action. Anxiety, too, stimulates action at low levels but cripples it at high levels (this suggests the unspecified emotional underpinnings of concepts like the U-curve describing the effects of repression on political mobilization). There is some evidence that bad moods improve decision-making—by increasing attention to detail and improving analysis (Schwartz and Bless 1991).

Whereas *moral* emotions we have about ourselves seem best classified under goals, those about others are probably better described as means (although the distinction blurs somewhat in these cases). Outrage and indignation are the emotions associated with blame: not only do we pity victims, we identify a perpetrator responsible for their suffering. Pity for victims does not by itself lead to action, until we also feel outrage toward the villain. Compassion shapes the goal, while outrage provides the spur to action.

Affect-control theorists have shown that one basic dimension of emotions is whether they are associated with dominance or with vulnerability, another is whether they are associated with activity or passivity (Morgan and Heise 1988). (The third basic dimension in this model is pleasant versus unpleasant.) Emotional states that are dominant and active, such as outrage, anger, and excitement, are presumably better spurs to political action than those that are vulnerable and passive, such as sadness (Lively and Heise 2004). Both moods and morals fit well in this picture.

David Hume carved out a large role for emotions when he portrayed them as the source of human goals, with rationality as mere means for attaining them. But we can see emotions as deeply permeating our means as well. By connecting us to a number of social and physical contexts, and providing immediate evaluations of those contexts, a number of different emotions are crucial means in political action. Just as it is difficult to understand political action without addressing its cultural dimensions, so it is almost impossible to understand culture without including its emotional components.

MORALITY

Moral Motivations

If cognition, emotion, and morality are three components of culture, morality has been especially slighted in recent theories—despite of or in reaction to Turner and Killian's (1957) and Smelser's (1962) early emphasis on values. Or rather, moral motives have been hidden through a division of labor in which religious movements are either studied separately from secular movements or are stripped of their religious content—as though all that mattered were their networks of recruitment, formal organizations, and so on. It is no accident that Christian Smith, a scholar of religion, should complain so sharply about sociology's inattention to morality. Sociological research, whether structurally or culturally oriented, has mostly avoided the issue of motivation altogether. He recognizes how thoroughly goals are shaped by culture. In his words (Smith 2003:145), any "cultural sociology worth pursuing" must articulate "a model of human personhood, motivation, and action in decidedly cultural terms." And for him, this means moral terms.

Morality is alive and well in the sociology of religion. Robert Wuthnow (1991) has investigated a number of ways in which religious faith and participation encourage "acts of compassion"—as well as some limitations to those effects. Sharon Erickson Nepstad (2004) showed how missionaries used church networks to focus Americans' attention on their government's policy in Latin America and to inspire protest by reminding Christians of fundamental tenets of their faith. James Aho (1990:15) analyzed the "politics of righteousness" that motivates a number of right-wing Christian groups in the United States, who feel they must do God's will by battling "a satanic cabal that has insidiously infiltrated the dominant institutions of society, especially the mass media, public schools, established churches, and state agencies like the Internal Revenue Service." What better "God term" than God Almighty himself? There could be no better motivating trope to fuse cognition, emotion, and moral duty.

Yet even scholars of religious movements tend to emphasize cognitive beliefs above emotional and moral motivations. Aho, for instance, highlights a dualistic view of history, a belief in conspiracy, and a sense of urgency because the Second Coming is imminent. These building blocks fit together into a coherent worldview, sometimes explicit and sometimes implicit, but the vision's motivating power presumably comes from the moral and emotional components, which are inseparable from the cognitive ones. Enumerating participants' beliefs is only the beginning of a full cultural explanation. The cognitive emphasis is necessary in part because secular scholars have trouble taking the right-wing religious beliefs seriously—one reason that so many scholars of religious movements themselves seem to be believers rather than doubters. But we need to recognize the moral and emotional dimensions.

Religion is not the only source of moral principles and intuitions. Jasper (1997:chap. 6) laid out a number of these, which often come into conflict with each other: political ideologies, professional ethics, community allegiances, and expectations of ontological or economic security. In all these cases, we have expectations about the social world, and when they are disappointed moral shocks may result that leave us indignant. Often we are not aware of our expectations until they are disappointed, and political activity helps us articulate what were previously inchoate moral intuitions. Some moral values attain fundamental importance, becoming what Taylor (1989) calls "hypergoods" that trump other goals.

As important as it is to recognize moral motivations, we cannot simply substitute them for material interests in another monocausal model of what drives human action—as Smith, for example, tends to do. Humans are not "fundamentally" moral any more than they are "fundamentally" materialist. They juggle many motivations and goals, some of which are in conflict and some of which are simply not comparable. The challenge, which I think only a cultural (i.e., rhetorical and strategic) approach could meet, is to understand why different goals become more prominent at different times. Emotions must be central to these models.

The Cultural Variety of Morality

Most moral intuitions and principles vary across groups, even if others seem universal. Changes over time are perhaps easiest to see. Inspired by Nietzsche, Michel Foucault (1998:379) famously commented on this variability: "We believe that feelings are immutable, but every sentiment, particularly the noblest and most disinterested, has a history." Foucault's genealogical approach was intended to demonstrate how moral intuitions and emotions come to feel as though they have emerged from our "gut level," from our bodies, an insight elaborated by Bourdieu (1984).

For instance compassion for the weak is a modern specialty. Movements to protect animals, children, or indigenous peoples, to take several examples, build upon a broad shift in moral and emotional sensibilities of the last 200 years, in which broad segments of the middle class have grown sentimental and compassionate about beings considered innocent and therefore easily portrayed as victims (Haskell 1985). If there were ever a movement that demanded attention to moral motivations, it is animal protection. Here, activists do not even belong to the same species as the beneficiaries of their activities (Jasper and Nelkin 1992; Garner 1993; Groves 1997).

Scholars have also examined international variations in morality, based on differences in national cultural traditions and institutions. Robert Bellah, another scholar of religion who broadened his focus to examine morality, worked with colleagues to investigate the languages Americans use to talk about their obligations to others (Bellah et al. 1985). Michèle Lamont (1992) probed the professional middle class in France and the United States for differences in the kinds of moral distinctions they made in daily life. But it is not always clear what kinds of political mobilization are precluded or made possible by the kinds of moral boundaries drawn in conversations with interviewers.

In using focus groups, William Gamson (1992) came a step closer to politics, observing the cultural meanings normal people use to elaborate political positions. In the conversations he organized, people drew on cultural understandings derived from the media, from their own experiences, and from popular wisdom as embodied in maxims. From these he was able to see what conditions allowed groups to begin to put together the necessary understandings for collective action, including a sense of moral injustice, a sense of agency that suggested it would be possible to alter policies or conditions through collective action, and a sense of collective identity about who would bring about these changes. Packed into this latter is also a sense of the identity of an adversary who must be influenced or stopped. Gamson could trace a number of themes related to the policy issues he raised with the groups.

In contrast to Gamson's work on the understandings that arise in small groups, Luc Boltanski and Laurent Thévenot (1991) have catalogued the kinds of arguments used to justify policies in public debates. In this way, they get at the intersection of cultural meanings, out there and available, and traditional rhetorical appreciation of messages designed to have effects on audiences. They identify the following "grammars of worth": "market" performance, "industrial" or "technical" efficiency based on technology and planning; "civic" solidarity; "domestic" trustworthiness based on personal ties; "inspiration" based on creativity and charisma; "renown" based on fame; and (added later: Lafaye and Thévenot, 1993) a "green" concern for ecological sustainability. So far, little research has related these grammars of worth to social movements (cf. Lamont and Thévenot 2000). But different institutional settings encourage different moral references.

Morality and Emotion

We can identify the many, culturally influenced motivations and goals that affect action, but what are the mechanisms by which they exert their effects? In the skeptical modern world, we assume that the pursuit of one's own material interests needs no explanation, but that the pursuit of distant ideals may. All goals are culturally shaped, of course, but less attention has been paid to the moral impulses. When we examine them closely, they may simply not be so "distant" after all. Acting morally is accompanied by a number of emotions that are directly satisfying.

I have used the concept of *moral shock* to highlight the emotions involved in responses to perceived injustice (Jasper 1997; Jasper and Poulsen 1995). When we learn or experience something that suggests the world is not morally as it seems, our indignation has a strong visceral aspect. We feel betrayed by the world as well as by other people. We rethink our moral stands and consider action to redress the wrong. Moral shocks can propel people into action, or at least predispose them to act if there is an opportunity to do so. They help us understand how morality actually moves us to action. They are a good example of a "precipitating event."

Researchers have found moral shocks in a variety of settings. Repressive regimes often stimulate more collective protest than they suppress, because of the moral shocks their brutality causes in "transformative events" (Hess and Martin 2006) and "revolutionary accelerators" (Reed 2004). Severe human rights abuses can shock foreign audiences, too, gaining their attention and sympathy (Stewart 2004). Other works trying to describe the emotional dynamics of protest have turned to moral shocks as a mechanism (Reger 2004; Satterfield 2004), for instance as a way of operationalizing Melucci's concepts (King 2004).

Acting collectively has its own accompanying moral feelings. We do the right thing for a variety of reasons, and prominent among them must be fear of the consequences of doing the wrong thing. We may fear public punishment for transgressions, or we may fear internal punishment such as guilt or shame. In between these extremes, and in a sense combining them, we may fear for our reputations among various relevant audiences. Fear is an ignoble motive, but surely it is a major form of glue enforcing the rules of any group.

We also enjoy a number of positive feelings that result from doing the right thing. *Deontological pride*, if we can call it that, is distinct from other feelings of pleasure. It is a sense that we have acted in a way we and others admire (and perhaps also signaling that we are the kind of person who should be admired). This feeling is often mixed with the pleasant anticipation of acclaim, but it need not be. It also contains an element of relief that we did not do the wrong thing, linking back to the potential fears. There are other forms of pride, of course, but deontological pride is central to collective action.

Deontological pride need not depend on external audiences. We can feel proud of ourselves for doing the right thing even if no one else knows, and even if we do not survive to enjoy any acclaim. When we are our own audience in this way, deontological pride comes close to a feeling of dignity, a key motivation for participation, even or especially in high-risk activities (Auyero 2003; Wood 2003). Honor is the form deontological pride takes in societies where there is agreement over the moral rules that determine pride and shame. Historically it has been more important than wealth, and even today reputation ranks as a goal far higher than most political theory recognizes. Reputations are fundamental human values.

Although it need not be, I nonetheless suspect that deontological pride is most often based on some collective identity. We have done something that either helps our imagined collectivity or which we think that collectivity would praise. Often, we expect positive reactions from individual members of that group, those who symbolize it for us in our face to face interactions. A sense of the collective provides both an imagined audience as well as a set of moral values.

There are additional feelings involved in various types of moral action. Most ideologies offer some hope for the future, suggesting that a situation can be improved through collective action. Hope feels good in itself, it is not simply an optimistic assessment about the chances of success (as process theories had it). In some collective action, compassion is an ingredient. Helping those in need is directly satisfying for most people. And let us not forget revenge, formed out of hatred and indignation: suicide bombers find their acts directly satisfying for this reason (and not necessarily because they altruistically strive for some public good, as rational-choice theorists would have it).

Blame is a moral and emotional concept crucial to strategic collective action (Jasper 1997:103–129; Jasper 2006b:48–53). If we believe that some adverse outcome could have been avoided, by an individual or group, we tend to become angry or indignant. If we cannot find someone to blame, framing what happened as an act of God or nature for instance, we are more likely to become sad—hardly a mobilizing mood (Nerb and Spada 2001). The boundaries and forms of blame are preeminently cultural constructions.

Even for an individual, few actions are driven by a single motive, aimed at a single goal. The goals of compound (collective) players are far more complicated. But just as we have the tools to get at elaborate cognitive understandings of the world, we have the tools to tease out complex combinations of motivations and of emotions. Morality can take its place alongside other factors, ready to be elaborated through empirical investigation. Goals, like the players themselves, need not be dictated in advance by our theories (on basic goals, see Jasper 2006b:chap. 3).

RETHINKING NONCULTURAL CONCEPTS

Structural and rationalist traditions have proven able to accommodate culture in the form of discrete variables, such as frames or collective identities. But a cultural approach in which human action is thoroughly permeated by meaning, emotion, and morality requires more than the addition of culture to other models. It demands that we rethink apparently noncultural concepts from a cultural point of view, demonstrating their meaningful character. Interpretation is required from start to finish. A fully cultural approach recognizes no factors that do not at least interact with our understandings, including biological variables as well as structural ones. And by reinterpreting them from a cultural perspective, I think we strengthen them.

Costs and Benefits

Rationalist traditions have featured rather stunted versions of humans, most interested in their own individual welfare, typically defined as material wealth. Olson (1965:61) famously recognized moral and emotional factors, only to exclude them from his model on the grounds that "it is not possible to get empirical proof of the motivation behind any person's action." Of course it is just as impossible to get proof that one is motivated by self-interest. Olson further muddied the waters by insisting, without evidence, that "most organized pressure groups are explicitly working for gains for themselves, not gains for other groups." Finally, in the same notorious footnote, he admits that affective groups—his examples are families and friendships—are probably best studied with other models than his. To the extent a protest group has affective ties, his model is inadequate.

Under the influence of the cultural revolution, scholars began to recognize the inadequacy of these early formulations, and to try to insert meanings as a patch (e.g., Ferejohn 1991). What seemed a simple supplement helped to transform the field, spawning experimental psychology and economics that could incorporate emotions, morals, and cognition—but which in the process undermined the mathematical precision that Olson had hoped to save. Crucially, the new behavioral economics has demonstrated that decision makers do not anticipate moves more than one or two rounds in advance, meaning they are more guided by their own culture and psychology than by the mathematical foresight needed to make optimal choices (Camerer 2003; Camerer, Loewenstein, and Rubin 2004).

Foremost, costs and benefits are defined and valued through cultural lenses. Jail time and other forms of repression are, from Olson's perspective, pure costs, but they contain many elements of benefit as well. For many, it is a badge of honor to have been imprisoned, increasing not only their reputations but their own deontological pride. Martyrs are difficult to understand through rationalist lenses, since they typically weigh group benefits so heavily. The sources of preferences, long dismissed by rationalists as exogenous to their models, also take us into the realm of culture. Rationalists have tried to incorporate this role of culture and psychology in constituting costs and benefits (Chong 1991, 2000), but only by turning rational choice into the platitudinous endeavor that Olson feared.

Culture does more than help to define costs and benefits. It tells players how much information should be collected to make a decision, a choice that cannot be made on purely logical grounds. It allows players to satisfice rather than maximize, partly by providing reference groups for players to decide what is satisfactory. It helps to shape the many decision-making heuristics and biases that cognitive psychologists and economists have described. Culture, and especially emotions, tell us what to do in situations of extreme uncertainty, where no single rational option could be derived but a decision must be made anyway. Finally, without culture we would have difficulty ranking different preferences, especially when we have noncomparable preferences such as hypergoods (Taylor 1989).

As experiments are beginning to show, culture influences how individuals try to balance their own personal interests with those of broader groups (see Camerer 2003 for summaries). Individuals are willing to give up monetary gains in order to punish players they believe are acting unfairly. (When they view the other player's unfair action as out of her control, they are less likely to punish her for it.) Radical economists Samuel Bowles and Herbert Gintis (Heirich et al. 2001, 2004) have studied cross-cultural differences in reciprocity, finding that roughly half the variation they observed was due to the relative development of markets and cooperation in the division of labor.

The ends, the means, and even the mistakes made in political action are thoroughly shaped by human interpretations of the world. These meanings provide the raw materials for any calculation of costs and benefits, advantages and disadvantages, and risks. Indeed, the real "work" of rationalist analysts is often in their interpretation of situations, not in the mathematics that follows. In game theory, seeing an interaction as a familiar game is the creative moment, often requiring an interpretive leap (especially about a player's goals). Culture is there from the bottom up, and always has been.

Organizations, Resources, and Leaders

One of the leading answers to Olson's challenge about how rational actors would come to engage in protest came from American "resource mobilization" theorists who focused on formal organizations and those who found and lead them. John McCarthy and Mayer Zald (1977) expressed this view most influentially, applying the metaphor of firms and industries and sectors to social movements. Like Olson, and perhaps because they were partly responding to him, they presented organizations and leaders as though they were little influenced by culture. But we can reread their position from an interpretive point of view.

Even the most formalized organizations rely on a range of cultural practices and understandings – as one strand of "new institutionalism" has stressed. They manipulate symbols and rituals to send signals about what kind of organizations they are (Meyer and Rowan 1977). They rely on cultural schemas about markets and societies (Dobbin 1994). Even the forms that protest organizations adopt reflect cultural schemas, often borrowed from other types of organization (Clemens, 1996). Organizations are never neutral, efficient means to pursue pre-given ends. They also embody *tastes in tactics* (Jasper 1997).

In McCarthy and Zald's metaphor of a firm, social movement organizations (SMOs) try to extract as much time and money from sympathetic populations as they can, competing with other SMOs (and other outlets for discretionary income) as they do so. But in their eagerness to reject older "grievance" models, McCarthy and Zald did not address the many rhetorical processes by which audiences are persuaded to part with contributions—precisely the gap that "framing" was later meant to fill. Ironically, by a seemingly cultural definition of a social movement as a "set of opinions and beliefs in a population for changing some elements of the social structure and/or reward distribution of a society," McCarthy and Zald precluded research on the sources of those opinions or how organizers might appeal to them. "Mobilization" is thoroughly imbued with culture.

So are resources. I prefer to define resources as purely physical capacities or the money to buy them (Jasper 1997), so that we can examine their relationship to the knowledge about how to use them, cultural scripts about when it is appropriate to use them, and decision-making processes that ultimately deploy them. Resources such as money, tear gas, and tanks allow certain kinds of actions, but they matter only through decisions and actions.

If SMOs are firms, their leaders are entrepreneurs, apparently doing what they do for the money. They see unmet preferences and needs, in the form of money that would be contributed to a new SMO were it founded, and they bear initial organizing costs with the prospect of recouping them later. Although giving a prominent place to leaders, McCarthy and Zald do not address the moral intuitions and principles, the emotional sympathies and antipathies, the cognitive framing and interpretation that make up potential followers' preferences, even though they highlight "conscience constituencies" who have moral rather than material interests in the cause being pursued.

Even a cultural observer like Alberto Melucci, as we saw, did not grasp the full cultural significance of leaders, instead following McCarthy and Zald in seeing leaders and their followers as exchanging benefits (1996a). But leaders have considerable cultural importance. They symbolize an organization or a movement, to insiders and outsiders (although often differently to these two audiences). This means that they transmit messages about a movement's intentions, power, trajectory, and tactics, but they also become the object of a variety of emotions. The love, admiration, and trust they inspire in members enhance mobilization and sacrifice; the trust they arouse in outsiders eases a movement's strategic efforts. The opposite feelings naturally have the opposite impacts.

Janja Lalich (2004) accomplishes this kind of updating in her rethinking of Hoffer's concept of a *true believer*. She compares Heaven's Gate, which gained notoriety in 1997 when three dozen of its members—including its aging leader—committed suicide in southern California in the hope of shedding their human traits and bodies and moving to a higher state of evolution via a passing spaceship, with a Marxist–Leninist–Maoist pre-party formation, also founded in the mid-1970s, that lasted a respectable decade. Charismatic leaders (another concept she revives) can demand such enormous sacrifices from their followers, she explains, by cutting recruits off from other social ties, people with other perspectives who might offer a critical view of the group's goals and means. They apply constant pressure to make participants see freedom in the ultimate transformation to come, in contrast to the current world of corruption. Charismatic leaders in these two groups lived apart, in ways that allowed followers to see them as embodying their ideals for living and thinking. The leaders and the groups they embodied came to be more important than the actual individuals who also comprised the groups—any of whom could be expelled at any moment. There was also paranoia about the outside world, making any internal criticism an act of betrayal as it could be used by those out to destroy the groups.

Much of this is classic Hoffer, but instead of damaged individuals seeking identity, Lalich discusses processes of cognition, culture, and social control that could operate in many different contexts and on anyone (although she is not clear about this). Today, it is easy for social scientists to recognize all the meaning work that goes into any political mobilization, from the most outlandish to the most mainstream. Groups construct identities for members, demonize opponents and outsiders, demand allegiance to the group above that to its individual members, find exemplary individuals (leaders or not) who inspire loyalty and action, and develop other ways to get work out of members. We need ways to study such mechanisms in a range of groups, finally overcoming the great intellectual divide, which has bedeviled political analysis for so long, between those who study groups they dislike and those who study groups they admire. Cognitive and emotional shaping occurs in all groups and organizations.

Structures, Opportunities, and Repression

Like resource mobilization, political opportunity models were an important strand of American research on movements in the 1970s and 1980s. One concentrated on the economics of protest organizations, the other on their political environments: the states and elites to which they appealed. But just as mobilization theorists ignored the cultural side of their favored processes, so political process theorists tended to view political environments in structural terms that equally ignored their cultural construction. Their belated efforts to add a few cultural variables were inadequate, and the paradigm collapsed rather abruptly at the turn of the millennium (Goodwin and Jasper 2003; McAdam et al. 2001).

Process theories included culture in the form of "cognitive liberation," intended to get at the moment when potential protestors believe they have a chance to succeed. For fifteen years, process theorists insisted on distinguishing between the existence of objective opportunities and the ability of protestors to perceive them—a distinction neatly demolished when

Kurzman showed that Iranian revolutionaries created opportunities by believing in them (1996). Today it is easier to see that there is some cultural interpretation at every stage or level of an opportunity (including a great deal of cultural work by elites during a crisis). Cognitive liberation involves emotions that might drive people to participate even when they do not think they can succeed.

In the dominant models, most structural opportunities involved cleavages among elites that either paralyze them or lead a faction to align with potential insurgents (Jenkins and Perrow 1977). Neither of these is automatic. Potential choices must be framed, symbols presented, emotions aroused. Political players persuade each other rhetorically to undertake certain actions. Alliances are a good example: they do not follow directly from material or "objective" interests. Cultural work goes into persuading players that they share interests, into instilling emotional solidarities, into imagining a certain kind of future together. At every step there are dilemmas to be finessed (Jasper 2006b).

Elites are important not only for the legal openings and physical resources they can provide, but also for their decisions about repression. When facing police or troops whose morale does not crack and who are well armed, insurgencies almost inevitably fail. But too often, repression was treated as though it were a structural capacity concerning resources, say the number of rifles or tanks available, rather than a matter of persuasion and choice. Commanders and troops at a number of levels must decide to follow orders, while weighing their moral principles and emotional loyalties and envisioning their futures under different regimes. There are many chances to defect, and many ways to do so. Elites interpret and persuade too.

Structures do little by themselves. They constrain because there are other players actively using resources, enforcing laws and other rules, occupying positions in organizations and other hierarchies, and generally working hard to pursue or protect their own advantages. In the heat of strategic engagement, these actions depend on a variety of emotional and cognitive processes. Few scholars today embrace the label structuralist, recognizing the open-ended nature of most structures (Kurzman 2003).

Mobilization and Networks

One of the most robust findings of movement research has been that participants are frequently recruited through personal networks—part of the structural imagery of the 1970s and 1980s. In the crudest formulations, often encouraged by methods of network analysis, the recruitment is almost mechanical. Attitudes do not seem to matter, only network ties. But David Snow and others (Snow et al., 1980) who helped demonstrate the importance of networks were quick to realize (Snow et al., 1983, 1986) that what mattered was largely the ideas (and I would add, the emotions) that flow through them. Networks consist of affective loyalties, not mechanical interactions. Networks and culture work together (Klandermans and Oegema, 1987).

The concept of biographical availability was used to help explain recruitment: supposedly structural traits such as lack of a regular job, a spouse, or children free individuals for the time commitment of protest (McCarthy and Zald, 1973, McAdam, 1988:chap. 2). But availability is a matter of low costs to protest, and as I argued above all costs must operate through the cultural and psychological filters of decisionmakers. For most the costs will be too high, but not for all. What we need to explain is these different interpretations of circumstances.

Bloc recruitment was also initially defined as a structural availability of an entire group or network that could be coopted to a new cause (Freeman, 1973; Oberschall, 1973). But just as individual recruitment through networks relies on activating affective loyalties and persuasive rhetoric, the same processes operate to draw the leader of a bloc to a new cause, then to keep her followers in the bloc (presumably, many are not persuaded: blocs rarely arrive in their entirety). Just as interactions with elites and other potential allies entails cognitive and emotional and moral persuasion, so does recruitment to the cause.

Theories of frame alignment were originally developed to explain exactly these processes of recruitment. Other cultural concepts, such as suddenly imposed grievances (Walsh, 1981) and moral shocks (Jasper, 1997; Jasper and Poulsen, 1995), were developed largely to get at the cultural spark necessary for networks to do their work—and to explain occasional cases of self-recruitment in the absence of networks. If we do not view protest exclusively or primarily as an effort to redress some recognized material or political lack, but recognize that it can also be an effort to impose cognitive, moral, and emotional order on the world, recruitment is more easily seen as a cultural exhortation than as a simple sharing of information.

Strategy as a Cultural Concept

Thanks to generations of game theorists, social scientists are accustomed to thinking about strategic choices as though they were calculations of advantages and payoffs, with little input from culture. Each player's choices are also narrowed, typically to a mere two possibilities, and communication—hence persuasion—is often barred. The result has been mathematical elegance at the expense of realism. One way to reinterpret strategy from a cultural perspective is to rethink costs and benefits, as we suggested above, but there are others.

Of the three main families of strategic action (I define strategy simply as trying to get others to do what you want them to)—coercion, payment, and persuasion (Jasper, 2006b)—the latter is most purely cultural. But the other two also contain elements of tradition, information, and even some persuasion. Coercion is frequently preceded by threat, for example; payment is typically followed by monitoring for performance. Most strategic engagements involve cooperation and communication, which have deep cultural dimensions. These include appeals to collective identities, emotional solidarities to prevent defections, and the elaboration of moral exemplars.

Decision making, reduced to a simple mathematical calculation in game theory, is a complex cultural and psychological process (Ganz 2000, 2003). Players rely on traditions and norms, on the cognitive heuristics that memory and media make available, and on their definitions of any given situation. And when it is groups rather than individuals who must arrive at decisions, persuasion becomes internal to a player, adding another layer of cultural process. Shared understandings, which help collective players operate smoothly, must be built up and negotiated.

When someone acts strategically, other players are audiences for those actions. They constantly interpret the intentions, feelings, commitments, the fragility of other players. They try to decide which words and actions are bluffs, which sincere. They make judgments about potential factions and fissures by assessing various motives. They estimate the utility of various kinds of resources and other advantages. They come up with theories about the "characters" of players, as a way to guess what they will do. They draw on their knowledge to invent new tactics when possible, based on their knowledge of what other players expect.

And as we saw above, the very creation of a strategic player is a cognitive and emotional accomplishment, a collective identity that requires continual reinforcement.

Two Ways to Think about Crowds

After this brief jaunt through so many basic concepts, we can return to the root metaphor of so much research on protest, namely crowds, to rethink them as well from a cultural perspective. In the old view, crowds stripped away cultural meanings, broader social ties, and long-term political projects, in order to get down to some "basic" form of interaction. In Durkheim, we see this in the notion that aboriginal gatherings somehow represented the "essence" of religion. As late as Smelser (1962), we see the same idea: that other forms of collective action, even the most complex value-oriented movements, are built up from basic forms of action, namely crowds. Because this long tradition lacked much empirical evidence, and because it relied on psychological mechanisms that were hard to observe, the structural tradition would dismiss it as myth—a cultural construction that served conservative political purposes. Those few who continued to study crowds were most interested in showing the structured microinteractions occurring, in order to demonstrate that crowds are not unified, rarely turn violent, are not composed of people with a predisposition toward violence, and so on (McPhail 1991).

Research on crowds is ready for a culturally oriented rebirth. For one thing, psychologists of emotion have demonstrated that the old notion of contagion contains some truth (Hatfield, Cacciopo, and Rapson 1994). Facial expressions of emotion are mimicked by those around one, a process that can spread salient emotions through an interacting crowd. More generally, Collins (2001) has elaborated the ritual component of crowds addressed by Durkheim. Seeking and receiving attention provide both goals and means for further action. The rituals of crowds are simply one example of interactions that generate attention and a number of emotions. The pleasures of crowds and other forms of coordinated movement go beyond social attention, however (McNeill 1995). And as Turner and Killian (1957) recognized, they are hotbeds of ideas. As Durkheim claimed, crowd actions interact with existing symbol systems, with each reinforcing the other through the emotions aroused. Crowds are not moments of madness, but moments of articulation.

Pamela Oliver (1989) argues that crowds are a corrective to the organizational metaphors and dynamics of most recent research. Events and gatherings have their own momentum and effects, not always under the control of formal organizations. In particular, how the events are understood (as successful or not, as promising, as fun) influences whether they are likely to be repeated. In addition, mutual reactions unfold through a strategic logic that often eludes formal organizations. Here too, crowds and culture come together.

METHODS OF RESEARCH

Case Studies

Scholars of social movements typically devote enormous time to mastering the diverse phenomena that comprise any movement, usually composed of many diverse groups, different kinds of members, various kinds of tactics and events, interactions with a number of other strategic players, and so on. The result is that most research consists of sustained *case studies*.

On the positive side, such close attention can allow an understanding of deep cultural meanings and feelings. On the negative, the same case is often used to develop new theories and concepts as well as to try them out empirically. For instance, each scholar derives a series of frames from her movement, without connecting them to frames in other movements or to broader cultural themes (Benford 1997; cf. Gamson 1992). We need more explicit *comparisons* of movements and settings: how is a frame adapted to a new movement; how does the same group reformulate its appeal for different audiences; how does it present its identity to outsiders and to insiders; when does it play the hero and when the victim. Comparisons over time and across groups or movements will help us isolate causal mechanisms by which meanings are created, disseminated, and affect action.

Noncultural Techniques

Many scholars have avoided the risks of case studies by looking at *events* instead of movements. Originally deployed in the study of riots, the use of events as units of analysis was especially helpful in the historical understanding of strikes and other contentious events for which newspaper reports but not richer information were available. The strength of this technique lies in tracking developments over time and checking correlations of protest with other variables such as unemployment or grain prices, but it remains largely wedded to newspaper accounts and does little to discern the meanings or feelings of protestors. The structural school used it to great effect in criticizing earlier crowd-based models (Shorter and Tilly 1974; Snyder and Tilly 1972), but they were forced to use proxies such as economic troubles to get at discontent. Long time series make sense primarily when there is an explicit or implicit theory of history lurking in the background.

Network analysis is another technique associated with structuralist assumptions about human action. An impressive number of studies have demonstrated the importance of networks for recruitment and collective action (Diani 2004 is a good summary). But all too often, such studies are content to describe the networks without theorizing exactly how networks allow or encourage action—often on the implicit assumption that bringing willing participants together is sufficient (structural models tend to assume that the grievances are already there, and only opportunities are lacking) (Fernandez and McAdam 1988). But more and more work argues that what travels across those networks is not only information about possibilities for action but affective bonds such as trust and collective identities and cognitive frames for understanding issues (Emirbayer and Goodwin 1994; Passy 2003). Mische (2003:259) even suggests that we view networks as "composed of culturally constituted processes of communicative interaction," in which understandings and decisions are negotiated. Unfortunately, the elaborate techniques developed for mapping networks are not the most subtle for getting at those meanings.

Surveys have the advantages of techniques developed across generations of social scientists, and they remain the premier tool for examining the distribution of beliefs in a population. Surveys can demonstrate a population's relative support for an issue or action, although cognitive agreement does little to explain who in the end actually participates in a protest action (Klandermans and Oegema 1987). They can identify clusters of ideas that form protestors' worldviews, such as the post-industrial values or the "new environmental paradigm" (Cotgrove 1982; Inglehart 1977, 1990, 1997; Milbrath 1984;). Surveys of protestors have also been used to identify cleavages within a movement, patterns of recruitment, and tactical preferences. They are especially good for tracing changes across time. They can also be used to gather basic descriptive information about organizations (such as Dalton 1994). Surveys are less adept for uncovering ideas unfamiliar to researchers or probing feelings that are difficult (or sensitive) to articulate (Klandermans and Smith 2002).

Interpretive Techniques

Focus groups redress these drawbacks by allowing deeper probing in a group setting in which new points of view might emerge that researchers had not initially recognized. We saw that Gamson (1992) used focus groups to show the raw cultural materials available for organizing, the common-sense understandings that are as important as media framings of events. Focus groups can also allow researchers to confront participants to observe their emotional as well as cognitive reactions, much as in Touraine's sociological interventions. As Kitzinger and Barbour (1999:5) observe, although with an overly cognitive emphasis, "Focus groups are ideal for exploring people's experiences, opinions, wishes, and concerns. The method is particularly useful for allowing participants to generate their own questions, frames and concepts, and to pursue their own priorities on their own terms, in their own vocabulary." They can also generate their own feelings.

Various forms of *content analysis* have looked at publicly expressed meanings, often formulating them as frames (Benford 1997; Johnston 2002). The advantage here is that the researcher need not probe subtle mental representations, only their public embodiments— although there remains some assumption of a connection between the two. Discourse analysis broadens the notion of what can be interpreted: not only written texts but spoken words and even—in poststructural fashion—all terms and practices (Laclau and Mouffe 1985). In this case, there is nothing outside discourse, in the sense of meaningful action. Even physical objects are meaningful only as part of a language game. In most cases, discourse analysis is essentially the study of rhetoric (Billig 1987; Steinberg 1998, 1999). Most often, it is used to decode the discourses of the powerful rather than those who challenge them, as in the relatively formal Critical Discourse Analysis (Fairclough 1995). Here, content analysis is not a search for static meanings but an effort to show how people *do things* with words.

The best way to get at the meanings and especially feelings of participants remains some form of involvement, through *ethnographic* observation, direct *participation*, depth *interviews*—or some combination of these. The lengthy time commitment allows adjustment between hypotheses and evidence, especially in the form of interrogating activists about what they think they are doing. Lalich's (2004) richly detailed study of Heaven's Gate and the Democratic Workers Party, for instance, was possible only through her unique (and extensive) contact with both groups: she belonged to the DWP and was one of its leaders for many years, and was a therapist and writer who worked with some of Heaven's Gate's former members and survivors. Of course, such access is costly to obtain. Nor do techniques like this help us understand movements of the past.

Semistructured interviews represent an effort to combine some of the representativity of surveys with the depth of open-ended interviews (Blee and Taylor 2002). Researchers can get at the feelings and understandings of participants, especially by adding some degree of context unavailable to most surveys. By carefully choosing whom to interview, researchers can get at something beneath the official statements of a group, for instance by probing factional disagreements. But as with surveys, the more structured the interview the less likely it is to reveal something entirely new to the researcher.

Several researchers have tried to get at the meanings and decisions of protestors by taking "the actors' point of view" (Bevington and Dixon 2005; Maddison and Scalmer 2006). Ethnographic and similar approaches share the assumption that only through our own participation can we fully understand what protestors are going through, what they are thinking and feeling. But there are two possible ways to adopt the actors' points of view. One is to sympathize with them, a natural stance for scholars who are also activists, as many are. The risk is that analyses of movements become moral cheerleading aimed at showing their arguments are right rather than at explaining them objectively. The other way to get inside actors' heads is simply to empathize, to understand their goals and sensibilities as well as possible, but to fit this empathy into rigorous causal models that would work whether the protestors' arguments are right or wrong. Besides, if sympathy is necessary, how can we understand opponents, state officials, and others who help determine the outcomes of struggle? And how do we study movements, as we'll see in a moment, for which we have little or no sympathy?

Introspection

Having reviewed methods commonly recognized as useful for the study of the cultural dimension of social movements—and some less useful for it—we turn finally to a method that is often used but rarely discussed, introspection. Still a staple among philosophers, introspection has a terrible reputation among social scientists. In psychology, experimentalism thoroughly vanquished it (Danziger 1990). Among scholars of social movements, it reeks of the "armchair theorizing" about crowds that prevented progress in understanding social movements for so long.

But armchair theorizing is not the same as introspection, unless those in the armchairs have participated in whatever process they are theorizing about. Today, many of those who write about social movements have participated extensively in them. They use introspection to derive theories on the basis of what they believe is plausible, although they usually seek independent evidence to test them. But since many scholars test their theories on the same movement from which they derived them, they do not always move very far from introspection. By being more explicit about our own introspection, we may be able to improve it by specifying which of our experiences we are drawing upon.

In his discussions of practices and habitus, Bourdieu regularly suggested that scholars who observe activities without participating in them tend to draw logical models of them that miss much of their driving force. Speaking of science, for instance, he warned, "One has to avoid reducing practices to the idea one has of them when one's only experience of them is logical" (2004:39). Meanings must be interpreted, and outsiders require empathy at the very least. Even then, they get things wrong a lot. Participation is useful because it allows introspection.

Introspection seems particularly appropriate for two areas of study, emotions and strategic choice. Emotions other than a handful of reflex emotions (see section on Emotions) are often difficult to discern from the outside. Combinations and sequences of emotions are even harder for an observer to interpret correctly, but cautious inspection of our own feelings may allow us to tease them out with a fair degree of complexity. We can actively examine and interrogate ourselves to try to understand our feelings, motives, and so on. Margaret Archer (2003) embraces this technique, rejecting the metaphor of a passive observer implied by "introspection."

Strategic choices often subtly balance a number of competing ends and means, in part because they involve innumerable tradeoffs. It is impossible to "see" decision making from the outside; at best one can observe collectives discussing and voting, but not the subtle calculations that occur inside each player's head. The creativity, motivations, and choices may not be entirely transparent even to those who make them, but participants have an enormous advantage over external observers. When player and analyst are the same person, scrutiny of one's mental processes can be disciplined, impulses and emotions can be labeled carefully, and rationales traced. No method is perfect, but introspection sometimes offers access to mental processes no other method does. We need to be explicit and systematic about it.

One drawback of introspection is that it is limited to our own experiences. We might have difficulty comprehending what it is like to be a suicide bomber, for instance. Another drawback is that we are not always honest with ourselves—but this is even more of a problem when we interview others.

Unpleasant Cases

Methodological challenges for getting at meanings and feelings are especially strong for those who study movements that are either extremely risky or repellent to the researcher. Revolutionaries are a case of the former, operating at war with authorities and thus putting a researcher at risk. No wonder revolutions have most often been studied through official records, or "the prose of counter-insurgency" (Guha 1983). Other "weapons of the weak" are also kept secret to protect the perpetrators from retaliation, and authorities often have an interest in suppressing publicity for fear that resistance will spread (Scott 1985, 1990). In many cases, researchers turn to the memoirs of revolutionary leaders who may not have similar motivations or experiences as their followers, often because they are from a different social class (Kriger 1992). Plus memoirs always have their own strategic purposes.

Other movements are simply offensive to the researcher. Only recently have sociologists begun to interview the far right, hate groups, and racist movements, after relying for many decades on content analysis of written materials (just as, until the 1960s, most leftist movements were treated from a distance). Here there is an additional challenge for the researcher: managing her own emotional displays so as not to disrupt the interview. She cannot show her own anger or disgust at what she hears without ending or distorting the interview (Blee 1998). Just as we must interpret an informant's performance of feelings or presentation of meanings, trying to see what is calculated strategic intention and what is less guarded, so we must put on a performance of our own. The more potentially hostile our audience, the more difficult this is.

Fortunately, the study of social movements has proven open to a variety of techniques rather than being wedded to any kind of methodological purity (Klandermans and Staggenborg 2002). Because feelings and meanings have both public and private sides, it is usually best to approach them with multiple methods.

UNANSWERED QUESTIONS AND FUTURE DIRECTIONS

Despite the enormous amount of excellent research into social movements during the past several decades, including its cultural dimensions, there are numerous questions that remain unanswered. I mention only a few.

The *first stirrings* of a social movement remain poorly understood. Given the sensibilities, ideas, values, and allegiances mixed together in different population segments, how does necessarily limited attention come to be focused on one set of issues rather than others? This is an eminently cultural process. A newsworthy event or death of a loved one may shock people into attention. These are often termed precipitating events. The zeitgeist may shift slightly, in enormously complex ways, bringing attention and sympathy to new arenas. News coverage also influences our emotional and moral attention. Typically, a small network of would-be leaders manages to set aside their normal lives to craft appeals to these understandings in order to recruit like-minded others (or they may be movement professionals whose work is to stimulate protest). Little is known about these initial processes.

We also know relatively little about the cultural dimensions of *how new tactics spread*, presumably as one individual moves from movement to movement or one individual learns from another (Soule 2004). Most work on diffusion has examined network ties and spatial patterns (Hedström 1994; Morris 1981) or the effects of media (Myers 2000). Tactics spread not only because they are effective (at least until opponents themselves innovate in response), but because they fit protestors' tastes in tactics (Jasper 1997), or fit with the way a problem is framed (Roggeband 2004).We know even less about the first creative spark that ignites a new tactic or understanding. I suspect these creative moments arise from the idiosyncracies of individuals finding new ways to deal with strategic dilemmas, typically under some sense of urgency in the heat of an engagement. Learning and choice are both cultural processes, and these are at the heart of tactical diffusion.

We still know too little about *cultural change*. How do the creators of meanings tinker with their frames and tropes? What is the interaction between creators and audiences? This seems an area where culture and strategy interact, as activists and their opponents try different ways to have their desired impacts. As I suggested, we still have a lot to learn about these processes from rhetorical traditions.

We know little about *strategic dilemmas and choices* made in facing them (Ganz 2000, 2003; Jasper 2004a, 2006b). These decisions are a cultural product, not a simple algorithm. Identities such as gender encourage people to answer strategic dilemmas in one way rather than another. Thus in her study of the civil rights movement Robnett (1991) showed women's tendency to reach in rather than reach out when faced with the ubiquitous Janus Dilemma. Groups trying to battle stigmatized identities nonetheless use those identities to mobilize supporters, in a dilemma fraught with risks. Culture and strategy are thoroughly entwined because strategic players are always audiences interpreting each other's words and actions.

Students of social movements, especially in sociology, have a lot to learn from *other disciplines*. For instance the rediscovery of emotions and morality in behavioral economics, reflecting the lagged influence of cognitive psychology, offers an opportunity for sociological students of collective action. Behavioral economists have criticized the rationalist and materialist traditions of their own discipline, showing that people value various forms of fairness. Psychology and social psychology, in addition, have their own insights into political action that are derived from the cognitive revolution (see Chapter 5 in this volume). Indeed, the interdisciplinary nature of this handbook promises this kind of cross-fertilization.

We also need further research in the *substance* of meanings. We need to think about basic sources of meaning such as time, place, and character. Are there tropes that reappear in diverse cultures? Are there certain parts of the social structure, for instance young people, new arrivals, rapidly growing cities, or the poor, that generate anxieties for a population (Jasper 1997:358–363)? Comparative research should help us lay out the variations in all these that suppress or encourage collective action. What tropes have emotional impacts that encourage confidence and action, which ones discourage them?

With the structural turn in movement theory, *leaders* fell from favor as a research topic, despite having once been prominent as the evil, demagogic force behind crowds. Yet there is a great opening today to rethink their role using the new tools of the cultural turn. Leaders are important in the decisions they make, but also in what they symbolize. They represent a group, not only to outsiders but to members as well (even after they are dead: Fine 2001). Part of this symbolic role consists in emotions they arouse both in and out of the group. They also convey important information in very practical ways. (For one effort to revive the concept, although not from an especially cultural perspective, see Barker, Johnson, and Lavalette 2001).

Numerous paths of research will return to noncultural mechanisms in order to interrogate and reinterpret them from a cultural perspective. I have barely touched on this kind of project. But if the social world is saturated with meaning, we need to see how culture operates in a number of areas that have hitherto been viewed as noncultural. Meanings and feelings must be seen as parts of strategic engagements in structured arenas, not floating mysteriously on their own. People have both passions and purposes. And when we figure out how these interact, we will be much closer to understanding social movements.

SUGGESTED READINGS

Bob, Clifford. 2005. *The Marketing of Rebellion*. Cambridge: Cambridge University Press.
Fine, Gary Alan. 2001. *Difficult Reputations*. Chicago: University of Chicago Press.
Gamson, William A. 1992. *Talking Politics*. Cambridge: Cambridge University Press.
Gitlin, Todd. 1980. *The Whole World Is Watching*. Berkeley: University of California Press.
Goodwin, Jeff, James M. Jasper, and Francesca Polletta, eds. 2001. *Passionate Politics*. Chicago: University of Chicago Press.
Jasper, James M. 1997. *The Art of Moral Protest*. Chicago: University of Chicago Press.
Laclau, Ernesto and Chantal Mouffe. 1985. *Hegemony and Socialist Strategy*. London: Verso.
Lalich, Janja. 2004. *Bounded Choice*. Berkeley: University of California Press.
McDonald, Kevin. 2006. *Global Movements*. Oxford: Blackwell.
Melucci, Alberto. 1996. *Challenging Codes*. Cambridge: Cambridge University Press.
Polletta, Francesca. 2006. *It Was Like a Fever*. Chicago: University of Chicago Press.
Touraine, Alain. 1978. *La voix et le regard*. Paris: Editions du Seuil. Translation: *The Voice and the Eye* (1981, Cambridge University Press).

REFERENCES

Adams, J. 2000. "Movement Socialization in Art Workshops: A Case from Pinochet's Chile." *Sociological Quarterly* 41:615–638.
Adorno, T. W. et al. 1950. *The Authoritarian Personality*. New York: Harper.
Aho, J. A. 1990. *The Politics of Righteousness: Idaho Christian Patriotism*. Seattle: University of Washington Press.
Alexander, J. C. 2006. "Cultural pragmatics: social performance between ritual and strategy". Pp. 29–90 in *Social Performance: Symbolic Action, Cultural Pragmatics, and Ritual*, edited by J. C. Alexander, B. Giesen, and J. L. Mast. Cambridge, UK: Cambridge University Press.
Alexander, J. C., Giesen, B. and Mast, J. L., eds. 2006. *Social Performance: Symbolic Action, Cultural Pragmatics, and Ritual*. Cambridge, UK: Cambridge University Press.
Alford, C. F. 1989. *Melanie Klein and Critical Social Theory*. New Haven, CT: Yale University Press.
——. 2006. "Hate and Love and the Other." Pp. 84–102 in *Emotions, Politics, and Society*, edited by S. Clarke, P. Hoggett, and S. Thompson. London: Palgrave-Macmillan.

Almond, G. A. and S. Verba. 1963. *The Civic Culture*. Princeton, NJ: Princeton University Press.

Althusser, L. 1969. *For Marx*. London: Allen Lane.

———. 1971. *Lenin and Philosophy*. New York: Monthly Review Press.

Althusser, L. and E. Balibar 1970. *Reading Capital*. London: New Left Books.

Archer, M. S. 2003. *Structure, Agency and the Internal Conversation*. Cambridge, UK: Cambridge University Press.

Auyero, J. 2003. *Contentious Lives*. Durham: Duke University Press.

Barber, B. R. 1984. *Strong Democracy*. Berkeley: University of California Press.

Barker, C., A. Johnson, and M. Lavalette, eds. 2001. *Leadership and Social Movements*. Manchester: Manchester University Press.

Bellah, R., R. Madsen, W. M. Sullivan, A. Swidler, and S. M. Tipton. 1985. *Habits of the Heart*. Berkeley: University of California Press.

Benford, R. D. 1997. "An Insider's Critique of the Social Movement Framing Perspective." *Sociological Inquiry* 67:409–430.

Bernstein, M. 1997. "Celebration and Suppression: The Strategic Uses of Identity by the Lesbian and Gay Movement." *American Journal of Sociology* 103:531–565.

Bevington, D. and C. Dixon. 2005. "Movement-Relevant Theory: Rethinking Social Movement Scholarship and Activism." *Social Movement Studies* 4:185–208.

Billig, M. 1987. *Arguing and Thinking*. Cambridge, UK: Cambridge University Press.

Blee, K. M. 1991. *Women of the Klan: Racism and Gender in the 1920s*. Berkeley: University of California Press.

———. 1998. "Managing Emotion in the Study of Right-Wing Extremism." *Qualitative Sociology* 21:381–399.

———. 2002. *Inside Organized Racism: Women in the Hate Movement*. Berkeley: University of California Press.

Blee, K. M. and V. Taylor. 2002. "Semi-structured Interviewing and Social Movement Research." Pp. 92–117 in *Methods of Social Movement Research*, edited by B. Klandermans and S. Staggenborg. Minneapolis, MN: University of Minnesota Press.

Blumenberg, H. 1983. *The Legitimacy of the Modern Age*. Cambridge, MA: MIT Press.

Bob, C. 2005. *The Marketing of Rebellion: Insurgents, Media, and International Activism*. Cambridge, UK: Cambridge University Press.

Boltanski, L. and L. Thévenot. 1991. *De la Justification*. Paris: Gallimard.

Bourdieu, P. 1984. *Distinction*. Cambridge, MA: Harvard University Press.

———. 2004. *Science of Science and Reflexivity*. Chicago: University of Chicago Press.

Bramwell, A. 1989. *Ecology in the 20th Century: A History*. New Haven, CT: Yale University Press.

Bruner, J. 1962. *On Knowing: Essays for the Left Hand*. Cambridge, MA: Harvard University Press.

Butler, J. 1990. *Gender Trouble: Feminism and the Subversion of Identity*. New York: Routledge.

Calhoun, C. 1982. *The Question of Class Struggle*. Chicago: University of Chicago Press.

———. 1993. "'New Social Movements' of the Early Nineteenth Century." *Social Science History* 17:385–427.

Camerer, C. F. 2003. *Behavioral Game Theory: Experiments in Strategic Interaction*. New York: Russell Sage Foundation.

Camerer, C. F., G. Loewenstein, and M. Rabin, eds. 2004. *Advances in Behavioral Economics*. Princeton, NJ: Princeton University Press.

Campbell, S. 1994. "Being Dismissed: The Politics of Emotional Expression." *Hypatia* 9:46–65.

Centre for Contemporary Cultural Studies (CCCS). 1978. *On Ideology*. London: Hutchinson.

———. 1980. *Culture, Media, Language*. London: Hutchinson.

Chong, D. 1991. *Collective Action and the Civil Rights Movement*. Chicago: University of Chicago Press.

———. 2000. *Rational Lives: Norms and Values in Politics and Society*. Chicago: University of Chicago Press.

Clemens, E. S. 1996. "Organizational Form as Frame: Collective Identity and Political Strategy in the American Labor Movement, 1880–1920." Pp. 205–226 in *Comparative Perspectives on Social Movements*, edited by D. McAdam, J. D. McCarthy, and M. N. Zald. Cambridge, UK: Cambridge University Press.

Clore, G. L., N. Schwarz, and M. Conway. 1994. "Affective Causes and Consequences of Social Information Processing." Pp. 323–417 in *The Handbook of Social Cognition*, 2nd edition, edited by R. S. Wyer and T. Srull. Mahwah, NJ: Lawrence Erlbaum.

Cohen, J. L. 1985. "Strategy or Identity: New Theoretical Paradigms and Contemporary Social Movements." *Social Research* 52:663–716.

Cohen, S. 1972. *Folk Devils and Moral Panics*. New York: St. Martin's Press.

Collins, R. 2001. "Social Movements and the Focus of Emotional Attention." Pp. 27–44 in *Passionate Politics*, edited by J. Goodwin, J. M. Jasper, and F. Polletta. Chicago: University of Chicago Press.

———. 2004. *Interaction Ritual Chains*. Princeton, NJ: Princeton University Press.

Cotgrove, S. 1982. *Catastrophe or Cornucopia*. New York: John Wiley & Sons.

Crane, D., ed. 1994. *The Sociology of Culture*. Oxford: Blackwell.

Crenson, M. A. and B. Ginsberg. 2002. *Downsizing Democracy: How America Sideline Its Citizens and Privatized Its Public*. Baltimore: Johns Hopkins University Press.

Dalton, R. J. 1994. *The Green Rainbow*. New Haven, CT: Yale University Press.

Dalton, R. J., S. C. Flanagan, and P. A. Beck, eds. 1984. *Electoral Change in Advanced Industrial Democracies*. Princeton, NJ: Princeton University Press.

Danziger, K. 1990. *Constructing the Subject: Historical Origins of Psychological Research*. Cambridge, UK: Cambridge University Press.

Davis, J. E., ed. 2002. *Stories of Change: Narrative and Social Movements*. Albany: State University of New York Press.

De Beauvoir, S. 1949. *Le Deuxiéme Sexe*. Paris: Gallimard.

Derrida, J. 1967. *Ecriture et la Différence*. Paris: Seuil.

———. 1978. "Structure, Sign and Play in the Human Sciences." Pp. 278–294 in *Writing and Difference*. Chicago: University of Chicago Press.

Diani, M. 2004. "Networks and Participation." Pp. 339–359 in *The Blackwell Companion to Social Movements*, edited by D. A. Snow, S. A. Soule, and H. Kriesi. Oxford: Blackwell.

Dobbin, F. 1994. *Forging Industrial Policy*. Cambridge, UK: Cambridge University Press.

Dosse, F. 1997. *History of Structuralism*. Minneapolis, MN: University of Minnesota Press.

Ekman, P. 1972. *Emotions in the Human Face*. New York: Pergamon.

Eliot, T. S. 1948. *Notes Towards the Definition of Culture*. London: Faber and Faber.

Elshtain, J. B. 1981. *Public Man, Private Woman: Women in Social and Political Thought*. Princeton, NJ: Princeton University Press.

Elster, J. 1992. *Strong Feelings*. Cambridge, MA: MIT Press.

Emirbayer, M. and J. Goodwin. 1994. "Network Analysis, Culture, and the Problem of Agency." *American Journal of Sociology* 99:1411–1454.

Epstein, B. 1981. *The Politics of Domesticity: Women, Evangelism, and Temperance in Nineteenth Century America*. Middletown, CT: Wesleyan University Press.

Eyerman, R. 2006. "Performing Opposition or, How Social Movements Move." Pp. 193–217 in *Social Performance: Symbolic Action, Cultural Pragmatics, and Ritual*, edited by J. C. Alexander, B. Giesen, and J. L. Mast. Cambridge, UK: Cambridge University Press.

Eyerman, R. and A. Jamison. 1998. *Music and Social Movements*. Cambridge, UK: Cambridge University Press.

Fairclough, N. 1995. *Critical Discourse Analysis*. Harlow: Longman.

Ferejohn, J. 1991. "Rationality and Interpretation: Parliamentary Elections in Early Stuart England." Pp. 279–305 in *The Economic Approach to Politics*, edited by K. R. Monroe. New York: HarperCollins.

Fernandez, R. and D. McAdam. 1988. "Social Networks and Social Movements: Multiorganizational Fields and Recruitment to Mississippi Freedom Summer." *Sociological Forum* 3:357–382.

Fine, G. A. 1995. "Public Narration and Group Culture." Pp. 127–143 in *Social Movements and Culture*, edited by H. Johnston and B. Klandermans. Minneapolis, MN: University of Minnesota Press.

———. 2001. *Difficult Reputations*. Chicago: University of Chicago Press.

Foucault, M. 1961. *Folie et Déraison*. Paris: Librairie Plon.

———. 1963. *La Naissance de la Clinique*. Paris: PUF.

———. 1966. *Les Mots et les Choses*. Paris: Editions Gallimard.

———. 1975. *Surveiller et Punir*. Paris: Gallimard.

———. 1976. *Histoire de la Sexualité. 1: la Volonté de Savoir*. Paris: Gallimard.

———. 1998. *Aesthetics, Method, and Epistemology*. Edited by J.D. Faubion. New York: The New Press.

Frank, R. H. 1988. *Passions within Reason*. New York: W. W. Norton.

Freeman, J. 1973. "The Origins of the Women's Liberation Movement." *American Journal of Sociology* 78:792–811.

Friedan, B. 1963. *The Feminine Mystique*. New York: W. W. Norton.

Futrell, R., P. Simi, and S. Gottschalk. 2006. "Understanding Music in Movements: The White Power Music Scene." *Sociological Quarterly* 47:275–304.

Gamson, J. 1995. "Must Identity Movements Self-Destruct? A Queer Dilemma." *Social Problems* 42:390–407.

———. 1997. "Messages of Exclusion: Gender, Movements, and Symbolic Boundaries." *Gender and Society* 11:178–199.

Gamson, W. A. 1992. *Talking Politics*. Cambridge, UK: Cambridge University Press.

———. 2004. "Bystanders, Public Opinion, and the Media." Pp. 242–261 in *The Blackwell Companion to Social Movements*, edited by D. A. Snow, S. A. Soule, and H. Kriesi. Oxford: Blackwell.

Ganz, M. 2000. "Resources and Resourcefulness: Strategic Capacity in the Unionization of California Agriculture (1959–1977)." *American Journal of Sociology* 105:1003–1062.

——. 2003. "Why David Sometimes Wins: Strategic Capacity in Social Movements." Pp. 177–198 in *Rethinking Social Movements*, edited by J. Goodwin and J. M. Jasper. Lanham, MD: Rowman and Littlefield.

Garner, R. 1993. *Animals, Politics and Morality*. Manchester: Manchester University Press.

Gilman, N. 2003. *Mandarins of the Future: Modernization Theory in Cold War America*. Baltimore: Johns Hopkins University Press.

Ginzberg, L. D. 1990. *Women and the Work of Benevolence: Morality, Politics, and Class in the 19th-Century United States*. New Haven, CT: Yale University Press.

Gitlin, T. 1980. *The Whole World Is Watching*. Berkeley: University of California Press.

——. 1987. *Sixties: Years of Hope, Days of Rage*. New York: Bantam Books.

Goldfarb, J. C. 1980. *The Persistence of Freedom: The Sociological Implications of Polish Student Theater*. Boulder: Westview.

Goodwin, J. 1997. "The Libidinal Constitution of a High-Risk Social Movement: Affectual Ties and Solidarity in the Huk Rebellion." *American Sociological Review* 62:53–69.

Goodwin, J. and Jasper, J. M., eds. 2003. *Rethinking Social Movements: Structure, Meaning, and Emotion*. Lanham, MD: Rowman and Littlefield.

——. 2004. "Caught in a Winding, Snarling Vine: The Structural Bias of Political Process Theory." Pp. 3–30 in *Rethinking Social Movements: Structure, Meaning, and Emotion*, edited by J. Goodwin and J. M. Jasper. Lanham, MD: Rowman and Littlefield.

——. 2006. "Emotions and Social Movements." Pp. 611–635 in *Handbook of the Sociology of Emotions*, edited by J. Stets and J. Turner. New York: Springer.

Goodwin, J., J. M. Jasper, and F. Polletta. 2000. "The Return of the Repressed: The Fall and Rise of Emotions in Social Movement Theory." *Mobilization* 5:65–84.

——. 2004. "Emotional Dimensions of Social Movements." Pp. 413–432 in *The Blackwell Companion to Social Movements*, edited by D. A. Snow, S. A. Soule, and H. Kriesi. Malden, MA: Blackwell.

Gordon, C. and J. M. Jasper. 1996. "Overcoming the 'NIMBY' Label: Rhetorical and Organizational Links for Local Protestors." *Research in Social Movements, Conflicts and Change* 19:153–175.

Gould, D. B. 2001. "Rock the Boat, Don't Rock the Boat, Baby: Ambivalence and the Emergence of Militant AIDS Activism." Pp. 135–157 in *Passionate Politics*, edited by J. Goodwin, J. M. Jasper, and F. Polletta. Chicago: University of Chicago Press.

——. 2003. "Passionate Political Processes: Bringing Emotions Back into the Study of Social Movements." Pp. 155–175 in *Rethinking Social Movements*, edited by J. Goodwin and J. M. Jasper. Lanham, MD: Rowman and Littlefield.

Griffiths, P. 1997. *What Emotions Really Are: The Problem of Psychological Categories*. Chicago: University of Chicago Press.

Groves, J. M. 1997. *Hearts and Minds*. Philadelphia: Temple University Press.

——. 2001. "Animal Rights and the Politics of Emotion: Folk Constructions of Emotion in the Animal Rghts Movement." Pp. 212–229 in *Passionate Politics*, edited by J. Goodwin, J. M. Jasper, and F. Polletta. Chicago: University of Chicago Press.

Guha, R. 1983. "The Prose of Counter-insurgency." In *Subaltern Studies II*. Oxford: Oxford University Press.

Gusfield, J. R. 1963. *Symbolic Crusade: Status Politics and the American Temperance Movement*. Urbana, IL: University of Illinois Press.

Hacking, I. 1999. *The Social Construction of What?* Cambridge, MA: Harvard University Press.

Hall, J. 1995. "Public Narratives and the Apocalyptic Sect: From Jonestown to Mount Carmel." Pp. 205–235 in *Armageddon in Mount Carmel*, edited by S. A. Wright. Chicago: University of Chicago Press.

Hall, S. 1980. "Encoding/Decoding." Pp. 128–138 in *Culture, Media, Language*, edited by S. Hall, D. Hobson, A. Lowe, and P. Willis. London: Hutchinson.

Hall, S. and T. Jefferson. 1976. *Resistance through Rituals*. London: Routledge.

Hartz, L. 1955. *The Liberal Tradition in America*. New York: Harcourt, Brace.

Haskell, T. L. 1985. "Capitalism and the Origins of the Humanitarian Sensibility, Parts I and II." *American Historical Review* 90:339–361, 547–566.

Hatfield, E., J. T. Cacciopo, and R. L. Rapson. 1994. *Emotional Contagion*. Cambridge, UK: Cambridge University Press.

Hebdige, D. 1979. *Subculture: The Meaning of Style*. London: Methuen.

Hedström, P. 1994. "Contagious Collectivities: On the Spatial Diffusion of Swedish Trade Unions, 1890–1940." *American Journal of Sociology* 99:1157–1179.

Heirich, J., R. Boyd, S. Bowles, C. Camerer, E. Fehr, and H. Gintis, eds. 2004. *Foundations of Human Sociality*. Oxford: Oxford University Press.

Heirich, J., R. Boyd, S. Bowles, C. Camerer, E. Fehr, H. Gintis, and R. McElreath. 2001. "Cooperation, Reciprocity and Punishment in Fifteen Small-Scale Societies." *American Economic Review* 91:73–78.

Heise, D. R. 1979. *Understanding Events.* Cambridge, UK: Cambridge University Press.

Hercus, C. 1999. "Identity, Emotion, and Feminist Collective Action." *Gender and Society* 13:34–55.

Hess, D. and B. Martin. 2006. "Repression, Backfire, and the Theory of Transformative Events. *"Mobilization* 11:249–267.

Hochschild, A. R. 1975. "The Sociology of Feeling and Emotion: Selected Possibilities." In *Another Voice: Feminist Perspectives on Social Life and the Social Sciences,* edited by M. Millman and R. M. Kanter. Garden City, NY: Anchor Books.

——. 1983. *The Managed Heart.* Berkeley: University of California Press.

Hoffer, E. 1951. *The True Believer.* New York: Harper and Row.

Hunt, L., ed. 1989. *The New Cultural History.* Berkeley: University of California Press.

Inglehart, R. 1977. *The Silent Revolution: Changing Values and Political Styles among Western Publics.* Princeton, NJ: Princeton University Press.

——. 1990. *Culture Shift in Advanced Industrial Society.* Princeton, NJ: Princeton University Press.

——. 1997. *Modernization and Post-Modernization.* Princeton, NJ: Princeton University Press.

Inkeles, A. and D. H. Smith. 1974. *Becoming Modern: Individual Change in Six Developing Countries.* Cambridge, MA: Harvard University Press.

Jasper, J. M. 1997. *The Art of Moral Protest: Culture, Biography, and Creativity in Social Movements.* Chicago: University of Chicago Press.

——. 2004a. "A Strategic Approach to Collective Action: Looking for Agency in Social Movement Choices." *Mobilization* 9:1–16.

——. 2004b. "Intellectual Cycles of Social Movement Research: From Psychoanalysis to Culture?" Pp. 234–253 in *Self, Social Structure, and Beliefs: Explorations in Sociology,* edited by J. C. Alexander, G. T. Marx, and C. L. Williams. Berkeley: University of California Press.

——. 2005. "Culture, Knowledge, and Politics." Pp. 115–134 in *The Handbook of Political Sociology,* edited by T. Janoski, R. Alford, A. Hicks, and M. A. Schwartz. Cambridge, UK: Cambridge University Press.

——. 2006a. "Emotions and the Microfoundations of Politics: Rethinking Ends and Means." Pp. 14–30 in *Emotion, Politics and Society,* edited by S. Clarke, P. Hoggett, and S. Thompson. London: Palgrave-Macmillan.

——. 2006b. *Getting Your Way: Strategic Dilemmas in Real Life.* Chicago: University of Chicago Press.

——. 2006c. "Motivation and Emotion." Pp. 157–171 in *Oxford Handbook of Contextual Political Studies,* edited by R. Goodin and C. Tilly. Oxford: Oxford University Press.

Jasper, J. M. and D. Nelkin. 1992. *The Animal Rights Crusade.* New York: Free Press.

Jasper, J. M. and J. Poulsen. 1993. "Fighting Back: Vulnerabilities, Blunders, and Countermobilization by the Targets in Three Animal Rights Campaigns." *Sociological Forum* 8:639–657.

——. 1995. "Recruiting Strangers and Friends: Moral Shocks and Social Networks in Animal Rights and Antinuclear Protest." *Social Problems* 42:401–420.

Jenkins, J. C. and C. Perrow. 1977. "Insurgency of the Powerless: Farm Worker Movements (1946–1972)." *American Sociological Review* 42:249–268.

Johnston, H. 2002. "Verification and Proof in Frame and Discourse Analysis." Pp. 62–91 in *Methods of Social Movement Analysis,* edited by B. Klandermans and S. Staggenborg. Minneapolis, MN: University of Minnesota Press.

Johnston, H. and B. Klandermans, eds. 1995. *Social Movements and Culture.* Minneapolis, MN: University of Minnesota Press.

Katzenstein, M. F. 1998. *Faithless and Fearless.* Princeton, NJ: Princeton University Press.

Kaufman, J. 2002. *For the Common Good: American Civic Life and the Golden Age of Fraternity.* Oxford: Oxford University Press.

Kemper, T. 1978. *A Social Interactional Theory of Emotions.* New York: John Wiley & Sons.

——. 2001. "A Structural Approach to Social Movement Emotions." Pp. 58–73 in *Passionate Politics: Emotions and Social Movements,* edited by J. Goodwin, J. M. Jasper, and F. Polletta. Chicago: University of Chicago Press.

Keniston, K. 1968. *Young Radicals.* New York: Harcourt, Brace, Jovanovich.

Kertzer, D. I. 1988. *Ritual, Politics, and Power.* New Haven: Yale University Press.

Kimeldorf, H., R. Meyer, M. Prasad, and I. Robinson. 2006. "Consumers with a Conscience: Will They Pay More?" *Contexts* 5:24–29.

King, D. 2004. "Operationalizing Melucci: Metamorphosis and Passion in the Negotiation of Activists' Multiple Identities." *Mobilization* 9:73–92.

Kitzinger, J. and R. S. Barbour. 1999. "Introduction: The Challenge and Promise of Focus Groups." Pp. 1–20 in *Developing Focus Group Research,* edited by R. S. Barbour and J. Kitzinger. London: Sage.

Klandermans, B. and D. Oegema. 1987. "Potentials, Networks, Motivations and Barriers: Steps Toward Participation in Social Movements." *American Sociological Review* 52:519–531.

Klandermans, B. and J. Smith. 2002. "Survey Research." Pp. 3–31 in *Methods of Social Movement Research*, edited by B. Klandermans and S. Staggenborg. Minneapolis, MN: University of Minnesota Press.

Klandermans, B. and S. Staggenborg, eds. 2002. *Methods of Social Movement Research*. Minneapolis, MN: University of Minnesota Press.

Kleinman, S. 1996. *Opposing Ambitions: Gender and Identity in an Alternative Organization*. Chicago: University of Chicago Press.

Kornhauser, W. 1959. *The Politics of Mass Society*. Glencoe, IL: Free Press.

Kriger, N. 1992. *Zimbabwe's Guerilla War: Peasant Voices*. Cambridge, UK: Cambridge University Press.

Kuper, A. 1999. *Culture: The Anthropologists' Account*. Cambridge, MA: Harvard University Press.

Kurzman, C. 1996. "Structural and Perceived Opportunity: The Iranian Revolution of 1979." *American Sociological Review* 61:153–170.

——. 2003. "The Poststructuralist Consensus in Social Movement Theory." Pp. 111–120 in *Rethinking Social Movements*, edited by J. Goodwin and J. M. Jasper. Lanham, MD: Rowman and Littlefield.

Laclau, E. and C. Mouffe. 1985. *Hegemony and Socialist Strategy*. London: Verso.

Lafaye, C. and L. Thévenot. 1993. "Une Justification Ecologique? Conflits dans l'Amenagement de la Nature." *Revue Française de Sociologie* 4:495–524.

Lafont, C. 1993. *La Razón Como Lenguaje*. Madrid: Visor.

Lalich, J. 2004. *Bounded Choice: True Believers and Charismatic Cults*. Berkeley: University of California Press.

Lamont, M. 1992. *Money, Morals, and Manners*. Chicago: University of Chicago Press.

Lamont, M. and L. Thévenot, eds. 2000. *Rethinking Comparative Cultural Sociology*. Cambridge, UK: Cambridge University Press.

Laraña, E., H. Johnston, and J. R. Gusfield, eds. 1994. *New Social Movements: From Ideology to Identity*. Philadelphia: Temple University Press.

Lazarus, R. S. 1999. "Hope: An Emotion and a Vital Coping Resource against Despair." *Social Research* 66:653–678.

Leacock, E. B. 1981. *Myths of Male Dominance: Collected Articles on Women Cross-Culturally*. New York: Monthly Review Press.

Le Bon, G. 1960/1895. *The Crowd*. New York: Viking.

Lee, R. E. 2003. *Life and Times of Cultural Studies*. Durham, NC: Duke University Press.

Lively, K. J. and D. R. Heise. 2004. "Sociological Realms of Emotional Experience. *American Journal of Sociology* 109:1109–1136.

Lofland, J. 1982. "Crowd Joys." *Urban Life* 10:355–381.

——. 1995. "Charting Degrees of Movement Culture." Pp. 188–216 in *Social Movements and Culture*, edited by H. Johnston and B. Klandermans. Minneapolis, MN: University of Minnesota Press.

Maddison, S. and S. Scalmer. 2006. *Activist Wisdom*. Sydney: University of New South Wales Press.

Madsen, D. and P. G. Snow. 1991. *The Charismatic Bond*. Cambridge, MA: Harvard University Press.

Martin, E. 1987. *The Woman in the Body*. Boston: Beacon.

McAdam, D. 1988. *Freedom Summer*. Oxford: Oxford University Press.

——. 2003. "Revisiting the U.S. Civil Rights Movement: Toward a More Synthetic Understanding of the Origins of Contention." Pp. 201–232 in *Rethinking Social Movements*, edited by J. Goodwin and J. M. Jasper. Lanham, MD: Rowman and Littlefield.

McAdam, D., J. D. McCarthy, and M. N. Zald, eds. 1996. *Comparative Perspectives on Social Movements*. Cambridge, UK: Cambridge University Press.

McAdam, D., S. Tarrow, and C. Tilly. 2001. *Dynamics of Contention*. Cambridge, UK: Cambridge University Press.

McCarthy, J. D. and M. N. Zald. 1973. *The Trend of Social Movements in America*. Morristown, NJ: General Learning Press.

——. 1977. "Resource Mobilization and Social Movements: A Partial Theory." *American Journal of Sociology* 82:1212–1241.

McNeill, W. H. 1995. *Keeping Together in Time: Dance and Drill in Human History*. Cambridge, MA: Harvard University Press.

McPhail, C. 1991. *The Myth of the Madding Crowd*. New York: Aldine de Gruyter.

Melucci, A. 1985. "The Symbolic Challenge of Contemporary Movements." *Social Research* 52:789–816.

——. 1988. "Getting Involved: Identity and Mobilization in Social Movements." *International Social Movement Research* 1:329–348.

——. 1994. "A Strange Kind of Newness." Pp. 101–130 in *New Social Movements: From Ideology to Identity*, edited by E. Laraña, H. Johnston, and J. R. Gusfield. Philadelphia: Temple University Press.

———. 1996a. *Challenging Codes*. Cambridge, UK: Cambridge University Press.

———. 1996b. *The Playing Self: Person and Meaning in the Planetary Society*. Cambridge, UK: Cambridge University Press.

Meyer, J. and B. Rowan. 1977. "Institutionalized Organizations: Formal Structure as Myth and Ceremony." *American Journal of Sociology* 83:53–77.

Milbrath, L. W. 1984. *Environmentalists, Vanguard for a New Society*. Albany: State University of New York Press.

Milgram, S. 1974. *Obedience to Authority: An Experimental View*. New York: Harper and Row.

Mische, A. 2003. "Cross-talk in Movements: Reconceiving the Culture-Network Link." Pp. 258–280 in *Social Movements and Networks*, edited by M. Diani and D. McAdam. Oxford: Oxford University Press.

Morgan, R. L. and D. Heise. 1988. "Structure of Emotions." *Social Psychology Quarterly* 51:19–31.

Morris, A. D. 1981. "Black Southern Sit-in Movement: An Analysis of Internal Organization." *American Sociological Review* 46:744–767.

———. 1984. *The Origins of the Civil Rights Movement: Black Communities Organizing for Change*. New York: Free Press.

Morris, A. D. and C. M. Mueller, eds. 1992. *Frontiers of Social Movement Theory*. New Haven: Yale University Press.

Mukerji, C. 1997. *Territorial Ambitions and the Gardens of Versailles*. Cambridge, UK: Cambridge University Press.

Mullaney, J. L. 2006. *Everyone Is NOT Doing It: Abstinence and Personal Identity*. Chicago: University of Chicago Press.

Myers, D. J. 2000. "The Diffusion of Collective Violence: Infectiousness, Susceptibility, and Mass Conditions." *American Journal of Sociology* 106:173–208.

Naples, N., ed. 1998. *Community Activism and Feminist Politics*. New York: Routledge.

Nepstad, S. E. 2004. *Convictions of the Soul: Religion, Culture, and Agency in the Central America Solidarity Movement*. Oxford: Oxford University Press.

Nerb, J. and H. Spada. 2001. "Evaluation of Environmental Problems: A Coherence Model of Cognition and Emotion." *Cognition and Emotion* 15:521–551.

Nicholson, L. J., ed. 1990. *Feminism/Postmodernism*. New York: Routledge.

Nussbaum, M. 2001. *Upheavals of Thought: The Intelligence of Emotions*. Cambridge, UK: Cambridge University Press.

Oberschall, A. 1973. *Social Conflict and Social Movements*. Englewood Cliffs, NJ: Prentice-Hall.

Oliver, P. 1989. "Bringing the Crowd Back In: The Nonorganizational Elements of Social Movements." *Research in Social Movements, Conflict and Change* 11:1–30.

Olson, M. 1965. *The Logic of Collective Action: Public Goods and the Theory of Groups*. Cambridge, MA: Harvard University Press.

Passy, F. 2003. "Social Networks Matter. But How?" Pp. 21–48 in *Social Movements and Networks*, edited by M. Diani and D. McAdam. Oxford: Oxford University Press.

Perrin, A. J. 2006. *Citizen Speak: The Democratic Imagination in American Life*. Chicago: University of Chicago Press.

Pichardo, N. A. 1997. "New Social Movements: A Critical Review." *Annual Review of Sociology* 23:411–430.

Pizzorno, A. 1978. "Political Exchange and Collective Identity in Industrial Conflict." Pp. 277–298 in *The Resurgence of Class Conflict in Western Europe Since 1968*, vol. 2, edited by C. Crouch and A. Pizzorno. London: Macmillan.

Polletta, F. A. 2006. *It Was Like a Fever: Storytelling in Protest and Politics*. Chicago: University of Chicago Press.

Polletta, F. A. and J. M. Jasper. 2001. "Collective Identity and Social Movements." *Annual Review of Sociology* 27:283–305.

Portes, A. 1998. "Social Capital: Its Origins and Applications in Modern Sociology." *Annual Review of Sociology* 24:1–24.

Potter, D. 1954. *People of Plenty*. Chicago: University of Chicago Press.

Putnam, R. D. 1993. *Making Democracy Work: Civic Traditions in Modern Italy*. Princeton, NJ: Princeton University Press.

———. 1995. "Bowling Alone: America's Declining Social Capital." *Democracy* 6:65–78.

———. 2000. *Bowling Alone: The Collapse and Revival of American Community*. New York: Simon and Schuster.

Reed, J. P. 2004. "Emotions in Context: Revolutionary Accelerators, Hope, Moral Outrage, and Other Emotions in the Making of Nicaragua's Revolution." *Theory and Society* 33:653–703.

Reed, T. V. 2005. *The Art of Protest*. Minneapolis, MN: University of Minnesota Press.

Reger, J. 2004. "Organizational 'Emotion Work' through Consciousness-raising: An Analysis of a Feminist Organization." *Qualitative Sociology* 27:205–222.

Robnett, B. 1991. *How Long? How Long? African-American Women in the Struggle for Civil Rights.* New York: Oxford University Press.

Roggeband, C. 2004. "'Immediately I Thought We Should Do the Same Thing': International Inspiration and Exchange in Feminist Action against Sexual Violence. *European Journal of Women's Studies* 11:159–175.

Rorty, R. 1993. "Human Rights, Rationality, and Sentimentality." Pp. 111–134 in *On Human Rights,* edited by S. Shute and S. Hurley. New York: Basic Books.

Roscigno, V. J. and W. F. Danaher. 2004. *The Voice of Southern Labor: Radio, Music, and Textile Strikes, 1929–1934.* Minneapolis, MN: University of Minnesota Press.

Rostow, W. W. 1960. *The Stages of Economic Growth, a Non-communist Manifesto.* Cambridge, UK: Cambridge University Press.

Rothwell, J. D. 1971. "Verbal Obscenity." *Western Speech* 35:231–242.

Rupp, L. and V. Taylor. 1987. *Survival in the Doldrums.* New York: Oxford University Press.

Ryan, M. P. 1990. *Women in Public: Between Banners and Ballots, 1825–1880.* Baltimore: Johns Hopkins University Press.

Satterfield, T. 2004. "Emotional Agency and Contentious Practice: Activist Dispute in Old-Growth Forests." *Ethos* 32:233–256.

Scheff, T. 1990. *Microsociology: Discourse, Emotion and Social Structure.* Chicago: University of Chicago Press.

——. 1994. *Bloody Revenge.* Boulder, CO: Westview Press.

——. 1997. *Emotions, the Social Bond, and Human Reality.* Cambridge, UK: Cambridge University Press.

Schmitt, C. 1976/1932. *The Concept of the Political.* New Brunswick, NJ: Transaction Press.

Schwartz, N. and H. Bless. 1991. "Happy and Mindless, but Sad and Smart? The Impact of Affective States on Analytic Reasoning." Pp. 55–71 in *Education and Social Judgments,* edited by J. P. Forgas. New York: Pergamon.

Scott, J. 1985. *Weapons of the Weak: Everyday Forms of Peasant Resistance.* New Haven, CT: Yale University Press.

——. 1990. *Domination and the Arts of Resistance: Hidden Transcripts.* New Haven, CT: Yale University Press.

Seidman, S. 1994. "Symposium: Queer Theory/Sociology: A Dialogue." *Sociological Theory* 12:166–177.

Shapiro, M. J. 1992. *Reading the Postmodern Polity: Political Theory as Textual Practice.* Minneapolis, MN: University of Minnesota Press.

Shorter, E. and C. Tilly. 1974. *Strikes in France, 1830–1968.* Cambridge, UK: Cambridge University Press.

Skocpol, T. 2003. *Diminished Democracy: From Membership to Management in American Civic Life.* Norman, OK: University of Oklahoma Press.

Smelser, N. J. 1962. *Theory of Collective Behavior.* New York: Free Press.

——. 1968. "Social and Psychological Dimensions of Collective Behavior." Pp. 92–101 in *Essays in Sociological Explanation,* edited by N. J. Smelser. Englewood Cliffs, NJ: Prentice-Hall.

Smith, C. 2003. *Moral, Believing Animals: Human Personhood and Culture.* Oxford: Oxford University Press.

Snow, D. A. 2001. "Collective Identity and Expressive Forms." Pp. 2213–2219 in *International Encyclopedia of the Social and Behavioral Sciences,* edited by N. J. Smelser and P. B. Baltes. London: Elsevier.

——. 2004. "Framing Processes, Ideology, and Discursive Fields." Pp. 380–412 in *The Blackwell Companion to Social Movements,* edited by D. A. Snow, S. A. Soule, and H. Kriesi. Oxford: Blackwell.

Snow, D. A. and R. D. Benford. 1988. "Ideology, Frame Resonance, and Participant Mobilization." *International Social Movement Research* 1:197–217.

——. 1992. "Master Frames and Cycles of Protest." Pp. 133–155 in *Frontiers in Social Movement Theory,* edited by A. D. Morris and C. M. Mueller. New Haven, CT: Yale University Press.

Snow, D. A., E. B. Rochford, Jr., S. K. Worden, and R. D. Benford. 1986. "Frame Alignment Processes, Micromobilization, and Movement Participation." *American Sociological Review* 51:464–481.

Snow, D. A., L. A. Zurcher, Jr., and S. Ekland-Olson. 1980. "Social Networks and Social Movements: A Microstructural Approach to Differential Recruitment." *American Sociological Review* 45:787–801.

——. 1983. "Further Thoughts on Social Networks and Movement Recruitment. *Sociology* 17:112–120.

Snyder, D. and C. Tilly. 1972. "Hardship and Collective Violence in France, 1830 to 1960." *American Sociological Review* 37:520–532.

Somers, M. R. 1995. "What's Political or Cultural about Political Culture and the Public Sphere? *Sociological Theory* 13:113–144.

Soule, S. A. 2004. "Diffusion Processes within and across Social Movements." Pp. 294–310 in *The Blackwell Companion to Social Movements,* edited by D. A. Snow, S. A. Soule, and H. Kriesi. Oxford: Blackwell.

Steinberg, M. 1998. "Tilting the Frame: Considerations of Collective Action Framing from a Discursive Turn." *Theory and Society* 27:845–872.

——. 1999. *Fighting Words.* Ithaca, NY: Cornell University Press.

Stewart, J. 2004. "When Local Troubles Become Transnational: The Transformation of a Guatemalan Indigenous Rights Movement." *Mobilization* 9:259–278.

Szreter, S. 2002. "The State of Social Capital: Bringing Back in Power, Politics, and History." *Theory and Society* 31:573–621.

Tarrow, S. 2003. "Paradigm Warriors: Regress and Progress in the Study of Contentious Politics." Pp. 39–45 in *Rethinking Social Movements*, edited by J. Goodwin and J. M. Jasper. Lanham, MD: Rowman and Littlefield.

Taylor, C. 1989. *Sources of the Self*. Cambridge, MA: Harvard University Press.

Taylor, V. 1989. "Sources of Continuity in Social Movements: The Women's Movement in Abeyance." *American Sociological Review* 54:761–775.

——. 1996. *Rock-a-bye Baby: Feminism, Self-help, and Postpartum Depression*. New York: Routledge.

Taylor, V. and N. Whittier. 1992. "Collective Identity in Social Movement Communities: Lesbian Feminist Mobilization." Pp. 104–129 in *Frontiers in Social Movement Theory*, edited by A. D. Morris and C. M. Mueller. New Haven, CT: Yale University Press.

Thompson, E. P. 1963. *The Making of the English Working Class*. London: Golancz.

Torfing, J. 1999. *New Theories of Discourse*. Oxford: Blackwell.

Touraine, A. 1969. *La Société Post-industrielle*. Paris: Editions Denoël S.A.R.L.

——. 1973. *Production de la Société*. Editions du Seuil.0

——. 1978. *La Voix et le Regard*. Paris: Editions du Seuil.

——. 1997. *Pourrons-nous vivre Ensemble? Egaux et Différents*. Paris: Arthème Fayard.

——. 1998a. "Can We Live Together, Equal and Different?" *European Journal of Social Theory* 1:165–178.

——. 1998b. "A Reply." *European Journal of Social Theory* 1:203–209.

Touraine, A., Z. Hegedus, F. Dubet, and M. Wieviorka. 1980. *La Prophétie Anti-nucléaire*. Paris: Editions du Seuil.

Touraine, A., M. Wieviorka, and J. Strzelecki. 1982. *Solidarité*. Paris: Arthème Fayard.

Touraine, A., M. Wieviorka, and F. Dubet. 1984. *Le Mouvement Ouvrier*. Paris: Arthème Fayard.

Trillin, C. 1968. *Eric Hoffer; An American Odyssey*. New York: Dutton.

Turner, R. H. and L. M. Killian. 1957. *Collective Behavior*. Englewood Cliffs, NJ: Prentice-Hall.

Turner, S. P. 1994. *The Social Theory of Practices*. Chicago: University of Chicago Press.

——. 2002. *Brains/Practices/Relativism*. Chicago: University of Chicago Press.

van Ginneken, J. 1992. *Crowds, Psychology, and Politics, 1871–1899*. Cambridge, UK: Cambridge University Press.

Walsh, E. J. 1981. "Resource Mobilization and Citizen Protest in Communities around Three Mile Island." *Social Problems* 29:1–21.

Warner, M., ed. 1993. *Fear of a Queer Planet*. Minneapolis, MN: University of Minnesota Press.

Whittier, N. 1995. *Feminist Generations: The Persistence of the Radical Women's Movement*. Philadelphia: Temple University Press.

Williams, R. 1958. *Culture and Society: 1780–1950*. New York: Columbia University Press.

——. 1977. *Marxism and Literature*. Oxford: Oxford University Press.

Williams, R. H. 2004. "The Cultural Contexts of Collective Action." Pp. 91–115 in *The Blackwell Companion to Social Movements*, edited by D. A. Snow, S. A. Soule, and H. Kriesi. Oxford: Blackwell.

Willis, P. 1977. *Learning to Labour: How Working Class Kids Get Working Class Jobs*. New York: Columbia University Press.

Wittig, M. 1992. *The Straight Mind and Other Essays*. Boston: Beacon Press.

Wood, E. J. 2003. *Insurgent Collective Action and Civil War in El Salvador*. Cambridge, UK: Cambridge University Press.

Wuthnow, R. 1991. *Acts of Compassion: Caring for Others and Helping Ourselves*. Princeton, NJ: Princeton University Press.

——. 1998. *Loose Connections: Joining Together in America's Fragmented Communities*. Cambridge, MA: Harvard University Press.

Young, S. 1997. *Changing the Wor(l)d: Discourse, Politics and the Feminist Movement*. New York: Routledge.

CHAPTER 4

Assessing the Politics of Protest

Political Science and the Study of Social Movements

DAVID S. MEYER AND LINDSEY LUPO

Social movements represent a challenge not only to more conventional political action, but also to academic analysis. To be sure, scholarly inquiry often does not neatly follow disciplinary boundaries. Topics, ideas, methods, and even scholars borrow move across disciplinary boundaries. Such disciplinary spillover figures to be even more pronounced in an area of inquiry like social movements, where the definitional boundaries are not well delineated and the questions to be explored are extremely diverse. As a discipline, political science touches on many aspects of social movements and the politics of protest

A few examples underscore this issue. If a social movement includes those who participate in it, individual motivations and activities are an appropriate focus of inquiry, and such concerns are often the province of social psychology, although political scientists do examine individual motivations. If social movements include the more permanent organizations that frequently stage, define, and represent collective action, then the sociology of organization seems like the most appropriate base of theoretical inquiry, but political scientists are attentive to political organizations, their tactics, and operations as well. If a scholar is concerned with the outcomes of protest, including policy reform, then the policy process and policy outcomes, normally the province of political science, provide most of the requisite tools for analysis. More broadly, as a discipline, political science emphasizes the connections among organized actors and their interests, state structures, and public policies (e.g., Lipset 1963).

Numerous and disparate definitions of the state fill the political science literature. Here, we refer to the state as a conceptual variable, and an autonomous actor that has goals, functions, and interests (Almond et al. 2004; Nettl 1968; Skocpol 1979). The state is always an actor, but not one that acts without internal and external constraints. States are defined by fundamental organizational structures that perform certain crucial functions, such as pursuit of the national interest, taxation, security, political communication, and policy adjudication (Almond et al. 2004; Morgenthau 1993; Waltz 1995). These functions are essential for state persistence; however, the functions are often performed by state and nonstate actors at the same time, making the state both a target and an instigator of action. Because there is generally a variety of interests and actors within contemporary states, particularly democratic states, the state itself is not only an actor, but also an arena for political action. Further, while the state often plays a critical role in political science social movement literature, state–movement interaction is not always the focus of the literature, as some outside the discipline might believe. If this were the case, then it could be said that political science successfully developed a distinct field of social movement studies, a suggestion that our argument counters.

In this chapter, we argue that although treatments of political movements appear regularly in the literature, the discipline has not developed a dominant paradigm for studying movements as a distinct set of political phenomena, and analyses in different subfields speak past each other. Indeed, although scholars within the discipline of political science engaged the area of social movements very productively in the late 1960s and early 1970s, by the middle of the 1970s the ground was largely ceded to sociology, and there have been missed analytical opportunities as a result. In this chapter, we review the distinct contributions that political science has made—and can make—to the study of social movements, then review selected cases in three of the four major subfields in American political science (American politics, comparative politics, and international relations), as well as a distinct area of inquiry, Women and Politics, which is rich with social movement studies. [We acknowledge analytical idiosyncrasies in the organization of the discipline in the United States, where "political theory" is a distinct subfield, and any report on politics outside the United States can be coded as "comparative politics."] At the same time, although political scientists have introduced important ideas and theoretical concepts for the analysis of social movements, including "resource mobilization" and "political opportunity" theories, most of the use and theoretical developments of those concepts have taken place outside the discipline, generally in sociology. This is particularly true among American political scientists; European political scientists have been more engaged with social movement theory. As a result of less explicit concern with developing social movement theory, the discipline as a whole has produced more in the way of useful analysis of problems and cases than a developed theory. Here, we call for reading and writing across subfields, emphasizing the potential contributions of a more integrated paradigm for inquiry.

Political scientists turned to study social protest in the 1960s, largely in response to unfolding events, particularly the movements for civil rights and against the war in Vietnam, in the United States, and the student and democracy movements globally. Previous work on social movements had emphasized mass irrationality, often a function of anomie, which was seen as a result of people acting out when conventional politics provided no routes for expressing influence (e.g., Kornhauser 1959). Political scientists from both the left and the right examined more contemporary phenomena and found the tenets of the old collective behavior approach did not withstand empirical examination, and saw both rationality and a connection with mainstream politics at the core of social movements.

Most directly, Frank Parkin (1968) surveyed activists in the British Campaign for Nuclear Disarmament (CND), and found that—in direct contrast to the assumptions of mass society theory—members were fully engaged in a range of more mainstream political groups, not disconnected from society or politics. In effect, joining a protest movement was an addition to, rather than a substitution for, more conventional political participation. In looking at revolutionary unrest around the world, Samuel P. Huntington (1968) emphasized the relationship of challenging movements and unrest to the stability of established political institutions, and indeed, the timing of "crystallization" of those institutions. At roughly the same time, in examining rent strikes and riots in urban politics, Michael Lipsky (1968, 1970) concluded that protest was not only a political strategy, but actually the one most likely to be effective for people with limited resources. Taken together, the attention to social capital, political institutions, and political strategy could have formed a foundation for a more integrated theory of social movements within political science. This didn't happen, partly a result of boundaries within subdisciplines. Social movements is an area of inquiry within three of the four major subfields of political science (American politics, comparative politics, international relations), but not a field in itself.

Consequently, individual authors concerned with social movements in political science tend to adapt paradigms from other disciplines to their topic, considering interest groups, race and ethnicity, voting, or power analysis in the context of the movement at hand. Alternatively, they may "cross over" to other disciplines, including history, anthropology, and particularly sociology, borrowing outside frameworks and speaking back to theory in another discipline. (Many scholars associated with social movements in political science maintain equal or greater profiles in the neighboring discipline of sociology, including Seymour Martin Lipset, Frances Fox Piven, Theda Skocpol, and Sidney Tarrow.)

As a result, the study of social movements in political science is less developed than it might be as an analytical perspective within the discipline. Political scientists don't use a specific social movement framework as a distinct area of study. The result is a less cumulative development of a paradigm of social movements than we see in sociology and other social sciences.

Political scientists study movements without a unified analytical paradigm; they also do not engage in routine communication about building such a paradigm. At the same time, the focus on institutions, the concern with political organization, the attention to institutional frameworks, and the focus on the policy payoff of different strategies of action can still contribute mightily to the study of social movements; these are all areas that are underdeveloped in the social movements literature (Meyer 2005). The discipline of political science should take up this challenge.

AMERICAN POLITICS

Political scientists wrote about protest in the context of broader debates, both theoretical and empirical, about the exercise of power in American life. In many ways, the development of research on social movements, and on social protest more broadly, played out against a developing literature on interest groups and pluralism. Whereas early work on interest groups presupposed—and then found—broad representation of different interests in mainstream American politics, much work on social movements focused on the systematic exclusion or, minimally, under-representation, of, first, poor and minority populations, and later, women.

Beginning with David Truman (1951), scholars saw the constellation of organized groups engaged in politics (through lobbying and electoral participation) as a reasonably approximate representation of interests in society at large. For Truman, new issues or constituencies created "disturbances" that produced new groups. At a system-wide level, this created—or restored–a kind of balance in American politics.

Although not explicitly about interest groups or social movements, Robert Dahl's work on power provided greater detail and explication of a nuanced pluralist perspective on power in American life. In his theoretical work, Dahl (e.g., 1956) looked at the ways in which the American political system, as designed by Madison, funneled social conflict into political institutions. The creation of multiple levels of government and the separation of powers among different branches of government both contributed to a situation in which all sorts of interests were essentially invited into a political struggle. The nature of American government made it very hard to use the state; at the same time, however, organized interests could effectively block initiatives they found unwelcome through multiple veto points built into the system. Dahl didn't explicitly consider the effects of the Madisonian system on the development of social movements in America (but see Meyer 2007), but his work provided a target for later students of social movements.

Empirically, Dahl (1963) examined the nature of political power within a community. In a detailed longitudinal study of politics in New Haven, Dahl traced the evolving competition among various interests. In most ways, the New Haven story follows outlines suggested by

Alexis de Tocqueville more than a century earlier. Groups of people with similar interests had to build coalitions to gain meaningful access to government. In doing so, they negotiated compromises among themselves and simultaneously bought into the larger political process. Importantly, virtually every constituency had some sort of resources to bring to bear on the political process, including money, information, cohesion, or numbers, as examples. In this way, organization and strategy became critical predictors for success. The work presumed that no significant group lacked *all* significant resources, and that effective tactics and organization could maximize the impact of any constituency.

Of course, pluralism endured extensive criticism. Bacharach and Baratz (1963) suggested that Dahl's work, and indeed pluralist analysis more generally, provided a fair read of the workings of the inside of the political arena. They questioned, however, the ready translation of social interests into organized political interests—in effect, directly questioning the translation of interests into organized actors. The second face of power, they contended, was the setting of the agenda, deciding what was to be decided. Later, political theorist Steven Lukes (2005 [1974]) suggested that power had a third, more insidious dimension, and that people who were generally excluded from meaningful political access were also victims of cultural hegemony that effectively determined how they considered their own interests. Political scientist and activist John Gaventa (1981) explored this third dimension of power in his classic study of miners' activism and (more frequently) quiescence. The episodic appearance of protest movements presented an explicit challenge to both the tenets of pluralist theory and the claims of its critics. If the system were relatively open, then movements would not be necessary; if the political system were completely insular from the interests of particular constituencies, then movements would not be able to emerge effectively in the first place. Treatments of social movements played out against this backdrop, initially focused on the connection between protest and public policy.

The critical conception of social movement politics was articulated most clearly by E.E. Schattschneider (1960)—although he was not writing about social movements. They key people to watch in any conflict, Schattschneider contended, were those who were not direct parties to the conflict, that is, the crowd or audience. By mobilizing support from outside actors, effectively calling in reinforcements or new resources, interested parties can alter the balance of power in a conflict in their favor. Schattschneider noted that it is the losers in any conflict who have an interest in expanding its scope, and bringing in new actors to the conflict. This is what social movements do. When social movements are successful, authorities and bystanders think not only about the political efforts of activists, but also about their demands and gripes. At the same time, institutional authorities, or organized interests in society that are well served, have a vested interest in minimizing the scope of a conflict, maintaining a power bias in their favor. Social movement politics is fundamentally a struggle about the composition of the field of actors within a conflict, with movement activists and their opponents actively working to construct the contest and its combatants in their favor. We see this conception develop in research on American politics and policy.

Public Policy

Schattschneider's theory inspired scholars seeking to explore the politics and policies affecting poor people. Michael Lipsky (1968), in examining politics, policy, and protest for poor people, explicitly questioned the openness of the political system and pluralism more generally. At the same time, his work may provide a foundation for developing a fuller and more nuanced account of pluralism and contemporary democracy. Lipsky argued that the policy responses poor people—even when mobilized—are able to extract from government, are primarily symbolic rather than substantive. He (1968:202) wrote, "It is literally fundamental because the kinds of rewards which can be obtained from politics, one might hypothesize, will have an impact upon the realistic appraisal of the efficacy of political activity." His critique of the pluralist model stems from his analysis of the rent strike movement of the early 1960s in New York City.

Following the critics of pluralism, Lipsky (1968, 1970) argued that many groups in the political system lack power and therefore cannot "get in the game"—the pluralist game that is—in an attempt to gain power and exercise influence. One resource they do have, however, is protest and this can make them active players, albeit not directly. He argued that rather than a direct relationship between unrest by the poor and policy responses, poor people need to mobilize third-party support, that is, the active sympathy of "bystander" publics. When activated, these bystander publics can pressure politicians to provide policy responses to the needs of poor people. Protest works, in effect, not as a direct exercise of influence, but as a means to appeal and promote sympathetic action from more powerful allies. To influence policy, activists need to tap into third-party support. The rent strike movement did so, but Lipsky cautioned that the somewhat successful case he studied is relatively unusual because activists were able to obtain resources, including talented leadership, committed participants, and financial support that most powerless groups generally find inaccessible. His approach to protest politics is predicated on the recognition of active groups consciously acquiring and applying resources to mainstream institutional politics. Protest, he asserts, is a political resource, one most attractive to those without other substantial resources—and it works by mobilizing more conventional political resources. Throughout, however, Lipsky asserts that the conditions that allowed the tenant activists he studied to be successful were rare. Although the work explicitly criticized pluralism, it also established a framework of countervailing resources, in which the mobilization, anger, and disruption of the poor could, under certain circumstances and at some time, effect influence.

Sociologists John McCarthy and Mayer Zald (1973, 1977) built on Lipsky's analysis—or at least his language, describing the phenomenon of social movements as a function of "mobilizing resources," but turned to broaden the analysis to different sorts of constituencies. In the process, they came to a somewhat different perspective. McCarthy and Zald (1973, 1977) posited that while grievances were essentially continual, social movement mobilization was episodic. They viewed the successful mobilization of opinion or action as the product of organizational success rather than political desperation and frustration. By broadening the scope of what they considered a social movement, they turned attention less to the actual conduct of protests, riots, or strikes, and more toward the creation and maintenance of social movement organizations. Clearly responding to Lipsky, the resource mobilization perspective nonetheless turned analytical focus away from the concerns about grievances and inequality that animated his research.

Other political scientists also tracked the fortunes of the poor through protest and policy. Following the concern with the political fate of poor people in the United States, Piven and Cloward (1971, 1977) afforded poor people the prospect for somewhat more direct influence on policy than Lipsky, but also somewhat less control. Lacking all meaningful conventional political resources, Piven and Cloward (1971) contend, poor people nonetheless have the capacity to disrupt daily life, including threatening governing coalitions. Authorities have an obvious interest in maintaining order, and can employ a range of tools for keeping poor people in line, including both direct and indirect repression. At the same time, offering both symbolic and substantive concerns, particularly public welfare payments, is a way to buy quiescence. They traced public spending on welfare to social unrest, and found that politicians increase spending on the poor during periods of unrest, and withdraw that support, sometimes dramatically, during periods of quiescence (Albritton's 1979 empirical test provides little support for their claims). The argument is clearly grounded in a Marxist theory of class and conflict, and their work is directed to political activists as well as scholars.

In *Poor Peoples' Movements* (1977), Piven and Cloward extend their argument about social movements through four extended case studies of social unrest generated by poor people. They are explicitly critical of pluralist frameworks, writing (1977:3), "Modes of participation and non-participation in electoral-representative procedures were not, as the pluralists had implied . . . freely made political choices of free men and women." In essence, they contend that protest is the only viable tool in the political arsenal of poor people, but that it is rarely employed and not always effective.

Piven and Cloward (1977) argued that opportunities for protest occur when there are broad social changes and a restructuring of institutional life. In other words, shifts in the political system break the chains of the poor and once freed from their shackles, the poor will utilize the opportunity to use the only power resource they have—protest. However, these "extraordinary occurrences" that are "required to transform the poor from apathy to hope, from quiescence to indignation," are few and far between. During normal circumstances, the exigencies of daily life take up all the time and energies of poor people, and only when daily life breaks down severely can protest emerge.

Organizers too often waste these extraordinary moments, building membership structures, cultivating elite support and tending to infrastructure. Piven and Cloward's (1977) study reads as a lesson plan for future poor people's movements, and a polemical one at that. Their lesson is simple: avoid the urge to organize and succumb to persuasive leaders and instead concentrate on staying mobilized and disruptive. Under the right circumstances, that is, when the governing coalition faces electoral instability and sees policy reforms as a route to maintaining or expanding its coalition, policy toward poor people may improve.

Social protest *can* help produce policy change favorable to those protesting, Piven and Cloward (1977) argue, but circumstances must be favorable. Importantly, the factors that give rise to protest are also often those that define a climate favorable to policy reform. When social unrest produces political instability, political authorities have a range of options for dealing with that instability. The first response is virtually always to ignore the disruption or to allow well-established social control mechanisms to manage the conflict. Repression is another option; another is policy concessions coupled with some sort of political inclusion. Although Piven and Cloward (1977) are not clear about just when unrest will generate concessions, they are clear that such concessions will be limited and may be withdrawn. Nonetheless, they contend, organizers undermine what limited impact they might have by quelling the disruption that affords them leverage and potential influence.

Piven and Cloward (1977) traced a path of inclusion and demobilization that is affected by both external circumstances and internal organizational dynamics. At the organizational level, they cite Michels' (1966 [1915]) "iron law of oligarchy," a well-established premise in political science. In a classic study of the German Social Democratic Party, Michels found that the leaders of a group committed to socialism and democracy developed interests and approaches toward politics that differed from those of the members. Power in organizations, Michels argued, inevitably concentrates in the hands of the few, who are available to negotiate deals with authorities that may serve the organization or those individuals better than those they purport to represent. At the external level, Piven and Cloward (1977) emphasized that authorities have a vested interest in offering sufficient concessions, including policy reforms and political inclusion, to negotiate a kind of settlement with at least some movement leaders who might broker a peace with their own rank and file.

As a result of these factors, Piven and Cloward (1977:xxii) argue, "organizers tended to work against disruption because, in their search for resources to maintain their organizations, they were driven inexorably to elites, and to the tangible and symbolic supports that elites could provide." The book emerges as a brief *against* organizations that might dampen protest. In effect, the authors pose a difficult dilemma for political leaders outside of government: they can build stable organizations and undermine their political influence OR they can abjure formal organization, stoke mobilization, recognizing that their disruption will be short-lived and unlikely to lead to substantial reform. It's a bleak view of the prospects for social change, even as it is wrapped in a framework that affords influence to grassroots activism of a sort.

Theodore Lowi (1971) offers a similar account of the trajectory of social movements and it is similarly bleak. His analysis is based more directly in the nature of American political institutions than in the nature of class conflict. Directly challenging the pluralist model, he points to the explosion of civil rights activism, including nonviolent and more disruptive activism, and the failure of pluralist theory to explain such phenomena. If power is even remotely balanced in the system, why do some groups fail to engage effectively conventional politics and structured political institutions and instead protest outside mainstream politics? Lowi contends that protest is sometimes the necessary recourse for a system that has failed in some way.

Like Piven and Cloward, Lowi argued that social movements emerge in response to some sort of change in the political system. Movements occur in the wake of institutional atrophy and act as the necessary counterpunch to a stagnated and routinized system. For both Piven and Cloward and Lowi, the arguments veer to the tautological. A social movement's goal is ostensibly to produce change in the system, but a change in the system is what's necessary for a social movement to arise.

For Lowi then, a social movement is a necessary outside-the-system means to promote public policy reforms. Social movements are disorders that rise up to challenge the "iron law of decadence"—Lowi's take on Michels's somewhat different "iron law of oligarchy." The iron law of decadence is "that tendency of all organizations to maintain themselves at the expense of needed change and innovation" (1971:5). Leaders become so entrenched in their routines that they collapse under the weight of their own idleness. Social movements provide the necessary revitalization, but the effects of the tonic will always be short lived. By the time social movements are recognized and institutionalized by mainstream politics, the dramatic action—and the effects—have passed.

Lowi claims that social movements create reform where institutions have failed. They hold the system accountable: "Governments in the United States—federal, state, and local—have never moved with greater certainty or with greater effectiveness than when pushed by movements" (1971:58). Thus, movements create change. The problem with movements is that—if successful—they also eventually routinize and become an ossified part of the system they once threatened. The movement eventually fades due to both its internal dynamics and the changing responses of mainstream politics. Eventually, any movement will organize, institutionalize, and negotiate some sort of implicit bargain with mainstream politics, prioritizing organizational survival and the expense of political influence. This is why, Lowi argues, society needs continuously to welcome disorder in the form of social movements; in addition to keeping the broader system at least somewhat fresh and flexible, movements provide the only real opportunity for policy innovation.

Whereas early scholars of policy and social movements focused on the effects of movements on policy and mainstream politics, Meyer (2005) explored the connections among them. Borrowing theoretical frameworks from policy studies (mostly developed in political science) and from social movement theory (mostly developed in sociology), he argues that influence moves back and forth between politics, policy, and protest movements. He lays out what we know about how policies affect movements (e.g., by creating causes or grievances) and how movements affect policies (e.g., by bringing new actors to the table). Meyer then describes how a broader model would epistemologically assist future social science research. His model, like Piven and Cloward's and Lowi's, suggests that social movements emerge when the prospects for political influence in other ways are weak. As a heuristic model, he sets the policy process at the beginning of the analysis of social movements. Following Baumgartner and Jones (1993), he suggests that most sets of policies are stable most of the time, supported by a relatively constant "policy monopoly," that is, a constellation of actors, inside and outside of government, with deep concern, often expertise, and potential influence, on those policies. Policy monopolies generally contain a great diversity of interest and opinion, and the stability of policies is often supported more by stalemate than satisfaction. Social movements provide the opportunity to mobilize new actors, draw public attention to issues that usually escape broad scrutiny, and to reconfigure the politics and policy of an issue area. He writes (2005:17), "Threats to the stability of a policy monopoly, which might arise from political, policy or other critical events (e.g., a foreign war, a nuclear reactor accident), create opportunities for mobilization that can reach a broader audience and for the potential renegotiation of the boundaries of the policy monopoly. Under such circumstances, political mobilization becomes more attractive to citizens because the pattern of institutional politics has changed." Ultimately, government responses fragment a movement's supporting coalition and make it more difficult for activists to mobilize protest.

Meyer, Jenness, and Ingram (2005) present a collection intended to focus social movement scholars' attention on the policy process. In their volume, scholars from political science, sociology, and other disciplines, examine the interaction of social protest and policy reform. Suzanne Mettler (2005, also see Mettler 2002), for example, analyzed the impact of the World War II-era GI bill had on providing resources and support for social engagement and mobilization in the future. Ellen Reese (2005) and Mary Katzenstein (2005) examined how grievances that come from welfare and criminal justice policies create (or block) the development of challenging movement coalitions, and provide targets for collective action.

Whereas work in political science on the protest of the poor focused on disruptive, and often violent, action, other studies turned to the processes by which disadvantaged groups, often ethnic or sexual minorities, have organized and tried to effect political influence. Frequently such works offer synthetic theoretical frameworks of movements, combining political analysis of participation with sociological notions of identity (e.g., see Garcia Bedolla 2005; Kim 2000; Rimmerman 2002). Another stream of work directed attention to the range of tactics that social movement organizations could mobilize, including the more conventional political participation that comprises the concern of much of political science. We next review literature on interest groups and on voting.

Interest Groups and Political Advocacy

Political scientists often studied social movement issues under the rubric of interest groups and political organizations. This area of inquiry is embedded in the debate about pluralism, stemming from James Madison's discussion of "factions" in Federalist Nos. 10 and 51. In modern political science, the inquiry begins with David Truman (1951), who viewed organized groups as the formal representation of the range of interests in American politics. Dahl (1963) provided additional empirical documentation and theoretical ballast for this perspective. Both scholars viewed the translation of interests into organizations as virtually always possible—if not automatic.

Economist Mancur Olson's (1967) critical work on the "free rider" problem in America problematized the translation of interests into organizations, much less effective organizations. Olson reasoned that each individual's contribution to the efforts of a group was unlikely to affect the prospects of success very much, although it could be personally costly—and that a rational individual would recognize this. The obvious thing to do in such a case, particularly in matters of "collective benefits," in which someone would receive advantages regardless of his or her individual participation, is to "free ride," that is, to do or contribute very little or nothing and to hope for the best. This free rider problem focused analytic attention on the process by which organizers mobilized support and activity anyway—over and against this rational calculation of costs and benefits.

Following Olson's suggestion, scholars analyzed the sorts of "incentives" the organizers provided to induce participation in collective action. Analysts parsed sorts of incentives into broad categories along two dimensions. First, in distinguishing between "collective" and "selective" benefits, they assessed whether citizens would receive the benefits of a policy reform even if they hadn't participated in collective action. If a group succeeds in promoting reforms that provide cleaner air and water, for example, even people who did not contribute to its efforts will derive benefits. Such benefits are distinguished from other benefits that are available only to group members, such as product discounts that come to members of a group. Second, they assessed the character of an incentive as being purposive (policy reform), material, or solidary (good feelings and human connections) (see Meyer 2007; Meyer and Imig 1993; Wilson 1995). Organizers had the job of finding meaningful inducements to inspire participation and support, and working with the constraints of the particular sets of resources available to them. Groups pursuing policy change without much to offer in the way of selective incentives would have the toughest time in mobilizing support, although the free rider principle represented more an elastic tendency, rather than a constant, one that shifted in response to political circumstances. Essentially, organizers had to provide something to participants in *exchange* for their support (Salisbury 1970).

One piece of the puzzle of incentives was effective political action, and subsequent scholars assessed the range of tactics available to groups that might promote effectiveness in pursuit of their policy aims. Beyond the generally accepted means of providing accurate information and campaign help to legislators (e.g., Berry 1977), under some circumstances, it made sense for groups to take their claims public, that is, to go outside of conventional political tactics to lobby publicly (e.g., Kollman 1998), in essence, to adopt the forms of social movements (Meyer and Tarrow 1998).

Most of the work was directed to the dynamics of interest groups, but a few scholars looked at the broader picture of representation. In his classic, *The Semi-Sovereign People*, Schattschneider (1960) had suggested that the fundamental flaw with pluralism was the under-representation of poorer people, memorably noting that the choir in the pluralist heaven sings with the accent of the upper class. Scholars examined this assertion empirically, finding predictable gaps and redundancies in representation (e.g., Imig and Meyer 1993; Schlozman 1984), severe disadvantages for advocacy on behalf of poor people (e.g., Imig 1996), and then shifts in the rules and practices of interest group life that made things even worse for all advocates of "public" interests (Berry 1999), and ultimately, the decline in grassroots participation altogether (Skocpol 2003). Taken together, they identify a trend in which the difficult task of counterbalancing the political advantages of those constituencies already advantaged in other ways got progressively more difficult over time, threatening not only the well-being of certain constituencies, but also democracy altogether.

Recognizing the rather bleak big picture, political scientists used the tools of their trade to look at the smaller pictures of mobilization and individual participation in politics, and the broader process of political institutionalization.

Voting and Mobilization

In analyzing the factors that contribute to the policy process, political scientists often turn to studies of mobilization. How do groups mobilize? How do they sustain this mobilization? Does the mobilization affect change in the power structure? It has been over two decades since Browning, Marshall, and Tabb (1984) reported that protest is not enough in the minority struggle for political access, and that while dramatic extrainstitutional action can work to set the policy agenda, effective representation over a longer haul is predicated on building inroads in mainstream political institutions. This oft-cited work has not really been replicated or extended. Importantly, the path toward secure institutionalization is far easier for groups with narrower claims and greater resources, as shown in Hansen's (1991) study of the evolution of the farm lobby.

Protest Is Not Enough centers on themes of minority mobilization, minority access, and political equality and asks three main questions regarding the openness of political systems, political incorporation, and policy response. In answering these questions, the authors drew on distinct literatures from several disciplines. Browning, Marshall, and Tabb addressed the openness of the urban political system by engaging the pluralist/elitist debate so prevalent in political science in the years just before, during, and just after the civil rights movement. Contrasting the two sides of the debate, the authors cite the political scientists commonly associated with their respective camps—pluralist Robert Dahl pitted against elite theorists like Murray Edelman (1971), Ira Katznelson (1982), and a host of other players. Browning, Marshall, and Tabb end up drawing on a more neutral theme, Nelson Polsby's (1967) notion of "pluralism2." Pluralism2 "asserts that power is relatively dispersed" and over time, the power dispersion will change (Browning, Marshall, and Tabb 1984:8). With regard to minority access, disadvantaged constituencies *can* achieve power and influence. Browning, Marshall, and Tabb contend that through building a serious institutional presence in local politics, minority communities can attain meaningful influence over relevant decisions, and not only elicit symbolic concessions.

In addressing how political incorporation works, however, and the extent to which minorities are actually a dominant coalition emerges, Browning, Marshall, and Tabb then leap frog over to the sociology literature. Here they address themes of group mobilization and conflict and therefore draw on prominent sociologists who study protest movements, particularly William Gamson (1990) and Charles Tilly (1978). The political scientists don't disappear entirely; Browning, Tabb, and Marshall engage the literature on minority strategies in urban politics. The authors therefore pull from distinct fields of literature from different disciplines in order to make their argument regarding mobilization, incorporation, policy, and ultimately, equality.

We might then ask, what is the result of using these disparate fields of study for their own analysis? The result is an incredibly extensive analysis of minority group mobilization.

Browning, Marshall, and Tabb ground their quantitative data in well described case studies of 10 Northern California cities and effectively move from an analysis of mobilization to incorporation and subsequently to policy. In thoroughly describing the process, from action to reaction, the authors step toward an inclusive theory of social mobilization. They allow the reader to consider essential questions about the outcomes of mobilization. In other words, what does it all mean? Will a higher level of political equality result from increased governmental response, which in turn results from mobilization?

The authors answer a resounding yes; demand-protest and electoral mobilization are two important resources that initiate a mobilization path that passes though minority incorporation and ends at policy response. Along the way, other resources come into play, most notably size of the minority population in the city and level of support for minority interests, particularly from white liberals (Lipsky's [1968] "bystanders" become partners in political coalition). They argue, "the combination of minority and white resources was the prerequisite for successful [liberal challenging] coalition" that eventually would replace the conservative coalition and lead to minority incorporation (Browning, Marshall, and Tabb, 1984:134). Theirs is an argument of resources, essentially about political entrepreneurs assessing those available to minority communities and how to use them. It harkens back to Dahl (1956), and ignores the critiques based on class that other scholars had advanced. Their theory of resources is predicated on an inclusive vision in which both bottom-up resources (such as demographic shifts) and top-down resources (such as the national civil rights movement) contribute to minority mobilization. For example, a few savvy Black leaders were able to harness the national civil rights movement's intensity, and to use it to spur action in their own cities. The result was a successful path of incorporation that began with mobilization and continued with policy change.

Whereas Browning, Marshall, and Tabb only tangentially mention the role of leaders, Rosenstone and Hansen's (1993) theory of participation is entirely couched in the notion that political leaders play a major role in individual political participation. Rosenstone and Hansen follow on the works of other analysts whom they accuse of telling only half the story regarding who participates and why. Individual interests, beliefs, and resources indeed contribute to participation but "people participate in politics not so much because of who they are but because of the political choices and incentives they are offered" (Rosenstone and Hansen 1993:5). In other words, individual characteristics explain the propensity to participate in politics, given contextual factors and mobilization efforts; the purposive efforts of leaders to mobilize explain who actually participates, when, and how.

Rosenstone and Hansen employ a rational choice model of political participation. Participation in politics is a cost not often worth incurring for individuals. Individuals are rational enough to calculate that the collective benefits of participation will still be bequeathed to them even if they don't participate ("the paradox of voting") and even if they wanted to participate, the learning process is too involved and complicated and they therefore won't even attempt it ("rational ignorance"). But people *do* participate and this parsimonious fact causes many scholars to debunk rational choice theory. However, Rosenstone and Hansen caution against throwing the baby out with the bath water. They argue that rational individuals won't participate given the high costs involved (they argue this is true for some more than others, for instance, poor, uneducated citizens will incur much higher costs and will therefore participate at far lower rates). Enter political leaders who alleviate the costs of participation and thereby mobilize the population.

Leaders will mobilize the population directly (building organizations, sponsoring rallies, circulating petitions) and indirectly (through social networks that spread the word through friends, neighbors, co-workers). They will then offer rewards to offset the costs of participation. Rewards come in many forms—attention, esteem, personal satisfaction, lack of sanctions. But theirs is not a rosy portrayal of political leaders consistently mobilizing all members of the citizenry and therefore contributing to the development of a fully integrated and equal society. Rather, Rosenstone and Hansen argue that the mobilization tactics of leaders are timed and strategic due to their own resource constraints. They don't mobilize all the time (only when they need it) and they don't mobilize everyone (only those who will help them). In effect, leaders' "efforts to move the organized, the employed, the elite, and the advantaged into politics exacerbate rather than reduce the class biases in political participation in America" (Rosenstone and Hansen 1993:33). The result is that those who were already more likely to participate because of their personal characteristics (wealth, education, time, knowledge) and the low level of participation cost associated with these characteristics, are even more likely to participate when leaders initiate their mobilization tactics.

Rosenstone and Hansen contend that one way in which leaders mobilize electoral participation is through social movements. Social movements "inspire" people "to vote, to persuade, to campaign, and to give" (Rosenstone and Hansen 1993:210). Their primary example of a social movement's ability to mobilize individuals is the national civil rights movement, which they argue, mobilized Blacks directly and indirectly. Directly, it mobilized because it was so forthright in its tactics "lawsuits, protests, marches, and sit-ins," not to mention voter registration, organization of voting blocs, and the forcing of political candidates (Rosenstone and Hansen 1993:192). Indirectly, the civil rights movement increased voter turnout and led to an increase in financial contributions. Both of these are likely effects of party mobilization—citizens were more likely during this time to be contacted by a political party and thus urged to vote and contribute. The result was that it wasn't just Blacks who were recruited; white participation increased as well. The movement was so prominent that knowledge increased (just one of the ways social movements decrease the cost of participation) and people were essentially forced to choose a "side" and participation in general rose.

Rosenstone and Hansen's model is strongly grounded in rational choice theory and the public choice field of political science. They view social movements as a variant in the class of political phenomena that include interest groups and community organizations, and contrasted with political parties and campaign organizations. Rosenstone and Hansen are less concerned with the meaning-making activity of social movements than their material existence and their traceable activities. Movements aren't necessarily a malleable organism, changing and responding to outside forces, but are instead an institutional tool political leaders can use to mobilize people.

Those who do the agenda-setting are often not those who can build institutions. The analysis of those agenda-setting events, particularly the disruptive urban riots of the 1960s, spurred research on a number of critical questions. Political scientists, for the most part, were more concerned with the causes and the effects of those riots than in analyzing their dynamics.

Urban Riots

Perhaps the most significant events in propelling scholarship on social movements were the urban riots of the 1960s. Unrest, often violent, swept across American cities throughout the decade, representing racial tensions and economic inequality, and spurred a raft of academic studies. Most focused on either why the riots emerged OR what impact those riots had on public policy. Both streams of research offered additional concepts that continue to animate research in other areas. Concepts developed in analysis of these riots are a lasting legacy of this wave of scholarship.

Peter Eisinger (1973) sought to explain why *some* American cities witnessed extensive riots about race and poverty during the late 1960s while others did not. Assuming a connection between protest in the streets and more conventional politics, Eisinger focused on the openness of urban governments to more conventional political inputs in formulating a theory of political opportunities. He found that cities with a combination of what he termed "open" and "closed" structures for citizen participation were most likely to experience riots. Cities with extensive institutional openings preempted riots by inviting conventional means of political participation to redress grievances; cities without visible openings for participation repressed or discouraged dissident claimants to foreclose eruptions of protest. The approach implicitly assumed constant pressures across urban America and treated the most proximate institutional arrangements as the key factors influencing the way political dissent emerged.

Tilly (1978) built upon Eisinger's (1973) work to offer the beginnings of a more comprehensive theory, suggesting national comparisons, recognizing changes in opportunities over time, and arguing that the structure of political opportunities would explain the more general process of choosing tactics from a spectrum of possibilities within a "repertoire of contention." For Tilly, tactical choice reflects activists optimizing strategic opportunities in pursuit of particular claims at a particular time. Like Eisinger, he contends that the frequency of protest bears a curvilinear relationship with political openness. When authorities offer a given constituency routine and meaningful avenues for access, few of its members protest because less costly, more direct routes to influence are available. At the other end of the spectrum of openness, authorities can repress various constituencies such that they are unable to develop the requisite capacity (whether cognitive or organizational) to lodge their claims. In this view, protest occurs when there is a space of toleration by a polity and when claimants are neither sufficiently advantaged to obviate the need to use dramatic means to express their interests nor so completely repressed to prevent them from trying to get what they want.

Tilly's empirical work traced the development of popular politics in relationship to state institutions. In his study of the development of democratic politics in Britain over nearly a century, for example, Tilly (1993) describes how a range of factors, including demographic and economic shifts and the opening of political institutions, led to a shift from local, direct, and particularistic political contention toward longer term, national, and routinized forms of politics. The development of a more democratic Parliament allowed popular politics to move indoors through the development of mass parties and electoral participation. In essence, Tilly traced the development of the same curve Eisinger postulated, in which protest is enabled, then channeled into less disruptive politics.

Taken together, Tilly and Eisinger offer models for cross-sectional comparisons and longitudinal studies. Eisinger's rather restrictive specification of opportunities focuses on formal institutional rules to explain the frequency of a particular behavior, riots. In contrast, Tilly's broader and more inclusive approach considers a wider range of variables to explain the range of expressions of popular politics over a long period. Both, however, agreed upon the fundamental curvilinear relationship of opportunities to protest politics. They also set out a spectrum of conceptual possibilities for subsequent scholars.

Although the concept of political opportunity structure clearly builds on basic premises in political science (Meyer 2004b), most influential in defining and promoting it as an analytical framework was sociologist Doug McAdam's (1982) treatment of the civil rights movement. McAdam's treatment opens with an assessment of the inadequacy of existing theoretical frameworks for the analyzing social movements; he even comments on the lack of dialogue between political scientists and sociologists. Sociologists, he argues, often fail to address the institutionalized political processes while political scientists often often fail to consider how a noninstitutional entity (a social movement) can effect change inside political institutions (McAdam 1982:2). McAdam attempts to bridge this divide by offering a *political process* model that borrows from resource mobilization theory as it developed in sociology and relies heavily and explicitly on the theory of political opportunities developed by Eisinger (1973) and Tilly (1978). This political process model emphasizes an interaction between external and internal forces. The constellation of political opportunity structures matter (external) but so does level of organization within the group (internal). Further, cognitive liberation and feelings of efficacy within the group matter (internal) but so does elite response to the insurgency (external). The interactive dynamics of all these factors can ultimately generate an insurgency that affects power relationships in the political system.

McAdam (1982) also raises fundamental doubts about the pluralist model of power distribution. If other issues divide social movement scholars (for instance, the importance of external versus internal factors to the success of the movement or the issue of whether organization is detrimental to the movement's success), one thing does seem to unite them: a rejection of simple pluralism. Pluralism as a theoretical construct emerged from political science under Robert Dahl (1956). As a theory, it tried to explain David Easton's (1953) "black box" of value conversion in the American political process and determined that many groups share power in the system. No one group held more power than others and all groups had the potential to achieve their goals. Social movement theorists attacked this theory as inappropriate and inaccurate for their studies. If all groups can achieve power under the pluralist model, then the model assumes social movements and protest politics to be irrational acts of insurgency that have unnecessarily skirted the more legitimate avenues of participation. Many social movement theorists then overcome their differences to conclude that this interpretation is not at all representative of movements.

Button's (1978) analysis of the outcomes of urban unrest also focuses on movement interaction with institutional politics. By tracking social expenditures by the federal government in the wake of urban riots, Button is able to consider the policy outcomes of protest. The findings are complicated and intriguing. Button found that under certain circumstances, determined at least partly by the president's potential political coalition, urban unrest produced expenditures targeted at the source of the unrest. Here the variance is provocative. Democratic president Lyndon Johnson's administration increased expenditures to areas hit by riots, while his successor, Republican Richard Nixon, cut spending in response to the very same stimulus of unrest.

Following the same set of questions, Herbert Haines (1988) examined the variable effects of disruptive action by a "radical flank" on the fortunes of a social movement, and found that it sometimes help and sometimes hurts. His radical flank model "focuses on many of the same variables [as resource mobilization theory and the political process model] in black collective action. It concentrates upon the formal and informal organizational features of the movement" (Haines 1988:3). He agrees with Lipsky (1968) that third-party support can be a crucial resource for social movement mobilization and maintenance. He writes, "the statements and actions of emerging militants might be expected to lead to changes in the willingness of various third parties to support moderates" (Haines 1988:13). In this way, a radical flank has created a social movement resource, third-party support. However, Haines also agrees with McAdam (1982; also see Piven and Cloward 1977) that external support is not the end all be all to movement sustainability, at least partly because of its volatility. Haines recognized the power of internal factors as laid out in McAdam's political process model. Specifically, interorganizational features play a role. Radicals and moderates form a symbiotic relationship, creating a positive radical flank effect that allows moderates to "maintain good relations with outside supporters by distancing themselves from radicals while at the same time profiting from the crises the radicals create" (Haines 1988:185). By employing both resource mobilization and political process models to portray how radical groups can benefit a social movement, Haines effectively rejects the moderate notions of a balanced pluralist system.

Ironically, it is a collaboration between political scientist Charles Hamilton and radical activist Stokely Carmichael (later known as Kwame Ture) that is most supportive of pluralism as a possibility—although *Black Power* at first glance seems to be radical in its analysis and prescriptions, explicitly indebted to Marxism, and calling for a "new consciousness among black people" (Ture and Hamilton 1992:xvi). It calls for nothing short of fundamental restructuring, modernization, and alteration of the current political system. Integration is not desirable and token rewards offered will not suffice. Further invoking Marxist thought, Carmichael (Ture) in his 1992 afterward refers to the historical dialectic and the United States' progression from slavery to civil rights and finally to major reform and the actual inclusion of blacks in the political process. This latter stage, argues Carmichael (Ture), has not yet been achieved. Nonetheless, the authors display ambivalence about both Marxist analysis and pluralism. Indeed, they argue, "SNCC has often stated that it does not oppose the formation of political coalitions *per se*; obviously they are necessary in a pluralistic society" (1992:59). They therefore see coalitions as necessary in what they see as a power struggle among groups. In this sense, they are accepting that pluralism might be the unchanging American way: "It should become clear that the advocates of Black Power do *not* eschew coalitions; rather we want to establish the grounds on which we feel political coalitions can be viable" (1992:60). What they do argue for is a complete restructuring of how the coalitions form. They should not be formed between Blacks and seemingly sympathetic groups (e.g., white liberal Democrats), but rather they should stem from four preconditions:

1. Recognition by the parties involved of their respective self-interests
2. Mutual beliefs that each party stands to benefit in terms of that self-interest from allying with the other or others
3. The acceptance of the fact that each party has its own independent base of power and does not depend for ultimate decision-making on a force outside itself
4. Realization that the coalition deals with specific and identifiable goals

These preconditions essentially restate fundamental pluralist ideas. Thus, for these social movement authors, a seemingly radical approach to power distribution actually begins to develop into a call for pluralism.

Boskin (1969), Rossi (1973), and Baldassare (1994) offer edited volumes that look at the urban riots of the 1960s. Boskin (1969) takes a historical approach to urban racial violence and analyzes a century of violence. He describes how riots before World War II were almost all initiated by Whites, and were therefore an expression of widespread racism (Boskin 1969). In contrast, the protest riots of the 1960s and 1970s were Black revolts that were responses to this racism. In this sense, he bases his approach on J-curve theories of rising expectations, one of the classical models criticized by McAdam (1982).

Rossi (1973:preface) approaches urban violence with an explicitly multidisciplinary approach: "It embodies rather a recognition that the social world cannot be easily carved into neat academic disciplines." The edited volume collects work from *Trans*action magazine (now known as *Society*) that apply social science theory to real world social problems. For instance, Lipsky and Olson (1977) analyze how the riot commissions that followed the riots of the civil rights movement were unable to effect change in the system due to their lack of real power in the larger political system. They contend that special commissions processed political conflict, taking up time and space and producing rhetoric rather than policy change.

Finally, Baldassare's (1994) edited volume on the 1992 Los Angeles riots examines the causes, dynamics, and consequences of what authors describe as a multicultural and multilayered riot. Whereas social movement theorists of the civil rights urban riots had to analyze the dynamics of a Black–White confrontation and struggle for power, the new social movement theorists studying the events of 1992 are forced to analyze the dynamics of all the mini-riots involved in the 1992 Los Angeles riot, Blacks, Whites, Asians, and Latinos all collided and each for differing reasons. As Sears (1994:251) suggests, "It seems apparent to me that no simple or single interpretation fits the 1992 events very well." Authors in this book attribute the "uprising" to class issues (Korean shop owners and Black consumers), ethnic competition (Latino in-migration), and injustice (White disrespect for Blacks as portrayed most egregiously by the Los Angeles Police Department). Sears writes the concluding chapter and determines that the 1992 Los Angeles riot was simply "several riots" in one.

Political scientists studied social movements in conjunction with public policy and urban riots primarily in the post-civil rights years. However, when the protests fizzled out, political scientists failed to develop social movement analysis alive as a distinct set of theoretical questions. Social movement studies became relegated to subdisciplinary areas and therefore dependent on alternate frameworks for study. Many of the scholars discussed in the preceding text reject the pluralist model of power distribution. However, beyond this rejection, the similarities disappear. There appears to be no single paradigm with which these authors write about social movements. They borrow from sociology, history, political science, and economics. The result is that political science has failed as a discipline to create a social movement framework distinct to the field.

Identity

Whereas the work on urban riots focused largely on structural and material aspects of politics, including interests, organizations, and tactics, more recent social movements have led scholars to consider the nature of the collective identity constructed and deployed by disadvantaged groups. Political scientists have generally seen collective identities constructed in response to the structural conditions of various constituencies, and much of the leading academic work has focused on the politics of race.

As example, Cathy Cohen's (1999) analysis of the reaction of Black urban communities to AIDS focuses on the construction of marginality. Cohen argues that structural conditions, including codified laws and practices that discriminate, can create marginality and distance from mainstream politics, to say nothing of social and economic inclusion. Paradoxically, such marginalization also produces the raw material that activists can use in creating community and a collective identity. Importantly, while structural exclusion can create marginalization and identity, such identities are often sustained even in the absence of sustained exclusion. Cohen's tale of the failure of the Black community to deal effectively with AIDS reflects the processes through which even marginal communities maintain their own boundaries. She cites a failure of leadership and prejudice, but the nature of exclusion enforcing collective identities has applications that extend well beyond her case.

Claire Kim (2000) examined similar issues by looking at the political divide between Blacks and Koreans in New York City at the end of the twentieth century. Kim contends that the racial divide in the United States continually reproduces itself. New immigrant groups are incorporated into a stratified order that keeps Blacks firmly at the bottom of this order, comprising almost a permanent underclass. By accepting this stratified system, "Korean immigrants may be said to be implicated in the American racial order to the extent that their positioning within it determines their opportunities and constraints, and, more specifically, to the extent that they benefit from Black marginalization and buy into American racial constructions" (Kim 2000:52).

Kim then argues that Black collective action against Korean immigrants in the latter decades of the twentieth century was thus not born out of irrational anger, but rather was in fact a response to the broader system of racial stratification in the United States. In describing this Black collective action (and the Korean immigrant response), Kim uses the sociological concept of framing and more specifically, frame repertoires. If frames can attribute a problem to a cause by making issue linkages clear for potential activists, then a frame repertoire is "a set of collective action frames that outlives specific movements, persists through time, and is continuously available to activists seeking to build a new movement" (Kim 2000:56). Frame repertoires are available only to groups who are persistently identified as such and who are consistently marginalized.

According to Kim, during a period of Black power resurgence in New York City at the end of the twentieth century, Blacks invoked two frame repertoires—Black power and community control. The former emerged in the 1960s and encouraged Blacks to be Black proud and to unite and forge a sense of community and solidarity. The latter, community control, follows from this sense of Black liberation and argues for Black control over Black communities, particularly in terms of retail establishments. In response to the resurgence of Black collective action, Korean immigrants employed their own frames— collective identity in defense of group interests and defense of the American creed (Kim 2000:163). Korean American leaders were successful in framing the conflict as anti-Korean and therefore racist, helping to "channel the community's strong transnationalist sentiments into the countermobilization effort" (Kim 2000:163). They were also able to frame the boycott against Korean owned stores as essentially anti-American, going against the ideals of "equal opportunity, fairness, and colorblindness" (Kim 2000:167). By invoking this latter frame, they therefore gathered supporters not only within the Korean community, but also from other racial, ethnic, and religious groups who sought to protect the "American dream" ideal of social mobility and opportunity. Kim's use of framing demonstrates how each group promoted its distinct identity in the service of political mobilization that ultimately maintained existing political and economic relations.

Studying Latino immigrant identity and political engagement on the other coast, Lisa Garcia Bedolla (2005) focused on the nature of resources available to disadvantaged groups, including psychological capital and contextual capital. Garcia Bedolla contends that although other disciplines have often studied the role of identity in minority behavior, political scientists have rarely focused on Latino identity in relation to political behavior (Garcia Bedolla 2005:16). Seeing this link as critical, she put the connection between identity and political behavior at the center of her analysis. She also problematized the construction of identity; if successful collective mobilization reflects strongly held collective identities, she asks, "where these kinds of mobilizing identities come from, why they exist for some group members and not others, [and] how to foster engagement by encouraging the creation of these kinds of identities" (Garcia Bedolla 2005:6).

Garcia-Bedolla's concept of a mobilizing identity is as a form of psychological capital, that is, "social capital that exists within the individual psyche and gives a person the motivation to act on behalf of the collective" (Garcia Bedolla 2005:6). In combination with contextual capital (the politics of the group's environment and social context), these two resources enhance "group members' feelings of agency and their political engagement" (Garcia Bedolla 2005:6). She found that identity and social context are important indicators of Latino political participation. For example, "in the case of East Los Angeles Latinos, affective attachment to their social group and feelings of group worth serve as sources of psychological capital, counterbalancing their sense of group stigma to motivate area residents to act politically" (Garcia Bedolla 2005:25). Understanding the interaction between identity and social and political context "can help us to better understand the political integration of subordinate groups in the United States" (Garcia Bedolla 2005:25). Political engagement for Latinos does not come from a mobilizing context alone, rather identity and a sense of group self-worth also contribute. This notion of self-worth is important, as it is not simply racial identification that matters in terms of mobilization, but "positive affective attachment to the racial group" (Garcia Bedolla 2005:174). Thus, Garcia Bedolla contributes to the political science literature in a way that other non-political scientists have already been doing, in the sense that she emphasizes the role that identity, *in addition to* political environment, plays in mobilizing minority groups to politically engage. The notion of identity as something constructed in the context of structural constraints and through the crucible of collective action is useful in examining the political development and influence of a range of social movements.

COMPARATIVE POLITICS

The study of social movements built deeper inroads in the area of comparative politics, as scholars borrowed from other fields to explain the problems they confronted analytically. [Here we adopt the odd norms of American political science, in which any study whose subject is outside of the United States is labeled "comparative," even if it is a single country study.) Importantly, comparative politics does not offer a unified paradigm for understanding social protest, and indeed, included a large divide between scholars concerned with social movements in advanced industrialized societies and others concerned with movements in the Global South. The content of those movements was, for the most part, very different, as was the borrowed literature. Scholars of the wealthy world studied, mostly, campaigns for such things as women's rights, the environment, and peace—very much like contemporary social movements in the United States and Europe. They borrowed literature from political sociology and opinion research conducted in both political science and sociology. In contrast, scholars concerned with unrest in poor countries studied disruptive movements that sought, and sometimes gained, state power, and therefore were heavily reliant on the literature on revolutions.

Developed World: Political Sociology

Both European and American political scientists working on European cases represent the greatest concentration of research on social movements in the discipline. Scholars in this area have used a range of methodological tools, focusing on both individual decisions and larger scale political formations, and have developed the political opportunity framework outlined in the preceding text.

Cross-sectional comparative studies, following Eisinger's (1973) model, trace the curve of opportunities across different contexts. For example, Herbert Kitschelt's (1986) study of antinuclear movements in four democracies—France, Sweden, the United States, and West Germany—uses political opportunity theory to explain the style and development of social movement politics, as well as their ultimate influence. Acknowledging a broad conception of opportunity, including resources, institutions, and historical precedents, Kitschelt nonetheless offers a narrower specification. He divides the four states along two dimensions: input structures (open or closed) and output capacity (strong or weak). The simple classification, he contends, explains the strategies employed by challengers in all four states. The options for participation determine strategy—*confrontational* in response to blockage, *assimilative* in response to openness. The capacity of the state determines influence—greater procedural innovation or substantive change in response to pressures in weaker states. This spare model offers an advantage of clarity, but at the cost of simplifying and flattening a broad range of factors critical to the development of a social movement over time.

Offering a more dynamic analysis, Tarrow (1989) applied a longitudinal model of political opportunities to explain the broad range of social movement activity over a tumultuous decade, 1965–1975, in Italian politics. His political process approach traced a "cycle of protest," including decline, by considering institutional politics along with social protest and disorder. In this case, government openings reduced the cost of collective action, and the initial mobilization of one constituency encouraged others to mobilize as well. Workers, students, religious reformers, and leftist factions within parties all took to the streets. Government responses initially encouraged additional mobilization, some of which turned violent. Violence and disorder legitimated repression, raising the costs of collective action, and diminishing protest. At the same time, some of the social movement actors turned their attention to more conventional political activity, reducing their claims and moderating their tactics, effectively institutionalizing dissent (Meyer and Tarrow 1998).

Methodologically, Tarrow (1989) developed "events data" analysis, a means of deriving information about the peaks and troughs of social movements, as well as their claims from a sampling of newspaper accounts. This method had been used by sociologists (including McAdam 1982), but political scientists extended the range of sources and developed new tools of analysis. This is particularly true of European political scientists, who mounted large-scale collaborative efforts to compile large data sets on comparative collective action (see especially Rucht, Koopmans, and Neidhardt 1999). Events data analysis would develop to compare political tactics over time and across contexts (e.g., Rucht 1990) and the claims that social movement actors made (Koopmans and Statham 1999a, b).

In his expressly theoretical overview of social movements (Tarrow 1998) emphasizes the connections between mainstream politics and protest movements. He argues that movements are best understood when studied in context, that is, the political context in which they are operating, following the political opportunity framework offered by Tilly (1978) and McAdam (1982) (Meyer 2004b). In *Power in Movement*, Tarrow (1998) argues that social movements are in constant interaction with the political system, both responding to it and altering it as the political system offers opportunities to an otherwise powerless group. Lacking in resources, and thus in power, social movements under normal circumstances lack the capacity to affect change. However, the political system, consisting of elites and their allocation of values, provides opportunities and incentives for the movement. He sees political opportunities as cues to the savvy movement activist that the system is open and susceptible to influence from below. Increased access, shifting electoral alignments, divided elites, and influential allies are all examples of political opportunities that Tarrow offers (Tarrow 1998:78–80).

However, social movements are not affected by politics only in the incipient phases. Rather, it is a continued relationship that advances the struggle at every stage. According to Tarrow, the social movement acts in "sustained interaction with elites, opponents, and authorities" (Tarrow 1998:4). In this way, the movement reacts to elite response and creates new opportunities. For instance, Tarrow discusses diffusion effects:

> Unlike conventional forms of participation, contentious collective action demonstrates the possibilities of collective action to others and offers even resource-poor groups opportunities that their lack of resources would deny them. This occurs when "early risers" make claims on elites that can be used by those with less daring and fewer resources. Moreover, collective action exposes opponents' points of weakness that may not be evident until they are challenged. It can also reveal unsuspected or formerly passive allies both within and outside the system. Finally, it can pry open institutional barriers through which the demands of others can pour. (Tarrow 1998:87)

But diffusion effects are just one way movements sustain themselves. The political system can also produce policy outputs in response to movements, and these outputs create a whole new set of political opportunities. Social movements socialize the participants to political practice, affect political institutions, and even shape the political culture of a system (Tarrow 1998:164). In this way, social movements become no longer outside of the institutional framework of the state, but rather become a part of a "complex policy network" (Tarrow 1998:25). For Tarrow then, to neglect the political system that social movements challenge is a critical mistake that undermines the possibilities of understanding a movement. Social movements receive incentives from, react to, and influence the political system, thereby creating a cycle of contention that continuously produces new outcomes.

Because of its reliance on the notion of the political system, Tarrow's argument is based firmly in political science. This critical piece is a theoretical work that discusses how social movements emerge and are sustained. The theory is not entirely without empirical evidence however, as Tarrow relied heavily on the writings of social movement scholars and particular movements. What he found is that these movements were heavily affected by (particularly in their incipient phases) openings in the political system, and in this way, he brought political science to a field otherwise dominated by sociologists. He agrees with sociologists that repertoires of contention and framing matter in the social movement cycle, and argues that these elements operate alongside and in conjunction with the state and its reaction to these elements. It's a theoretical piece that crosses disciplinary perspectives and that should prove informative for social science and humanities scholars across many fields of study.

European political scientists have been more active in studying social protest movements, and in providing comprehensive synthetic theoretical frameworks for doing so. Particularly influential has been Hanspeter Kriesi and his collaborators. Kriesi and his colleagues (Kriesi, Koopmans, Duvydenak, and Giugni 1995) combined the complexity and nuance of the longitudinal studies with the analytical leverage of cross-sectional studies, comparing "new social movements" [the "family" of left-libertarian movements in advanced industrialized states (see della Porta and Rucht 1995)] across four European states (France, Germany, the Netherlands, and Switzerland) over time. Opportunity structures include the nature of political cleavages, institutional structures, alliance structures (here, the openness and political position of the organized left), and prevailing strategies of social movements. By focusing on the effects of two factors, the configuration of power on the left and its presence or absence in government, they offer a fuller picture of citizen mobilization as it responds to political opportunity.

By thinking of movement participation as including less disruptive and confrontational protest, they examine the full range of expressions that activists employ to make claims. They remind the reader that the state can invite action by facilitating access, but it can also provoke action by producing unwanted policies and political threats, thereby raising the costs of inaction. State action affects not only the volume of participation but also its form and location. They show that when normalized for population size, Switzerland has by far the highest level of social mobilization, but it is largely concentrated in conventional political participation and membership in social movement organizations. In contrast, France offers the lowest volume of participation, including the smallest numbers of protest events and members of social movement organizations, but the most confrontational and violent action, which declines when the left is in power. The explanation is more comprehensive than Kitschelt's (1986), but also much more complicated and harder to translate simply to other cases. The work underscores the importance, and the difficulty, of developing a useable theory of political opportunity that can inform a variety of empirical investigations, many conducted by Kriesi's collaborators.

Writing about the rise of the so-called new social movements" in West Germany at the end of the twentieth century, Koopmans (1995) found that this new form of contentious politics can be attributed to the German political system. Various aspects of the system's nature and development, from the defeat of Nazism to elite use of repression to its federalist structure, led to the rise of strong, ideological, and at times violent movements in West Germany, particularly in comparison to other countries. In describing protest in West Germany, Koopmans explicitly rejects certain social movement theories which he sees as misguided and which only produce common misconceptions. Specifically, he criticizes the classical model (which relies on grievances and relative deprivation to explain protest) and resource mobilization theory, instead turning to a political approach. The political approach, he writes, says that "the development and characteristics of protest are shaped by the available political opportunities for mobilization" (Koopmans 1995:13).

In seeking a parsimonious explanation, Koopmans consciously sought to simplify his explanation, reducing some of the complexity involved in social movement analysis. Therefore, he concentrates "on one set of factors of particular relevance: the interaction between social movements and the political system" (1995:230). This perspective, he argues, best explains German social movement development in the latter half of the last century. Koopmans employs a modified form of the political process model, focusing specifically on the role of the political opportunity structure, imbued with something of a theory of motivation, which is also tied to the political process. To trace the translation of structure into agency, that is, the connection between broad political opportunities and activist agency, Koopmans introduces the concept of "concrete opportunities" (consisting of chances of success, reform/threat, repression, and facilitation) which have motivational consequences for the movement. Koopmans therefore uses an explicitly political approach to describe the social movement process as it developed during the final years of Cold War West Germany.

In their edited volume, *Policing Protest: The Control of Mass Demonstrations in Western Democracies*, della Porta, Reiter, and their contributors analyze the relationship between police and protestors in Western democracies; in effect, police represent a proximate element of the structure of political opportunities activists face. The protest policing style that emerges in a polity, they found, is influenced by the political system. In their introduction, Della Porta and Reiter describe their model for protest policing styles and argue that it is directly influenced by the political opportunity structure. They further describe the notion of a political opportunity structure as having a stable context with institutional features such as police organization, law codes, constitutional rights and a volatile context whereby the government and the movement (as well as other interested actors such as the media) are in constant interaction and struggle for power. In addition, both the stable and volatile opportunities and their effect on protest policing styles are mediated by what they refer to as police knowledge—"the police's perception of their role and of the external reality" (1998:22). It refers to the images they hold, both about their responsibilities and about the external challenges they face (1998:229). The level of control they use becomes an issue of police image—what do they perceive to be true (1998:24)? Police decisions regarding protest are therefore influenced by the political opportunity structure, both its institutional and volatile features, but also by police knowledge. Using this perspective regarding protest policing, most contributors in the book, as noted by Marx in the afterward, argue that "there has been a leavening of police response to protest, regardless of the country" (1998:254). In other words, there is a higher degree of tolerance on the part of the police. This trend, Della Porta and Reiter argue in the introduction, can be attributed to the political opportunity structure of each country as well as the intervening concept of police knowledge.

Giugni (2004) also uses political opportunity structure to explore the consequences of social movements, namely, the effect they have on policy. Whereas many other pieces on social movements focus on strategy and internal characteristics, Giugni argues that not only should strategies be taken into account, but also structures. However, in addition to the political opportunity structure, Giugni also looks to the role of public opinion. Therefore, he credits two factors, both of which are external to the movement, with affecting change in a political system: political opportunity structure and public opinion. With regard to the former, he concentrates on formal structures and the configuration power, but he gives particular emphasis to the role of political alliances (for instance, what role do parties on the left play?). With regard to public opinion, he looks at the effects of social movements on public opinion. Social movement activists, he argues, direct their action not just toward powerholders but also to the public and in this way, they affect public opinion. In turn, the government pays attention to public opinion, thus the role of public opinion in social movement outcomes is crucial, according to Giugni (2004:26).

Giugni's inclusion of public opinion in his model, and his use of polling data, follows well-established practices in political science. As Giugni claims, the role of public opinion is often studied in the United States but usually in the context of legislative change. Giugni (2004) argues for its inclusion in social movement studies as "the existing literature has largely neglected how the media covers, frames, and interprets social movements" (2004:27). Public opinion and political alliances (one element of a broader political opportunity structure) both become resources for the movement, confirming his hypothesis that "interactions among protest activities, political alliances, and public opinion, increase the likelihood that social movements bring about policy changes" (2004:220). It's important to note this interaction, as he finds that public opinion on its own does not hold much explanatory power. Rather, it is the *interaction* of public opinion, political alliances, and protest action (his so-called "joint-effect") that affects policy change. His study is very sociological in the sense that he utilizes political opportunity structure theories; however, it turns toward political science with its inclusion of public opinion as a movement resource and interacting factor.

Well-established senior scholars Doub McAdam, Sidney Tarrow, and Charles Tilly initiated a collaboration in an effort to build a theoretical framework based on the analyses of political processes that would transcend—or unite—the Global North and Global South. The authors argue that by the 1980s, most North American students of social movements had agreed on a model, in effect a new "classic social movement agenda" (McAdam, Tarrow, and Tilly 2001:16). Disagreements, if any, were on functional aspects, which component was more important at any given moment of the movement. The classic model involves mobilizing structures, framing processes, repertoires of contention, and opportunity and threat. The model is useful, they contend, for explaining the mobilization and demobilization of single-actor social movements in the west. However, it has a "narrow concentration," is static, and doesn't particularly explain for instance, contentious politics outside of democracies (McAdam, Tarrow, and Tilly 2001:18).

The authors then examine combinations and sequences of mechanisms (a delimited class of events, for example, resource depletion as an environmental mechanism) that lead to particular outcomes for contentious politics. In doing so, the authors use epistemological advancements in the area of social movements to draw conclusions about other forms of contention, including democratization, nationalism, and fundamentalism. For example, they contribute to the democratization literature by applying their political process framework, designed to explain Western social movements, to democratization. They find that "democratization occurs through the same kinds of mechanisms we found in social movements, cycles of contention, revolutions, and nationalism" (McAdam, Tarrow, and Tilly 2001:304). Their expanded research makes social movements just one form of contention in the political world. This piece appears to be in response to the rise in democratization and nationalism literature. If social movement scholars had come to some concrete and thoroughly tested conclusions about movement mobilization and sustainability, then what could these conclusions contribute to studies of other forms of contentious politics? To discover this, the authors classify social movements as just one form of contention, compare it to others, and find that similar mechanisms are operating across the board.

Whereas most of the political sociology work focuses on large-scale political formations, public opinion research addresses individual decisions about protest and politics.

Developed World: Public Opinion

Karl-Dieter Opp (1989) offers a social theory of political protest explicitly rooted in the moral philosophies of Adam Smith and David Hume, as well as others. It is a rational choice model of political protest based on variables such as preferences for public goods, constraints, and opportunities in predicting the conditions for protest. Simply put, individuals weigh the costs and benefits of protest participation and decide on an outcome that will maximize their own utility (Opp 1989:44). Opp distinguishes himself from other economics-based theories of collective action, notably Olson's (1966) "orthodox rational choice theory," that focus on the irrationality of protest. Instead, Opp argues that *group* protest might just be rational, given that the likelihood of success is higher than if an individual protested alone, in other words, assuming a certain engaged critical mass. This comprises what Opp calls the "collectivist conception of rationality" (Opp 1989:77).

This notion of protest success ties into Opp's discussion on the incentives to protest. Normative expectations, expected sanctions, norms of protest behavior, and feelings of efficacy are just some of the nonmaterial incentives Opp describes and that he argues other rational choice modelers don't consider. For instance, with regard to efficacy, does a person's belief that dissident groups helped or hindered a cause affect protest levels? In fact it does, particularly with regard to legal protest. These feelings of efficacy (or inefficacy) become incentives for protest. The incentives are weighed against costs (perceived sanctions if one acts) and lead a person to determine if their actions will be influential in the distribution of public goods. If so, this is an incentive to protest.

Opp addresses other political protest models, such as relative deprivation and resource mobilization theory. By the time of his writing, relative deprivation had been criticized ubiquitously and replaced by the resource mobilization paradigm (following Lipsky 1968; McCarthy and Zald 1973, 1977). He doesn't disregard either outright but rather argues that elements of these theories enter into his rational choice model. In this way, relative deprivation might actually be a rational choice variable if it refers to perceived costs and benefits. Similarly, he doesn't reject resource mobilization theory, claiming instead that the "general background theory of resource mobilization theory is the rational choice model" (Opp 1989:28). He argues that the basic variables in resource mobilization theory (opportunity and constraint) are similar to those in his own model. In the end, he finds that some of resource mobilization theory's assumptions are not "acceptable" to rational choice theories but that resource mobilization theory is not entirely incompatible with rational choice. Thus, Opp borrows heavily from economics (with cost–benefit analysis as the primary element of political protest) but also links his own model to current sociological explanations of social movements.

In *Citizen Politics*, Dalton (1988) explores public opinion and political behavior by studying four advanced, industrial democracies and finds a "new pattern of citizen political power" and a "new pattern of political thought and action" (Dalton 1988:9). Specifically, there have been recent changes in political participation (citizens are less likely to be passive), values and attitudes (advanced industrial societies are increasingly addressing post-materialist values more than economic ones), and partisan politics (increased citizen dealignment from political parties). This creates increased strain on the "traditional political order" as these democracies face increased citizen skepticism, volatility, social movements, and protest (Dalton 1988:10). This strain creates a democratic paradox: new issues mean that democracies have become more inclusive, but at the same time, people are increasingly critical of the government that is including them. The mobilization of increased numbers of demanding political actors makes it harder and harder for democracies to develop policies that satisfy their populations, in effect, inviting distrust (Meyer and Staggenborg 1996; Meyer and Tarrow 1998). In direct response to elite theorists who claim the downfall of democracy due to these disruptive elements, Dalton spins the "paradox" into a positive new trend. If anything, it is a step closer to Dahl's ideal notion of democracy—democracy beyond polyarchy. Dalton (1988:72) writes, "I favor a Jeffersonian view of the democratic process"; in his telling, active citizens make for a stronger democracy.

Dalton's "New Politics Perspective" accepts citizen dissatisfaction with the political system. Dalton explains that this perspective embraces first, the changing nature of citizen politics and second, a new style of representation. He argues that citizens have become more demanding, a result of better information and better skills (which can be contributed to positive economic transformations in the advanced industrial democracies). As to the second, we are witnessing an "explosion of citizen interest groups, social movements and other social groups in recent decades [and] these groups represent a new style of interest representation" (Dalton 1988:254). In essence, citizen distrust has led to an increase in political activism, particularly modes of participation that were previously unconventional (Meyer and Tarrow 1998). This is a rejection of Putnam's (2000) notion of the erosion of social capital and activism. It's not the level of activity that's changed, argues Dalton; rather it's the types of action employed. Protest politics is on the rise as it becomes more acceptable (Dalton 1988:72). It also becomes less disruptive (Meyer and Tarrow 1998).

Thus, Dalton criticizes theorists who proclaim a crisis of democracy due to too much citizen participation. Dalton embraces more of a pluralist approach to political participation and social movements. In this way, he uses an interest group framework to describe social movements; social movements are analytically flattened into a sort of interest group. Deeply rooted in political science, he nonetheless draws on social movement theory from sociology as well. Social movements and protest become another political resource, "like voting, campaign activity, or communal activity" (Dalton 1988:66). His description of social movements provides the reader with an example of how citizens have changed the way we do politics. Previously unconventional modes of participation are on the rise and therefore it might be that social movements are actually becoming conventional forms of political participation. His treatment of social movements is situated in an analytic context of political organizations and pluralist politics; protest is one form of activity employed by some number of competing groups.

The authors in Dalton and Kuechler's (1990) *Challenging the Political Order* look specifically at these "new social movements." These movements are based in "post-materialist" thought (see Inglehart 1977) and furthered by new forms of political activism. The combination of new political interests, beyond conventional economic issues, and new styles of participation, including increased activism and unconventional politics, resulted in the emergence of new social movements. These new movements challenge the traditional political order. For instance, party politics are affected as advanced, industrial democracies experience a rise in "movement parties" which reflect these new criticisms of the prevailing order (Dalton and Kuechler 1990; also see Schwartz 2005).

In this volume, Dalton is more critical of resource mobilization theory, arguing that the theory omits the role of ideology in explaining social movements. Dalton and Kuechler (1990:282) conclude that new social movements create an ideological bond between members, uniting them in a "radical idealistic critique of prevailing norms and values on the individual." Focusing particularly on individuals rather than groups, they contend that resource mobilization theory fails to account for the power of ideology. The 1980s experienced an increase in post-materialist values as the Cold War came to an end and this new ideology unites citizens and creates a new type of social movement, one that "represents a qualitative change in political goals and the pattern of interest representation" (Dalton and Kuechler 1990:10). In this sense, it's an expose of social movements that relies heavily on political science analysis. Social movements, as they define them, are ideologically driven and they behave like interest groups in the way that they can permanently alter the political system (especially in the political party arena), and built relatively permanent places for themselves in mainstream politics.

The issues confronted and even the methods employed are very different in looking at what is termed social movements in nondemocratic or democratizing societies. Analysts of movements in the developed world, particularly the new (non–class-based) social movements, treat economic growth and modernization mostly as enablers of "post-materialist" thinking and purposive social action. In the developing world, in contrast, economic inequality sets the terrain of the political struggle.

Developing World: Repression

The empirical material scholars address understandably affects the theoretical literature they engage. Well-established theoretical literatures set the boundaries of much inquiry on certain topics. Interestingly, most of the literature that deals with social movements and state repression doesn't engage the social movement literature so much as theories developed in studies of democratization, such that the topic is defined less by analysis of process than by a focus on a particular desired outcome. The democratization literature tends to focus on top-down, elite-initiated transitions and authors often issue warnings about too much citizen mobilization during a transition from authoritarian rule. Democratic transitions are particularly vulnerable to the threats posed by violent action. Most analysts see moderation, or the rejection of radical mass mobilization, as the preferable choice during the untenable transition process; these authors promote temperate progress: negotiations, pacts, and peace agreements. Protest, political violence, and radical mobilization are framed as potential hindrances and obstacles to successful democratization. Disruption is a threat rather than a subject of inquiry.

However, in a critical piece on democratization, Dankwart Rustow (1970) disagrees. For Rustow, struggle is a necessary part of the democratic transition: "What infant democracy requires is not a lukewarm struggle but a hot family feud" (1970:355). In a tribute to Rustow, Nancy Bermeo (1999:136) agrees:

> Democracy can be created despite so-called 'extremist' demands and despite high levels of mobilization in civil society. In many cases, a 'hot family feud' may, indeed, provide the proper environment for the forging of a new democracy.

Pointing to proponents of the "moderation argument," Bermeo criticizes their "fear of the masses" and their propagation that the threat from below must be moderated. While acknowledging that cases do exist in which violence disrupted the transition process, "these negative cases do not in themselves make an argument for moderation" (Bermeo 1999:127). In contrast, she cites the cases of Spain, Portugal, Peru, and South Korea, where instances of political violence did not mean a derailing of the transition to democracy. Bermeo (1999:131) explains, "Moderation is not a prerequisite for the construction of democracy; the parameters of tolerable mobilization are broader than we originally anticipated. In many cases, democratization seems to have proceeded alongside weighty and even bloody popular challenges."

Bermeo contends that the myopic focus on moderation is based in the well-regarded assumption that if the ruling regime *perceives* the costs of tolerance to be higher than the costs of suppression, they will continue to suppress the people and halt the democracy process, but she suggests shifting the focus to the perception of threat. She argues that proponents of the moderation argument have mistakenly assumed that "the costs of toleration are a simple function of the presence or absence of extremism" (1999:132). Arguing that it is essential to unpack the process of assessing costs, Bermeo contends that it is not the *presence* of extremist activity per se, but rather the *elite calculation* of the potential effects of the violence that matters. For instance, if pivotal elites predict that the extremists will not win in the new democratic setting, they are likely to allow the transition to progress forward despite continued extremist activity. They might even welcome democratic elections as a tool to legitimate their claims to government power. In this sense, "neither the presence or the scope of extremist activities is as important an element in elite calculations as their estimates of what the effects of extremism will be" (1999:132). Radical popular mobilization, according to Bermeo, *might* harm the potential for a successful transition. However, it is not in and of itself a detrimental factor. Bermeo then writes of social movements from a democratization prospective; she takes a "response" approach (rather than directly drawing on social movement literature)— responding to the democratic transition literature and the persistent calls for moderation.

Elisabeth Jean Wood (2000) also formulates a democratization argument based on elite perception of mass mobilization. Hers is a class-based argument that uses El Salvador and South Africa as examples of successful democracy movements forged from below by the insurgency of poor people. (She does not refer to scholars who have looked at activism of the poor in democratic settings.) The insurgency, she argues, reshapes economic interests and opportunities and forces economic elites (and eventually regime elites) to share power and/or wealth (Wood 2000). She relies heavily on economic theories of elite calculation to drive her argument, and augments these theories with her analysis of the democratization literature and ethnographic studies of two insurgencies in different societies. In this sense, the tools she uses come from economics, anthropology, and political science.

Like Bermeo, Wood discusses democratization in terms of the effect of extremist activity on elite perception (although it should be noted that Bermeo primarily discusses regime elites whereas Wood primarily refers to economic elites). In the discussion of El Salvador, Wood writes that the civil war transformed the political economy of the state, thereby reshaping the interests of the economic elites. Structural transformations, such as a decline in economic production, a decline in export agriculture, and capital flight, were largely the result of a sustained unrest (primarily by the guerilla group Farabundo Marti National Liberation Front (FMLN)). These transformations then caused economic elites to rethink their perception of the repressive state. Neo-liberal economic policies and a market economy, rather than a coercive state, became better choices for disciplining the labor force. In addition, she writes, the "war-induced transformation of the economy shifted the balance of power within economic elites toward those who came to favor compromise over recalcitrance" (2000:52). In the face of sustained war and a subsequent shifting political economy, the better choice for economic elites was a peace agreement and a relenting of the repressive state. The rise of the compromise-oriented National Republican Alliance (ARENA) party, the primary articulator of elite interests, helped to advance the democratization peace process in El Salvador.

Similar processes occurred in South Africa; Wood again links mass mobilization to modified elite interests. Domestically, there were rising strikes, township unrest, and increased militancy of the unions. This led to international sanctions against South Africa and inevitably their economy felt the pressure. A shift in capital, decreasing elite confidence and investment, an increase in capital intensiveness, and international sanctions shifted the economy to one in which the economic logic of apartheid no longer held up against neo-liberal theories of a free market economy. The economic advantages that business elites enjoyed under apartheid began to erode. Business elites began negotiating with Nelson Mandela's African National Congress (ANC) party; both sought political change albeit for different reasons. Whereas the ANC sought a settlement to advance the interests of its constituency, business elites sought to limit their losses. Wood quotes one business elite's perception of the sustained mobilization of township blacks: "Because [workers] did not have a way to express political freedom, they used the labor situation, the shop floor, to do that. And that was an important pressure point on business" (Quoted in Wood 2000:172). In both El Salvador and South Africa, "after insurgency transformed elite economic interests away from coercive institutions, the economic interdependence of the principal antagonists provided the structural underpinnings for a resolution of the conflict based on a transition to both liberal capitalism and political economy" (Wood 2000:204). Wood, like Bermeo, views mass mobilization as a power force in a democratic transition not because of its sheer force, but because of its ability to transform elite perception. Elites undertake democratic reforms in response to social movements because they begin to think it is in *their own* best interest to do so. Disruptive action affects their calculations about their interests.

But neither Bermeo nor Wood reference social movement literature directly. Their writing draws primarily on democratization literature from political science. In contrast, Vincent Boudreau (2004) bridges the social movement and transition to democracy literature in his study of Burma, Indonesia, and the Philippines. He compares the repressive strategies of these states and the subsequent modes of collective action and resistance that arose in response to these strategies. Whereas resistance movement literature has often treated state repression as a one-dimensional independent variable, Boudreau unpacks repression and explores the different options available to elites as well as the strategies they choose to effect repression. The repressive strategies elites employ don't just stoke or dampen mass mobilization, they sculpt it. Boudreau (2004:251) writes, "Democracy movements rise when the states established repressive strategy, for some reason can no longer contain social challengers." In the Philippines, Marcos' strategies simply became ineffective. In Indonesia, *keterbukaan* (their own form of *glasnost*) in the 1980s relaxed restrictions on activists and allowed for more institutionalized resistance activity. The military leaders in Burma never found themselves in a position where the social challengers couldn't be contained and repression not only continued, but it intensified.

Boudreau writes in critical response to the democratization literature, which tends to focus on the macrostructural aspects of a transition. The top-down, elite and government initiated perspective of most transition literature is not surprising given that it is written almost entirely by political scientists. The literature tends to reduce the transition to a process involving government hard-liners and soft-liners involved in a series of moderate negotiations and pacts. Nongovernment opposition groups sometimes enter the democratization literature as actors or players but if they do, they are often treated as tangential groups operating on the outskirts of the true transition process and dealings. Boudreau instead focuses on interactions: "The key to understanding contention in such settings rests in the logic of its interactions, rather than in identifying events that touch off collective action" (2004:253). In this way, he draws from the social movements literature, particularly on McAdam, Tarrow, and Tilly (2001), applying their focus on mechanisms to Southeast Asian democracy movements:

> The political process model, with its careful attention to the conditions that trigger and shape mobilization provides important signposts for our analysis, but we must still rethink how this processes [sic] unfolds in the different contexts of the global South . . .The usefulness of these Southeast Asian case is not, therefore, in their utter uniqueness, but rather that state repression and social resistance in Southeast Asia interacted to produce particularly salient patterns that may have broader theory building and comparative utility" (Boudreau 2004:18–19).

Boudreau's focus is on precisely these interactions between resistance and repression. He argues the patterned interaction creates particular modes of contention that act in relationship to modes of coercion.

Like Bermeo and Wood, Boudreau argues that mobilizing groups can and do play a role in promoting a transition to a liberal society. For instance, where the democratization literature tends to start with the liberalization of the regime stage, both Wood and Boudreau argue that political mobilization often starts *before* liberalization and can even *shape* subsequent liberal reforms undertaken by the state. Both authors also suggest the constructivist element of insurgency and counterinsurgency as each responds to the other, thereby moving the transition forward (or deeper into repression as in the case of Burma). Wood (2000:51) writes, "the civil war [in El Salvador] was thus the product of varying processes of insurgency and counterinsurgency, processes whose unintended as well as intended consequences eventually laid the foundations for political compromise." Similarly, Boudreau (2004:3) comments that his study analyzes "how particular modes of state attack encourage specific patterns of political contention." By "patterns of political contention," Boudreau is referring to "interactions between state repression and movement response" (p. 4). Bermeo, Wood, and Boudreau all refer to this notion of interaction, a cycle whereby groups mobilize, the government responds, and elite perception shifts. Transformations occur as insurgency erupts and a response to that insurgency develops.

Political scientists have also engaged a large literature on revolutions, sometimes employing terms and concepts from social movement theory.

Developing World: Revolution and Rebellion

Tracing the evolution of theories of revolution over 100 years, Jack Goldstone (2003) describes three major theoretical approaches in the introduction to his edited volume. Goldstone outlines problems inherent in the first two generations of theory; the first generation of theory emerged in the 1920s and 1930s and the second, in the 1960s and 1970s. Both focused on a very small number of cases: the cases of collective action that ended in successful and substantial regime change. Acknowledging deficiencies in the work, Goldstone also identifies some important epistemological contributions of these early works. The first two generations of revolutionary theory weren't wrong so much as they were limited in scope yet overgeneralized. Still, epistemologically, they provided key pieces of information as to why groups might revolt (e.g., resources and opportunities), but they failed to take us further; "all the general theory approaches had certain problems in explaining where and how revolutions occurred" (Goldstone 2003:6). He seems to favor a third set of theories that emerged in the beginning of the twenty-first century, structural approaches that consider the disparate nature of state structures across cases.

Structural theories show that revolutions "begin from some combination of state weakness, conflicts between states and elites, and popular uprisings" (Goldstone 2003:6). Where previous theories of revolutions tended to focus on the opposition, structural theories bring in the role of the state. The opposition is still viewed as a key component of revolution, but it is recognized that a state with weakened structural capabilities and a predilection for conflict between the state and the elites will be prone to revolution. When this combines with pervasive popular uprisings, revolution becomes more likely. When the grievances of peasants or urban dwellers meet with "conducive structural conditions," such as landlord vulnerability or weakly policed cities, there is the possibility of effective revolutionary action (2003:10–11). Further, when conflict between the state and powerful elites coincides and connects with the structural conditions and popular uprisings, revolution becomes even more likely.

In describing the role of popular uprisings, Goldstone hints at some of the contributions and findings of the previous generations of theories. Again, this appears to indicate that theories of revolution have indeed progressed in their explanatory power, building off one another. First, in speaking of peasant revolts, Goldstone emphasizes the importance of solidarity and organization in translating grievances to action, a direct reference to Tilly's version of resource mobilization theory. Second, in looking at urban uprisings, Goldstone (2003:11) describes the role of grievances and writes, "Two grievances stand out as the chief causes of revolutionary urban tumults: the cost of food and the availability of employment." Here he directly addresses the relative deprivation or psychological theories (also part of the second generation of theories) that emerged in the 1960s and 1970s. Therefore, the current structural theories of revolutions build on and improve earlier theories. It should be noted that Goldstone also describes an emerging fourth generation of scholarship on revolutions, process theories that explore the agency and path dependency characteristics of a revolution.

In general, Goldstone builds on Huntington (1968), accepting and adopting his focus on the role of political institutions, and particularly their decay, in the makings of a revolution. Goldstone writes, "A marked imbalance between the demands of a changing population on the economy and the government, and the ability of the government to respond creates a situation of declining political stability. Whenever such imbalances become widespread, so too does the risk of revolutions" (Goldstone 2003:18). In other words, when the capability of the political system is outweighed by the political demands and challenges of the populace, political decay (and revolution) is likely to occur.

For the last two decades, political scientists studying revolutions have devoted a great deal of attention to the revolutions of 1989 in Eastern Europe. They are a heterogeneous group of revolutions, as Vladimir Tismaneanu (1999) argues in his edited volume on this year of revolutions. However, they are inextricably linked together by their result: the displacement and denigration of the state communist systems of totalitarian control. The first part of this edited text focuses on causes of the revolutions, but interestingly, despite political scientist contributions to other chapters of the book, none of them appear in this particular section. Given that a revolution at its most fundamental level is defined by a transformation of the *political* order, this omission speaks to our argument regarding political science's contribution, or lack thereof, to the study of social movements.

In his chapter on the causes of the revolutions, Daniel Chirot attempts to turn to established theories of revolution but finds that "most widely accepted sociological models of revolution are of limited help in explaining what happened" (Chirot 1999:35). Here is precisely where political science models of social movements could have proven invaluable. Instead, Chirot utilizes an idiosyncratic model; in particular he looks to the moral and political climate of the time to explain the events of 1989. What he finds is that while economic reasons played a role in all of the revolutions—he points particularly to the inefficiencies of the socialist system—they are not the sole contributors. Rather, he describes the way in which the system had fundamentally lost legitimacy. The people living under the communist regimes had simply lost confidence and "utter moral rot" ensued (Chirot 1999:38).

Similarly, in his piece on the East European revolutions of 1989, Jeff Goodwin (2003) lays out certain structures and practices (personalist dictators, racially exclusive regimes) that made the communist regimes "unreformable" and thus made revolution more likely, especially when combined with economic stagnation, subsequent economic liberalization, and repression. However, Romania is his exception case in that it doesn't fit any of the general theories Goodwin presents regarding other "revolutions" in East Europe (Poland, Hungary, USSR, Czechoslovakia, East Germany). Perhaps this is why Romania had the most violent and bloody revolution of 1989.

Martyn Rady (1992) offers a deeper look at Romanian Christmas Revolution. He explores whether Romania's history explains the unfolding of political events at the end of the twentieth century. He describes a culture of falsehood, illusion, and violence that led the Romanian people to embrace fascism in the interwar years. Later, the rise of communism in Romania is attributed not to the Romanian culture, but to the Soviet domination in Romanian politics after World War II. But how does a country move from a repressive, totalitarian state to a bloody revolution, especially in light of the relatively peaceful transitions of their neighbors? On this, Rady is unclear. He writes of increasing riots and "disorganized popular protests" in the late 1980s, the fame of a Hungarian pastor (Laszlo Toekes) who preaches for justice and somehow survives the watchful eyes of Ceausescu's *securitate*, and a bloody crackdown on protestors in the city of Timisoara just a week before the eventual revolution. Timisoara, Rady writes, pushed the population into further opposition and stories leaked on foreign television channels only fueled the flames. Full demonstrations against the government began mid-December, but it's unclear how. For a country with a weak civil society, that is, a dramatically underdeveloped set of organizations, interpersonal networks, and autonomous connections among individuals, a surge in protest seems unlikely and even impossible. Indeed, Ceausescu's totalitarian and sultanistic regime was committed to undermine the emergence of such civil society based on the belief that its absence would secure the regime's survival.

Indeed, the Romanian revolution appears to defy everything we know about social movements. Certainly grievances were present and the events in Poland, Hungary, East Germany, and Czechoslovakia in the months just before provided useful intelligence and inspiration. The Soviet Union was not responding to political unrest, which incipient activists had to regard as a positive cue. But to whom did this political opening cue a revolution? In other words, what mobilized the protestors and eventual revolutionaries? Rady (1992:204) writes that in the days leading up to the revolution, "in university halls of residence and in a number of work places, committees were formed to coordinate the swelling movement of protest." However, the manner in which ubiquitous grievances were translated into action remains a mystery. Organization of the opposition might be linked in some way to the fact that some elites ("old guard" members of the communist party, parts of the army and *securitate*) were coordinating a successor government even before Ceausescu's execution or to the fact that many members of the *securitate* were switching to the opposition in the final days of the Ceausescu regime. As Tarrow (1998) argues, the presence of divided elites and influential allies can certainly make for ripe political opportunities. However, the dearth of official documentation of the events of December 21–25, 1989 makes it difficult to know. Therefore, Rady's political analysis of the Romanian revolution set in a historical context tells us *why* the movement occurred, but fails to tell us *how*.

The studies in comparative politics point to the importance of the international system, including both military and economic relationships above the state, as providing opportunities and constraints for domestic social movements (see Gourevitch 1978). The literature in international relations explores some of these relationships. It is clear that social movements within a state—and the authorities they challenge—cannot operate with a free hand, but are constrained and enabled by extranational forces.

INTERNATIONAL RELATIONS

Without explicit reference to social movement theory, Theda Skocpol's (1979) classic work on revolutions argued that the prospects for success of a revolutionary effort were largely dependent upon the international context that authorities within the state faced. External challenges could weaken their capacity to deal with dissent, making the state vulnerable. The recognition of the connection between international and domestic politics is evident throughout the literature on international relations but systematic research on how social movements are affected by international politics, or how they can affect international relations, are underdeveloped. The literature addresses three sets of questions: first, as noted in the preceding text, the role the international context plays in setting the environment for social movements (e.g., Gourevitch 1978; Imig and Tarrow 2001; Meyer 2004a); second, the impact of social movements on international relations by their effect on states' foreign and security policies; and third, the changing international context for cooperation about social movement actors. We first address the question of the role of international context and setting the environment for social movements and then we focus particularly on the second and third set of questions.

The question of how the international context, particularly supranational politics, affects social movements is a newer one, and Doug Imig and Sidney Tarrow (2001) tackle it in an edited volume that explores the effects of European integration on contentious politics in and across the states of the European Union. They were interested in "contentious politics *within* Europe, on the part of citizens who might support an integrated Europe, oppose it, or have no opinion about its desirability, but whose interests and values led them to focus on Europe as the source of their grievances and to make claims intended to affect its policies or its institutions" (Imig and Tarrow 2001:233). What they found was that most Europeans "continue to protest about domestic issues and against domestic targets" (2001:34). They refer to this as the continuance of routine domestic protests, "familiar from the literature on national social movements and has little or no relation to European policy-making" (2001:18).

At the same time, they find changes in European-focused contention in the sense that transnational contention is an increasing phenomenon. European policy-making can elicit protest and when it does, it most often comes in domesticated forms, particularly when "domestic groups target national or subnational agents in response to their claims against the European Union" (Imig and Tarrow 2001:18). However, "the largest proportion of contentious political responses to the policies of the European Union takes domestic rather than transnational form" (p. 47). This means that states will continue to play a key role in the sense that protest action still overwhelmingly occurs within the domestic arena and also in the sense that even protests against EU policies and agents take place against national institutions and on domestic soil. Protestors might increasingly voice opinions regarding the EU, but they will ask their national governments to act as their representative, thereby continuing to give their state a leading role.

The book is framed around larger political science (and particularly international relations) theories of European integration. Eschewing the common theories, Imig and Tarrow (2001:4) claim that their theory to be "neither a neofunctionalist, a neorealist, nor a constructivist perspective but an *interactionist* one" which focuses on the "long-term outcome[s] of conflict and cooperation between and among nonstate and public actors" (p. 4). Other models of European integration, they argue, limit "attention to elite transactions within policy networks and leave no space for the examination of the possible role of nonelites in the broader European system" (p. 15). Instead, theirs focuses on citizen activism and their role in and response to European integration. What they find is that traditional social movement theories (which often focus on interaction between protestors and the political environment) go far in explaining European-centered protest, most notably because the protest remains so thoroughly domesticated.

We now turn to the question of the impact of social movements on states' foreign and security policies. Just as social movements affect domestic policy making, social movements can also affect state policy decisions when they regard the international arena. Jeffrey Knopf (1998) asks whether or not citizen mobilization is an important contributor to state decision making in foreign policy. To answer the question, he looks at peace movements and tests their impact on U.S. decisions to pursue arms control negotiations with the USSR. What he finds is that mobilization indeed affected decisions to engage in these talks.

His theoretical approach is traditional in the sense that he draws on both classic international relations theories (domestic structure approach, liberalism) and classic domestic policymaking models (mass electoral pressure, shifting elite coalitions). However, his approach is unconventional in the sense that he combines the two. He sees the utility in international relations theories but finds they fall short or aren't appropriate for the question at hand; thus, he turns to more general theories of American politics. In this way, he uses the domestic structure approach to address the foreign policy question at hand, but expands it and develops his own framework that also includes traditional models of domestic policymaking. He notes that domestic structure studies are typically interested in policy networks, particularly ones that link state and society. His model expands on this and fills in some gaps by identifying the mechanisms that are driving the policy networks. The three influence mechanisms he identifies and examines (electoral pathway, shifting elite coalitions, and bureaucratic use of movement ideas) are commonly well-established and analyzed processes in the study of American politics.

For instance, in studying the nuclear freeze movement's impact on President Reagan's decision to engage in a new set of talks with the Soviets, Knopf finds that "an overall U.S. preference for cooperation had definitely emerged by 1984, in large part due to domestic activism" (Knopf 2000; see also Meyer 1990). The freeze movement activated two of the three influence mechanisms. First, citizen activism altered the electoral incentives of government officials. Second, there was a shift in the elite coalition patterns. The first mechanism was activated when public mobilization successfully interacted with broader public opinion. While the government continued to use rhetoric and dismiss arms control, surveys continued to show public support for a freeze. The disjunction between the two opened up the electoral pathway and "created the promise of significant benefits to those politicians who could first get themselves identified with the freeze" (Knopf 2000:214). The second mechanism was activated when many members of Congress "became interested in using the legislative process to pull US policy back to a more centrist position on the arms buildup versus arms restraint spectrum" (p. 215). The freeze movement had landed at Congress' doorstep and many legislators became interested in associating with it. Therefore, as Knopf argues, both mechanisms had taken place within congressional debate and both ultimately made activism a source of state preference in foreign policy. The link is indirect; the freeze movement affected policy to be sure, but did so by activating traditional influence mechanisms.

Perhaps what is most interesting to note about Knopf's research is his virtual neglect of social movement literature and theories for his research. He argues that mobilization on behalf of arms control is best viewed as a social movement, but that social movement theories are not able to describe the process as it occurs in his case:

> Social movement research has not focused on how such movements gain influence. Instead social movement theory seeks mostly to explain the rise and nature of movements, rather than their impact on policy. The few studies that do focus on political impact, moreover, generally define the question as the determinants of movement success or failure. That is inappropriate in this case. Failure to obtain its own stated objectives need not mean that a movement has failed to exert any influence on state preferences. In the case studies, the important question is whether there is change from an existing policy baseline (in particular, one that initially does not favor arms talks).

We might see this rejection as a flaw in Knopf's reading across subfields in political science, but it is more productive, we think, to see this neglect as a function of subdisciplinary boundaries in political science that have proved to be obstacles in developing a comprehensive approach to social movements. If Knopf, working within the field of international relations, had consulted literature from American politics research to address his research question, his findings could also be bolstered by existing American social movement literature. Lowi (1971) and Piven and Cloward (1977) appear direct relevant to Knopf's argument. Instead, he ignores a social movement framework and turns straight to traditional international relations and American institutions theories.

Keck and Sikkink (1998) are concerned with the patterns of action and influence of dissidents operating cross-nationally. They study the interaction of nonstate actors in an increasingly globalized world. In particular, they analyze transnational advocacy networks (TANs), the networks of nonstate actors "distinguishable largely by the centrality of principled ideas or values in motivating their formation" and who act to "multiply the channels of access to the international system" (Keck and Sikkink 1998:1). In addition to policy change, they seek value change and do so by engaging in consistent information exchange with each other.

Keck and Sikkink ask four main questions: What is a TAN? Why and how have they emerged? How do TANs work? Under what conditions do they have influence? What they find is that one reason TANs emerge is that the domestic channels of participation are blocked or hindered and thus "the international arena may be the only means that domestic activists have to gain attention to their issues" (Keck and Sikkink 1998:12). They label this the "boomerang pattern" whereby "international contacts can amplify the demands of domestic groups, pry open space for new issues, and then echo back theses demands into the domestic arena" (p. 13). To do so, TANs rely on a number of tactics (such as the use of symbols, leverage, information dissemination, holding governments accountable) to carry and frame ideas. The TANs then attempt to influence domestic politics by pressuring governments and enforcing international norms (p. 199). For example, Keck and Sikkink describe the impact of TANs on the issue of violence against women. When the issue of women's rights was left off the agenda of the 1993 World Conference on Human Rights, groups mobilized and began to apply the human rights methodology (a method that says that change can be advanced by reporting facts and holding groups accountable) to the women's rights cause. In doing so, the network successfully utilized two tactics: information politics and accountability politics. Information was not only disseminated effectively, it successfully held particular groups and governments accountable through the use of careful documentation and powerful stories of bodily harm. At the UN Conference on Women in Beijing just two years later, women's rights was a centerpiece and one of four issues given top prominence. Keck and Sikkink argue that nonstate actors, and TANs in particular, have increased influence in this new global order as norms are changing, new procedures and protections are being implemented, and national politics are being pressured to place international issues onto their national agendas.

Just as Knopf rejects the divide between international relations and American politics, Keck and Sikkink bridge the divide between international relations and comparative politics. With regard to international relations theory they use a "neo-medieval" (a form of constructivism) approach, rejecting neo-liberalism and neo-realism as explanations for TAN emergence and influence. From comparative politics, they draw upon classic social movement theories, borrowing from sociology in their discussion of framing and identity and interests. They refer to their approach as a "network theory," built heavily on constructivist models of international relations: "Network theory can thus provide a model for transnational change . . . [in] which the preferences and identities of actors engaged in transnational society are sometimes mutually transformed through their interactions with each other" (Keck and Sikkink 1998:214). Finally, they also use domestic policy studies models, particularly those from American political science. In this regard, they draw from traditional interest group models, albeit rejecting what they call the reductionist theories of both elite and pluralist theories. They put an interactive spin on interest group theory and explore how interaction within networks leads to interest shaping.

Thomas (2001) also analyzes international norms and their effects. He studies human rights norms, as developed by the Helskinki Accords of 1975, during the Cold War and argues that the act's "formal commitment to respect human rights contributed significantly to the demise of Communism and the end of the Cold War" (Thomas 2001:4). A number of social movements (particularly the mobilized dissident groups in Eastern Europe) emerged following Helsinki and Thomas argues that their impact needs to be given as much, if not more, credit for the fall of communism than traditional theories of a collapsed "Old Guard."

Thomas argues that prior to Helsinki, protecting human rights was not a norm in East-West relations. In the early 1970s, both Nixon and Brezhnev deliberately ignored the issue and it wasn't until the European Community began publicly pushing for human rights, linking it to its own internal identity, that the issue was put on the international agenda. After more than two years of negotiation, the Helsinki final act emerged with 35 states agreeing to respect human rights. The immediate reaction in Eastern Europe was one of increased dissident activity. Initially Eastern European governments were successful in framing the Accords as legitimating the current state of affairs; indeed, many conservative groups inside the United States criticized their government for signing onto it. Yet, dissident activity in Eastern Europe increased, asking for their own governments to live up to the language, and this almost quite activism began to discredit claims that the act essentially didn't change anything. Instead, word spread among dissident groups in Eastern Europe and "some began to see it not as a ratification of Communist rule but as an opportunity to challenge the repressive regimes" (p. 98). With increased activity, new international norms emerged and became the foundation for even more dissident mobilization. Where domestic channels were blocked, groups used the "boomerang pattern" as nonstate actors in the East used the Helsinki norms as an ideational frame with which to engage the attention of non-state and substate actors in the West" (p. 122). A Helsinki network arose and it, in conjunction with the new norms and the creation of the U.S. Helsinki watch group. Organized activism across borders pushed the issue of human rights, and kept the issue on the United States' foreign policy agenda. Thomas recognizes that external pressure and top-down liberalization contributed to the fall of communism, but he argues that citizen mobilization also played a crucial role in pressuring the governments to adhere to changing international norms regarding human rights.

Like both Knopf and Keck and Sikkink, Thomas rejects "realism" outright, focusing on bringing nonstate actors into the analysis. In contrast to Keck and Sikkink, however, Thomas argues that constructivism also falls short. Thomas handles this lack of theoretical explanation by utilizing both liberal and constructivist theories. He uses liberalism to explain some findings and constructivism to explain others, and at times combines the two. His contribution here is that both theories should perhaps be revised to include more specific assumptions regarding formal international norms. In this way, he explains social movements as a result of international norms, which can legitimate and thus encourage dissident mobilization. As word spread in Eastern Europe that the cost of opposition was low (in other words, communist tolerance was increasing), then more mobilization occurred. His piece is very clear as to how mobilization flourishes, it is less clear, however, as to how it first arises. More explicit use of social movement theory would allow his analysis to consider the origins of dissident organizations and networks.

Recently, scholars have begun to argue that transnational activism has increased, and indeed, become a common form of political contention. Increased economic and political integration, vastly improved communication networks, and a generally increased cosmopolitanism have made it both increasingly attractive and increasingly possible for activists to organize transnationally—although it is not clear whether this increase represents a change in kind or in degree of transnational activism (Rucht 2000; Tarrow 2005). Others have argued that intensifying corporate globalization has imposed a new set of grievances that can only be effectively challenged through transnational organization (e.g., Bandy and Smith 2004; Smith, Chatfield, and Pagnucco 1997). For the most part, however, political scientists have been more concerned with drawing from diverse theories of social movements to address the problem at hand, rather than to develop a more comprehensive framework for understanding movements themselves as a form of meaningful politics.

WOMEN AND POLITICS

Scholars of ethnic, minority, and gay politics have often borrowed social movement theories, often from sociology as well as political science, to explain their cases (eg., Garcia Bedolla 2005; Kim 2000; Rimmerman 2002), but they don't always speak back to social movement theory. The use and synthesis of social movement theory has probably been most extensive and most successful in the area of gender politics, often crossing all of the empirical subfields of political science. Indeed, crossing this transgression of subdisciplinary boundaries has probably contributed to the development of a more comprehensive approach to social movements. Still, initially writing about women's movements and politics developed apart from the major paradigms that sought to explain social movements more generally.

As example, Jo Freeman's (1975) comprehensive study of the second wave of the women's movement in the United States astutely considered changing demographics (particularly the increased movement of women into the workforce), cultural norms, and mainstream politics. Analyzing the development and processing of women's dissent, Freeman's empirical work most clearly resembles, and improves upon, a political process or political opportunity approach. Apparently unaware of this emerging perspective, she terms her framework "modified relative deprivation." As a result, although the book has become a classic because of its empirical treatment of the women's movement, it is rarely cited for its theoretical insights or development.

Similarly, Jane Jenson (1982) writes about the modern women's movement by studying three western European countries: Italy, France, and Great Britain. Her analysis recognizes the contributions of the social strain/social change theories of social movements whereby rapid social change creates societal stress which in turn leads to unusual forms of political expression, but her argument centers on the idea that social change theory does not, in and of itself, explain the women's movement very well. Rapid change might be the source of discontent, but it is the political context in which this discontent arises that will affect the trajectory of the movement.

She finds that broader social change was a source of the movement in all three countries, but that varied political contexts led to different outcomes in all three countries. She writes, "The configuration of the party system and the reactions of Left parties in each country as well as the kind of opposition to the demands of the women's movement, affected its forms of expression, organization, and viability" (Jenson 1982:343). In other words, in order to find success, the movement had to form a relationship with the Left and this interaction (particularly how the Left reacted) shaped the outcome of the movement to a large degree. The women's movement proved to be a daunting challenger to the Left as it "challenged their leadership of the 'progressive position'" (Jenson 1982:372). For instance, in Britain, the women's movement challenged the governing Left (the Labour Party), a party whose leaders argued that through their efforts in developing the welfare state they had basically taken care of women's issues. However, Jenson argues that the Labour party platform was actually full of contradictions. Thus, a new dialogue began between the women's movement and the Left and this led to many of the women being identified as active players and as "fragments" of the

Left (370). In other words, the Left's response to the women's movement led to the women themselves becoming part of the bargaining process. Jenson's piece emphasizes not so much the outcome of these political dialogues, but rather the process. At the same time, it is most clearly related to the political process perspectives then in development in sociology.

Joyce Gelb (1989) uses a similar comparative approach, studying how culture and institutions have shaped feminist movements in the United States, Great Britain, and Sweden. She studies the "context evolution" of the feminist movements and finds that movement development is "largely dependent on external factors such as political environment and available resources" (Gelb 1989:5). Policy in the different countries might be similar but the impact of the policy will depend on the political context. In her contrast of the United States and Great Britain, Gelb finds the former is greatly distrustful of centralized politics while the latter is highly centralized. The result is that the United States has a form of "interest group feminism" while Great Britain has more of an "ideological feminism." The British system of ideological feminism stems mostly from its closed, centralized system that does not favor lobbying and interest group politics; the result is that in Great Britain there is "a reluctance to work with groups espousing different viewpoints" (p. 4). Gelb then concludes by arguing that "the character of feminism has been shaped by the character of the state" (p. 179). The strong focus on the role of the state, whether centralized as in Great Britain or decentralized as in the United States, or a state that co-opts women's concerns into public policy as in Sweden, is again strikingly similar to political process approaches, albeit without the nomenclature of the theory.

Jane Mansbridge (1986) conducted a similarly process-oriented case study of the failure of the Equal Rights Amendment (ERA) in America. The ERA passed both houses of Congress in 1972 but by 1982 it had fallen short of the required three-quarters of state legislatures. Mansbridge contends that opponents of the amendment had a good understanding of the constraints and opportunities of the American constitution and the politics of the time. Taking advantage of their need to stop rather than promote change, they devised and implemented a strategy based on exaggerating the likely effects of the ERA, shifting the discourse from a principle of equality to specific hot-button issues, including drafting women, abortion, homosexuality, and a chimerical same-sex bathroom. Advocates of the ERA were complicit in exaggerating the effects of the ERA, as they felt compelled to heighten the stakes of their efforts in order to mobilize support. Initially, support for the ERA was virtually ubiquitous as most citizens supported the basic tenets of equal rights. However, Mansbridge argues that ERA proponents began accreting new claims to the ERA, sometimes endorsing radical claims. The pro-ERA coalition was loosely managed, and a wide range of actors supported an ERA that matched each one's personal ideology. At the same time, a conservative movement that joined political and social conservatives emerged and used the campaign against ERA to build its own base of support. Opponents were more tightly organized than the larger pro-ERA movement. The battle over ERA in state legislatures became a proxy fight for changing American values, and ERA supporters were unable to generate the supermajorities necessary for ratification.

Where Gelb (1989) analyzes political opportunity structure and finds that structural limits in all three countries affect the feminist movement, Mansbridge focuses more on the ways in which group tactics are influenced by understanding political context. Ultimately, Mansbridge comes to make a strategic organizational argument, offering her analysis as a lesson for the women's movement.

Anne Costain (1992) considers the failure of the ERA in a longitudinal study explicitly modeled after McAdam's (1982) treatment of the civil rights movement, although she is more directly concerned with the policy process than her colleague in sociology. Costain's self-consciously adapts and defends a political process model, then, she argues, little known outside of Sociology. She (Costain 1992: xvi) writes, "To analyze the women's movement this way means incorporating political process theory from sociology into political science . . . it is still not well known in the political science discipline as a whole." Costain imported both conceptual and methodological (political process; events data analysis) tools from another discipline because "in the case of the women's movement, the relationships among Congress as an institution, the social movement, and public opinion cannot be examined within the framework of rigid political models" (p. 134). Using these tools, she writes about the movement's trajectory, identifying openings in the political structure that encouraged, supported, and ultimately swallowed a women's movement.

Lee Ann Banaszak (1996) considers both tactical choices and opportunities in her comparative study of women's suffrage movements in the United States and Switzerland, separated by more than 50 years (Swiss women got the vote in 1971). Specifically, she seeks to explain why the two movements had such different trajectories with the Swiss lagging far behind in granting women the right to vote. Banaszak argues that tactics matter and American and Swiss activists often chose the same tactics but employed them differently. Tactical choices reflected the state of values, beliefs, and culture in each country at the time of the movement's challenge. These collective beliefs and values ("framing") in turn affected perception within the movement, effectively acting as a lens that filtered information to the movement about political strategies available (Banazak 1996:33). She writes, "I contend that beliefs and values may aid a movement, as they did in the case of the U.S. suffrage movement, by predisposing it to take advantage of opportunities. On the other hand, these same factors may explain why a movement forgoes existing opportunities as in Switzerland" (p. 27).

Banaszak is also cognizant of the role of opportunities in movement development. In fact, she uses resource mobilization theory and political opportunity theory to begin her argument. However, it is the collective beliefs and values theory that provides the most explanatory power in her study. Resources are indeed important, as are political opportunity structures, she argues. Yet as theories they don't take us far enough (the term "resources" is vague, she argues, and political opportunities don't offer analytical leverage on strategic decisions without explicit consideration of activists' perception's of opportunities). She turns to a theory of collective beliefs and values to explain the disparate paths of the women's suffrage movement in the United States and Switzerland, focusing on the different beliefs, values, and tactics in each country. In emphasizing these cultural dynamics, she underscores the role that activist perception plays in shaping a movement. Banaszak (1996:217) writes, "Swiss activists' perceptions of available tactics were frequently biased, incomplete or inaccurate, and their values also caused them to reject strategies that might have been effective." What she finds in the United States is an opposite effect. She therefore argues that all three frameworks (resource mobilization, political opportunity structure, and collective beliefs and values ("framing") contributed to the differences between the movements, but that the latter has the most explanatory power.

Karen Beckwith (1996) focuses on a single-issue women's group at the grassroots level, the Lancashire Women against Pit Closures, to portray the importance of context in women's collective action. Women, mostly married to miners, formed the group in 1992, in response to the British government's announced intention to close the majority of Britain's deep coal mines. In studying this group, Beckwith looks first at women's movement location (how much of a role does gender play in setting or bounding the resources, opportunities, and claims of this movement?) and second, at articulation of movement standing (do the women articulate their presence and are they accepted as legitimate stakeholders by others?). She finds is that the perception of standing, a concept of legitimacy borrowed from public law, affects movement success. The Lancashire WPAC group created its own standing, first, by claiming an immediate relationship to the men, as wives, daughters, and mothers. They also claimed a concern for the larger working class community in which they lived, which would suffer if the pit closures took place. The group was very successful "in constructing a primary, relational standing in the anti-pit closure struggle, even though they were indirectly located in the movement" (Beckwith 1996:1051).

Beckwith uses the political opportunity literature, but adapts the framework to her own purposes. Rather than focus on "political institutions and their practices as major structuring devices that condition the possibilities of success and failure of collective action" (Beckwith 1996:1036), she instead explores noninstitutional factors, culture, discourse, and collective identity. Her focus is primarily on the intersection between political standing and identity and Beckwith argues that the collective identity literature has not "recognized the necessity of standing construction in linking identity with agency" (p. 1063). Her use of the political opportunity structure therefore relies more on collective identity and its relationship to political standing, the latter of which affects movement success. The group was dramatic, but ultimately unsuccessful.

In contrast, Katzenstein (1998) explores activists who were less visible and often less radical, but sometimes achieved greater influence. Indeed, she is particularly interested in finding women's activism in unlikely places, a legacy, she argues, of more visible feminist activism earlier. She focuses specifically on institutional protest and how female activists have affected change in some of America's male-dominated institutions, picking the very hard cases of the military and the Catholic Church. Feminist protest inside these two organizations caused disruption, but did so through tactics that were designed for the distinct context each institution offered. Military activists used "moderate, interest-group, influence-seeking" tactics whereas the church activists used "discursive radicalism" (1998:16). She defines the military groups' tactics as interest group activism because they first, had specific "interests," and second, had concrete demands that required compromise and bargaining that is so familiar to traditional interest groups (p. 47). She defines the church groups' activism as discursive because it involved reflection and reformulation in the form of words, images, songs, writings, and plays. There was more of a focus on ideas rather than policies, because they had no access to challenge policies in a meaningful way. Those tactics arose was primarily the result of one intervening political opportunity, the law.

Katzenstein (1998:23) argues that the law "shapes how those vying for power think about themselves and others, and how they define the meaning of the world around them." She argues that political opportunity structure theories don't go far enough in explaining social movement development, because the institutional settings and opportunities provided by the context, including the law, "does provide an opportunity for activism; but it does so in part by shaping the values, beliefs, and preferences that activists hold" (p. 33). Both Katzenstein and Banaszak (1996) thus argue that political opportunity structures are important, but not determinative. Mobilization and political outcomes are the produce of the interaction of opportunities with organization, collective identities, tactics, and beliefs.

Robin Teske and Mary Ann Tetreault (2000), who both work primarily in international relations, adopt a more explicitly feminist framework in their edited volume on feminist approaches to social change and the different strategies and tactics used by activist groups. The contributors include activists and academics, and span many disciplinary backgrounds, but all assign the state a central role in their analyses. It's also clear that Teske and Tetreault aim to contribute to both academic literature and activist practice.

Five key concepts unify the various authors in Teske and Tetreault: feminism, power, social movements, community, and civil society. For instance, Meyer draws on feminist theory in his analysis of social movement protest, arguing that social movements are defined by connecting self and community and "feminist scholarship emphasizes the relationship between these two worlds" (2000:38). Feminist scholarship, he argues, can contribute to social movement theory by broadening the tools used, including origins, tactics, and influence. In addition, like many of the authors already discussed here, Meyer also refers to political opportunity structures in describing the trajectory of social protest. Opportunity structures range from government structures to political rhetoric but all are potentially important in shaping the trajectory of a movement. The movement responds to the structures, and later, when policy emerges, future opportunity structures will be altered.

Drawing from comparative politics and public policy, as well as feminist scholarship, S. Laurel Weldon (2002) compares government responsiveness to violence against women across 36 democratic countries. She examines a number of possible determinants, such as culture, level of development, and the women's movement, and finds that the "form and strength of social movements and political institutions determine government responsiveness to violence against women" (Weldon 2002:xi). Most significantly, the presence of an active women's movement, which serves as a "catalyst" for government action, is most important in getting the issue of violence against women on the agenda. She writes, "strong, independently organized women's movements improve government responsiveness to violence against women" (2002:61). In fact, she refers to them as a necessary condition. However, they are effective in influencing policy only through interaction with mainstream political institutions. Thus, when these rules and structures interact with the movement there is a reinforcement of each. The movement can "improve the institutional capabilities of government to address women's issues," gain leverage over government departments, coordinate policy action, and provide research support (Weldon 2002:140). Likewise, the government departments will seek to avoid conflict with the movement and will allow more access and will thus increase the movement's leverage. Weldon's argument is based entirely on this notion of interaction: "Most policies to address violence against women are thus products of partnerships between women's movements and sympathetic insiders" (2002:163).

In writing about this interaction, Weldon employs an explicitly structural approach. Like many of the authors here, she argues that the political opportunity structure theories don't fully account for this interaction effect. She refers to Gelb (1989) as a classical political opportunity structure theorist who speaks of how external factors shape a movement. What Gelb and other political opportunity theorists miss, according to Weldon, is that "social movements sometimes create their own political opportunities . . .so the idea that social movements arise in response to political opportunities does not recognize the impact of social movements on the political opportunity structure itself" (Weldon 2000:178). Her structural approach, she contends, best captures the interaction between movements and the institutions that she deems crucial to movement success. This approach takes her beyond traditional policy analysis, which she argues doesn't account for this dynamic interaction.

In an exemplary collective effort, Banaszak, Beckwith, and Rucht (2003) coordinate a group of scholars in directed comparative analysis of interactions between movements and states that change around them. Considering the development and influence of women's movements in advanced industrialized countries engaging in neoliberal reforms, the editors devise a political process approach that focuses on interaction. Their introduction observes a secular shift of women's movements in the western, democratic countries since the 1970s from radical and autonomous to moderate and state-involved. The reasoning can be attributed to a different type of interaction with a "new" and reconfigured state. Even as women—and other organized groups—made significant inroads in institutional politics in national states, the states themselves have ceded much of their own policy-making autonomy to other levels of government. In essence, women's movements have won access to levers of power that are now less meaningful. Since the 1970s, there has been a rearrangement of formal power and policy responsibility, leading to structural changes within the states and a changed relationship between the state and civil society. In describing this relationship between states and movements, Banaszak, Beckwith, and Rucht specifically reject the structural approach as taken by Weldon. Instead, they argue that "states are not necessarily stable and homogeneous structures but are rather composed of, or represented by, various sets of actors who engage in diverse and dynamic relationships with social movements" (2003:16). Thus, their approach is based on the idea of a dynamic state, acting in interaction with a similarly changing movement.

This idea of a dynamic state is most fully developed in Rucht's (2003) chapter in this volume. Studying the specific patterns of movement-state interaction in Germany, Rucht finds that the German women's movement in the 1970s lacked interaction with the state and the relationship was therefore rather antagonistic and confrontational. By the 1980s and 1990s, the relationship had changed as interaction increased and there was then a shift from confrontational to assimilative (2003:255). But other movements, such as the labor movement and the peace movement in Germany, developed different relationships with the state. Why the different trajectories and outcomes? Rucht argues that despite the fact that all the movements were interacting with one state, they were actually interacting with different states as the state changed; he contends, "only in a very formal sense was the same state involved. On closer inspection we see that any given state is not a uniform machinery with similar parts following the same principle" (Rucht 2003:255). Rucht sees the importance of state–movement interaction and emphasizes that it is not just the interaction that shifts, the players themselves shift and "reconfigure" as well.

Whether the authors are using resource mobilization, political process, political opportunity, or structural approaches (and, as seen above, all are recalled), all the authors note the role of state–movement interaction. None of the authors above seem to view the state or the movement as either a static or unitary actor; rather, each author appears to emphasize the dynamic relationship between the political world and the women's movement. Each of the above authors notes the importance of movement reaction to and shaping of the political context. Therefore, this theme of interaction ties them all together. In this sense, the women and politics literature seems to have the most consensual and comprehensive approach to social movements within political science: political context matters as it shapes the movement and the movement in turn shapes the macropolitical world. In the two decades since Jenson wrote about political context, this is a strong level of agreement amongst a disparate group of scholars (who encompass a range of disciplines).

CONCLUSION

Political scientists study social movements, but for the most part, the discipline as a whole has missed opportunities to build a more comprehensive framework to examine the politics of protest. To be sure, such a broad indictment requires many qualifications. First, many scholars are not strictly bound by disciplines. At least three of the authors discussed in this chapter—Seymour Martin Lipset, Frances Fox Piven, and Theda Skocpol—have held very high office in the American Political Science Association AND the American Sociological Association.

A far larger number of scholars hold cross-disciplinary appointments and read and publish across disciplines, mostly political science and sociology. Moreover, European political scientists have actively engaged social movement theory, often working with American sociologists.

At the same time, key concepts for the analysis of social movements originated in political science, but were far more fully developed in sociology. Michael Lipsky (1968) coined the term "resource mobilization," but McCarthy and Zald (1973, 1977) developed the concept into a broad theoretical framework that animated a great deal of additional research. Peter Eisinger (1973) coined the phrase "political opportunity structure," and it has been employed across disciplines, but far more extensively in sociology (Meyer 2004b). The disciplinary organization of political science, particularly in the United States, has worked to frustrate the development of an integrated perspective on social movements. Even when scholars read across fields and borrow concepts from others working in different areas, the work rarely speaks back to those concepts in political science. (In contrast, sociology in the United States has identified social movements as a distinct area of study.)

On the one hand, disciplinary homes are less important than the quality of analysis. On the other hand, we can view a series of missed opportunities in the analysis of social movements. Political scientists, by vaunt of their disciplinary training, focus on state structures, laws, and public policy. These critical issues have, in our view, gotten short shrift in the analysis of social movements, and there is work to be done.

REFERENCES

Albritton, Robert B. 1979. "Social Amelioration through Mass Insurgency: Re-Examination of the Piven and Cloward Thesis." *American Political Science Review* 73:1003–1011.
Almond, Gabriel, G. Bingham Powell, Kaare Strom, and Russell Dalton, eds. 2004. *Comparative Politics Today: A World View,* 8th edition. New York: Longman.
Bacharach, Peter and Morton S. Baratz. 1963. "Decisions and Nondecisions: An Analytical Framework." *The American Political Science Review* 57:632–642.
Baldassare, Mark ed. 1994. *The Los Angeles Riots: Lessons for the Urban Future.* Boulder: Westview Press.
Banaszak, Lee Ann. 1996. *Why Movements Succeed or Fail: Opportunity, Culture, and the Struggle for Woman Suffrage.* Princeton, NJ: Princeton University Press.
Banaszak, Lee Ann, Karen Beckwith, and Dieter Rucht, eds. 2003. *Women's Movements Facing the Reconfigured State.* Cambridge, UK: Cambridge University Press.
Bandy, Joe and Jackie Smith, eds. 2004. *Coalitions across Borders: Transnational Protest and the Neoliberal Order.* Lanham, MD: Rowman & Littlefield.
Baumgartner, Frank and Bryan D. Jones. 1993. *Agendas and Instability in American Politics.* Chicago: University of Chicago Press.
Beckwith, Karen. 1996. "Lancashire Women against Pit Closures: Women's Standing in a Men's Movement." *Feminist Theory and Practice* Summer:1034–1068.
Bermeo, Nancy. 1999. "Myths of Moderation." Pp. 120–139 in *Transitions to Democracy,* edited by Lisa Anderson. New York: Columbia University Press.
Berry, Jeffrey. 1984. *Lobbying for the People.* Princeton, NJ: Princeton University Press.
———. 1999. *The New Liberalism: The Rising Power of Citizen Groups.* Washington, DC: Brookings.
Boskin, Joseph, ed. 1969. *Urban Racial Violence in the Twentieth Century.* Beverly Hills, CA: Glencoe Press.
Boudreau, Vincent. 2004. *Resisting Dictatorship: Repression and Protest in Southeast Asia.* Cambridge, UK: Cambridge University Press.
Browning, Rufus P., Dale Rogers Marshall, and David H. Tabb. 1984. *Protest Is Not Enough: The Struggle of Blacks and Hispanics for Equality in Urban Politics.* Berkeley, CA: University of California Press.
Button, James W. 1978. *Black Violence: Political Impact of the 1960s Riots.* Princeton, NJ: Princeton University Press.
Carmichael, Stokely (Kwame Ture) and Charles V. Hamilton. 1992 [1967]. *Black Power: The Politics of Liberation in America.* New York: Vintage Books.

Chirot, Daniel. 1999. "What Happened in Eastern Europe in 1989?" Pp. 19–50 in *The Revolutions of 1989*, edited by Vladimir Tismaneanu. London and New York: Routledge.

Cohen, Cathy J. 1999. *The Boundaries of Blackness: AIDS and the Breakdown of Black Politics*. Chicago: University of Chicago Press.

Costain, Anne N. 1992. *Inviting Women's Rebellion: A Political Process Interpretation of the Women's Movement*. Baltimore: The Johns Hopkins University Press.

Dahl, Robert A. 1956. *A Preface to Democratic Theory*. Chicago: University of Chicago Press.

——. 1963. *Who Governs: Democracy and Power in the American City*. New Haven, CT: Yale University Press.

Dalton, Russell J. 1988. *Citizen Politics: Public Opinion and Political Parties in Advanced Industrial Democracies*. New York: Chatham House Publishers.

Dalton, Russell J. and Manfred Kuechler, eds. 1990. *Challenging the Political Order: New Social and Political Movements in Western Democracies*. New York: Oxford University Press.

della Porta, Donatella and Herbert Reiter, eds. 1998. *Policing Protest: The Control of Mass Demonstrations in Western Democracies*. Minneapolis, MN: University of Minnesota Press.

della Porta, Donatella and Dieter Rucht. 1995. "Left-libertarian Movements in Context: A Comparison of Italy and West Germany, 1965–1990." Pp. 229–272 in *The Politics of Social Protest*, edited by J. Craig Jenkins and Bert Klandermans. Minneapolis, MN: University of Minnesota Press.

Easton, David. 1953. *The Political System*. New York: Knopf.

Edelman, Murray. 1971. *Politics as Symbolic Action: Mass Arousal and Quiescence*. New York: Markham.

Eisinger, Peter K. 1973. "The Conditions of Protest Behavior in American Cities." *The American Political Science Review* 67(1):11–28.

Freeman, Jo. 1975. *The Politics of Women's Liberation: A Case Study of an Emerging Social Movement and its Relation to the Policy Process*. New York: David McKay.

Freeman, Joseph F. 1992. *Government Is Good: Citizenship, Participation, and Power*. Columbia, MO: University of Missouri Press.

Gamson, William A. 1990 [1975]. *The Strategy of Social Protest*, 2nd edition. Belmont, CA: Wadsworth.

Garcia Bedolla, Lisa. 2005. *Fluid Borders: Latino Power, Identity, and Politics in Los Angeles*, Berkeley, CA: University of California Press.

Gaventa, John. 1981. *Power and Powerlessness: Quiescence and Rebellion in an Appalachian Valley*. Carbondale, IL: University of Illinois Press.

Gelb, Joyce. 1989. *Feminism and Politics: A Comparative Perspective*. Berkeley, CA: University of California Press.

Giugni, Marco. 2004. *Social Protest and Policy Change: Ecology, Antinuclear, and Peace Movements in Comparative Perspective*. Lanham, MD: Rowman & Littlefield.

Goldstone, Jack, ed. 2003. *Revolutions: Theoretical, Comparative, and Historical Studies*. Belmont, CA: Wadsworth/Thomson Learning.

Goodwin, Jeff. 2003. "The East European Revolutions of 1989." Pp. 255–261 in *Revolutions: Theoretical, Comparative, and Historical Studies*, 3rd edition, edited by Jack A. Goldstone. Belmont, CA: Wadsworth.

Gourevitch, Peter. 1978. "The Second Image Reversed: The International Sources of Domestic Politics." *International Organization* 32:881–912.

Haines, Herbert H. 1988. *Black Radicals and the Civil Rights Mainstream, 1954–1970*. Knoxville, TN: University of Tennessee Press.

Hansen, John Mark. 1991. *Gaining Access: Congress and the Farm Lobby, 1919–1981*. Chicago: University of Chicago.

Huntington, Samuel P. 1968. *Political Order in Changing Societies*. New Haven, CT: Yale University Press.

Imig, Douglas R. 1996. *Poverty and Power: The Political Representation of Poor Americans*. Lincoln, NE: University of Nebraska Press.

Imig, Douglas R. and David S. Meyer. 1993. "Political Opportunity and Peace and Justice Advocacy in the 1980s: A Tale of Two Sectors." *Social Science Quarterly* 74:750–770.

Imig, Douglas R. and Sidney Tarrow, eds. 2001. *Contentious Europeans: Protest and Politics in an Emerging Polity*. Lanham, MD: Rowman & Littlefield.

Inglehart, Ronald. 1977. *The Silent Revolution: Changing Values and Political Styles among Western Publics*. Princeton, NJ: Princeton University Press.

Jenson, Jane. 1982. "The Modern Women's Movement in Italy, France, and Great Britain." *Comparative Social Research* 5:341–375.

Katzenstein, Mary Fainsod. 1998. *Faithful and Fearless: Moving Feminist Protest inside the Church and Military*. Princeton, NJ: Princeton University Press.

——. 2005. "Rights without Citizenship: Activist Politics and Prison Reform in the United States." Pp. 236–258 in *Routing the Opposition: Social Movements, Public Policy, and Democracy*, edited by David S. Meyer, Valerie Jenness, and Helen Ingram. Minneapolis, MN: University of Minnesota Press.

Katznelson, Ira. 1982. *City Trenches*. Chicago: University of Chicago Press.

Keck, Margaret E. and Kathryn Sikkink. 1998. *Activists beyond Borders: Advocacy Networks in International Politics*. Ithaca, NY: Cornell University Press.

Kim, Claire Jean. 2000. *Bitter Fruit: The Politics of Black-Korean Conflict in New York*. New Haven, CT: Yale University Press.

Kitschelt, Herbert P. 1986. "Political Opportunity Structures and Political Protest: Anti-Nuclear Movements in Four Democracies." *British Journal of Political Science* 16:57–85.

Knopf, Jeffrey W. 1998. *Domestic Society and International Cooperation: The Impact of Protest on US Arms Control Policy*. Cambridge, UK: Cambridge University Press.

Kollman, Ken. 1998. *Outside Lobbying: Public Opinion and Interest Group Strategies*. Princeton, NJ: Princeton University Press.

Koopmans, Ruud. 1995. *Democracy from Below: New Social Movements and the Political System in West Germany*. Boulder, CO: Westview Press.

Koopmans, Ruud and Paul Statham. 1999a. "Challenging the Liberal Nation-state? Postnationalism, Multiculturalism, and the Collective Claims Making of Migrants and Ethnic Minorities in Britain and Germany." *American Journal of Sociology* 105:652–696.

——. 1999b. "Political Claims Analysis: Integrating Protest Event and Political Discourse Approaches."*Mobilization* 4:40–51.

Kornhauser, William. 1959. *The Politics of Mass Society*. Glencoe, IL: Free Press.

Kriesi, Hanspeter, Ruud Koopmans, Jan Willem Duvydenak, and Marco G. Giugni. 1995. *New Social Movements in Western Europe: A Comparative Analysis*. Minneapolis, MN: University of Minnesota Press.

Lipset, Seymour Martin. 1963. *Political Man*. New York: Anchor.

Lipsky, Michael 1968. "Protest as a Political Resource." *American Political Science Review* 62:1144–1158.

——. 1970. *Protest in City Politics: Rent Strikes, Housing and the Power of the Poor*. Chicago: Rand McNally and Company.

Lipsky, Michael and David J. Olson. 1977. *Commission Politics: The Processing of Racial Crisis in America*. New Brunswick, NJ: Transaction.

Lowi, Theodore J. 1968. *Private Life and Public Order: The Context of Modern Public Policy*. New York: W. W. Norton.

——. 1971. *The Politics of Disorder*. New York: Basic Books.

Lukes, Steven. 2005 [1974]. *Power: A Radical View*, 2nd edition. New York: Palgrave Macmillan.

Mansbridge, Jane J. 1986. *Why We Lost the ERA*. Chicago: University of Chicago Press.

McAdam, Doug. 1982. *Political Process and the Development of Black Insurgency, 1930–1970*. Chicago: University of Chicago Press.

McAdam, Doug, Sidney Tarrow, and Charles Tilly. 2001. *Dynamics of Contention*. New York: Cambridge University Press.

McCarthy, John D. and Mayer N. Zald. 1973. *The Trend of Social Movements in America: Professionalization and Resource Mobilization*. Morristown, NJ: General Learning Press.

——. 1977. "Resource Mobilization and Social Movements: A Partial Theory." *American Journal of Sociology* 82:1212–1241.

Mettler, Suzanne. 2002. "Bringing the State Back in to Civic Engagement: Policy Feedback Effects of the G.I. Bill for World War II Veterans." *American Political Science Review* 96(2):351–365.

——. 2005. "Policy Feedback Effects for Collective Action: Lessons from Veterans' Programs." Pp. 211–235 in *Routing the Opposition: Social Movements, Public Policy, and Democracy*, edited by David S. Meyer, Valerie Jenness, and Helen Ingram. Minneapolis, MN: University of Minnesota Press.

Meyer, David S. 1990. *A Winter of Discontent: The Nuclear Freeze and American Politics*. New York: Praeger.

——. 2000. "Social Movements: Creating Communities of Change." Pp. 35–55 in *Feminist Approaches to Social Movements, Community, and Power, Vol. I: Conscious Acts and the Politics of Social Change*, edited by Mary Ann Tetreault and Robin L. Teske. Columbia, SC: University of South Carolina Press.

——. 2004a. "Political Opportunity and Nested Institutions." *Social Movement Studies* 2:17–35.

——. 2004b. "Protest and Political Opportunity." *Annual Review of Sociology* 30:125–145.

——. 2005. "Social Movements and Public Policy: Eggs, Chickens, and Theory." Pp. 1–25 in *Routing the Opposition: Social Movements, Public Policy, and Democracy*, edited by David Meyer, Valerie Jenness, and Helen Ingram. Minneapolis, MN: University of Minnesota Press.

——. 2007. *The Politics of Protest: Social Movements in America*. New York: Oxford University Press.

Meyer, David, Valerie Jenness, and Helen Ingram, eds. 2005. *Routing the Opposition: Social Movements, Public Policy, and Democracy*. Minneapolis, MN: University of Minnesota Press.

Meyer, David S. and Douglas R. Imig. 1993. "Political Opportunity and the Rise and Decline of Interest Group Sectors." *Social Science Journal* 30:253–270.

Meyer, David S. and Suzanne Staggenborg. 1996. "Movements, Countermovements, and the Structure of Political Opportunity." *American Journal of Sociology* 101:1628–1660.

Meyer, David S. and Sidney Tarrow, eds. 1998. *The Social Movement Society*. Lanham, MD: Rowman & Littlefield.

Michels, Roberto. 1966 [1915]. *Political Parties*. New York: Free Press.

Morgenthau, Hans J. 1993. *Politics Among Nations*. New York: Knopf.

Nettl, J.P. 1968. "The State as a Conceptual Varialbe." *World Politics* 20(4):559–592.

Olson, Mancur. 1967. *The Logic of Collective Action*. Cambridge, MA: Harvard University Press.

Opp, Karl-Dieter. 1989. *The Rationality of Political Protest: A Comparative Analysis of Rational Choice Theory*. Boulder, CO: Westview Press.

Parkin, Frank 1968. *Middle-Class Radicalism*. Manchester, UK: Manchester University Press.

Piven, Frances Fox and Richard A. Cloward. 1971. *Regulating the Poor*. New York: Vintage.

Piven, Frances Fox and Richard A. Cloward. 1977. *Poor People's Movements: Why They Succeed, How They Fail*. New York: Vintage Books/Random House.

Polsby, Nelson 1967. *Community Power and Political Theory*. New Haven, CT: Yale University Press.

Putnam, Robert 2000. Bowling Alone: *Bowling Alone: The Collapse and Revival of American Community*. New York: Simon and Schuster.

Rady, Martyn. 1992. *Romania in Turmoil: A Contemporary History*. London: IB Tauris & Company.

Reese, Ellen. 2005. "Policy Threats and Social Movement Coalitions: California's Campaign to Restore Legal Immigrants' Rights to Welfare." Pp. 259–287 in *Routing the Opposition: Social Movements, Public Policy, and Democracy*, edited by David S. Meyer, Valerie Jenness, and Helen Ingram. Minneapolis, MN: University of Minnesota Press.

Rimmerman, Craig A. 2002. *From Identity to Politics: The Lesbian and Gay Movements in the United States*. Philadelphia: Temple University Press.

Risse-Kappen, Thomas, ed. 1995. *Bringing Transnational Relations Back In: Non-State Actors, Domestic Structures, and International Institutions*. Cambridge, UK: Cambridge University Press.

Rossi, Peter H., ed. 1973. *Ghetto Revolts*. New Brunswick, NJ: Transaction Books.

Rucht, Dieter. 1990. "The Strategies and Action Repertoires of New Movements." Pp. 156–175 in *Challenging the Political Order: New Social and Political Movements in Western Democracies*, edited by Russell J. Dalton and Manfred Kuechler. New York: Oxford University Press.

Rucht, Dieter. 2000. "Distant Issue Movements in Germany: Empirical Description and Theoretical Reflections." Pp. 76–105 in *Globalizations and Social Movements: Culture, Power, and the Transnational Public Sphere*, edited by John A. Guidry, Michael D. Kennedy, and Mayer N. Zald. Ann Arbor, MI: University of Michigan Press.

———. 2003. "Interactions between Social Movements and States in a Comparative Perspective." Pp. 242–274 in *Women's Movements Facing the Reconfigured State*, edited by Lee Ann Banaszak, Karen Beckwith, and Dieter Rucht.Cambridge, UK: Cambridge University Press.

Rucht, Dieter, Ruud Koopmans, and Friedhelm Neidhardt. 1999. *Acts of Dissent: New Developments in the Study of Protest*. Berlin: Sigma.

Rustow, Dankwart.1970. "Transitions to Democracy: Toward a Dynamic Model." *Comparative Politic* 2:337–363.

Salisbury, Robert H. 1970. *Interest Group Politics in America*. New York: Harper & Row.

Schattschneider, E.E. 1960. *The Semi-Sovereign People*. New York: Holt, Rinehart & Winston.

Schlozman, Kay Lehman. 1984. "What Accent the Heavenly Choir? Political Equality and the American Pressure System." *Journal of Politics* 46:1006–1032.

Schwartz, Mildred. 2005. *Party Movements in the United States and Canada: Strategies of Persistence*. Lanham, MD: Rowman & Littlefield.

Sears, David O. 1994. "Urban Rioting in Los Angeles: A Comparison of 1965 with 1992." Pp. 237–254 in *The Los Angeles Riots: Lessons for the Urban Future*, edited by Mark Baldassare. Boulder, CO: Westview Press.

Skocpol, Theda. 1979. *States and Social Revolutions: A Comparative Analysis of France, Russia, and China*. New York: Cambridge University Press.

———. 2003. *Diminished Democracy: From Membership to Management in American Civic Life*. Norman, OK: University of Oklahoma Press.

Smith, Jackie, Charles Chatfield and Ron Pagnucco, eds. 1997. *Transnational Social Movements and Global Politics: Solidarity beyond the State*. Syracuse, NY: Syracuse University Press.

Tarrow, Sidney G. 1989. *Democracy and Disorder: Protest and Politics in Italy, 1965–1975*. Cambridge, UK: Cambridge University Press.

———. 1998. *Power in Movement: Social Movements and Contentious Politics*, 2nd edition. Cambridge, UK: Cambridge University Press.

———. 2005. *The New Transnational Activism*. New York: Cambridge University Press.

Teske, Robin L. and Mary Ann Tetreault, eds. 2000. *Feminist Approaches to Social Movements, Community, and Power, Vol. 1: Conscious Acts and the Politics of Social Change*. Columbia, SC: University of South Carolina Press.

Thomas, Daniel C. 2001. *The Helsinki Effect: International Norms, Human Rights, and the Demise of Communism*. Princeton, NJ: Princeton University Press.

Tilly, Charles. 1978. *From Mobilization to Revolution*. Reading, MA: Addison-Wesley.

———. 1993. "Contentious Repertoires in Great Britain, 1758–1834." *Social Science History* 17:253–280.

Tismaneanu, Vladimir, ed. 1999. *The Revolutions of 1989*. London and New York: Routledge.

Truman, David. 1951. *The Governmental Process*. New York: Knopf.

Walker, Jack L. 1983. "The Origin and Maintenance of Interest Groups in America." *American Political Science Review* 72:390–406.

Weldon, S. Laurel. 2002. *Protest, Policy and the Problem of Violence against Women: A Cross-National Comparison*. Pittsburgh, PA: University of Pittsburgh Press.

Wilson, James Q. 1995. *Political Organizations*, 2nd edition. Princeton, NJ: Princeton University Press.

Wood, Elisabeth Jean. 2000. *Forging Democracy from Below: Insurgent Transitions in South Africa and El Salvador*. Cambridge, UK: Cambridge University Press.

CHAPTER 5

Individuals in Movements

A Social Psychology of Contention

JACQUELIEN VAN STEKELENBURG AND BERT KLANDERMANS

INTRODUCTION

Social psychology is interested in how social context influences individuals' behavior. The prototypical social psychological question related to collective action is that of why some individuals participate in social movements while others do not, or for that matter, why some individuals decide to quit while others stay involved. The social psychological answer to these questions is given in terms of typical psychological processes such as identity, cognition, motivation, and emotion. People—social psychologists never tire of asserting—live in a perceived world. They respond to the world as they perceive and interpret it, and if we want to understand their cognitions, motivations, and emotions we need to know their perceptions and interpretations. Hence, social psychology focuses on subjective variables and takes the individual as its unit of analysis.

Taking the individual as the unit of analysis has important methodological implications. If one wants to explain individual behavior, one needs to collect data at the individual level: attitudes, beliefs, opinions, motives, affect and emotions, intended and actual behavior, and so on. Face-to-face interviews, survey questionnaires (paper and pencil or online), experiments, and registration and observation of individual behavior are the typical devices applied in social psychological research. Whatever the method employed, the point of the matter is that answers, measures, and observations must be unequivocally attributable to one and the same individual. This is important because the fundamental methodological principle in social psychological research is the coincidence of two observations in one individual. Such methodological individualism is not to say that people do not interact or identify with groups. Obviously, people *are* group members and *do* interact. In fact, group identification and interaction within groups is among the key factors in any social psychological explanation. It only is a consequence of an approach that takes the individual as the unit of analysis.

Taking the individual as the unit of analysis has important epistemological implications as well. It implies, inter alia, that questions that take a unit of analysis other than the individual (e.g., a movement, a group, a region, or a country) require disciplines other than social psychology to formulate an answer to that question. Hence, social psychology should fare fine in explaining why individual members of a society participate or fail to participate in a movement once it has emerged, but is not very helpful in explaining why social movements emerge or decline in a society or at a specific point in time. How individual decisions and choices accumulate and result in a more or less successful movement is the subject of other disciplines. The rise and fall of social movements and their impact on politics are topics that take the movement as the unit of analysis. Sociology, political science, and history are better suited for such analyses. Similarly, social psychology should be able to explain why individuals identify with a group, and why strong group identification reinforces someone's willingness to take part in protest on behalf of that group. However, sociology and especially anthropology are better suited for a study of the collective identity of a group, where the group is the unit of analysis. Finally—to give a last example—social psychology is good in analyzing why specific beliefs and attitudes foster participation in a movement, but the question of how such beliefs and attitudes are distributed in a society is a study topic that social geography and sociology are better equipped for.

Taking the individual as the unit of analysis alludes to the limits of structural explanations. Unless all individuals who are in the same structural position display identical behavior, a shared position can never provide sufficient explanation of individual behavior, and even if people do display identical behavior, the motivational background and the accompanying emotions may still be different. Indeed, this is exactly what a social psychology of protest is about—trying to understand why people who are seemingly in the same situation respond so different. Why do some feel ashamed of their situation, while others take pride in it? Why are some aggrieved, while others are not? Why do some define their situation as unjust, while others do not? Why do some feel powerless, while others feel strong? Why are some angry, while others are afraid? These are the kinds of questions social psychology students of movement participation seek to answer.

Before we move along, a remark must be made about the assumptions regarding individual behavior that underlie social movement studies. Although anthropology, sociology, political sciences, history, and social geography usually do their analyses at levels different than that of the individual, they do build their reasoning on assumptions about individual behavior. These assumptions are not necessarily in sync with state-of-the-art social psychological insights. This is not to say that every social scientist must become a social psychologist first, but it *is* to say that it is worth the effort to specify the social psychological assumptions that underlie the analyses and to see whether they fit into what social psychologists know these days about individual behavior.

About this Chapter

The principal part of this chapter consists of a discussion of social psychology of movement participation. The first section deals with four fundamental social psychological processes as they are employed in the context of social movement participation: social identity, social cognition, emotions, and motivation. Identity, cognition, emotion, and motivation are presented as the processes at the individual level that link collective identity and collective action. We elaborate on each of these constructs, discuss how they are employed in the study of social movement participation, and describe exemplary studies that take them as their explanatory focus. Thereafter we deal with the phenomenon of social movement participation. We discuss such matters as what we mean by movement participation; movement participation within the broader spectrum of the dynamics of contention; short-term versus sustained participation; and the dynamics of disengagement (an often forgotten aspect of the dynamics of movement participation). The concluding section of the chapter, we assess where we stand and propose directions to proceed. However, before we start with where we (as social psychologists) are, we will go back to the past.

Back to the Past

For a long time social movement scholars outside of social psychology tended to equate social psychology to relative deprivation theory, and indeed, relative deprivation is a key concept in any grievance theory. Since Runciman's (1966) classical study, relative deprivation, and more specifically fraternalistic relative deprivation, has featured in social movement literature as explanation of movement participation. Feelings of relative deprivation result from comparisons of one's situation with some standard of comparison—be it one's own past, someone else's situation, or some cognitive standard (Folger 1986). If such comparisons result in the conclusion that one is not receiving the rewards or recognition one deserves, the feelings that accompany this assessment are referred to as relative deprivation. Runciman proposed to use the concept of egoistic deprivation if the comparison concerns someone's personal situation. He proposed the concept of fraternalistic deprivation if the comparison concerns the situation of a group someone belongs to. It was assumed that especially fraternalistic relative deprivation is relevant in the context of movement participation (Major 1994; Martin 1986).[1]

However, while fraternalistic deprivation is regarded as the more valid explanation of collective action, the relationship between fraternalistic deprivation and collective action is moderate at best (Guimond and Dubé-Simard 1983). Indeed, while many minority group members recognize their group's discrimination, relatively few are involved in collective action (Wright, Taylor, and Moghaddam 1990). Thus, the almost singular focus on fraternalistic deprivation does not appear to provide an adequate psychological explanation for collective action (Foster and Matheson 1999). Foster and Matheson argued that an expanded understanding of the role of perceived relative deprivation may be gained from alternative theories of group behavior, namely theories of *group consciousness raising* (e.g., Stanley and Wise 1983), which suggest that individuals act to benefit their group once they acknowledge that "the personal is political."

To capture the connection between individual (personal) and group (political) oppression, it may be informative to consider the much ignored notion of *double relative deprivation* (Foster and Matheson 1999), the perception of both personal and group deprivation (Runciman 1966). It is suggested that people who feel both egoistic deprivation and fraternalistic deprivation may report a qualitatively different experience that may be more strongly associated with action-taking than the experience of either egoistic or fraternalistic deprivation alone. Foster and Matheson (1999) showed that when the group experience becomes relevant for one's own experience, there is a greater motivation to take part in collective action.

---

[1] Social psychologists have not been the only ones who applied relative deprivation theory in the context of social movements. Political scientists used relative deprivation theory as well. The concept features prominently in the work of Gurr (1970, 1993). See Lupo and Meyer in this volume.

Akin to relative deprivation theory but featuring less prominently in social movement literature has been frustration–aggression theory (Berkowitz 1972). The idea is that when the achievement of some goal is blocked by some external agency, this results in feelings of frustration. Among the possible reactions to such feelings of frustration are acts aiming at the external agency to lift the blockade or simply punish the agency for blocking goal achievement. Being a general theory about human behavior the frustration–aggression framework has been applied in the context of movement participation and political protest as well (Berkowitz 1972; see for a review of the literature on union participation Klandermans 1986).

Both relative deprivation theory and frustration–aggression theory are examples of grievance theories. In an attempt to develop a more systematic grievance theory, Klandermans (1997) distinguished between illegitimate inequality, suddenly imposed grievances, and violated principles. Illegitimate inequality is what relative deprivation theory is about. The assessment of illegitimate inequality implies both comparison processes and legitimating processes. The first processes concern the assessment of a treatment as unequal, the second of that inequality as illegitimate. Suddenly imposed grievances refer to an unexpected threat or inroad on people's rights or circumstances (Walsh 1981). The third type of grievance refers to moral outrage because it is felt that important values or principles are violated. We can find each of these kinds of grievances embodied in various movements. The women's movement, for example, attempts to redress years of unequal treatment in society; the toxic waste movement is a response to suddenly imposed grievance, and the pro-life movement is a reaction to what its participants see as a violation of a moral principle, the commandment "Thou shall not kill." Klandermans takes the three types or grievances together as feelings of injustice, which he defines as "outrage about the way authorities are treating a social problem" (p. 38).

Since the appearance of resource mobilization theory, grievance theories have lost the attention of many a movement scholar. Grievance theories were associated with so-called breakdown theories, which were discredited for portraying social movements and movement participation as irrational responses to structural strain. Moreover, the resource mobilization approach took as its point of departure that grievances abound and that the question to be answered was not so much why people are aggrieved but why aggrieved people mobilize. As a consequence, the social movement field lost its interest in grievance theory and because of the association of grievance theory with social psychology it lost its interest in social psychology as well. Klandermans (1984) was among the first to observe that in so doing it had "thrown the baby out with the bathwater." He began to systematically explore and disseminate what social psychology has to offer to students of social movements. He demonstrated that grievances are necessary but certainly not sufficient conditions for participation in social movements and proposed social psychological mechanisms that do add sufficient explanation. He argued and demonstrated that there is much more available in social psychology than relative deprivation. His example was followed by a small but growing number of social psychologists who have gradually expanded Klandermans' models. This chapter takes stock of what they accomplished so far: of what we have and where we are today.

A SOCIAL PSYCHOLOGY OF MOVEMENT PARTICIPATION

Movement participation is participation in collective action. Such collective action is generally assumed to root in collective identity. In the words of Wright (2001): "It is simply obvious that in order to engage in collective action the individual must recognize his or her membership in the relevant collective" (p. 413). This section elaborates on four basic social psychological mechanisms—social identity, cognition, emotion and motivation—that mediate between collective identity and collective action. Figure 5.1 provides a schematic representation of the four social psychological mechanisms, on the one hand, and the two collective phenomena, collective identity and collective action, on the other. The two arrows at the left and right (e) indicate that not only collective action roots in collective identity, but also that collective action influences collective identity. As the Elaborated Social Identity Model (Reicher 1996a, 1996b) holds: "identities should be understood not simply as a set of cognitions but as practical projects. In this account, identities and practice are in reciprocal interaction, each mutually enabling and constraining the other" (Drury et al. 2005: p 310). There is something active about identity; it is not just there; it is not a thing (Jenkins 2004); it is constant in motion. In other words, collective identities are constantly "under construction" and collective action is one of the factors that shape collective identity.

Acting collectively requires some collective identity. Sociologists were among the first to emphasize the importance of collective identity in collective action participation. They argued that the generation of a collective identity is crucial for a movement to emerge (Melucci 1989; Taylor and Whittier 1992). Collective identity is conceived as an emergent phenomenon. In the words of Melucci, "Collective identity is an interactive, shared definition produced by several individuals that must be conceived as a process because it is constructed and negotiated by repeated activation of the relationships that link individuals to groups " (Melucci 1995: p 44).

Individuals engage in collective action, "any time that they are acting as a representative of the group and the action is directed at improving the conditions of the entire group" (Wright 2001: p 995). As social psychologists we must emphasize that it is individuals who construct collective identity and it is individuals who stage collective action. Individuals, however, live in a perceived reality. In the end, it is individuals who react to their social

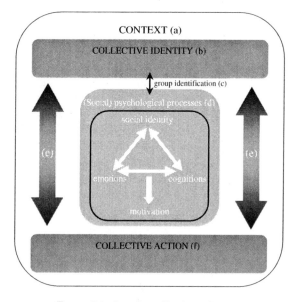

FIGURE 5.1. A road to collective action.

environment as they perceive it and who are motivated (or not) to take part in collective action. Social psychologists have proposed four fundamental mechanisms to explain the relationship between collective identity and collective action participation: *social identity, social cognition, emotion,* and *motivation*. In practice, these concepts are thoroughly interwoven, resulting in a motivational constellation, but the distinction is useful analytically. In Figure 5.1 they are depicted in the inner square (d).

Identification with the group involved appears to be a strong predictor of collective action participation (de Weerd and Klandermans 1999; Haslam 2001; Hercus 1999; Kelly 1993; Kelly and Breinlinger 1996; Simon et al. 1998; Stürmer et al. 2003). Besides the direct effects of group identification on collective action, group identification also indirectly influences collective action participation through its impact on social identity, cognition, emotions, and motivation. Depersonalization of the self is the fundamental process that determines this indirect link: "Through depersonalization self-categorization effectively brings self-perception and behavior into line with the contextually relevant in-group prototype, and thus transforms individuals into group members and individuality into group behavior" (Hogg, Terry, and White 1995:261). Individuals think, act, and feel like group members because they incorporate elements of a collective identity into their social identity. The mechanism in between is group identification. The black arrow (c) between collective identity and the small square in Figure 5.1 reflects the role of group identification. Group identification influences what people feel, think, and do. Collective identity, however, is also shaped by what people feel, think, and do with regard to the collective. Therefore, the arrow points in both directions.

What makes the proposed social psychological mechanisms all point in the direction of a readiness for action? Indeed, group identification makes people have ideas, feelings, and interests similar to others, yet this does not necessarily imply a readiness for action. Group members have to experience a growing *consciousness* of shared grievances and a clear idea of who or what is responsible for those grievances. Consciousness refers to a set of political beliefs and action orientations arising out of this awareness of similarity (Gurin, Miller, and Gurin 1980:30). It involves correct identification in one's group or category and the location of that group in the structure, as well as a recognition that one's group's interests are opposed to those of other groups. Tajfel (1974, cited by Gurin, Miller, and Gurin 1980) stresses that the transformation of social categorization into a more developed state of consciousness is enhanced by conflict and structural factors. In his view, people will engage in a number of cognitive reinterpretations that provide the critical components of consciousness if mobility out of a socially devalued category is structurally constrained. This brings us to the context were the collective struggle is fought out.

All the processes depicted in Figure 5.1 do not operate in a social vacuum. Contrary to this, collective identities are created and constructed in a social and political context, and group interests and values are defended in intergroup situations (see Figure 5.1a). Indeed, although the emphasis in social psychology is on the individual level, the dynamics of collective action participation do take place in a social and political context. As Klandermans (1997: p 9) states: "Movement organizations, multiorganizational fields, political opportunities, and social and cultural cleavages affect the route that individual participants take towards or away from the movement." The collective struggle is, by definition, fought out in the social or political intergroup context. Figure 5.1 can be read as if *one* of these group processes is placed under a magnifying class; obviously, these processes take place in a wider social, cultural, and political context. Thus, although we acknowledge the influence of this wider context, we focus on the more social psychological mechanisms in the sections to come.

Figure 5.1 is to a large extent a roadmap for the sections to come. We elaborate on the separate constructs as they feature in social psychological research on movement participation and describe exemplary research taking these constructs as the key explanatory factors.

Group Identification

Group identification seems to be the fundamental social psychological answer to the question of what drives people to engage in collective action. Identification with the group involved seems a powerful reason to participate in protest on behalf of that group, be it identification with women or workers (Kelly and Breinlinger 1995; Kelly and Kelly 1994), the elderly or gay (Simon et al. 1998; Stürmer and Simon 2004a, 2004b; Stürmer et al. 2003), farmers (de Weerd and Klandermans 1999; Klandermans, Sabucedo, and Rodriguez 2004; Klandermans et al. 2002), former East Germans (Mummendey et al. 1999), feminists (Liss, Crawford, and Popp 2004), or obese individuals (Stürmer et al. 2003). These studies report consistently that group identification and collective action participation are correlated. They report moderately positive correlations between the two variables, roughly between .20 and .30: the more people identify with the group involved, the more they are motivated to participate in collective action. This relationship also proved to be important meta-analytically (van Zomeren, Postmes, and Spears 2006). Apparently, identification with a group is an important reason why people participate in protest on behalf of that group. To understand why, we need to elaborate the concept of identity.

Identity

The clearest definition of social identity that has been located in the social psychological literature is presented by Tajfel. According to Tajfel (1978b:63), identity is "that *part* of an individual's self-concept which derives from his knowledge of his membership of a social group (or groups) together with the value and emotional significance attached to that membership." The concept, thus, contains a cognitive (awareness of membership), an evaluative (the values associated with the membership), and an emotional/affective (feelings toward one's group membership as well as others standing in relation to the group) element (see Tajfel 1978a). Identity is our understanding of who we are and of who other people are, and, reciprocally other people's understanding of themselves and others (Jenkins 2004). Hence, the notion of identity involves two criteria of comparison between people: sameness and difference-ness, which led Simon (1999) to define identity succinctly as a place in the social world. Importantly, though, identity is not a given fact; identity is in process. Identifying ourselves or others is a matter of meaning, and meaning always involves interaction: agreement and disagreement, convention and innovation, communication and negotiation (Jenkins 2004).

At the psychological heart of social identity theory (Tajfel and Turner 1979) lies the assumption that people strive for a positive self-evaluation (Turner 1999:8). This self-evaluation concerns two components: personal and social identity. *Personal identity* refers to self-definition in terms of personal attributes, whereas *social identity* refers to self-definition in terms of social category memberships. Social identity is seen as a cognitive entity; that is to say, if social identity becomes more salient than personal identity, then people see themselves less as unique individuals and more as the prototypical representatives of their in-group category. Indeed, people are inclined to define their personal self in terms of what makes them different from others, whereas they tend to define their social identities in terms of what makes them similar to others. In other words, it is the cognitive transition from an "I" into a "we" as a locus of self-definition that transforms personal identity into collective identity. When social identity becomes more salient than personal identity, people think, feel, and act as members of their group (Turner 1999). In their striving for a positive self-evaluation, it is important that the membership of groups has a positive influence on one's self-evaluation. Therefore people want to be members of high-status groups.

Because people strive for a positive self-evaluation, membership in a low-status group spurs them to undertake action in order to acquire a higher group status by leaving the group or changing its status. Tajfel and Turner (1979) formulate social structural characteristics controlling intergroup behavior. The first characteristic is *permeability of the group boundaries*, that is, the possibilities perceived by the individual to attain membership in a higher status group. When people see membership in a higher status group as a possibility, they will try to leave the lower status group. As a consequence, their commitment to the lower status group declines. The second characteristic is *stability*. Stability refers the extent to which status positions are stable or variable. People who conceive of status positions as variable perceive collective action as a possible strategy to realize higher group status, which implies that they are inclined to participate in collective action on behalf of the group. Such an inclination is fostered when the low group status is perceived as *illegitimate*. To sum up, according to social identity theory, people will participate in collective action to improve group status if they are not able to leave the group, if they believe that this status position is variable, and when the low status is perceived as illegitimate.

GROUP IDENTIFICATION: THE LINK BETWEEN COLLECTIVE AND SOCIAL IDENTITY.

Acting collectively requires some *collective* identity or consciousness (Klandermans and de Weerd 2000). Although collective identity and social identity are related concepts, they refer to different aspects of group life. Collective identity concerns cognitions shared by members of a single group (Taylor and Whittier 1992), whereas social identity concerns cognitions of a single individual about his or her membership in one or more groups (Tajfel and Turner 1979). *Group identification* forms the link between collective and social identity. Group identification can be seen as a product of *self-categorization*—a cognitive representation of the self as a representative of a more inclusive category (Brewer and Silver 2000). This cognitive representation is accompanied by an awareness of similarity, in-group identity, and shared fate with others who belong to the same category. Polletta and Jasper (2001), however, emphasize that group identification is more than a cognitive process; in their words, "a collective identity is not simply the drawing of a cognitive boundary [. . .] most of all, it is an emotion" (p. 415). It is difficult to imagine that an identity is purely cognitive yet strongly held. The "strength" of an identity comes from its affective component. Thus where self-categorization theory emphasizes the cognitive side of identification paletta and Jasper reminds us of the more affective side of group identification (see Ellemers 1993 for a similar argument).

Self-categorization theory proposes that people are more prepared to employ a social category in their social identity the more they identify with that category. Thus, the stronger the group identification, the more the shared beliefs and fate comprising the group's collective identity are incorporated in the individual's social identity. However, individuals do not incorporate the complete picture but rather a selection of what a collective identity encompasses. These idiosyncratic remakes of collective beliefs at the individual level create a variety in the *content* of the social identity. Indeed, not all farmers, obese, workers, women, feminists, or gays have identical social identities, yet they do feel like farmers, obese individuals, and so on.

A group's collective identity can be studied in its own right by examining such phenomena as the group's symbols, rituals, beliefs, and the values its members share. An individual's identification with a group can be studied in its own right as well by examining the individual's beliefs, sentiments, commitment to the group, use of symbols, participation in rituals, and so on. Thus, group identification can be assessed in all kinds of ways, but any operationalization of group identification refers somehow to what it means to an individual to belong to the group in point and will thus implicitly or explicitly refer to the pride of being a member of the group, to the symbols, values, and fate shared by the group members. Therefore group identification is akin to commitment to the group (Ellemers, Spears, and Doosje 1999; Goslinga 2002). Huddy (2001) argued that it is not group identification per se but the strength of such identification that influences group members' readiness to view themselves and act in terms of their group membership. Huddy (2001) criticized social identity literature for neglecting the fact that real-world identities vary in strength; identifying more or less strongly with a group, she argues, may make a real difference, especially in political contexts. Linked to this point is the fact that identity strength is related to identity choice (Huddy 2003). Huddy distinguishes between *ascribed* and *acquired* group membership; ascribed identities are "quite difficult to change, and acquired identities are adopted by choice" (p. 536). Group identification tends to increase in strength when it is voluntary. Membership in a social movement organization can be seen as a prototypical example of a voluntarily acquired, and hence strong, identity.

De Weerd and Klandermans (1999) broke group identification down into an affective and a behavioral component. The affective component refers to the degree of attachment to the group (farmers in this study) or category, and the behavioral component refers to membership in identity organizations (being a member of a farmers' organization). In a longitudinal study, they investigated the causal relationship between the affective and behavioral identity components and collective action participation. It should not come as a surprise any longer that identification with farmers stimulated collective action participation. While both the affective and the behavioral components impacted on people's willingness to participate in political protest, only the behavioral component stimulated actual participation directly. According to de Weerd and Klandermans, that makes sense: "Being organized implies communication networks, access to resources, interpersonal control, information about opportunities when, where and how to act, and all those other things that make it more likely that intentions materialize" (p. 1092).

The opposite assumption, that participation strengthens group identification, was confirmed for behavioral but not affective identification. These findings suggest that at least in the case of behavioral identification causality between identification and action participation goes in both directions (Klandermans et al. 2002).

The question remains as to why people who participated in collective action are more inclined to participate in farmers' organizations than people who did not participate. A possible answer might be that actual participation enhances feelings of belonging and collective empowerment (Drury and Reicher 1999; Drury et al. 2005) or makes the shared grievances or claims more transparent. In other words, actual participation influences which aspects of collective identity are appropriated. Indeed, although this study can be seen as an important first step in investigating the dynamic interaction between group identification and collective action participation, a great many questions remain unanswered.

SALIENCE. The fact that people have many collective identities raises the question of why some collective identity become central to mobilization while others do not. People have many identities that remain latent most of the time. Self-categorization theory (Turner et al.

1987) hypothesizes that, depending on contextual circumstances, the transition from an "I" to a "we" as the locus of self-definition occurs. A particular identity is said to be salient if it is "functioning psychologically to increase the influence of one's membership in that group on perception and behavior" (Turner et al. 1987:118). Salience is context dependent (Turner 1999). What makes a dormant identity salient and spurs action on behalf of that identity? Besides contextual factors and direct reminders, the presence of other in-group members can be a potent reminder of someone's social identity, the more so if the members are aiming at a common goal. The presence of an outgroup will also remind people of their in-group identity. Another effective prompt is being treated as a member of a minority. Although all these reminders can make a social identity salient, probably the most powerful factor that brings group membership to mind is conflict or rivalry between groups.

The social identity approach suggests that salient social identity spurs several social–psychological processes that facilitate group-serving behavior. For example, when group members define themselves in terms of their collective identity, they focus on the similarities between themselves and fellow in-group members with references to experiences, needs, interests, or goals. As a result, "my" experiences and "your" experiences, needs, and so forth are transformed into "our" experiences and needs. The perception of shared problems or grievances, or of interchangeable needs, goals, and interests, is an important first step toward politicization of a group's collective identity (Simon and Klandermans 2001).

IDENTITY: WHERE DO WE STAND AND HOW TO PROCEED. The foregoing demonstrated the role of identity in spurring collective action participation. Indeed, collective action is contingent on seeing the self as part of a group, while acting collectively requires some *collective* identity or consciousness (Klandermans and de Weerd 2000). It shows that the role of identification in spurring collective action participation is not simply a matter of an on/off switch. Indeed, the influence of identity strength, identity salience, and identity changes over time, revealing that the role of identity on collective action participation is dynamic and multifaceted.

However, there remains a lot to be explained regarding the role of identity in the context of movement participation. To be sure, the basics are clear, but so far we have emphasized the direct effects of identification on collective action participation, but through its influence on values, interests, and emotions identification may also have an indirect effect on collective action participation (Hogg, Terry, and White 1995). The stronger someone's group identification, the more shared beliefs, grievances, emotions, and fate comprising the group's collective identity are incorporated in the individual's social identity. These indirect effects of group identification on participation are far from understood. Moreover, people have multiple social identities that can reinforce or work against each other in motivating people to take the streets. Furthermore, to allude to yet another unsolved issue, little is known about the relationship between collective identity and the idiosyncratic remake of this into someone's social identity. Indeed, more systematic research into the role of collective identity is needed.

Cognition

As mentioned previously, people engage in collective action "any time that they are acting as a representative of the group and the action is directed at improving *the conditions* of the entire group" (Wright 2001). This definition obviously refers to cognition as it implies that people *know* about the conditions of their group. Certainly, the political arena is a domain in which cognitions and the cognition formation are important phenomena. The social psychological study of how people make sense of the social world, or more precisely, of the way in which they interpret, analyze, store, and use information about the social and political world might shed light on how cognition and cognition formation are linked to collective action, particularly, "because social cognition emphasizes the cognitive processes that mediate between environmental stimuli and interpersonal responses and [...] links cognition to action" (Carlston 2001:2). Take, for example, the process of politicization of collective identity as conceptualized by Simon and Klandermans (2001). According to the authors, the process begins with the *awareness* of shared grievances. Next, an external enemy is *blamed* for the group's predicament, and *claims* for compensation are leveled against this opponent. Group members' *perception* that they share grievances is an important first step toward collective social and political action. These emphases make clear that there is an important *cognitive component* (in addition to a motivational and an emotional component) in how people react to their social and political environment.

For more than two decades, social cognition and social psychology were almost synonymous, reflecting how the discipline was transformed by the cognitive revolution (Mischel 1998). The cognitive revolution has had a strong impact on political psychology as well (McGraw 2000). The cognitive approach in political psychology is characterized by the deceptively simple premise that information about the outside political world is organized in internal memory structures, and that these memory structures determine how people interpret and evaluate political events and make political decisions (McGraw 2000).

Despite the pervasive influence of cognition within social and political psychology, remarkably little is known about how cognition translates into collective action participation. Indeed, there is an abundance of cognitive approaches to voting behavior and leadership representation (see McGraw 2000 for an overview) but collective action participation got a raw deal. To be sure, people's cognitions regarding their social environment were often — directly or indirectly—subjects of investigation of students of protest. Moral shocks (Jasper 1997), suddenly imposed grievances (Walsh 1981), frame alignment (Benford and Snow 2000), relative deprivation (Kawakami and Dion 1993), social construction of reality (Gamson 1992), political knowledge (Verba, Schlozman, and Brady 1995), and justice judgments (Tyler and Smith 1998), to give only a few examples, are all cognitive concepts shown to be related to engagement in collective action. However, *what* people know of social and political situations (the content) cannot be easily separated from *how* they process information (the cognitive process, Shweder and Bourne 1984). The processes of interpreting, analyzing, storing, and using information in the context of movement participation are understudied. Cognitive and social psychological information processing approaches, as we hope to be able to show, may introduce new methodologies and new theories to investigate information processing in the context of collective action participation.

REALITY CONSTRUCTION. How do individuals make sense of their complex social environment? What are the underlying mechanisms that determine our understanding of the social world? And how does this understanding relate to action, specifically, collective action? Social cognition literature—the study of the cognitive processes that are involved when we think about the social world—attempts to answer these questions.

What kind of information do people pay attention to? When does political discourse rise enough above the abundance of messages for people to be noticed? Three broad types of information are identified that may be of special concern to people as they form opinions about their social and political environment: (1) the material interests that people see at stake,

(2) the sympathies and resentments that people feel toward groups, and (3) commitment to the political principles that become entangled in public issues (Sears and Funk 1991; Taber 2003). Previous research also showed that attention is automatically allocated to negative information or information inconsistent with existing schemata (Stangor and Ruble 1989), unexpected events (Wyer and Srull, 1986), or information that activates the (social) self (e.g., Bargh 1994). Moreover, as people tend to base their inferences on information from people they trust, interpersonal trust creates an information shortcut (Brewer and Steenbergen 2002). So far these findings are not related to collective action participation. However, we may assume that individuals who interpret information from people they trust as having more unexpected negative consequences for their personal or social self, either because their material interests are at stake or because it is against their principles, are more inclined to take to the streets.

COGNITIVE MISERS.   Individuals are "cognitive misers" (Wyer and Srull 1986), that is, they are seen as having limited processing capacity with which to deal with an infinitely complex and ever-changing environment. They must therefore make the best possible use of these resources and treat them in a miserly manner. For instance, individuals utilize mental shortcuts, called *heuristics,* that reduce the amount of cognitive energy used in decision-making (Kahneman, Slovic, and Tversky 1982). An example of a heuristic is majority rules; in other words, individuals confronted with uncertainty will seek fast and frugal group decision heuristics. A simple majority rule qualifies as such a fast and frugal heuristic. Another cognitive energy-saving device is a *prototype*, which is an abstract mental representations of the central tendency of members of a category (Cantor and Mischel 1977). When people shift from their personal to their social self, self-perception and behavior are effectively brought into line with the contextually relevant in-group prototype. Thus, just relying on the cognitive prototype of the relevant in-group makes people feel, think, and do as group members. How events go by is cognitively represented by *scripts*, or event schemas (Schank and Abelson 1977). Activists, for instance, will have a highly accessible script on how demonstrations go by. The last example of cognitive structures represents a person's knowledge about an object, person, or situation, including knowledge about attributes and relationships among those attributes, or so-called *schemata* (Rumelhart 1980). Justice scholars, for example, were wondering whether individuals have justice schemata (Tyler 1994). If so, it would be interesting to investigate whether individuals with highly elaborated justice schemata are more inclined to participate in collective action than those without.

More recently, the cognitive miser metaphor has been stretched even further in the literature on automaticity (Bargh 1994). In this literature, thought and judgment are viewed as being beyond conscious control. Automatic cognitions are determined and shaped by dominant expectations, schemas, and scripts. However, "one rarely sees explicit mention of automaticity [in political psychology]" (Taber 2003:462). Indeed, investigation of political information processing and accordingly political behavior may take a leap forward by taking automatic processes into account.

DUAL-PROCESS MODELS.   These different processes refer also to a longstanding distinction drawn by psychologists between two distinct ways of information processing—so-called dual process models. One process concerns the unconscious learning of regularities, whereas the other concerns the assessment of unique or novel events (Smith and DeCoster 2000).

Examples of such models abound: the Heuristic Systematic Model (HSM, Chaiken 1980); the Elaboration Likelihood Model (ELM, Petty and Cacioppo 1986), experiential versus rational thinking (Epstein et al. 1996), reflective and impulsive processes (Strack and Deutsch 2004), associative and rule-based processes (Sloman 1996; see Smith and DeCoster 2000 for an extensive overview and conceptual integration of dual-process models in social and cognitive psychology). Moore and Loewenstein (2004), for example, found that self-interest and concern for others influence behavior through different cognitive systems. Self-interest is automatic, viscerally compelling, and often unconscious, while understanding one's ethical obligations to others involves a more thoughtful process. Take, for example, Omoto and Snyder's (1995) distinction between more self-focused and other-focused motivations in their studies of types of motivations of AIDS volunteers (buddies). Indeed, dual-process models may generate new insights into how information processing influences motivational constellation and how it translates into collective action participation.

COGNITIVE ABILITY. Characterizing social cognition as learning what matters in the social world highlights the fact that social-cognitive principles exist because they are adaptive, even necessary, for human survival. They provide essential *benefits* to self-regulation and social regulation. But this is not the whole story, The principles come with *costs* by producing errors and biases in memory, judgments, and decision-making (Higgins 2000). Taber (2003) relates these costs and benefits to information processing and political opinion and concludes that "there is little question that people use heuristics to simplify their information processing; there is considerable question that such short-cuts allow them to behave competently" (p. 459). Taber is one of the scholars who conclude that humans are incapable of analytically interpreting, analyzing, storing, and using political information, and instead rely on a variety of heuristics, which reduce their competence. These scholars depart from the notion that people are cognitive misers. But specifically in relation to complex social and political information, it is the *ambiguity* or *shortage* of information rather than an *abundance* that makes it hard to get an idea of what is going on or who is to be blamed. Indeed, social reality is seldom sufficiently transparent to arrive at one single interpretation.

However, despite these difficulties some authors hold that people are very well capable of conducting political debates and employing political cognition. These authors reason that opinion formation is not only a result of employing individual heuristics to interpret, store, and remember social and political information, but also that people are constantly and actively engaged in a complex and socially situated process of reality construction. Gamson (1992) is an example of the latter from the field of movement studies. He wonders how it is that so many people become active in social movements if people are so generally uninterested and badly informed about (political and social) issues. Gamson designed a study to explore the construction of political understanding and how that may or may not support participation in collective action. Gamson conceived of reality construction as a socially situated process and therefore collected data created in a socially situated setting: focus group interviews. Gamson reported the results of a study of conversations conducted within various social networks. He asked groups of friends and acquaintances to discuss such issues as the Israeli–Arab conflict and affirmative action. One of his most interesting findings was that in these conversations people use any kind of information source available: newspapers, movies, advertisements, novels, rumor, their own and others' experiences, and so on. He claims that a mix of experiential knowledge, popular knowledge, and media discourse develop into so-called collective action frames. In Gamson's words (1992) a *collective action frame* is "a set of action-oriented beliefs and meanings that inspire and legitimate social movement activities and campaigns" (p. 7). They comprise three components—injustice, agency, and identity. The *injustice* component refers to moral indignation. It is not just a cognitive judgment, but also one that is laden with emotion (i.e., a hot cognition). The *agency* component refers to the awareness that it is possible to alter conditions or policies through collective action. The *identity* component refers to the process of defining a "we" and some "they" that have opposing interests and values. Combination of the data sets revealed that media discourse provides information about who is to be blamed for the situation. Experiential knowledge helped to connect the abstract cognition of unfairness with the emotion of moral indignation. Gamson has pioneered new approaches to the study of political understanding, developing new conceptual and methodological tools for thinking about how groups actually formulate political understandings. Instead of treating media content as a stimulus that leads to some change in attitude or cognition, he treated it as an important tool or resource that people in conversation have available, next to popular wisdom, and experiential knowledge.

COGNITION: WHERE DO WE STAND AND HOW TO PROCEED.   The study by Gamson addresses the construction of social reality and how this translates into collective action, which makes it an important contribution to the social psychology of protest. It emphasizes both individual and social aspects of cognition in relation to collective action. However, this study mainly takes the *content*, in other words what people know about their social reality, as its starting point, which leaves many questions addressing the cognitive *process* in relation to collective action unanswered. These cognitive processes and how they relate to collective action participation are insufficiently studied.

The traditional information-processing approach focused on the individual, assuming that cognition was something that concerns the individual brain. However, it is recognized more and more that cognition forms within social groups, rather than individual brains (e.g., Gamson 1992; Smith and DeCoster 2000; Taber 2003). Indeed, people acquire "shared cognitions." How do people come to share information; whom do they trust as a source of information and whom not? Individual members of a collectivity incorporate a smaller or larger proportion of the views supported by "their" organization; but there is an abundance of frames in our social and political environment, so why would people adopt certain frames while neglecting or paying less attention to others? The challenge for collective action scholars will be to account for the social influence on individual cognition formation. Indeed, because the cognitive approach rests on methodological individualism (Fiske et al. 1998) it ignores the fact that many psychological processes are the result of commitment with a given group. Social networks, for example, intervene by shaping the individual preferences or perceptions that form the decision-making process and bring potential activists to collective action (Passy 2003). Moreover, social comparison theory tells us that "an opinion, a belief, an attitude is "correct," "valid," and "proper" to the extent that it is anchored in a group of people with similar believes, opinions, and attitudes" (Festinger 1950:272). In addition, social identification processes underlie the general finding that persuasive messages from in-group sources are more effective than messages an out-group source (Festinger 1950:272). There also appears to be a clear link between the development of shared cognition and shared identity in that a social identity can be both the product of, and precursor to, the development of shared cognition (Swaab: 2007 PSPB, 33, p. 187-199). Finally, consensus formation is also the result of an interpretation process, and personal networks strongly influence this interpretation process (Klandermans 1988). Potential adherents of social movements "attribute meanings to events and interpret situations" before they decide to join a social movement organization and engage in collective action (Klandermans 1992:77). Indeed, socially structured cognition is a new and inviting field in relation to collective action, which is a social phenomenon by nature.

Another theme that requires much more insight is the formation and role of grievances. Why are people aggrieved about one state of affairs and not about another, and why are some grievances the beginning of a mass movement while others never become a reason to mobilize? In addition, the relationship between grievances and emotions is yet to be specified. It is obvious that grievances evoke emotions, but which emotions and how and why is unclear.

Emotions

Politics—and especially politics of protest—are full of emotions. People are *fearful* about terrorism, *angry* about proposed budget cuts, *shocked* about senseless violence, and *proud* about their national identity. Clearly, there is an emotional component in how people react to their social and political environments. Yet, amazingly little is known about where emotions exactly fit into the context of movement participation. In collective action research, emotions are a novice with a long history. In the first half of the previous century, emotions were at the center of collective action studies. Collective action was seen as an irrational response to discontent and emotions were equated with irrationality. As a reaction to these approaches, the dominant academic analyses on collective action participation shifted to rationalistic, structural, and organizational explanations. Such phenomena as moral shocks (Jasper 1997) or suddenly imposed grievances (Walsh 1981) were approached primarily from a cognitive point of view whereas few researchers paid attention to the complex emotional processes that channel fear and anger into moral indignation and political activity. Frame alignment is yet another example of an approach that deals entirely with the cognitive components (but for an exception see see Robnett 2004; Schrock, Holden, and Reid 2004). As a result, emotions as they accompany protest were neglected altogether. The rational trend has now been reversed and we see emotions back on the research agenda of collective action scholars (Goodwin, Jasper, and Polleta 2001, 2004; Jasper 1997, 1998; van Zomeren, Postmes, and Spears, 2004).

To understand engagement in collective action, one must understand emotions—what they are, how they work, and how they interact with motivation, identification, and cognition. Over the past several decades, emotions have become an important topic for research in social psychology. Some of this research concerns the nature of emotion itself: types of emotions, their causes, and their properties. Other research concerns how emotions influence social phenomena: their effects on thought and behavior, their social functions. Importing social psychological expertise on emotions in the sociology-dominated field of collective action may help to understand the role of emotions in protest behavior.

The purpose of this section is to provide some background for the study of emotions and their importance in collective action. We explain why emotions and protest are inextricable phenomena and summarize social psychological emotion theories and research on emotions that—in our view—might be of help by explaining protest behavior, and describe some exemplary studies of the influence of emotions on the dynamics of protest.

EMOTIONS AND PROTEST.   Emotions permeate protest at all stages: recruitment, sustained participation, and dropping out (Jasper 1998 and this volume). Goodwin, Jasper, and Polletta (2001:13) argue that "emotions are socially constructed, but that "some emotions are more [socially] constructed than others, involving more cognitive processes." In their view, emotions that are politically relevant are more socialy constructed. For these emotions, cultural and historical factors play an important role in the interpretation (i.e., perception) of the state of affairs by which they are generated. Emotions, these authors hold, are important in the growth and unfolding of social movement and political protest. Obviously, emotions can be manipulated. Activists work hard to create moral outrage and anger and to provide a target against which these can be vented. They must weave together a moral, cognitive, and emotional package of attitudes. Also in the ongoing activities of the movements do emotions play an important role (Jasper 1997, 1998). Anger and indignation are emotions that are related to a specific appraisal of the situation. At the same time, people might be puzzled by some aspects of reality and try to understand what is going on. They may look for others with similar experiences, and a social movement may provide an environment to exchange experiences, to tell their stories and to express their feelings.

SOCIAL PSYCHOLOGICAL PERSPECTIVES ON EMOTION.   The study of emotions has become a popular research area in social psychology. Such was not always the case. As rational approaches were the state of the art, emotions were often regarded as some peripheral "error term" in motivational theories. But emotion states and their influence on motivation were not about to be so easily explained away. Indeed, emotions have the power to override even the most rational decisions. Several strands of emotion theories were developed since then.

Valence Theories of Emotions.   According to valence theories, emotions are the means by which living creatures are motivated to "approach" and "avoid" (Marcus 2003). However, while it is certainly the case that we all can readily respond to instructions to classify our perceptions into binary oppositions, such as liking/disliking, good/bad, or warm/cold that does not mean that emotional experiences are fully and adequately captured by such a reduction in presumptive structure. Despite this conceptual problem the methodology of binary oppositions is widely practiced in, for instance, semantic differentials and feeling thermometers.

Two-Dimensional Theories.   The two-dimensional theories of emotions are an improvement over the one-dimensional theories in the sense that emotions are characterized not only by approach/avoidance tendencies but by the level of *arousal* as well. To account for both approach and avoidance and arousal, two-dimensional theories propose that emotions fall in a circular order around the perimeter of the space defined by a bipolar valence dimension (pleasantness versus unpleasantness) and an orthogonal dimension labeled activation or arousal (low versus high arousal). These two dimensions define a circumplex, that is, a model in which emotion descriptors can be systematically arranged around the perimeter of a circle (Watson et al. 1999). Although there is an infinite set of possibilities to label the two dimensions, two competing dimensional theories of emotion emerged in social psychology. One is associated with Russell and colleagues (Russell 1980), labeling the dimensions respectively low versus high arousal and unpleasant versus pleasant emotions, and the other with Watson and collaborators (Watson and Tellegen 1985), labeling the dimensions respectively low versus high negative affect and low versus high positive affect.

Underlying Adaptive Systems Theories of Emotions.   Adaptive systems theories all incorporate the idea that two (adaptive) systems are core elements in the regulation of behavior. One system deals with appetitive motivation and approach behavior; the other system deals with aversive motivation and avoidance behavior. According to these theories the vast majority of emotional experiences derive from the same two motives or action tendencies (Carver, Sutton, and Scheier 2000). Much discussion of this link focuses on two aspects of it: the first is that emotions motivate; they prod people to act. The second is that specific emotions prompt actions that have different aims, aims relevant to the particular emotion being experienced. Several relatively distinct theoretical and empirical streams reach a surprising degree of consensus (see Carver, Sutton, and Scheier 2000 for an overview) regarding approach and avoidance processes underlying two kinds of self-regulation, and that these two kinds of self-regulation are paralleled by distinct feeling qualities. A few examples are the behavioral activation system (BAS) and the behavioral inhibition system (BIS) (Gray 1990), promotion of self-regulation and prevention of self-regulation (Higgins 1997), and appetitive and aversive motivational systems (Lang 1995).

Marcus and colleagues translated this line of thought into political psychology with the theory of affective intelligence, which describes the role of emotions in the making of political judgments (Marcus, Neuman, and MacKuen 2000). They believe that emotional responses to political candidates cannot be modeled simply by attaching an affective tag to cognition; they assume that emotions are the result of a dual process: a behavioral inhibition system (i.e., a surveillance system) and a behavioral approach system (i.e., a dispositional system, Marcus and MacKuen 1993).

The theory of affective intelligence adopts a dynamic view of judgment and, further, argues that anxiety is the particular emotion that shifts people from one mode of judgment to the other (and back). When anxiety is low, the disposition system allows people to rely on existing "heuristics" or "predispositions" because low anxiety signals that the environment is safe, familiar, and predictable. On the other hand, when anxiety is high—signaling that the environment is in some fashion uncertain and unsettled—reliance on prior learning with its presumption of predictable continuity would not be a strategically sound course. In such situations, it would likely be potentially dangerous to ignore contemporary information and to rely thoughtlessly on preexisting courses of action. In these environments, the surveillance system pushes people to eschew reliance on existing predispositions, turn to consideration of contemporary information, and make a judgment.

Marcus, Neuman, and MacKuen (2000) tested these effects using evaluation of political candidates and National Election Studies data. Political candidates generate emotions, and in conditions in which anxiety is generated, learning is enhanced. Enthusiasm, on the other hand, does not lead to greater learning or make individuals more careful in processing information. The authors did find, however, that enthusiasm led to greater campaign involvement. It would be worthwhile to investigate under what conditions anxiety or enthusiasm lead to political collective action participation. Indeed, this dual system of emotion approach suggests a more complex set of relationships, with different emotion systems having different impacts not only on the expression of feelings but also on various aspects of cognition and behavior (Marcus 2003).

Discrete Theories of Emotions.   Discrete theories of emotion attribute emotion to the application of multiple cognitive evaluations. It is the personal meaning we give to ambiguous stimuli through *appraisals* that determines emotions we feel. People are continuously evaluating or "appraising" the relevance of their environment for their well-being and appraisals help account for different emotions (Arnold 1960). Lazarus proposed the distinction between "primary appraisal" of an event's implications for one's well-being and "secondary appraisal" of one's ability to cope with the situation (Lazarus 1966). After a fast and automatic evaluation of the first two appraisal dimensions that establishes the impact of the event on the person's general well-being, the other appraisal dimensions are evaluated: How does the event influence my goals? Who or what caused the event? Do I have control and power over the consequences of the event? Are the consequences of the event compatible with my personal values and (societal) norms? Two persons can thus appraise the same event differently and have different emotional responses.

A growing body of appraisal theories of emotions has emerged, each specifying a set of appraisal dimensions in an attempt to better predict the elicitation and differentiation of emotions see (Roseman, Antoniou, and Jose 1996) for a theoretical overview and integration). Nerb and Spada (2001) conducted three experimental studies to investigate the relation between the cognitive appraisal of environmental problems, the development of distinct emotions (anger and sadness), and the resulting action tendencies. The participants in their studies read a fictitious but realistic newspaper report about an environmental problem (a tanker running aground in a severe storm and spilling oil into the North Sea). Different experimental conditions were realized: (1) the tanker did not fulfill the safety guidelines—the damage could have been avoided (high controllability); or (2) the tanker did fulfill the safety guidelines—the damage could not have been avoided (low controllability). It turned out that the more controllable the event the more angry people were and, important for our discussion, the more willing to participate in a boycott (Nerb and Spada 2001). However, if the participants were to believe that the damage could not have been avoided, they were sad, which did not translate into action preparedness.

Group-Based Appraisal Theories of Emotions.   Appraisal theory was developed to explain personal emotions experienced by individuals. Yet, "the self" implicated in emotion-relevant appraisals is clearly not only a personal or individual self. If group membership becomes part of the self, events that harm or favor an in-group by definition harm or favor the self, and the self might thus experience affect and emotions on behalf of the in-group. With such considerations in mind, Smith (1993) developed a model of intergroup emotions that was predicated on social identification with the group. Since collective action is by definition a group phenomenon and group identification appears to be an important factor in determining collective action, we will elaborate on the possible implications of group-based emotions on protest behavior.

The main postulate of intergroup emotion theory (as spelled out by Smith in 1993) is that when a social identity is salient, situations are appraised in terms of their consequences for the in-group, eliciting specific intergroup emotions and behavioral intentions. In three studies Mackie, Devos, and Smith (2000) tested this idea. Participants' group memberships were made salient and the collective support apparently enjoyed by the in-group was measured or manipulated. The authors then measured anger and fear (Studies 1 and 2) and anger and contempt (Study 3), as well as the desire to move against or away from the out-group. Participants who perceived the in-group as strong were more likely to experience anger toward the out-group and to desire to take action against it. Participants who perceived the in-group as weak, on the other hand, were more likely to experience fear and to move away from the out-group. The effects of perceived in-group strength on offensive action tendencies were mediated by anger. Results of these three studies confirm that when a social identity is salient, appraisals of events in terms of consequences for the salient in-group lead to specific emotional responses and action tendencies toward the out-group.

Smith and colleagues investigated the salience of an identity predicting social emotions. Recently we have seen studies addressing the role of social identification in a more explicit way (Dumont et al. 2003; Gordijn, Wigboldus, and Yzerbyt 2001; Yzerbyt et al. 2002, 2003). These scholars argue that "people can, under certain conditions, be connected to others in such a way that they are likely experience emotions even though they themselves are not directly confronted with the triggering situation" (p. 535), in their words: "I feel for us" (p. 533).

These studies suggest that the same emotion processes (i.e., appraisals, emotions, and action tendencies) operating at the individual level and in interpersonal situations operate in intergroup situations. Moreover, people do experience emotions on behalf of their group membership. Since intergroup emotion theory is based on the presumption that the group is incorporated in the self ("the group is in me," thus "I feel for us"), one would assume that the more the group is in me (i.e., the higher the group identification) the more people experience group-based emotions. Yzerbyt et al. (2003) showed that indeed emotional reactions fully mediated the impact of categorization context and identification on action tendencies. In other words, the salience of similarity was found to generate angry feelings among participants only to the extent that they strongly identified with the relevant category. Thus people will experience group-based emotions when the social category is salient *and* they identify with the group at stake.

EMOTIONS: WHERE DO WE STAND AND HOW TO PROCEED.   This brief overview suffices to demonstrate that emotions matter. They warn people of threats and challenges and propel (collective) behavior. Indeed, demands for change begin with discontent. Moreover, affective measures, such as affective commitment (Ellemers 1993) and affective injustice (Smith and Ortiz 2002; van Zomeren et al. 2006), have the largest impact on someone's (collective) behavior. As mentioned previously, phenomena such as moral shocks (Jasper 1997) or suddenly imposed grievances (Walsh 1981) are approached primarily from a cognitive point of view. Few researchers paid attention to the complex emotional processes that channel fear and anger into moral indignation and political activity.

Although emotion terms abound, so far, injustice is approached mainly from a cognitive point of view. Fortunately, the growing attention for emotions in social psychological research also affected injustice scholars (Guimond and Dubé-Simard 1983; Olson and Hafer 1994; Scher and Heise 1993). It is also clear that further investigation of the nature of the justice motive is needed (van Zomeren 2006). Of particular importance is an understanding of the psychological processes underlying various forms of justice, since recent studies suggest that these processes may differ (Tyler 1994). There may very well be other, neglected, aspects of justice to be explored. One suggestion flowing from both general social psychology and the specific literature on retributive justice is that affective models need to receive greater attention.

In the social psychological approaches of emotions, anger is seen as *the* prototypical protest emotion. For those of us who have been part of protest events or watched reports on protest events in the news media, this is hardly surprising. Indeed, it is hard to conceive of protest detached from anger. But other emotions may be relevant in stimulating protest participation. Indignation is one of those emotions that "puts fire in the belly and iron in the soul" (Gamson 1992:32) and, therefore, stimulates protest participation. Ekman (1993) defines indignation as anger about the mistreatment of someone or something; this makes indignation the most political of feelings (Reichenbach 2000). Indeed, the role of indignation in stimulating protest behavior deserves to be investigated (see Jasper 1997, 1998; Kim 2002; Reichenbach 2000).

Another important matter concerns the possibility to do something about goal obstructions. Research suggests that emotions result not only from the appraisal of the implications of an event for goals of the individual but also from his or her ability to cope with the consequences of the event (Scherer and Zentner 2001). Thus, strong political efficacy seems to elicit anger, while weak political efficacy elicits sadness (conforms with the argument of Scherer and Zentner 2001). Further research is needed to shed light on this.

In closing this section, we want to allude to two new potentially interesting directions research is taking. Rahn (2004) has argued that people also experience mood as a result of group membership. This so-called public mood "provides feedback to people about how the group (i.e., the political community) is faring p 7." Research has demonstrated that people in a positive mood display more self-efficacy, are more optimistic, and show more associative cognitive processes, while a negative mood, conversely, is related to higher risk perception, pessimism, and more rule-based cognitive processes (Forgas 2001). In other words, the "emotional barometer" in a country might trigger different (risk) perceptions, cognitive styles, and emotions. This suggests that public mood might influence the claims social movement organizations make, the way problems are framed, the emotions that are experienced, and the motivations to participate in collective action.

Finally, recent work has explored to what extent coping activates certain brain areas known to be related to the aforementioned behavioral inhibition system and the behavioral activation system (BIS/BAS). In a recent study by Harmon-Jones et al. (2003), participants were led to believe that the research concerned reactions to radio broadcasts. Evaluative responses to the broadcast were assessed and brain activity was measured (Harmon-Jones et al. 2003). The participants (all college students) were led to believe that a tuition increase was either certain or merely under consideration. The researchers found that when conflict was less pronounced and action is possible (i.e., when tuition increase is merely planned and petitions are being handed out), greater relative left frontal activation is to be observed than in a situation in which conflict cannot be resolved and action is impossible (i.e., when tuition increase is certain). Furthermore, among those who thought that the increase was merely under consideration, relative left frontal activity predicted both self-reported anger in response to the tuition increase message and coping behavior (signing and taking petitions). Thus, the possibility to act to ameliorate a situation activated the behavioral activation system, resulting in anger and collective action behavior, whereas a seemingly unsolvable problem activated the behavioral inhibition system, resulting in withdrawal (Harmon-Jones et al. 2003).

Consciousness: The Interlock between Individual and Context

We proposed that the social psychological concepts identification, emotions, cognitions and motivation mediate between two collective phenomena: collective identity and collective action. Obviously, in practice all these concepts are interwoven but, as we argued, the distinction is analytically useful. For example, several previously mentioned strands of research show that social identity and emotions seem to work in concert (e.g., Dumont et al., 2003; Mackie, Devos, and Smith, 2000; Smith, 1993) and the same appears for social identity and cognitions (e.g., Swaab et al. 2007). Emotions and cognitions also work together in explaining collective action participation. Originally relative deprivation theory proposed that collective actions are propelled by profound justice-related emotions. However, empirical work in the 1980s and the 1990s began to focus more on people's perceptions or cognitive interpretations of inequality. Yet, in line with the traditional assumptions of RDT Relative Deprivation theory , studies found that although *cognitions* of group-based deprivation did predict collective action, *justice-related emotions* of deprivation such as dissatisfaction, resentment, and group-based anger were a more powerful motivator for action, both empirically (Guimond and Dubé-Simard 1983) as well as meta-analytically (Smith and Ortiz 2002; van Zomeren et al. 2006).

Thus social psychological research reveals that at least the combination of identity/ emotions, identity/cognitions, and cognitions/emotions work together to motivate collective action. But how do these concepts act together in concert such that they all create a nutritious breeding ground for motivation to engage in collective action? In other words, how do group affiliation and the meaning and related feelings that individuals give to a social situation become a shared definition implying collective action?

Following, for example Gamson (1992), Foster and Matheson (1999), and Duncan (1999) we propose *consciousness* as a concept that connects individual and collective processes so that individual processes such as identification, cognition, and emotion all synthesize into a motivational constellation preparing people for action.[2] Political consciousness generally represents a shift from a victim perspective, through which people accept their status, to a sense of discontent and withdrawal of legitimacy from the present social or political situation. Consciousness is defined as politicized identification, that is, an identification with a category coupled with a collective political ideology around issues concerning that category (Duncan 1999). This definition is based on stratum consciousness (Gurin, Miller, and Gurin 1980), which involves four independent elements: (1) a sense that one's fate is linked to that of other members of a group or category (gays, farmers, women, blacks); (2) discontent with the power and influence of the group; (3) a belief that power differentials are a result of structural rather than individuals factors; and (4) a collective orientation toward redressing these inequities. Hence, consciousness involves a mesh between individual and cultural levels (Morris 1992:55) or between individual beliefs about the social world and cultural belief systems and ideologies.

Meaning structures at the individual level can be investigated with concepts such as *heuristics, prototype, scripts,* or *event schemas* and (*justice*) schemata and the meaning structures of the collective level can be examined with concepts such as beliefs, symbols, ideologies, and rituals. Of course, we can learn something of value from work that focuses on a single level, but "neither is adequate by itself if we want to understand the kind of political consciousness that affects people's willingness to be quiescent or to engage in collective action" (Morris 1992:65). Taken alone, both the individual level approaches and the collective level approaches seem incomplete. As Gamson (1992, p. 67) puts it: "students of social movements need a social psychology that treats consciousness as the interplay between two levels—between individuals who operate actively in the construction of meaning and sociocultural processes that offer meanings that are frequently contested". He argues that the concept of *framing* offers the most useful way of bridging these levels of analysis (Benford and Snow 2000; de Weerd 1999; Gamson 1992; Hercus 1999; Snow and Benford 1992).

FROM COLLECTIVE IDENTITY TO POLITICIZED COLLECTIVE IDENTITY. Awareness of a collective identity does not necessarily make that identity politically relevant; collective identity must politicize to become the engine of collective action. Politicization of collective identity and the underlying power struggle unfold as a sequence of politicizing

---

[2] The concept of consciousness is related to Tajfel's (1971) concept of *social change orientation* (solving group problems through group actions), in that it indicates the process of investing the self in the group and can be understood as a form of collective identity that underlies group members' explicit motivations to engage in such a power struggle. The same process is described as cognitive liberation (McAdam, 1982) and recently referred to as politicized collective identity (Simon and Klandermans, 2001).

events that gradually transform the group's relationship to its social environment. Typically, this process begins with the awareness of shared grievances. Next, an external enemy is blamed for the group's predicament, and claims for compensation are leveled against this enemy. Unless appropriate compensation is granted, the power struggle continues. If in the course of this struggle the group seeks to win the support of third parties such as more powerful authorities (e.g., the national government) or the general public, collective identity fully politicizes (Simon and Klandermans 2001).

What distinguishes politicized collective identity from collective identity? The first distinction is raised consciousness: "the growing awareness of shared grievances and a clearer idea of who or what is responsible for those grievances reflect a distinct cognitive elaboration of one's worldview providing group members with a meaningful perspective on the social world and their place in it" (Simon and Klandermans 2001:327). The second distinction is about the relation with other groups. A politicized identity provides antagonistic lenses through which the social world is interpreted. This intergroup polarization defines other groups in the social and political arena as "pro" or "con," thus as allies or opponents. The third distinction concerns the unique behavioral consequences of politicized collective identity, namely, politicized group members should be likely to engage in collective action directed at the government or the general public to force them to intervene or to take sides.

CONSCIOUSNESS: WHERE DO WE STAND AND HOW TO PROCEED. Although Gurin came up with the concept of consciousness as an important prerequisite of collective action three decennia ago, not much collective action researchers took up this idea (for exceptions see Duncan 1999, Gamson 1992, and Morris 1992). A focus on consciousness might shed a light on what connects cognitions, emotions, and motivation. Indeed, the politicization of both individual social and collective identities can be seen as a spiral process of consciousness raising by interpretation and reinterpretation in which cognitions and emotions all will act in concert to reinterpret social and political situations aimed at redressing a perceived social or political injustice. Hence, the politicization of both collective and individual identities can be seen as a dynamic process in which the individual-based consciousness as described by Gamson (1992) interacts with the more collectively based consciousness as mentioned by Morris (1992).

However, little is known about the dynamic processes of politicization of the collective identity and how this may change the content of the social identities. Another related identity issue is causality. For example, it seems plausible that people with a stronger politicized identity are more inclined to join a social movement and accordingly have strong action preparedness. Indeed, the (causal) dynamic relation between collective identities and politicized identities is underexplored and deserves attention.

How may this relate to group identification and politicization of that identity? The findings in classic and recent research indicate that people who identify with a group (1) perceive themselves to be more similar to each other (Allen and Wilder 1975; Mackie 1986); (2) are more likely to act cooperatively (Back 1951); (3) feel a stronger need to agree with group opinion (Deutsch and Gerard 1955; Mackie, Gastardo-Conaco, and Skelly 1992; Wilder 1990); (4) perceive in-group messages to be of higher quality (Brock 1965; Mackie, Worth, and Asuncion 1990); and (5) conform more in both behavior and attitude (French and Raven 1959; Wilder and Shapiro 1984); even more strongly in time of intergroup conflict owing to polarization of group attitudes and behavior (Mackie 1986). This is exactly what Oegema (1993) shows in his study on the peace movement in the Netherlands, in times of intergroup conflict (when the Dutch government decided to deploy the cruise missiles) cognitive consistency proved to increase.

Motivation

Demands for change are rooted in a notion of belonging (identification), and an experienced grievance (cognition) in combination with feelings related to this (collective) grievance. Consciousness-raising turns an individual experienced grievance into a collective grievance. Consciousness generally includes an action orientation: "the view that collective action is the best means to realize the group's interests" (Gurin, Miller, and Gurin 1980:31). Hence, it includes the *motivation* to solve collective grievances with collective action. This brings us to our last proposed social psychological concept mediating between collective identity and collective action: motivation.

Motivation is the desire to achieve a goal, combined with the energy to work toward that goal. What motives do people have for taking part in collective action? So far, social psychologists have proposed three participation motives: instrumentality, identity, and group-based anger. We feel, however, that an important element is missing here, namely ideology (van Stekelenburg, Klandermans, and Dijk 2007a). The triad of instrumentality, identity, and *ideology* has a long history in functional theories of attitudes and behavior (Sears and Funk 1991; Sears, Hensler, and Speer 1979), and related triads have been proposed in the literature as antecedents of attitude importance (Boninger, Krosnick, and Berent 1995) and cooperative behavior (Tyler and Blader 2000). Therefore, we propose to add ideology as a fourth motive for participation in social movements. In the sections that follow we elaborate on these four motives.

INSTRUMENTAL MOTIVES. Instrumentality became the focus of the literature on movement participation when resource mobilization and political process theory became the dominant paradigm of the field. It was emphasized that movement participation is as rational or irrational as any other behavior. Movement participants were seen as people who believed that a situation can be changed at affordable costs. In other words, movement participation was seen as a rational choice following from the expectation that protest will yield certain outcomes and the value of those outcomes.

The instrumental motive is theoretically rooted in Klandermans's (1984) social psychological expansion of resource mobilization theory. Klandermans noted that resource mobilization theory had nearly abandoned the social–psychological level of analysis of collective actions and underestimated the significance of grievances and ideology as determinants of participation in collective actions (Klandermans 1984:584). He argued, furthermore, that in their decision to participate in collective action, people take reactions of others into account; indeed, costs and benefits of participation are not assessed in a social vacuum. To cure these flaws, Klandermans (1984) presented a *social–psychological expansion* of resource mobilization theory as an explanation of why some aggrieved people participate in protest, while others do not.

The model he proposes is a fusion of expectancy value theory and collective action theory. Expectancy value theory explains the motivation for specific behavior by the value of the expected outcomes of that behavior (Klandermans 1984). The core of the social–psychological expansion of resource mobilization theory is the individual's expectation that specific outcomes will materialize multiplied by the value of those outcomes for the individual. In line with expectancy-value approaches (Feather and Newton 1982), expectations and values stand in a multiplicative relationship. A goal might be valuable, but if it cannot be reached, it is unlikely to motivate behavior. If, on the other hand, a goal is within someone's reach, but it is of no value, it will not motivate behavior either.

Expectancy-value theory thus assumes a rational decision maker. However, collective action theory (Olson 1965) maintains that rational decision makers, if they must decide to take part in collective action, are faced with a dilemma, the collective action dilemma. Collective actions, if they succeed, tend to produce collective goods that are supplied to everybody irrespective of whether people have participated in the production of the collective good. Thus, if the collective good is produced people will reap the benefits anyway. Collective action theory predicts that under those circumstances rational actors will choose to take a free ride, unless selective incentives (i.e., those incentives that depend on participation) motivate them to participate. However, if too many people conclude from that assessment that they can afford to take a free ride, the collective good will not be produced.

Klandermans (1984) argued that information about the behavior of others can help to overcome the dilemma. However, when the decision to participate must be taken it is usually not known what the others will do (but see Zhao, 1998 for an interesting example of a mobilization campaign where people did have information about the behavior of others). In the absence of factual information, people must rely on expectations about the behavior of others. Such expectations can be based on past experience, interaction between potential participants, newspaper accounts, and so on. This is walking a thin line. If someone expects that few will participate his motivation to take part will be low. If someone feel that many people participate he may conclude that he can afford to take a free ride. Organizers will, therefore, try to make people belief that their participation does make a difference.

The model Klandermans built on the basis of these considerations, therefore, contained expectations about the behavior of others. Collective action participation is explained by the following parameters: *collective benefits* and *social* and *non-social selective incentives*. Collective benefits are a composite of the value of the action goal and the expectation that the goal will be reached. This expectation is broken down into expectations about the behaviors of others, expectations that the action goal will be reached if many others participate, and the expectation that one's own participation will increase the likelihood of success.

Combining collective action theory with expectancy value models appeared to be a fruitful approach for a systematic analysis of the variety of beliefs, expectations, and attitudes that are involved in the decision to take part in collective action (Klandermans 1984). However, others have doubted whether movement participation could be fully explained by such rational considerations (Kelly and Breinlinger 1996; Klandermans 2003, 2004; Schrager 1985). Kelly and Breinlinger (1996) argue that the assumption of rationality is especially strained in cases of protracted disputes. In these cases, activists often bear the financial and social burden of extreme hardship and are usually fully cognizant of the fact that benefits, if gained at all, may be slight. A major limitation of this account is its neglect of the *social* and *ideological* aspects of collective action. As Schrager (1985:859) points out, "collective action is more than the sum of economistic calculations: social and ideological factors figure powerfully in people's willingness to act."

Simon and colleagues observed that the instrumental approach proposed by Klandermans (1984) ignores the fact that people's decisions are influenced by their membership of groups and inter-group dynamics (Gamson 1992; Kelly 1993; Stürmer and Simon 2004b). As a result, it misses key factors encountered in social movement contexts. Understanding the influence of group membership on participation requires a broader perspective, one that goes beyond individualistic analyses and takes the relationship between the individual and the group into account (Haslam 2001; Simon et al. 1998). Identity theories offer such a perspective.

IDENTITY MOTIVES.   The basic hypothesis regarding the identity motive is fairly straight-forward: a strong identification with a group makes participation in collective political action on behalf of that group more likely (see Huddy 2003; Simon 2004; Stryker, Owens, and White 2000 for a comprehensive treatment of the subject). As mentioned in the identification section, the available empirical evidence overwhelmingly supports this assumption.

Identity motives refer to the circumstance that people identify with the others involved. For people taking the identity path to collective action participation, the focus changes from what "I" want to what "we" want (Brewer and Gardner 1996). Collective action participation is seen as a way to show who "we" are and what "we" stand for. Moreover, group members have the idea that "we" have much in common (by way of shared grievances, aims, values or goals). This participation motive is theoretically rooted in the identity pathway to collective action proposed by Simon et al. (1998).

Simon and colleagues (1998) proposed a *dual path model* to collective action participation in which they distinguished between an instrumental pathway, guided by calculative reasoning that concentrates on the costs and benefits of participation, and an identity pathway guided by processes of identification. Two levels of identification were measured. The first concerned the broader social category from which a social movement typically recruits its supporters, the second the specific social movement organizations themselves. It was expected that identification with the social movement organization would be a better predictor than identification with the broader social category. This should be the case because the former is more directly tied to activist identity, which implies a readiness to act (Kelly 1993).

In a series of studies, Simon and his colleagues assessed the influence of identification on collective action participation net of instrumental motives. The studies clearly confirmed the hypothesized role of both instrumental and identity motives (Simon et al. 1998). Moreover, identification with the social movement (the German Grey Panthers, the gay movement, or the fat acceptance movement) appeared to be a better predictor of movement participation than identification with the broader recruitment category (aged people, gays, or fat people). These results underscore the importance of the more politicized form of collective identification with the social movement itself. They suggest that identification with a disadvantaged group increases group members' willingness to participate in collective action only to the extent that it is transformed into a more politicized form of activist identification (Simon and Klandermans 2001).

The research program of Simon et al. has taught us a lot about the working of instrumental and identity motives. First, it showed that both instrumental and identity motives account independently for willingness to participate. Rather than replacing instrumentality as an explanatory paradigm, identity adds to the explanation as a second parameter. Next, the program revealed the importance of identity salience. Yet, although salience is an essential condition, it is not enough; it is salience combined with a strong group identification that turns individuals into committed group members. Third, the research of Simon et al. showed that in times of relative peace primarily those who are strongly identifying members of the social movement organizations are prepared to mobilize, whereas in more conflictual times those who identify with the broader category are also prepared to take the streets.

Identity processes appear to have both *indirect* and *direct* effects on collective action participation (Stürmer 2000, cited by Klandermans and de Weerd 2000): direct effects because collective identity creates a shortcut to participation—participation stems not so much from the outcomes associated with participation but from identification and solidarity with other group members involved (Klandermans 2000); indirect effects because collective identity influences instrumental reasoning; it makes it less attractive to take a free ride—high levels of group identification increase the costs of defection and the benefits of cooperation. Moreover, if people identify more with their group, their grievances are stronger (Kawakami and Dion 1993; Tropp and Wright 1999), instrumental reasoning becomes more influential (McCoy and Major 2003), threats to values are more strongly felt (Branscombe et al. 1999), as are emotions (Yzerbyt et al. 2003), and they believe more in the collective efficacy of their group to organize and execute the courses of action required to produce given attainments (Kelly 1993).

GROUP-BASED ANGER MOTIVES.   Sociologists of emotions were the first to discuss the emotional aspects of collective action, but students of emotions in social psychology followed suit. Van Zomeren and colleagues (2004) proposed an emotional pathway to collective action next to the instrumental pathway; hence they also propose the notion of a dual pathway in their approach to collective action participation. Central in the model are so called group-based appraisals.

They took the appraisal theory of emotion (Lazarus 1991) as their point of departure. This theory conceives of appraisal, emotion, and action as the means by which people cope with events in their social world. It makes a distinction between problem-focused and emotion-focused coping. According to Lazarus (2001:48), a person engages in problem-focused coping when he "obtains information on which to act and mobilizes actions for the purpose of changing the reality," while "the emotion-focused function is aimed at regulating the emotions tied to the situation." Following Smith (1993), van Zomeren, Postmes, and Spears (2004) propose an extrapolation of the appraisal theory of emotion to the group level. They argue that group members who perceive disadvantages as collective appraise events in group rather than individual terms. They relate problem-focused coping to the instrumental pathway to collective action and emotion-focused coping to the emotional pathway, the so-called group-based anger pathway.

On the instrumental pathway *group efficacy* and *action support* play a central role. Group efficacy is the belief that group-related problems can be solved by collective efforts. When people take the instrumental path to political protest, they participate "for the purpose of changing reality" (Lazarus 1991:48). Collective action is seen as an instrumental strategy to improve the situation of the group. Action support implies the perceived willingness of other group members to engage in collective action. That, hence, increases a sense of efficacy.

In the group-based anger pathway *unfairness* and *social opinion support* play a central role. In line with social psychological grievance literature, van Zomeren et al. hold that it are more often procedures deemed unfair, than outcomes deemed unfair that upset people. In addition to perceived procedural unfairness, social opinion support is proposed as a mechanism that helps to define the experienced unfairness as shared. Social opinion support refers to the perception that fellow group members share the experienced unfairness. Appraisals such as unfairness and social opinion support are believed to promote collective action because they evoke emotions such as anger. Action participation allows people to regulate their emotions through action, which makes participating in collective action with a group-based anger motive a goal in itself.

Van Zomeren and colleagues tested their model in three experiments. They predicted and found that when a group is collectively disadvantaged (which makes salient individuals' social identity), (1) group-based appraisals of procedural unfairness and social opinion support promote collective action tendencies through group-based anger (so-called "emotion-focused coping") and (2) group-based appraisal of social action promotes collective action tendencies through group efficacy (so-called "problem-focused coping"). Moreover,

(3) because people can use both ways of coping, both group-based anger and group efficacy independently predict collective action tendencies (i.e., the dual pathway model to protest).

The study of Van Zomeren, Postmes, and Spears (2004) confirms the importance of emotions as motivators without replacing the instrumental pathway. Indeed, both pathways go together and reinforce one another and are conceptualized as equally rational ways of coping with collective disadvantage. However, besides emotional coping (i.e., emotion regulation) we want to emphasize another function for how emotions impact on protest behavior. We hold that emotions function as *accelerators or amplifiers*. Accelerators make something move faster, and amplifiers make something sound louder. In the world of protest *accelerating* means that because of emotions, motives to enter, stay, or leave a social movement translate into action faster, while amplifying means that these motives are stronger.

The importance of these concepts in explaining protest participation is also demonstrated in a meta-analysis (van Zomeren, Postmes, and Spears 2006). The authors conducted a meta-analysis of 172 independent studies. Three areas of subjective perception are deduced from the social psychological literature on protest: perceived injustice, perceived efficacy, and a sense of social identity (see Gamson 1992; Klandermans 1997; van Zomeren, Postmes, and Spears 2004). At least three important conclusions can be drawn from this meta-analysis. First, a sense of injustice, efficacy, and identity each has an independent, unique effect on collective action. Second, politicized measures of identity resulted in stronger effect sizes than nonpoliticized measures (see Simon and Klandermans 2001; Stürmer and Simon 2004a). The third conclusion is that the affective component of injustice is more predictive of collective action than the cognitive component of injustice. This relates to another important development in the social psychological injustice and relative deprivation literature that shows exactly the same, namely, that emotions play a crucial role in predicting collective action participation.

IDEOLOGY MOTIVES. The fourth motive, wanting to express one's views, refers at the same time to a longstanding theme in the social movement literature and to a recent development. In classic studies of social movements the distinction was made between instrumental and expressive movements or protest (see Gusfield 1963; Searles and Williams 1962). In those days, instrumental movements were seen as movements that aimed at some external goal, for example, the implementation of citizenship rights. Expressive movements, on the other hand, were seen as a goal in itself, for example, the expression of anger in response to experienced injustice. Movement scholars felt increasingly uncomfortable with the distinction, because it was thought that most movements had both instrumental and expressive aspects and that the emphasis on the two could change over time. Therefore, the distinction lost its use.

Recently, however, the idea that people might participate in movements to express their views has received anew attention, this time from movement scholars who were unhappy with the overly structural approach of resource mobilization and political process theory. These scholars put an emphasis on such aspects as the creative and cultural aspects of social movements, narratives, emotions, and moral indignation (Goodwin, Jasper, and Polleta 2001, 2004). People are angry, develop feelings of moral indignation about some state of affairs or some government decision, and want to make that known. They participate in a social movement not necessarily to enforce political change, but to gain dignity and moral integrity in their lives through struggle and moral expression.

The ideology path to protest participation refers to people's values and the assessment that these values have been violated. A fundamental assumption on which this path relies is that people's willingness to participate in political protest depends to a significant extent on their perception of a state of affairs as illegitimate (see van Zomeren et al. 2004), in the sense that it goes against fundamental values. An individual's personal set of values is believed to strongly influence how, for example, a proposed policy, its ends and means, is perceived and evaluated.

According to Rokeach (1973:5), a "*value* is an enduring belief that a specific mode of conduct or end-state of existence is personally or socially preferable to an opposite or converse mode of conduct or end-state of existence. A *value system* is an enduring organization of beliefs concerning preferable modes of conduct or end-states of existence along a continuum of relative importance." For Schwartz (1992:4), "values (1) are concepts of beliefs, (2) pertain to desirable end states or behaviors, (3) transcend specific situations, (4) guide selection or evaluations of behavior and events, and (5) are ordered by relative importance. Values, understood this way, differ from attitudes primarily in their generality or abstractness (feature 3) and in their hierarchical ordering by importance (feature 5)." In principle, then, the distinction between attitudes and values is clear. "Attitudes refer to evaluations of specific objects while values are much more general standards used as basis for numerous specific evaluations across situations" (Feldman 2003:481).

Conceptualized this way, values are matters about which people have strong feelings. They defend them and react strongly when their values are challenged (Feather and Newton 1982). Indeed, "values are standards employed to tell us which beliefs, attitudes, values, and actions of others are worth challenging, protesting, and arguing about, or worth trying to influence or change" (Rokeach 1973:13). Participating in collective action is one of the possible reactions to a perceived violation of one's values.

MOTIVATIONAL CONFIGURATIONS.   We began our section on motives with a discussion of instrumental motives, and within that context we referred to the debate about the free rider dilemma. Having discussed now the three other motives of participation we are in a position to reconcile the free rider debate. Within the instrumentality framework there are two ways to overcome the dilemma—selective incentives and optimistic but not too optimistic expectations about the behavior of others. The identity, ideology, and emotion framework implies additional ways to overcome the free rider dilemma. In all three frameworks, the working of inner drives functions to neutralize the dilemma. In the case of identity, identification with others involved generates a felt inner obligation to behave as a "good" group member (Stürmer et al. 2003). These authors show that, when self-definition changes from personal to social identity, the group norm of participation becomes salient; the more one identifies with the group, the more weight this group norm will carry and the more it will result in an "inner obligation" to participate on behalf of the group. Ideology motives create a sense of inner *moral* obligation for reasons of moral integrity maintenance. Maintaining one's moral integrity incites an inner moral obligation to oneself, as compared to an inner social obligation to other group members incited by group identification. Group-based anger, finally, points to emotion regulation or catharsis as yet another mechanism to overcome free riding. After all, "the emotion-focused coping function is aimed at regulating the emotions tied to the situation" (Lazarus 1991:48), and one way to regulate these personally experienced emotions is to participate in collective action. Therefore emotional-focused coping makes free riding less likely, because one might take a free ride on the production of a *collective* good, but one cannot take a free ride on regulating one's own *personal* emotions. The free rider literature tends to focus on external pull factors, such as goal achievement and selective benefits, but neglects the internal factors or felt inner obligations that push individuals toward participation.

MOTIVATION: WHERE DO WE STAND AND HOW TO PROCEED.   Research of the last two decennia has taught us a great deal about the working of motivation. It showed that people have several motives to take part in collective action. It started of with instrumental motives followed by identity motives. Recently emotion regulation and ideological motives are added as reasons to take part. However, the current social psychological literature on protest participation does not elaborate on which of the participation motives proposed so far will prevail for whom, when, and why. In other words, for whom will what pathway to collective action prevail, and why? Why are people attracted to one social movement organization rather than another? Why are some people inclined to take the instrumental path whereas others take the ideological path? More generally, the combined working of the motives to participate is far from clear, let alone the way the motivational configuration might differ for different movements, in different contexts, or at different times. We are currently in the process of publishing research in which we focus on various motivational constellations as a result of the mobilizing context (van Stekelenburg, Klandermans, and v. Dijk. 2007a, 2007b, 2007c).

We also have pointed to the role of inner obligations. The social psychological importance of inner obligations is that one cannot take a free ride on inner obligations. This makes them important in the process of mobilization. But how such inner obligations are generated and how the various inner drives differ in their working or how they interact is not clear, let alone how they interact with group identification and consciousness-raising.

Instead of focusing on people who *are* motivated to participate, we might learn much from people who do *not* participate. Does the motivational constellation of nonparticipants differ from that of participants? And how about cognitions and experienced emotions? Is the consciousness of people who do not participate lower than that of people who do participate? All these kinds of questions are interesting and can tell us a much about why (or why not) people take to the streets.

COLLECTIVE ACTION PARTICIPATION

In this section, we deal with the phenomenon of collective action participation. We discuss such matters as what we mean by movement participation, movement participation within the broader spectrum of the dynamics of contention, short-term versus sustained participation, and the dynamics of disengagement (an often forgotten aspect of movement participation).

The Process of Participation

Participation in social movements is a multifaceted phenomenon. Indeed, there are many different forms of movement participation. Two important dimensions to distinguish forms of participation are *time* and *effort*. Some forms of participation are limited in time or of a once-only kind and involve little effort or risk—giving money, signing a petition, or taking part in a peaceful demonstration. Examples in the literature are the demonstration and petition against cruise missiles in the Netherlands (Klandermans and Oegema 1987; Oegema and Klandermans 1994). Other forms of participation are also short-lived but involve considerable effort or risk—a sit-in, a site occupation, or a strike. Participation in the Mississippi Freedom Summer (McAdam 1988) and participation in the Sanctuary movement (Nepstad and Smith 1999) are cases in point. Participation can also be indefinite but little demanding—paying a membership fee to an organization or being on call for two nights a month. Pichardo, Alman-zar, and Deane (1998) studied a variety of such forms of participation in the environmental movement. Finally, there are forms of participation that are both enduring and taxing, such as being a member on a committee or a volunteer in a movement organization. Examples are the members of neighborhood committees (Oliver 1984) and the members of underground organizations (Della Porta 1988, 1992). From a social psychological viewpoint, taxonomies of participation are relevant because one may expect different forms of participation to involve different motivational dynamics. Let us give two illustrative examples. Long-term, taxing forms of participation are typically of the kind for which you need a few people who are willing to do the job. Once you have mobilized those few you do not really need more par-ticipants. Indeed, more participants might even create problems. This is typically the situation where people can and in fact do take a free ride (Marwell and Oliver 1993). Oliver (1984) shows that the few who participate in these activities are usually fully aware of the fact that they are giving a free ride to most sympathizers, but it doesn't bother them. In fact, this is part of their motivation: if I do not do it nobody else will do it, they reason. Compare this to a strike. For a strike you need some minimal number of participants. As long as this threshold is not passed all effort is in vain. In terms of the motivation of participants, the problem to be solved is to make people believe that the threshold will be reached.

Knowing that you are giving many others a free ride or knowing that a threshold must be reached are two completely different cognitions. The two examples illustrate that different forms of participation imply different motivational dynamics. More obvious is the impact of costs. Higher costs will reduce participation. This is indeed what we found in studies of two campaigns of the Dutch peace movement (Klandermans and Oegema 1987; Oegema and Klandermans 1994). Although the numbers of sympathizers at the two points in time were the same, as was the proportion of the sympathizers that was targeted by mobilization attempts, the campaign for the petition resulted in the participation of more than 50 percent of the sym-pathizers while that for a demonstration in not even 5 percent. In one of the rare comparative studies of types of movement participation, Passy (2001) found indeed that the motivational dynamics of various forms of participation were different.

Demand, Supply, and Mobilization

Social psychology might be interested in individual level processes such as movement partic-ipation, but this is not to say that the other disciplines have nothing to say about participation. To illustrate this it is important to understand that movement participation has a demand side and a supply side. *Demand* refers to the potential in a society for protest; it relates to the inter-est in a society in what a movement stands for. Is the movement addressing a problem people are worried about? Is there a need for a movement on these issues? Usually, the people who participate in a movement are only a small proportion of those who care about the issue. This is not necessarily a sign of weakness. On the contrary, for a movement to be viable, a large reservoir of sympathizers is needed to nourish its activists. *Supply* refers, on the other hand, to the opportunities staged by organizers to protest. It relates to the characteristics of the move-ment. Is it strong? Is it likely to achieve its goals at affordable costs? Does it have charismatic leaders? Is it an organization people can identify with? Does it stage activities that are appeal-ing to people? Demand and supply do not automatically come together. In the market econ-omy marketing is employed to make sure that the public is aware of a supply that might meet its demand. *Mobilization* is the marketing mechanism of the movement domain.

Empirical research into these aspects of the dynamics of participation addresses different phenomena. The demand-side of participation requires studies of such phenomena as socialization, grievance formation, causal attribution, emotions, and (the formation of) collective identity. The study of the supply-side of participation concerns such matters as action repertoires, the effectiveness of social movements, the frames and ideologies movements stand for, and the constituents of identification they offer. The study of mobilization concerns such matters as the effectiveness of (persuasive) communication, the influence of social networks, the implied costs and benefits of participation, and frame resonance.

Studies of participation tend to concentrate on mobilization and to neglect the development of demand and supply factors. Yet, there is no reason to take either for granted. To be sure, grievances abound in a society, but that does not mean that there is no reason to explain how grievances develop and how they are transformed into a demand for protest. Nor does the presence of social movement organizations in a society mean that there is no need to understand their formation and to investigate how they stage opportunities to protest and how these opportunities are seized by aggrieved people.

Between the social sciences, a division of labor exists in terms of the study of demand, supply, and mobilization. Social psychology is well equipped to study demand and mobilization, whereas sociology and political science typically study supply factors. The interplay of demand, supply, and mobilization leads to different configurations in different local and national settings. Therefore, comparative, preferable interdisciplinary, studies are the proper way of exploring demand, supply, and mobilization.

DEMAND. Our treatment of the dynamics of movement participation builds on the previously described three fundamental motives of why movement participation is appealing to people: people may want to change their circumstances (instrumentality), they may want to act as members of their group (identity), or they may want to express their views and feelings (ideology). Indeed, we mentioned group-based anger motives too, but we take a slightly different approach to emotions than van Zomeren, et al. (2004) do. We do not conceptualize group-based anger as a separate motive; we rather assume that there is no protest participation without emotions. Following Jasper (1997), we assume that emotions "give [all] ideas, ideologies, identities and even interests their power to motivate" (p. 127). Or, as we argued, emotions function as amplifier or accelerator for each of the three motives. Therefore we hold that instrumentality, identity, and ideology (amplified by emotions) together account for most of the demand for collective political action in a society.

Social movements may supply the opportunity to fulfill these demands, and the better they do, the more movement participation turns into a satisfying experience. In the section on the social psychology of movement participation, we elaborated extensively on the demand side of the motives. In the current section we briefly illustrate how movements shape the supply side of participation.

SUPPLY

Instrumentality. Instrumentality presupposes an effective movement that is able to enforce changes or at least to mobilize substantial support. Making an objective assessment of a movement's impact is not easy (see Giugni 1998, 2004; Giugni, McAdam, and Tilly 1999), but of course movement organizations will try to convey the image of an effective political force. They can do so by pointing to the impact they have had in the past, or to the powerful allies they have. Of course, they may lack all this, but then, they might be able to show other signs of strength.

A movement may command a large constituency as witnessed by turnout on demonstrations, or by membership figures, or large donations. It may comprise strong organizations with strong charismatic leaders who have gained respect, and so on. Instrumentality also implies the provision of selective incentives. The selective incentives of participation that can be made available may vary considerably between movement organizations. Such variation depends on the resources a movement organization has at its disposal (McCarthy and Zald 1976; Oliver 1980).

Identity. Movements offer the opportunity to act on behalf of one's group. This is most attractive if people identify strongly with their group. Movements and movement organizations may be, and in fact often are, controversial. Hence, becoming a participant in a movement organization does not mean taking a respected position upon oneself (Linden and Klandermans 2006, 2007). Within the movement's framework, this is, of course, completely different. There the militant does have the status society is denying him. And, of course, for an activist in-group–out-group dynamics may turn the movement organization or group into a far more attractive group than any other group "out there" that is opposing the movement. Indeed, it is not uncommon for militants to refer to the movement organization as a second family, a substitute for the social and associative life society was no longer offering them (Orfali 1990; Tristan 1987). Movement organizations supply, make salient, or even create sources of identification. Moreover, they offer all kinds of opportunities to enjoy and celebrate the collective identity: marches, rituals, songs, meetings, signs, symbols, and common codes (see Stryker, Owens, and White 2000 for an overview).

A complicating matter is the fact that people have multiple identities while movements tend to emphasize a single collective identity. This may imply competing loyalties, as Oegema and Klandermans (1994) demonstrated with regard to the Dutch peace movement. The movement's campaign against cruise missiles brought many a citizen who sympathized with the movement but was affiliated the Christian Democratic Party, which stood opposite the movement, under cross-pressure. Movement organizations can be more or less successful in coping with multiple identities. Kurtz (2002) describes how clerical workers of Columbia University struggled but succeeded to reconcile gender, ethnic, and class identities. Beckwith (1998), however, explains how women in the Pittston Coal Strike were denied the possibility to act on their gender identity. Very little systematic attention has been given in the social movement literature to the issue of multiple identity, yet it is to be assumed that every movement somehow must deal with the problem, and depending on how this is accomplished is more or less attractive to various constituencies.

Ideology. Social movements play a significant role in the diffusion of ideas and values (Eyerman and Jamison 1991). Rochon (1998) makes the distinction between "critical communities" where new ideas and values are developed and "social movements" that are interested in winning social and political acceptance for those ideas and values. "In the hands of movement leaders, the ideas of critical communities become ideological frames" (p. 31), Rochon argues. Social movement organizations, then, are carriers of meaning. Through processes such as consensus mobilization (Klandermans 1984), framing (Snow et al. 1986), or dialogue (Steinberg 1999) they seek to disseminate their definition of the situation to the public at large. Indeed, participating because of common interests or ideologies requires a shared interpretation of who should act, why, and how. Movements affect such interpretations by the information they disseminate, a process known as *framing* (see Benford and Snow 2000; Snow and Benford 1988, 1992). Gerhards and Rucht's study (1992) of flyers produced by the various groups and organizations involved in the protests against the

International Monetary Fund and the World Bank in Berlin is an excellent example in this respect. These authors show how links are constructed between the ideological frame of the organizers of the demonstration and those of the participating organizations in order to create a shared definition of the situation. Such definitions of the situation have been labeled *collective action frames* (Gamson 1992; Klandermans 1997).

Social movements do not invent ideas from scratch; they build on an ideological heritage as they relate their claims to broader themes and values in society. In so doing they relate to societal debates that have a history of its own and that history is usually much longer than that of the movement itself. Gamson (1992), for example, refers to the "themes" and "counterthemes" that in his view exist in every society. One such pair of a theme and countertheme he mentions is "self-reliance" versus "mutuality," that is, the belief that individuals must take care of themselves versus the belief that society is responsible for its less fortunate members. In a study of the protests about disability payment in the Netherlands we demonstrated how in the Netherlands these two beliefs became icons that galvanized the debates (Klandermans and Goslinga 1996). While "self-reliance" became the theme of those favoring restrictions in disability payment, "mutuality" was the theme of those who defended the existing system. For decades, Marxism has been such an ideological heritage that the past movements identified with, positively by embracing it or negatively by distancing themselves from it. In a similar vein, fascism and nazism form the ideological heritage that right-wing extremism must comes to terms with, either by identifying with it or by keeping it at a distance (Klandermans and Mayer 2006).

Satisfying Demand.   Social movement organizations are more or less successful in satisfying demands for collective action participation and we may assume that movements that are successfully supplying what potential participants demand gain more support than movements that fail to do so. More specifically, movement organizations may gain support in case of a "fit" between the fundamental reasons why people participate (more instrumental, identity of ideological reasons) and what social movement organizations have to offer, that is, supply. Surprisingly, little systematic comparison of the characteristics of movements, movement organizations, and campaigns in view of the supply side of participation can be found in the literature (but see Klandermans 1993; Klandermans and Mayer 2006).

MOBILIZATION.   When an individual participates in collective action staged by a social movement organization, this is the result of a sometimes lengthy process of mobilization. Successful mobilization brings demand and supply together. Mobilization is a complicated process that can be broken down into several conceptually distinct steps. Klandermans (1984) proposed to break the process of mobilization down into consensus and action mobilization. Consensus mobilization refers to dissemination of the views of the movement organization while action mobilization refers to the transformation of those who adopted the view of the movement into active participants.

In their frame alignment approach to mobilization Snow and Benford and their colleagues elaborated consensus mobilization much further (see Benford 1997 for a critical review and Snow 2004), while Klandermans and his collaborators focused on the process of action mobilization. They broke action mobilization further down into four separate steps (Klandermans and Oegema 1987). Each step brings the supply and demand of collective political action closer together until an individual eventually takes the final step to participate in an instance of collective political action. The first step accounts for the results of consensus mobilization. It distinguishes the general public into those who sympathize with the cause and

FIGURE 5.2. Four steps toward participation.

those who do not. The more successful consensus mobilization has been, the larger the pool of sympathizers a mobilizing movement organization can draw from. A large pool of sympathizers is of strategic importance, because for a variety of reasons many a sympathizer never turns into a participant. The second step is equally obvious as crucial; it divides the sympathizers into those who have been target of mobilization attempts and those who have not. The third step concerns the social psychological core of the process. It divides the sympathizers who have been targeted into those who are motivated to participate in the specific activity and those who are not. Finally, the fourth step differentiates the people who are motivated into those who end up participating and those who do not (Figure 5.2).

In our research on the mobilization campaign for a peace demonstration (Klandermans and Oegema 1987) we found that three quarters of the population of a small community south of Amsterdam felt sympathy for the movement's cause. Of these sympathizers three quarters were somehow targeted by mobilization attempts. Of those targeted, one sixth were motivated to participate in the demonstration. Finally, of those motivated one third ended up participating. The net result of these different steps is some (usually small) proportion of the general public that participates in collective action. With each step smaller or larger numbers drop out. The better the fit between demand and supply the smaller the number of dropouts.

Sustained Participation

Most research on collective action concerns a comparison of participants and nonparticipants in a specific instance of participation at a specific point in time—be it a demonstration, a boycott, a sit-in, a rally, or a petition. In terms of our typology of forms of participation, this concerns short-term, most of the time low-risk or little-effort participation, sometimes high-risk or -effort. We argued that such short-term activities have different motivational dynamics than sustained participation, be it low- or high-risk or -effort.

Sustained participation is surprisingly absent in the social movement literature, which is surprising, because long-term participants keep the movement sector going. A movement has only a limited number of core activists. For example, 5 to 10 percent of the membership of the Dutch labor unions are core activists (Klandermans and Visser 1995; Nandram 1995), while the Dutch peace movement at its heyday counted approximately 500 core groups with

15 to 20 members (Oegema 1993). Empirical evidence suggests that most core activists are perfectly aware of the fact that they are giving 90 percent or more of the movement's supporters a free ride, but do not care. On the contrary, this is what seems to motivate them to take the job (Klandermans and Visser 1995; Oliver 1984). They are the true believers who care so much for the movement's cause that they are prepared to make that effort knowing that most others won't. Indeed, Nandram (1995) found that for 29 percent of the core activists within Dutch unions this was the single most important motivation for their participation.

Sustained participation need not necessarily take the form of the same activity all the time. People often go from one activity to another, sometimes even from one movement to another, and in so doing build activist careers.

THE DYNAMICS OF SUSTAINED PARTICIPATION. Becoming a long-term activist is to a large extent a matter of biographical availability. After all, sustained participation requires discretionary time for an extended period. The concept of biographical availability was proposed by McAdam (1986) in his study of participation in the Mississippi Freedom Summer. What McAdam had in mind was freedom from other societal commitments. "If college students are uniquely free of life-course impediments to activism, the Freedom Summer applicants were freer still. And the actual volunteers were the freest of all" (Goldstone and McAdam 2001). Indeed, participants in the Mississippi Freedom Summer Campaign were students who were biographically available. But in terms of a life history there is more than available time, there is also mental availability, that is, a readiness for the ideas a movement is propagating. In trying to understand the interplay of socialization, long-term activism, and the social and political context, we propose to use the concepts of biographical continuity and conversion.

Biographical continuity describes a life history whereby participation appears as the logical result of political socialization from someone's youth onwards (Roth 2003). *Conversion*, on the other hand, implies a break with the past. Critical events are supposed to play a crucial role in both situations (see also Blee 2002). In the context of biographical continuity, the event means the last push or pull in a direction in which the person is already going, whereas in the context of conversion the event means an experience that marks a change of mind. Obviously, such conversion does not come out of the blue. It is rooted in a growing dissatisfaction with life as it is. The critical event is the last push toward change. Teske (1997) describes the example of a journalist who ends up in front of the gate of a nuclear weapons plant and whose experience with the authorities' suppressive response to that demonstration turns him into an activist. The story of this journalist made clear that on the one hand it was no accident that he ended up at that gate, but on the other hand had the demonstration not taken that dramatic turn it would not have had this impact on his life.

By way of illustration, we refer to life history interviews we conducted with extreme right activists (Klandermans and Mayer 2006). Three patterns of mobilization emerged from those interviews: continuity, conversion, and compliance. The first pattern concerned interviewees who had always been interested in politics, some of them from very early on. Interestingly, all reported that they have always been interested in right-wing politics. All but one were from a politically conservative milieu; the remaining interviewee was from a social democratic milieu. The converts had not been particularly interested in politics in the past, but later became involved in the extreme right. They can perhaps be best described as politically displaced persons who found a new political home. They could no longer identify with the parties they voted for, or they felt that politics or the government was not addressing the real problems of society. In terms of their parental milieu, no clear picture emerged. Some are from a social democratic background, some from a conservative background. There seems to be a generational pattern here: the latter interviewees were from an older generation and became involved in politics later in their lives, obviously, as they are the ones whose right-wing activism is a matter of conversion. The former were from a younger generation and were attracted to politics on the extreme right from the very beginning. They seem to constitute some kind of "new right" reacting to the new social movements of the 1980s (see also Minkenberg 1998). This group's political life history can be described in terms of biographical continuity, that is, at least the way they do it themselves. Compliants are people who were pulled into activism more or less despite themselves. Sometimes a partner, a friend, or a brother asked them to assist or accompany them to a meeting and gradually they became more involved in the extreme right.

The Dynamics of Disengagement

The dynamics of sustained participation in social movements have a clear counterpart, namely, the dynamics of disengagement. Indeed, the sustainability of a fit between demand and supply is by no means obvious. Why do people defect from the movement they have worked for so very hard? Surprisingly little attention has been given to that question. Compared to the abundant literature on why people join movements, literature on why they exit is almost nonexistent (but see Klandermans 2003; van der Veen and Klandermans 1989). The guiding principle of our discussion of disengagement is the simple model shown in Figure 5.3.

Insufficient gratification in combination with declining commitment produces a growing intention to leave. Eventually, some critical event tips the balance and makes the person quit. Obviously, the event itself only triggers the final step. Against that background, its impact may be overestimated. After all, it was the decline in gratification and commitment that causes defection; the critical event only precipitated matters.

INSUFFICIENT GRATIFICATION.   In the previous sections, we distinguished three fundamental motives to participate. A movement may fall short on each of these motives. Most likely it is for movements to fall short in terms of instrumentality. Although it is difficult to assess the effectiveness of social movements, it is obvious that many a movement goal is never reached. Opp (1988) has argued that indeed people are very well aware of the fact that movement goals are not always easy to achieve, but they reason that nothing happens

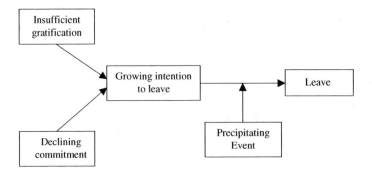

FIGURE 5.3. The dynamics of disengagement.

in any event if nobody participates. Yet, sooner or later some success must be achieved for the instrumentality motive to continue to fuel participation (M. Schwartz 1976). In addition to not being achieved, movement goals may lose their attraction to people. They may lose their urgency and end lower at the societal agenda. Finally, the individual costs or risks of participation may be too high compared to the attraction of the movement's goals. Repression adds to the costs and might make participation too costly for people (Tilly 1978).

Movements offer the opportunity to act on behalf of one's group. This is most attractive if people identify strongly with their group. But the composition of a movement may change and as a consequence people may feel less akin to the others in the movement (Klandermans 1994; Whittier 1997). Indeed, Klandermans showed how activists from other movements flocked in increasing numbers into the Dutch peace movement, and thus estranged the original activist who had a church background. Schisms are another reason why movements fail to satisfy identity motives. Schisms are not uncommon in the social movement domain (Gamson 1975). Sani and Reicher (1998) demonstrate that schisms result from fights over the core identity of a movement and that people who leave no longer feel that they can identify with the movement (see also Catellani, Milesi, and Crescentini 2006). Finally, people occupy a variety of positions in society. Each position is shared with other people and therefore (most of the time) comes with a latent collective identity. A change in context may make the one collective identity more and the others less salient, and therefore identification with a movement may wither. For example, in our study of farmers' protest in the Netherlands and Spain, we observed that in Spain during a campaign for local and provincial elections the identification with farmers declined (Klandermans et al. 2002).

Social movements provide the opportunity to express one's views. This is not to say that they are always equally successful in that regard. Obviously, there is not always full synchrony between a movement's ideology and a person's beliefs. Indeed, many a movement organization ends in fights between ideological factions and schisms and defection as a consequence (Gamson 1975).

DECLINING COMMITMENT.   The concept of commitment roots in the fields of organizational psychology and the social psychology of union participation, where a lively debate on commitment has taken place over the last two decades (Goslinga 2002). Movement commitment does not last by itself. It must be maintained via interaction with the movement, and any measure that makes that interaction less gratifying helps to undermine commitment. Downton and Wehr (1991;1997) discuss mechanisms of social bonding that movements apply to maintain commitment. Leadership, ideology, organization, rituals, and social relationships, which make up a friendship network, each contribute to sustaining commitment, and the most effective, is, of course, a combination of all five.

Although not all of them are equally well researched, each of these five mechanisms is known from the literature on union and movement participation as factors that foster people's attachment to movements. For example, it is known from research on union participation that involving members in decision-making processes increases commitment to a union (Klandermans 1986, 1992). For such different groups as the lesbian movement groups (Taylor and Whittier 1995) and a group called Victims of Child Abuse Laws (Fine 1995) it was demonstrated how rituals strengthen the membership's bond to the movement. Unions and other movement organizations have developed all kind of services for their members to make membership more attractive. Selective incentives may seldom be sufficient reasons to participate in a movement, but they do increase commitment.

THE ROLE OF PRECIPITATING EVENTS.   When gratification falls short and commitment declines an intention to leave develops. Yet, this intention to leave does not necessarily turn into defection. Many participants maintain a marginal level of participation for extended periods until some event makes them quit. For example, Goslinga (2002) calculated that a stable 25 percent of the membership of Dutch labor unions considered leaving. As the event is the immediate cause of disengagement it draws disproportionate attention as explanation of exit behavior, but note that the event has this impact only in the context of an already present readiness to leave. Such critical events can have many different appearances that sometimes even appear trivial. When some decades ago Dutch labor unions changed to a different system of dues collection and members had to sign to agree with the new system, quite a few members chose not to sign. A change of address may be seized as an opportunity to leave the movement simply by not renewing contacts in the new place of residence. More substantial reasons might be a conflict with others in the organization, disappointing experiences in the movement, a failed collective action, and so on. Such events function as the last drop that makes the cup run over.

COLLECTIVE ACTION PARTICIPATION: WHERE DO WE STAND AND HOW TO PROCEED.   Movement participation is a phenomenon that has always intrigued social scientists. Why are people prepared to spend a lifetime as activists and to sacrifice wealth, a pleasant and carefree life, or sometimes even their lives for a common cause? Why are at some points of time hundreds of thousands taking to the streets, while at other moments mobilization fails? We have argued that participation is preeminently a topic of social psychology. In this section we have focused on the phenomenon of collective action participation and analyzed how it fits into the dynamics of contention. We have proposed that individual participation results from the successful interplay of demand factors, supply factors, and mobilization. The more successfully the three combine, the more individuals will participate and the more sustainable participation will be. At the individual level mobilization is successful if people decide to participate.

Admittedly, much of what has been mentioned so far concerns the demand-side of participation. There remains a whole array of unanswered questions about how the demand-side of participation relates to the supply-side and how the two influence mobilization processes. One of the unsolved puzzles has to do with the role of the organizers of protest (Boekkooi 2006). Obviously some people have to take the initiative to start organizing and mobilizing an event and thereby create the supply of collective action (Klandermans 2003, 2004). How do they mobilize for an event and what choices do they make? And what is the role of negotiations in these mobilization processes? Importing the large (social psychological) literature on group dynamics and negotiations into the study of mobilization processes might be helpful.

A SOCIAL PSYCHOLOGY OF CONTENTION: WHERE DO WE STAND AND HOW TO PROCEED

In the previous sections, we discussed group identification, cognition, emotions, and motivation as explanatory frameworks of collective action participation. Obviously, a comprehensive master frame that brings these elements together is still to be built. Yet, compared to 20 years ago, the social psychology of protest has become richer, more sophisticated, and more rooted in state-of-the-art social psychology. Students of social movements have for too long neglected social psychology. At the same time, social psychologists have for too long neglected to study such phenomena as social movements and collective action. As a consequence, social movement scholars are not aware of new developments in social psychology, while social psychologists are unaware of the many unanswered questions to which they could help find answers. We hope to have been able to build bridges between social psychology and the other social science disciplines. This is not to say that the social psychological approach to social movements is without any flaws. On the contrary, in the next and final section we will go into some of the limitations and challenges of a social psychological approach to social movement participation.

Limitations of a Social Psychology of Contention

The most obvious limitation of a social psychological approach to social movements and collective action lies in its level of analysis and its methodological individualism, as mentioned in the introductory section. Social psychology is good in explaining individual behavior but not in explaining the rise and fall or the success of failure of social movements. Because of its universalistic theories it also tends to be a-historical. Social psychological theories are not always good in taking the context of individual behavior into account and in theorizing about how contextual factors impact on social psychological mechanisms. Nonetheless, collective phenomena such as social movements and political protest are also composed of individual behavior. One may quarrel about the degrees of freedom individuals have when they choose to participate or not in protest activities, but in principle individuals do have a choice.

Challenges of a Social Psychology of Contention

We hope our "roadmap" has been useful in exemplifying what social psychology has to offer to the study of social movements, where we stand, and where we think the lacunas are. What are the challenges a social psychology of movement participation faces? We will mention a few and there might be more. Probably, the most important challenge is the integration of the proposed concepts. In that regard, moving from static to more dynamic explanations of protest participation is important. A more dynamic approach would provide the opportunity to study concepts such as identification, participation motives, efficacy, emotions, and feelings of injustice as consequence and antecedent of collective action. "From an investigational point of view, it is difficult to deal with a variable that, at the same time, can be a dependent and an independent variable, can develop over time or change across contexts" (Ellemers, Spears, and Doosje 1999:3). Yet, studying protest participation in a more dynamic way would do more justice to the theoretical and empirical richness of the concepts and may be crucial to gain better insights into the processes at hand.

Little social–psychological research has focused on the subjective experience of more objective macro-level factors (Klandermans 1997). This is not to say that social–psychological analyses of collective action should return to the "objective" social reality, but we think it is possible to identify variables at the meso- or macro level that are important in affecting peoples' subjective interpretations of their collective disadvantages in terms, for example, of identities, opportunities, or constraints and injustice. Recently, for example, it has been acknowledged that the dynamics of participation are created and limited by characteristics of the national contexts in which people are embedded (Koopmans and Statham 2000). The key point is that people still have to perceive characteristics of this context and translate it to their individual situation (Roggeband 2002, 2004).

Moreover, the relationship between individual and collective processes explaining collective action is begging for exploration, be it socially shared cognitions, group-based emotions, idiosyncratic remake of collective identities, or individual versus collective consciousness. How the individual and collective processes relate to each other is far from clear. Interdisciplinary approaches might be a good step in resolving these puzzles.

In sum, we see a future for a dynamic (interdisciplinary) social–psychological approach to collective action exploring both individual as well as collective processes in social movement participation that goes beyond a static individual level of analysis.

SUGGESTED READINGS

We start the suggested readings section with a few preceding books on the social psychology of protest, starting with a classic followed by more contemporary books.

Toch, H. 1965. *The Social Psychology of Social Movements*. Indianapolis, IN: Bobbs-Merrill.

Morris, A. D. and C. McClurg-Mueller. 1992. *Frontiers in Social Movement Theory*. Binghampton, NY: Vail-Ballou Press.

Klandermans, B. 1997. *The Social Psychology of Protest*. Oxford: Blackwell Publishers.

Identity appears to play a key role in social movement participation and the following books are excellent sources to get a grip on how social psychologists study and interpret the concept identity more in general and in the context of collective action.

Ellemers, N., R. Spears, and B. Doosje. 1999. *Social Identity: Context, Commitment, and Content*. Oxford: Basil Blackwell.

Simon, B. 2004. *Identity in Modern Society. A Social Psychological Perspective*. Oxford: Blackwell Publishers.

Stryker, S., T. J. Owens, and R. W. White. 2000. *Self, Identity, and Social Movements*. Minneapolis, MN: University of Minnesota Press.

It is hard to conceive of social movement participation without feelings of injustice; the following reference give an outstanding review of the social–psychological literature on justice and social movements.

Tyler, T. R., and H. J. Smith. 1998. "Social Justice and Social Movements." Pp. 595–629 in *Handbook of Social Psychology*, edited by D.Gilbert, S. T. Fiske, and G. Lindzey. New York: McGraw-Hill.

We argued that in collective action research emotions are a novice with a long history. We consider socially structured emotions a new and inviting field in relation to collective action, which is a social phenomenon by nature. Therefore we suggest two key readings in this field:

Mackie, D. M. and E. R. Smith. 2002. (eds) *From Prejudice to Intergroup Emotions: Differentiated Reactions to Social Groups*. Philadelphia: Psychology Press.

Tiedens, L. Z. and C. W. Leach. 2004. (eds) *The Social life of Emotions*. Cambridge, UK: Cambridge University Press.

Finally, we refer to two more general edited volumes in which chapters elaborate on the (social psychology) of social movement participation.

Sears, D., L. Huddy, and R. Jervis. 2003. *Oxford Handbook of Political Psychology*. New York: Oxford University Press.

Snow, D. A., S. A. Soule, and H. Kriesi. 2004. *The Blackwell Companion to Social Movements* Oxford: Blackwell Publishing.

REFERENCES

Allen, V. L. and D. A. Wilder. 1975. "Categorization, Belief Similarity, and Intergroup Discrimination." *Journal of Personality and Social Psychology* 32:971–977.

Arnold, M. B. 1960. *Emotion and Personality*. New York: Columbia University Press.

Back, K. W. 1951. "Influence Through Social Communication." *Journal of Abnormal and Social Psychology* 46:9–23.

Bargh, J. A. 1994. "The Four Horsemen of Automaticity: Awareness, Efficiency, Intention, and Control in Social Cognition." Pp. 1–40 in *Handbook of Social Cognition* (vol. 2), edited by J. R. S. Wyer and T. K. Srull. Hillsdale, NJ: Lawrence Erlbaum.

Beckwith, K. 1998. "Collective Identity of Class and Gender: Working Class Women in the Pittston Coal Strike." *Political Psychology* 19(1):147–167.

Benford, R. 1997. "An Insider's Critique of the Social Movement Framing Perspective." *Sociological-Inquiry* 67(4):409–430.

Benford, R. D. and D. A. Snow. 2000. "Framing Processes and Social Movements: An Overview and Assessment." *Annual Review of Sociology* 26:11–39.

Berkowitz, L. 1972. "Frustrations, Comparisons, and Other Sources of Emotion Aroused as Contributors to Social Unrest." *Journal of Social Issues* 28:77–92.

Blee, K. M. 2002. *Inside Organized Racism: Women in the Hate Movement*. Berkeley: University of California Press.

Boninger, D. S., J. A. Krosnick, and M. K. Berent. 1995. "Origins of Attitude Importance: Self-Interest, Social Identification, and Value Relevance." *Journal of Personality and Social Psychology* 68(1):61–80.

Branscombe, N. R., N. Ellemers, R. Spears, and B. Doosje. 1999. "The Context and Content of Social Identity Threat." Pp. 35–58 in *Social Identity; Context, Commitment, Content*, edited by N. Ellemers, R. Spears, and B. Doosje. Oxford: Basil Blackwell.

Brewer, M. B. and W. Gardner. 1996. "Who Is This 'We'? Levels of Collective Identity and Self Representations." *Journal of Personality and Social Psychology* 71(1):83–93.

Brewer, M. B. and M. D. Silver. 2000. "Group Distinctiveness, Social identification, and Collective Action." Pp. 153–171 in *Self, Identity, and Social Movements* (vol. 13), edited by S. Stryker, T. J. Owens, and R. W. White. Minneapolis, MN: Minnesota University Press.

Brewer, P. R. and M. R. Steenbergen. 2002. "All Against All: How Beliefs about Human Nature Shape Foreign Policy Opinions." *Political Psychology* 23(1):39–58.

Brock, T. C. 1965. "Communicator-Recipient Similarity and Decision Change." *Journal of Personality and Social Psychology* 1:650–654.

Cantor, N. and W. Mischel. 1977. "Traits as Prototypes: Effects on Recognition Memory." *Journal of Personality and Social Psychology* 35:38–48.

Carlston, D. E. 2001. "Social Cognition: The Things That Define Us." *Social Cognition* 19(1):1–8.

Carver, C. S., S. K. Sutton, and M. F. Scheier. 2000. "Action, Emotion, and Personality: Emerging Conceptual Integration." *Personality and Social Psychology Bulletin* 26(6):741–751.

Catellani, P., P. Milesi, and A. Crescentini. 2006. "One Root, Different Branches: Identity, Injustice and Schism." Pp. 204–223 In *Extreme Right Activists in Europe. Through the Magnifying Glass*, edited by B. Klandermans and N. Mayer. London and New York: Routledge.

Chaiken, S. 1980. "Heuristic versus Systematic Information Processing and the Use of Source versus Message Cues in Persuasion." *Journal of Personality and Social Psychology* 39:752–766.

Della Porta, D. 1988. "Recruitment Processes in Clandestine Political Organizations: Italian Left-Wing Terrorism." Pp. 155–172 in *From Structure to Action*, edited by B. Klandermans, H. Kriesi, and S. Tarrow. Greenwich, CT: JAI Press.

———. 1992. "Institutional Responses to Terrorism: The Italian Case." *Terrorism and Violence* 4:151–170.

Deutsch, M. and H. B. Gerard. 1955. "A Study of Normative and Information Social Influences upon Individual Judgement." *Journal of Abnormal and Social Psychology* 51:629–636.

de Weerd, M. 1999. *Social-Psychologische Determinanten van Boerenprotest: Collectieve Actie Frames, Onvrede, Identiteit en Effectiviteit (Social Psychological Determinants of Farmer Protest: Collective Action Frames, Dissatisfaction, Identity and Efficacy)*. Unpublished dissertation, Vrije Universiteit, Amsterdam.

de Weerd, M. and B. Klandermans. 1999. "Group Identification and Political Protest: Farmers' Protest in the Netherlands." *European Journal of Social Psychology* 29:1073–1095.

Downton, J., Jr. and P. Wehr. 1991. "Peace Movements: The Role of Commitment and Community in Sustaining Member Participation." *Research in Social Movements, Conflicts, and Change* 13:113–134.

——. 1997. *The Persistent Activist: How Peace Commitment Develops and Survives.* Boulder, CO and London: Westview.

Drury, J., C. Cocking, J. Beale, C. Hanson, and F. Rapley. 2005. "The Phenomenology of Empowerment in Collective Action." *British Journal of Social Psychology* 44:309–328.

Drury, J. and S. Reicher. 1999. "The Intergroup Dynamics of Collective Empowerment: Substantiating the Social Identity Model of Crowd Behavior." *Group Processes Intergroup Relations* 2(4):381–402.

Dumont, M., V. Yzerbyt, D. Wigboldus, and E. Gordijn. 2003. "Social Categorization and Fear Reactions to the September 11th Terrorist Attacks." *Personality and Social Psychology Bulletin* 29:1509–1520.

Duncan, L. E. 1999. "Motivation for Collective Action: Group Consciousness as Mediator of Personality, Life Experiences, and Women's Rights Activism." *Political Psychology* 20(3):611–635.

Ekman, P. 1993. "Facial Expression and Emotion." *American Psychologist* 48(4):384–392.

Ellemers, N. 1993. "The Influence of Socio-structural Variables on Identity Management Strategies." Pp. 27–58 in *European Review of Social Psychology* (vol. 4,), edited by W. Stroebe and M. Hewston. Chichester, UK: John Wiley & Sons.

Ellemers, N., R. Spears, and B. Doosje. 1999. "Introduction." Pp. 1–5 in *Social Identity: Context, Commitment, Conten,* edited by N. Ellemers, R. Spears, and B. Doosje. Oxford: Basil Blackwell.

Epstein, S., R. Pacini, V. Denes-Raj, and H. Heier. 1996. "Individual Differences in Intuitive-Experiential and Analytical-Rational Thinking Styles." *Journal of Personality and Social Psychology* 71(2):390–405.

Eyerman, R. and A. Jamison. 1991. *Social Movements. A Cognitive Approach.* Cambridge, MA: Polity Press.

Feather, N. T. and J. W. Newton. 1982. "Values, Expectations, and the Prediction of Social Action: An Expectancy-Valence Analysis." *Motivation and Emotion* 6(3):217–244.

Feldman, S. 2003. "Values, Ideology, and the Structure of Political Attitudes." Pp. 477–508 in *Oxford Handbook of Political Psychology,* edited by D. Sears, L. Huddy, and R. Jervis. New York: Oxford University Press.

Festinger, L. 1950. "Informal Social Communication." *Psychological Review* 57:271–282.

Fine, G. A. 1995. "Public Narration and Group Culture: Discerning Discourse in Social Movements." Pp. 127–143 in *Social Movements and Culture,* edited by H. Johnston and B. Klandermans. Minneapolis, MN: University of Minnesota Press.

Fiske, A. P., S. Kitayama, H. R. Markus, and R. E. Nisbett. 1998. "The Cultural Matrix of Social Psychology." Pp. 915–981 in *Handbook of Social Psychology* (vol. 2), edited by D. T. Gilbert, S. Fiske, and G. Lindzey. New York: McGraw-Hill.

Folger, R. 1986. "Rethinking Equity Theory: A Referent Cognitions Model." Pp. 145–162 in *Justice in Social Relations,* edited by H. W. Bierhoff, R. L. Cohen, and J. Greenberg. New York: Plenum Press.

Forgas, J. P.,ed. 2001. *The Handbook of Affect and Social Cognition.* Mahwah, NJ: Lawrence Erlbaum.

Foster, M. D. and K. Matheson. 1999. "Perceiving and Responding to the Personal/Group Discrimination Discrepancy." *Personality and Social Psychology Bulletin* 25(10):1319–1329.

French, J. R. P. and B. H. Raven. 1959. "The Bases of Social Power. Pp. 150–167 in *Studies in Social Power,* edited by D. Cartwright. Ann Arbor, MI: University of Michigan Press.

Gamson, W. A. 1975. *Strategy of Social Protest.* Homewood, IL: The Dorsey Press.

——. 1992. *Talking Politics.* New York: Cambridge University Press.

Gerhards, J. and D. Rucht. 1992. "Mesomobilization: Organizing and Framing in Two Protest Campaigns in West Germany." *American Journal of Sociology* 98:555–596.

Giugni, M. G. 1998. "Was It Worth the Effort? The Outcomes and Consequences of Social Movements." *Annual Review of Sociology* 85:1017–1042.

——. 2004. *Social Protest and Policy Change.* Lanham, MD: Rowman and Littlefield.

Giugni, M., D. McAdam, and C. Tilly, eds. 1999. *How Social Movements Matter.* Minneapolis, MN: University of Minnesota Press.

Goldstone, J. and D. McAdam. 2001. "Placing Contention in Demographic and Life-Course Context." Pp. 195–221 in *Silence and Voice in the Study of Contentious Politics,* edited by R. Aminzade, J. Goldstone, D. McAdam, E. Perry, J. William Sewell, S. Tarrow, and C. Tilly. New York and London: Cambridge University Press.

Goodwin, J., J. M. Jasper, and F. Polleta. 2001. *Passionate Politics. Emotions and Social Movements.* Chicago: The University of Chicago Press.

——. 2004. "Emotional Dimensions of Social Movements." Pp. 413–432 in *The Blackwell Companion to Social Movements,* edited by D. A. Snow, S. A. Soule, and H. Kriesi. Oxford: Blackwell Publishing.

Gordijn, E., D. Wigboldus, and V. Yzerbyt. 2001. "Emotional Consequences of Categorizing Victims of Negative Outgroup Behavior as Ingroup or Outgroup." *Group Processes and Intergroup Relations* 4:317–326.

Goslinga, S. 2002. *Binding aan de Vakbond (Union Commitment).* Unpublished doctoral dissertation. Vrije Universiteit, Amsterdam.

Gray, J. A. 1990. "Brain Systems that Mediate Both Emotion and Cognition." *Cognition and Emotion* 4:269–288.

Guimond, S. and L. Dubé-Simard. 1983. "Relative Deprivation Theory and the Quebec Nationalist Movement: The Cognition-Emotion Distinction and the Personal-Group Deprivation Issue." *Journal of Personality and Social Psychology* 44:526–535.

Gurin, P., A. H. Miller, and G. Gurin. 1980. "Stratum Identification and Consciousness." *Social Psychology Quarterly* 43(1):30–47.

Gusfield, J.1963. *Symbolic Crusade: Status Politics and the American Temperance Movement.* Urbana, IL: University of Illinois Press.

Harmon-Jones, E., J. D., Sigelman, A. Bohlig, and C. Harmon-Jones. 2003. "Anger, Coping, and Frontal Cortical Activity: The Effect of Coping Potential on Anger-Induced Left Frontal Activity." *Cognition and Emotion* 17:1–24.

Haslam, S. A. 2001. *Psychology in Organizations: The Social Identity Approach.* London: Sage.

Hercus, C. 1999. "Identity, Emotion and Feminist Collective Action." *Gender and Society* 13(1):34–55.

Higgins, E. T. 1997. "Beyond Pleasure and Pain." *American Psychologist* 52(12):1280–1300.

——. 2000. "Social Cognition: Learning About What Matters in the Social World." *European Journal of Social Psychology* 30(1):3–39.

Hogg, M., D. Terry, and K. White. 1995. "A Tale of Two Theories: A Critical Comparison of Identity Theory with Social Identity Theory." *Social Psychology Quarterly* 58:255–269.

Huddy, L. 2001. "From Social to Political Identity: A Critical Examination of Social Identity Theory." *Political Psychology* 22(1):127–156.

——. 2003. "Group Identity and Political Cohesion." Pp. 511–558 In *Oxford Handbook of Political Psychology,* edited by D. O. Sears, L. Huddy, and R. Jervis. Oxford: Oxford University Press.

Jasper, J. 1997. *The Art of Moral Protest. Culture, Biography, and Creativity in Social Movements.* Chicago: The University of Chicago Press.

——. 1998. "The Emotions of Protest: Affective and Reactive Emotions in and Around Social Movements." *Sociological Forum* 13(3):397–424.

Jenkins, R. 2004. *Social Identity,* 2nd edition. London and New York: Routledge.

Kahneman, D., P. Slovic, and A. Tversky. 1982. *Judgment Under Uncertainty: Heuristics and Biases.* Cambridge, UK.: Cambridge University Press.

Kawakami, K. and K. L. Dion. 1993. "The Impact of Salient Self-Identities on Relative Deprivation and Action Intentions." *European Journal of Social Psychology* 23:525–540.

Kelly, C. 1993. "Group Identification, Intergroup Perceptions, and Collective Action." Pp. 59–83 In *European Review of Social Psychology,* edited by W. Stroebe and M. Hewstone. Chichester, UK: John Wiley & Sons.

Kelly, C. and S. Breinlinger. 1995. "Identity and Injustice—Exploring Womens Participation in Collective Action." *Journal of Community and Applied Social Psychology* 5(1):41–57.

——. 1996. *The Social Psychology of Collective Action: Identity, Injustice and Gender.* London: Taylor and Francis.

Kelly, C. and J. Kelly. 1994. "Who Gets Involved in Collective Action?: Social Psychological Determinants of Individual Participation in Trade Unions." *Human Relations* 47(1):63–88.

Kim, H. 2002. "Shame, Anger, and Love in Collective Action: Emotional consequences of Suicide Protest in South Korea, 1991." *Mobilization: An International Journal* 7(2):159–176.

Klandermans, B. 1984. "Mobilization and Participation: Social-Psychological Expansions of Resource Mobilization Theory." *American Sociological Review* 49(5): 583–600.

——. 1986. "Psychology and Trade Union Participation: Joining, Acting, Quitting." *Journal of Occupational Psychology* 59:189–204.

——. 1988. "The Formation and Mobilization of Consensus." Pp. 173–196 In *From Structure to Action: Comparing Social Movement Research across Cultures* (vol. 1), edited by B. Klandermans, H. Kriesi and S. Tarrow. Greenwich, CT: JAI Press.

——. 1992. "The Social Construction of Protest and Multiorganizational Fields." Pp. 77–103 in *Frontiers in Social Movement Theory,* edited by A. D. Morris and C. M. Mueller. New Haven, CT: Yale University Press.

——. 1993. "A Theoretical Framework for Comparisons of Social Movement Participation." *Sociological Forum* 8(3):383–402.

——. 1994. "Transient Identities? Membership Patterns in the Dutch Peace Movement." Pp. 168–184 In *New Social Movements: From Ideology to Identity,* edited by E. Larana, H. Johnston and J. R. Gusfield. Philadelphia: Temple University Press.

——. 1997. *The Social Psychology of Protest.* Oxford: Blackwell.

——. 2003. "Collective Political Action." Pp. 670–709 in *Oxford Handbook of Political Psychology,* edited by D. O. Sears, L. Huddy and R. Jervis. Oxford: Oxford University Press.

——. 2004. "The Demand and Supply of Participation: Social-Psychological Correlates of Participation in Social Movements." Pp. 360–379 in *The Blackwell Companion to Social Movements,* edited by D. A. Snow, S. A. Soule, and H. Kriesi. Oxford: Blackwell Publishing.

Klandermans, B.and M. de Weerd. 2000. "Group Identification and Political Protest." Pp. 68–92 in *Self, Identity, and Social Movements,* edited by S. Stryker, T. J. Owens, and R. W. White. Minneapolis, MN: University of Minnesota Press.

Klandermans, B. and S. Goslinga. 1996. "Media Discourse, Movement Publicity, and theGeneration of Collective Action Frames: Theoretical and Empirical Exercises in Meaning Construction in Comparative Perspectives on Social Movements." Pp. 312–337 in *Political Opportunities, Mobilizing Structures, and Cultural Framings,* edited by D. McAdam, J. D. McCarthy, and M. N. Zald. New York: Cambridge University Press.

Klandermans, B. and N. Mayer,. eds. 2006. *Extreme Right Activists in Europe. Through the Magnifying Glass.* London and New York: Routledge.

Klandermans, B. and D. Oegema. 1987. "Potentials, Networks, Motivations, and Barriers: Steps Toward Participation in Social Movements." *American Sociological Review* 52:519–531.

Klandermans, B., J. M. Sabucedo, and M. Rodriguez. 2004. "Inclusiveness of identification among farmers in The Netherlands and Galicia (Spain)." *European Journal of Social Psychology* 34(3):279–295.

Klandermans, B., J. M. Sabucedo, M. Rodriguez, and M. de Weerd. 2002. "Identity Processes in Collective Action Participation: Farmers' Identity and Farmers' Protest in the Netherlands and Spain." *Political Psychology* 23(2):235–251.

Klandermans, B. and J. Visser, eds. 1995. *De Vakbeweging na de Welvaartstaat.* Assen: Van Gorcum.

Koopmans, R. and P. Statham, eds. 2000. *Challenging Immigration and Ethnic Relations Politics: Comparative European Perspectives.* Oxford: Oxford University Press.

Kurtz, S. 2002. *All Kinds of Justice: Labor and Identity Politics.* Minneapolis, MN: University of Minnesota Press.

Lang, P. J. 1995. "The Emotion Probe: Studies of Motivation and Attention." *American Psychologist* 50:372–385.

Lazarus, R. S. 1966. *Psychological Stress and the Coping Process.* New York: McGraw-Hill.

——. 1991. *Emotion and Adaptation.* New York: Oxford University Press.

Linden, A. and B. Klandermans. 2006. "Stigmatization and Repression of Extreme-Right Activism in the Netherlands." *Mobilization: An International Journal* 11(2): 213–228.

——. 2007. "Revolutionaries, Wanderers, Converts, and Compliants: Life Histories of Extreme Right Activists." *Journal of Contemporary Ethnography* 36:184–201.

Liss, M., M. Crawford, and D. Popp. 2004. "Predictors and Correlates of Collective Action." *Sex Roles* 50(11–12): 771–779.

Mackie, D. M. 1986. "Social Identification Effects in Group Polarization." *Journal of Personality and Social Psychology* 50(4):720–728.

Mackie, D. M., T. Devos, and E. R. Smith. 2000. "Intergroup Emotions: Explaining Offensive Action Tendencies in an Intergroup Context." *Journal of Personality and Social Psychology* 79(4):602–616.

Mackie, D. M., M. C. Gastardo-Conaco, and J. J. Skelly. 1992. "Knowledge of the Advocated Position and the Processing of In-group and Out-Group Persuasive Messages." *Personality and Social Psychology Bulletin* 18:145–151.

Mackie, D. M., L. T. Worth, and A. G. Asuncion. 1990. "Processing of Persuasive In-group Messages." *Journal of Personality and Social Psychology* 58:812–822.

Major, B. 1994. "From Social Inequality to Personal Entitlement: The Role of Social Comparisons, Legitimacy Appraisals, and Group Memberships." *Advances in Experimental Social Psychology* 26:293–355.

Marcus, G. E. 2003. "The Psychology of Emotions and Politics." 182–221 In *Oxford Handbook of Political Psychology.* edited by D. O. Sears, L. Huddy, and R. Jervis. Oxford: Oxford University Press.

Marcus, G. E. and MacKuen, M. 1993. "Anxiety, Enthusiasm, and the Vote." *American Political Science Review* 87:688–701.

Marcus, G. E., W. R. Neuman, and M. MacKuen. 2000. *Affective Intelligence and Political Judgment.* Chicago: The University of Chicago Press.

Martin, J. 1986. "The Tolerance of Injustice." 217–242 In *Relative Deprivation and Social Comparison: The Ontario Symposium* (vol. 4), edited by J. M. Olson, C. P. Herman, and M. P. Zanna. Hillsdale, NJ: Lawrence Erlbaum.

Marwell, G. and P. Oliver. 1993. *The Critical Mass in Collective Action: A Micro-Social Theory.* Cambridge, UK: Cambridge University Press.

McAdam, D. 1982. *Political Process and the Development of Black Insurgency, 1930–1970.* Chicago, IL: The University of Chicago Press.

——. 1988. *Freedom Summer.* New York: Oxford University Press.

McCarthy, J. D. and M. N. Zald. 1976. "Resource Mobilization and Social Movements: A Partial Theory." *American Journal of Sociology* 82:1212–1241.

McCoy, S. K. and B. Major. 2003. "Group Identification Moderates Emotional Responses to Perceived Prejudice." *Personality and Social Psychology Bulletin* 29(8):1005–1017.

McGraw, K. M. 2000. "Contributions of the Cognitive Approach to Political Psychology." *Political Psychology* 21(4):805–832.

Melucci, A. 1989. *Nomads of the Present: Social Movements and Individual Needs in Contemporary Society.* London: Hutchinson Radius.

———. 1995. "The Process of Collective Identity." Pp. 41–63 in *Social Movements and Culture*, edited by H. Johnston and B. Klandermans. Minneapolis, MN: University of Minnesota Press.

Minkenberg, M. 1998. *Die neue adikale Rechte im Vergleich, USA, Frankreich, Deutschland.* Opladen/Wiesbaden: Westdeutscher Verlag.

Mischel, W. 1998. "Metacognition at the Hyphen of Social-Cognitive Psychology." *Personality and Social Psychology Review* 2(2):84–86.

Moore, D. A. and G. Loewenstein. 2004. "Self-interest, Automaticity, and the Psychology of Conflict of Interest." *Social Justice Research* 17:189–202.

Morris, A. D. 1992. "Political Consciousness and Collective Action." Pp. 351–373 in *Frontiers in Social Movement Theory*, edited by A. D. Morris and C. McClurgMueller. Binghampton, NY: Vail-Ballou Press.

Mummendey, A., T. Kessler, A. Klink, and R. Mielke. 1999. "Strategies to Cope With Negative Social Identity: Predictions by Social Identity Theory and Relative Deprivation Theory." *Journal of Personality and Social Psychology* 76(2):229–245.

Nandram, S. S. 1995. *Het Beredeneerd aan- en Afmelden als Kaderlid: Een Studie naar het Vrijwilligerswerk Binnen de Vakbond (Deliberate Entrance and Exit Behavior in the Context of the Union).* Unpublished doctoral dissertation, Vrije Universiteit, Amsterdam.

Nepstad, S. E. and C. Smith. 1999. "Rethinking Recruitment to High-Risk/Cost Activism: The Case of the Nicaragua Exchange." *Mobilization: An International Journal* 4(1):25–40.

Nerb, J. and H. Spada, H. 2001. "Evaluation of Environmental Problems: A Coherence Model of Cognition and Emotion." *Cognition and Emotion* 15(4):521–551.

Oegema, D. 1993. *Tussen Petitie en Perestrojka: De Nadagen van de Nederlandse Vredesbeweging.* Unpublished doctoral dissertation, Vrije Universiteit, Amsterdam.

Oegema, D. and B. Klandermans. 1994. "Why Social Movement Sympathizers Don't Participate: Erosion and Nonconversion of Support." *American Journal of Sociology* 49:703–722.

Oliver, P. 1984. "Rewards and Punishments as Selective Incentives: An Apex Game." *Journal of Conflict Resolution* 28(1):123–148.

———. 1980. "Rewards and Punishments as Selective Incentives for Collective Action. Theoretical Investigations." *American Journal of Sociology* 85(6):1356–1375.

Olson, J. M. and C. L. Mafer. 1996. "Affect, Motivation and Cognition in Relative Deprivation Research." Pp. 85–117 In Handbook of Motivation and Cognition: the interpersonal context, edited by R. M. Sorrentino and E. T. Higgins. Newyork: Guilford.

Olson, M. 1965. *The Logic of Collective Action: Public Goods and the Theory of Groups.* Cambridge, MA: Harvard University Press.

Omoto, A. M. and M. Snyder. 1995. "Sustained Helping Without Obligation: Motivation, Longevity of Service, and Perceived Attitude Change among AIDS Volunteers." *Journal of Personality and Social Psychology* 68:671–686.

Opp, K. D. 1988. "Grievances and Social Movement Participation." *American Sociological Review* 53(6):853–864.

Orfali, B. 1990. *L'Adhésion au Front National, de la Minorité Active au Mouvement Social.* Paris: Kimé.

Passy, F. 2001. "Socialization, Connection, and the Structure/Agency Gap: A Specification of the Impact of Networks on Participation in Social Movements." *Mobilization: An International Journal* 6(2):173–192.

———. 2003. "Social Networks Matter. But How?" Pp. 21–49 in *Social Movements and Networks. Relational Approaches to Collective Action*, edited by M. Diani and D. McAdam. Oxford: Oxford University Press.

Petty, R. E. and J. T. Cacioppo. 1986. "The Elaboration Likelihood Model of Persuasion." Pp. 123–205 in *Advances in Experimental Social Psychology* (vol. 19), edited by L. Berkowitz. San Diego, CA: Academic Press.

Pichardo, N. A., H. S.-C. Almanzar, and G. Deane. 1998. "Is the Political Personal. Everyday Behaviors as Environmental Movement Participation." *Mobilization: An International Journal* 3(2):185–205.

Polletta, F. and J. M. Jasper. 2001. "Collective Identity and Social Movements." *Annual Review of Sociology* 27(1):283–305.

Rahn, W. M. 2004. *Feeling, Thinking, Being, Doing: Public Mood, American National identity, and Civic Participation.* Paper presented at the Annual Meeting of the Midwest Political Science Association, Chicago.

Reichenbach, R. 2000. *The Scandalised Self.* Paper presented at the Association of Moral Education (AME), Glasgow, Scotland.

Reicher, S. 1996a. " 'The Battle of Westminster': Developing the Social Identity Model of Crowd Behaviour in Order to Explain the Initiation and Development of Collective Conflict." *European Journal of Social Psychology* 26:115–134.

——. 1996b. "Social Identity and Social Change: Rethinking the Contexts of Social Psychology." Pp. 317–336 in *Social Groups and Identities: Developing the Legacy of Henri Tajfel*, edited by P. W. Robinson. Oxford: Butterworth Heinemann.

Robnett, B. 2004. "Emotional Resonance, Social Location, and Strategic Framing." *Sociological Focus* 37(3):195–212.

Rochon, T. R. 1998. *Culture Moves: Ideas, Activism, and Changing Values*. Princeton, NJ: Princeton University Press.

Roggeband, C. M. 2002. *Over de Grenzen van de Politiek. Een Vergelijkend Onderzoek naar de Opkomst en Ontwikkeling van de Vrouwenbeweging tegen Seksueel Geweld in Nederland en Spanje (Passing the Borders of Politics. A Comparative Study of the Rise and Development of the Women's Movement Against Sexual Violence in the Netherlands and Spain)*. Assen: Van Gorcum.

——. 2004. "Instantly I Thought We Should Do the Same Thing. International Inspiration and Exchange in Feminist Action against Sexual Violence." *European Journal of Women's Studies* 11:159–175.

Rokeach, M. 1973. *The Nature of Human Values*. New York: Free Press.

Roseman, I. J., A. A. Antoniou, and P. E. Jose. 1996. "Appraisal Determinants of Emotions: Constructing a More Accurate and Comprehensive Theory." *Cognition and Emotion* 10(3):241–278.

Roth, S. 2003. *Building Movement Bridges. The Coalition of Labor Union Women*. Westport, CT: Praeger.

Rumelhart, D. E. 1980. "Schemata: The Building Blocks of Cognition." 38–58 In *Theoretical Issues in Reading and Comprehension*, edited by R. J. Spiro, B. Bruce, and W. F. Brewer. Hillsdale, NJ: Lawrence Erlbaum.

Runciman, W. G. 1966. *Relative Deprivation and Social Justice*. London: Routledge.

Russell, J. A. 1980. "A Circumplex Model of Affect." *Journal of Personality and Social Psychology* 39:1161–1178.

Sani, F. and S. Reicher. 1998. "When Consensus Fails: An Analysis of the Schism within the Italian Communist Party 1991." *European Journal of Social Psychology* 28:623–645.

Schank, R. C. and R. Abelson. 1977. *Scripts, Plans, Goals, and Understanding*. Hillsdale, NJ: Lawrence Earlbaum.

Scher, S. J. and D. R. Heise. 1993. "Affect and the Perception of Injustice." *Advances in Group Processes* 10:223–252.

Scherer, K. R. and M. R. Zentner. 2001. "Emotional Effects of Music Production Rules." Pp. 361–392 in *Music and Emotion: Theory and Research*, edited by P. N. Juslin and J. A. Sloboda. Oxford: Oxford University Press.

Schrager, L. S. 1985. "Private Attitudes and Collective Action. Comment on Klandermans, ASR. 1984." *American Sociological Review* 50:858–859.

Schrock, D., D. Holden, and L. Reid. 2004. "Creating Emotional Resonance: Interpersonal Emotion Work and Motivational Framing in a Transgender Community." *Social Problems* 51:61–81.

Schwartz, M. 1976. *Radical Protest and Social Structure: The Southern Farmers' Alliance and Cotton Tenancy, 1880–1890*. New York: Academic Press.

Schwartz, S. H. 1992. "Universals in the Content and Structure of Values: Theoretical Advances and Empirical Tests in 20 Countries." *Advances in Experimental Social Psychology* 25:1–65.

Searles, R. and J. A. Williams. 1962. "Negro College Students' Participation in Sitins." *Social Forces* 40:215–220.

Sears, D. O. and C. Funk. 1991. "The Role of Self-interest in Social and Political Attitudes." Pp. 1–91 in *Advances in Experimental Social Psychology* (vol. 24), edited by M. P. Zanna. New York: Academic Press.

Sears, D. O., C. Hensler, and L. Speer. 1979. "Whites' Opposition to "Busing": Self-Interest or Symbolic Politics?" *American Political Science Review* 73:369–385.

Shweder, R. and E. Bourne. 1984. "Does the Concept of the Person Vary Cross-culturally?" Pp. 158–199 in *Culture Theory*, edited by R. Shweder and R. LeVine. Cambridge, UK: Cambridge University Press.

Simon, B. 1999. "A Place in the Social World: Self and Social Categorization. Pp. 47–69 in *The Psychology of the Social Self*, edited by T. R. Tyler, R. M. Kramer and O. P. Johns. Mahwah, NJ: Lawrence Erlbaum.

——. 2004. *Identity in Modern Society. A Social Psychological Perspective*. Oxford: Blackwell.

Simon, B. and B. Klandermans. 2001. "Politicized Collective Identity: A Social Psychological Analysis." *American Psychologist* 56(4):319–331.

Simon, B., M. Loewy, S. Sturmer, U. Weber, P. Freytag, C. Habig, et al. 1998. "Collective Identification and Social Movement Participation." *Journal of Personality and Social Psychology* 74(3):646–658.

Sloman, S. A. 1996. "The Empirical Case for Two Systems of Reasoning." *Psychological Bulletin* 119:3–22.

Smith, E. R. 1993. "Social Identity and Social Emotions: Toward New Conceptualizations of Prejudice." Pp. 297–315 in *Affect, Cognition, and Stereotyping: Interactive Processes in Group Perception*, edited by D. M. M. D. L. Hamilton. San Diego: Academic Press.

Smith, E. R. and J. DeCoster. 2000. "Dual-Process Models in Social and Cognitive Psychology: Conceptual Integration and Links to Underlying Memory Systems." *Personality and Social Psychology Review* 4(2):108–131.

Smith, H. J. and D. Ortiz. 2002. "Is It Just Me? The Different Consequences of Personal and Group Relative Deprivation." Pp. 91–118 in *Relative Deprivation,* edited by I. Walker and H. J. Smith. New York: Cambridge University
Press.

Snow, D. 2004. "Framing Processes, Ideology and Discursive Fields. Pp. 380–412 in *The Blackwell Companion to
Social Movements,* edited by D. A. Snow, S. A. Soule, and H. Kriesi. Oxford: Blackwell Publishing.

Snow, D. A. and R. D. Benford. 1988. "Ideology, Frame Resonance, and Participant Mobilization." *International
Social Movement Research* 1:197–217.

——. 1992. "Master Frames and Cycles of Protest." Pp. 133–155 in *Frontiers of Social Movement Theory,* edited by
A. Morris and C. Mueller. New Haven, CT: Yale University Press.

Snow, D. A., E. B. Rochford, S. K. Worden, and R. D. Benford. 1986. "Frame Alignment Processes, Micromobilization, and Movement Participation." *American Sociological Review* 51:464–481.

Stangor, C. and D. N. Ruble. 1989. "Strength of Expectancies and Memory for Social Information: What We
Remember Depends on How Much We Know." *Journal of Experimental Social Psychology* 25:18–35.

Stanley, L. and S. Wise. 1983. *Breaking Out: Feminist Consciousness and Feminist Research.* London: Routledge
and Kegan Paul.

Steinberg, M. W. 1999. "The Talk and Back Talk of Collective Action: A Dialogic Analysis of Repertoires of Discourse among Nineteenth-Century English Cotton Spinners." *American Journal of Sociology* 105:736–780.

Strack, F. and R. Deutsch. 2004. "Reflective and Impulsive Determinants of Social Behavior." *Personality and Social
Psychology Review* 8(3):220–247.

Stryker, S., T. J. Owens, and R. W. White, eds. 2000. *Self, Identity, and Social Movements* (vol. 13). Minneapolis,
MN: University of Minnesota Press.

Stürmer, S. and B. Simon. 2004a. "Collective Action: Towards a Dual-Pathway Model." *European Review of Social
Psychology* 15:59–99.

——. 2004b. "The Role of Collective Identification in Social Movement Participation: A Panel Study in the Context
of the German Gay Movement." *Personality and Social Psychological Bulletin* 30(3):263–277.

Stürmer, S., B. Simon, M. Loewy, and H. Jörger, H. 2003. "The Dual-Pathway Model of Social Movement Participation: The Case of the Fat Acceptance Movement." *Social Psychology Quarterly* 66(1):71–82.

Swaab, R. I., T. Postmes, I. Van Beest, and R. Spears. 2007. "Shared Cognition as a Product of, and Precursor to,
Shared Social Identity: Studying the Role of Communication in Negotiations. *Personality and Social
Psychology Bulletin* 33:187–199.

Taber, C. S. 2003. "Information Processing and Public Opinion." Pp. 433–476 in *Handbook of Political Psychology,*
edited by D. O. Sears, L. Huddy, and R. Jervis. London: Cambridge University Press.

Tajfel, H. 1978a. "Interindividual Behaviour and Intergroup Behaviour." Pp. 27–60 in *Differentiation between Social
Groups,* edited by H. Tajfel. London: Academic Press.

——. 1978b. "Social Categorization, Social Identity and Social Comparison." Pp. 61–76 in *Differentiation between
Social Groups,* edited by H. Tajfel. London: Academic Press.

Tajfel, H. and J. C. Turner. 1979. "An Integrative Theory of Intergroup Conflict." 33–47 In *The Social Psychology of
Intergroup Relations,* edited by S. Worchel and W. G. Austin. Chicago: Nelsan-Hall Publisher.

Taylor, V. and N. E. Whittier. 1992. "Collective Identity in Social Movement Communities: Lesbian Feminist
Mobilization." Pp. 104–129 in *Frontiers of Social Movement Theory.* edited by A. Morris and C. Mueller.
New Haven, CT: Yale University Press.

——. 1995. "Analytical Approaches to Social Movement Culture: The Culture of the Women's Movement in
Social Movements and Culture." Pp. 163–187 in *Social Movements and Culture,* edited by H. Johnston and
B. Klandermans. Minneapolis, MN: University of Minnesota Press.

Teske, N. 1997. *Political Activists America. The Identity Construction Model of Political Participation.* Cambridge,
UK: Cambridge University Press.

Tilly, C. 1978. *From Mobilisation to Revolution.* Reading, MA: Addison-Wesley.

Tristan, A. 1987. *Au Front.* Paris: Gallimard.

Tropp, L. R. and S. C. Wright. 1999. "Ingroup Identification and Relative Deprivation: an Examination across
Multiple Social Comparisons." *European Journal of Social Psychology* 29(5–6):707–724.

Turner, J. C. 1999. "Some Current Themes in Research on Social Identity and Self-Categorization Theories."
Pp. 6–34 in *Social Identity: Context, Commitment, Content,* edited by N. Ellemers, R. Spears, and B. Doosje.
Oxford: Blackwell.

Turner, J. C., M. A. Hogg, P. J. Oakes, S. D. Reicher, and M. S. Wetherell. 1987. *Rediscovering the Social Group:
A Self-Categorization Theory.* Oxford: Blackwell.

Tyler, T. and S. L. Blader. 2000. "Psychological Engagement with the Group." Pp. 179–213 in *Cooperation in
Groups: Procedural Justice, Social Identity and Behavioral Engagement,* edited by T. Tyler and S. L. Blader.
Philadelphia: Psychological Press.

Tyler, T. R. 1994. "Psychological Models of the Justice Motive: Antecedents of Distributive and Procedural Justice." *Journal of Personality and Social Psychology* 67(5):850–863.

Tyler, T. R. and H. J. Smith. 1998. "Social Justice and Social Movements." Pp. 595–629 in *Handbook of Social Psychology*, edited by D.Gilbert, S. T. Fiske, and G. Lindzey. New York: McGraw-Hill.

van der Veen, Gerrita and B. Klandermans. 1989. "Exit Behavior in Social Movement Organizations." Pp. 179–198 in *Organizing for Change: Social Movement Organizations In Europe and the United States,* edited by B. Klandermans. Greenwich, CT: JAI Press.

van Stekelenburg, J., B. Klandermans, and W. W. v. Dijk. 2007a. "Demonstrating for Imperiled Interests or Violated Values." *Journal of Social Issues*. Manuscript submitted for publication.

——. 2007b. "Different Motivational Configurations as a Function of Mobilizing Context." Manuscript to be submitted for publication.

——. 2007c. "Justice-related Emotions: Anger versus Indignation in the Context of Collective Action." Manuscript submitted for publication.

van Zomeren, M., T. Postmes and R. Spears. 2006. "Collective Action: A Meta-Analysis." Manuscript to be submitted for publication.

van Zomeren, M., R. Spears, A. H. Fischer, and C. W. Leach. 2004. "Put Your Money Where Your Mouth Is! Explaining Collective Action Tendencies Through Group-Based Anger and Group Efficacy." *Journal of Personality and Social Psychology* 87(5):649–664.

Verba, S., K. L. Schlozman, and H. E. Brady. 1995. *Voice and Equality: Civic Voluntarism in American Politics.* Cambridge, MA: Harvard University Press.

Walsh, E. J. 1981. "Resource Mobilization and Citizen Protest in Communities Around Three Mile Island." *Social Problems* 29(1):1–21.

Watson, D. and A. Tellegen. 1985. "Toward a Consensual Structure of Mood." *Psychological Bulletin* 98(2):219–235.

Watson, D., D. Wiese, J. Vaidya, and A. Tellegen. 1999. "The Two General Activation Systems of Affect: Structural Findings, Evolutionary Considerations, and Psychobiological Evidence." *Journal of Personality and Social Psychology* 76(5):820–838.

Whittier, N. E. 1997. "Political Generations, Micro-cohorts, and the Transformation of Social Movements." *American Sociological Review* 62:760–778.

Wilder, D. A. 1990. "Some Determinants of the Persuasive Power of In-group and Out-groups: Organization of information and attribution of independence." *Journal of Personality and Social Psychology* 59:1202–1213.

Wilder, D. A. and P. N. Shapiro. 1984. "Roles of Out-group Cues in Determining Social Identity." *Journal of Personality and Social Psychology* 47(2):342–348.

Wright, S. C. 2001. "Strategic Collective Action: Social Psychology and Social Change." Pp. 409–430 in *Intergroup Processes: Blackwell Handbook of Social Psychology* (vol. 4), edited by R. Brown and S. Gaertner. Oxford: Blackwell Press.

Wright, S. C., D. M Taylor., and F. M. Moghaddam. 1990. "Responding to Membership in a Disadvantaged Group: From Acceptance to Collective Protest." *Journal of Personality and Social Psychology* 58:994–1003.

Wyer, R. and T. Srull. 1986. "Human Cognition in Social Context." *Psychological Review* 93(2):322–342.

Yzerbyt, V., M. Dumont, E. Gordijn, and D. Wigboldus. 2002. "The Impact of Self-categorization on Reactions to Victims of Harmful Behavior." Pp. 67–88 in *From Prejudice to Intergroup Emotions: Differentiated Reactions to Social Groups,* edited by D. M. Mackie and E. R. Smith. Philadelphia: Psychology Press.

Yzerbyt, V., M. Dumont, D. Wigboldus, and E. Gordijn. 2003. "I Feel for Us: The Impact of Categorization and Identification on Emotions and Action Tendencies." *British Journal of Social Psychology* 42(4):533–549.

Zhao, D. 1998. "Ecologies of Social Movements: Student Mobilization During the 1989 Pro-democracy Movement in Beijing." *American Journal of Sociology* 103:1493–1529.

Anthro[...] [...]dy
of S[...]

TON S[...]

When Barrington Moore († 20[...] [...]ience and Revolt addressed the question of why [...]ften accept their lot, and only in exceptional circumstances take to the barricades, he underscored what anthropologists had been discovering whenever they studied social movements: to understand collective action, the political and "grievances" focuses will not do. It is impossible to analyze social movements if one confines the effort to making an analysis of political power relations, or if one trusts on the automatism that, in the end, accumulated frustration and anger will produce insurrection. Moore's approach was anthropological in the sense that he explicitly took account of the aspirations and doubts, and the adherence to the "lived normality," of the rank and file of the people who, if at all, make social movements. His study of the harsh lot of industrial workers in early twentieth century Germany attempted to explain why overwhelming majorities were hesitant to rebel, and why, if they did, they often demanded piecemeal improvements rather than radical, structural changes. The participant's vantage point and *culture*, at the micro-level of lived and shared daily life, took central stage in his analysis.

His approach to the emergence of social protests and movements, in this regard, was exemplary of at least *part* of what anthropologists are able to contribute to our understanding of such movements. We would, however, do the anthropologists' participation in the study of social movements injustice if we were to suggest that in Moore's work it all, in a rudimentary way, is there. Rather, as Escobar (1992:400) remarked, Moore's book was one of the "historically oriented political economy" studies, which only incipiently gave a systemic role to the "problems of meaning and identity that are essential for understanding (. . .) forms of protest" (pp. 400–401). In anthropology, ideally, this *is* done more systematically. In such efforts, as we will see, also other issues such as "the cultural and symbolic aspects of (. . .) social movements" (p. 403), and the cultured "dispositions" of the various agents in play, crop up. As a consequence of these research efforts, both in and outside of anthropology, the very concept of "culture" (as a given ingredient of social movements or as a constituting axis of society) also comes under scrutiny.

We will not make a plea for any exclusive or unique role of anthropology in studying social movements—anthropology's specific contribution to or modification of the study of social movements, we believe, cannot be captured in one sloganesque phrase. We illustrate the complementary contribution of anthropology's approach in analyzing the multilayered phenomenon of people's collective action by indicating that such contributions often came about in cross-disciplinary research and theoretical explorations. To orient ourselves, however, we suggest that anthropology's contribution to the study of social movements entails four crucial dimensions: first, in anthropological approaches *culture* takes central stage. Culture, as elaborated below, is an complex matter, and questions revolving around the connection between "culture" and "social movements" touch on manifold themes such as the cultural characteristics of societies at large, influencing both protesters and authorities, such as cultural traits explicitly being contested by social movements because of their alleged unjust character, and a movement's *proper* cultural narratives to justify their case and recruit supporters Rodriguez 1994. In addition, as elaborated in the second section, culture emerged as an extremely complex notion in the very effort to identify new social movements against the backdrop of analyses of postindustrial societies. Some, for instance, argued that the nature of social (or, for that matter, historical) movements had become cultural since it was no longer the production order, but the basic cultural groundwork of societies that had become the pivotal issue. We address these various dimensions and appearances of culture in this chapter—introducing the phenomenology of some of these items in the remainder of this Introduction, and addressing the theoretical debates in the second section.

Second, we argue that anthropology (including some non-anthropology fields inspired by its approaches), through its emphasis on cultural dimensions, contributed to clarifying the recurrent debate between more structuralist and more agency-focused approaches of social movements Bouvdieu 1972. Culture is the product of history, but having emerged, whereby emergence is an ongoing process, it obtains properties of its own. Culture is man-made—but culture is able to shake off its makers, and impact on them beyond their control or consciousness. In its analyses and reconstructions of the adventures of social movements and the people participating in them, anthropology has been able to contribute to insights in the ways these processes occur. This idea is addressed more extensively in the third section and throughout the chapter.

Third, we believe that anthropology is strong in taking the analysis to the site of the individual and group's *perceptions*. To understand the participant's and nonparticipant's considerations, doubts, meaning-giving and aspirations, and their own wording and interpretations, anthropology has much to offer. In analyzing sociocultural phenomena, anthropology distinguishes between *emic* and *etic* viewpoints. These neologisms refer to the different contexts in which assertions about cultural features are expressed, or to the different nature of the information that is articulated. The emic perspective focuses on the intrinsic cultural distinctions that are meaningful within that society. It searches for the words, distinctions, and labels that the people in that society use and recognize as well as judge the validity of such descriptions and concepts. The etic perspective searches for the concepts and categories that have meaning among scientists. These concepts are often not directly recognized, or even known, among the people and the society they attempt to depict. But they enable scientific dialogue and comparison. In most (social) scientific accounts, the concepts and *verbatim* wording of the people, the emic dimension, has disappeared. Consequently, this language and the meanings it holds are no longer part of the analysis. Anthropology often will try to preserve the emic accounts, and make them part of the appraisal of the facts. In social movement research, this is of crucial importance. Finally, anthropology is often depicted as a "holistic social science." Although controversial, the core idea remains valuable. It claims that anthropology is the "study of mankind as a whole" that professes "systematically to research all the manifestations of the human being and of human activity in a unified way" (Hoebel 1972). It integrates political science, economics, architecture, musicology, and other disciplines into the study of mankind as a whole. Anthropology would thus be lifted to the status of a crowning "science." Whatever one may think of that, more recently Nash (2005:22), in her introduction to a volume dedicated to the anthropological study of social movements, has also stressed that holistic analysis of such movements is the hallmark of the anthropological approach. Holism entails that a phenomenon will be studied "in its social whole." A specific feature—a religious ritual, a particular symbol, a patrilinear inheritance system, a political upheaval—will be analyzed taking into account the different dimensions of a society: the economic, religious, gender, political, kinship, and other spheres that co-constitute the issue under study and give it its—emic— significance, magnitude, value, and corollary. In social movement research, it is beyond any doubt important to take into consideration the societal features that surround and penetrate the events. Economic and societal orders, dominant religious convictions, kinship relations, and existing communication media, among others, will inevitably have an impact on the course of events with regard to the conflict at stake, and will definitely have a bearing on local perceptions and valuations of it. This feature of the anthropologist's approach will surface throughout the chapter, as it is intimately connected to the very nature of the key idea of culture.

Social movements are a multilayered and complex phenomenon. One would therefore need more than just the help of one discipline or focus; one would need a political science approach (Campbell 2005; Tarrow 1998), a focus on societal structures (Díaz 1993; Touraine 1985), a sociology and an episodical and longitudinal historical analysis (Thompson 1966), a social–psychology approximation (Stryker, Owens, and White 2000), and probably more, to account for their developments. Culture, however, is beyond doubt a key component in social movements. But culture is fickle.

We reiterate that we do not believe there exists a quasi-ontological, isolated, bounded cultural layer underneath concrete action and manifest opinions of social movements and their participants (which would be the exclusive subfield for the anthropological discipline), nor do we want to ontologize unfathomable strata of culture that actors are subordinated to, and that rob them of their agency and sovereignty (Salman 2002b). Rather, we suggest taking account of the *cultured features* of social movement manifestations. These entail collective memories, body attitudes and "bodily memory" (Roodenburg 2004:219), *le sens pratique* (Bourdieu 1980), contested legitimising narratives and cosmologies, habitus, collective identities, and much more. One thing can already be inferred from this haphazard record: culture reaches beyond the discursive realm. We therefore need to account for the fact that "a society's symbolic violence can (not) be defeated by a *prise de conscience*" (Roodenburg 2004:223). Culture, moreover, crops up in multifarious ways in social movement emergence and actions.

Structure of the Chapter

In the remainder of this first section, we, to begin with, introduce the anthropological discipline in a quite straightforward way. Next, we explore, in a rather phenomenological mode, various facets of culture's presence in social movement formation and action, touching on culture's *locus* in social movements, on culture's "materialization," and on the problem of the time perspective of culture in relation to the time perspective of social movements.

In the second section, we deal with the "cultured constellation" of social movements and elaborate on the important theoretical shifts in this regard from the 1970s onward. In this section, we intend not only to demonstrate the cultural layers of social movement manifestations, but also to suggest that the very conceptualization of the cultural dimension underlying societal changes and concomitant movement's motivations and goals was, in the course of the recent decades, radically altered. We dedicate the second section of this chapter to these developments, and address some of the crucial transformations in the understanding of these cultural features of social movements' *raison d'être*, among which is a discussion of the newness of the new social movements.

In the third section, attention is given to two important facets of anthropology's approach to social movements: the issue of the structure/agency balance and anthropology's inclination to highlight (but maybe sometimes overstate) the sociocultural stake, at the cost of the political and strategic stakes. With regard to the first facet, the main issue is the recasting of the debate on the role of structure and of agency once culture is brought into play. With regard to the second facet, the crucial importance of underscoring the cultural and identity dimensions is discussed, as well as the concomitant risk to "forsake" politics.

In the fourth section, we discuss culture as natural input for social movements. Culture is society's and social movements' natural habitat and their struggles main resource. This is the field of the cultural "stuff" social movements tap, or collide against, to make their point. In the movements' emergence, their mobilization practices, and their success in obtaining participants' commitments, much more than just actual grievances, shared fates, and societal and political opportunities come into play. The (often constrained) possibilities to contest; the recognition of collective identities; the revitalization or invention of collective (combative) memories; and the allusion to appealing historical examples, heroes, and icons are integrative features of movements' trajectories. These are eminently *cultural* facets, and often analyzed in symbolic, ritual, and ceremonial terms. They, however, also include the "natural" justifications, in institutions, meaning schemes, and political repertoires present in any society. As such, they are often highlighted in anthropologists' accounts of social movements' histories.

In this section we also pay attention to the explicitly contested cultural features and meanings. This is the dimension of the challenge these movements embody *vis á vis* the cultural "arrangements" that legitimize and uphold established political, religious, social, and gendered inequalities (Alvarez, Dagnino, and Escobar 1998a). It is about their attempt to create alternative cultures, to resignify hardened significances. In recent years, for instance, the contents of the concepts of "citizenship," "civil obligations," "free markets," and "governability" have come under scrutiny in movements' accusations regarding the concealing effects of the meanings attached to these terms by oligarchic or neoliberal spokespersons and discourses. In this realm, then, *meaning* is the stake of social movements' actions. We also come to speak about social learning processes, and about ethnic, gender, or religious identity converted into a source of pride to foster movement participation.

Finally, in the fifth section, we will attention to perhaps the most (stereo)typical characteristic of anthropology's approach to social movements: its contribution to the study of social movements employing its methodological asset of fieldwork and participant observation. These methods result in *ethnographies* of social movements that complement the understanding of social movements' whereabouts in crucial ways. Here, the aspirations, doubts, and life histories of the rank and file of participants in such movements take central stage, often shedding new light on the successes and failures of the strategies and mobilization initiatives of leaders and ideologues.

Anthropology: Introducing a Discipline

Before discussing in more detail anthropology's role in the study of social movements, and the specific consequences this had for anthropology's own—and ongoing—reflections on culture, we first briefly introduce the discipline's main characteristics and its attempts to grasp the essentials of this cultural dimension.

Anthropology, the "study of man," is often said to have been born in the nineteenth century, with strong roots in the Anglo-Saxon world and in the Enlightenment. This is not fully correct since the Greeks and Romans already studied the "barbarians" but above all because travels to the Near and Far East, and later the discovery and conquest of the New World, gave rise to studies of the customs and social organization of its inhabitants. Although this did not result in the emergence of a distinct discipline, independent from philosophy, theology, and juridical theorizing, which at that time were quite mixed up at any rate, it is also certain that the colonial encounter gave rise to descriptions and attempts at explanation of social facts that constituted what later would be labeled "anthropology," a discipline concerned with the study and understanding of "different" societies and "other" cultures. Such efforts to "understand," just to remind ourselves, were often just as much inspired by problems and self-perceptions of the colonizers as by the actual features of the peoples being conquered (Lemaire 1986). The nineteenth century saw the rise of cultural evolutionism, soon followed by diffusionism while the early twentieth century witnessed the institutionalization of the discipline, named cultural anthropology in the United States, social anthropology in Britain, and ethnology in France.

Enlightenment and John Locke's attempt to prove that at birth the human mind was an "empty cabinet" provided the groundwork for the late nineteenth century attempts at formal definitions of "culture," of which Edward Tylor's 1871 formulation is the most quoted in anthropological textbooks: "Culture or Civilization, taken in its wide ethnographic sense, is that complex whole which includes knowledge, belief, art, morals, law, custom and other capabilities and habits acquired by man as a member of society." Culture here emerges not as the intellectual or spiritual development of the individual, as in humanist understandings, but as the way of life of a whole society (Crehan 2002:46), although societies, at the time, were often still considered to be hierarchically ordered and "cultures" were thought to be of a higher or lower rank. Culture, as this definition however highlights, is not innate, but acquired or learned behavior and "man" came to be regarded as a culture-creating and culture-bound animal, possessor of a "treasure of signs" that sets him and her apart from all other animals: a signifying animal and as such the object of anthropology in its different guises.

Cultural relativism is a notion of the early twentieth century, but remained fairly insignificant in broader society until well into that past century. Even more stubborn was the romantic idea of cultures as coherent, organic, primordial traditions. This view holds the notion that cultural contacts "contaminate" these traditions and bereave them of their authenticity. Although there have been many attempts to define culture as holistically as possible, including artistic, symbolic, and religious features; customs and habits; knowledge and science; morals; laws; and politics, the Geertzian idea (Geertz 1973) that culture is principally a coherent "whole," a "web of significance"—penetrating all other realms of life—is still strong. Only recently is the idea that culture is not something like a body of symbolic and societal features defended more and more (Kuper 2000). Kuper warns against the idea that culture might actually *explain* things (Kuper 2000:xi). We should, he asserts, not separate out a cultural sphere and use it as explanation. Rather, Kuper (2000:247) insists, "unless we separate out the various processes that are lumped together under the heading of culture, and then look beyond the field of culture to other processes, we will not get far in understanding any of it." Following this advice, we avoid reifying culture or present it as an unequivocal "cause" of anything Bhabha 1996. We instead take into account the hybrid and often contradictory nature of cultural formations and try to show how the crucial dimension of (contested) meaning, in concrete ways, penetrates into the decisions taken by the agents involved in social and political configurations triggered by social movements. Nevertheless, we do not disregard that culture is not something people easily dispose of; culture shapes our shaping of ourselves, even in attempts to escape it.

There is an additional important caveat: in the midst of these de- and reconstructions of the notion of culture, in folk knowledge "culture' " is a taken-for-granted dimension of most any society. Worldwide, all peoples have discovered they "have" a culture. And folk self-references and explanations for very diverse events often call upon "our culture." "The cultural self-consciousness developing among imperialism's erstwhile victims is one of the most remarkable phenomena of world history in the later twentieth century" (Marshall Sahlins cited by Kuper 2000:2). This is true for these erstwhile victims, but also for social movements. Inside, or emic, explanations of social movement features will also often invoke "culture" (Brysk 2000; Quintanilla 1996)—and often in a fairly essentialist mode. This, then, has to be part of our efforts to account for the cultural presence in the vicissitudes of these movements as well, and is addressed further below.

Culture's Manifold Presence in Social Movements' Emergence and Actions

To address more systematically the possible role of anthropology in social movement studies, we first need to explore the terrain of social movement studies as such, to determine the dimensions of the studies to which cultural anthropology might be able to contribute. Bader (1991) made a very valuable attempt to understand this terrain, and was able—if not to answer all theoretical and domain-related distinctions and concomitant questions—to determine what type of questions need to be posed and what theoretical challenges we face with regard to the different stages or dimensions of social movement performances. His schemes (Bader 1991:45, 55) make it possible to distinguish, for instance, between the preconstruction episodes, the articulation episodes, and the mobilization and conflict episodes. The former logically precede the episodes of actual mobilization and confrontation, but of course are not necessarily previous to or fully accomplished once the manifest confrontation erupts. Paraphrased, Bader distinguishes between the episode that entails the structural social, economic, ethnic, or other changes, or given specific unequal access to recourses, that account for a *potential protest group*; the episode in which this group's further development is decisively influenced by *habitus* to crystallize in a *collective identity* of a specific nature; the emergence of awareness of *grievances* and *interests* and of articulated *ideologies or utopias*; the role of a minimum level of *organization*, and *leadership*; and the possible subsequent *mobilization* and the recruitment of resources. It is important to stress that this is not intended to present the actual course and sequence of things. Many episodes will, in real circumstances, overlap, and feedback effects occur all the time and have decisive impacts on the other episodes.

The point in reflecting on Bader's suggestions is not to unravel the whole complex of factors and aspects relevant in such research, but to be reminded about the crucial role cultural dimensions play in the various rounds of the emergence and action of the movement, and in the responses of authorities and opponents. Most obvious and irrefutable is this role in episodes such as the formation of habitus and collective identity. It is, however, also present in the concrete evolvement of episodes such as the framing of interests, and the design of utopias and concomitant slogans. It becomes also manifest in the construction or invention of historical myths and exemplary heroes and events, And resonates in the forms of leadership and mobilization patterns (Díaz Barriga 1998:261; Lazar 2006; Nuijten 1992). Even models of confrontation, and expectations and anticipations about risks, about the possible counteractions of the opponent and about choices to go for concessions or for "all or nothing" are informed by culture. Culture accompanies the whole course of the life of social movements, and enables to link the different episodes to features of the surrounding society, where specific culturally embedded arrangements suggest specific forms of bringing about the movement.

A focus on culture in the study of social movements (see Escobar 1992) moreover enables us to connect social movements' actions to the quotidian "going on" (Giddens 1991:35) and the taken for granted, habitual, and routine of everyday. This everyday culture constitutes the "submerged reality which is the latent or less readily observed side" of collective action (Foweraker 1995:47, see also Díaz Barriga 1998:261–264 Salman 1998). It is a social tissue, the nature of which is of central importance to understand both the emergence— or the absence thereof—of social protest formations, as well as the reach and limitations of the changes they strive for.

This is not an argument to culturalize or de-politicize the social movements. Social movements, as Foweraker (1995:61*ff*) has stressed, are not phenomena that remain confined to the culturally saturated civil society, even if that is where their meaning's cradle is. They explicitly relate to political issues and the polity, and can therefore not be studied as if they were mainly sociocultural phenomena. According to Foweraker, they are political both in the sense that they politicize new issues, and in the sense that they "enter the political and institutional arena (and engage) in strategic interaction with the state" (p. 62; we return to this issue in the fourth section). Nevertheless, as also Foweraker underscores, in understanding social movements it is crucial not only to focus on the explicitly and discursively politicized dimensions, but also to take into account the "submerged reality" of "subcultures, alternative milieu, issue-specific publics, movement networks and social movement sectors" (p. 47, see also Baño 1984) that constitute their groundwork. This cultural background of the rise of organizations and movements is crucial to understand their fate—where political, discursive, and structural factors do not suffice to do so (Alvarez, Dagnino, and Escobar 1998a). To be able to obtain access to the cultural features of social movement actions, we need anthropology.

Second, culture is important to study in relation to social movements because it corrects our understanding of the very idea of cultures as "discrete and bounded entities" (Crehan 2002:36). Studying social movements reminds us of an insight that has been growing in contemporary cultural anthropology and currently haunts its theoretical debates (García Canclini 1992, 1995; Kuper 2000), namely that culture should not be interpreted as a self-contained realm of a group of people's significations, symbols, rituals, and traditions—more or less detached from or overarching society's internal heterogeneity, strives, and inequalities. Culture is plural, contested, and fragmented—as is any society. That is precisely the reason it plays such an important role in societal frictions and discords. Culture doesn't merely have some bearing on conflicting political actors; it is an *integral part* of their very constitution and identities—which, to reiterate, does not mean these identities can be reduced to culture. (De la Cadena 1990). One's societal position, access to resources, role in power configurations, gender, age, and so forth, *also* make identities. Already Gramsci pointed out that the cultural worlds of what he termed the subaltern were part and parcel of the societal machinery reproducing inequalities (Gramsci 1971:334–343; see also Carroll and Ratner 1994; Crehan 2002:7). Culture, then, appears as intimately engaged with, and providing significations for, political and economic realities, and as a societal praxis that does not homogenize, but rather divides, and keeps divided, societies. Culture, in Bourdieu's (1986) later and famous words, *distinguishes* within societies. Eric Wolf elaborated on the argument, stressing it would be mistaken to trust, in any given society, "the efficacy of symbols, (. . .) the workings of logics and aesthetics in the movement toward integration or reintegration, as if these cognitive processes were guided by a *telos* all their own"(Wolf 1982:229). Instead, Wolf argues, "[p]ower is implicated in meaning through its role in upholding one version of significance as true, fruitful, or beautiful, against other possibilities that may threaten truth, fruitfulness, or beauty". And therefore, "symbolic work is never done" (p. 230). Social movements are one of the protagonists of this perseverance of the "symbolic work." Thus, culture not only is the shared discursive and practical backdrop for the parties in (political) conflict, but it also, in its heterogeneous and contested nature, is one of the very substances of the conflict. And conversely, " . . ..[m]ovements of squatters, women, marginal people, and others also set into motion cultural forces" (Alvarez, Dagnino, and Escobar 1998b:6). In Escobar's (1992:408) words: "questions about daily life, democracy, the state, and the redefinition of political practice and development are closely interrelated and (. . .) social movements might be a particularly suitable arena in which to explore these interrelations." In the second section we return to this theme.

A third reason to include (a dynamically, heterogeneous, stratifying rather than homogenizing conceptualization of) culture in our attempts to comprehend social movements is the fact that social movements often explicitly and deliberately recur to cultural symbols to strengthen and legitimize their case. Their discourse taps (counter)culture, to justify, or give appeal, to their calls and complaints. Studying such cultural backing is crucial in understanding both the layers of meaning that provide for the attractiveness, and for assessing the effectiveness of such strategies.

Fourth, there are the ethnic movements, and the identity politics of social movements (including all the specific intricacies connected to them like the tendency to mistake "a group position for a 'culture' " (Bernstein 2005:50; Findji 1992 Assies et al. 2000). In such movements, the ways in which dominant cultures constrain the reproduction and public presence of minority groups becomes an explicit motive for and element of the struggle. Often, the rights of a particular culture become the central bone of contention in conflicts in which such movements partake.

One of the additional, paradoxical ways in which culture surfaces in social movements is that often the poor do not mobilize but resort to hidden forms of resistance (Scott 1990), not challenging but engaging in small-scale undermining of the incumbent hierarchies and impositions. Such forms of protest, obviously, are also heavily influenced by cultural characteristics of the "sneakily" protesting group. But in this case, these characteristics do no help explain a movement, but its omission—or transformation in "decentered" micro-protests.

Although the preceding discussion was not exhaustive, it can help us imagine the many ways in which the presence of culture in social movements becomes manifest, as illustrated below.

The Concrete Incarnation of Culture in Social Movements

Culture surfaces in the coming about and in the actions of social movements in various ways. Two illustrations might help to envision more concretely how this becomes tangible. In the first place, in taking into account the life histories of the actors in social movements, we learn to avoid taking social movements as given aggregates once they ubiquitously perform, or as phenomena inevitably triggered off by adverse circumstances or the worsening of living conditions, or, alluding to yet another research strategy, as launched by the mere injection of a discourse made available by third parties or by a charismatic leader. In all these cases, the actors are, often implicitly, portrayed as available components. We hold that an analysis of social organizations' and movements' emergence and development needs to include that the actors involved—or, for that matter, the actors who had the chance but declined becoming involved—have life histories, and solidified capabilities and inabilities, and views and judgments, and knowledge and networks (Espinoza 1993 Salman 2000), and are therefore not infinitely flexible. They have in a specific manner been prepared, both on the level of conscious memories and conceptions and concrete faculties, and on the level of unconscious routines, self-images, and notions of societal differences and inequalities, to react to organizational opportunities and propositions—to react maybe affirmatively, maybe declining, but neither one of these possibilities is *random*. Sensibility toward the cultural features of the make-up of the people these social movements try to motivate to participate decisively enriches our analysis. Movement leaders, of course, try to connect as well as possible to the people they try to mobilize, and find the most powerful incentives, the most appealing images, the skills and characteristics that most speak to people's self-esteem and pride.

In the second place, and getting more concrete, various studies suggested that, *before* explicit protests occurs, people often try to convince the authorities in more "elegant" and socially conventional ways of their needs. In, for instance, their valuation of official petitions and a formal, stately, grandiloquent and cultivated language used in them, the poor, in an indirect manner, express their high esteem of respectful, obliging, and polite interaction with authorities. Incumbent politico–cultural arrangements, thus, often seem to convince, initially at least, the poor, or to be accepted as "natural." In addition, in asking to be heard *on the authorities' conditions,* they stress their hankering after a respectful and equal treatment (cf. Moore 1987). Peasants, workers, and poor dwellers of shantytowns often also tend to value very much the formal and legal correctness of their initiatives: first you lay down and have acknowledged your "articles of association," before you begin to act (albeit that in situations of harsh repression the logics of organization formation are of course often different). The devotion to official forms and procedures is equally remarkable. This expresses that often the poor *want* to expect that both local leaders and politicians act "regardless of persons, rejecting particularism" (Burgwal 1995:168). A similar conclusion was reached by Lehmann, who states that the poor want institutions to "operate according to the rules" (Lehmann 1990:96). In all these wishes and expressions (which, by the way, easily go together with patron/ client practices and strategies [Menéndez-Carrión 1986] and with cunningly or unsuccessfully playing the clientelist game), a set of values and standards is present in which the image "of a dignified and respectful citizen suffering neither exploitation nor humiliation" (Lehmann 1990:96) prevails. Hence, popular culture does not merely echo the subordination to insecurity, fate and power, it—between the lines—also expresses the "model" the poor adhere to *underneath* their resourceful and inventive adaptation to adverse and unpredictable circumstances. It is only when dignity and respect is denied them that the poor or subjugated recur to means that, implicitly or explicitly, challenge the culture they first embodied and identified with. Culture, it seems, needs to fail before it is questioned. Social movements emerge when elements of that—culturally codoned—social order became unacceptable.

These examples, among many other possible ones, illustrate the need to look at the specific, and concrete, cultural features of the premovement circumstances, to be able to understand social movements. These cultural features include encompassing the cultural dimensions of the fundamental religious, ethnic, or, for instance, caste societal arrangements; the ways these arrangements "harden" in people's memories, identities and aspirations—but they also include the ways people initially often resign to given societal orders, and, only in specific cases, the ways they develop and support the counter- and subcultures that challenge these arrangements.

The presence of culture in social movements' actions thus is broad and varied – as will become even clearer in the subsequent sections. There is, however, another conceptual matter to be resolved before we address, in the second section, the question of the nature of "culture" in social movement studies: the traditionally quite different vocabularies and approaches of the study of culture on the one hand, and the ones most often dominating the studies of social movements, especially with regard to time, or *durée*, on the other.

The Distinct "Temporalities" of Culture and Protest Actions

In a way, culture sits uneasily with the study of social movements. Whereas the first often is assumed to be about longitudinal, largely unintended, and broadly conceptualised meaning-laden features of—albeit contested—determined social formations, the latter is about specific, often short episodes, strategic and goal-focused action, and specific collective acts. The translation of long-term, partially nonintentional and subconscious processes into a short-term sequence of often strategically triggered events can of course not be a one-dimensional one, like in the metaphor of the eruption of accumulated grief. There is no direct or causal link between culture (or, for that matter, people's perceptions of societal injustices, memories, and sub-conscious awareness of daily "going on") and collective action. There is, however, we insist, a strong and "organic" relationship. But in connecting "slow" cultural traits with the explicit, visible episodes of social movements' and organizations' actions, a conceptual problem crops up: the constitutive and backdrop factors accounting for the organizations' and movements' vicissitudes are stretched in time and complexity, whereas the movements, to the contrary, are often episodic (Espinoza 1994). If the "ingredients" to explain movement's actions reach into the long interludes of time that passed before anything identifiable as a social formation emerged, and also reach into de layers of culture and routine the actors are unaware of, then how do we link the one with the other?

To do so, we need to link these lesser visible and ascertainable dimensions of the culture of those involved in social organizations and movements with their concrete, episodical involvement in concrete actions. It seems important to clarify precisely what we understand by these social (protest-)formations—or at least, we need to reflect upon the common feature of confining them to a specific lapse of time. We will argue that we should and can avoid turning this issue into one that leads to a "yes-it-is-one" or "no-it-is-not-one" verdict. Too often, in our view, has this question guided case research, and such research has focused on determining the movement level of certain forms of collective action, lapsing into arbitrary labeling (Salman 1997:2–5, 216). Although we therefore argue against a research strategy that takes a certain definition or inventory of what a social movement should be as a point of departure to decide about the degree in which a certain collective action episode fulfils the requirements, we cannot simply disregard the issue. What we do argue, however, is that we should renounce from a perspective that detaches the factual period of action and protest from the broader sociocultural life-world of the people or groups involved in it, or from the societal politico–cultural hegemonies in which protests emerged. In our analysis of the actual protests we therefore include the long-term history of the societal context in which these protests take place. We thus methodologically, for instance, argue in favor of including life histories—and everything contained in them—of the people mobilized in the analysis.

Social movements then, in our view, are informal or more formalized groups of people or small-scale organizations aimed at social change. In the case of small-scale organizations, these pursued changes may be local and related to specific issues, but a challenge of dominant structures and stratifications is nevertheless discernible. In large-scale mobilizations, such challenges are mostly explicit. In their pursuits, these groups embody cultural features of the surrounding society regarding power, authority, and signification—and will often contest the symbols, rituals and otherwise legitimizing characteristics of this power, this authority, and these impositions of meaning. In all cases, neither the participants nor the movements simply "begin from scratch." In addition, social movements also themselves construe and embody shared values, styles, conduct, vocabularies, and/or other forms of group definition. The discursive layer of such cultured features articulates the movement's character explicitly. There is, however, also an unspoken dimension in this movement's culture, which often accounts for the feelings of belonging the participants might encounter in it. This movement culture deliberately distinguishes itself from the dominant culture of the society it aims to change. But often, it will also in certain respects echo this dominant culture. These cultural dimensions of the movements' identities, discourses, and actions should be taken into account in social movements analysis.

This emphasis on the cultural dimensions of social movements allows and invites one not to have a strict and exclusionary definition of what is and is not social movement— and less so in terms of its exact duration. Maybe exaggerating the point, Hetherington (1998:10/11) remarks that "[t]o analyse expressive identities and identity politics as other than new social movements, (. . ..) we have to move from trying to locate them in some linear sense of time". . . .(we need to avoid turning) social movements into a single picture rather than a multiple assemblage." Different manifestations of collective action qualify as relevant and worthwhile if "culture" is the subject of the central questions. Different manifestations of social movements represent different forms of interest-promotion, self-help, public-opinion-influencing, protest, learning processes, culture- and lifestyle-defense strategies, and the like. To study them with a lens on culture, it is fruitful to conceptualize them *in their differences* and their respective qualities and imitations. In its definitional-comprising quality, the concept of 'social movement' obfuscates rather than clarifies the specific cultural features and settings of collective action – and it should therefore be employed in a critical rather than contracting manner.

We have identified four terrains on which an anthropological approach can enrich our understanding of social movements (focus on "culture," intervening in the structure/ agency-debate, bringing in an "emic" perspective, and taking a holistic view), and we have introduced the most salient features of the anthropological discipline. We also explored the multifarious ways in which culture "shows" in social movements and reflected on the consequences of the apparent mismatch between culture's "slow time" and movements' "rapid time." In the next section we reflect on the changing conceptualizations of "culture" in the course of the involvement of anthropology with political issues.

THE CULTURED CONSTELLATION
OF SOCIAL MOVEMENTS

In this section, we first address how, in the course of the discipline's more recent history, the notion of culture evolved alongside the development of a more *political* anthropology. Subsequently, we will focus on how in the debates on "new" social movements, culture again was reframed as the, almost, synthesizing dimension of social movement's raison d'être and identity struggles, Alvarez, Dagnino and Escobar, 1998a, 1998b ending with new questions on the links between these views and the focuses on resource mobilization, globalization, and right-wing movements.

Since its inception and institutionalization, anthropology has traveled through time and space. If initially culture and civilization, as in "primitive cultures," were used as virtually coterminous, albeit with strong evolutionist connotations, the notion of "civilization" gradually faded to the background or was dropped altogether as cultural relativism made headway.[1] The very notion of "cultures" as patterned and bounded wholes came under scrutiny and attention shifted to mixing and hybridity but also the strident defense of culture and identity in a globalizing world where roles and functions become increasingly destabilized as sources of meaning, identification, and identity that appear to become more and more a matter of choice, self-construction, or construction of the "self" (Castells 1997). Rather than being the reflection of a role or function in society, identity is said to have become a culturally constructed performance, related to consumption and life-styles rather than to positions in the production process. As notions and concepts, or what more pretentiously are called paradigms, have come and faded because they became worn and exhausted and/or failed to address newly arising questions, anthropology also traveled in space and sort of "came home" and turned its eye on what used to be considered "not so different." Whereas "alien" cultures/societies had been the traditional object of study it was found that enterprise or corporate company cultures might be quite "alien" and could be studied through an "anthropological lens." Neither anthropology nor anthropological studies of social movements should therefore any longer be identified with a *regional* emphasis, for example, with studies being conducted in "the South." Anthropologists, today, possibly have studied "Western" movements as often as they traveled "South."

Perhaps this development has to do not only with the possibility that anthropologists were running out of subject matter and jobs as decolonization proceeded, but also with the allegedly increased "self-reflexivity" of postindustrial societies where culture itself became a battlefield where "wars of interpretation" were being fought. Things like an "anthropology of democracy," an "anthropology of citizenship," or, for that matter, an "anthropology of social movements" were thought up and took shape in interaction with other "disciplines" as multi- and interdisciplinarity came in vogue.

Social Movements: The Oldies

Social movements, as we shall see, have been defined and redefined in the course of time, and interpretative frameworks have varied and incorporated something as elusive as "culture" in different ways and under different denominations, for example as "ideology" or "discourse." Traditionally anthropologists studied movements closest to their traditional objects of study, the peoples they came across in the colonial encounter and who reacted to this encounter

---

[1] The story is rather complicated, in fact. French Positivism developed the evolutionist scheme of stages in human evolution, which allegedly went from the savage stage, through barbarism to civilization, a scheme that also influenced Morgan and through him Engels and Marx, to become canonized in Stalin's "historical materialist" scheme of stages. Meanwhile, the notion of culture or *Kultur* had been appropriated by the German Counter-Enlightenment and nationalist movement, a move that paved the way not only for reactionary and conservative thinking but also for cultural -relativism and its critique of alleged Western superiority and white supremacy through Boas. Although we should alert the reader to the vagaries of the culture-civilization binomium, it is not the place here to tease it out.

through various forms of protest, rebellion, and revolt. Such reactions took a variety of forms. Millenarianism, often led by a messianic leader who promises his or her followers that an end will come to all evil, is one form. By the end of the nineteenth century and the beginning of the twentieth the South Pacific saw the rise of cargo cults. People abandoned their fields, destroyed their ancestral masks, replaced old rituals with new ceremonies, created new symbols, and built wharfs and miniature landing strips to receive the goods that white colonizers possessed in abundance. In the United States at the end of the nineteenth century the Ghost Dance spread through the Plains, where buffalos had vanished, lands were taken, and the native population had been decimated by measles and smallpox. It was believed that all whites would be destroyed by some (super)natural disaster after which the natives would live happily ever after. A number of Sioux, who were thought to have turned the movement into one of more active resistance, were massacred in 1890 at Wounded Knee by panicking whites and dumped in a mass grave.

These were the stories of disruption of "old ways of life" and the reaction thereto. The Inca resistance in Peru led by Tupac Amaru I, who was beheaded by the conquering Spanish in 1572, gave rise to the Inkarrí myth according to which the decapitated head would, once underground, unite with the body again and rise up to bring about the end of a historical cycle or *pachacuti*, turn the world upside-down, or rather down-side up, and restore the order and social justice disrupted by the invaders (Andrien 2001). Such are the collective memories that may feed into present-day "social movements" as exemplified by the rhetoric of Bolivian Indian leader Felipe Quispe when he asserts that Tupak Katari, the leader of a late eighteenth century revolt against colonial rule, "lives and will return . . .damn it" as the title of a booklet published, significantly, under the emblem of *Pachakuti*: the world turned downside-up. Elsewhere, as in the United States, Gerónimo, Sitting Bull, and Red Cloud would become icons of the "red power" movement.

While such stories may be a delight for anthropologists Worsley's (1957) account of cargo cults in Melanesia is significant in that the author, an anthropologist, can be regarded as an exponent of one current in social movement studies. During the post-war years Marxism became an important source of inspiration in social movement studies, albeit in different guises in Britain, France, and Germany.

British Cultural Marxism

Worsley's work provides a bridge to what might be called an epistemic community or more concretely to postwar cultural Marxism in Britain (Dworkin 1997). While, as an anthropologist, Worsley was particularly concerned with Third World issues, other participants in this epistemic community focused on the contentious actions that accompanied the transition from feudalism to capitalism, the consolidation of industrial capitalism, and the emergence of the modern state in Europe.[2] E. P. Thompson's *The Making of the English Working Class* (1986), first published

---

[2] For anthropology, Marxism was particularly important, on the one hand, in allowing to situate the objects of their studies in the context of a capitalist (colonial or imperialist) world system and thus to break away from the artificial construction of the object as some isolated, bounded and unique "culture" and, on the other hand, in reframing the study of peasant societies in terms of class relations, including those within the "communities." As Bloch (1983:139) has noted, this was part of a wider theoretical development influenced by the theories of historians and economists such as Emanuel, Sweezy, Dobb, Hobsbawn, and Wallerstein. In North American anthropology this development was reflected in the work of people such as Eric Wolf, for example, in his *Peasant Wars of the Twentieth Century* (1973, first published in 1969), and Sidney Mintz, who both stressed the importance of (the critique of) political economy and history for the anthropological endeavor.

in 1963, is one of the well-known examples of such studies that sought to write "history from below" and often emphasized stories of "lost rights" in the transition to capitalism as a motive for revolt (Dworkin 1997). On the one hand, Thompson sought to counter structural functionalism, which regarded class consciousness as an "unjustified disturbance symptom," and on the other hand he distanced himself from orthodox "latter-day" Marxism in emphasizing that class is not a "thing" that can be almost mathematically deducted from productive relations and only has to be made aware of its real interests, as they "ought to be" as disclosed by a party, a sect, or a theorist. In his preface Thompson stated that his book has a "clumsy title" but one that meets its purpose since *making* refers to the study of an active process, which "owes as much to agency as conditioning. The working class did not rise like the sun at an appointed time. It was present in its own making" (Thompson 1966:8–13).

Eric Hobsbawm, another participant in this epistemic community, introduced the distinction between prepolitical and political movements in his discussion of "primitive rebels," first published in 1959 and which for quite some time has been influential in the analysis of social movements. With this distinction he sought to capture the transformation in political culture that accompanied the emergence of industrial capitalism. Prepolitical movements, Hobsbawm (1978:3) wrote, are those of people who come into capitalism as its "first generation immigrants, or what is even more catastrophic, it comes to them from outside . . ." Social banditry, the rise of the mafia, various types of millenarianism, the city mob, and labor sects were phenomena of the *transition* to industrial capitalism. Established industrial capitalism, in contrast, saw different movements. The nature of the state changed with the nationalization of governmental action that paralleled the nationalization of the economic process. Politics itself was transformed through changes in the forms of organization, propaganda, and mobilization and, finally, the language of politics changed through secularization.[3] For Hobsbawm, as for later British "cultural Marxists," the socialist movement, with its labor unions, parties, and secular aspirations, is the emblematic social movement of industrial capitalist society. "Primitive rebels" were people who sought to cope with the changes that came over them, but yet had to develop a way of thought to confront them.

Such studies inspired the development of the notion of "moral economy" to explain the protests that frequently accompany processes of capitalist penetration and state making. The increasing predominance of the cash nexus and the coming of new forms of taxation undermined a subsistence ethic that operated through patron–client relationships, reciprocity, and redistributive mechanisms and provided a sort of social insurance. The undermining of the precapitalist "moral economy" thus could be a reason for protest and revolt.

These are but a few examples of the typically British approach to working class culture, which, in contrast to the more pessimistic views of the Frankfurt School on mass culture, was regarded as potentially subversive. Such work paved the way for the emergence of "cultural studies" in the early 1970s. British cultural Marxism can be said to clearly tend toward a humanist Marxism that was critical of orthodox theorizing and its reductionist views and base/superstructure dichotomy. It is not surprising that the work of Antonio Gramsci became an important source of inspiration since it allowed seeing culture and ideology as a field of conflict between dominant and subordinate groups while the concept of hegemony made it possible to see more than mere domination.

---

[3] On this transformation, though from a non-Marxist perspective, see also Tarrow (1994:32), who refers to the work of Charles Tilly.

Structuralist Marxism and Urban Movements

Although French structuralism and linguistics would influence cultural studies, given their humanist background, British Marxists tended to be weary of the structuralist Marxism that arose in France around Louis Althusser. One of Althusser's major contributions was his recasting of the concept of ideology as the imaginary forms and representation through which people live their real conditions of existence. Culture or ideology is not regarded as an expression or reflection of lived experience but as its precondition, the foundation of consciousness and subjectivity. Though innovative in many ways, structuralist Marxism left very little room for human agency and tended to become overly scientist.

For our purposes it is important that structuralist Marxism became influential in theorizing urban social movements, particularly through the work of Manuel Castells (1977). Castells was astonished by the prominence of urban–environmental issues in the 1970s, at a time when in his view waves of anti-imperialist struggle were sweeping across the world and working class action reemerging. He sought to theorize "the urban" as part of the economic process, namely the *reproduction* of labor power. The urban unit is to the process of reproduction what the company is to the productive process. The new prominence of the urban question in advanced capitalist countries, Castells argued, has to do with the increased significance of "collective consumption," that is, the organization of the collective means of reproduction of labor power. In this context urban planning is regarded as a political intervention to ensure the extended reproduction of the urban system in the interest of the dominant social class. Urban social movements, in contrast, are systems of practices that tend toward a structural transformation of the urban system or the power relations in the class struggle. Whereas planning is concerned with regulating contradictions, social movements are the source of true innovation and change.

Urban contradictions, Castells argued, are "pluri-class" in nature in that they affect different classes and they are secondary to the principal contradiction between labor and capital. Hence urban contradictions are an important occasion for interclass alliance making. In cities one can observe different types of mobilization, and Castells reserved the denomination of *urban social movement* for those mobilizations that directly link up with the class struggle at a political level. Castells was one of the people who intervened in a lively debate about the potential of urban movements and their relationship to the class struggle and structural or revolutionary social change, of which the *pobladores* movement in Chile was one of the oft cited examples.

The interpretation of urban struggles and of their potential significance in bringing about structural change received a particular twist in Latin America, where it was argued that under conditions of "dependent" or "peripheral" capitalism no working class similar to the European counterpart comes into existence since the laboring population is marked by structural heterogeneity. In such circumstances the site of reproduction—the neighborhood or the slum—rather than the site of production may become an important front in the anticapitalist struggle.

Critical Theory

Drawing on the work of Marx and Weber, the Frankfurt School of critical theorists dedicated quite some effort to the fate of the working class under "postcompetitive" capitalism. Notions of alienation and commodity fetishism along with rationalization and the feeling that Enlightenment had gone awry and succumbed to instrumental reason informed their diagnosis of late capitalism and the forms of authoritarianism that accompanied it. Of particular interest here is their view of the "culture industry" as producing debased mass entertainment for passive consumers, thus undermining their autonomy and capacity for independent critical thinking. The culture industry thus was attributed a key role in gaining the acquiescence of the masses, a view that contrasts with that of the British Marxists and their more optimistic assessment of popular culture and its potentially subversive elements.

While critical theorists shared the view on the centrality of the working class in bringing about a societal transformation with the other currents of European Marxism, they were quite pessimistic about the capacities and willingness of the working class to engage in revolutionary action. In his *One Dimensional Man,* Herbert Marcuse argued that the antagonisms of capitalist society had been superseded by forms of rationality that turned problems into individual issues instead of clarifying their collective character. Nonetheless, he argued that the gap between the promises of capitalist society and what it actually was delivering was growing and that that might fuel dissent, particularly among groups on the periphery of the system, such as minorities and poor whose basic needs are not even satisfied, or among students and intellectuals who might escape established social controls and thus might act as catalyst groups that stir the working class into action.

Jürgen Habermas in a way carried forward the critical theory program in his theorizing about the colonization of a life-world of communicative interaction by the systemic media of money and power. Somewhat similar to Marcuse, he draws attention to the potential for protest of those at the periphery of late capitalist society. He argues, however, that neither the bourgeois emancipation movements nor the struggles of the organized labor movement can serve as a model for this protest and that historical parallels are more likely to be found in the social–romantic movements of the early industrial period. Only the feminist movement, Habermas argues, stands in the tradition of the bourgeois–socialist liberation movements and can be regarded as an offensive emancipatory movement, while the others are defensive resistance or withdrawal movements that seek to defend communicatively structured domains, but not to conquer new territory (Habermas 1989:393).

Well into the 1970s the study of social movements was strongly linked to unorthodox Marxist theorizing of different brands, as we have outlined in the foregoing. An implication was that class analysis played a central role in such approaches, together with political economy at a world scale. The working class was regarded as "the" social movement of industrial capitalist society and other movements were often assessed in their relationship to the full-fledged working class movement in one way or another. This transpires in the distinction between prepolitical and political movements as well in the distinction between protest and social movement in urban movement studies. Whereas protests would be spontaneous eruptions of disorder, social movements are forms of more sustained collective action. This distinction can be regarded as two poles of a continuum with various intermediate forms and where social movements are those that effect significant structural change. For Castells (1977) urban movements were capable of becoming urban social movements only if they linked up with the working class movement and adopted a "correct line."

Second, whereas the British historians and anthropologists distinguished themselves by their vivid descriptions of culture, not merely as a "whole way of life" but, as E. P. Thompson put it, "the whole way of struggle" (cf. Dworkin, 1997:102), French structuralism was more inclined to theorizing about ideology, and a principal aim of Castells' early work was to unmask the "urban ideology." In Germany the focus tended to be on the culture industry and the capacity of the welfare state compromise to encapsulate the working class. When he assessed the feminist movement as the only movement to stand in the tradition of bourgeois–socialist liberation movements, Habermas (1989:393) enumerated a plethora of other movements but argued that their potentials for protest are very difficult to classify, because scenes, groupings, and topics change very rapidly. He mentions the antinuclear and environmental movements; the peace movement; single-issue and local movements; the alternative movement (which includes squatters and alternative projects and rural communes); minorities such as the elderly, handicapped, and so forth; the psychoscene; and religious fundamentalism as well as autonomy movements struggling for regional, linguistic, cultural, and also religious independence. These movements are seen as movements of resistance or withdrawal that at times are strongly sensitized to the self-destructive consequences of capitalist growth. According to Habermas, these movements find their historical parallel in the "social–romantic" movements of the early industrial period, that is, the movements that so much intrigued the historians among the British cultural Marxists. However, the latter tended to stress that although the movements they studied might be "primitive," "archaic," or "pre-political" they also pointed out that they were not mere continuations of medieval forms of social protest but rather were groping to come to terms with the new realities of emerging industrial capitalism and as such could also be regarded as precursors of the "political" movement of the working class. Habermas, by contrast, does not regard the movements he enumerates as a breeding ground for viable counter-institutions (Habermas 1989:396). Others, however, saw the movements enumerated by Habermas as precursors of something new: the new (or a new) social movement(s).

Recasting the Debate: Emerging New "Paradigms"

The 1970s and 1980s saw a shift in the debate on social movements, or rather a construction of "social movement studies" as a sort of "discipline" in its own right, informed by and "superseding" contributions from a variety of "established disciplines," such as sociology, political science, social psychology, history, and anthropology. The waning of the Cold War imagery and the transition to a postindustrial society provided the "conditions of emergence" of movements that could not be easily classified in terms of the working class centred approach in Europe, while in the United States dissatisfaction grew with the functionalist and psycho–social approaches propounded by the Chicago School and its emphasis on the rural/urban and community/society dichotomies that tended to represent protests as reflections of irrational maladjustment to inevitably changing conditions. In Europe this gave rise to the emergence of what became known as the "new social movements" approach while in the United States it gave rise to the "resource mobilization" approach. These approaches have sometimes been regarded as "competing paradigms" but can also be viewed as "complementary," and we can observe attempts to "synthesize" the two approaches in recent years. We will try to outline some of the main features of both approaches and the mutual attempts to incorporate such features. We then will move on to the impact of this evolving general debate on social movements in "the South." We will argue that although anthropology made important contributions, social movement studies became sort of an undisciplined "discipline" in its own right. New themes emerged, and in interaction with other "disciplines," anthropologists contributed to the debate while at the same time redefining their "professional identity" and, again, the place and contents of "culture."

New Social Movements

By the 1970s many had become disenchanted with the transformative potential of the working class, which came to be regarded as culturally and ideologically co-opted by "regulated capitalism," underpinned by Fordist production techniques and Keynesian welfare state economics. Nonetheless, as Habermas noted, forms of protest were not absent. In contrast to Habermas, however, scholars such as Alain Touraine (1981, 1985) argued that they were the first manifestations of a *new* unified *social movement*. Whereas the *old social movement* reflected the class contradiction between workers and managers of industrial society—whether capitalist or socialist—the emergence of these new forms of social protest, Touraine argued, indicated the transition to a qualitatively new type of society, the postindustrial or programmed society. They were to be regarded as the first manifestations of a unified social movement, the "self management" movement in opposition to the technocrats—and as such embodied a struggle over a "cultural model."[4] The conflict not only involves two new "classes" he argued, but also evolves on a different level than the conflict of industrial society. Those conflicts had revolved around issues of distribution at an institutional or political level, but the movement of the postindustrial society addresses *cultural* issues on what Touraine calls the "level of historicity" or the self-producing capacity of society. Whereas in the preceding types of modern society—commercial and industrial society—organizational processes and political institutions had been challenged, in postindustrial society cultural orientations such as the meta-narrative of "progress" have become open to challenge. With the advent of postindustrial society the highest level of reflexivity and capacity for self-production of society has been reached, and this is what the "self management" movement is involved in. Cultural orientations have become the terrain and object of struggle as we enter the age of counter-culture in which the identity of social actors corresponds to their capacity for self-reflection.

Touraine (1985), who was involved in making different movements aware of being part of the (unified) "new social movement" of postindustrial or informational society, sought to situate his "sociology of action" by contrasting it to various other approaches to collective action in vogue at the time: Talcot Parsons' functionalism, which viewed protest and conflict essentially as a dysfunction and regards society as classless; strategic or rational choice theories that focus on self-interested and instrumentally rational calculating actors without taking account of the cultural orientation that shapes their choices; and (structuralist) Marxism, which supposes that each class has an ideology of its own. Instead, Touraine argued that society is divided into classes or social movements struggling over the appropriation/alienation of a cultural model: preindustrial, industrial, or postindustrial. Social movements, according to Touraine, therefore are not involved in structural transformation of society but pertain to its synchronic dimension. He distinguishes between modes of production (commercial, industrial, and postindustrial) and modes of development (capitalist, socialist, etc.). Social movements, then, reflect the conflict inherent in a mode of production. Under industrial capitalism the conflict is between workers and managers, independent of the mode of development. Thus the conflicts and social movements in capitalist or socialist industrial societies are essentially the same: they are between workers and managers. And the conflicts and social movements of

---

[4] Social movements, according to Touraine, are defined by three principles: identity, adversary, and control of a cultural/societal model.

postindustrial or programmed society (and here "modes of development" seem to fade as into an "end of history") oppose self-management to technocracy. Conflicts over distribution give way to conflicts over cultural issues such as "progress," or as Habermas signals without drawing similar conclusions about a "new social movement" of postindustrial society, "growth."

Such conflicts between two social movements or classes of a mode of production, Touraine insists, are about the social direction of historicity or the interpretation of the cultural model specific to a mode of production and not about the transformation of society. They belong to the synchronic axis in contrast to the modes of development, which belong to the diachronic axis and involve politics and the state. Social movements are thus located in the civil society sphere. This view leads Touraine to assert that in the developing countries, like those of Latin America, one does not find real social movements because these societies are dominated by issues of development, that is, the transition from one mode of production to another through statism or capitalism. Politics thus, as it were, crowds out social movements.

Similar to Touraine, Alberto Melucci (1980, 1985) viewed social movements as a specific type of collective action and insists that they transcend institutionalized norms and the rules of the political system. Although he also suggests that the new movements act in the field of culture rather than on the economic–industrial plane, he points to their fragmented character and their network-like forms, based in the submerged networks of daily life and permitting multiple and partial participation and a plurality of significations and forms of action. The form of movements by itself is a message and a symbolic challenge. Rather than fulfilling a long-term "universal mission" the new, or rather contemporary, movements can be regarded as "nomads of the present" responding to expressive needs: the movement as message.

Touraine and Melucci can be regarded as major exponents of what have become known as "new social movement theories," which initially were formulated in the 1970s and evolved over time. Theorizing about postindustrialism and the advent of the information society came to be complemented by the theorizing about globalization. A good example is the work of Manuel Castells, who in 1983 renounced his earlier structuralist Marxism and embraced the approach advocated by Touraine, albeit with the twist that Castells regards statism and capitalism as modes of production while industrialism and informationalism are viewed as modes of development (Castells 1983, 1996:14). In his 1983 *The City and the Grassroots* the focus shifted from "the urban" to the city; urban meaning became a central notion linked to urban function and urban social movements are viewed as involved in the transformation of urban meaning. Class relations and the class struggle were no longer viewed as the only primary source of urban social change as Castells now acknowledged the autonomous role of the state, gender relationships, ethnic and national movements, and citizens' movements as alternative sources of urban social change (Castells 1983:291). Among the case studies presented in this book, the Madrid citizens' movement, which emerged in the 1960, is presented as the archetypical urban social movement in its effects on the provision of collective consumption goods, political self-management, and cultural revitalization and community life.

In his monumental study on the information age and its economy, society, and culture, Castells further elaborated his new approach (Castells 1996, 1997, 1998) and highlighted the dramatic technological, economic and social changes occurring at the end of the second millennium. In this confusing environment of change, he stresses, "people increasingly organize their meaning not around what they do but on the basis of what they are, or believe they are" (Castells 1996:3). Societies become structured around a bipolar opposition between the Net and the Self. For our purposes the second volume of this study, entitled *The Power of Identity* (Castells 1997), is particularly relevant. In this volume Castells focuses on identity and meaning in the network society. He discusses religious fundamentalism, both Islamic and

American Christian, and renewed nationalisms in the context of the break-up of the Soviet Union and the Spanish autonomy movements, as well as ethnic/racial communalism, as defensive reactions to prevailing social trends and as alternative sources of meaning. These are examples of defensive reactions in the globalization age that aim to shrink back a world becoming too large to be controlled (Castells 1997:66 Bauman 1992).

In his study, Castells (1997) differentiates between *resistance identity*, *legitimizing identity*, and *project identity*. Resistance identity is exemplified in the reactions to globalization mentioned before, which draw on God, the nation, family, and community to mount a counter offensive against the culture of real virtuality (Castells 1997:66). Resistance identity, which builds on cultural communes, brings about a crisis of legitimizing identity that relies on civil society as it was constructed during the industrial era and the nation-state as the main sources of identity formation. Instead, it relies on a negation of civil societies and political institutions in a defensive and reactive posture that may "transform communal heavens into heavenly hells" (Castells 1997:67), an enclosure of cultural resistance in the boundaries of communes. Project identity, in contrast, may emerge from resistance and the crisis of civil society and the nation-state as a potential source of social change in the network society; new *proactive* subjects may emerge from the *reactive* cultural communities.

This approach leads Castells to the affirmation that social movements have to be understood in their own terms, perhaps echoing Melucci's "the movement is the message," "they are what they say they are" and, second, that social movements may be "socially conservative, socially revolutionary, or both, or none," because there is no predetermined directionality in social evolution and, therefore, from an analytical perspective there are no "good" or "bad" social movements. Third, Castells categorizes social movements according to Touraine's framework of identity, adversary, and vision or societal goal (Castells 1997:70–71).

Such affirmations lead Castells to examine a sample of social movements against globalization, which are rather different in their identity, goals, ideology, and their relation to society, but similar in their opposition to the new global "order": the Zapatista movement in Mexico, the American militia—self-identified as *The Patriots*—, and the Japanese *Aum Shinrikyo*, which in 1995 attacked the Tokyo subway with sarin gas. The structure of "values and beliefs" of such movements is summarized in Table 6.1. Nonetheless, while Castells characterizes these movements as basically reactive and denies any predetermined directionality in history, he also identifies some proactive movements such as environmentalism and feminism. The environmental movement, in all its diversity and varieties of expression or

TABLE 6.1. **Structure of Values and Beliefs of Insurgent Movements against Globalization**

Movement	Identity	Adversary	Goal
Zapatistas	Oppressed, excluded Indians/Mexicans	Global capitalism (NAFTA), illegal PRI government	Dignity, democracy, land
American militia	Original American culture	New world order, U.S. federal government	Liberty and sovereignty of citizens and local communities
Aum Shirinikyo	Spiritual community of delivered bodies and believers	United world government, Japanese police	Survival of apocalypse

Source: Castells (1997:105).

what Castells (1997:112) calls "the creative cacophony of environmentalism," is producing a deep cultural change by dramatically reversing the ways in which we think about the relationship between economy, society, and nature. The themes it puts forward directly correspond to the fundamental structures of the emerging network society: "science and technology as the basic means and goals of economy and society; the transformation of space, the transformation of time; and the domination of cultural identity by abstract global flows of wealth power, and information constructing real virtuality through media networks" (Castells 1997:122). It is, he argues, a science-based movement but it subverts the conventional understanding of science in using science to oppose science on behalf of life and the wisdom of a holistic vision. It furthermore defends the "space of places" from the "space of flows," privileging the local where social meaning can be constructed and political control can be exercised, hence its strong links with grass roots and participatory democracy as a political model. Similarly, the perception of time is challenged, both the "clock time" of industrial society and the "timeless time" of the network society, in that the environmental movement introduces a "glacial time" perspective of intergenerational solidarity that merges ourselves with our cosmological self. Through their struggles over the appropriation of science, space, and time the movement induces the formation of a new socio–biological identity, a culture of the human species as a component of nature (Castells 1997:126). Environmentalism in action seeks to reach minds through witness-bearing attitudes that restore trust and enhance ethical values. Environmentalists do so by making extensive use of the media—feeding them with images that speak louder than words—and the new communications technologies. The multifaceted movement seeks to tame capital and "courts" the state by lobbying for environmental legislation. All sorts of social struggles become infused with environmentalism and the notion of environmental justice, which hints at a superseding of the "exhausted social movements of industrial society" and a resumption, under historically appropriate forms, "the old dialectics between domination and resistance, between *realpolitik* and utopia, between cynicism and hope" (Castells 1997:133).

The other proactive movement that profoundly challenges entrenched forms of domination is the women's movement and feminism, which although present for quite some time have now caught fire (Castells 1997:136). Castells argues that this is so due to (1) transformations in the economy, the labor market, and education opportunities; (2) the growing control over child bearing and reproduction; (3) the climate created by the social movements of the 1960s and the emergence of the "personal as political"; and (4) the rapid diffusion of ideas in a globalized culture. This combination of elements underpins a questioning of gender relations and poses a profound challenge to patriarchalism, although Castells (1997:242) also points to the patriarchalist backlash and restorationism and, once again, underlines that there is no predetermined directionality in history. Patriarchalism may be in crisis and it may be strongly challenged, but it also lashes out in the defense of values that once seemed to be taken for granted, eternal, natural, or divine.

With this overview, which of course hardly can do justice to an extremely rich and multistranded debate, we have sought to at least outline some of the main characteristics of the "new social movements approach" as it emerged from, and is indebted to, the poststructuralist and post-Marxist trends of the 1970s in Europe, in particular. As we shall see, a different perspective emerged from mainly U.S.-based thinking about collective action but by now it will not come as a surprise that in times when ideas travel increasingly harder and faster some sort of exchange, dialogue, and cross-pollination occurs. What we see from this overview is that only a partial break took place with "grand theorizing" about the role and place of social movements in industrial and postindustrial society and their contribution or potential contribution to the "progress of humanity," the "emancipation from domination," or "societal transformation." The theme of defensive/reactive versus progressive/proactive movements remains important, though it is increasingly emphasized that people are making history, rather than merely "doing it" as ossified "Marxism" sometimes would have it. Some of the features underscored in the new social movement approach, besides "identity" and the ways it can be constructed rather than performed, is that these movements address "post-material" or "cultural" issues in a context of "postindustrialism." Another, related, feature is that these movements in a sense are "postpolitical." Rather than addressing the state or seeking political power, civil society has become a terrain and object of struggle. The rediscovery of the work of Antonio Gramsci on hegemony and (popular) culture helped to theorize this aspect. This also means that the new movements would be regarded as "expressive" rather than instrumentalist in orientation, as reflected in Melucci's view of the "movement as the message."

Mobilizing Resources for Collective Action

In 1976 James Scott published *The Moral Economy of the Peasant* in which he sought to explain peasant rebellions and revolutions in Southeast Asia by focusing on the subsistence logic of the peasant economy and argued that the transformations brought about by colonial rule had systematically violated the peasants' "moral economy": "their notion of economic justice and their working definition of exploitation—their view of which claims on their product were tolerable and which intolerable" (Scott 1976:3). Three years later Samuel Popkin (1979) countered with his *The Rational Peasant* in which he develops a "political economy" approach that focuses on individual decision making, investment logic, and cost–benefit calculation, which also applies to collective action. Whereas, he argues, moral economists have regarded rebellion and protest as reactive responses to declining situations such collective action should better be viewed as responses to new opportunities and depend on the ability of a group or class to organize and make demands, hence also his interest in "political entrepreneurs" and the "free rider" problem. With this argument Popkin placed himself within the North American debate on collective behavior and the critique of the Chicago School tradition and in particular its theorizing about "mass societies" and structural–functionalist explanations of collective behavior, which tended to depict collective, or *crowd*, behavior as abnormal and as an irrational somewhat trampling herd-like reaction to social change.[5]

Where it come to theorizing social movements as a form of collective *action*—rather than "behavior"—this critique gave rise to what has become known as the resource mobilization approach, often presented as an alternative to the "new social movement approach" discussed earlier. The resource mobilization approach looks at rational choices—initially perhaps conceived in rather narrow "cost–benefit" terms[6]—and looks at organization, strategies,

---

[5] In this respect Popkin (1979) perhaps overstates his case in targeting the "moral economy" approach which, as we saw, has strong roots in European non-orthodox Marxism, rather than in "crowd psychology." One might say that rather than being rooted in a psychology of irrational and unorganized response to grievance the moral economy approach looks at culturally established action repertoires and the ways in which they change under changing circumstances, as in Hobsbawm's (1978) *Primitive Rebels*, or for that matter Tarrow's (1994) discussion of action repertoires from a resource mobilization perspective.

[6] As we have seen, Touraine sought to position himself by stressing that "rationality" is culturally embedded and cannot be reduced to some sort of decontextualized "economic" interest calculation.

resources, strategizing, and opportunities for mobilization. Social movements, then, come to be viewed as a form of collective action and more precisely as *contentious* collective action or, as Tarrow (1994:3) puts it, "collective challenges by people with common purposes and solidarity in sustained interaction with elites, opponents and authorities." Over time, as noted, a cross-pollination with other perspectives has taken place and eventually McAdam, McCarthy, and Zald (1996) proposed to group the main features of the resource mobilization perspective under the rubrics of political opportunities, mobilizing structures, and cultural framings, which they regarded as elements of an emerging synthesis (McAdam, McCarthy, and Zald 1996:2).

A basic idea in the resource mobilization approach, to put it crudely, is that the amount of discontent in any given society is a constant. What has to be explained is when and how discontent erupts into contentious collective action, how it is framed, and what its effects are. Movements, as Tarrow (1994:1) puts it, are created when political opportunities open up for social actors who usually lack them and, after reviewing the literature—which owes much to political process theorizing—McAdam et al. (1996:27) lists four dimensions of political opportunity:

1. The relative openness or closure of the institutional political system
2. The stability or instability of that broad set of elite alignments that typically undergird a polity
3. The presence or absence of elite allies
4. The state's capacity and propensity for repression

In contrast to the new social movement approach and its tendency to stress the "postpolitical," resource mobilization theory thus explicitly takes institutional politics into account. Changes in the political opportunity structure can be used by people who lack regular access to institutions. "Early risers" grab the opportunity and that sets in motion a "protest cycle" with a dynamics of its own, since new opportunities are created in the process and new groups join the bandwagon. The protest cycle then may result in outcomes that can range from repression, through absorption into institutional politics, to revolution (Tarrow, 1994:24–25). However, as Tarrow (1994:8) points out, the effects of a protest cycle go beyond such immediately visible results as they leave behind permanent expansions in participation, popular culture, and ideology.

The attempt to break with grievance-based conceptions of social mobilization furthermore led to a focus on the mobilization process and *mobilizing structures* that can account for *sustained* movement activity. This directs the attention toward the more or less formal organization patterns and networks that provide the resources for movement emergence and persistence. Informal networks, similar to Melucci's "submerged networks," like friendships, neighborhoods, or work networks or more formal organizations like churches, unions, or professional organizations can provide the conditions of emergence for movements, but sustained activity rather depends on informal activist networks, affinity groups, and memory communities and more formal social movement organizations, protest committees, and movement schools (McAdam et. al 1996). The attention then goes to the development of such informal and formal mobilizing structures and the internal dynamics of the formal movement structures, for example, the questions internal democracy, participation, decision-making processes, modes of leadership, or the workings of the "iron law of oligarchy."

Opportunity structures and mobilization structures, however, remain insufficient to account for collective action. *Framing processes* are the mediating element. They bring in the element of shared meaning and definitions, an element that was long neglected in the resource mobilization tradition as it relied on cost–benefit analysis while, in contrast, new social movement scholars tended to highlight this dimension. Framing is about sociocultural perceptions and the construction of shared understandings that justify, dignify, and motivate collective action. Framing processes draw on and modify the available cultural stock, such as images of justice and injustice, as well as the repertoires of contention and models of action. They are about building consensus for action, but building consensus can be a competitive and even conflictive process.

The two approaches to social movements outlined here—according to rather conventional lines—sometimes are presented as competing "paradigms" while at other times they are viewed as potentially complementary. While the new social movement approach focuses on structural preconditions for movement emergence and particularly emphasizes the difference between industrial and postindustrial society, resource mobilization approaches drew attention to problems of mobilization, organization, and strategizing. And while the new social movement approach with its focus on identity and cultural issues often tended to reduce politics to a "residual category or to a transmission belt" (Foweraker 1995:18), resource mobilization approaches put such issues at the forefront. Such differences in emphasis, along with a growing body of empirical research, have contributed to an enrichment of social movement studies, which gradually became sort of a "discipline" in its own right. Thus, if anthropologists contributed to the study of social movements they did so against the background or in the context of this discursive community and its ongoing debates.

A second point that should be made is that much of the theorizing outlined in the preceing text reflects conditions in the "central" capitalist countries. This certainly is not to say that it is irrelevant, but that in the "periphery" conditions are different and specific themes require attention or should be framed in a different way. Drawing inspiration from the new social movements approach, Mainwaring and Viola (1984), for example, listed a series of social movements that could be regarded as "new" in the Latin American context: the ecclesiastical base communities of the Catholic Church, the women's movement, ecological associations, human rights organizations, and neighborhood associations. These movements were new, they asserted, in that they are inclined toward affective concerns, expressive relations, group orientation, and horizontal organization, in contrast to the "old" movements that were characterized by an inclination toward material concerns, instrumental relations, an orientation toward the state, and vertical organization. Of course, such assertions about "newness" would soon be scrutinized and questioned, among others by anthropologists.[7] Mainwaring and Viola (1984) also argued that the values and emergence of the new movements reflected four conditions: the adverse political consequences of the military regimes under which they emerged, the crisis of the traditional left, the questioning of the populist style of politics that preceded the military regimes, and the development of new social movements in the North. To be sure, while valuable and suggestive the list presented by Mainwaring and Viola (1984) is limited and should be expanded to include the indigenous movements that have become such prominent sociopolitical actors in Latin America as well as the *Movimento Sem Terra*—the Movement of the Landless—in Brazil and its emulations in other Latin American countries. The case of the indigenous peoples' movements and, for that matter, of Black peoples' movements, furthermore points to the importance of the colonial legacy and the issue of "internal colonialism" as well as to the debate over subaltern agency triggered by "post- colonial" theorizing, initially centered in India.

Largely absent from Mainwaring and Viola's (1984) account is the question of structural adjustment policies and neoliberalism, which triggered rounds of riots and more sustained

---

[7] Mainwaring and Viola (1984) themselves pointed out that the base communities and the neighborhood movements were furthest from their "ideal type," but that these were also the most "popular."

protests from the mid-1970s onward (Walton 1989). Neoliberalism and globalization have become prominent foci of conflict and social protest that have been met with repression and the criminalization of protest—which took on even more uncanny features after the 9/11 attacks[8]— leading Seoane (2003) to speak of "neo-liberalism in arms." The "Water War" in the Bolivian city of Cochabamba in early 2000 Assies 2003 is a good example of the more recent protests against neoliberal privatization policies. A central argument in the protest was that water should be considered a public good, rather than a commodity, and that access to it is a human right.

The counterpart of neoliberal globalization is "globalization from below" through the creation of social movement networks involved in cosmopolitan politics and giving rise to a "global civil society" (Cohen and Rai 2000; Smith and Guarnizo 1998). Most visible have been the large-scale protests that accompanied the meetings of the World Trade Organization and the IMF and the creation of the World Social Forum which first met in the Brazilian city of Porto Alegre and brought together activists from all over the world to discuss common problems and to devise common strategies to counter the process of globalization from above. However, apart from such highly visible manifestations the new communication technologies have created opportunities for new forms of networking and "witnessing at a distance" since the activities of protest movements and, more importantly the attempts at repression, can be transmitted in "real time." The use of cyberspace by the Zapatista movement is one of the most eloquent examples of summoning support of global civil society to curb the efforts of the Mexican government at a "military solution" to the conflict.

Finally, as we have seen, Castells (1997) discusses the Zapatista movement in Mexico, the American militia, and the Japanese *Aum Shinrikyo* as examples of contemporary social movements, albeit of the "reactive" variety, and points out that the notions of pre-determined progress or teleological views of history and the role of social movements have come under scrutiny, to say the least. The sample he discusses is a rather mixed bag indeed and it is suggestive of a further turn in social movement studies. As Melucci (make it:1985) has argued, social movements should be considered a type of collective action that breaks through the system's compatibility limits, besides invoking solidarity and making manifest a conflict. And he goes on (Melucci 1996:31) by saying that "[U]p to this point, social movements literature has been mainly devoted to oppositional movements, revealing an explicit bias of the majority of students of collective phenomena. With some important exceptions, much less attention has been paid to what we can call *reaction*, that area of collective action where solidarity is employed to defend social order even by breaching the system limits." Thus right-wing movements, counter-movements, or backlash movements come under the purview of social movement studies. To be sure, this view of "reaction" as backlash is a bit different from Castells' view of reaction as basically a defense of "community" in times of globalization. Nonetheless, it is suggestive of a shift in social movement studies in the sense that less "sympathetic" movements or less "progressive" movements have become an object of social movement studies at a time when the very notion of "progress" has become hedged in with uncertainties.[9]

---

[8] A case in point is the criminalization of Mapuche protests against forest plantations that encroach upon their lands in Chile and that the Chilean state inappropriately classifies as "terrorism" under legislation stemming from the Pinochet dictatorship, as has also been denounced by UN Special Rapporteur on indigenous issues Rodolfo Stavenhagen.

[9] Even if Castells' (1997) distinction between proactive and reactive movements resounds with Habermas' (1989) argument, which is clearly rooted in Enlightenment thinking and sees the feminist movement as the sole remaining carrier of the Enlightenment emancipation project of expanding rational communicative interaction in the face of the colonization of the life-world by power and money as means of exchange.

An interesting instance of this shift is Nash's (2005) anthology of anthropological studies of social movements. Although in her introduction to the volume Nash asserts that her "main preoccupation in organizing this anthology is to document, through studies of social movements, their ongoing task of building the institutional networks needed to transform the policies required to ensure social justice in the globalization process" (Nash 2005:4) the volume includes various studies, by "certified"—and "disciplined"(?)—anthropologists, of "right-wing" social movements such as the state-sponsored Village Scout Movement in Thailand or fundamentalist reactions to secularization in Afghanistan, Egypt, West Papua, and Sri Lanka. And we might add the elite-driven regionalist movement in Bolivia, whose contribution to social justice in the globalization process is rather questionable (Assies 2006). While anthropologists certainly can, and *should*, contribute to the study of such movements and social movement theorizations provide important tools to approach them we should at least be aware of the distinction between proactive and reactive, progressive and reactionary movements, despite the confusion over terms that obviously is in need of clarification.

In either case, we are dealing with societal sectors rejecting incumbent social orders, or reacting against groups challenging these orders. And in both cases, the question about the possibility to articulate such resistance (rather than accommodate and adapt to the dominant order) crops up. It brings us to the question about the reach and scope of agency in structured and culturally solidified societal arrangements. This question is addressed in the next section.

THE STRUCTURED AGENT
AND THE CULTURALIST PROCLIVITY

Introduction

Possibly the most "classical," but certainly not the only way in which anthropology has been engaged in social movements studies, is by means of its methodological stronghold: anthropologists go to the grass roots and do participant observation. Thus, anthropologists often contributed with insights about the rank and file participants (and bystanders). Their participant observation and often longitudinal involvement with the microdynamics of movement construction and action provided important knowledge about people's perceptions of and attitudes toward the framing discourses, the leaders' appeal, the movement's strategies, and the actual actions and mobilizations. This is crucial information: looking "from above," social movements might appear as homogeneous and determined entities, consciously striving and mobilizing to obtain their goals. In actual fact, they seldom are. Often, participation is wavering, the participants heterogeneous, the motives varied and sometimes improper, and people's aspirations more modest, or more impatient, than those of the movements' spokespersons and slogans. To understand the "voyages" of social movements, it often is crucial to *also* know about these grass roots' characteristics. Moreover, as Turner (1994[1957]) and in his wake Gledhill (1994) assert, looking at particular, crisis-generating incidents affecting the lives of individuals and small groups often reveals something of "society's basic value systems and organizational principles"(Gledhill 1994:130). But the issue triggers two important theoretical issues. First, we sketch the debate on the delineation of the space for individual freedom of judgements and actions in cultural constellations, and second, we will briefly reconstruct, in the subsequent paragraph, the debate on "the cultural sphere" as, in the eyes of some, the realm per excellence where social movements ought to give battle.

Social Movements and Structure, Agency, and Culture

To assess the position and role of individual participants in social movements, and to evaluate anthropology's contribution in this respect, we must first address the debates that have been taking place about an old moot point in social sciences: the debate on the balance between more general societal structures and patterns on the one hand, and the agency in individual and local decisions on the courses of actions and protests on the other hand. Traditionally, social science scholars have oscillated between more structuralist and more actor- or subject-oriented (or "interpretative") approaches. In our view, in recent decades anthropologists—among others—have contributed substantially to this puzzle. To begin with, they have, in their conceptualization of the "determining structures," given much more emphasis to the cultural features. Culture, in a way, became the way through which the organizing structures of a society "transmitted" to the subject. Giddens (1984) "anthropologized" a bit when he elaborated on his structuration theory. In this work, he suggests that human agency and social structure are in an ongoing relationship with each other. Individuals *repeat* their act; there is a *pattern* in actions. We do not start anew acting every day, in all known or "comprehensible" settings and not even in many new situations. We recur to known repertoires and routines; we are in a "flow of conduct." This (re)produces the structure. This structure, embodied in traditions, routines, institutions, moral criteria, and action patterns, for example, in culture, informs individual performance. But it is not unchangeable. People can resist it or alter the routine way of doing things. The case is that they don't often do this, because it would require a constant "highly active," reflective consciousness. Such a "rationalizing consciousness" emerges only when the routine fails to function. Then, "actors mobilize their efforts and focus their thoughts on responses to problems that will diminish their anxiety, and ultimately bring about social change" (Giddens 1984:134). Subjective reflexivity thus has a crucial place in Giddens' thinking, but at the same time he emphasizes the "weight" of quotidian praxis. This (structured) praxis, in actual fact, guides most of our (inter)action.

Such a line of thought inevitable brings in "culture." It helps us to understand a little bit better the ongoing fine-tuning between, on the one hand, systems of values and norms, institutions, structured power relationships and symbolized and ritualized prescriptions on "right" and "wrong," and on "realistic" and "unrealistic," and, on the other hand, subjectivity partly subjugated to the "imposition of actual reality" and partly enabled by it to ask questions and to disobey. Such notions are crucial in any attempt to explain grass roots conduct and the instances in which the "flow of conduct" is interrupted, for instance in events of mobilization to protest.

Giddens, however, is decisively influenced by (post)modern, Western universes. This makes him overstate the reflexive "victory over tradition," and makes him overlook crucial cultural differences. Although Giddens admits that "the sureties of tradition and habit have (not) been replaced by the certitude of rational knowledge" (Giddens 1991:2/3), and introduces *doubt* as the most crucial instance for that statement, he still tends to skip the dimension Bourdieu (see below) stressed: the stubbornness of unreflected patterns of evaluation, taste, gestures, and subscribing oneself to his or her "natural place." Patterns that are nestled in culture.

Giddens emphasizes that "because of the 'openness' of social life today, the pluralisation of contexts of action and the diversity of 'authorities', lifestyle choice is increasingly important in the constitution of self-identity and daily activity. Reflexively organized life-planning, which normally presumes consideration of risks as filtered through contact with expert knowledge, becomes a central feature of the structuring of self-identity" (p. 5). "Choice," "consideration," and "reflexivity" all suggest control over and availability of the ingredients and processes of self-constitution. He evades stretching his point too far, because he refers to "differential access," to exclusion and to marginalization. But do these qualifications of the reflexivity account for the involuntary inabilities people with the explicit will to change themselves or the relationships surrounding them, display? Giddens tends to insufficiently elaborate the dimension of un-freedom connected to culture and the burden of the past. This— also persisting in modern society—"weight" of the past, internalized in people and institutions, and residing in layers of identity not directly available to reflexive scrutiny, counters the idea of an individual's relation to the world in which "external criteria (kinship, social duty, or traditional obligation) have become dissolved" (p. 6). A similar thing is at stake with regard to Giddens' claim about the "reflexive mobilization" (p. 7) of the body. In confining his argument to "bodily regimes" as a example of attempts to construct and control the body, he leaves out the unconscious self-regulation of bodily gestures, ways of doing, and even physical awareness of feeling good or feeling uncomfortable.

It thus seems as if Giddens' account of the "maneuvering space" of the reflexive actor is out of balance. It insufficiently helps us to understand the (effects and consequences of) sociocultural formations that are *both* individually reflected on and influenced by this reflection, *and* in part unreachable for reflexive penetration by the "subjects" of these formations. Archer (1995, 1996) presents a similar argument against what she calls Giddens' "central conflation" (1996:72*ff*, 1995:101*ff*). Her main argument is that "the 'parts' (of a societal structure and culture) and the 'people' are *not* co-existent through time and therefore any approach which amalgamates them wrongly foregoes the possibility of examining the interplay between them over time" (1996:xiv, italics in original). Although her obsession—as Giddens'—is to relate structure and agency (cf. Jessop 1996:121*ff*), she envisions the two dimensions of structure and agency respond to different logics, and should therefore not be conflated downwards, which refers to explaining behavior out of the system, nor upwards, in which "cultural properties are simply formed and transformed by some untrammelled dominant group or placed at the mercy of capricious renegotiation by unconstrained agency" (p. xv), nor through "central" conflation (which in Archer's view applies to Giddens), where the two levels "mutually constitute one another" (p. 97). In this latter view, according to Archer, "the two elements cannot be untied and therefore their reciprocal influences cannot be teased out in cultural analysis" (p. 98). Archer's point, based on the idea of a "Cultural System," in her own words, is that

> [a]s an emergent entity the Cultural System has an objective existence and autonomous relations amongst its components (theories, beliefs, values, arguments, or more strictly between the propositional formulations of them) in the sense that these are independent of anyone's claim to know, to believe, to assert or to assent to them. At any moment the Cultural System is the product of historical Socio-Cultural interaction, but having emerged (emergence being a continuous process) then *qua* product, it has properties of its own. Like structure, culture is man-made but escapes its makers to act back upon them. (1996:107, italics in original)

The quintessence of Archer's contention is that the systemic cultural features respond to other rules and logics than do the agents' rules and logics. "Analytical dualism" (1995:15) is therefore required, in which the logics of the sequences of action should not be reduced to the logics of the "autonomous properties (which) exert independent causal influences in their own right" (p. 14).

On a different level and applying a different vocabulary, Eric Wolf is another theorist who contributed to the reflection on the structure/actor connection. His primarily historical focus accounts for his fascination for human agency in social evolution. He highlighted the formative force of culture, but evaded reifying it. Culture is historical, and constantly transforming. Power relations—and the resistance against them—often trigger these transformations. He therefore rejects "to view any given culture as a bounded system or as a self-perpetuating 'design for living' " (Wolf 1982:19). Against the teleological consequences of such an approach, Wolf wants to bring in, as a complement, "human consciousness and history" (p. 401). His proposition is to look at the entanglement of structure and agency in "historical configurations of relationships" (p. 21). History is a process shaped by people, albeit that these people are shaped and constrained by forces of wider range. This latter element accounts for the fact that cultures have a "coherent logic or pattern" (Crehan 2002:182). Citing Kroeber, Wolf insists that culture is "an accommodation of discrete parts, largely inflowing parts, into a more or less workable fit" (quoted in Crehan 2002:182). But, from a radical *world*-history perspective, there is no such thing as a homogeneous (capitalist) steamroller overdetermining local outcomes ("downward conflation," in Archer's terms). By "decentering" history (Gledhill 2005:44), Wolf opens space for taking into account different "layers" of social transformations and local contexts, which is exactly where the unforeseen and not externally overdetermined outcomes come into the picture. And it is the place where the "implausible" rebellion of the subaltern takes root— even though the rebellion cannot escape its "shaping" by structured culture. The difference in emphasis with Archer are there—but they are gradual rather than of kind.

Sherry Ortner, inspired by among others Clifford Geertz, also reflected on "subjectivity" in anthropological research, defining this subjectivity as "the ensemble of modes of perception, affect, thought, desire, fear, and so forth that animate acting subjects. But I always mean as well the cultural and social formations that shape, organize and provoke those modes of affect, thought, and so on" (Ortner 2005:31). She thus, on the one hand, insists upon the impossibility to "stand outside of culture" or to evade its experience-shaping power, but on the other hand stresses that "consciousness (. . ..) is always multi-layered and reflexive, and its complexity and reflexivity constitute the grounds for questioning and criticizing the world in which we find ourselves"(p. 46). As with Wolf and Giddens, however, the main instance to counter the "structuring power" is consciousness. As we suggested in our elaboration of Giddens' position, it seems likely that such an idea insufficiently addresses the subconscious dimensions of people's embeddedness in sociocultural structures.

The theoretically most influential scholar on the subject with a clear anthropological sensitivity is, arguably, Pierre Bourdieu. In particular his concept of "habitus" is important. Bourdieu's elaboration of habitus emphasizes various aspects. It is something learned in socialization, and socialization is structured, first and foremost, by class—in cultural disguises. Socialization solidifies in patterns of judgment, valuation, and appreciation of social reality, which in turn produce specific dispositions for thinking and acting. Owing to a process of slow but inevitable internalization of the patterns of the sociocultural world one grows up in, people come to "coincide" with that world. Habitus thus functions as a "glue" between the individual and the social environment, as the principal orienting scheme of one's actions, and as the mechanism to recognize oneself and one's peers in daily interaction. It makes one aware of the differences in "styles" between one's own group, and "the others." Because of its very nature, it is not easily undone or unlearned; it is something that sunk into the subconscious, and something responsible for feelings of "ease" or "unease"—at a different level than discursive knowledge or skills can accomplish that. It explains why, in spite of dominating all the discursive and consciously learned capabilities and being competent in a specific domain of knowledge one finds oneself in, professionals of lower class background, often for a lifetime, feel less at ease in the "higher" cultural worlds they have obtained access to thanks to their schooling. "The habitus is necessity internalised and converted into a disposition that generates meaningful practices and meaning-giving perceptions" (Bourdieu 1986:170) "[The schemes of the habitus] engage the most fundamental principles of construction and evaluation of the social world, those which most directly express the division of labour (between the classes, the age groups and the sexes) or the division of the work of domination, in divisions between bodies and between relations to the body which borrow more features than one, as to give them the appearances of naturalness, from the sexual division of labour and the division of sexual labour" (Bourdieu 1986:466; see also Roodenburg 2004).

Habitus is not "a set of unquestioned rules" on how to do things. It is the pattern of judgement underlying people's evaluations of situations, and their subsequent actions. This makes habitus something beyond mere "determination" of one's lot, whereas at the same time it entails something not easily disposed off. This is the case both because the direct environment tends to confirm the "correctness" of one's judgment and behavior, and also because one feels "at home" and one feels "oneself" applying them. In this sense they become the "unacknowledged conditions of action" (Livesay 1989) also in social movements and collective actions. These conditions refer to the *barriers* for change even among those seeking change or criticizing the status quo. People are subconsciously attached to their habitual "reality" even in their efforts to change it. This is a crucial insight for social movement research, and a potential bridge between structuralist and more agency-emphasizing viewpoints. It makes it possible to understand peoples' resistance to prevailing situations of domination, and at the same time understand their troubles to rise above the "heavy reality" of such relations. Instead of dichotomising structure and agency, habitus allows us to focus on their entanglement: ". . . . all knowledge, and in particular all knowledge of the social world, is an act of construction implementing schemes of thought and expression—(. . ..) between conditions of existence and practices or representations there intervenes the structuring activity of the agents, who, far from reacting mechanically to mechanical stimulations, respond to the invitations or threats of a world whose meaning they have helped to produce" (Bourdieu 1986:467).

All these theoretical exercises learn us that old, "hardened" directive guides do not disappear easily, and they constitute an important element in explaining the possibilities and impossibilities for change in times of turbulence or radical revolutions in political or social circumstances. The more profound strata of group and class culture that the concept of habitus reveals, help to account for the fact that—in the context of social movements' performances—proclaimed social and political aims, and passionately avowed changes in self-esteem are in the end often not met.

As the final or sufficing clue, however, the habitus concept will not do. The reason therefore is that it is primarily fit to explain the non-change; it is the concept to explain the solidity *tout court*, not *slowness*. "Habitus seems to stand for the inertia in social structures, for the persistence of inexorable traditions" (Roodenburg 2004:224). One of the few sections in Bourdieu's work that explicitly deals with the relationship between the habitus and the possibility of collective action, for precisely that reason, is one of the few sections that does not come up to the mark of precision and clarity. In *Le sens pratique* Bourdieu remarks that the failure to take into account "the dialectics between dispositions and 'opportunities' (is) one of the reasons (. . .) for missed chances in efforts to mobilize (people)" (Bourdieu 1980:100). That is a mere programmatic warning, and does not live up to the suggestion associated with "habitus" to go beyond similar admonishing advertisements. We suspect that the inability of the habitus-idea to analyze *slow* learning and change processes, and even less to explain for sudden shifts in behavior, surfaces here. Whereas the habitus concept is very fruitful in analyzing the reproductive patterns of behavior of the "class-unconsciousness," it is much less helpful when change-aimed action and atypical conduct are at stake.

Moreover, the habitus concept suffers of more flaws. It suggests unity within classes, or, to be more precise, it does not provide for explaining differentiation (beyond mere individual variety) within classes. It reduces differences to the one "axis" of ("cultured") class. Habitus, however, also takes shape in patterns of socialization marked by gender, religion, region, urban/rural, and the like. A multistratified embodiment of habitus thus appears more realistic. This idea, moreover, might also be applied to the study of specific capacities for resistance or change. Fields of socialization, for instance, less confined to particular (geographic, religious, or other) settings, might allow for wider margins for change.

Hence, habitus is too global, too container-like, to analyze different, multiple subconscious and conscious layers that might at times reinforce each other, but also at times contradict each other (Bader 1991:103). People cross permanently the borders of class and cultural fields, in their work, though education, media, leisure, and the like. Habitus, then, is not only a class phenomenon, but also is constructed and challenged in socialization patterns and encounters that are related to gender, ethnicity, religion, region, to urban versus rural contexts, and so forth. We have to take into consideration this multilayeredness of habitus if we want to give habitus the content it pretends to have: culture in the flesh.

For these reasons, it seems necessary to recast the habitus concept. It ought to have not only a dimension that accounts for what steers the "only-available program," but also a dimension that allows for a change potential, on the basis of its multicentred source material. It also is important to remind ourselves that what is a stake is more than mere "adaptation" in an—almost—biological–evolutional sense; what we are dealing with is a cultural re-creation, re-construction, and re-structuration of both the new or changing environment, and of the subjective resources and action patterns, mediated by the "cultural (in)formation" in which the subject is immersed. Next, the habitus concept would have to be situated in a constellation that could offer insights in the multitemporality of change. In such a constellation, a place would have to be reserved for processes of change that might occur relatively fast, and others that take more time. Crucial is that in such research strategies the focus should not primarily address the larger constellation in which enter *all* the dimensions that are external to the actors' constitution—such as political opportunities, structural settings, third parties' attitudes, the whole of the situational circumstances, institutional innovation, changes of authorities and policies, reshuffling of political alliances, changes in political culture, and the like—in short, the configuration that would make up the theoretical toolkit for someone who wants to tell the *whole* story of a collective action (*cf.* Bader 1991)—but also the smaller constellation that focuses on the various forces that account for the actors' dispositions, actions, and reactions. These include ideologized convictions and political, religious, or other tenets, pragmatic—but very consciously applied rules of conduct, the more quotidian strategies of interaction with representatives of different strata of society, memories of former conflicts and their outcomes, "crises" of steady daily routines, exposures to or the conquest of new spaces and social circles, as well as the less cognizant dimensions that are, up to a larger or smaller degree, relatively immune to abrupt changes in societal and political conditions and stimuli: habitus, homemaking patterns of daily interchange, routines, and "practical senses."

Currently, many anthropologists working in the field of social movement studies observe, in general terms, these insights. They make sure not to overstate or belittle the maneuvering space of the agents, they are well aware of the intricacies of processes of and efforts to obtain change, and they attempt to take into account the complexity of cultural universes and the multilayered ways in which culture is embodied in individuals and groups.

The Cultural Sphere as the Acting Ground
for Social Movements' Participants

An extra impulse was given to the already existing anthropological focus on social movements *fieldwork* when, around the mid-1980s, a plea for focusing on the social movements' social and cultural rather than their political achievements became louder and louder. In an attempt to evade both the sterility of structuralism recognizing only societal contradictions whose "social bases" would subsequently act, and the strategic-action approach merely seeing a flow of strategic interactions without taking into account any structural setting, the "new social movement" approach gained terrain, and obtained its strongest defenders among those who highlighted the subjective, cultural, and identity-focused dimensions of the social movements of a new generation: the postmaterialist, horizontal and informal, expressive and anti-institutional *new* social movements (Almeida et al. 1996; Bustos 1992; Falk 1987; Kärner 1983). At was claimed by Melucci cited in the second, new movements act in the field of culture rather than on the economic–industrial plane.

This sociocultural focus in the study of social movements (sometimes referred to as the identity-oriented paradigm) was defended in a time of low appreciation of "alienating" institutional and formal politics. Involvement in such politics would probably "stain" the movements, whose principal goal was another one: " . . ..it is (. . ..) about new forms of social relations and organization: what is being transformed or raised is, more than a political, a social renewal" (Jelín 1985:17).

Evers (1985) radicalized this idea, by stretching the contents of the political. He explicitly rejected the political sphere as a mere "power play," and suggested that the cultural stakes of social movements ought to alter the very quintessence of politics: "by reclaiming politics as a constant element within social life and not separated from it, this socio-cultural potential of the new social movements may turn out to be not less, but more political than action directly oriented towards existing power structures" (Evers 1985:51). The political reaches into the identities of people, and it is at this level of identities that the counter-potential lies: "At the very fundamental level, this means a reassertion of one's own human dignity, vis à vis the everyday experience of misery, oppression and cultural devastation" (p. 56). It is this coming together of identity, social and cultural life, and politics that forms the very kernel of the identity-oriented approach (Castells 1997; Cohen 1985:690; Touraine 1988). The ways in which social movements struggled expressed the great importance they assigned to mutual respect and participation. In this way they, *in actu,* challenged the intrusion of power in human relations.

The problem with this approach is the risk to suggest that power (could) stop at the threshold of identity. Evers, although from time to time apparently aware of the problem, strengthened this impression by talking about an "identity of its own" and stating that "any domination is a theft of identity" (p. 55). In terms of movement developments, this suggested a possibility to intervene in power relations, without letting "power" into one's ways of doing things. It also suggested that identities in which no power interventions whatsoever occurred were possible. More recently, the idea that not even a given "we-ness" but the "experience of difference" accounts for the emergence of movements has been brought forward. Such movements would not share an identity, but "a situation" (McDonald 2004: 575, 589). In most of these analyses, it was suggested that movements should remain "in themselves," because the outside (politically institutionalized) world was incapable of dealing with the "real problems" or would endanger the emancipatory potential of the movements (Edelman 2001). Sheth (1983:2) illustrated the first point when referring to the "all too obvious incapacity of the existing institutions to successfully tackle the contemporary crisis in the human condition," and Kothari (1985:543) illustrated the second point when judging that invitations to "participate" often "get translated into clientage" or make that the poor "get trapped into this closed pyramid of participation." Melucci unwillingly expressed the stalemate when he, in for him unusually vague terms, suggested that the movements "make society hear their message and translate these messages into political decision making, while the movements maintain their autonomy"(Melucci 1985:815). However, in the course of time, doubts about the movements' ability to *replace* or make superfluous the old political institutions increased.

These were the problems subsequent research and theorizing tried to deal with. Cohen (1982) and others have criticized the anti-institutional thrust of such identity-oriented theorizing. Civil society, the terrain in which movements ought to operate "horizontally," according to the identity oriented thinkers, she asserts, is not at all un-institutional, and should not be considered the antipode of "dirty politics." Society is full of institutions, of continuities, and of established bodies of reproduction. This is the principal terrain of social movements: in fighting for institutions that do express identities, that do include the subaltern, that do give voice to the poor, the movements can change societal patterns, and *therefore* change politics. Politics does not stand apart; it answers to societal articulations of interests and identities. Here, the gap between movements/civil society on the one hand, and the polity on the other, can be narrowed. The vehicle to do so is not only the message, but also the institutional logic.

This can be done in various ways. Movements might question the terms that direct institutions and the divisions of rights and prerogatives embodied in them. The intervention in the political culture, in such cases, would not remain confined to messages, but include proposals regarding institutions (Alvarez, Dagnino, and Escobar 1998b:10). Movements might also intervene in the debates on "co-government" and *concertación* in urban shanty towns. They can undermine the proposals of authorities that often try to make local settlers co-responsible without offering real influence, by suggesting *other* arrangements with regard to proceedings and mandates of these co-governing bodies. This, ideally, would not be done as a mere power game, but incorporate criticisms with regard to the identities and capabilities the authorities impose on the "bottom-up" participation in decision making. Processes of discovering and articulating shared identities and interests on the basis of emic perceptions instead of ideological proposals could be fostered by such processes (Dagnino 1989; Foweraker 1995:22–23). Women's movements may, for instance, challenge customary local arrangements to distribute land when these increasingly tend to disadvantage them, by recurring to legal resources, to their own increased capital to buy land, and to other tactics confronting authorities and clans with the dramatic consequences of their tradition-justified decisions, as they do in Uganda (Tripp 2004). Such and likewise findings help to account for the simultaneous cultural and political, identity and strategic, autonomous, and institutionally embedded dimensions of the actions of social movements. Various researchers have also done empirical work to illustrate the point (Assies 1992; Banck and Doimo 1988; Burgwal 1995; Downs and Solimano 1988; Sall 2004; Tripp 2004). This empirical work inevitably took them to the grass roots, the "ants-work" of social movement participants—to be elaborated in the fifth section of this chapter. For now, it seems justified to conclude that, as in the debate on the entangledness of structure and agency, the developments in this discussion also demonstrate a plausible, albeit inconclusive, way out of the impasse that the overly culturalist stance ended up in.

SOCIAL MOVEMENTS: THE PRESENCE
OF CULTURE AS ASSET, AND AS CONSTRAINT

Culture is not merely a dimension *accompanying* social movements' emergence and an enlivening component of our analyses. It is also something that very graphically, tangibly, and sometimes deliberately enters the struggles social movements fight. This can take various forms. It can become an explicit theme of debate and controversy in, for instance, struggles over normative issues such as homosexuality and gender equality. Conservative, culturally legitimized positions often resist emancipation struggles, and such moral convictions then become the cultural bone of contention. In other cases, alleged cultural features of the mobilizing group are celebrated and highlighted as appealing elements to recruit followers. This may entail the glorifying remembrance of historical events or personalities, the deployment of images of bravery or perseverance of the group, or the use of motivating and incentivating rituals preceding rallies or other public acts. In these cases, culture is an asset for the mobilizing group. Culture here becomes a resource. In yet other cases, culture takes the shape of a collective trait hampering effective mobilization. This can, for instance, be the case when clientelism has been internalized to such an extend that people do not manage to resist the divide-and-rule strategies of the challenged authority—and, once again, prefer the short- term reward above the long-term change of power relationships. It can also be the case when internal distrust, often stimulated by the incumbent authorities, produce petty bickering about leadership or strategies. Here, culture becomes a constraint for successful mobilization.

In this section, we first look into some examples of culture as asset. To illustrate the different facets of the issue, after the introductory paragraph, we pay attention to the "intimate relationship" between injustices and the cultural form in which these are perceived, named, and rejected. We also address how cultural "material" is put to use in efforts to "make sense" of experienced injustice and exploitation people cannot express because no acknowledged cultural vocabulary exists. Subsequently, we elaborate on how "culturalized" forms of expressing protest and rejection contain at the same time an explicit political message.

Next, we explore illustrations of culture as constraint. After introducing some conceptual issues, we discuss the enormous effort it takes to develop and publicly present an equally plausible and evenly matched (cultural) alternative to a hegemonic "narrative about the truth."

The final part of this section is dedicated to the possibilities to turn cultural constraints into assets.

Culture as *A*sset

In the early morning of January 1, 1994, Mexican president Carlos Salinas de Gortari was celebrating New Year's Day and the entering in vigor of the North American Free Trade Agreement (NAFTA), which according to government propaganda meant that Mexico entered the First World by one stroke of a pen. The atmosphere at the party was jubilant. While the president danced with his daughter a somber-looking presidential aide entered the room and walked up to them to whisper something in the president's ear. Salinas left the party and was informed by his Defense Minister that in the remote southern state of Chiapas a rebel army, calling itself the Zapatista National Liberation Army, had seized various cities and threatened to march straight to Mexico City to topple the government. The news spoiled the party.

One of the most significant social movements of the late twentieth century had erupted upon the scene to tell the world: "*Today we say, enough! We are the heirs of those who truly forged our nationality. We the dispossessed are millions, and we call on our brothers to join in this call as the only path in order not to die of hunger in the face of the insatiable ambition of a dictatorship for more than 70 years led by a clique of traitors who represent the most conservative and sell-out groups in the country.*"[10] The several thousand Maya rebels, armed with anything from machetes to AK-47 guns, reminded the people of Mexico that they were the "product of 500 years of struggle."

The Zapatistas are one of the most expressive instances of what anthropologist Lynn Stephen (2002) calls "cultural politics." In her comparison between rural communities in the state of Chiapas and in the neighboring state of Oaxaca she shows how different views of the nation are shaped by local identities and histories and, in turn, redefine and reconstitute the nation. Emiliano Zapata, who led the indigenous peasantry of the central Mexican state of Morelos in their agrarian revolt during the Mexican revolution (1910–1917), is one of those icons of Mexican history and Mexican nationalism that have been appropriated in different ways. As Stephen puts it:

> While all four communities may share specific symbolic images and metaphors with the government—specifically, Emiliano Zapata and the Mexican Revolution– the contextual meaning of these symbols varies with each place and forms a key part of reactions to contemporary state policy such as the end of agrarian reform, efforts to promote privatization of communally held land, and NAFTA. If nationalism is constructed in regionally and locally distinct manners from below, then ideas about how one belongs to the nation are also variably understood (Stephen 2002:xxxv).

In fact, president Salinas had used the figure of Emiliano Zapata—until then the emblematic symbol of redistributive agrarian reform—to market the end of agrarian reform. Where Zapata had promised his followers "Land and Liberty" Salinas promised "Liberty and Justice for the Countryside" to promote the individualization and privatization of commonly held lands. But just as elite constructions of national symbols change over time, local narratives change over time and vary according to place. Dissenting discourses are forged by rearticulating symbolic resources and constructing counter-narratives while drawing on a pool of symbols and collective memories. Such discourses or cultural framings underpin and justify decisions to act or not to act. The Mexican Zapatista movement is one example of an extremely effective cultural politics, not only through the creation of a discourse for internal use and movement cohesiveness but also in addressing the Mexican and global public at large through its cybercultural politics. Subcommander Marcos and the ski-masked indigenous warriors from the Lacandona forest have themselves become icons in the struggle against neoliberal globalization worldwide.

If such are the elements for forging movement identity and identification cultural elements can also be evoked to picture the adversary. To stick with the Mexican example, President Carlos Salinas soon was depicted as a reincarnation of the *chupacabras*, a sort of bat- or dragon-like animal that according to popular lore attacks goats and other domestic animals and sucks them dry. Small boys wearing Salinas masks with huge pointed ears and dressing up in bat costumes appeared at traffic lights all over Mexico City to do juggling acts or stand as human pyramids to earn their daily *tortilla*. Earlier, in 1992, on the occasion of Columbus Day thousands of people, most of them indigenous, had flooded the town of San Cristóbal de las Casas to protest 500 years of colonialism and oppression. Under loud cheers, they tore down the statue of conquistador Diego de Mazariegos. It is believed that this was the first manifestation of the Zapatista movement.

---

[10] *Declaración de la selva lacandona*, January 1, 1994. Translation by John Womack Jr.

Popular nationalism and imageries of the nation and ways of belongingas well as images of the anti-nation as personified in the *chupacabras* who sucks the nation dry through his neoliberal policies—are an important element in the cultural politics of social movements. Indigenous peasants invading, or in their view rather repossessing, large estates in the Peruvian Andes in the 1960s invariably planted a Peruvian flag on the land. But identifications also may change. Whereas flying the official national flag was an important statement in mobilizations in Andean countries in the 1960s, from the late 1960s onward a new imagery was constructed evoking the heroes of the great late eighteenth century rebellions, particularly Tupac Katari in Bolivia, where the Katarista movement reclaimed the Indian identity that had officially been submerged in a generic peasant identity in the context of the nation-building efforts in the wake of the 1952 nationalist revolution. The new indigenous movements that arose now stated that "as Indians we are oppressed and as Indians we will liberate ourselves." A new imagery was forged and symbols such as the *wiphala*, the multi-colored flag of the Inca empire, now held to symbolize multiculturalism, was retrieved and now is prominently present in manifestations and marches in countries such as Bolivia and Ecuador. Similarly, rituals and ceremonies have been reinstituted or reinvented and nowadays it is not even unusual that the UN forums dealing with issues concerning indigenous peoples—not only from Latin America but from all over the world—are inaugurated with some indigenous cleansing ceremony to ensure the well-being of all participants and to make the event prosper.

Such movement-building efforts require the creation of "sameness" in the face of "the other," which may result in essentialist discourses and a continuous tension between the need to project unitary identities and the constant negotiation of identities within organizations. Although essentializing may be a strategic necessity in the process of "self" representation and creation of symbolic capital, and not only for indigenous movements, anthropologists drawing on the classic work of Barth (1969) have highlighted the dynamic character of such processes and have sought to assess them critically, pointing to the constant contingent processes of reorganization and redefinition without which movements and, for that matter, their constituencies cannot survive (De la Peña 2006; Sierra 1997; Van Cott 2005; Yashar 2005; Zuñiga 2000).

When people face situations they cannot or will no longer bear, when they become enraged because of injustice being done, or when that are called upon to rally or organize, they thus inevitably recur to cultured memories and images for support for their decisions and actions—or their decision not to act. In individual, and in the case of organizing activities even stronger so in collective memories, people find examples, inspiration, and symbols that inform their stand.

In a recent, important article Rubin (2004) argues that social movements (and states, for that matter) need to be analyzed in their historical and cultural dimensions, rather than as merely political phenomena. The risk of taking actors like social movements as "pre-existing subjects"(Rubin 2004:108) or simply "rational actors"(p. 137) is large, if one does not take into account "the diverse pieces of representation and meaning that come together in political actors" (p. 136). The point is illustrated by referring to movements such as the indigenous COCEI ("Coalition of Workers, Peasants and Students of the Isthmus") in southern Mexico (here again), the Zapatistas, and the Pan-Maya movement in Guatemala. The more specific point about the role of the cultured dimensions of gender, beauty, and sexuality is additionally illustrated by referring to the Afro-Reggae Cultural Group in Brazil. A movements' appeal, according to Rubin, stems not only from the "adequate" wording of a political or livelihood problem or the "convincing" strategy to solve these problems. A movement also needs to be attractive and promise, one way or the other, "pleasure," and it does so by (re)signifying the cultural components of its make-up. Finally, he stresses that movements inevitably essential-ize, to be able to represent and make claims. He adds, however, that this does not mean all participants endorse these "essential" features; peoples' beliefs and experiences might very well differ from these prescripts. Such tensions, Rubin asserts, are the "ambiguities and contradictions inherent in cultures and movements" (p. 128). In his conclusion, Rubin argues for acknowledging and studying the ways in which movements "arise out of multiple histori-cal and cultural pathways, involve interweavings of culture and politics, construct authority in interaction with gender, beauty, and sexuality, and routinely essentialize" (p. 135). Only in this way can we account for the ways in which identities, interests, and political goals actually come into being, before and during the actual conflicts movements often engage in.

Many social movements recur to icons and (historical) heroes to strengthen their case. Sometimes these heroes were tragic figures, murdered for their cause, such as Inca heir to the throne *Manco Capac* resisting the Spanish conquest, *Tupac Amaru* fighting exploitation and land theft in eighteenth century Peru, and *Tupac Katari* in Bolivia. Others were rediscovered as predecessors and are currently venerated as inspirational historical figures, such as eighteenth century Belle van Zuylen for the Dutch feminist movement. Others, such as Sacco and Vanzetti, because of their fate have become inspirational for movements in the United States denouncing classist and racist justice. The names of Zapata, Sandino, Rosa Parks, Bobby Sands, and Ernesto Che Guevara and many more have become even more famous owing to the movements that later acted in their names or individuals who honored them in songs, clothing, novels, and oral storytelling.

Why are such heroes important to movements? Why and how do they use them? Accord-ing to Navarette and Oliver (2000), heroes must embody liminality; their fame and legendary status makes them transcend the times in which they lived and make them "fit" the role of example in later times. It is this very characteristic that accounts for the mixture of history and myth in the stories about their lives and deaths. Finally, they must embody both something "ordinary," being a typical example of their groups' lives in their times, and something out of the ordinary, related to their rebellious character, visionary ideas, or exceptional courage. Of course, to have appeal or charisma, the hero should preferably belong to the same group that is being mobilized—but in globalized eras, Argentinean Che Guevara inspires Europeans, North Americans, and rebelling Africans alike.

A hero might very well have ended tragically, but a necessary ingredient is his courage. Rodriguez (1996) pointed out that a doubtless "masculinity" seems to be a decisive feature of the suitability as hero. Women heroes, so it seems, can inspire only female-dominated or feminist movements.

A hero complying with these characteristics is often called upon by protest movements. In such a hero, they find inspiration for their discourses, and legitimacy for their cause. The injus-tice once fought for by the hero, it is often claimed, yet has to be undone. The achievements of the hero, although he in the ended mostly was defeated, strengthen the belief that the opponent can be defeated. And his words often still arouse enthusiasm and incite the people fighting for his, or a similar cause. A hero can help a group identify with a cause, with the group as such, and can help to clarify the need to fight the adversary.

Cultural politics are, hence, not the monopoly of indigenous movements. Popular envi-ronmentalism, though it sometimes also is a feature of indigenous movements, also heavily relies on representations of local ways of life that have permitted the forging of alliances with transnational environmentalism, which often tended to advocate the creation of conservation units from which the local population was to be removed in order to preserve "nature" as perceived by Northern Hemisphere urbanites. A case in point is the rubber tappers' movement in the Brazilian Amazon, which eventually found an ally in U.S.-based organizations such as the Environmental Defense Fund, the Sierra Club, and the National Resources Defense Council. These organizations had singled out a World Bank funded highway construction project to mount a campaign against the destruction of the Amazon forest, without giving much thought to local forest dwellers, such as the rubber tappers, who were involved in a struggle against the expansion of cattle ranches. Their leader, Chico Mendes, became an icon in the struggle to defend the rainforest and the rubber tappers' way of life. The alliance between rubber tappers and transnational environmentalism resulted in the creation of extractive reserves managed by the rubber tappers.

Culture can serve social movements in other ways. Mothers, stressing their role as mothers, have been in the forefront of human rights movements in the struggle against Latin American dictatorships. The silent protests of the Mothers of the Plaza de Mayo in Buenos Aires, Argentina, who demanded the "alive reappearance" of the disappeared—in the active mode—are perhaps the best-known example. Initially, they were regarded by many as crazy for demanding the impossible. But the fact that they were women made it difficult to repress their manifestations, even for one of the cruelest military regimes. Their continuing protests when democracy was restored and even after the military had been granted an amnesty, which made further protests seem hopeless, have against all odds contributed to the recent reopening of processes against the military.

A final theme to be mentioned is the importance of ritual. Rituals in which leadership is installed and reaffirmed is one example: on the 21st of January 2006, Evo Morales was ritually invested as Bolivia's new president during a colorful ceremony in *Tiwanaku*, an archeological site that is a powerful symbol of the expanding indigenous presence in Bolivia's public and political realm. Morales' investiture as *mallku*—"condor" or indigenous "governor"—at that particular site is symbol saturated. The united indigenous people revitalized, and partly reinvented, instauration protocols, symbols, and wordings, to highlight something unprecedented in the continent: an indigenous president was accredited and paid tribute to, by "his people," in an act neither acknowledged by the nation's political code of rules nor enacted since colonization. The uniqueness of the event was underscored by a highly ritualized act.

In addition, movements' manifestations and actions are often either preceded by ritualized ceremonies, or themselves take a ritual form. The weekly silent walks of the Mothers of the Plaza de Mayo in Buenos Aires, Argentina, are an example.

The Intimacies of Injustices and Culture

There is yet another dimension to this issue, best exemplified by the work of James Scott (1985, 1990). In his work, he emphasizes that the poor and subaltern often refrain from overt, provocative resistance. Instead, they recur to "hidden" forms of opposition, insubordination, sabotage, or obstruction. Gossip and mockery, malingering, folk songs, jokes, and many more testify to the fact that hegemonic discourses and imposed social orders do not bereave the subaltern of mechanisms to demystify and subvert those orders. Scott thus engages in debates within Marxism on the "overdetermination" of consciousness, inspired by authors such as Gramsci, Lukacs, Hobsbawn, and Thompson. But more importantly, he stresses the cultured ways in which opposition takes shape: rarely are dominant orders challenged in direct, explicit, confronting ways, based on elaborated counter-discourses "matching" the one sustaining the incumbent social stratifications. Rather, counter-acts are fragmented, disrupting rather than completely undermining, teasing rather than head-on defying. The means of such subversions are often cultural: in using words with double meaning, in imitating exaggerating authority's speech and gestures, in quasi-obedience, and the like.

At the same time, the notions of "justice," fairness, rights, and the moral order are shaped by the dominant constellation. People "learn" what is fair, what they can aspire for, in the course of their dealings with authorities and social structures. Their perception of what is "right" is hence often shaped in a situation of systematic denial of equal rights. As it is composed of both of these elements, the cautiously disrupting one, and the one constituted by the impositions of dominants orders, counter-efforts crop up.

One of the countries most notorious for a quotidian practice of the non-application of equal rights, in spite of constitutional guaranties, might be Ecuador (Salman 2002a). Peoples' lives are full of experiences such as being denied first aid in a hospital after an accident because of being unable to guarantee the payment afterwards, in spite of the fact that the law stipulates that every health institution has the obligation to attend someone who needs first aid. People know that after an accident it is not a good idea to call upon the police to establish who was wrong, because bribes rather than the *ley de tránsito* determine one's culpability, and because your car being towed away might result in endless efforts to get it back, and in getting it back stripped of all its accessories. People know that after having been in a cue for many hours they might lose their turn because a friend of the counter clerk, or simply a well-off or "important" person shows up. People know that the police beat up detainees, and that afterwards the complaint results in an investigation that invariably acquits the police officer. People know that counter clerks can with impunity ignore them, insult them, and send them back home in spite of fulfilling all the prerequisites for a bureaucratic formality. People know that they have to pay their fines whereas people "with influence" usually don't. Also, people know that all these things are forbidden and violations of the law. But they don't have the means to ensure that the law stands.

People learn to cope with the systematic inequality and build their responses, individually and collectively, upon these experiences. On a limited and often quite ineffective scale the poor too try to mobilize friends, or friends of friends. They, instead of demanding their rights, try to apply the rule of "affirming the authority in his power," imploring him or her to yield for the petitioners' vulnerability: *no sea malito, señor. . . .*(I beg you not to be harsh, sir . . .). In addition, they try to avoid "unpersonal encounters" with the law and its representatives, knowing that only "personal" relations might change no's into yes's.

The internalization of these experiences and the incompetence to deal with instances and institutions in a direct, universal, and impersonal (Weberian) manner in which the "anonymous individual" is a bearer of "rights" leads to meeting the citizen discourse with suspicion, or in the best case with skepticism. Asking someone to renounce from all the strategies that serve not to suffer too much in daily interactions with state or institutional representatives is like asking someone to expose himself in his most vulnerable stature. For the poor, affirming the power inequalities in their encounters with power bearers is a much more promising way to proceed then challenging the unjustified and unjust hierarchies and privileges. The constitution and the law as instances to call upon in case their rights have been denied are beyond their reach.

Thus, the notion of universal equality and citizenship[11] exists as a latent awareness alongside the daily practices to cope with the endemic violations of civil and social rights.

---

[11] Citizenship has, in recent decades, become a hotly debated notion. Its status and contents changed in the process in which the market mechanism is converted into the new hegemonic device. The reverse side of this societal model is a lack of sensitivity to the inequities that it generates. Whereas sectors living in extreme poverty may become objects

The latter, however, is a much stronger and more important guide in daily interactions. This also informs people about how to understand and, in case it is stimulated or seems useful, request the fulfilment of their citizenship. Instead of insisting on the universality of rules and regulations, or on their equal rights in relation to the rights—or privileges—of the more powerful and the wealthier, people rather will insist on being treated *con respeto* (respectfully), or simple being attended. This is a culturally informed "translation" of one's citizen's rights. When we asked a *poblador* in Quito how he thought of *participation*, he explained that that would be a good thing, because more contact would mean that he had more friends at the municipality, which would make things much easier in case he went there for some *asunto*, some bureaucratic errand. Hence, giving shape to citizenship in a society permeated by clientelism results in emphasis on "more and easier access" to the levels and circuits where one has to settle his affairs. The particularism is not abjured; people try to modify and "improve" it. Not the individual autonomy, right, and dignity, but the amelioration and optimization of personalized relationships and interactions is seen as bringing closer citizens' rights.

This does not mean, however, that the notions and parameters of the "classical" concept of citizenship are absent. They form the background for the insistence on the amplification of access, the demand for respect, and the persistence of the query to be attended, but are in this process transformed into a mere reference pillar under struggles for a more equitable negotiation. The systemic character of social and economic segregation therefore stays out of range in the ways the poor strive for the fulfilment of civil rights. Insisting on a "clean" interaction pattern between (poor) citizens and state institutions would deprive them of exactly the only weapon within their reach: making pleas, and using brokers and "friends."

In addition, the particular traditional character of the Latin American welfare programs and legal "integrationalism" is deeply ingrained in the strategies and orientations of the poor supposed to benefit from these programs. As a consequence, the "purist" notions of citizenship often called upon in the discourses of politically informed (and nongovernment organization [NGO]-supported) social movements might meet with distrust among the rank and file participants. Their "imaginative horizon" does not include a citizenship model in which their old strategies would be inapplicable. This is what makes the current interest in and struggles for ("more," or "real," or even "participative") citizenship an ambivalent notion for many poor Latin Americans. And this, in turn, influences social movement participation.

This is even strengthened by the economic adjustment programs in vogue in many countries in the South. Whereas on the one hand the poor experience that the (deficient) welfare programs and "compromise states" are withering, they can, on the other hand, not (yet?) incorporate and put to use individualized strategies and opportunities for obtaining rights and benefits. The absence or, in some cases, gradual disappearance of a state that could—sometimes, being lucky—be a help in obtaining urban services, and which, in the case of

---

of attention and "targeted intervention," it is assumed that the remainder of society is essentially a "level playing field" upon which all participants have the same opportunities. Reality, however, is somewhat different because new forms of precariousness produce "low-intensity citizenship". While the developmentalist model at least held out some hope of integration in which the state functioned as a "hope-generating machine" (Nuijten 1998), this entity now seeks to shed this function. In this context, new forms of state, para-state, and privatized violence and coercion flourish and, in the eyes of some, the "double transition"—to electoral democracy and free marketeering—may well usher in a democratization of violence. "Citizenship-as-strategy," rooted in the "right to have rights," was invented to counter just such a scenario. Civil society was revealed as an object and a terrain of struggle, while citizenship became a device for questioning a broad range of injustices and exclusions considered signs of "non-citizenship," which become the object of political practice that contests the dominant meanings of citizenship.

labourers in the formal sector, could owing to its corporatist nature be a guarantee in obtaining (modest) social security, leaves them even more empty-handed when simultaneously the clientelistic and corporatist strategies they are familiar with are now questioned even in the circles where they would traditionally find support for their problems: leftist political parties, NGOs, the Church. More then ever before, the illusion of social mobility is in danger. And much more, thus, it seems necessary to employ all possible means to open the state's institutions' doors, to obtain collective goods, which runs exactly opposite to the individual citizens' rights' discourse. Learning new "culture" takes more time than learning clear-cut new skills.

The Political Layer of Cultural Features

Quite a different, but fascinating, albeit controversial contribution to the exploration of the cultured layers of resistance is the work of Michael Taussig. Especially in his book *The Devil and Commodity Fetishism in South America* (1980), he reveals an original way of linking beliefs on evil, the devil, and individuals who managed to accumulate wealth, to perceptions of how capitalist modes of production, and even more of producing social relations, destroy local communities. The research is on miners in Bolivia (based, to a large extend, on June Nash's research among these miners; see Nash 1979), and on plantation workers in the Cauca Valley in Colombia. Stories and metaphors revolving around the devil and devilish powers, in Taussig's interpretation, refer to the way these communities try to make sense of the penetration of "cold," socially void wage labor, exploitation, and monetarization of their worlds. Wealthy people the workers have grown dependent upon are believed to have struck a deal with the devil. In Bolivia, the rituals through which the miners express their linkage to, dependency on, and worship of the "mine devil," *el tío*, contain a similar mechanism: the merciless mine, on which at the same time the people are dependent for their survival, can be portrayed and represented only as a devilish entity. Thus, the vocabulary through which people express their relationship with the entity of their livelihood at the same time coins this entity as an evil one. In such choices of metaphors, a deep rejection of the current living conditions is embodied—even if it only occasionally leads to actual collective protests. In his later work (1987, 1993) Taussig is faithful to his style of analysis. A recurring theme is the way in which political (counter)stances are expressed in ritual, symbolic, and religious practices. People tap their cultural repertoire, not only to denominate and "call" the vicissitudes of their lives, but also to value and criticize, and even demonize them.

Such "cultural layers" and cultural identities of socials movements take completely different shapes. The punk movement, across the globe, ranges from groups consistently involved in political actions against urban real estate speculation, world free-trade negotiations, political summits, and racist right-wing movements to groups merely expressing their "punkist" affiliation through music, clothing, and hair style. What they, in general, share is a wish to radiate an a-conventional, dissenter attitude, expressed primarily in clothing. Conformity is explicitly, and categorically, rejected. Personal freedom and direct action, often with anarchist overtones, prevail. The explicit political action priorities, however, vary from squatting through badgering and pestering authorities of whatever kind, through street protest against economic and political high-level meetings "jeopardizing" the fate of the poor and powerless, and the world as a whole, to the mere exhibition of "awkward" clothing styles. In many cases, political activity has faded altogether, and punks confine to expressing discontent through their music, attire, jewelry, and body modification, and "provocatively scruffy" meeting loci. To a significant extend, their message is a cultural one: they challenge the sleekly "brushed-up" world for its hypocrisy, materialism, and greed. Although largely complying with "the movement is the message" (Castells 1983), it must nevertheless be emphasized that this cultural message expressed in externalities obtains its full significance only because it is backed by the explicit, and sometimes fierce, political actions of punks. This is what makes people's reactions completely different from those triggered by, for instance, the Hare Krishnas. That is why, in most studies, the political contents of the movement are emphasized alongside its expressive and cultural ones. Thompson (2004) maybe goes furthest in this, interpreting the punk movement as, primarily, an anticapitalist one. Others (Hebdidge 1979) have stressed the resistance contents of punk styles. Leblanc (1999) highlighted yet another aspect: where often male dominance in subcultures is taken for granted, she went on to give the microphone to punk girls, discovering they are often mixed up not only in resentful relationships with their parents and society, but also with their dominant, sometimes "piggish" male peers. Resistance to subjugating social relationships acquires an ambiguous stature in the punker's worlds. Maybe this is why punk has a strong political resonance, but a hazy political stand. The case, however, again, illustrates the entangledness of the political and the cultural.

Culture as a Constraint?

Invoking cultural ingredients can, as we saw, foster movements—or at least echoes in their articulations of what grieves them. But cultural features can also hinder the development of such movements. Sometimes authorities will attempt to "exploit" specific cultural images to delegitimize social movements. Sometimes specific characteristics of a dominant discourse on the movement's nature and goals will deter its development. As, for instance, we have noted in the theorizations about social movements, especially those of the 1970s and early 1980s, great emphasis was placed on their extrainstitutional character and the ways in which they breach the limits of "the system" and act outside the usual modes of political regulation, which are considered to be concerned with "normalization" and "discipline." Eventually, much of such theorizations filtered into the discourse and self-representation of would-be social movements themselves (Assies 1999). Anthropologists like Ruth Cardoso (1983), however, were quick to point out that realities on the ground often were much more ambiguous, not to say messy. Mobilizations and urban protests that were labeled "social movements" and that were attributed a great potential for bringing about momentous change and breaching the political system—as their own rhetoric often suggested—were found to be engaged in much more complex and ambiguous power games involving both contestation and engagement in clientelist give-and-take courses of action. Such movements, as Foweraker (1995) makes clear, confront the state and the political system as an adversary but to achieve their goals also engage it as an interlocutor. Cardoso points out that urban movements in Brazil, which emerged in the context of the "democratic transition," only partly managed to break away from the political clientelism that had characterized an earlier generation of neighborhood organizations. Rather than radically breaking with this earlier pattern, the "new" movements extended their margins of autonomy and room for maneuver. Things were changing, but the change was often much more piecemeal than the early enthusiastic accounts of the new urban movements had suggested. The overrated belief in "extra-institutionality" did, beyond any doubt, foster the limited scope and success of the movements. A less radical adherence to the "autonomy" might have helped these movements to challenge the dominant political routines in a more pressing way.

If the "external relations" of movements with the state and the political system often are complex, "internal processes" also have come under scrutiny. Undeniably, participation in a movement often has empowering effects, as Díaz Barriga (1998) underscores. But he also suggests that such effects may be more limited than has too often been assumed. Participation at the grass roots teaches people to speak out and it allows them to move outside the circumscribed realm of the domestic unit, which affects established gender relations. Nonetheless, grass roots organization is not simply a practicing ground for democracy. Mobilization to obtain a concrete material benefit, like a primary school, requires all sorts of efforts. When finally the objective of mobilizations is reached and the school, in this case, has been inaugurated disputes often arise about who is going to be employed in the school. Jobs are scarce and people who somehow participated in the mobilization often expect to be rewarded according to their self-perceived input. Envy, slander, and backroom politics often are part and parcel of movement activity. In addition, it is not rare that people's inclination to subdue to "authority"—also the product of a long history of hierarchical social and political relations—is echoed in neighborhood-based organizations. "Micro-despotism" has often harmed local initiatives. The reasons why such initiatives were so vulnerable to such dangers are, at least in part, cultural in nature.

Unequal relations can also help to explain some of the less successful aspects of the Ecclesial Base Communities that, promoted by Liberation Theologians, came to play such a prominent role in grass roots organizing in countries like Brazil. Such Base Communities would organize their gathering according to the principle of "seeing, judging—in the light of the Holy Script—, and acting." A problem or an injustice would be identified and analyzed and then a remedy would be sought. However, using the Bible as a source of inspiration and reading a passage to shed light on a problem at hand also meant that those who did not read easily or not at all would be in an uncomfortable position. For them Pentecostalism might then become an alternative option. In this case, thus, the "progressive option" lost terrain to an often more conservative one, owing to its insistence on an emancipatory strategy that did not connect to local cultures and skills.

Even the culture of self-help and empowerment generated by grass roots organization can eventually become problematic, as Schild (1998) and Paley (2001) have shown. Neoliberal discourse emphasizes responsibility and participation, which allow the state to shed its responsibilities. Discourses and concepts that were designed, and initially used to foster self-awareness and emancipation, sometimes were hijacked by authorities or ideologues of the adversary, and then backfired: women's pleas for "autonomy," for recognition of their decisive role in keeping families afloat in times of crisis, and for acknowledgment of their crucial role in founding the self-help organizations that were the only real alternative in times of repression, now see themselves confronted with discourses in which the state embraces such self-help philosophies and connects them with those women's (and citizens' generally) "liberation from state patronizing." From there, it is a small step to measures reducing the state's involvement in subsidies, social housing, and, more in general, redistribution. In cases like these, counter-cultural creations proved vulnerable to being captured by the adversaries, and in the end sabotaged to quest for emancipation.

Lucy Taylor (1998) has argued that specific societal conceptions of politics, citizenship and rights are in part produced by particular political systems and political cultures (Badev 1995). Such conceptions obviously include imageries of what people can expect from their politicians, of what people perceive to be their "rights" in daily encounters with state representatives, and of what, in times of emerging discontent, people actually challenge or defy: "habits" of slight by the police or state functionaries, "routines" of patronizing or populist styles of politicians, "established" micro-corruption, and systematic manipulation by politicians of terms like *el pueblo* ("the people"), "the greatness of the nation," and the like. Here, dominant cultural patterns are a constraint because of their very nature of having obtained an almost "natural" status. Any challenge to what is "natural" runs the risk of being marginalized and ridiculed as "absurd," abnormal, and eccentric. The next part of this section addresses the difficult tasks social movement face when attempting to deconstruct such a "culturally normalized" status quo.

The Tentative Nature of Counter-Cultures

In social movement research, often the challenger's demands directly or indirectly referring to notions of justice, participation, rights, equality, and the like, are part of the analysis. Just as often, however, such notions are more or less taken for granted—especially when they explicitly emerge as part of the movement's discourse. Yet, it might be worthwhile to delve a little deeper into what the various sectors of movement participants exactly understand on these notions. Among many poor, for instance, a "non-standard" perception of citizenship exists. Whereas on the one hand they internalized the awareness (which is incessantly reaffirmed in most official political discourse) that everybody is equal in terms of the law, and that every citizen of the nation has the same rights and obligations, on the other hand their experience taught them that in many cases this equality does not exist. Only latently is there a consensual demand for the realization of what is supposedly the *rule*. Although many people are aware of the friction, a systematic demand for the application of what "ought to be" is not always the case. This phenomenon has to be explained by the enormous weight and impact of a whole life of experiences of denial of rights. Not only the poor embody such learning processes leading to "deviant" perceptions of the relation with politics and the polity, of one's rights, and of "natural societal hierarchies," but also women and ethnic or religious minorities—and in some cases majorities—often personify notions on the social order that are highly skewed. Demands by social movements, albeit not always explicitly, frequently challenge such legacies. The most illustrative example might be the feminist movement. Simultaneously, however, the "culture battle" fought by this social movement also reveals a controversial issue. Epstein (2002), on the women's movement in the United States, notes that "[t]o some degree this expansion of various forms of consciousness going way beyond the borders of the movements in which they first emerged shows the lasting influence of those movements. But it also has to do with what appears to be the decline of political and protest movements, and the difficulty of finding compelling forms of political engagement. The tendency of the political to collapse into the cultural, even as it connotes a measure of triumph, weakens the left." Does a movement's "victory" in terms of changing consciousnesses and "hegemonizing" culture mean its political strength withers? Or is it the other way around: does the fact that issues addressed by the movement, and later accepted in mainstream consciousness and policies, mean that the movement has been a success? And is not the feminist movement the most conspicuous example of this? In most Western societies at least, the taken-for-grantedness of women's equal rights in educational and job opportunities, in sexual and reproductive matters, in family affairs and in public and political spheres, is atleast formally acknowledged. This was not the case in the 1950s and 1960s. The change has not only taken place in the realm of political measures and legislation—which were of course among the prominent demands of the feminist movement—but also in the realm of "societal consciousness," for example, the cultural embeddedness of dominant views on gender roles and identities. The point, moreover, underscores that the delineation of what is, and what is not "a movement," is nebulous: its effects extend well beyond the direct impact of its actions and manifestations. Sociological research might be able to register and measure the shifting opinions on such matters, but ethnographic research is needed to unpack the processes of change in societal interactions and people's "signification" of issues such as gendered patterns of behavior and aspirations.

Attention to gendered aspects of social movement has also resulted in a theoretical reconsideration of the "given" distinction between the public and the private, or domestic. Various authors have pointed out that it was precisely women's "traditional" obligations in the domestic realm that brought them to participation in social movements: if their possibilities to comply with these obligations were blocked by economic or political circumstances, they would often reach out to "unconventional" activities such as political action, association, and the labor market to be able to fulfil their domestic, nurturing tasks (Chuchryk 1989; Molineux 1985; Salman 2002a; Valdés 1986). In an important contribution, Díaz Barriga (1998) pointed out that such "trespassing" from the domestic into the public is accompanied by a challenge of the "traditional mores" of this public realm. It is about cultural images, about "creating alternatives to traditional notions of 'woman as housewife' and 'man of politics' " (Díaz Barriga 1998:264). More generally, the "expansion of the domestic sphere into politics" (p. 265) brought about a reimagination of politics in which traditional mores like clientelism and corruption are no longer accepted as conventional ways to proceed. The very dichotomy of the domestic and the public is thus questioned: women enter, interpret, and act in the world of politics with—heterogeneous— skills and tools they developed earlier, and create "borderlands" (Díaz Barriga 1998) in which they "navigate the intersections of social experience" (p. 254). In the process, the clear distinction between the domestic and the public blurs—and cultured patterns of the "fitting" behaviour in each of these spheres are problematized. The effects of the social movements thus go beyond the concrete and palpable new policies or authority's concessions; they penetrate cultural hegemonies. Whether or not this is accompanied by, or has any causal relationship with, the movement's strength and cohesion in the narrower sense of the word is therefore dubious.

In other words, the very attempt to challenge hegemonic cultural images is often accompanied by various problems: the spokespersons of this dominant imagery will often strike back by poking fun at the eccentric and ridiculous ideas of the challengers. Besides that, the movement as a political pressure force often loses its strength and "urgency" when, slowly, their alternative suggestions are accepted by majorities.

Transforming Constraints into Assets: Building an Alternative Cultural Repertoire

Cultural repertoires can support social movements—and can also hamper them. Can constraints be transformed into assets, and if so, how? Social movements have, at times, been interpreted as "practice grounds for democracy" (cf. Assies 1990:82). In optimistic accounts, the participation in local organizations or social movements was seen as a trajectory toward an increased political consciousness, increased social and political cohesion among the poor (Valdés 1986), and as an escape from dependency and fatalism. More recent studies have revealed that such a unilineary logic does not exist (Vélez Ibañez 1983). Whereas on the one hand the experiences of the poor in such associations should not be underestimated in the sense that they do indeed produce important learning processes, on the other hand the ability of the governments and the dominant classes to maintain the structures of economic inequalities and exclusionary politics is vast, especially in view of the fact that protest issues often are not very suitable for "upscaling" toward systemic political characteristics.

These findings have stimulated a broadening of the research focus, away from a concentrated "movementist" entrance, toward a contextualization of the organizations' and movements' activities (Oxhorn 1991) in the light of overreaching themes such as democracy and citizenship Oxhorn 1994. In a way, the experiences people collect when participating in social movements doubtlessly contribute to their capacities and skills. People become more articulate, people learn how to express their viewpoints in public, and people learn how to seek consensus on priorities and strategies. Cultural learning, with all its "slowness" and distortions, does indeed take place (Salman 1998) . Acquiring such informal technical qualifications often boosts people self-confidence (Abers 2000). In this sense, movement participation is an ideal learning school for citizenship. But (often short-term, fragmented, haphazard) experiences in social movements of course compete with the heavy-weighing experiences outside these movements. No radically new, politically skilled people emerge out of movement participation. Nevertheless, a culture of "voluntary" abstention, a culture of meekness vis à vis the given authorities, and a culture of unquestioned acceptance of subalternity can be eroded by participation (Oxhorn 1994).

A different aspect is that of the discovery of alternative protest forms. Gal (2002) beautifully describes how women, less articulate in defying elaborate political discourse, can recur to silence, to colloquial forms of speech, or to wordless actions such as making obscene gestures in front of a politician. Protest, thus, not always has to be a verbal match to the authority's or patriarchy's speech. Silence itself can be an act of protest, and a worthwhile ingredient of a repertoire of demonstrating rejection.

However, sometimes protests containing a challenge of dominant (political) cultures do indeed result in growing self-esteem, and in the gradual emergence of a full-blown alternative. Where initially only timid signs of discontent with the cultural and conceptual a priori's of the dominant order are expressed, these might eventually develop into a self-confident defiance of this order. A case in point might be developments in recent decades in various Latin American countries. Traditionally, Andean countries coined their national identities, their economic parameters, and their political systems largely in "Western" terms. The taken-for-grantedness of these terms has weakened during the last decades Parker 1993. To begin with, political pressure triggered constitutional reforms in most of the countries, resulting in the formal acknowledgment of the "multinational, pluricultural and/or multiethnic" make-up of their societies (Assies, van der Haar and Hoekema 2000).

Recent developments suggest the process continues: candidates for political functions explicitly referring to their indigenous roots or cosmologies either won, or came close to winning high political positions (e.g., Peru, Bolivia). Also the criticism toward deficient, and corrupt political practices increasingly draws upon indigenous criteria about proficient and honorable leadership; and finally the criticism toward neoliberal economic models and free-trade treaties increasingly draws on indigenous notions of livelihood security, the ecologically superior small-scale agriculture, reciprocity, and cosmologically embedded environmental harmony.

In broader terms, the ongoing "indigenous emancipation" is accompanied by strength-gaining insistence upon the legitimacy of these—hitherto marginalized in public space—indigenous notions on how to conceptualize national identity and sovereignty, on how to envisage a nation's peoples' future, and how to govern "beyond" party systems and representative, institutionalized democracy. This tendency is supported by nonindigenous voices questioning the adequacy of Western-styled democracy models for the particular Latin American realities. In various countries, the traditional party systems and the authority of presidential positions are in crisis, and calls for deliberative democracy and "peoples' assemblies" abound. Even acknowledging that these development might relapse in a type of neo-populism, these trends trigger the question of whether Latin America, and in particular the Andes, is in the process of developing and implementing new models and "rearranging" its societies. Often, historical, ethnic, and territorial ingredients enter into such increased indigenous assertiveness, and combine with cross-national networking. On the indigenous Mapuches in Chile, for instance, Boccara (2006) remarks that "[t]he re-emergence of indigenous territorial conceptualizations happens to be central to the reconstruction of Mapuche identity and polity. Those renovated modes of territorial ordering result in the reactivation of collective memory. New forms of organizing transnational mobilization contribute to the emergence of Mapuche networks that connect local leaders, activists and intellectuals. Creating an identity of objective interests and subjective perception of the political and cultural issues at stake, indigenous transnationalism works as integrative mechanism."

In such cases, culture becomes the central arena of the discord. Demands not only contain political changes, but also include a counter-discourse to important elements of the prevailing culture. The legitimacy of this culture to define the terms of the "setting" in which the discontent is voiced, is defied. And room is claimed for the cultural currents that hitherto only had a marginal place in the national public space. Claims, today, are often accompanied by references to the "courage and resilience of women," or the "millenarian traditions of biodiversity stewardship by indigenous peoples." Culture here became a treasure, to guard and to summon against threats.

Such developments, however, should of course be situated in the context of globalization, in which calls upon one's "proper" cultural traditions have become more commonplace. Worldwide, the awareness that globalization processes alter cultural traditions with unprecedented speed, has triggered initiatives to protect, secure, or purify one's cultural heritages (Eriksen 2002). Whereas anthropologists have meanwhile reached agreement on the dynamic and hybrid nature of all cultures, and have even sometimes problematized the very idea of distinct cultures as such (Kuper 2000), people claim cultural authenticity and value in more rigid terms then ever before (see special issue *Etnofoor* journal XVII (1/2), 2004). Bringing in "culture" as a (central) issue in social movements' struggles of course has to be interpreted in this context.

Culture as the explicit *subject* of social movement manifestations, then, can be addressed from various angles. The tension between political and cultural effects of social movements is often an issue in social movements circles themselves, triggering the question of whether successes in the realm of public opinion "depoliticize" and appease militants. The "counter-question" is the one asking for movements' ability to politicize hitherto "domestic" societal arrangements.

Another matter are the cultural "vehicles" deployed in actions and manifestations. Some of these embody "deviant" meanings attached to the issues implicitly or explicitly at stake, such as in the case of one's rights, others refer to "demonizing" naming of the elements of the social order people reject. And yet others are explicitly chosen, such as provocatively visible dresses and accessories, that symbolize the refutation of the dominant codes and standards.

Often, rebellion is more fragmented, less articulate, and more inchoate than the contested order. No unidirectional "logic of maturation" can be assumed. Nevertheless, sometimes protests that begin hesitantly and inarticulately for alternatives develop into self-conscious, well elaborated criticisms of the moral and political premises of the dominant societal rule.

A final important caveat is that culture as a "prideful possession" of the mobilizing group has become much more commonplace. In view of the fact that globalization-driven processes are often equated with fears for homogenization and loss of tradition, protesting groups increasingly call on "their culture" to justify their stand. Culture here, apart from always already being an "inevitable ingredient" of protest formation and actual actions, becomes a dimension the protesting groups reflects upon and deploys in its strategies. The often "essentializing" side effects of such calls on culture, should be taken into account in studying its "application."

In this section on culture as a dimension backing, or obstructing the emergence, development, and success of social movements, we saw that ways in which movements try to "use" culture all serve to attract followers and gain legitimacy. The way they do this may vary. Sometimes icons or heroes are called upon for their appealing power. Sometimes rituals are performed to obtain a more emotional and self-assertive commitment of the participants. Sometimes the "hypocritical" ways in which authorities try to force through their standards become a central theme—and illustrate the ambivalence with which people understand and use elments of the prevailing discursive hopes such as citizenship and equality. People thus recur to strong but contentious cultural repertoire to denounce injustices they feel but cannot explain. And sometimes people behave in a *culturally* unconventional way, to make a *political* statement.

Culture as a constraint surfaced in images and practices that are present in "folk" beliefs, which actually obstruct a movement's development. These images vary from leadership myths to ideologies on the "purity" of the movements itself. Another shape constraints take is when concepts and demands originally coined by the protest movement, are later usurped by the authorities, and then used against the original "inventers." Finally, we addressed the problem that hegemonic cultural narratives are often so strong and omnipowerful that it is almost impossible to develop a full fledged counter-discourse. The discourse that challenges the status quo is therefore often of a more incipient and fragmented nature than the one it addresses.

Finally, we made note of the fact that learning processes, and growing self-esteem and assertiveness, can, sometimes, convert initial constraints into assets.

RESEARCH AT THE GRASS ROOTS

We claimed that anthropology's *forte* in social movement research is also its ability to touch ground with the rank and file participants, to be able to take into account the "before" and 'after' processes of mobilizations, in terms of social cohesion, significations, feelings of belonging, memories (Turner 1995), micro-networking, sense-making of circumstances and events, vocabularies and knowledge to build counter-discourses (Siegel 1997), and other emic issues, in other words: cultural framing. To substantiate this claim, we need to explain, in a somewhat more methodological vocabulary, in what this practice of anthropology consists.

Emic Accounts: The Views of the Rank and File

Moore's findings on the modest demands of the German workers in the midst of radical collective action that we mentioned at the begining of this chapter are prototypical for the contribution grass root focuses can bring to the study of social movements. Paradoxically, however, the results of such research has been that Moore's findings should not be generalized.

Studies of how structural constraints and the inputs of creative and innovative agency worked out among the rank and file participants in social movements did not always reveal the bases' reluctance to adhere to the more encompassing or radical demands of movement leaders; occasionally it was even the other way round: in such cases protesters on the street forced the leaders to radicalize or focus their discourses on specific (sub)issues. This, for instance, was the case during recent protests in Bolivia, in 2005, when rallies organized by movements demanding the overhaul of a bill on increased state participation in the exploitation of the country's natural gas reserves turned out calling for the stepping down of the sitting president, whose wavering stance people would no longer accept (Salman 2006). They made leaders adopt the new demand, even though these leaders had never suggested it and were unprepared for the subsequent step. The point became clear during intensive talking with the protesters on the street: many protested against the bill *as such*, because they refused to trust *any* government initiative on the matter. Journalists and international observers often coincided in criticizing these protests for being "for the sake of protest" and for mobilizing people who could not even state what was at stake in the referendum on the issue. What they missed hearing in the people's angry exclamations were expressions of systematic distrust in all governmental propositions with regard to something that has become a poor Bolivian's hope for a better future, namely enormous reserves of natural gas. Their fear of being deceived won over their awareness that they were indeed unable to answer the question about what alternative would be possible. The source of this stand was a collective memory dating long back. It is *this* that many Bolivians had learned in the dealings with their fatherland's politics. And it is the point the political scientists and other "top down" observers failed to spot.

The dynamics between the "guidance" from above and the multiple developments simultaneously taking place among the "ordinary participants" can take many different forms. Jeffrey Rubin (1998), for instance, in his analysis of COCEI ("Coalition of Workers, Peasants and Students of the Istmus"), a radical grass roots movement in the Zapotec city of Juchitán, in southern Mexico, denied a simple coincidence between, on the one hand, the sort of "progressive politics" publicly forwarded by social movements such as COCEI, and cultural emancipation in the sphere of relationships among the movement's participants. His findings suggested that left-wing politics as embodied in COCEI's stands, even if combined with mobilization power, and autonomy from political parties, does not necessarily mean that also the authoritarianism in the movement's make-up is overcome. To the contrary, he found that *caudillismo*, threatening with violence, applying tactics like warning for an "explosion" of the rough and indomitable "indian," and repression of women were part and parcel of COCEI's character. Racism, sexism, and authoritarianism characterized not only the status quo, but also the victims of these traits united in a strong social movement. In his explanation Rubin emphasized that such traits, on the one hand, do indeed dominate much of the popular culture protest allegedly is rooted in, whereas on the other hand COCEI simultaneously with employing these traits allowed for ambiguity and "decentered-ness" in its actual performance and relations with its supporters. It was this ambivalence that, in the minds and hearts of many participants who were marginalized in its centralized actions, made COCEI attractive.

Rubin stressed that, apart from helping to explain the success of movements that do not "fully" express people's convictions, his findings also suggested that "culture" remains an unruly dimension in social movements' mobilizations. People are not easily "molded" into the progressive (or not so progressive) cultural standards the movements advocate. People's motivations might therefore be partly dissimilar to those the movements' leaderships foster. This, in turn, suggests that cultural features might even be *shared* between the movement and the established structures and powers it challenges. Specific values "making it worthwhile to fight for" may exist both among the powers that be and protesters. The exact dynamics of such somewhat "chaotically" distributed cultural beliefs and practices can be revealed only by thorough field-research among the "ordinary" participants.

Orin Starn's work (1992) is another case in point. He also came to the conclusion that social movements do not necessarily unite and homogenize the populations they mobilize or culturally strive to "emancipate." Moreover, basing his conclusions on research among the *rondas campesinos* (nightly vigilances) in the mountains of northern Peru, he pointed to the unscrupulous mix of "authentic" and "alien" components in acclaimed new collective action practices. Like Rubin, he also encountered features within the movements that did not fit the progressive, and "politically correct" or "culture-oppositional" image they have. He found that the concrete forms the peasants chose to make their *rondas* reflected both endogenous and external sources. The *rondas*, originally, were nightly vigilances to stop cattle thieves. They came into being because the peasants were deeply disappointed with the state's ability and/or willingness to stop the thefts. In the course of time, the *rondas* became "autonomous" community organizations with the tasks to judge internal conflicts, family violence, and local crime. They set up local "courts" to deal with these problems. The *rondas* introduced a sort of idiosyncratic "uniform," with *ponchos* and hats. The idea of the uniforms came from military service; it gave status to the *rondistas*. The actual garments were local and partially the "reinvention" of traditional attires. The courts embodied both traditional mores and customs, such as community-broad deliberation, but also appropriated elements such as the alternation between attorneys and prosecutors. Court hearings were set up as formal ones: dignitaries behind a table; the bible and (often outdated) books of law within the dignitaries' and judges' reach; and proceedings according to formal lawsuits, with prosecutors, solicitors, defendants, and witnesses taking the floor. On the other hand, the course of events often was not that formal, with people taking the opportunity to express all sorts of complaints unrelated to the case, gossiping, mocking, and making fun. The *rondas* thus, in Starn's view, embody a political message, but at the same time a cultural practice and statement inspired by both local, "remembered" forms, and by forms stemming from greater society to give the whole thing more standing. Among the rank and file participants of the *ronda* movement, thus, no such thing as a categorical rejection of everything outside the Andean traditions emerged. This "de-essentializing" thrust of Starn's work would have been impossible without his ethnographic work in the Peruvian highlands.

Schönwalder's (2002) book on Peru was another valuable contribution. In his view, the really important issue is not whether, but how, the interaction between social movements and "third parties" transpires. The book presents a detailed analysis of the relationships between urban movements and local governments and their dependencies, political parties (especially on the left), NGOs, and the central governments' agencies responsible for urban development matters, focusing on Lima, Peru, in the period from 1980 to 1992. The book is divided into two parts. The first part deals with theory, addressing the autonomy question, and making a plea for combining rather than contrasting the traditionally competing focuses on strategy and identity, because this much better fits the dynamics "on the ground." In the analysis, the attitudes and strategies of the Peruvian left on the local political level in the 1980s are highlighted, because they co-shaped the responses of neighborhood organizations. The book thus interlocks the viewpoints, strategies, and perceptions of the various "levels" and actors in play. Maybe Schönwalder does not fully illustrate our point, because in his account we hear relatively little about the perceptions, ambitions, and doubts of the "ordinary participant." The "smallest" level of analysis is not that of the individual participant (or nonparticipant, for that matter), but the level of the organizations, movements, and their spokespersons. Nevertheless, the analysis contributes to a meticulous unpacking of the not-at-all straightforward opposition between grass root, and more meso- and macro-levels of interaction.

Vélez-Ibañez's (1983) book *Rituals of Marginality* offers more detail on what exactly takes place in the houses and conversations of the dwellers of a marginal neighborhood in the city of Netzahualcoyotl Izcalli, close to Mexico city. He presents a detailed account of the course of events in a confrontation (ending for the most part in co-optation) between a neighborhood organization and political authorities. Focusing on the scarce resources of the local population, he concludes that their vulnerability to get caught up in "rituals of marginality" is immense. He suggests that local reciprocity networks, to decrease individual family's vulnerability, do not necessarily express proper cultural traditions (Vélez-Ibañez 1983:2); rather they often express the limited access to formal political spheres. In addition, the author stresses that no such thing as a mere "political conviction" accounts for people's involvement in local organizations. People take such decisions in a complex network of dependencies and reciprocity. These networks constitute people's individual and collective identities, and their "place," their belonging, and the reproduction mechanisms of such places and belongings. Not necessarily do people "believe" in the politician they vote for or try to approach for solutions to their misery, and not necessarily do they agree with the discourses upheld by (local) politicians and/or the neighborhood "brokers" and leaders. Their decisions, rather, are also based on loyalties, reciprocities, language codes, and residential affinity (p. 240 *ff*). Not always, then, do movement discourses and actions coincide with the views of the participants. This ambiguity is a prerequisite for the movements because they need to be able to highlight specific features of identities and interests, and downplay the other dimensions of the participants' "selves," if they want to be successful in the first place. The ambiguity, however, also affects the solidity of the movement: when the mismatch between movement versions and participant versions becomes too large, the movement will lose mobilization strength.

Salman (1997), in his research on the Chilean shantytown organizations during the later years of Pinochet's dictatorship, found that the overwhelming majority of the participants in these organizations did not share the opinion of the spokespersons and optimistic NGO researchers about a new social movement (and a "new democracy") coming into being. Contrary to what these optimistic voices proclaimed, the majority of the participants to the self-help organizations did not have any political ambitions, did not want to shift aside the traditional (and indeed quite bureaucratic and hierarchical) political parties, and did not even aspire to continue their organizational efforts once employment opportunities would improve again, for example, once they *individually* would be capable again of providing for their families. Behind these modest outlooks were a number of factors. First of all, the fact that mainly women managed these organizations gave them a character of their own. Most of the participants were not trained, and reluctant, to translate their efforts into political projects. Their motivations were of a practical nature, and attempted to mitigate practical problems rather than searching for political visibility. The male absence was excused by the (often unemployed) poor city-dwellers in concomitant terms: they felt uneasy about the fact their families needed to be "helped," and were very hesitant about stepping in organizations that did not *demand* for improvements in their lot. An organization that would not address the state, that would not seek for political emancipation, and that would not affirm their class pride and identity, was something they found hard to sympathize with. In spite of the misery and lack of prospects, they preferred the ongoing search for odd jobs above stepping into the "defensive" subsistence efforts of their spouses.

Precisely the fact that the phenomenon was so massive, and that it was "new" and included so many people who never before had been involved in collective action, stimulated observers and scholars to speculate about its future. Many came to the conclusion that a renewal of politics was at stake, and that the political landscape in Chile, after the return of democracy, would be changed. It turned out otherwise: the organizations proved to be not a decisive political force after all, and the traditional political parties proved unwilling to give up their prominent role in the transition and the make-up of democracy.

But—and this is the second reason for the mismatch between the optimistic assessments and the situation on the ground—it was not only *because* of the parties' regained protagonism that the organization failed to "change politics." It was also due to the fact that too few scholars—and "leaders," for that matter—had critically asked the participating women about their ambitions and perceptions of "politics." No doubt many of these women impatiently awaited the return of democracy, but this was not so much because of aspiring to an active role in it. Rather, the women hoped the new democratic polity would be more responsive to their needs and problems. Whereas many of the men, in pre-dictatorial Chile, had been socialized in a more politicized manner and still maintained images about striving for a share of power in politics and the state, the women, even after their experiences in these organizations, and even well aware of the "political" significance of their collective efforts as "anti-dictatorship," still were much more reluctant to view a political role for themselves. Instead, as Worsley (1984:219) has observed, "[p]reoccupied with problems of immediate survival and individual betterment, the poor perceive and treat the political system as another resource to be exploited." This attitude of hoping for a more responsive state, instead of self-consciously demanding a role in it, had largely been overlooked by the theorists announcing the transition from grass roots organizations to innovative social movements at the moment of Chile's democratic transition.

Besides the "divergences" visible in the relationships between leaders, discourses, and official strategies on the one hand, and participants' priorities and perceptions on the other, another dimension of "mismatch" between these participants and the authorities or the polity they address calls for attention. The representatives of movements in closer contact with the authorities often try to adapt to the language and the strategic rules of the game of these political authorities they are challenging. In doing so, they run the risk of alienating themselves from the views of the people in whose interest they emerged in the first place. Many anthropologists have reported a gap between the life worlds of the poor and the language of politics. Many poor, many women, many indigenous, and the like believe that in reality "politicians know nothing about us" (Baño 1984; García Canclini 1995]; Piña 1987). Lehmann (1990) specifies this and states that what the poor (in his case, informal workers in Mexico and Ecuador) really reject is the vices and untrustworthiness of politicians and public authorities: they are "pick-pockets," cunning people, liars, and in political relationships, a poor person "risks humiliation and personal dependence" (Lehmann 1990:93). The contacts and negotiations between their spokespersons and these authorities are often also looked upon with distrust.

Often, people have trouble connecting experiences of humiliation, injustice, and misery to structural features of society. "Politics" are associated with "mighty people" rather than with a system, or a structure of inequality. What, in people's accounts of their problems, is therefore *not* so explicitly rejected, or is not mentioned at all, are the structures, the organization and transparency of the state, and the representational institutions. This might in part be a self-incapacitation, a denial of self-competence with regard to the world of politics, but it also illustrates how "normal" it is to reduce experiences of injustice and humiliation to the immoral behavior of *persons*, and not so much to the underlying causes (Piven and Cloward

1977:21). This helps explain why rallies against "the system" or mobilizations "for reform" are often only reluctantly supported: for the poor, that is often not where they feel the core problem is. Moreover, it is about a world they, in their own perception, have no knowledge of and no capacity for.

Worsley confirms many of the finding of Barrington Moore on the limited aspirations of movement participants—even during the highpoints of conflict. As our elaboration on the scope of agency in structured settings might help explain, people will in their utterances sometimes endorse quite radical demands—and sometimes even force their leaders into even more uncompromising or "revolutionary" positions. But often their more profound ambitions, and their very *ability* for change, will be more modest. Often, the poor perceive of politicians and civil servants as the most powerful in society. Most often, there is no overall aversion toward the system (Worsley 1984:219), even if at times people prove willing to mobilize, in cases in which their opportunities for subsistence shrink or when they feel treated disrespectful. In such cases, even radical discourses voiced by movements' leaders might be backed. But often, in the end, the poor will act acknowledging they have a stake in the system. Most often, signs of radical ideology, or propensity to revolutionary action, are completely absent. Instead, the poor make a rational adaptation to the rules of the political game, distinguishing which kinds of political action are rewarded by the authorities and which kind are likely to be ignored or violently repressed. The poor often do not respond to poverty ideologically, but instrumentally (p. 220). Paradoxically, this is in part a *cultural* phenomenon.

It is hard to reveal an unequivocal trend, or theoretically testable hypotheses, in the findings of anthropological research among the rank and file of social movements. Some ethnographies find radicalism exceeding the demands of the official spokespersons; many more find more modest, more diffuse, and more "conservative" aspirations. Some find attachment to traditions and customs the movement is officially contesting as part of its transformation wishes; others find rejections of the negotiations their leaders are involved in, because people have lost confidence in concession by the authorities *tout court*. Some find attempts to overcome traditional submissiveness in violent attacks on official buildings and symbols; others find that some participants loath the confrontations their neighbours engage in with the police, because their houses and family security are endangered. To translate this diversity in "informed guesses" about (causal) relationships between different aspects of the phenomenon, is complicated. What the diverse stories do tell us, however, is that, in our attempts to understand the movements' fortunes, the perceptions, reactions, and ambitions of those who hardly ever obtain a microphone are just as crucial as are the easier detectable public statements and strategies. Without anthropology, social movements research risks instrumentalizing and functionalizing what these movements, through the actions of the ordinary participants, actually do. It risks being teleological and normative in its assessments of the changes movements strive for and obtain. To be able to analyze these changes beyond normativism and modernization prejudices, we need to include culture. Only then can we avoid to merely "discover" the contrast between the aims of movements in terms of democracy, rights, participation, justice and citizenship, and the situation against which they rally. A characterization in its own right of what is going on in such movements, their participants, and in their relationships with the political sphere would then remain out of sight. Change, to the contrary, should be measured in etic, but also in emic terms, we don't want to lose sight of its locally constructed and construed significance.

FUTURE RESEARCH

It seems that two major tasks lie ahead for anthropologists' involvement in social movement research. First, the job of thoroughly and systematically accounting for the participants' perceptions, reactions, and ambitions with regard to the movement's goals and strategies has only just begun. Much too often, movements are still conceptualized as if they were "the unity of analysis." Thus, the public statements and strategies, the rallies, and the slogans are taken as representative of what *makes* the movement. This is problematic. The so-called "actor-oriented approach" needs to be radicalized: not the movements-as-actor, but the actors that make the movements need to be studied much more intensively. Insights into the doubts, aspirations, motivations, and even "improper" considerations of these participants will help us to understand the movements as a polyvalent, multilayered phenomenon, and will contribute to our insights in their successes and failures. The only way to avoid the functionalist approach of these movements is through the attitudes and actual actions of the ordinary participants. Much more ethnographic research among these participants is therefore needed. And much more questions need to be asked revolving around collective and individual memories; around the emotional significance of mottos, metaphors, and rituals; around the role of social networks as recruiting vehicles; around the pursuit for *belonging* as a motivational factor; around images of "a good life"; and around the fears brought about by rapid or unpredictable changes in the social, economic, and political life conditions. Questions and questionnaires confining themselves to motivational dimensions, formulating these in explicit, discursive modes, will not be able to bring to light the complexities of people's reasons and motivations to be part—or to decline being part. Only research into de dimensions referred to in the preceding text will be able to reveal the entangledness of the *cultural* contents of *political* struggles.

Second, some theoretical and conceptual issues triggered by the outcomes of such research need further attention. One of them is—once again—the intricate nature of culture. Today's paradox is that, whereas scholars have become convinced of the fluid, dynamic, and heterogeneous make-up of cultures, and extensively study the ways in which local cultural transformations, and local political conflicts, are at least partially "fashioned" outside the local setting, at the same time the invocation of traditional and "authentic" local cultures increasingly becomes one of the motivational pillars of many movement's emergence and self-legitimating discourses. Scholars of social movements or of "cultural defenses" today all insist on the transnational, or at least trans-local, character of such initiatives, and show how the very assembling of countervailing discourses is decisively influenced by external input. In the eyes of the people concerned, however, there is nothing "alien" in their pleas for acknowledgment of, for instance, indigenous rights, their pleas for the revival of local rituals and celebrations, or their claim that the protection of biodiversity is something "natural" to indigenous populations. The denial of the external impact upon such "assertive" narratives of local dignity and tradition is, beyond doubt, partially a strategic maneuver—it is, however, also part and parcel of genuine local views upon the emergence of these struggles. Where other scholars of social movements are possibly well-equipped to *demystify* these images of domestic roots of local discourses, anthropology might be able to help decipher such mechanisms of reification of local ancestry, and help reveal the impulses that propel people away from the recognition of their own hybridity and heterogeneity, toward believing in "proper" and authentic identities.

Another issue future research, in our view, should take up is the cultural dimension of "framing processes." Our understanding of such framing processes, as one of the crucial intermediating mechanisms between "conditions" and actual mobilization, has increased over time. But our insights in the ways in which (also "pre-conscious") cultural elements account for the successes and limitations of such framing processes is still limited. Such cultural dimensions beyond doubt include the icons, heroes, and rituals we mentioned above, but they probably also include, for instance, styles, and modes of leadership, and of specific types of "social glue" responsible for the abilities of movements to get their supporters out on the streets. One might, for instance, suspect that in some cases "soft" and democratic leadership (consistent with the movement's own claims about inclusive and participatory democracy) might be less successful than charismatic and "caudillo-like" leadership— because the latter fits local political cultures better. To be able to understand how such schemes work, we need the accounts of the participants, rather than a mere typology of leadership styles. Subsequently, we need a thorough reflection on the linkages (or mismatches) between participant's expectations and "familiar modes" of social interaction on the one hand, and the characteristics of framing discourses on the other hand.

A final suggestion for further research efforts is the theme of cultural ambiguity. Contrary to political statements or stands, which most of the time leave little room for haziness about the contents or intentions, cultural phenomena tend to leave more room for interpretation. It is, for instance, not rare to have two people explain a cultural trait in a society in quite different ways. Self-ascribed cultural characteristics, the explanation and justification of traditions, and the culturally condoned inequalities between men and women, may all sound confusing when conveyed to an observer by different members of such societies. It is, as Rubin (1998) stressed, a very important, and often *facilitating* feature of cultural phenomena: it allows for adherence to movements by people radically different in their convictions about a range of issues— including the ones the movements did put on the agenda. A movement's insistence upon the "original, pure and millenarian" indigenous traditions, to criticize government measures and strengthen one's political position, will in the views of the indigenous people often seamlessly go together with images about access to "modern" and high-tech facilities and services. Cultural expressions and "properties" allow sharing of things, while differing on exact meanings and consequences. The effects of this phenomenon need further scrutiny: it may enhance our understanding of social movements to analyze the combination of political and cultural vocabularies and repertoires, and to reveal the ways in which political diagnoses and demands merge with narratives about unity and belonging that permit the divergent to differ, and simultaneously feel companionship.

SUGGESTED READINGS

Alvarez, Sonia E., Evelina Dagnino, and Arturo Escobar, eds. 1998. *Cultures of Politics, Politics of Cultures— Revisioning Latin American Social Movements.* Boulder/Oxford: Westview Press.

Assies, Willem, Gerrit Burgwal, and Ton Salman. 1990. *Structures of Power, Movements of Resistance—An Introduction to the Theories of Urban Movements in Latin America.* Amsterdam: CEDLA.

Bourdieu, Pierre. 1977. *Outline of a Theory of Practice.* Cambridge, UK: Cambridge University Press.

Castells, Manuel. 1997. *The Information Age: Economy, Society and Culture* (vol. II): *The Power of Identity.* Oxford: Blackwell Publishers.

Escobar, Arturo. 1992. "Culture, Practice and Politics; Anthropology and the Study of Social Movements." *Critique of Anthropology* 12(4):395–432.

Evers, Tilman. 1985. "Identity: The Hidden Side of New Social Movements in Latin America." in *New Social Movements and the State in Latin America,* edited by David Slater. Amsterdam, CEDLA, 43–72.

Melucci, Alberto. 1985. "The Symbolic Challenge of Contemporary Movements." *Social Research* 52(4):789–815.

Nash, June, ed. 2005. *Social Movements: An Anthropological Reader.* Malden, Oxford, Carlton: Blackwell Publishing.

Paley, Julia. 2001. *Marketing Democracy—Power and Social Movements in Post-Dictatorial Chile.* Berkeley/ Los Angeles/London: University of California Press.

Salman, Ton. 1997. *The Diffident Movement—Disintegration, Ingenuity and Resistance of the Chilean Pobladores, 1973–1990.* Amsterdam: Aksant.

Scott, James. 1990. *Domination and the Arts of Resistance: Hidden Transcripts.* New Haven, CT: Yale University Press.

Turner, Christena L. 1995. *Japanese Workers in Protest. An Ethnography of Consciousness and Experience.* Berkeley: University of California Press.

Vélez Ibañez, Carlos. 1983. *Rituals of Marginality: Politics, Process, and Culture Change in Central Urban Mexico, 1969–1974.* Berkeley: University of California Press.

REFERENCES

Abers, Rebecca. 2000. *Inventing Local Democracy.* Boulder/London: Lynne Rienner Publishers.

Almeida, José, Freddy Rivera, N. Alejandra Maluf, José Sánchez-Parga, and Luis Verdesoto 1996. *Identidad y Ciudadanía—Enfoques teóricos,* Quito: FEUCE, ADES and AEDA.

Almond, Gabriel A. and Sidney Verba. 1965. *The Civic Culture.* Boston: Little, Brown.

Alvarez, Sonia E., Evelina Dagnino, and Arturo Escobar, eds. 1998a. *Cultures of Politics, Politics of Cultures— Revisioning Latin American Social Movements.* Boulder/Oxford: Westview Press.

———. 1998b. "Introduction: The Cultural and the Political in Latin American Social Movements." Pp. 1–29 in *Cultures of Politics, Politics of Cultures—Revisioning Latin American Social Movements,* edited by Sonia E. Alvarez, Evelina Dagnino, and Arturo Escobar. Boulder/Oxford: Westview Press.

Anderson, Benedict. 1983. *Imagined Communities—Reflection of the Origins and Spread of Nationalism.* London/New York: Verso Books.

Andrien, K. J. 2001. *Andean Worlds: Indigenous History, Culture, and Consciousness Under Spanish Rule, 1532–1825.* Albuquerque: University of New Mexico Press.

Archer, Margaret S. 1995. *Realist Social Theory: The Morphogenetic Approach.* Cambridge, UK: Cambridge University Press.

———. 1996. *Culture and Agency: The Place of Culture in Social Theory* (revised edition 1996; first published in 1988). Cambridge, UK: Cambridge University Press.

Assies, Willem. 1990. "Of Structured Moves and Moving Structures." Pp. 9–98 in *Structures of Power, Movements of Resistance—An Introduction to the Theories of Urban Movements in Latin America,* edited by Willem Assies, Gerrit Burgwal, and Ton Salman. Amsterdam: CEDLA.

———. 1992. *To Get Out of the Mud—Neighbourhood Associativism in Recife 1964–1988.* Amsterdam: CEDLA.

———. 1999. "Theory Practice and 'External Actors' in the Making of New Urban Social Movements in Brazil." *Bulletin of Latin American Research* 18:211–226.

———. 2003. "David Fights Goliath in Cochabamba: Water Rights, Neoliberalism and the Renovation of Social Protest in Bolivia. *Latin American Perspectives* 30(3):14–36.

———. 2006. "La 'Media Luna' sobre Bolivia: Nación, región, etnia y clase social." *América Latina Hoy* 43:87–105.

Assies, Willem, Gemma van der Haar, and André Hoekema, eds. 2000, *The Challenge of Diversity: Indigenous Peoples and Reform of the State in Latin America.* Amsterdam: Thesis Publishers.

Bader, Veit M. 1991. *Collectief Handelen.* Groningen: Wolters-Noordhoff.

———. 1995. *Rassismus, Ethnizität, Bürgerschaft—Soziologische und Philosophische Überlegungen.* Münster, Westfälisches Dampfboot.

Banck, Geert. 1994. "Democratic Transparency and the Train of Joy and Happiness—Local Politicians and the Dilemmas of Political Change in Brazil." Pp. 135–156 in *Transactions. Essays in Honor of Jeremy Boissevain,* edited by Jojada Verrips. Amsterdam: Spinhuis.

Banck, Geert and Ana María Domino. 1988. "Between Utopia and Strategy: A case study of a Brazilian Urban Movement", Pp. 71–87, in Banch, Geert & Kees Koonings (eds.) *Social Change in Contemporary Brazil. Politics, Class and Culture in a Decade of Transition.* Amsterdam: CEDLA.

Baño, Rodrigo. 1984. *Lo social y lo político: Consideracines acerca del movimiento popular urbano* (vol. I and II). Santiago, FLACSO: Documento de Trabajo 208.

Barth, Frederick. 1969. *Ethnic Groups and Boundaries: the Social Organization of Culuture Difference.* London: George Allen & Unwin.

Bauman, Zygmunt. 1992. *Intimations of Postmodernity.* London: Routledge.

Bernstein, Mary. 2005. "Identity Politics." *Annual Review of Sociology 2005* 31:47 –74.

Bhabha, Homi K. 1996. "Culture's In-Between." Pp. 53–60 in *Questions of Cultural Identity*, edited by Stuart Hall and Paul de Gay. London/Thousand Oaks/New Delhi: Sage.

Boccara, Guillaume. 2006. "The Brighter Side of the Indigenous Resistance." *Nuevo Mundo* (WebJournal) 6, at http://nuevomundo.revues.org/document2484.html

Bourdieu, Pierre. 1972. *Esquisse d'une théorie de la pratique, précédé de trois études d'ethlogie Kabyle*. Genéve/Paris: Librairi DROZ.

——. 1980. *Le sens pratique*. Paris: Les Editions de Minuit.

——. 1986. *Distinction—A Social Critique of the Judgement of Taste*. London: Routledge and Kegan Paul.

Brysk, Alison. 2000. *From Tribal Village to Global Village: Indian Rights and International Relations in Latin America*. Stanford: Stanford University Press.

Burgwal, Gerrit. 1995. *Struggle of the Poor: Neighborhood Organization and Clientelist Practices in a Quito Squatter Settlement*. Amsterdam: CEDLA.

Bustos, Guillermo. 1992. "Quito en la transición: Actores colectivos e identidades culturales urbanas (1920–1950)." Pp. 163–188 in *Enfoques y estudios históricos—Quito a través de la historia*, edited by Paul Aguilar et al. Quito: Municipio de Quito, Dirección de Plani°ficación.

Cadena, Marisol de la. 1990. "De utopías y contrahegemonías: El proceso de la cultura popular." *Revista Andina* 8(1):65–76.

Campbell, John. 2005. "Where Do We Stand? Common Mechanisms in Organisations and Social Movements Research." Pp. 41–67 in *Social Movements and Organization Theory*, edited by Gerald F. Davis, Doug W. McAdam, Richard Scott, and Mayer N. Zald. Cambridge, UK: Cambridge University Press.

Canel, Eduardo. 1992. "Democratization and the Decline of Urban Social Movements in Uruguay. A Political-Institutional Accounts", Pp. 276–290, in *The Making of Social Movements in Latin America*, edited by Sonia Alvarez and Arturo Escobar, Boulder: Westview Press.

Cardoso, Ruth. 1983. "Movimentos sociais urbanos: balanço crítico." Pp. 215–239 in *Sociedade e políca no Brasil pós 64*, edited by B. Sorj and M. H. T. de Almeida. São Paulo: Brasiliense.

Carroll, William K. and R. S. Ratner. 1994. "Between Leninism and Radical Pluralism: Gramscian Reflections on Counter-Hegemony and the New Social Movements." *Critical Sociology* 20(2):3–26.

Castells, Manuel. 1977. *The Urban Question: A Marxist Approach*. London: Edward Arnold.

——. 1983. *The City and the Grassroots*. London: Arnold Publishers.

——. 1996. *The Rise of the Network Society, The Information Age: Economy, Society and Culture* (vol. I). Cambridge, MA; Oxford, UK: Blackwell Publishers.

——. 1997. *The Information Age: Economy, Society and Culture*, (vol. II): *The Power of Identity*. Oxford: Blackwell Publishers.

——. 1998. *The End of the Millennium, The Information Age: Economy, Society and Culture* (vol. III). Cambridge, MA; Oxford, UK: Blackwell Publishers.

Chuchryk, Patricia. 1989. "Feminist Anti-authoritarian Politics: The Role of Women's Organizations in the Chilean Transition to Democracy." Pp. 149–184 in *The Women's Movement in Latin America—Feminism and the Transition to Democracy*, edited by Jane Jaquette. London: Ed. Unwin Hyman.

Cohen, Jean. 1982. "Between Crises Management and Social Movements: The place of Institutional Reform", *Telos* 52, Pp. 21–40.

Cohen, Jean. 1985. "Strategy or Identity: New Theoretical Paradigms and Contemporary Social Movements." *Social Science Research* 52(4) 663–716.

Cohen, Jean L. and Andrew Arato 1992. "Social Movements and Civil Society." Pp. 492–563 in *Civil Society and Political Theory*, edited by Jean L. Cohen and Andrew Arato. Cambridge, MA: MIT Press.

Cohen, Robin and Shirin M. Rai, eds. 2000. *Global Social Movements*. London, New Brunswick: The Athlone Press.

Comaroff, Jean. 1985. *Body of Power, Spirit of Resistance*. Chicago: University of Chicago Press.

Crehan, Kate. 2002. *Gramsci, Culture and Anthropology*. London/Sterling, Virginia: Pluto Press.

Dagnino, Evelina. 1989. "Culture, Citizenship and Democracy: Changing Discourses and Practices of the Latin America left". 33–63, in *Cultures of Politics, Politics of Cultures—Revisioning Latin American Social Movements*, edited by Sonia E. Alvarez, Evelina Dagnino and Arturo Escobar. Boulder Oxford: Westview press.

De la Peña, Guillermo. 2006. "A New Mexican Nationalism? Indigenous Rights, Constitutional Reform and the Conflicting Meanings of Multiculturalism." *Nations and Nationalism* (12)2:279–302.

Díaz, Alvaro. 1993. "Estructuras y movimientos sociales—La experiencia Chilena entre 1983–93." *Proposiciones* 22:13–20.

——. 1998. "Beyond the Domestic and the Public: Colonas Participation in Urban Movements in Mexico City." Pp. 252–277 in *Cultures of Politics, Politics of Cultures—Revisioning Latin American Social Movements*, edited by Sonia E. Alvarez, Evelina Dagnino, and Arturo Escobar. Boulder/Oxford: Westview Press.

Downs, Charles and Giorgio Solimano. 1988. "Alternative Social Policies from the Grassroots: Implications of Recent NGO Experience in Chile." *Community Development Journal* 23(2):63–72.

Dworkin, R. 1997. *Taking Rights Seriously.* London, Duckworth.

Edelman, Marc. 2001. "Social Movements: Changing Paradigms and Forms of Politics." *Annual Review of Anthropology* (30):285–317.

Eder, Klaus. 1985. "The 'New Social Movements': Moral Crusades, Political Pressure Groups, or Social Movements?" *Social Research* 52(4) 869–890.

Epstein, Barbara. 2002. "Feminist Consciousness after the Women's Movement." *Monthly Review* 54(4), at http://www.monthlyreview.org/0902epstein.htm.

Eriksen, Thomas Hylland. 2002. *Ethnicity and Nationalism.* London: Pluto Press.

Escobar, Arturo. 1992. "Culture, Practice and Politics; Anthropology and the Study of Social Movements." *Critique of Anthropology* 12(4):395–432.

Espinoza, Vicente. 1993. *Social Networks Among the Urban Poor. Inequality and Integration in a Latin American City.* Santiago: SUR: Documento de Trabajo 139, 42 pp.

——. 1994. "Tiempos cortos y largos en el movimiento poblacional." *Proposiciones* 24:246–250.

Etnofoor, Journal of Anthropology. 2004. University of Amsterdam, no. XVII (1/2): *Authenticity*. Münster: LIT Verlag 43–72.

Evers, Tilman. 1985. "Identity: The Hidden Side of New Social Movements in Latin America." in *New Social Movements and the State in Latin America*, edited by David Slater. Amsterdam: CEDLA.

Falk, Richard. 1987. "The Global Promise of Social Movements: Explorations at the Edge of Time." *Alternatives* XII:173–196.

Findji, Maria Teresa. 1992. "From Resistance to Social Movements: The Indigenous Authorities Movement in Colombia." in *The Making of Social Movements in Latin America: Identity, Strategy and Democracy*, edited by Arturo Escobar and Sonia Alvarez. Boulder/San Francisco/Oxford: Westview Press 112–133.

Foweraker, Joe. 1995. *Theorizing Social Movements.* London/Boulder, Colorado: Pluto Press.

Gal, Susan. 2002. "Between Speech and Silence." Pp. 213–221 in *The Anthropology of Politics—A Reader in Ethnography, Theory, and Critique*, edited by Joan Vincent. Malden/Oxford: Blackwell Publishers.

García Canclini, Nestor. 1995. *Cultural híbridas. Estrategias para entrar y salir de la modernidad.* Buenos Aires: Grijalbo.

——. 1995. *Consumidores y ciudadanos—Conflictos multiculturales de la globalización.* México D.F.: Grijalbo.

Geertz, Clifford. 1973. *The Interpretation of Cultures.* New York: Basic Books.

Giddens, Anthony. 1982. *Profiles and Critiques in Social Theory.* Berkeley and Los Angeles: University of California Press.

——. 1984. *The Constitution of Society: Outline of the Theory of Structuration.* Berkeley: University of California Press.

——. 1991. *Modernity and Self-Identity: Self and Society in Late Modern Age.* Cambridge, MA: Polity Press.

——. 1993. *Sociology*, 2nd edition. Cambridge, MA: Polity Press.

Gledhill, John. 1994 (2nd edition 2000). *Power and Its Disguises— Anthropological Perspectives on Politics.* London/ Ann Arbor, MI: Pluto Press.

——. 2005. "Some Histories Are More Possible than Others—Structural Power, Big Pictures and the Goal of Explanation in the Anthropology of Eric Wolf." *Critique of Anthropology* 25(1):37–57.

Gramsci, Antonio. 1971. *Selections from the Prison Notebooks.* Edited and translated by Hoare, Quintin and Geoffrey Nowell Smith. London: Lawrence and Wishart.

Habermas, Jürgen. 1989. *The Structural Transformation of the Public Sphere.* Cambridge, MA: Polity Press.

Hebdidge, Dick. 1979. *Subculture: The Meaning of Style.* London: Methuen.

Hellman, Judith Adler. 1990. "The Study of New Social Movements in Latin America and the Question of Autonomy." *LASA Forum* XXI(2):7–12.

——. 1995. "The Riddle of New Social Movements: Who They Are and What They Do." Pp. 165–183 in *Capital, Power, and Inequality in Latin America*, edited by Sandor Halebsky and Richard L. Harris. Boulder/ San Francisco/Oxford: Westview Press.

Hetherington, Kevin. 1998. *Expressions of Identity. Space, Performance, Politics.* London: Sage.

Hobsbawm, E. J. 1978. *Primitive Rebels.* Manchester: University of Manchester Press.

Hoebel, E. A. 1972. *Anthropology: The Study of Man.* New York: McGraw-Hill.

Jelín, Elizabeth. 1985. *Los nuevos movimientos sociales.* Buenos Aires: Biblioteca Política Argentina.

Jessop, Bob. 1996. "Interpretive Sociology and the Dialectic of Structure and Agency." *Theory, Culture and Society* 13(1):119–128.

Kärner, Hartmut. 1983. "Los movimientos socials: Revolución de lo cotidiano." *Nueva Sociedad* 64. 25–32.

Kuper, Adam. 1999. *Culture—The Anthropologists' Account.* Cambridge, MA: Harvard University Press.

Kothari, Rajni. 1984. "Party and State in Our Times: the Rise if Non-party Political Formations", in *Alternatives* IX, Pp. 541–564.

Lazar, Sian. 2006. El Alto, Ciudad Rebelde: Organisational Bases for Revolt. *Bulletin of Latin American Research* 25 183–199.

Leblanc, Lauraine. 1999. *Pretty in Punk: Girls' Gender Resistance in a Boys' Subculture*. New Brunswick, NJ: Rutgers University Press.

Lehmann, David. 1990. "Modernity and Loneliness: Popular Culture and the Informal Economy in Quito and Guadalajara." *The European Journal of Development Research* 2(1):89–107.

Lemaire, Ton. 1986. *De Indiaan in ons bewustzijn*. Baarn: Ambo.

Livesay, Fell. 1989. "Structuration Theory and the Unacknowledged Conditions of Action", in *Theory, Culture and Society* 6, Pp 263–292.

Lowe, Stuart. 1986. *Urban Social Movements: The City After Castells*, Houndmills Besingstoke, Hampshire, London: Macmillan.

Melucci, Alberto. 1996. *Challenging Codes: Collective Action in the Information Age*, Cambridge, Cambridge University press.

Mainwairing, Scott. 1987. "Urban Popular Movements, Identity and Democratization in Brazil." *Comparative Political Studies* 20(2) 131–159.

Mainwairing, Scott and E. Viola. 1984. "New Social Movements, Political Culture and Democracy." *Telos* 6:17–54.

McAdam, Doug, John D. McCarthy, and Mayer N. Zald. 1988. "Social Movements." in *Handbook of Sociology*, edited by N. J. Smelser. Newbury Park, CA: Sage 695–739.

Mc Adam, Dong, John D. Mc Carthy and Mayer N. Zald (eds) 1996. *Comparative Perspectives on Social Movements: Political Oppertunities, Mobilizing Structures, and Culutural Framings*. Cambridge, New York, Melbourne: Gambridge University Press.

Mc Adam, Dong. 1996. "Conceptual Problems, Current Problems, Future Directions", in (4), Pp. 141–151.

McCarthy, John D. 1996. "Constraints and Opportunities in Adopting, Adapting and Inventing", in (4), Pp. 141–151.

McDonald, Kevin. 2004. "Oneself as Another: From Social Movement to Experience Movement." *Current Sociology* 52(4):575–593.

Melucci, Alberto. 1980. "The New Social Movements: A Theoretical Approach." *Social Science Information* 9(2):199–226.

——. 1985. "The Symbolic Challenge of Contemporary Movements." *Social Research* 52(4):789–815.

Menéndez-Carrión, Amparo. 1986. *La conquista del voto en el Ecuador*. Quito: Corporación Editora Nacional.

Molineux, Maxine. 1985. "Mobilization without Emancipation? Women's Interests, State and Revolution in Nicaragua." *Feminist Studies* 11(2):227–254.

Moore, Barrington. 1987. *Injustice: The Social Bases of Obedience and Revolt*. White Plains, NY: M.E. Sharpe.

Nash, June. 1979. *We Eat the Mines and the Mines Eat Us*. New York: Columbia University Press.

——. ed. 2005. *Social Movements: An Anthropological Reader*, Malden, Oxford, Carlton: Blackwell Publishing.

Navarette Linares, Federico and Guilhem Oliver. 2000. *El héroe entre el mito y la historia*. México D.F.: UNAM.

Nuijten, Monique. 1992. "Local Organization as Organizing Practices— Rethinking Rural Institutions." Pp. 189–207 in *Battlefields of Knowledge—The Interlocking of Theory and Practice in Social Research and Development*, edited by Long, N and Long, A. London and New York: Routledge.

——. 1998. *In the Name of the Land; Organization, Transnationalism, and the Culture of the State in a Mexican Ejido*, Wageningen: WAU.

Offe, Claus. 1985. "New Social Movements: Challenging the Boundaries of Institutional Politics." *Social Research* 52(4) 817–868.

Ortner, Sherry. 2005. "Subjectivity and Cultural Critique." *Anthropological Theory* 5(1):31–52.

Oxhorn, Philip. 1991. "The Popular Sector Response to an Authoritarian Regime: Shantytown Organizations Since the Military Coup." *Latin American Perspectives* 18(1):66–91.

——. 1994. "Where Did All the Protesters Go? Popular Mobilization and the Transition to Democracy in Chile." *Latin American Perspectives* 21(3):32–48.

Paley, Julia. 2001. *Marketing Democracy—Power and Social Movements in Post-Dictatorial Chile*. Berkeley/Los Angeles/London: University of California Press.

Parker, Cristián. 1993. *Otra Lógica en América Latina—Religión popular y modernización capitalista*. Santiago: Fundo de Cultura Económica.

Perlman, Janice. 1976. *The Myth of Marginality: Urban Poverty and Politics in Rio de Janeiro*. Berkeley: University of California Press.

Piña, Carlos. 1987. " 'Lo popular': Notas sobre la identidad cultural de las clases subalternas. in *Espacio y poder—los pobladores*, edited by Jorge Chateau et al. Santiago de Chile: FLACSO 259–291.

Piven, Frances and Richard A. Cloward. 1977. *Poor People's Movements—Why They Succeed, How They Fail.* New York: Pantheon Books.

Popkin, Damuel. 1979. *The Rational Peasant: The Political Economy of Rural Society in Vietnam.* Berkeley: University of California Press.

Quintanilla, M. Soledad. 1996. "La historia local vista por sus protagonistas: un eje para comprender la organización comunitaria." *Proposiciones* 27:174–185.

Rodriguez, Ileana. 1996. *Women, Guerrillas and Love: Understanding War in Central America.* Minneapolis, MN: University of Minneapolis Press.

Rodríguez, Lilia. 1994. "Barrio Women: Between the Urban and the Feminist Movement." *Latin American Perspectives* 21(3):8–31.

Roodenburg, Herman. 2004. "Pierre Bourdieu—Issues of Embodiment and Authenticity." *Etnofoor* XVII (1/2): 215–226.

Rubin, Jeffrey W. 1998. "Ambiguity and Contradiction in a Radical Popular Movement." Pp. 141–164 in *Cultures of Politics, Politics of Cultures—Revisioning Latin American Social Movements,* edited by Sonia E. Alvarez, Evelina Dagnino, and Arturo Escobar. Boulder/Oxford: Westview Press.

Rudi, George. 1981. *The Crowd in History, 1930-1848,* London: Lawrence and Wishart (revised edition)

——. 2004. Meanings and Mobilization: A Cultural Politics Approach to Social Movements and States" *Latin Amenrican Research Review* 39(3):106–142.

Sall, Ebrima. 2004. "Social Movements in the Renegotiation of the Bases for Citizenship in West Africa." *Current Sociology* 52(4):595–614.

Salman, Ton. "Between Orthodoxy and Euphoria: Research Strategies on Social Movements: A Comparative Perspective." Pp. 99–161 in *Structures of Power, Movements of Resistance—An Introduction to the Theories of Urban Movements in Latin America,* edited by Willem Assies, Gerrit Burgwal, and Ton Salman. Amsterdam: CEDLA.

——. 1997. *The Diffident Movement—Disintegration, Ingenuity and Resistance of the Chilean Pobladores, 1973–1990.* Amsterdam: Aksant.

——. 1998. "La base social persistente. Nuevos movimientos sociales en América Latina: Cambio, resistencia y lentitud." *Proposiciones* 28:88–115.

——. 2000. "Politico-cultural Models and Collective Action Strategies—The Pobladores of Chile and Ecuador." Pp. 192–216 in *The Collective and the Public in Latin America,* edited by Luis Roniger and Tamar Herzog. Brighton/Portland: Sussex Academic Press.

——. 2002a. "Modelos políticos y organización barrial: Chile y Ecuador." *Proposiciones* 34:219–232.

——. 2002b. "De onschuld ontgroeid—Nieuwe en stedelijke organisaties en bewegingen in Latijns Amerika." Pp. 137–161 in *Voorheen de Derde Wereld—Ontwikkeling anders gedacht,* edited by Bas Arts, Paul Hebinck, and Ton van Naerssen. Amsterdam: Mets and Schilt.

——. (with Willem Assies and Marco Calderón). 2005. "Citizenship, Political Culture and State Transformation in Latin America." Pp. 3–26 in *Citizenship, Political Culture and State Reform in Latin America,* edited by Willem Assies, Marco Calderón, and Ton Salman. Amsterdam: Dutch University Press/Zamora: El Colegio de Michoacán.

——. 2006. "The jammed Democracy: Bolivia's Troubled Political Learning Process". *Bulletin of Latin American Research* 25(2):163–182.

Schild, Veronica. 1998. " 'New Subjects of Rights? Women's Movements and the Construction of Citizenship in the 'New Democracies.' " Pp. 93–117 in *Cultures of Politics, Politics of Cultures – Re-visioning Latin American Social Movements,* edited by Sonia E. Alvarez, Evelina Dagnino, and Arturo Escobar. Boulder/Oxford: Westview Press.

Schönwälder, Gerd. 2002. *Linking Civil Society and the State—Urban Popular Movements, the Left, and Local Government in Peru, 1980–1992.* University Park, PA: The Pennsylvania State University Press.

Sheth, D.L. 1983. "Grass-roots Stirrings and the Future of Politics", in *Alternatives* IX, Pp. 1–24.

Scott, James. 1976. *The Moral Economy of the Peasant: Rebellion and Subsistence in Southeast Asia.* New Haven, CT: Yale University Press.

——. 1985. *Weapons of the Weak: Every Forms of Peasant Resistance.* New Haven, CT: Yale University Press.

——. 1990. *Domination and the Arts of Resistance: Hidden Transcripts.* New Haven, CT: Yale University Press.

Seoane, José (comp.). 2003. *Movimientos sociales y conflicto en América Latina.* Buenos Aires: CLACSO.

Siegel, Janes T. 1997. *Fetish, Recognition, Revolution.* Princeton, NJ: Princeton University Press.

Sierra, María Teresa. 1997. "Esencialismo y autonomía: Paradojas de las reivindicaciones indígenas." *Alteridades* 7(14):131–143.

Smith, Michael Peter and Luis Eduardo Guarnizo, eds. 1998. *Transnationalism from Below.* New Brunswick, NJ: Transaction Publishers.

Starn, Orin. 1992. " 'I Dreamt of Foxes and Hawks'—Reflections on Peasant Protest, New Social Movements, and the *Rondas Campesinas* in Northern Peru." Pp. 89–111 in *The Making of Social Movements in Latin America: Identity, Strategy and Democracy*, edited by Arturo Escobar and Sonia Alvarez. Boulder: Westview Press.

Stephen, Lynn. 2002. *Zapata Lives! Histories and Cultural Politics in Southern Mexico*. Berkeley, Los Angeles, London: University of California Press.

Stryker, Sheldon, Timothy J. Owens, and Robert W. White, eds. 2000. *Self, Identity and Social Movements*. Minneapolis, MN: University of Minnesota Press.

Tarrow, Sidney. 1994. *Power in Movement. Social Movements, Collective Action and Politics*. Cambridge, UK: Cambridge University Press.

Taussig, Michael T. 1980. *The Devil and Commodity Fetishism in South America*. Chapel Hill, NC: University of North Carolina Press.

——. 1987. *Shamanism, Colonialism and the Wild Man: A Study in Terror and Healing*. Chicago: University of Chicago Press.

——. 1993. *Mimesis and Alterity: A Particular History of the Senses*. London/New York: Routledge Press.

Taylor, Lucy. 1998. *Citizenship, Participation and Democracy: Changing Dynamics in Chile and Argentina*. London: Macmillan.

Thompson, E. P. 1986. *The Making of the English Working Class*. London: Vintage Books.

Thompson, Stacy. 2004. *Punk Productions: Unfinished Business*. Albany, NY: State University of New York Press.

Touraine, Alain. 1981. *The Voice and the Eye*. Cambridge, UK: Cambridge University Press.

——. 1985. "An Introduction to the Study of Social Movements." *Social Research* 52(4): 747–789.

——. 1988. *Return of the Actor: Social Theory in Postindustrial Society*. Minneapolis, MN: University of Minneapolis Press.

Tripp, Aili Mari. 2004. "Women's Movements, Customary Law, and Land Rights in Africa: The Case of Uganda." *African Studies Quarterly* 7(4):1–19.

Turner, Christena L. 1995. *Japanese Workers in Protest. An Ethnography of Consciousness and Experience*. Berkeley: University of California Press.

Turner, Victor. 1994 (1957). *Schism and Continuity in an African Society*, Oxford: Berg.

Valdés, Teresa. 1986. *El movimiento poblacional: La recomposición de las solidaridades sociales*. Santiago: FLACSO, Documento de Trabajo.

Van Cott, Donna Lee Van. 2000. *The Friendly Liquidation of the Past: The Politics of Diversity in Latin America*. Pittsburgh: University of Pittsburgh Press.

——. 2005. *From Movements to Parties in Latin America: The Evolution of Ethnic Politics*. Cambridge, UK: Cambridge University Press.

Vélez Ibañez, Carlos. 1983. *Rituals of Marginality: Politics, Process, and Culture Change in Central Urban Mexico, 1969–1974*. Berkeley: University of California Press.

Walton, John. 1989. "Debt, Protest and the State in Latin America." Pp. 299–328 in *Power and Popular Protest: Latin American Social Movements*, edited by Susan Eckstein. Berkeley and Los Angeles: University of California Press.

Whisnant, David E. 1995. *Rascally Signs in Sacred Places— The Politics of Culture in Nicaragua*. Chapel Hill and London: The University of North Carolina Press.

Wolf, Eric. 1982. *Europe and the People without History*. Berkeley/Los Angeles/London: University of California Press.

Womach, John. 1999. *Rebellion in Chiapas: An Historical Reader*. New York: The New press.

Worsley, Peter M. 1957. *The Trumpet Shall Sound: A Study of "Cargo" Cults in Melanasia*, London: Macgibbon and Kee

Worsley, Peter. 1984. *The Three Worlds—Culture and World Development*, London: Weidenfeld and Nicolson.

Yashar, Deborah. 2005. *Contesting Citizenship in Latin America, the Rise of Indigenous Movements and the Postliberal Challenge*. Cambridge, UK: Cambridge University Press.

Zuñiga, Gerardo. 2000. "La dimension discursiva de las luchas étnicas. Acerca de un artículo de María Teresa Sierra." *Alteridades* 10(19):55–67.

CHAPTER 7

Historians and the Study of Protest[*]

BRIAN DILL AND RONALD AMINZADE

THE DISCIPLINE OF HISTORY

In reflecting on the distinctive way in which historians have approached the study of social movements and collective action, we call attention to a number of issues that have been addressed in the literature on history as a discipline. A distinction that has often been made between the disciplines of history and the social sciences concerns the general and the particular. Historians are purportedly more concerned with context-dependent generalizations, offering findings that are relevant only to the particular context they are studying and overly cautious in making inadequately contextualized generalizations based on evidence from a particular time and place. However, historians cannot avoid the use of general concepts, such as revolution or social movement; hence they necessarily generalize. Such concepts select certain instances as "facts" and make their descriptions more meaningful by suggesting causal analogies to phenomena in other times and places that may also be labeled revolutions or social movements. Nevertheless, the types of generalizations and levels of generality with which historians are typically comfortable are those that apply to a relatively limited number of cases delimited in time and space, rather than the decontextualized general laws to which social scientists sometimes aspire. As a discipline, historians are organized along the lines of time and space, and most historians focus their research on a particular place during a delimited period of time. Philip Abrams (1982:194) contrasts the historians' "rhetoric of close presentation (seeking to persuade in terms of a dense texture of detail)" with the sociologists' "rhetoric of perspective (seeking to persuade in terms of the elegant patterning of connections seen from a distance)."

In their efforts to offer context-dependent generalizations, historians rely on what Kai Erikson (1970) labels "professional reflexes." This refers to the distinctive set of working arrangements, vocabularies, and "standards of explanation" to which students are exposed during their professional socialization, and that are enforced by a variety of disciplinary gatekeepers, from journal editors to grant reviewers. Because historians typically work in a

[*] The authors would like to thank Charles Tilly, Thomas Wolfe, Bert Klandermans, and Conny Roggeband for comments on an earlier draft.

context of data scarcity rather than da ta abundance, their working arrangements are less concerned with sampling from a large population and more focused on close attention to matters of texture and detail. Erikson also observes that professional climates and reflexes involve different criteria for what constitutes a plausible explanation. Historians typically explain an outcome by telling a credible story about the sequence of events leading up to it or the motives that impelled it, providing a plausible and persuasive plot that has a sense of dramatic inevitability, rather than viewing an outcome as explained if it is connected to institutions and forces in the surrounding environment.[1] Historians typically see storytelling, or the use of narratives, as a central defining feature of their work, an integral part of writing history that makes possible close attention to actors and events. Narratives, then, are a key vehicle for addressing the relationship between the particular and the general.

Another distinction relates to the nature of the evidence that historians typically use. Historians usually rely on documentary evidence available in archives, residues of the past that are filtered down to the present, typically through the operation of large-scale organizations, such as churches and states (Tilly 1970:434–466). Unlike social scientists, most historians do not go out and generate their own data, but rely on already existing data. Although social scientists sometimes adopt a critical approach to their sources, historian's reliance on archival sources has meant treating sources as suspect and paying greater attention than is often the case among social scientists to questions concerning the social construction of knowledge, that is, to why, how, and under what conditions documents were created and their authenticity. A reliance on archival sources requires interpretation, that is, the processing and evaluation of data by the individual researcher, whose reconstruction of the past is inevitably shaped by her language, culture, values, and historical location.

A final distinction that observers have made between the disciplines of history and the social sciences concerns temporal scopes. The focus of social scientists on the present often means a narrow concern with short-term causes and short-term consequences. Historians' focus on the past provides an opportunity to study not just short-term sequences but also the *longue durée* and long-term processes of change, such as industrialization, urbanization, or demographic transitions. Many historians do not seize this opportunity and most historical research tends to focus on the in-depth study of relatively short periods of time, but an attentiveness to long-term processes of change and to the temporal boundaries demarcating different historical periods can help to ascertain the scope conditions, or boundaries, of theoretical generalizations and to identify key turning points in processes of change.

Are these features simply disciplinary stereotypes or are they actually reflected in the work that historians do? The extent to which historians of social movements actually do develop context-dependent generalizations, highlight temporal rather than lateral connections, take long-term rather than short-term approaches to the study of social protest, utilize the connotative vocabulary of the narrative, and rely on archival data is an empirical question that we address in our subsequent analysis of historian's research on social movements. Our concern is not with whether historical and the social scientific studies of movement *should* merge as a common endeavor or the benefits that each side might derive from such a marriage, but the actual disciplinary practices of historians who study social movements.

---

[1] Although the so-called "historic turn" in the social sciences (McDonald 1996) and the rise of an event-centered historical sociology have blurred this distinction, these disciplinary reflexes still appear to be dominant, at least in the major journals of the disciplines. In recent years, social scientists have rediscovered narrative and argued for the importance of analytic narrative in social science explanations (Abbott 1990; Abrams 1982; Adams, Clemens, and Orloff 2005; Aminzade 1992; Griffin 1993; Hart 1992; Kiser 1996; Stryker 1996).

HISTORICAL METHODS

Because historians work with such a wide variety of archival and nonarchival sources-including physical remains, personal documents, organizational records, and oral accounts, and adopt different approaches to the use of these sources, it is difficult to specify a single historical method. Yet three key features of the historians' approach to data, including close attention to detail and context, a critical interrogation of sources and of the institutional processes that produced them, and the use of narrative to capture structure and agency as mutually constituted over time have important theoretical implications. First, close attention to detail and context can serve as an antidote to broad generalizations that fail to adequately specify the temporal and spatial scope conditions of claims and can foster more context-dependent generalizations, greater attentiveness to connections among events, and concern for the micro-dynamics of mobilization and claims-making. Close attention to details and context can lead to fortuitous and unexpected discoveries, including the discovery of key silences in existing accounts. Second, the skeptical and judicious questioning of sources via internal and external criticism to assess the authenticity and credibility of evidence need not lead to a positivist effort to find "the true account." The key question may not be whether or not an account is true, for example, whether it provides an accurate report of the size of crowds, but rather how and why this account was produced. Situating historical sources in the social location of the observer or the social conventions of the organization can lead to the posing of new questions about "biased" sources to reveal how and why actors created the data and what it tells us about their interests and values and about the social contexts of power and inequality in which accounts have been produced. Finally, the use of narrative can help prevent the pitfall of structuralist approaches to social protest in which agency disappears and actors simply respond to the overpowering constraints of a political opportunity structure or capitalist class structure. It can also mitigate against the static use of before and after snapshots and inferences about change based on their comparison in favor of more event-centered accounts which take time seriously, trace the contingent and often path-dependent character of movement trajectories, and identify turning points in movement histories.

Some of the benefits of adopting an historical approach to the study of social movements stem not from the particular methodological approach of the historian but from the nature of social movements. The latter have an interest in minimizing public knowledge of their internal divisions and disputes and maintaining an appearance of unity and solidarity to the outside world. Thus the divisions and conflicts that may play a key role in strategic decision-making or framing processes may become available only long after the demise of the movement or it protagonists, as memoirs, letters, and other documents that record divisions and conflicts among those struggling for change become available for scholarly analysis.

THE CONTRIBUTION OF HISTORIANS
TO THE STUDY OF SOCIAL MOVEMENTS

Social scientists are typically skeptical about the ability of historians to contribute to the conceptual and theoretical developments in the social sciences. For example, Hamilton and Walton (1988) argue that the actual disciplinary practices of historians involve a focus on sources rather than theories or methods. "Among historians," they write (1988:184), "data collection rests on finding and mastering a body of primary sources about a clearly delineated topic. . . . competition to be an expert in an area promotes ever more refined historical specializations, more exhaustive treatments of increasingly narrow topics, and a revisionist orientation based on ever closer readings of primary sources." They contrast this with the work of sociologists, for whom "the preference is always for breadth and not for depth of coverage, because it is the scope of coverage that tests the generality of theories . . ." (1988:184–185). The problem with this analysis, however, is that it presumes a relative unity of the discipline of history when in fact all disciplines, including history, contain numerous fields, some of which have more in common with fields in neighboring disciplines than with each other. "The notion of disciplinary unity," argues Julie Thompson Klein (1993:191), "is triply false: minimizing or denying differences that exist across the plurality of specialties grouped loosely under a single disciplinary label, undervaluing connections across specialties of separate disciplines, and discounting the frequency and impact of cross-disciplinary influences."

Historians in certain areas of the discipline, such as demographic and economic history, adopt analytic rhetorics and readily cross disciplinary boundaries to engage in theoretical and methodological dialogues with other disciplines (Levine 2001; Ruggles 1987). Most historians, however, limit their generalizations to limited time and place contexts rather than generalize about structures and processes regardless of time and place. The discipline of history is organized around such temporal and spatial boundaries. In the study of social protest, as we argue below, the main contribution of historians has not been to develop new theories or concepts or even to assess critically the core concepts of social movement theories. The central contribution has been to develop context dependent analyses that provide innovative interpretive accounts of events, augment the historical record by extending the temporal or spatial boundaries of particular movements, and correct existing accounts by challenging official or established views of events.

A number of historians, most of whom define themselves as "social historians" and
m were part of the social movements of the 1960s and 1970s, have a produced
f studies on the history of a variety of movements, from the civil rights to the
labor movements to peasant rebellions. Some of these studies have directed our
he existence of "free social spaces" within which the microdynamics of mobi-
place (Evans 1986) and shed light on early debates among scholars about
ind solidarity theories (Hobsbawm 1969; Rude 1964). Historians have also
erly structuralist misreadings of peasant protest by highlighting the agency of
s who had been presumed to be at the mercy of large-scale structural forces over
iad little control (Isaacman 1993). In addition, they have analyzed the cultural
of working-class collective action and the moral codes that shaped protests
1963) and called attention to the role of popular memory and oral traditions in
t. Historical research has carefully documented the sources of nineteenth century European artisans' revolutionary collective actions and the roots of their grievances in transformations of capitalist production (Johnson 1975; Jones 1983).

Explanations of social change must be based on accurate understandings of how events unfold over time, which means that in order to answer the question of why, and develop explanations of sequences of events, scholars must first answer the question of how. Genuinely historical work in the social sciences, notes Charles Tilly (1984:79), must acknowledge that "the existing record of past structures and processes is problematic, requiring systematic investigation in its own right instead of lending itself immediately to social-scientific synthesis." As our subsequent discussion of the civil rights movement reveals, historian's research on social movements has contributed to this task of carefully interrogating the historical record in at least three ways: by reinterpreting protest events, by expanding our knowledge of movements and their temporal and spatial scope, and by correcting problematic claims and assumptions. This work of interpreting, expanding, and correcting existing accounts may engender new explanatory challenges that can provide the basis for conceptual and theoretical revisions and innovations. For example, by reinterpreting, expanding, and correcting the historical record and clarifying the concrete sociocultural context in which movements unfold, historical research can inform current theorizing based on contemporary contentious politics by questioning taken-for-granted assumptions about the existence of liberal-democracy, secular politics, instrumental rational action, modern temporal orientations, and universal literacy. This may prompt important questions concerning various meanings of opportunity and threat; alternative definitions and valuations of resources; the emotional dynamics of protest; conceptions of time as something other than a scarce resource; and the use of diverse means of communication, including music, and dance, and oral traditions, to promote collective identity and solidarity. These are opportunities for conceptual and theoretical progress that arise from the study of history, but whether historians or nonhistorians take advantage of these opportunities is an empirical question.

In recent years there has been a lively debate among social scientists concerning the dominant paradigms informing social movement research and the concepts derived from these approaches (e.g., see Goodwin and Jasper 2004). Resource mobilization has focused on the organizational basis of mobilization while political process theory highlights the sociopolitical contexts shaping movements, whereas cultural and cognitive theories have emphasized the creation of collective identities and framing of goals. Each tradition has produced a variety of concepts that have generated research and debate, including mobilization, professionalization, political opportunity structures, repertoires, cycles of protest, framing, and collective identity. Has this lively debate and the concepts and theories implicated in it affected how historians study social movements? Some scholars have claimed that historical research on social movements "begins by questioning its core concepts" (Clemens and Hughes 2002). This statement is prescriptive, directed toward a social science audience, rather than descriptive, illustrating the practice of historians. To what extent, then, do historians who research social movements and collective action address the core concepts of social movement theory and question their applicability to past protest? Which, if any, of the core concepts do historians employ in their analyses? How self-conscious are they in applying the concepts and theories of social movement scholars to the particular cases they study? Have they used the study of past protest to challenge core concepts and dominant theories? Does their work address long-term processes of change? Are the professional reflexes described above evident in the work of historians of social and political protest or have they disappeared as historians challenge disciplinary boundaries and professional reflexes? These are the questions we address in this chapter.

HISTORICAL STUDIES OF SOCIAL MOVEMENTS AND COLLECTIVE ACTION

To understand how historians have studied the phenomena of social movements and collective action, we sampled a wide range of articles published by historians on the subject. Given the enormous body of historical literature that has investigated innumerable examples of social protest in different times and places, a comprehensive review of all the books and articles published on the subject is not possible in a single book chapter. We therefore opted for a preliminary analysis of a limited number of publications that would enable us to make some tentative observations about the way in which historians approach the study of social protest.

In selecting journal articles, we used a sampling frame that is both practical and representative of the work that has been done by historians.

Initially, we thought to limit our investigation spatially, temporally, or thematically. Upon further consideration, however, we found that each approach was untenable. Limiting the investigation to social movements and collective action in North America or Western Europe, for example, may tell us little about how historians have studied these phenomena in the global South. Similarly, an examination of only those movements occurring in the twentieth century may not allow us to speak to the challenges, in terms of data and methods, facing historians concerned with contentious politics in previous eras. Finally, the body of literature on specific types of movements, such as the labor movement, women's movement, or peasant movements, is too large to allow a comprehensive review. Limiting our purview to prominent episodes or examples of contentious action—for example, the French Revolution, the American civil rights movement—would also suffer from being unwieldy and unrepresentative. Historians have produced an enormous amount of material on most well-known movements, thus making it impossible to cover all that has been written about even one. Furthermore, the extensive discussion and debate concerning the most renowned movements suggests that researchers investigating them have had the luxury of employing very different data and methods than their colleagues studying less well researched movements.

In an effort to understand how contemporary historians have approached the study of social movements, we decided to sample journal publications temporally, spatially, and thematically. Temporally, our sample contains journal articles published over a 31-year period (1970–2000). Spatially, we have chosen to include in our investigation the study of social movements occurring around the world. In an effort to capture the richness and diversity of social movement activity, our sample includes ten articles for each of the following five regions: North America, Europe, Latin America, Africa, and Asia. This broad geographic scope has allowed us not only to investigate scholarly work concerned with less prominent movements, but also to understand whether and to what extent scholars of movements in the global South utilize concepts similar to and/or different from those created and used to explain social movement activity in North America and Western Europe. Finally, we have sought to increase the breadth of our sample by including articles with a particular thematic focus: women's movements. Specifically, our sample integrates ten articles about women's movements that have occurred across different geographical regions. We have sampled a minimum of three journals for historical research on North America, Europe, Latin America, Africa, Asia, and women's movements. In sum, we have examined a total of 60 articles from 20 journals over a 31-year period.[2]

There are advantages and disadvantages associated with each sampling frame we could have employed. As already noted, we have sought to strike a balance between sampling in a manner that is not only representative of historical work on social movements and collective action, but also realistic in terms of analysis. The chief merits of the approach we have taken, then, are that it captures the breadth of historical research on contentious episodes and does so in a manner that is practical. But we recognize the limitations of our sample as well, the

---

[2] For a complete list of the 60 journal articles in our sample, see the references cited in the reference list that are identified by an asterisk. The 20 journals from which we selected these articles were: *Past and Present, Journal of African History, Canadian Journal of African Studies, Modern Asian Studies, Modern China, Journal of Contemporary History, Journal of Modern History, Russian Review, Journal of Latin American Studies, Journal of Latin American History, Journal of American History, Journal of Southern History, Radical History Review, Journal of Negro History, Journal of British Studies, International Journal of African Historical Studies, African Studies Review, New England Quarterly, American Historical Review,* and *Journal of Palestinian Studies.*

most important of which relates to Erikson's (1970) point about "professional reflexes." History is often viewed as a discipline that is more oriented toward books than articles. By sampling articles, we run the risk of drawing conclusions about the practice of history that are more appropriately applied to only a certain aspect of the discipline. By analyzing a form of published work that is, by design, short, concentrated, and succinct, we may come away with a distorted or limited view. Scholars clearly have much more freedom in a book. Rather than limit the claims they make in an effort to produce a minimally publishable unit, such as an article for a peer-reviewed journal, authors of books have the latitude to approach the events under investigation from multiple perspectives. Temporal scopes that are quite narrow in a 50-page journal article might become much broader in a 300-page book. These caveats notwithstanding, we believe that our sample is sufficient to allow us to make robust claims about the ways in which historians approach the study of social movements and collective action.

CENTRAL ISSUES AND QUESTIONS WITHIN THE DISCIPLINE OF HISTORY

This section addresses what we have identified as four central issues that relate to historians' study of social movements and collective action: (1) the extent to which historians either limit the claims they make to the particular context they are studying or seek to generalize to other times and places; (2) the temporal scope that informs historical studies; (3) the extent to which the core concepts that have informed social science research are employed as tools in the historical study of social movements and collective action; and (4) the nature of the evidence used by historians and the extent to which this places limitations on their analyses.

To illustrate each of these four issues, we provide numerous examples from the articles sampled for this chapter. As noted in the preceding text, these articles differ significantly from one another in terms of their temporal, spatial, and/or thematic focus. Thus, to reinforce our argument, we take the additional step of demonstrating our main points by referring to a single, well-known social movement: the American civil rights movement. In the interest of clarity, we present the examples concerning this movement in boxes separated from the main text. The first of these boxes (see Box 7.1) presents a conventional summary of the civil rights movement.

Context-Dependent Generalizations

The historical study of social movements and collective action is replete with general concepts. Strikes, riots, peasant insurrections, labor movements, and rebellions defy the spatial and temporal boundaries that otherwise circumscribe particularistic historical studies. Historians have chronicled "labor strikes," for example, among both Brazilian porters in the mid-nineteenth century (Reis 1997) and West African railway workers just after World War II (Cooper 1996); similarly, they have examined "riots" directed toward suburban railways in Brazil in the mid-1970s (Moises and Martinez-Alier 1980) and Muslims in Sri Lanka a half century earlier (Kannangra 1984). But for a few exceptions, concern with the general ends at the conceptual level; historians tend to employ general concepts only insofar as they facilitate the organization and construction of narratives that are context specific. As we will discuss in a later section of this chapter, these concepts are neither problematized nor operationalized; reference is rarely, if ever, made to the concept's usage in the sociological literature or by other analysts of social movements and collective action.

Box 7.1.   The Conventional View of the American Civil Rights Movement

The American civil rights movement generally refers to events that took place in the Southern United States over the course of 14 tumultuous years: 19551968. During this period, numerous individuals and organizations undertook a wide range of activities in an effort to eliminate public and private discrimination against African Americans. Conventional wisdom holds that the civil rights movement began on December 1, 1955, when a 42-year-old African American woman named Rosa Parks boarded a city bus in Montgomery, Alabama. She refused to relinquish her seat to a white passenger as required by local ordinance and was subsequently arrested, tried, and convicted of disorderly conduct. In response, African American leaders, most notably Dr. Martin Luther King, Jr., gathered and organized what is commonly referred to as the Montgomery Bus Boycott. For 381 days, African American residents of Montgomery refused to ride the public bus, thereby pressuring local authorities to overturn the ordinance segregating whites and African Americans on public buses.

   The civil rights movement that unfolded over the next decade and a half was punctuated by a series of contentious actions that have been the focus of voluminous historical writings. Thoroughly researched and discussed events include, but are certainly not limited to: the sit-ins staged by four African American college students at a segregated lunch counter Greensboro, North Carolina in 1960; the March on Washington in 1963, where Dr. Martin Luther King delivered his famous "I have a dream" speech; and the 1964 "Freedom Summer," which involved more than one hundred white, northern college students traveling to Mississippi in order to register voters and to teach in "Freedom Schools." The vast majority of these events took place in a handful of Southern states commonly referred to as the "Deep South."

   The final years of the civil rights movement witnessed both legislative accomplishments and personal tragedy. In terms of the former, the federal government passed three acts that meant to insure equality and opportunity for all Americans: the Civil Rights act of 1964 banned discrimination in employment practices and public accommodations; the Voting Rights Act of 1965 restored voting rights to African Americans; and the Civil Rights Act of 1968 prohibited discrimination in the sale or rental of housing. In terms of the latter, the movement's iconic figure, Dr. Martin Luther King, Jr., was assassinated in Memphis, Tennessee on April 4, 1968.

   The articles sampled for this chapter corroborate the view that historians tend to offer findings that are relevant only to the particular context they are studying and rarely make claims that could be readily applied to other times and places. Painting with a broad brush, we find that historical analyses of social movements and collective action exhibit concern with the particular in one of three ways. First, historians characterize their task as **interpretative**; that is, they attempt to establish not only the "actuality" of an event by constructing a textual account of it, but also its meaning by providing a detailed description of its causes, scope, and outcomes, as well as of the parties involved, their motives, and their accomplishments (cf. McDonald 1996). A second approach is **expansive**. Scholars working in this vein seek to augment the historical record with respect to established events, legitimating their particular contribution to the literature by showing how it fills a gap or omission. This typically takes the form of extending the spatial or temporal boundaries of a documented social movement, revolution, and so forth. Third, historians of social movements and collective action portray their narrative accounts of particular events as **corrective**. This often involves providing an interpretation that challenges the official or established view of an event. For example, corrective narratives might illuminate resistance where it was thought to be absent, argue that non-elite protagonists had well understood and legitimate grievances, or situate a social movement in a broader context.

Before turning to our data to illustrate each of these context-specific approaches to the historical study of social movements and collective action, we should note that the division between **interpretive, expansive**, and **corrective** is neither rigid nor claimed by the authors themselves, but rather is flexible and intended for analytic purposes only. There is considerable overlap among these three aspects. Moreover, whereas some of the articles sampled for this chapter fall into more than one category, others do not fit neatly into any specific one.

HISTORY AS AN INTERPRETIVE EXERCISE.   Historiography, that is, "the craft of writing history and/or the yield of such writing considered in its rhetorical aspect" (Hexter 1971:15), is first and foremost an **interpretative** exercise. This is the case regardless of whether the emphasis is on elites and institutionalized politics, as prevailed in earlier historical writing, or on the "history from below" that gained momentum during the 1960s and 1970s. Historical accounts of social movements and collective action are no exception. The number of contentious actions that might qualify as significant historical events is myriad. To complicate matters, these "events" have no innate boundaries; "observers draw lines around them for their own analytic convenience" (Tilly 1995:1601). The task of the historian, then, is to discern which events warrant exposition, to categorize them by reference to general concepts, and to interpret them in a manner that comports with the requirements of narrative accounts. For some, this consists of providing a sequential account of an event that is sensitive to the context-specific processes that led to its occurrence and makes a case for its broader significance: "What follows is a modest attempt to interpret the event in terms of these interacting processes and thereby to indicate some of the illuminating contexts in which the tense story of the Cape Town police strike can be told and its significance appreciated" (Nasson 1992:302). Other historical articles surveyed for this chapter, however, take a different approach. They interpret contentious actions by delineating the parties involved, describing their motives, highlighting their accomplishments, and noting their context-specific significance. In her analysis of the Russian peasant movement that emerged in the first decade of the twentieth century, Perrie (1972) provides an example of this mode of interpretation:

> The disastrous course of the war in the Far East precipitated a revolutionary situation in which the Russian peasantry was to play a major rle. This paper will attempt to assess that rle in terms of the social composition of the participants in the peasant movement, and the extent to which they were influence by the revolutionary forces in the towns. (p. 123)

It should be noted that the articles we have categorized as "interpretive" do more than simply document an event and describe its protagonists; they typically aim to lay out the meaning of the event under investigation—a meaning that is often counterintuitive—particularly in terms of how it affected the context in which it occurred. Charkrabartry's (1981) analysis of labor riots in Bengal is a good example of an interpretive article:

> The events that caused such a sudden reversal of official attitude in 1895 are the subject of this essay. They took the form of a series of riots and disturbances that broke out unexpectedly among the jute mill operatives of Bengal between the years 1894 and 1897. Interestingly, most of these riots turned around religious and community sentiments and not around purely economic issues. (p. 141)

In sum, interpretation is central to the entire enterprise of historical work. That is, rather than view history as either the "actual" or the "recorded" past, history, as an intellectual endeavor, should be understood as the active process of creating a "written" past (McDonald 1996). This requires, first and foremost, interpretation of the documents and other materials that comprise the "recorded" past. As Gareth Stedman Jones (1976:296) notes:

> [T]he historian investigates or reconstructs not the past, but the residues of the past which have survived into the present. [. . .] The historian, in other words, constructs historical problems on the basis of an argued case for their relevance to historical analysis, and then, through the critical use of extant residues (or even a search for new ones), attempts to provide a solution to them.

Given the diversity of "actual" events, "recorded" materials, and underlying research questions, the interpretive aspect of historiography manifests itself in many ways. In this subsection of the chapter, we have provided a few examples of how historical work on social movements and collective action is both **interpretive** and context specific (see Box 7.2). Rather than simply catalog or describe contentious events that occurred in the past, historians of social movements seek to make sense of these events, to imbue them with meaning, to note their context-specific significance.

Box 7.2.   Interpreting the Events of the Civil Rights Movement

Many of the myriad events that are collectively referred to as the American civil rights movement attracted scholarly attention because of their dramatic qualities. The Greensboro sit-ins of 1960, for example, demonstrated the injustice of segregation in a spectacular way, inspiring similar actions in dozens of cities in adjacent states. Likewise, the 1963 March on Washington raised public awareness of the movement and its goals by bringing hundreds of thousands of demonstrators to the streets. But events can have multiple interpretations and thereby speak to different aspects of complex movements. Whereas the Greensboro sit-ins reveal the power of audacious and novel tactics, they also highlight the importance of preexisting social structures to the initiation and spread of collective action (Morris 1981). And while one can reasonably view the March on Washington as an indicator of the strength of the civil rights movement and a harbinger of legislative gains, historian Scott Sandage (1993) **interprets** the event somewhat differently: as one of two key occasions that African Americans consciously and strategically used the Lincoln Memorial to "link the black political agenda to the regnant cultural nationalism of the era" (1996:159). The first event, he argues, was in 1939 when a Black, female contralto, named Marian Anderson, sang "My country 'tis of thee" at the Memorial, after having been denied the opportunity to do so at other venues; the second event was the March on Washington. Rather than **interpret** these two rallies as straightforward organic expressions of African-American solidarity, Sandage (1993:159) takes the position that civil rights leaders deliberately chose the venue and "a compelling universe of national symbols" in an effort to frame their goals in a way that resonated with a broader nationalist sentiment. Specifically, Sandage claims that:

> This essay argues that African Americans' struggles to hold a series of rallies at the Lincoln Memorial between 1939 and 1963 constituted a tactical learning experience that contributed to the civil rights movement's strategies of nonviolent action. Black

> protestors refined a politics of memory at the Lincoln Memorial. . . . Blacks strategi-
> cally appropriated Lincoln's memory and monument as political weapons, in the
> process layering and changing the public meanings of the hero and the shrine."
> (Sandage, 1993:136)

Through the **interpretive** exercise of "writing" history, Sandage gives these events meaning that they do not possess as "actual" occurrences in time or as basic components of
"recorded" history. Moreover, his analysis is very context-specific insofar as it provides an
interpretation of particular aspect of a specific social movement; the author does not seek
to apply his findings to other movements or even other events within the American civil
rights movement.

HISTORY AS EXPANSIVE.   While documentation and interpretation are central to all historical work, many historians seek specifically to expand our knowledge or understanding of
recognized events. The stated purpose of narratives that we characterize as **expansive** is to
supplement the historical record with respect to particular episodes of contentious action. The
events themselves are not in question; however, the conventional understanding of them may
be too narrow and thus subject to reexamination. There are three distinct approaches to this.

    First, historians may seek to extend the generally accepted **spatial boundaries** of a
known social movement, revolution, series of riots, and so forth (see Box 7.3). That is, the
aim is to show that the events under investigation occurred in locales that the dominant dis-

---

Box 7.3.   Expanding the Spatial Boundaries of the Civil Rights Movement

With the exception of events that occurred in the nation's capital, most notably the 1963
March on Washington, the historical record of the American civil rights movement has
tended to highlight the defining episodes that took place in the Deep South at the expense
of those that happened in other parts of the country. And yet some historians have consciously sought to challenge this conventional understanding of the **spatial boundaries** of
the movement.

    In his analysis of racial protest in Seattle, for example, Taylor (1995) provides an alter-
native to a literature that he believes has been geographically too broad or too narrow in
its focus. In contrast to studies that have emphasized either high-profile national leaders
and organizations or local organizations in the South, he argues that:

> The movement should be viewed as a national transformation, an energizing of small
> and large African American communities throughout the country, inspired by national
> goals and leadership, but which pursued distinctly local agendas. For these people the
> Movement was not simply a television report of fire hoses and police dogs set on
> demonstrators in distant Birmingham. It was instead the campaign to end job bias or
> school segregation in the local communities. . . . (p. 1)

Goldberg's (1983) analysis of the civil rights activities in San Antonio, Texas is also
emblematic of such efforts to contribute to the literature by showing how the movement
had a broader geographic presence than commonly acknowledged:

> Despite the plethora of material the movement remains only partially explored.
> Television cameras and scholarly studies have focused selectively upon the civil rights

> struggle in the Deep South where segregation was most vigorously defended and violence was an all-too-frequently-chosen instrument of resistance. But, what occurred in the towns and cities outside the Deep South? [. . .] A case study of the San Antonio integration effort provides an important opportunity to investigate a neglected facet of the civil rights movement in its least publicized environment. (pp. 349–350)
>
> By expanding the spatial boundaries of the civil rights movement, Goldberg is able to provide a more nuanced understanding the transformations it occasioned and the process through which they unfolded. While much of the action that took place in the Deep South is marked by punctuated contentious episodes, Goldberg claims that several key factors in San Antonio created a situation whereby the process of integration was much less radical than elsewhere: a small black population, a sizable Mexican American population, and "Especially important in explaining the absence of racial tension and rigidity were the actions of the city government" (p. 353). In short, the article shows that the local government's acceptance of the basic tenets of civil rights, as well as their capacity and desire to proceed slowly, resulted in a protracted but peaceful process of racial integration.

course has overlooked. Instances of efforts to expand our **spatial understandings** of a social movement abound. For example, Edelman (1985:260) focuses on a specific part of the Ukraine as a site of contentious action in order to address what he views as a critical gap in the literature concerning the peasant revolts of 1905. He argues that, in spite of the high level of discontent that manifest itself in three provinces on the west bank of the Dnieper River, scholars have tended to direct their attention to only those regions where the majority of contentious episodes occurred: "In short, the previous scholarly focus on central Russia should be modified to include the right bank Ukraine as a significant area of the peasant movement during the first Russian Revolution." Welch (1995:162) similarly expands the generally accepted spatial boundaries of a well-known social movement in Brazil, arguing that while there is widespread agreement in the historical literature concerning the role that rural labor militancy played in stimulating agrarian elites to support the overthrow of the president, "the literature suffers from regional imbalances." Whereas most studies emphasize events in the northeast, this article aims to highlight the activities of a state in the center South.

Second, in a similar vein historians may challenge the more or less arbitrary **periodization** of contentious action. While all historians divide the past and/or the objects of study into chronological periods, those taking an expansive approach to the study of social movements and collective action seek to extend the **temporal boundaries** of the particular movement or event under investigation (see Box 7.4). This often involves either shifting one's analytical gaze to the years or decades immediately prior to the established onset of movement activity or focusing on the movement's long-term effects.

An excellent example of extending the conventional time frame so as to include the relevant actions that occurred both before and after the seminal event is Monson's (1998) investigation of the "Maji Maji" rebellion in colonial Tanganyika. She argues that, in contrast to the accepted nationalist interpretation of this well-known peasant rebellion, which characterizes it as temporally limited and directed exclusively against colonial authorities, "Maji Maji represents a larger complex of political relationships, tensions and grievances that spanned the late precolonial and early colonial periods" (Monson 1998:96). That is, rather than see "Maji Maji" as encompassing only an uprising against German colonial rulers from 1905 to 1907, it is better understood as a

---

Box 7.4.   Expanding the Temporal Boundaries of the Civil Rights Movement

As noted in Box 7.1, the conventional understanding of the American civil rights movement is that it unfolded over the course of fourteen tumultuous years: 1955–1968. But it hardly seems controversial to suggest that the struggle for racial equality did not begin and end with the spectacular acts of resistance and violence, most notably the arrest of Rosa Parks and the assassination of Dr. Martin Luther King, Jr., that often serve to bookend the movement. Just as the years leading up to 1955 arguably helped to prepare the ground for the more visible episodes of contentious action that we associate with the civil rights movement, so have the decades since 1968 witnessed ongoing efforts to bring about equality and justice for all Americans.

An example of extending a movement's **temporal boundaries** forward includes Korstad and Lichtenstein's (1988) questioning of the origins of the civil rights era:

> Most historians would agree that the modern civil rights movement did not begin with the Supreme Court's decision in *Brown v. Board of Education.* Yet all too often the movement's history has been written as if events before the mid-1950s constituted a kind of prehistory, important only insofar as they laid the legal and political foundation for the spectacular advances that came later. . . . But such a periodization profoundly underestimates the tempo and misjudges the social dynamic of the freedom struggle. (p. 786)

To counter what they view as a rather narrow periodization, Korstad and Lichtenstein (1988:788) argue that to understand the true origins of the civil rights movement, one must examine the involvement or incorporation of blacks into labor unions in the 1940s: "The essay explores two examples of the workplace-oriented civil rights militancy that arose in the 1940s – one in the South and one in the North." The authors show how union activity not only catalyzed black political and social consciousness in the 1940s, but also brought about significant gains for black workers. They also show how the anticommunist sentiment and the mechanization of production in the 1950s resulted in the decline of the movement, leading to a lull in black activism and social and political gains that would not be reversed until the emergence of well-documented activism of the 1960s.

Clearly other **temporal** dimensions of the civil rights movement remain worthy of investigation, and its prominence in American history begs the question as to the long-term significance of black activism in the 1960s. Noting a gap in the historical literature, Minchin (1999:809) stresses the importance of examining the enduring effects of the civil rights movement: "Scholars have concentrated primarily on protest efforts, especially on organizations and leaders during the 'heroic period' of activism between 1955 and 1965, and less attention has been focused on economic aspects of the movement and its effect on southern workers." To this end, the author considers the effects that the passage of the Civil Rights Act of 1964 had upon the Southern textile industry in subsequent years.

---

protracted struggle catalyzed by land pressure and intertribal conflicts that extended over decades. While the article seeks to expand the boundaries of what is referred to as "Maji Maji," it maintains the importance of the actual rebellion itself, noting that it was a consequence of alliances, grievances, and environmental changes that were long in the making.

Third, historians have approached the study of social movements in a way that expands the roster of relevant actors. That is, they extend the **participatory boundaries** (see Box 7.5). Researchers have found, for example, that conventional accounts of a wide range of contentious

Box 7.5.   Expanding the Participatory Boundaries of the Civil Rights Movement

Countless individuals and organizations were involved in the American civil rights movement. And yet the historical record has, by emphasizing the achievements of a few notable examples, tended to overlook the actions of the many. In terms of individual participants, the spotlight has long been dominated by male leaders of the movement. With the exception of Rosa Parks, those most closely associated with the national struggle for racial equality are all men: Dr. Martin Luther King, Jr., Malcolm X, Robert Williams, Stokely Carmichael, and Medgar Evers, to name but a few. In terms of organizational actors, historical narratives have taken a similarly narrow view, emphasizing the role played by national institutions that were formed and led by African-Americans but calling much less attention to those of sympathetic whites.

Recently, however, historians of the civil rights movement have sought to expand the roster of relevant **participants**. Gyant (1996), for example, endeavors to correct what is arguably the most glaring omission in the historical record of individual contributors to the movement, namely, the critical role played by African American women. She notes that:

> When one looks at the history of the civil rights movement, one would think that there were only a few women involved—Rosa Parks, Fannie Lou Hamer, Daisy Bates, Ella Baker. However, recent research shows that there was a large contingent of women who participated in the civil rights movement. . . . This essay discusses some of the characteristics of women who participated in the movement as well as their motivation, leadership roles, and attitudes toward traditional men's roles. (p. 630)

Historians have also begun to investigate those organizations that were involved in the civil rights movement, but, thus far, have received limited academic or popular attention. In contrast to the welter of studies concerned with the actions and achievements of pivotal African-American organizations such as the Southern Christian Leadership Conference (SCLC), the Student Nonviolent Coordinating Committee (SNCC), and the National Association for the Advancement of Colored People (NAACP), much less has been published about white (or predominantly white) organizations that also contributed to the movement. Findlay's (1990) article about the shifting involvement of mainline Protestant churches in the civil rights struggle is a welcome exception. Specifically, he examines the National Council of Churches and their participation in advocating on behalf of the Civil Rights Act of 1964. Rather than simply document their contributions, however, the article probes their limitations, in particular by highlighting the extent to which their moral commitments were in tension with the system of racial discrimination in which they were embedded.

> Demonstrating an idealism and sense of moral concern stemming from their moral commitments, in 1963 and 1964 the mainline churches spoke out in a sustained and constructive way on the central dilemma of our national domestic life. . . . Soon they fell back into traditional ways or seemed paralyzed, especially in the late sixties, by tumult and confusion. In their actions church people for a short time led, but then simply did little more than reflect, the general course of the nation in race relations. (Findlay, 1990:92)

Both of these articles are representative of recent historical work that seeks to expand the **participatory boundaries** of the American civil rights movement.

events have tended either to exclude or to downplay the significance of certain racial (Echeverri-Gent 1992), ethnic (Escobar 1993), and class (Basu 1998; Neeson 1984) groups. Historical narratives have been skewed with respect to gender as well (Johnson 1982). Among the ten articles on women's movements sampled for this chapter, we find that half sought to question the established understanding of the class composition of such movements. For example, both Vincent (1999) and Evans (1980) challenge traditional assertions that women's movements were exclusively populated and directed by middle-class women. The latter argues, for example, that "the fight for women's suffrage was led not by middle-class, but by working-class women, and the largest and most determined women's suffrage organizations were not the liberal feminist societies of the bourgeoisie, but the mass socialist movements of the working class" (Evans 1980:534). Similarly, Stevenson (1979:80) defends a counterintuitive position, namely that women were actively involved in campaigns and organizations opposed to women's suffrage: "Historians of the early twentieth-century suffrage campaign have neglected to credit women with their place in anti-suffragist ranks." She argues, in other words, that the participatory boundaries of the anti-suffragist movement need to be expanded to include women. The implication is that, in the absence of considering this hitherto overlooked group, we are left with an incomplete account of this historical movement.

Scholarly work that we have characterized as **expansive** seeks to augment the historical record with respect to established contentious events and/or social movements. While well-known examples of collective action may have generally agreed upon boundaries, it is important to remember that these boundaries are not innate but rather are demarcated by historians according to intellectual interests or analytical convenience. For that reason, they are subject to reconfiguration by subsequent analysts. As illustrated in the preceding text, this expansion typically takes the form of challenging the **spatial**, **temporal**, or **participatory boundaries** of a documented social movement, revolution, episode of contention, and so forth. This expansion should not be confused with generalization, however; for such work seeks to extend our understanding of events that are rooted in specific contexts, not to apply findings or interpretations related to these events to those observed elsewhere.

HISTORY AS CORRECTIVE.   In addition to being interpretive and expansive, historians who study social movements often portray their work as being **corrective**. In some cases, the intended correction consists of providing an explanation that explicitly challenges the official or established view of an event (see Box 7.6). In other cases, the desired alteration of the historical record is more innocuous, the aim being simply to reinterpret the event by situating it

---

Box 7.6.   Correcting the Record of the Civil Rights Movement

The history of the American civil rights movement reads like a tactical handbook of modern contentious politics. Activists employed a wide range of tactics, including marches, boycotts, sit-ins, "freedom rides," and other means of nonviolent action, in an effort to raise public awareness of pervasive racism, to gain support for the movement that sought to challenge it, and to bring about tangible changes to American society. But, as noted above, this "written" history of the movement has more often than not concentrated on its most visible years. This conventional but circumscribed time frame also applies to analyses of the movement's tactics, a tendency that one can observe in both the historical and sociological literatures. McAdam's (1983) well-known article on movement tactics exemplifies this approach in sociology, stating in the very first paragraph that it "studies the relationship between *tactical interaction* and the pace of black insurgency between 1955 and 1970" (p. 735, emphasis in original).

Sandage (1993) offers a **corrective** view of the civil rights movement's tactics. He argues that the movement leaders' commitment to nonviolent tactics—that is, those dramatic approaches for which the movement is known – did not simply emerge in 1955, but rather developed over the course of decades and was underpinned by a conscious appropriation of nationalist ideology and imagery. Specifically, the active use of American symbols began with a concert at the Lincoln Memorial, initiating a "formula" that activists would reemploy more than one hundred times in subsequent years. Sandage (1993:136) summarizes his argument as follows:

> Tactically, the modern civil rights movement came of age on Easter Sunday 1939. The concert was not the first African-American political use of Lincoln's memory, nor even the first civil rights gathering at his memorial. But it was, significantly, the first black mass action to evoke laudatory national publicity and earn a positive place in American public memory. . . . In an era obsessed with defining Americanism, activist successfully portrayed their adversary as un-American. . . . Memory and ritual have been central concepts in the writing of cultural history but remain mostly unexplored in studies of black activism after 1940; this essay looks toward a cultural history of the civil rights movement. It is necessarily a dual inquiry into not only political tactics but also political imagery—in particular, the ambivalent relationship between African Americans and the icon called Abraham Lincoln.

Goldberg's (1983) analysis of civil rights activities in San Antonio, Texas also **corrects** the prevailing view of how the struggle for racial equality manifested itself. In contrast to the numerous and well-documented violent confrontations that characterize the tumultuous years of movement activity, which witnessed police dogs and fire hoses being turned on peaceful demonstrators, Goldberg presents the process of legal and social transformation as much less contentious:

> Unlike the Deep South, the finished portrait of the San Antonio situation is without sharp contrasts. The line between right and wrong, heroes and villains, is not obvious. The San Antonio example also sheds light upon the relationship between minorities. Included in the San Antonio equation were not only blacks and whites but a large Mexican American population. (p. 350)

By **expanding** the **spatial boundaries** of the movement (see Box 7.3), Goldberg (1983) is able to offer a **corrected** portrait of the complex ways in which it unfolded.

in a broader context. This differs from efforts to **expand** the **temporal, spatial**, or **participatory boundaries** of a social movement as illustrated in the previous section; rather than shift the time frame, broaden the geographical location, or increase the pool of actors of a documented social movement, **corrective** narratives typically argue that the movement is better understood as being a component of a larger movement. Examples of the former (i.e., challenging the official view) often include narrative accounts of contentious actions in which the targets of claims are colonial authorities or their proxies (e.g., see Hanson 1994; Osborne 1978; Turton 1972). In such instances, the popular view of those making claims is that they are politically immature, influenced by elites, and are engaged in mob violence rather than coordinated protest. The correction, then, consists of arguing that claim makers engage in collective action in order to ameliorate well-understood and legitimate grievances. Basu's (1998) portrayal of riots and strikes in late nineteenth- century Calcutta is a good example of what we refer to as a **corrective** narrative:

> This article attempts to re-evaluate the strikes and riots in the mill towns and Calcutta in the 1980s in order to explain the nature of workers' politics in the period. . . . [C]olonial officials regarded the western European proletariat as a model against whom they measure the political and social 'maturity' of the Indian factory labour force. Viewed from such perspective, political protests of Indian workers appeared to be effervescent outbursts of anger and frustration of migrant peasants who were lacking in political maturity. . . . This article visualizes workers as the makers of their own politics rather than as passive clients of the politics of the Hindu or Muslim elites." (Pp. 950–953)

In addition to restoring agency to protagonists and meaning to their claims, corrective narratives also aim to situate the events under investigation in a broader social and political context. Rather than offer generalizations, however, such approaches remain committed to unraveling the particular. In his analysis of a massive railway strike in French West Africa, Cooper (1996) exemplifies the efforts of historians to locate and understand a particular event vis-à-vis a broader context. By unpacking the connection of the labor movement to the independence struggle, he aims to show how "the two were both complementary and in tension with one another" and "to re-examine the question of how to locate the railway strike in the history of post-World War II West Africa and to point to questions that need further research" (Cooper 1996:81–82). In other words, while the article is built around the explication of a critical event in the labor history or French West Africa, the author seeks to correct the conventional understanding of it; rather than view the railway strike as a straightforward labor dispute, he argues, it is better understood as a direct challenge to France's colonial authority.

The articles discussed in this subsection illustrate the point that historians tend to offer findings that are relevant only to the particular context they are studying and rarely make an effort to apply them to other times and places. With numerous examples, we have shown how historical analyses of social movements and collective action exhibit concern with the particular in three ways. First, history is inherently **interpretive**, in that its purpose is to reconstruct the "actual" and "recorded" past into a "written" account of that past. With regards to social movements and collective action, historical narratives that we characterize as interpretive seek to convey the context-specific meaning of a single transformative event or series of contentious episodes. Second, historical analyses are **expansive**; that is, they augment the historical record with respect to a documented social movement or episode of contention by extending the temporal, spatial, and/or participatory boundaries typically associated with it. Third, historical accounts of protest are often **corrective**, providing an interpretation that disputes or modifies the established view of a given protest, riot, revolution, and so forth. We now turn to a discussion of the temporal scope that informs historical studies of social movements and collective action.

Temporal Scope

How far back must one go to locate the origins of a social process? How long does it take for meaningful change to occur? The answers to these questions depend on how the researcher frames the object of analysis. In the case of sectarian or ethnic conflict, for example, the analyst will invoke different temporal scopes according to whether s/he seeks to document and understand the immediate events that precipitated short-term riots (Chakrabarty 1981), or tease out the long-term environmental and demographic changes that underpinned a protracted, multi-faceted struggle (Monson 1998). The causes and consequences of analytic interest, in other words, may unfold rapidly, catalyzed by a rare concatenation of proximate variables, or very slowly, taking years, decades, or even centuries to work themselves out. The point is that temporal scopes—that is, the period of time over which change occurs—are not inherent elements of social processes, but rather are analytic constructs imposed by the researcher. In this section of the chapter, we examine historians' use of temporal scopes in the study of social movements and collective action. Given their concern with events that "actually" occurred in the past, do historians avail themselves of the opportunity to concentrate on long-term processes of change? Or are they more narrowly focused on short-term causes and consequences?

Notwithstanding the obvious variability in the causes and consequences of social processes and the latitude the researcher has in delimiting them, Pierson (2003:178) argues that social scientists tend to employ restricted temporal horizons in their analyses: "In choosing what we seek to explain and in searching for explanations, we focus on the immediate; we look for causes and consequences that are both temporally contiguous and rapidly unfolding." As a result, he continues, researchers either overlook important information or misinterpret the evidence gathered. While this tendency may be true for a good deal of contemporary social research, historically oriented social scientists have taken a different approach to the study of social movements and collective action. Following the pioneering work of Charles Tilly (1964), contemporary sociological analyses of contentious action tend to emphasize long-term temporal scopes. For example, in a recent volume on the study of contentious politics, two prominent contributors to the field argue that four temporal rhythms are "highly relevant to an understanding of the emergence, development, and decline of political contention" (McAdam and Sewell 2001:89). Three of these rhythms require extended time frames to occur: long-term change processes, cycles of contention, and cultural epochs of contention. Only the fourth temporal rhythm, transformative events, is short and punctual rather than long and continuous. (For an excellent discussion of "eventful temporality" see Sewell 1996.)

How, then, does the discipline of history approach temporal scopes? At first glance, the tendency of professional historians to define themselves in terms of temporal and spatial dimensions—for example, claiming expertise in medieval Europe, colonial Latin America, or modern China—suggests that they might take a temporally and spatially circumscribed view of contentious action. However, the inclination of historians to assume that when and where something occurs affects how it occurs suggests that they might seek to ground their explanations in long-term processes of change (cf. Tilly 1990). Our analysis of the articles sampled for this chapter reveals that historical accounts of contentious action array themselves across the temporal continuum. Some focus on short-term causes and consequences, referring to and/or explicating long-term processes only insofar as it is necessary to contextualize the social movement or collective action under investigation. Others, however, go to great lengths to establish the origins or unravel the consequences of the event in long-term change processes. Let us now turn to some illustrative examples.

More than half of the articles analyzed for this chapter focused on the short-term causes and consequences of a given social movement or particular example of collective action. These articles reflect both the spatial and temporal diversity of the broader sample. One can observe a narrow temporal focus, for example, in historical analyses of industrial riots in colonial India (Basu 1998), the women's movement in early twentieth-century Palestine

(Fleishmann 2000), and the Chicano movement in late-1960s North America (Escobar 1993). This diversity also extends to those analyses that we have characterized as being interpretive, expansive, and corrective (see above); examples of each exhibit a similar concern with the short term.

The grievances impelling collective action and the structural conditions facilitating mobilization are two examples of causal variables that can exist or unfold within narrow temporal horizons. Kannangara's (1984:131) recounting of riots in Sri Lanka is characteristic of work that seeks to explain contentious action by reference to proximate rather than distant causes:

> I shall then argue that while certain economic grievances against the Muslims were of long standing, they are very far from providing a sufficient or even main explanation of the riots. The fears and resentments aroused among the Buddhists by the procession dispute were far more significant in the genesis of the riots than has been recognized.

Whereas this article, as well as Stevenson's (1979) investigation of women anti-suffragists, highlights the catalyzing power of immediate grievances, Escobar's (1993:1486) analysis of the Chicano movement in Los Angeles focuses on the relatively longer-term opportunity structures that created the conditions for and shaped the character of mobilization:

> While the Chicano movement developed in response to a historically unique set of grievances and generated distinctive solutions to those grievances, it emerged within and benefited from the broader currents of social protest that existed in the sixties. The black civil rights movement of the fifties and early sixties set the stage by focusing on public attention on the issue of racial discrimination and legitimizing public protest as a way to combat discrimination.

We should note that historians who invoke short-term causes and consequences to explain a particular episode of contentious action do not entirely neglect or overlook long-term change processes. While migration patterns (Reis 1997) or the geographic spread of commercialization (Echeverri-Gent 1992) may not figure prominently as explanatory variables, historians are often at pains to describe these and other processes in order to contextualize the event under investigation. Their discussion of long-term processes provides a background or context for the events in question, rather than serves as integral part of explanation. This point about the discipline of history has also been made by William Roy (1987:55):

> When large-scale processes are examined within a given time/place setting, they can be examined only as part of the setting rather than as the object of one's research. Large-scale structural concepts become sensitizing rather than explanatory concepts. They frame assumptions rather than generate issues for data to arbitrate.

Moreover, temporality is not a dichotomous variable, with analysts forced to choose between competing and mutually exclusive temporal scopes. Historians whose scholarly pursuits include the investigation of social movements and collective action often attend to both short- and long-term processes of change; their causes and consequences also exhibit temporal variability. Basu's (1998:954–955) discussion of riots in Calcutta is a case in point. In an effort to understand workers' politics during a very contentious year in the city's industrial history, the author examines both the immediate, tangible catalysts of a series of riots and the deeply rooted, longer-term colonial relationships that escalated their frequency and degree:

> This article shows that frequent strikes in the jute mills in the 1890s were products of the tightening work discipline in the factory which led to a curtailment of holidays on the occasion of religious festivals. . . . Furthermore, this article draws upon the social perspectives of the

functionaries of the colonial state in order to explain certain biases in police operations that influenced the pattern of unfolding of communal riots.

The roots of many social movements or episodes of contention are to be found in long-term change processes. Colonization, industrialization, migration, and urbanization, for example, may act singly or in combination to alter existing power structures, produce widespread grievances, and/or create new opportunities for people to mobilize. There is, however, an unfortunate deterministic or teleological bent to some explanatory accounts of contentious action that invoke the *longue durée* (McAdam and Sewell 2001:101; Sewell 1996); implicit in explanations that emphasize long-term change processes is often a sense of dramatic inevitability. Without acknowledging the contribution of other short-term causes or the capacity of actors to understand, define, and respond to their grievances, one is left to conclude that the historical event under investigation was simply an unavoidable consequence of long-term processes. Osborne's (1978:236) portrayal of peasant protest in colonial Cambodia, for example, is arguably deterministic in its account of the movement's origins:

> Quite in contrast to the explanations offered by the colonial officials of the day, the apparent coordination of peasant protest in 1916 may be judged to have sprung less from planning than from the existence of a generally unsettled peasant society throughout rural Cambodia. Increasing interference by the French administration had left a situation in which a single protest in Khsach Kandal was all that was required to bring forth a broad reaction.

Positing the existence of an aggrieved population, in other words, is seemingly, if mistakenly, sufficient to understanding the emergence of a widespread movement. Not all analyses that anchor explanation to long-term change processes resort to deterministic language, however. Forman's (1971:3–4) analysis of peasant movements in Brazil, for example, discusses macro-level, long-term processes as creating the conditions for change (i.e., collective action) without leading inexorably to the change itself:

> Our basic hypothesis is that urbanization, industrialization and subsequent commercialization in agriculture created demands for increased production and consumption in rural areas which ultimately lead to a breakdown in traditional forms of behavior and to widespread discontent. . . . The accoutrements of a rationalized internal marketing system—vastly improved transport and communications facilities – make mass recruitment of peasants, and thus mass movements possible. In essence, we are arguing that economic rationalization leads to political radicalization.

A similar approach can be found in Andrien's (1990) investigation of a particular event in Latin American history: the Quito insurrection of 1765. The author views this event as the "first in a wave of violent popular protests against colonial rule" (1990:105) that, over the course of fifteen years, occurred in other locations under Spanish control. This article is a good example of how the object of analysis largely determines the temporal horizon employed by the researcher. The author in this particular case hopes to locate the factors that contributed to the broader "cycle of riot and rebellion" (ibid.) rather than probe the unique causes and consequences of the event under investigation. As a consequence he focuses his analytic attention on long-term socioeconomic trends that prompted the rebellion, namely the "structural changes [that] narrowed economic opportunities, heightened social tensions and sharpened the political consciousness of the city's elite and plebian sectors by 1765, when the crown attempted to raise tax levies" (p. 106). The expectation is that these same long-term factors were responsible for the broader cycle of contention.

Historians utilize different temporal scopes when studying social movements and collective action. As the preceding examples illustrate, the temporal scope employed by a researcher is a function of the questions motivating her or his research. Historians concerned with interpreting key, transformative events tend to focus on the short-term causes and consequences of those events; those who seek to understand broader episodes or trajectories of contention ground their analyses in long-term change processes. Notwithstanding the variance one would expect to find in the broader historical literature on social movements and collective action, the majority of the articles sampled for this chapter focus on origins and outcomes of contention that are short-term. That is, the historical narratives we have analyzed are more likely to provide a detailed analysis of events rather than to unravel long-term processes (see Box 7.7). This finding may be an artifact of our sampling strategy. As noted previously, we have chosen to investigate historical studies published as journal articles but not as books. The space constraints of journal articles place limits on a researcher's ability to undertake a detailed investigation of long-term processes; books offer more appropriate venues to consider long-term processes as explanatory variables.

Box 7.7.   Temporal Scopes and the Civil Rights Movement

The roots of the American civil rights movement are to be found in long-term change processes (McAdam 1999; McAdam and Sewell 2001). That is, while the dramatic episodes of contention that characterize the movement's most tumultuous years were often responses to sudden disruptions or injustices, they were also underpinned by processes that took a long time to unfold. The profound economic and demographic shifts that resulted from the collapse of the Southern cotton economy and the expansion of northern industrial capacity, for example, not only exacerbated relations between Whites and Blacks in the South, but also strengthened the educational and organizational capacity of African American leaders. In particular, the migration of African Americans from rural to urban areas, as Burgess (1965) noted, was a necessary condition for the emergence of the movement:

> It is in the city that the greatest educational opportunities have become available to the Negro. It is here that expanding occupational opportunities have been possible, and that a rise in income and standard of living have gradually been realized. In the urban black belts, Negro institutions . . . have flourished. These social institutions provide the breeding ground for a new kind of leadership trained in the values and skills of the middle class. (p. 344, cited in McAdam and Sewell 2001:92)

And yet, the handful of articles sampled for this chapter have not availed themselves of the opportunity to explore the long-term change processes that led to the civil rights movement. While some of the articles attempt to situate the particular events under investigation in the *longue durée*, no where do we find a deep analysis of long-term processes. None of the articles, in other words, investigates the ways in which the decline of the cotton economy, the shift of African Americans to urban areas, or the ideological struggles of the Cold War set the stage for a concentrated struggle for racial justice over the course of 14 years. Instead, they examine in detail the actual short-term processes involved with bringing about the desired legal and social changes in specific spatial and temporal contexts, such as San Antonio, Texas from 1960 to 1965 (Goldberg 1983), or Seattle, Washington from 1960 to 1970 (Taylor 1995).

This is not to suggest that all authors adhered to the conventional periodization of the movement. As noted earlier (see Box 7.4), Korstad and Lichtenstein (1988) shifted the temporal boundaries of the movement, examining the involvement and incorporation of

African Americans into labor unions in the 1940s rather than the later period of high activity. But while their analysis concerned the involvement of black workers in labor unions in the North and South, they did not look to the profound socioeconomic changes wrought by the Great Depression, World War II, etc., that provided new opportunities and incentives for African Americans to organize, as key explanatory variables. The purpose of the article was to understand how context-specific unionization efforts unfolded over a short period of time.

We suggest two reasons for our seemingly counterintuitive finding that historians of the civil rights movement focus on short-term rather than long-term change processes. Both reasons, we believe, are related to our sampling strategy. First, journal articles, which tend to be shorter than 50 pages, do not readily lend themselves to a detailed investigation of long-term processes. Analyses of such breadth are better left to much longer books. Second, the brief, dramatic events that characterize the civil rights movement are of sufficient complexity as to warrant an investigation of them alone. The interpretive demands of "writing" history place limits on what can be explored in a journal article.

Core Concepts

Three key concepts have, over the course of nearly four decades, guided the lion's share of sociological research on social movements and collective action. **Political opportunities** refer to conditions in the broader political environment that create and sustain the potential for collective action. Early proponents of this concept (Jenkins and Perrow 1977; Tarrow 1994) argued that the emergence of a movement is not simply a consequence of accumulated grievances, but rather is contingent upon changes in the external political system. **Mobilizing structures** consist of "those collective vehicles, informal as well as formal, through which people mobilize and engage in collective action" (McAdam, McCarthy, and Zald 1996:3). Scholars using this concept work from the assumption that grievances and opportunities alone are insufficient to produce a social movement; instead, they argue that preexisting social structures, such as informal social networks and formal organizations, are crucial to the initiation and spread of collective action (Morris 1981). Finally, **collective action frames** are interpretive tools that individuals call upon to make sense of their situation, identify the sources of their grievances, and formulate ways to address them (Snow and Benford, 1992; Snow et al. 1986). Frames include not only those existing cultural codes and understandings that orient protagonists, but also those that they actively construct over the course of engaging in contentious action.

In recent years, there has been extensive debate among social scientists about the utility and limitations of these concepts (cf. Goodwin and Jasper 2004). The first two, for example, have come under spirited attack for being excessively structural and static, and for downplaying the role that human agency plays in social movements and collective action (Morris 2004). Critics of the third concept have pointed to its use in an all-encompassing manner and a failure to distinguish among frames, framing, and ideology (Benford 1997; Oliver and Johnston 2000). But the concept does emphasize the active choices and efforts of movement actors rather than their structural locations. As social movement theory has developed over the years, researchers have increasingly sought to assimilate both structure and agency into their explanations. To be sure, concern with the tension between structure and agency is longstanding in both the humanities and the social sciences. Both historians and social scientists share an interest in the problematic of agency and structure. As Abrams (1980:7) notes, "It is the problem of finding a way of accounting for the human experience which recognizes simultaneously and in equal measure that history and society are made by constant, more or less purposeful, individual action and that individual action, however purposeful, is made by history and society."

To what extent have the three core concepts listed above informed historical research on social movements and collective action? And to what extent have historians used them in a critical manner? Given that much of this research has been undertaken in the wake of the "social history" that gained momentum during the 1960s and 1970s—that is, history that sought to reconstruct the experiences of ordinary people—is there greater emphasis placed on agent-centered concepts? In this section of the chapter we review historians' use of social movement concepts. We show that while each of the three core concepts is used by historians, their usage is quite limited. Among the 60 articles sampled for this chapter, nine made specific reference to the political opportunities that made collective action possible; seven focused on the mobilizing structures, primarily formal organizations, that played a key role in aggregating and seeking to remedy grievances; and just five articles highlighted the collective action frames protagonists employed to articulate their demands. Moreover, the assumptions underlying these concepts remain unexplored. We find that historians tend not to interrogate the theoretical origins and implications of the concepts. We also find that historians tend to deploy the concepts of **political opportunities** and **mobilizing structures** in a manner that downplays the agency of movement protagonists. However, those who use the concept of **collective action frames** tend to focus on the agency of leaders but not on the social construction of grievances; that is, they tend to impute grievances to actors by virtue of their structural location.

POLITICAL OPPORTUNITIES.   Many researchers of social movements and collective action have made use of the concept of political opportunities to account for the origins and outcomes of contentious episodes (Jenkins and Perrow 1977; Tarrow 1994). The central assumption is that, given their inherently weaker structural position, potential claimants are unlikely to engage in collective action in the absence of new opportunities. The existence of grievances, in other words, does not lead inexorably to riots, strikes, labor movements, or peasant insurrections; changes must first occur in the broader political environment. These changes, which can be real or perceived, may consist of transformations that are unique and significant, such as a loss in the state's capacity and propensity for repression (McAdam 1996:27), or relatively routine and minor, such as the change in political administrations or the enactment of a specific policy.

Historians who research social movements and collective action incorporate various political opportunities into their explanatory narratives. Some of these opportunities evolve from a profound rupture in the political, economic, and social fabric of the context in question. In an analysis of peasant resistance in Ethiopia, for example, Tareke (1984:77) argues that the emergence of the rebellion was contingent on very specific opportunities presenting themselves to an aggrieved population, namely the expulsion of the Italians from the country and the subsequent actions of the postcolonial government during the next two years: "The causes of the revolt were the complex interaction of existing social structures within the political events of 1943, which, by creating new opportunities, reinforced the capacity of the participants for collective action." Carr (1996) makes a similar point in his narrative account of strikes that occurred among Cuban sugar workers in the years between the first and second world wars. The article argues that a profound shift in power created new opportunities for labor mobilization:

> The *insurgencia* was also crucially shaped by developments in the larger society that facilitated a temporary alteration in the balance of class forces; the serious weakening of the state apparatus for a brief but important period between August and October 1933; the destruction of the old army officer corps in the sergeants' revolt of 4 September; and the appearance of civilian militias which tolerated and even supported worker actions. The institutional, coercive and legal structures serving the sugar mills did not function very well in August-October 1933, and this was as important in explaining the sugar worker insurgency as the role of parties and ideology. (p. 130, emphasis in original)

Other historical narratives link both mobilization and successful outcomes to opportunities that come about as a consequence of periodic shifts within political institutions, such as a change in leadership or the enactment of new legislation. Examples from the French labor movement illustrate this point. In terms of mobilization, for example, Berlanstein (1992:677) notes that Parisian gas workers responded to specific opportunities that led to a surge in union membership:

> Stokers rushed into the Gas Workers Union. Over 1,400 may have joined between September 1898 and May 1899. The stokers were probably responding to favorable trends in the Parisian job market as a result of preparations for the next (1900) international exposition as well as to the climate of strife created by a large general strike by construction workers and ditch diggers.

As for successful outcomes, Berlanstein (1992:674) highlights the opportunities that Parisian gas workers gained as a result of a fortuitous change in the city's political administration:

> Opportunities for gas workers to improve their bargaining position with their employer received support from an exceptional political development. The municipal election of 1890 returned a left-leaning council that was enthusiastically committed to addressing the 'social question'. . . . Whereas labor issues had not arisen at any earlier discussions between the PGC and the city, the aldermen now insisted on an improved situation for the gas personnel.

As a consequence of this political opportunity, gas workers were, for the first time, in a position to demand and receive wage increases, pensions, and profit sharing.

The preceding examples suggest that historians do apply the **political opportunity** concept to the study of past protest. This should not come as a surprise given the extraordinary attention to detail and the construction of logical narratives that characterizes the craft of writing history. By unpacking the events under investigation, historians are able to devote considerable attention to the context-specific transformations (i.e., political opportunities) that enable actors to engage in collective action (see Box 7.8). We should note, however, that political opportunity is one concept among many that historians employ to construct their narratives; it is not typically the central focus of the analysis, but rather one element of the broader story; its function, then, is supplementary not explanatory. In none of the articles sampled for this chapter is the political opportunity concept problematized or operationalized. Moreover, no reference is ever made to the concept's usage in the sociological literature or by other analysts of social movements and collective action. In short, historians use this concept in a manner that is distinct from the meaning it has vis-à-vis a larger theoretical framework.

MOBILIZING STRUCTURES. Social movement scholars have recognized that political opportunities alone do not produce a social movement or other forms of collective action. While the political environment may create the structural potential for protagonists to make claims, the extent to which this potential will be tapped is contingent on the organization of the aggrieved group. Morris (1981), for example, argues in his classic article that black churches and colleges played a critical role in the emergence of the student sit-in movement,

Box 7.8.   Political Opportunities and the Civil Rights Movement

In the beginning of the twentieth century, African Americans were structurally in a weak position from which to pursue collective goals. Their ability to demand the elimination of racist policies and practices, particularly those that prevented them from exercising their constitutionally guaranteed rights, was tempered by the fetters of institutionalized segregation, endemic poverty, and limited educational and employment opportunities. But the emergence of specific **political opportunities**, both before and after the peak period of civil rights movement activity, enabled African Americans to make significant gains in the struggle for racial equality.

Korstad and Lichenstein (1988), for example, stress the importance of specific labor policies that were developed and implemented in the years bracketing the Second World War. Specifically, they claim that:

> the rise of industrial unions and the evolution of late New Deal labor legislation offered working-class blacks an economic and political standard by which they could legitimate their demands and stimulate a popular struggle. The 'one man, one vote' policy implemented in thousands of National Labor Relations Board (NLRB) elections, the industrial 'citizenship' that union contracts offered once-marginal elements of the working class, and the patriotic egalitarianism of the government's wartime propaganda—all generated a rights consciousness that gave working-class black militancy a moral justification in some ways as powerful as that evoked by the Baptist spirituality of Martin Luther King, Jr. a generation later. (p. 787)

Both the mental and legal opportunities occasioned by labor legislation and nationalist rhetoric gave African Americans an organizing capacity they did not have hitherto and, as a consequence, significant gains were made for African American workers.

A second example of **political opportunities** comes from an article concerned with the activities of Southern African Americans in what is largely considered to be the post-civil rights era. Minchin (1999) argues that legislative gains made during the "heroic" period of civil rights activism created new opportunities for African Americans to demand equality at the workplace. Specifically, he focuses on the effects that the passage of the Civil Rights Act of 1964 had upon the Southern textile industry:

> Both black men and women used the passage of the Civil Rights Act to fight discrimination in the textile industry. Across the South, African American textile workers were acutely aware of the act's passage, and they were determined to enforce its non-discrimination mandate. The act led to an upsurge of militancy as black workers used the machinery provided by the act to unite and protest against discrimination. (p. 821)

Through examination of data from numerous court cases brought against employers by African American employees and those seeking employment, the author shows how the victories attained helped to radically reconfigure the workforce. The article goes on to suggest not only that this **political opportunity** was the only one at the disposal of African Americans at the time, because unions, comprising less than ten percent of the workforce, were relatively weak, but also that it has had an enduring significance: "Today these workers recognize the central importance of the Civil Rights Act in ensuring this change. Across the South, they recall the legislation of 1964 as the watershed between the status quo of racial discrimination and an era of increased opportunity in Southern employment practices" (p. 844).

transforming opportunities into action. The organization of potential claimants need not be formalized, however; a wide range of preexisting social structures has been shown to facilitate movement activity (Freeman 1973; McAdam 1982).

Historians of social movements and collective action are clearly amenable to casting mobilizing structures in a central role. Several of the articles sampled for this chapter devote considerable space to discussing the organizations that mobilized aggrieved populations and made claims on their behalf (cf. Escobar 1993; Forman 1971; Garvin 1982; Krikler 1999; Smith 1978; Taylor 1995; Turton 1972). This attention to organizations may, as noted in the preceding text, be a function of the evidentiary constraints faced by historians; that is, their reliance on evidence that is more often than not produced, collected, and disseminated by organizations may cause them to focus analytical attention on these organizations. Some social movement organizations may have, during the course of making claims, created documents of significant interest to historians; those that continue to exist, such as large, national organizations that have endured for decades, may even maintain their own collections (Clemens and Hughes 2002:203).

In situations where the organization in question was transitory or otherwise prevented from producing documentary evidence of its activities, such as those that were formed on an ad hoc basis or operated in the context of repressive regimes, historians may be compelled to highlight them for a different reason: to dismiss the notion of popular politics as irrational reactions to temporary strain. Basu (1998), for example, seeks to correct the prevailing historical interpretation of this view of labor unrest by restoring some semblance of agency to the striking workers. In contrast to other historical work on the subject, which either portrays this particular group of protests as little more than politically immature mob violence, or as being heavily influenced by elites, this article argues that workers organized and protested in order to ameliorate well understood and legitimate grievances. Moises and Martinez-Alier (1980) make a similar point in their analysis of a series of riots directed at the suburban railways in Brazil. In this case, however, organizations are absent. The authors argue repeatedly that one should view the lack of organization observed among the various spontaneous strikes as a rational strategy given the environment in which they emerged:

> Since 1964, the Brazilian working class has lacked independent organizations for social and political representation through which it can express its grievances in an organized manner. . . . Only on the surface do the riots appear 'irrational', 'anarchic' though inevitable reactions to hardship. Their spontaneity and violence are the consequence of the working class's *formal* exclusion from politics. The people reacted in the way that they did, not out of any historically determined political backwardness, but because, in the circumstances in which they found themselves, this was the only means available to them to make themselves heard. (p. 182, emphasis in original)

Broadly speaking, historians of social movements and collective action employ the concept of mobilizing structures in a manner similar to other social scientists. They portray both informal and formal structures as vital to the initiation and spread of collective action. Johnson's (1982) discussion of anticolonial activism among Nigerian women, for example, illustrates the importance of a wide range of social ties among protagonists. The efforts of women's organizations to mobilize constituents were successful, she argues, largely because they were able to tap a variety of social networks:

> Depending on the issue, the NWP could mobilize huge demonstrations of women, often numbering in the thousands. Family and ethnic connections, trans-organizational membership, school ties, business relationships, and religious networks ensured a broad-based solidarity of women, just as they did in the male-dominated parties. An individual woman might belong to several organizations at the same time, thus increasing the chances for cooperation among groups. (p. 145)

While the use of the mobilizing structures concept is similar to political opportunities discussed above—that is, it tends to play a supplementary rather than an explanatory role in the narrative – there are notable exceptions. In his analysis of striking porters in Brazil, Reis (1997) makes an explicit link between mobilization and organization:

> The central argument of this article is that the *ganhadores* mobilised the strike on the basis of labour organisations that preceded the movement and were built up on the basis of the ethnic and cultural characteristics of those Africans. African ethnic identity and cultural practices, had very clear political dimensions, both in their daily occupations and at the times when they broke with those daily routines, as in the case of the strike and the other conflicts that preceded it. (p. 357, emphasis in original)

Without the presence of overlapping formal and informal structures, one is left to conclude that the dramatic strike that erupted in urban Brazil would have been unlikely to occur or endure. Mobilizing structures, in other words, helped to ensure that aggrieved porters were transformed into a striking sector of the labor force.

Mobilizing structures take many forms, ranging from informal interpersonal networks to formal national organizations. Regardless of whether collective action is facilitated by structures resembling either the former or the latter, the key insight made by social movement scholars is that potential claimants require more than just an opportunity to engage in collective action; they also require some kind of organizing structure to facilitate that action (see Box 7.9).

Box 7.9.   Mobilizing Structures and the Civil Rights Movement

Organizations were the driving force behind the American civil rights movement. Churches, colleges, business groups, and advocacy organizations all played key roles in the local and national struggles for racial equality, undertaking activities that spanned decades, included innumerable participants, and brought about significant legislative and social gains. To focus on the **mobilizing structures** that facilitated action is not to discount the importance of iconic figures such as Dr. Martin Luther King, Jr., Rosa Parks, Malcolm X, and Medgar Evers, but rather to note that behind these individuals stood a network of formal organizations.

Since the 1970s, historians have devoted considerable attention to the civil rights organizations that achieved national prominence, producing extensive biographies of most of the movement's leading organizations. Meier and Rudwick's (1975) analysis of the Congress for Racial Equality (CORE) was an early and oft-cited analysis of one of the movement's first noteworthy organizations. A decade later, Adam Fairclough (1987) recounted the history of Southern Christian Leadership Conference (SCLC). Similarly, Carson (1981) and Zinn (1964) highlighted the important contributions made by the Student Nonviolent Coordinating Committee (SNCC), the organization that played a central role in the Freedom Rides in 1961, the March on Washington in 1963, and the Mississippi Freedom Summer campaign in 1964. More recently, Jonas and Bond (2004) have produced the first comprehensive account of the National Association for the Advancement of Colored People (NAACP).

But the civil rights movement consisted of more than national organizations and their efforts to bring about federal legislative reforms; many of the most tangible changes occurred at the state or city levels and were catalyzed by local organizations. Among the articles sampled for this chapter, two focus on the local organizations that sought to advance the cause of civil rights in particular urban areas. Taylor (1995), for example, examines the civil rights movement in Seattle, Washington, a city which, in spite of its distance from the struggles that engulfed the Deep South, had to confront its own legacy of racial discrimination. By focusing on the emergence and activities of a local civil rights organization that brought together community leaders from a variety of prominent national organizations, Taylor (1995:3) is able to show how the issues of concern in Seattle were both similar to and distinct from those observed elsewhere:

> Local civil rights leaders reached a broad consensus on a strategy and tactics which eluded their national counterparts throughout the 1960s. The created the Central Area Civil Rights Committee (CACRC) to provide one voice on civil rights issues and determine the civil rights agenda. Included in this group [was] Edwin Pratt, Executive Director of the Seattle Urban League. . . . June Smith, President of the Seattle Branch of the National Association for the Advancement of Colored People (NAACP), and Walter Hundley of the Congress of Racial Equality (CORE) were also members.

One can also observe the importance of local **mobilizing structures** in Goldberg's (1983) analysis of the struggle for desegregation in San Antonio, Texas. As in other Southern cities, African Americans in San Antonio were constantly reminded of their second-class status by the visible (and legal) segregation of lunch counters in downtown department stores. Efforts to change the status quo in this context, as elsewhere, required the mobilization of aggrieved African Americans. An important insight of Goldberg (1983:356), however, is that mobilizing structures also played a critical role in getting Whites to accept the change of an entrenched practice: "The store owners finally agreed to serve blacks at lunch counters but demanded several safeguards. To defuse a potential white counterreaction, the businessmen asked Catholic, Jewish, and Protestant clergymen present to mobilize the religious community in support of integration."

Both Taylor's (1995) and Goldberg's (1983) articles highlight the role of local mobilizing structures in bringing about a change to racist laws, policies, and practices. But whereas the former investigates those that enabled African Americans to make claims, the latter considers those that helped to ensure that whites accepted them.

COLLECTIVE ACTION FRAMES. Framing is about action. It emphasizes the active choices of potential claimants rather than their structural locations. The concept conveys agency, in that it consists of protagonists actively defining a situation as unjust or otherwise unacceptable, attributing blame for the condition in need of correction, and suggesting a course of action to remedy it (Snow and Benford 1992). To explore the extent to which and manner in which historians use this concept in their studies of social movements and collective action, we focus on two aspects of contentious action that are potential sites of agency: **leadership** and **grievances**. In terms of **leadership**, we want to know how historians portray what leaders do. Social scientists have long noted that social movement leaders play an important and active role in framing and articulating issues, activating networks, and mobilizing supporters (Aminzade, Goldstone, and Perry 2001:127). Do historians also ground their explanations in the view that leaders' actions shape the course and outcomes of contentious action? Or do they downplay leaders' capacity for agency by characterizing them as simply responding to larger structural forces? In terms of **grievances**, our aim is to understand whether and to what extent historians characterize them as socially constructed or structurally determined. Proponents of **collective action frames** emphasize the agency of protagonists in defining grievances as injustices and transforming them into demands (Snow and Benford 1992; Snow et al. 1986). This view contrasts with earlier approaches to the study of social movements and collective action, which asserted a direct link between dissatisfaction and action (Zald 1992:328). How do historians characterize the relationship between grievances and action? Do they follow the tack of early collective behavior theorists, explaining collective action in terms of intensified grievances? Do they impute grievances to actors by virtue of their structural location? Or do they explore the manner in which protagonists actively interpret grievances and use this interpretation as the basis for making claims?

Leadership.   A number of scholars have recently emphasized the importance of leadership as a complex phenomenon that affects the origins and outcomes of movements (Aminzade, Goldstone, and Perry 2001; Morris 2004). They point to different types of leadership and how their goals and relationships can produce different outcomes, such as when the choices of dynamic leaders in fluid and ambiguously defined situations determine the trajectory of a movement (Aminzade, Goldstone, and Perry 2001:129–133, 147). Many of the articles sampled for this chapter suggest that historians take an agent-centered approach to leadership. While leadership was certainly not a central feature of all 60 of the contentious episodes in question, those narratives that did focus on leaders tended to emphasize the active choices they made, their efforts to aggregate and mobilize aggrieved groups, their relationship with followers, and their influence on movement trajectory.

In his analysis of peasant movements in Brazil, for example, Forman (1971) devotes considerable attention to Francisco Julião, the proclaimed leader of the peasant leagues in the northeast of the country. The article highlights the choices he made in terms of actively seeking out a constituency to mobilize and speculates that his choice of peasants was strategic not only in terms of mobilization, but also, and more importantly, in terms of his political career. Julião clearly plays a central role in shaping the peasant movement, essentially determining its origins insofar as he,

> was aware that different land tenure systems and productive arrangements produced different peasant subtypes which could be expected to react differently to appeals for political mobilization. . . . It was the peasant, he believed, who presented the best conditions for waging a protracted struggle against the latifundia, and he appealed to them to join together in the building of an effective agrarian society. (Forman 1971:10)

Consistent with the social science usage of the collective action frame concept, historians convey the agency of movement leaders by documenting their efforts to frame the world in which they were acting, by interpreting grievances, defining the aggrieved, attributing blame, and making claims. Smith's (1978:110) analysis of a revolt among agricultural workers in southern France is illustrative:

> Undeniably, Marcelin Albert's calls for social unity in the face of the wine crisis in 1907 grew out of these persisting class conflicts in the larger villages of the region. Indeed the demands from the desperate strikes of 1905–6 were even directly transferred to the mass meetings of 1907—in their words 'the right to work in the vineyards'—an issue which Albert skillfully broadened to become a generalized 'right to live from the vine' which was the basis for much of his appeal to all wine producers, and not only the vine-workers, at the meetings of 1907.

Holton's (1994) contribution is also representative of how movement leaders employ collective action frames to define a social condition as problematic and to articulate a strategy for challenging it. The article focuses on the actions of one individual, Elizabeth Cady Stanton, and the leaders she assembled around her, to show how they were instrumental in advancing the women's suffrage movement, both in Britain and the United States. Holton

(1994:1121) highlights the efforts of the leadership to frame the issue and their approach, noting that it can be a contentious process: "The central suffrage leadership remained cautious nonetheless, and the disunity this provided among her British colleagues provided another trial for Elizabeth Cady Stanton during this visit. At the heart of the discord was the question of whether or not to include married women in the demand for the vote."

Numerous other examples of the active role of social movement leaders abound. In short, the articles sampled for this chapter suggest that, when constructing narratives about social movements or collective action, historians emphasize the role of leadership in a way that is consistent with social scientists; that is, they portray leaders' actions as shaping the course and outcomes of collective action.

Grievances.   Implicit in all accounts of social movements and collective action is a sense of underlying grievances. In the absence of an unpleasant, unjust, or unacceptable social condition, it makes little sense to expect that individuals would have the impetus to engage in collective action; making claims can be a time-consuming, hazardous, and uncertain enterprise. But while all episodes of contention are rooted in grievances, their presence does not adequately account for movement activity. Grievances are a pervasive component of social life; contention is relatively rare. As Trotsky (1959:249) noted long ago, if grievances were sufficient to cause an insurrection, then one would expect the masses to be in constant revolt. How, then, have scholars characterized the relationship between grievances and action? More specifically, how have historians approached this question?

Whereas early collective behavior theorists presumed a strong relationship between intensely felt grievances and engagement in some form of collective action, later generations of scholars have sought to show that grievances are socially constructed. Klandermans (1992:85), for example, emphasizes the agency of potential protagonists by arguing that interpretive processes underlie action: "situations are defined as unjust and grievances are transformed into demands." This analytical shift owes a tremendous debt to David Snow and his colleagues, who were among the first to lament the widespread "neglect of the fact that grievances or discontents are subject to differential interpretation, and the fact that variation in their interpretation across individuals, social movement organizations, and time can affect whether and how they are acted upon" (Snow et al. 1986:465). While the framing literature has usefully highlighted the importance of ideas, perceptions, and understandings for inspiring action, it has been criticized for taking little account of where these ideas come from. Schurman and Munro (2006), for example, attempt to address this shortcoming by focusing on the process of grievance formation; rather than simply interpret social conditions, movement leaders, they argue, play an important role in generating the ideas that produce grievances and, subsequently, collective action.

All of the historical articles sampled for this chapter make explicit reference to the grievances underlying the contentious event in question. Striking workers, for example, are portrayed as demanding wage increases and the dismissal of unpopular factory supervisors (Basu 1998), reacting to layoffs and inequitable sick pay (Berlanstein 1992), and challenging racial discrimination in hiring (Minchin 1999). With the notable exception of one article, however, historians explain these grievances, and the consequent collective response to them, as structurally determined rather than socially constructed. That is, they largely impute grievances to actors by virtue of their structural position; there is virtually no discussion of the manner in which protagonists actively frame social conditions and use this interpretation as a basis for making claims. They do not, in other words, interrogate the relationship between the observed activity (e.g., strike, riot, peasant movement) and the conditions thought to have catalyzed it.

Two examples illustrate this observed tendency among historical approaches to the study of social movements and collective action. The first focuses on a week-long police strike in Cape Town, South Africa. Nasson (1992) highlights the ways that economic contraction and the nationalization of the police force negatively impacted wages; he also discusses how difficulties in rural areas, paired with the participation of many British officers in World War I, created both the incentives and opportunities for poor, rural Afrikaners to join the force, which profoundly impacted the overall expectations, interests, and grievances of the officers. He does not, however, examine the manner in which these grievances were interpreted by the officers:

> But rank-and-file police discontent had more to do with debt and drudgery than with the anticipated despotism and illiberalism of new state service which occupied and alarmed those of increasingly mournful Cape liberal inclinations. . . . Second, and of more importance in shaping the strike pressures of 1918, was the issue of rates of pay. Not only was the South African Police the lowest paid 'of any of the larger Forces within the Empire'; levels of remuneration and conditions varied between regions in the Union. . . . Effective wage cuts triggered immediate dissatisfaction and seemed a long-term prescription for trouble. . . . For Cape Town policemen, the Local Allowance system became an immediate and principal cause for grievance. (pp. 303–304)

The second article is grounded on a single event: the May Day protest of 1917 in Rio de Janeiro. Meade's (1989:264) focus, however, is not on this particular event per se, but rather on the three decades of community-based protests which led up to it: "The general strike should be viewed in relationship to the years of protest that had preceded it." To make this point, the author highlights a number of smaller riots, protests, campaigns and movements in the decades leading up to 1917, showing the consistency in grievances and tactics. In doing so, she presumes a direct link between grievances and action:

> In addition to taxes and high food prices, grievances relating to housing, sanitation, health care, education and the distribution of public services were the motivation for demonstrations, riots and other forms of collective action. . . . The extent to which the crowds had vandalized the transport system was not surprising since hatred of the transport companies was something of a long-standing tradition in Rio. Appallingly erratic service, poor wages and terrible working conditions for drivers and ever-escalating fares for passengers had caused a steady stream of strikes and protests during the Empire as well as under the Republic. (pp. 245, 249–250)

In contrast, the article by Escobar (1993) is noteworthy for its emphasis on the manner in which people actively interpret a problematic condition of their life and frame it as an injustice that needs to be remedied. The author examines the Chicano movement in Los Angeles, in an effort to expand historical analysis of militant protest and official repression in the 1960s.

> The Chicano movement of the late sixties challenged many of the previous generation's assumptions and tactics. . . . They developed a nationalist concept of *chicanismo* to signal that they rejected assimilation. They declared that as a result of their Mexican ancestry and their experiences in the Southwest, they had an identity and a heritage that they intended to keep intact. Moreover, Chicanos declared themselves a nonwhite minority in solidarity with other oppressed racial groups throughout the world. Like members of other nonwhite racial groups, they saw themselves as victims of white racism and argued Chicanos could achieve equality only through collective social and economic empowerment." (p. 1491)

By actively framing their grievances vis-à-vis a specific nationalist identity, movement leaders were able to mobilize specific constituents and to demand particular reforms.

Grievances are an ineluctable factor of social, economic, and political life. By themselves, however, grievances do not typically produce collective action or lead to broader social movements.

Getting people to perceive particular grievances as unjust and in need of resolution requires that individuals actively frame them as such (see Box 7.10). While this insight emerged in sociological studies of collective action in the 1980s, it appears to have not yet taken root in the research of historians of social protest. That is, although grievances play a central role in all of the narratives sampled for this chapter, the active process of understanding or framing these grievances is under explored. As a consequence, readers are left assuming that individuals have grievances simply by virtue of their structural location, and that these grievances are a given rather than something requiring interpretation.

Box 7.10.   Collective Action Frames and the Civil Rights Movement

Long before Rosa Parks refused to give up her bus seat in Montgomery, Alabama, African Americans were arguably the most aggrieved group of American citizens. Pervasive and often violent racism, first manifesting itself in the institution of slavery, later reemerging as the softer segregation of Jim Crow laws, had interfered with African Americans' right to life, liberty, and the pursuit of happiness for centuries.

Given such pervasive and long-standing grievances, it is obvious, as suggested above, that the struggle for racial equality did not begin in 1955. African Americans had sought to attain their liberty and assert their rights since their arrival in North America. National organizations committed to eliminating racism, most notably the National Association for the Advancement of Colored People (NAACP), had emerged decades before Rosa Parks's act of resistance. But the campaign did enter a more active phase from 1955 to 1968 as African Americans sought to bring the injustice of their situation to the attention of the broader public through marches and street protests, sit-ins and boycotts. What led to this rapid proliferation of civil rights activity and the eventual legislative gains it facilitated? More importantly, what enabled African Americans to cultivate the support of essential white allies?

Scott Sandage's (1993) article about the use of ritual and memory asserts that African Americans' success came about as a result of their ability to **frame** their grievances in a way that appealed to the broader American public. Specifically, he argues that civil rights leaders learned over time to tap into the nationalist sentiment that was widespread in the United States immediately prior to World War II and throughout the Cold War. Rather than appeal to whites' common humanity, African Americans found that their message was more readily received once they appealed to whites' sense of common citizenship. In a direct challenge to those who argue that the agenda of African Americans was co-opted by white progressives, Sandage (1993:138) takes the position that African Americans were in the driver's seat, actively framing their struggle in a way that appealed to whites:

> Such views overlook exactly what studies of ritual and memory can show – that it was often activists who did the co-opting. Protesters mobilized mainstream symbols to further alternative ends, to constitute (not just reflect) shared beliefs, and to open spaces for social change. It was precisely the unrelenting nationalism that reigned from the 1930s to the 1960s that finally offered black activists a cultural language to speak to white America and to elicit support. (p. 138)

By employing a collective action frame readily understood by all Americans, not just African Americans, civil rights leaders were able to communicate forcefully why the *status quo* was unjust and what needed to be accomplished in order to remedy it.

Nature and Use of Evidence

A final feature of historical analysis is its overwhelming reliance on evidence produced, collected, organized, and disseminated by others. The vast majority of this evidence takes the form of written material, though there are exceptions for those engaged in historical scholarship of either the most recent or most distant past (Tilly 1990:689). The articles sampled for this chapter utilize a wide range of written documents, including, but not limited to: government policies, reports, and memoranda; judicial records of arrests, trials, convictions, and executions; newspaper and magazine articles; organizational records, membership lists, and promotional materials; official and private correspondence; photographs, maps and political cartoons; and various secondary materials, typically monographs produced by the historians who first documented the events under investigation. This wealth of written and visual material creates tremendous **opportunities** for and places extreme **restrictions** on historians studying social movements and collective action. **Opportunities** derive from the volume and range of data gathered by a variety of actors over time, as well as the intriguing possibility of locating new data sources. **Restrictions** result from reliance upon data that are **limited**, produced by organizations with self-serving agendas; **silent**, in terms of capturing the perspectives and motives of those making claims; and **absent**, with regards to the actual object (e.g., strike, riot, labor movement, peasant insurrection, etc.) of analysis. Let us now examine each of these opportunities and restrictions in turn.

The range of existing and potential data sources available to historians of social movements and collective action offers distinct **opportunities**. First, for those concerned with prominent episodes of contentious action, the locations and composition of relevant data archives are well known. The task of the researcher, then, is to gain access to these archives and undertake the often tedious task of plowing through the established files. Second, researchers of well-known movements can also turn to a large body of published historical work, such as books, theses and articles. For example, a surfeit of secondary materials is available to historians of the American civil rights movement or the French revolution. This, however, is a mixed blessing, insofar as it complicates the historian's task of making an original contribution to the literature (see Box 7.11). Third, researchers who are able to construct their narratives from government documents and newspaper articles benefit from "the consistency and range of data gathered every year, every decade, or at every occurrence of a particular type [of event], such as a strike or an arrest" (Clemens and Hughes 2002:206).

Box 7.11.   Evidence and the Civil Rights Movement

Historians of the American civil rights movement have at their disposal a tremendous amount of primary and secondary evidence. The surfeit of primary materials derives from the fact that the movement, at least its most active phase, occurred during birth of the world's first truly multimedia era. In addition to the government documents, judicial records, and newspaper and magazine articles that are standard fare for historians, the civil rights movement was also captured by myriad radio and television broadcasts. Historians and non-historians alike have already been exposed to or can readily access audio and visual materials that exhibit the movement's most heroic moments of resistance and solidarity, as well as some of the most ignominious responses to its claims by the authorities. Who hasn't heard, for example, Dr. Martin Luther King Jr.'s "I have a dream" speech,

---

which he delivered from the steps of the Lincoln Memorial during the March on Washington? And who can forget the violent images from Birmingham, Alabama, where peaceful protesters were assaulted by the police using dogs, batons, and water cannons?

In terms of secondary evidence, one would be hard pressed to find a more thoroughly researched social movement. Historians have seemingly produced studies covering every aspect of the movement, including, but not limited to, the policies of presidential administrations (Brauer 1977; Burk 1984; McCoy and Reutten 1973), biographies of its leading figures (Cone 1991; Garrow 1986; Grant 1998; Oates 1982) and national organizations (Carson 1981; Fairclough 1987; Jonas and Bond 2004; Zinn 1964), the decisions of federal courts (Kluger 1976; Wilkinson 1979), and even the opponents of the movement (Bartley 1969; McMillen 1971).

At first glance, the welter of primary and secondary materials is a boon to scholars of the American civil rights movement. Much of the onerous work of locating appropriate materials and developing a general sense of the origins and outcomes of the movement has already been done. But the extent to which primary sources have been scrutinized by others and the very comprehensiveness of the secondary literature makes it difficult for contemporary scholars to make new contributions to the field. Nevertheless, given the volume of potential materials, it would be folly to suggest that all sources of data have already been tapped by researchers. In addition to reviewing the large body of literature on the civil rights movement and Southern textile workers, Minchin (1999:812), for example, recently made use of unexplored records from the various legal suits brought by African American workers following the passage of the Civil Rights Act:

> During the years when the industry's workforce was being integrated, there was generated an extensive body of material that has not been previously utilized by historians. . . . In particular, the letters that black workers wrote to the Equal Employment Opportunity Commission (EEOC), which was created by the 1964 act, together with their depositions and trial testimony, are vivid statements of their grievances. This account is the first to use the records, and it suggests a number of new arguments about the racial integration of Southern textile plants.

Finally, the variety of recognized historical evidence provides researchers with both an incentive to, and the possibility of, utilizing and/or locating new sources of data. Historians attempt to differentiate themselves from their predecessors by noting that their analyses are based on evidence that has been overlooked, underutilized, or misinterpreted by previous scholars. In his analysis of nineteenth-century migration from the Senegal River valley, for example, Hanson (1994:39) links the strength of his narrative to his unique combination of evidence: "Only a few historians have consulted Pulaar oral accounts about the migrations, and no one has attempted to integrate information and perspectives from Arabic, Pulaar and French materials in a synthesis of the *fergo Nioro*." In addition, claims to present a historical event in a new light or with a different interpretation are given a tremendous boost when one is able to allege that her/his article draws on data that are newly available. This is often the case with recently declassified government documents, as evidenced by Osborne (1978):

> Until recently, only partial comparison could be made of the limited published commentaries on the 1916 Affair with the official but confidential reports prepared by the French administrators who held responsibility for Cambodia, and Indochina as a whole. Some of the vital archival records have been open to investigation for a number of years, but other important documents became available to scholars only very recently. (pp. 217–218)

While data abundance is perhaps the rare exception to the rule of data scarcity, the merit of the historical enterprise hinges on the ability of the researcher to construct a plausible narrative about the events under investigation. Often the available evidence places **restrictions** on this ability. That is, with few exceptions, historians must **limit** the questions they ask and the meanings they ascribe to the data available in archives and the published works of other historians. As noted in the preceding text, most existing data are the products of large-scale organizations such as churches and states (Tilly 1970). While these organizational documents can prove to be a gold mine for assiduous researchers, reliance upon them is also fraught with danger, insofar as "they may omit or distort crucial information in order to present the organization more favorably, for the sake of present legitimacy or future legacy" (Clemens and Hughes 2002:204). Indeed, this particular **limitation**, namely, the risk of potential bias, is particularly salient with regard to social movements and collective action, where the targets of claim making are often the producers of historians' documentary evidence. It was in the self-interest of colonial administrations, for example, to characterize the contentious actions of their subjects, particularly the grievances motivating them, as having endogenous roots, lest they lose the support of the citizens in the *metropole*. In his analysis of a Cambodian peasant movement, Osborne (1978) argues that, contrary to the interpretation of the French colonial administrators at the time, it was features of the administrative system that aroused discontent among the population.

Historians interested in social movements and collective action face an additional evidentiary constraint. Not only must they, like all historians, confront organizational limitations in the data they employ, but they are also restricted by the **silence** of the data (i.e., data scarcity) with regard to the subjects of their narratives. In many of the articles sampled for this chapter, the protagonists (i.e., individuals and groups engaging in protest, participating in strikes, fomenting rebellion, or otherwise making claims) were the illiterate subjects of colonial administrations. As a consequence, they often lacked the capacity to create and preserve the documentary evidence that would shed light on the grievances, motives, tactics, goals, and accomplishments related to their collective action. This gap in the historical record is noted by Reis (1997:390), who, in an analysis of a labor strike in Bahia, Brazil, laments the lack of written testimonies or oral records from any of the African participants:

> Unfortunately, we lack the testimony of the *ganhadores* themselves. The *ganhadores* simply communicated their feelings throughout the city by word of mouth. . . . Thus, there was not police investigation, with arrests and interrogations, which would furnish the type of documents that might provide insight (however distorted) into the movement's internal workings. We must content ourselves with reading between the lines. (p. 390)

There are exceptions to this, of course. For example, researchers concerned with relatively recent historical events may have the luxury of gathering data through oral interviews with surviving participants and eyewitnesses (e.g., see Fleischmann 2000; Johnson 1982; Monson 1998). But even this has its limitations, insofar as the respondents might either portray themselves and the cause they fought for in rather sanguine terms, downplay divisions and conflicts within their ranks, or refuse to say much at all. In her analysis of the Palestinian Women's Movement, for example, Fleishmann (2000:202) found that "informants were reluctant to discuss it even almost sixty years after the event."

In addition to confronting data that are silent with respect to the perspectives and motives of those making claims, historians also often bump against the stark reality of constructing narratives from thin or **absent** data. This is a particularly vexing problem for analysts of contentious episodes, in that it requires them to speculate about how the event actually unfolded and to impute motives to the individuals and groups making claims. This is problematic for two fundamental reasons. First, as suggested in the preceding text, fragmentary data tends to privilege the organizations responsible for their production; that is, states, churches, and other targets of claims often have a vested interest in documenting and/or interpreting collective action in a way that is neither sympathetic to nor reflective of claimants' interests, demands, or goals. Second, it forces historians to extrapolate to events from understandings which are beyond the range of verifiable knowledge. That is, historians must attribute motives to those making claims in the absence of empirical evidence. This is of particular importance, because, as we will discuss below, historians of social movements and collective action tend to ground their interpretations on an assessment of the potential grievances catalyzing action. In contrast to many sociologists, who assume that grievances are chronic and that mobilization is contingent on the presence of political opportunities, mobilizing structures, and/or collective action frames, historians, as noted in the preceding text, tend to portray an unencumbered relationship between grievances and action. In the absence of claimants establishing this link in their own voices, the validity such inferences are questionable. Bernal's (1981:159) assessment of social movement activity in Vietnam is representative of this practice: "Although there is no documentary evidence to suggest it, the form the movement launched in 1930 leads me to believe that the ICP leaders hoped to establish in Indo-China the rights to organize and demonstrate which had been achieved by the French Communist Party."

To be fair, many of the historians surveyed for this chapter are not only keenly aware, but also forthcoming when faced with the reality that their data are thin and that their narrative may be based more on speculation than actual hard evidence. For example, one analyst of communal riots in Bengal notes: "The sources used here are conventional: mainly government documents, police reports and newspaper accounts. The evidence is scrappy. Much of what I say is conjectural in nature" (Chakrabarty 1981:142). A similar claim is made by a historian studying the development of the labor movements in Costa Rica and Honduras: "There is a marked lack of surviving documentation on the black West Indian population that worked in Honduras and Costa Rica. . . . Regrettably, surviving historical material only provides the briefest outline concerning this particular strike" (Echeverri-Gent, 1992:284–289).

In their efforts to create "written" accounts of the past, historians analyze a wide range of materials that constitute the "recorded" past (cf. McDonald 1996). The tremendous volume of potential materials (e.g., written, audio, and visual) offers unique opportunities to historians studying social movements and collective action. Given a surfeit of evidence, one can approach a particular episode of contention from numerous viewpoints and thereby produce a rich and nuanced interpretation of its origins, the process through which it occurred, and its outcomes. But the nature of historical evidence also places restrictions on researchers. The data which are available may be limited (recording only one, self-serving view of the "actual" past), silent (failing to capture the perspective of claimants), and/or absent (missing with regard to the event in question). Navigating the opportunities and restrictions afforded by historical evidence is, in short, a fundamental element of the entire historical endeavor.

CONCLUSION: CONTRIBUTIONS, SILENCES, AND DISCIPLINARY BOUNDARIES

Individuals with an abiding interest in social movements and collective action owe a tremendous debt to historians. Academic and amateur historians have, over the course of several decades, produced a vast body of rich and nuanced research detailing the origins, dynamics, and outcomes of what has recently been referred to as "contentious politics" (McAdam,

Tarrow, and Tilly 2001). Our sample of 60 journal articles, which is merely the tip of the scholarly iceberg, suggests that the intellectual curiosity of historians has been boundless, insofar as it has led not only to an examination of large-scale social movements operating in the context of modern nation-states, but also to the investigation and documentation of small, isolated contentious events occurring in numerous locations around the globe during different time periods. But while these articles illustrate the many ways in which historical work contributes to our understanding of social change, they also reveal the areas in which historians remain silent. By highlighting both the contributions and silences of historical research on social movements and collective action, this conclusion lends support to those who argue for greater collaboration among historians and social scientists. History and the social sciences, in our opinion, stand to benefit from the recurring efforts of researchers to cross disciplinary boundaries.

What have we learned about the discipline of history? On the one hand, our findings support William Roy's (1987:55) assessment of how disciplinary specialization shapes historical research:

> Historians, by defining themselves in terms of time and place and orienting their work toward others who share their interest in a particular time and place, thereby tend to narrow their endeavor to gathering new evidence on old questions or making new interpretations of old issues or recutting the historical pie into new time/place slices. The social boundaries among different time/place specialties deter comparisons between different times and places. Working within a particular time and place, one holds constant large-scale structural processes, restricting the agenda to changes within a region and era.

Although our data preclude us from generalizing to the entire discipline of history, they show rather convincingly that historical studies of social movements and collective action reflect both Roy's (1987) observation that historians tend to offer limited context-dependent generalizations and Erikson's (1970) contention that the practice of history is shaped by "professional reflexes." The articles sampled for this chapter rarely make claims that could be readily applied to other times and locations nor do their authors attempt to do so. Rather, the various narratives that we have characterized as interpretive, expansive, and/or corrective tend to offer context-specific analyses of contentious episodes. With few exceptions, studies analyzing labor movements, peasant insurrections, or religious riots in one context neither reference nor seek to compare themselves to those found in other spatial or temporal locations.

We also find that, in line with an evidentiary distinction that is often made between history and social science, historians rely heavily on documentary evidence found in archives. As amply captured by exhaustive footnotes, historical studies analyze a wide range of written and visual materials that have been produced, collected, organized, and disseminated by others. This observation is neither unexpected nor particularly noteworthy. Of greater interest, however, is the finding that historians dealing with events that occurred relatively recently have availed themselves of the opportunity to produce their own data. Employing a methodology usually associated with social scientists, historians have begun to conduct oral interviews with the surviving participants of the events under investigation (see, e.g., Cooper 1996; Fleishman 2000; Monson 1998). This approach yields unique data that have not been mediated or picked over by countless others, thereby bolstering an historian's claim to making a new contribution to the literature.

On the other hand, we find that the articles included in our sample defy the expectation that historians employ broad temporal scopes when producing their narratives. Rather than focus on long-term processes of change, the majority of the studies analyzed for this chapter explored the short-term origins and outcomes of particular events. Why might this be the case? We suggested above that this finding may, to a certain extent, be a product of our sampling strategy: journal articles do not readily lend themselves to detailed analyses of the *longue durée*; broad temporal scopes are more likely to be a feature of books that run several hundred pages. As a consequence, long-term change processes such as colonization, industrialization or urbanization tend to emerge as background variables rather than as explanatory variables. But a comparison of the articles sampled for this chapter and the books produced by the same authors suggests that most of these historians of social protest have not taken the opportunity to extend the temporal scopes of their analyses in books and that not all of those who have written books have used them to expand the temporal scope of their analyses. Of the 60 contentious events that were the focus of the articles, only 21 were developed further in books. Of those 21 books, 14 sought to situate the events under investigation in long-term change processes; the remaining 7 used the additional space afforded by a book-length manuscript to provide a more comprehensive narrative account of the event without extending its temporal scope. In sum, less than one-quarter of the articles examined for this chapter were subsequently developed into books in which long-term change processes featured prominently as explanatory variables. Thus, we do not feel that our sampling strategy compromises our finding that historians tend to employ relatively narrow temporal scopes when analyzing social movements and collective action.

The tendency of historians to explicate short-term processes may also derive from the practice, at least in journal articles, of providing detailed analyses of particular, temporally delimited events—that is, "those occurrences that come to be imbued with at least some degree of public visibility and significance" (McAdam and Sewell 2001:123) instead of comprehensive accounts of broader movements. Events are often of significant complexity and concentrated activity to warrant such a detailed interpretation of their immediate causes and consequences.

In addition to confirming some of the basic assumptions about the discipline of history, our analysis also lends support to those scholars who question predictions of a merger of history with other social sciences, such as sociology, into a common enterprise. We find, for example, that historical research on social movements and collective action lacks attention to the key concepts that have generated research and theory construction in other disciplines. Historians of social movements tend not to interrogate the theoretical grounding of these concepts, but rather employ them in a somewhat uncritical sense. Should historians of social protest make greater efforts to address the issues debated by scholars in the disciplines of sociology and political science? Should social scientists do more to ground their generalizations in specific historical contexts? We believe that there are a number of reasons why both efforts should be encouraged.

Social science stands to benefit from a deeper understanding of the specific context in which social movements unfold or collective actions occur. Because the bulk of the theories and concepts informing social movement research are based on studies of the present, or the relatively recent past, deeper historical knowledge would enable social scientists to better understand the scope conditions of various theories, thereby fostering more context-dependent theory. Social scientists, most notably Charles Tilly, have argued that the study of social movements requires expert historical knowledge and the grounding of generalizations in historical contexts. "By and large," he writes (2003:9–10), "students of contemporary social movements fail to recognize that they are analyzing an evolving set of historically derived political practices. Either they assume that social movements have always existed in some form or they treat social movements as contemporary political forms without inquiring into their historical transformations." Consider, for example, the distinction made in the both the historical and social science literatures between "pre-modern" or "reactive" movements and those deemed to be "modern" or "proactive" (cf. Hobsbawm 1956; Tilly 1978). Whereas the former are characterized as being spontaneous, irrational, and nonideological responses to immediate and tangible grievances, such as "food riots" or "machine-breaking sprees" (Tilly 1986), the latter are viewed as organized and ideologically driven actions, such as "strikes," that are geared towards attaining long-term goals. "Reactive" collective actions are thought to occur in rural areas or in territories without strong, centralized states; "proactive" movements, in contrast, tend to occur in modern, industrialized societies and be the purview of urban factory workers.

While this distinction between the "pre-modern" and "modern" may be both intuitive and useful at a very general level, historically grounded research, which affords a close attention to detail, reveals that many examples of collective action, particularly those occurring in non-Western contexts, exhibit both "reactive" and "proactive" elements (cf. Meade 1989; Reis 1997; Yokohama 1975). In their analysis of a series of riots directed toward the suburban railways in Brazil in the mid-1970s, Moises and Martinez-Alier (1980), for example, found that, contrary to theoretical expectations, these riots were spontaneous although they occurred in the country's leading industrial centers. Their conclusion, that "in a context where political rights have been reduced to a minimum, riots are after all one of the few possible forms of popular political expression" (1980:182), is robust and should serve to modify the scope conditions of subsequent research. Similarly, Carr's (1996) analysis of Cuban sugar workers illustrates the "pre-modern" activities of an ostensibly "modern" labor force:

> The Cuban mill occupations of summer 1933 clearly show the limitations of this approach. The radicalism of the sugar workers did not necessarily prefigure a post-capitalist order as the term soviet might imply. . . . In most cases workers did not challenge the longer-term legitimacy of private control over the enterprises in which they worked. (p. 130)

In sum, the close attention to detail that comes from grounding research in a particular temporal and spatial context, research that characterizes the work of historians, should serve to improve the explanatory power of social science theories. To that end, social scientists should heed Charles Tilly's (1989:142) suggestion that they ground their inquires in sources rather than theories in an effort to overcome their "unawareness of the historical limits to their observations."

The onus to cross disciplinary boundaries does not fall on social scientists alone, however. If "written" history should be an essential element of the social scientific study of social movements, then we must avoid what seems to be the current problematic division of labor in which historians labor in the trenches of the archives in order to provide a storehouse of data for social scientists but make relatively little effort to move beyond the historical particulars to theoretical generalization. Although we did not find much evidence to suggest that historians have begun to engage with theory, McDonald (1996), analyzing a much larger and broader sample of published work beyond the study of social protest than we have done for this chapter, claims that theory has become a common feature of history. He notes that, while it is common to characterize historians as reluctant borrowers of social science theory,

> this view is contradicted by analysis of the actual use of social science literature by the most popular and widespread of the 'new' histories – the 'new' urban and social history. . . . [Data] reveal that this encounter between history and the social sciences was broad-based, overwhelmingly theoretical, primarily sociological, mostly middle range, and, unsurprisingly, only minimally Marxist. (p. 99)

These findings complement a point that we made earlier, namely, that some areas of the discipline of history have engaged with theoretical debates in the social sciences and crossed disciplinary boundaries more than others. The extent to which historians engage with other disciplines varies greatly, as does the range of disciplines that have become part of a growing cross-disciplinary dialogue. However, there seems to be more dialogue and borrowing across the disciplinary boundary between history and anthropology (cf. Kertzer 1986) than between history and either sociology or political science, the two disciplines which have made the most important contributions to social movement theory and research.

One of the questions addressed in this paper concerns whether historians who study social movements, most of whom self-identify as social historians, have engaged in relevant theoretical debates and made conceptual and/or theoretical contributions. Our negative answer to this question suggests the need not only for more dialogue between historians and social movements scholars in other disciplines but also, and perhaps more importantly, the need for dialogue across the intradisciplinary boundaries separating social, political, economic, and cultural history. In the discipline of sociology, recent efforts to identify silences in research and expand the research agenda of social movement scholarship has involved crossing intradisciplinary boundaries that divide important areas of the discipline—for example, the sociology of emotions, sociology of religion, and life course sociology—from social movement research (Aminzade et al. 2001). A similar boundary crossing endeavor among historians might prove extremely fruitful, as cultural, economic, demographic, and political historians lend their voices and insights to the study of a phenomenon that has mainly attracted the attention of social historians.

A variety of common concerns also suggest the viability of more permeable disciplinary boundaries and more interdisciplinary dialogues. In addition to their common concern with assessing continuity and change, historians and social scientists also share a concern with the problematic of agency and structure. As Abrams states (1980:5), "both seek to understand the puzzle of human agency and both seek to do so in terms of processes of social structuring." To the extent that historians utilize narratives in a more analytically self-conscious manner, disciplinary rhetorics constitute an opportunity rather than an obstacle. Historian's careful attention to the particularities of specific times and places is a necessary prerequisite to developing the historically grounded context-dependent generalizations that sociologists and political scientists who study social movements are seeking.

Given that the problem is one of institutional mechanisms of professional socialization rather than the logic of knowledge, the obvious solution involves institutional change to foster collaborative interdisciplinary, or trans-disciplinary, research and transform graduate education in a manner that challenges established disciplinary divisions of labor and professional reflexes and rhetorics. Although a number of "hybrid disciplines" already exist and are even expanding (Monkkonen 1994), no hybrid discipline for the study of historical contentious politics exists. We are not so naïve as to suggest that there will be an institutionalization of such a hybrid discipline in the near future, but at the very least, greater disciplinary collaboration and borrowing of concepts, theories, and methods by historians of social movements might lead to a more critical approach to the established categories that have informed social movement research.

SUGGESTED READINGS

Cooper, Frederick. 1996. *Decolonization and African Society: The Labor Question in French and British Africa.* Cambridge: Cambridge University Press.

Cronin, James E. 1984. *Labour and Society in Britain, 1918–1979.* New York: Schocken Books.

Duberman, Martin. 1994. *Stonewall.* New York: Plume.

Evans, Sara M. 1980. *Personal Politics: The Roots of Women's Liberation in the Civil Rights Movement and the New Left*. New York: Vintage Books.

Goodwyn, Lawrence. 1978. *The Populist Movement: A Short History of Agrarian Revolt in America*. Oxford: Oxford University Press.

Hanagan, Leslie Moch, and Wayne te Brake, eds. 1998. *Challenging Authority. The Historical Study of Contentious Politics*. Minneapolis, MN: University of Minnesota Press.

Hobbsbawn, E. J. 1964. *Primitive Rebels*. Manchester: Manchester University Press.

Isaacman, Allen F. 1993. "Peasants and Rural Social Protest in Africa." Pp. 205–317 in *Confronting Historical Paradigms: Peasants, Labor, and the Capitalist World System in Africa and Latin America*, edited by Frederick Cooper, Allen F. Isaacman, Steve J. Stern, Florencia E. Mallon, and William Roseberry. Madison, WI: University of Wisconsin Press.

Koenker, Diane and William G. Rosenberg. 1989. *Strikes and Revolution in Russia, 1917*. Princeton, NJ: Princeton University Press.

Mallon, Florencia. 1983. *The Defense of Community in Peru's Central Highlands: Peasant Struggle and Capitalist Transition, 1860–1940*. Princeton, NJ: Princeton University Press.

Meier, August and Elliot Rudwick. 1973. *CORE: A Study in the Civil Rights Movement, 1942–1968*. New York: Oxford University Press.

Montgomery, David. 1987. *The Fall of the House of Labor: The Workplace, the State, and American Labor Activism, 1865–1925*. Cambridge, UK: Cambridge University Press.

Perrot, Michelle. 1987. *Workers on Strike: France, 1871–1890*. New Haven, CT: Yale University Press.

Perry, Elizabeth. 1993. *Shanghai on Strike: The Politics of Chinese Labor*. Stanford, CA: Stanford University Press.

Roseberg, C. G. and J. Nottingham. 1966. *The Myth of Mau Mau: Nationalism in Kenya*. Stanford, CA: Hoover Institution Press, Stanford University.

Rudé, George. 1964. *The Crowd in History*. New York: John Wiley & Sons.

Ryan, Mary P. 1992. *Women in Public: Between Banners and Ballots, 1825–1880*. Baltimore and London: Johns Hopkins University Press.

Sewell, William H. Jr. 1980. *Work and Revolution: The Language of Labor from the Old Regime to 1848*. New York: Cambridge University Press.

Stern, Steve J. 1993. *Peru's Indian Peoples and the Challenge of Spanish Conquest: Huamanga to 1640*. Madison, WI: University of Wisconsin Press.

Thompson, E. P. 1963. *The Making of the English Working Class*. New York: Pantheon Books.

REFERENCES

Abbott, Andrew. 1990. "Conceptions of Time and Events in Social Science Methods: Causal and Narrative Approaches." *Historical Methods* 23:140–150.

Abrams, Philip. 1980. "History, Sociology, Historical Sociology." *Past and Present* 87:3–16.

——. 1982. *Historical Sociology*. Ithaca, NY: Cornell University Press.

Adams, Julia, Elisabeth S. Clemens, and Ann Shola Orloff, eds. 2005. *Remaking Modernity*. Durham, NC: Duke University Press.

*Adelman, Jeremy. 1993. "State and Labour in Argentina: The Portworkers of Buenos Aires, 1910–21." *Journal of Latin American Studies* 25(1):73–102.

Aminzade, Ronald. 1992. "Historical Sociology and Time." *Sociological Methods & Research* 20(4):456–480.

Aminzade, Ron, Jack Goldstone, and Elizabeth Perry. 2001. "Leadership Dynamics and Dynamics of Contention." Pp. 126–154 in *Silence and Voice in the Study of Contentious Politics*, edited by Ronald R. Aminzade, Jack A. Goldstone, Doug McAdam, Elizabeth J. Perry, William H. Sewell, Jr., Sidney Tarrow, Charles Tilly. Cambridge, UK: Cambridge University Press.

*Andrien, Kenneth J. 1990. "Economic Crisis, Taxes and the Quito Insurrection of 1765." *Past and Present* 129:104–131.

*Awuah, Emmanuel. 1997. "Mobilizing for Change: A Case Study of Market Trader Activism in Ghana." *Canadian Journal of African Studies* 31(3):401–423.

Bartley, Numan V. 1969. *The Rise of Massive Resistance: Race and Politics in the South During the 1950s*. Baton Rouge: Louisiana State University Press.

*Basu, Subho. 1998. "Strikes and 'Communal' Riots in Calcutta in the 1890s: Industrial Workers, Bhadralok Nationalist Leadership and the Colonial State." *Modern Asian Studies* 32(4):949–983.

Benford, Robert. 1997. "An Insider's Critique of the Social Movement Framing Perspective." *Sociological Inquiry* 67:409–430.

*Berlanstein, Leonard R. 1992. "The Distinctiveness of the Nineteenth-Century French Labor Movement." The *Journal of Modern History* 64(4):660–685.

*Bernal, Martin. 1981. "The Nghe-Tinh Soviet Movement 1930–1931." *Past and Present* 92:148–168.

*Bevir, Mark. 1999. "The Labour Church Movement, 1891–1902." *The Journal of British Studies* 38(2):217–245.

Brauer, Carl M. 1977. *John F. Kennedy and the Second Reconstruction*. New York: Columbia University Press.

*Bric, Maurice J. 1983. "Priests, Parsons and Politics: The Rightboy Protest in County Cork 1785–1788." *Past and Present* 100:100–123.

Burk, Robert Fredrick. 1984. *The Eisenhower Administration and Black Civil Rights*. Knoxville, TN: University of Tennessee Press.

*Carr, Barry. 1996. "Mill Occupations and the Soviets: The Mobilisation of Sugar Workers in Cuba 1917–1933." *Journal of Latin American Studies* 28(1):129–158.

Carson, Clayborne. 1981. *In Struggle: SNCC and the Black Awakening of the 1960s*. Cambridge, MA: Harvard University Press.

*Chakrabarty, Dipesh. 1981. "Communal Riots and Labour: Bengal's Jute Mill-Hands in the 1890s." *Past and Present* 91:140–169.

*Chatterjee, Partha. 1986. "The Colonial State and Peasant Resistance in Bengal 1920–1947." *Past and Present* 110:169–204.

*Chen, Joseph T. 1970. "The May Fourth Movement Redefined." *Modern Asian Studies* 4(1):63–81.

Clemens, Elisabeth S. and Martin D. Hughes. 2002. "Recovering Past Protest: Historical Research on Social Movements." Pp. 201–230 in *Social Movement Research*, edited by Bert Klandermans and Suzanne Staggenborg. Minneapolis, MN: University of Minnesota Press.

Cone, James H. 1991. *Martin and Malcolm and America: A Dream or Nightmare*. Maryknoll, NY: Orbis Books.

*Cooper, Frederick. 1996. "'Our Strike': Equality, Anticolonial Politics and the 1947–48 Railway Strike in French West Africa." *The Journal of African History* 37(1):81–118.

*DuBois, Ellen Carol. 1987. "Working Women, Class Relations, and Suffrage Militance: Harriot Stanton Blatch and the New York Woman Suffrage Movement, 1984–1909. " *The Journal of American History* 74 (1):34–58.

*Echeverri-Gent, Elisavinda. 1992. "Forgotten Workers: British West Indians and the Early Days of the Banana Industry in Costa Rica." *Journal of Latin American Studies* 24(2):275–308.

*Edelman, Robert S. 1985. "Rural Proletarians and Peasant Disturbances: The Right Bank Ukraine in the Revolution of 1905." *The Journal of Modern History* 57(2):248–277.

*Ellner, Steve. 1999. "Obstacles to the Consolidation of the Venezuelan Neighbourhood Movement: National and Local Cleavages." *Journal of Latin American Studies* 31(1):75–97.

Erikson, Kai T. 1970. "Sociology and the Historical Perspective." *The American Sociologist* 5(4):331–338.

*Escobar, Edward J. 1993 "The Dialectics of Repression: The Los Angeles Police Department and the Chicano Movement, 1968–1971." *The Journal of American History* 79(4):1483–1514.

*Evans, Richard J. 1980. "German Social Democracy and Women's Suffrage 1891–1918." *Journal of Contemporary History* 15(3):533–557.

Evans, Sara M. and Harry C. Boyte. 1986. *Free Spaces: The Sources of Democratic Change in America*. New York: Harper and Row.

Fairclough, Adam. 1987. *To Redeem the Soul of America: The Southern Christian Leadership Conference and Martin Luther King, Jr*. Athens, GA: University of Georgia Press.

*Fleischmann, Ellen L. 2000. "The Emergence of the Palestinian Women's Movement, 1929–39." *Journal of Palestine Studies* 29(3):16–32.

*Forman, Shepard. 1971. "Disunity and Discontent: A Study of Peasant Political Movements in Brazil." *Journal of Latin American Studies* 3(1):3–24.

Freemon, Jo. 1973. "The Origins of the Women's Liberation Movement." *American Journal of Sociology* 78:792–811.

*Furedi, Frank. 1973. "The African Crowd in Nairobi: Popular Movements and Elite Politics." *The Journal of African History* 14(2):275–290.

Garrow, David J. 1986. *Bearing the Cross: Martin Luther King, Jr. and the Southern Christian Leadership Conference*. New York: Quill.

*Garvin, Tom. 1982. "Defenders, Ribbonmen and Others: Underground Political Networks in Pre-Famine Ireland." *Past and Present* 96:133–155.

*Goldberg, Robert A. 1983. "Racial Change on the Southern Periphery: The Case of San Antonio, Texas, 1960–65." *The Journal of Southern History* 43(3):349–374.

Goodwin, Jeff and James M. Jasper, eds. 2004. *Rethinking Social Movements: Structure, Meaning and Emotion*. Oxford: Rowman & Littlefield Publishers.

Grant, Joanne. 1998. *Ella Baker: Freedom Bound.* New York: John Wiley & Sons.

*Green, James R. 1973. "The Brotherhood of Timber Workers 1910–1913: A Radical Response to Industrial Capitalism in the Southern U.S.A." *Past and Present* 60:161–200.

Griffin, Larry J. 1993. "Narrative, Event-Structure Analysis, and Causal Interpretation in Historical Sociology." *American Journal of Sociology* 98(5):1094–1133.

Hamilton, Gary G. and John Walton. 1988. "History in Sociology." Pp. 181–199 in *The Future of Sociology,* edited by Edgar F. Borgatta and Karen Cook. Newbury Park, CA: Sage.

*Hanson, John H. 1994. "Islam, Migration and the Political Economy of Meaning: Fergo Nioro from the Senegal River Valley, 1862–1890." *The Journal of African History* 35(1):37–60.

Hart, Janet. 1992. "Cracking the Code: Narrative and Political Mobilization in the Greek Resistance." *Social Science History* 16(4):631–668.

Hexter, J. H. 1971. *Doing History.* Bloomington, IN: Indiana University Press.

Hobsbawm, E. J. 1969. *Bandits.* New York: Delacorte Press.

*Holton, Sandra Stanley. 1994. "'To Educate Women in Rebellion': Elizabeth Cady Stanton and the Creation of a Transatlantic Network of Radical Suffragists." *The American Historical Review* 99(4):1112–1136.

Isaacman, Allen F. 1993. "Peasants and Rural Social Protest in Africa." Pp. 205–317 in *Confronting Historical Paradigms: Peasants, Labor, and the Capitalist World System in Africa and Latin America,* edited by Frederick Cooper, Allen F. Isaacman, Steve J. Stern, Florencia E. Mallon, and William Roseberry. Madison, WI: University of Wisconsin Press.

Jenkins, Craig J. and Charles Perrow. 1977. "Insurgency of the Powerless: Farm Workers' Movements (1946–1972)." *American Sociological Review* 42:249–268.

*Johnson, Cheryl. 1982. "Grass Roots Organizing: Women in Anticolonial Activity in Southwestern Nigeria." *African Studies Review* 25(2/3):137–157.

Johnson, Christopher. 1975. "Economic Change and Artisan Discontent: The Tailors' History, 1800–1848." Pp. 87–114 In Revolution and Reaction: 1848 and the Second French Republic, edited by Roger Price. London: C. Helm.

Jonas, Gilbert and Julian Bond. 2004. *Freedom's Sword: The NAACP and the Struggle Against Racism in America, 1909–1969.* New York: Routledge.

Jones, Gareth Stedman. *Languages of Class: Studies in English Working Class History, 1832–1982.* Cambridge: Cambridge University Press.

*Kannangra, A. P. 1984. "The Riots of 1915 in Sri Lanka: A Study in the Roots of Communal Violence." *Past and Present* 102:130–165.

*Keep, John. 1977. "The Agrarian Revolution of 1917–1918 in Soviet Historiography." *Russian Review* 36(4):405–423.

Kertzer, David. 1986. "Anthropology and History." In "History and Anthropology: A Dialogue." *Historical Methods* 19:119–120.

Kiser, Edgar. 1996. "The Revival of Narrative in Historical Sociology: What Rational Choice Theory Can Contribute." *Politics and Society* 24(3): 249–271.

Klandermans, Bert. 1992. "The Social Construction of Protest and Multiorganizational Fields." Pp. 77–103 in *Frontiers in Social Movement Theory,* edited by Aldon D. Morris and Carol McClurg Mueller. New Haven, CT: Yale University Press.

Kluger, Richard. 1976. *Simple Justice: The History of Brown v. Board of Education and Black America's Struggle for Equality.* New York: Vintage Books.

*Korstad, Robert and Nelson Lichtenstein. 1988. "Opportunities Found and Lost: Labor, Radicals, and the Early Civil Rights Movement." *The Journal of American History* 75(3):786–811.

*Krikler, Jeremy. 1999. "The Commandos: The Army of White Labour in South Africa." *Past and Present* 63:202–244.

*Kulik, Gary. 1978. "Pawtucket Village and the Strike of 1824: The Origins of Class Conflict in Rhode Island." *Radical History Review* 17:5–37.

Levine, David. 2001. *At the Dawn of Modernity: Biology, Culture, and Material Life in Europe after the Year 1000.* Berkeley, CA: University of California Press.

*Marks, Robert B. "The World Can Change!: Guangdong Peasants in Revolution." *Modern China* 3(1):65–100.

*Mather, Charles. 1993. "The Anatomy of a Rural Strike: Power and Space in the Transvaal Lowveld." *Canadian Journal of African Studies* 27(3):424–438.

*Mayhall, Laura E. Nym. 2000. "Defining Militancy: Radical Protest, the Constitutional Idiom, and Women's Suffrage in Britain, 1908–1909." *The Journal of British Studies* 39(3):340–371.

McAdam, Doug. 1982. *Political Process and the Development of Black Insurgency, 1930–1970.* Chicago: University of Chicago Press.

McAdam, Doug, John D. McCarthy, and Mayer Zald, eds. 1996. *Comparative Politics on Social Movements: Political Opportunities, Mobilizing Structures, and Cultural Framings.* Cambridge, UK: Cambridge University Press.

McAdam, Doug and William H. Sewell, Jr. 2001. "It's About Time: Temporality in the Study of Social Movements and Revolutions." Pp. 51–88 in *Silence and Voice in the Study of Contentious Politics,* edited by Ronald R. Aminzade, Jack A. Goldstone, Doug McAdam, Elizabeth J. Perry, William H. Sewell, Jr., Sidney Tarrow, and Charles Tilly. Cambridge, UK: Cambridge University Press.

McCoy, Donald and Richard T. Reutten. 973. *Quest and Response: Minority Rights and the Truman Administration.* Lawrence, KS: University of Kansas Press.

McDonald, Terrence J., ed. 1996. *The Historic Turn in the Human Sciences.* Ann Arbor: University of Michigan Press.

McMillen, Neil R. 1971. *The Citizens' Council: Organized Resistance to the Second Reconstruction, 1954–64.* Urbana, IL: University of Illinois Press.

*Meade, Teresa. 1989. "'Living Worse and Costing More': Resistance and Riot in Rio de Janiero, 1890–1917." *Journal of Latin American Studies* 21(2):241–266.

*Minchin, Timothy J. 1999. "Black Activism, the 1964 Civil Rights Act, and the Racial Integration of the Southern Textile Industry." *The Journal of Southern History* 65(4):809–844.

*Moises, Jose Alvaro and Verena Martinez-Alier. 1980. "Urban Transport and Popular Violence: The Case of Brazil." *Past and Present* 86:174–192.

Monkkonen, Erik. 1994. *Engaging the Past. The Uses of History Across the Social Sciences.* Durham, NC: Duke University Press.

*Monson, Jamie. 1998. "Relocating Maji Maji: The Politics of Alliance and Authority in the Southern Highlands of Tanzania, 1870–1918." *The Journal of African History* 39(1):95–120.

Morris, Aldon. 1981. "Black Southern Sit-in Movement: An Analysis of Internal Organization." *American Sociological Review* 46:744–767.

———. 2004. "Reflections on Social Movement Theory: Criticisms and Proposals." Pp. 233–246 in *Rethinking Social Movements: Structure, Meaning and Emotion,* edited by Jeff Goodwin and James M. Jasper. Oxford: Rowman & Littlefield.

*Nasson, Bill. 1992. "'Messing with Coloured People': The 1918 Strike in Cape Town, South Africa." *The Journal of African History* 33(2):301–319.

*Neeson, J. M. 1984. "The Opponents of Enclosure in Eighteenth-Century Northamptonshire." *Past and Present* 105:114–139.

Oates, Stephen B. 1982. *Let the Trumpet Sound: The Life of Martin Luther King, Jr.* New York: Harper & Row.

Oliver, Pamela E. and Hank Johnston. 2000. "What a Good Idea! Ideologies and Frames in Social Movement Research." *Mobilization* 4:37–54.

*Osborne, Milton. 1978. "Peasant Politics in Cambodia: The 1916 Affair." *Modern Asian Studies* 12(2):217–243.

*Perrie, Maureen. 1972. "The Russian Peasant Movement of 1905–1907: Its Social Composition and Revolutionary Significance." *Past and Present* 57:123–155.

Pierson, Paul. 2003. "Big, Slow-Moving, and . . .Invisible." Pp. 177–207 in *Comparative Historical Analysis in the Social Sciences,* edited by James Mahoney and Dietrich Rueschemeyer. Cambridge, UK: Cambridge University Press.

*Reis, Joao Jose. 1997. " 'The Revolution of the Ganhadores': Urban Labour, Ethnicity and the African Strike of 1857 in Bahia, Brazil." *Journal of Latin American Studies* 29(2):355–393.

*Rogers, Nicholas. 1978. "Popular Protest in Early Hanoverian London." *Past and Present* 79:70–100.

Roy, William G. 1987. "Time, Place, and People in History and Sociology: Boundary Definitions and the Logic of Inquiry." *Social Science History* 11(1):53–62.

Rude, George. 1964. *The Crowd in History.* New York: John Wiley & Sons.

Ruggles, Steven. 1987. *Prolonged Connections: The Rise of the Extended Family in Nineteenth-Century England and America.* Madison, WI: University of Wisconsin Press.

*Sandage, Scott A. 1993. "A Marble House Divided: The Lincoln Memorial, the Civil Rights Movement, and the Politics of Memory, 19391963." *The Journal of American History* 80(1):135–167.

Schurman, Rachel and William Munro. 2006. "Ideas, Thinkers, and Social Networks: The Process of Grievance Construction in the Anti-Genetic Engineering Movement." *Theory and Society* 35(1):1–38.

Sewell, William H. Jr. 1996. "Three Temporalities: Toward an Eventful Sociology." Pp. 245–280 in *The Historic Turn in the Human Sciences,* edited by Terrence J. McDonald. Ann Arbor, MI: University of Michigan Press.

*Smith, J. Harvey. 1978. "Agricultural Workers and the French Wine-Growers Revolt of 1907." *Past and Present* 79:101–125.

Snow, David A. and Robert D. Benford. 1992. "Master Frames and Cycles of Protest." Pp. 133–155 in *Frontiers in Social Movement Theory*, edited by Aldon D. Morris and Carol McClurg Mueller. New Haven, CT: Yale University Press.

Snow, David A., E. Burke Rochford, Steven K. Worden, and Robert D. Benford. 1986. "Frame Alignment Processes, Micromobilization and Movement Participation." *American Sociological Review* 51:464–481.

*Stevenson, Louise L. 1979. "Women Anti-Suffragists in the 1915 Massachusetts Campaign." *The New England Quarterly* 52(1):80–93.

*Strom, Sharon Hartman. 1975. "Leadership and Tactics in the American Woman Suffrage Movement: A New Perspective from Massachusetts." *The Journal of American History* 62(2):296–315.

Stryker, Robin. 1996. "Beyond History Versus Theory." *Sociological Methods & Research* 24(3):304–352.

*Suguru, Yokoyama. 1975. "The Peasant Movement in Hunan." *Modern China* 1(2):204–238.

*Tareke, Gebru. 1984. "Peasant Resistance in Ethiopia: The Case of *Weyane*." *The Journal of African History* 25(1):77–92.

Tarrow, Sidney. 1994. *Power in Movement: Social Movements, Collective Action and Politics*. Cambridge, UK: Cambridge University Press.

*Taylor, Quintard. 1995. "The Civil Rights Movement in the American West: Black Protest in Seattle, 1960–1970." *The Journal of Negro History* 80(1):1–14.

Thompson, E. P. 1963. *The Making of the English Working Class*. New York: Pantheon Books.

——. 1976. "On History, Sociology and Historical Relevance." *British Journal of Sociology* 27(3):287–402.

Thompson Klein, Julie. 1993. "Blurring, Cracking, and Crossing: Permeation and the Fracturing of Discipline." Pp. 185–211 in *Knowledge: Historical and Critical Studies in Disciplinarity*, edited by Ellen Messer-Davidow, David R. Shumway, and David J. Sylvan. Charlottesville, VA: University of Virginia Press.

Tilly, Charles. 1970. "Clio and Minerva" in *Theoretical Sociology*, edited by John C. McKinney and Edward Tiryakian. New York: Appleton-Century-Crofts.

——. 1984. *Big Structures, Large Processes, Huge Comparison*. New York: Russell Sage Foundation.

——. 1988. "How (and What) Are Historians Doing?" *American Behavioral Scientist* 33(6):685–711.

——. 1989. "History, Sociology and Dutch Collective Action." *Tijdschrift voor sociale geschiedenis* 2:142–153.

——. 1995. "To Explain Political Processes." *American Journal of Sociology* 100(6):1594–1610.

——. 2006. "How and Why History Matters" Pp. 417–437 in *Oxford Handbook of Contextual Political Analysis*, edited by Robert E. Goodin and Charles Tilly. Oxford: Oxford University Press.

Trotsky, Leon. 1959 (1932). *The History of the Russian Revolution*. Edited by F. W. Dupre. New York: Doubleday.

*Tsurumi, Kazuko. 1970. "Some Comments on the Japanese Student Movement in the Sixties." *Journal of Contemporary History* 5(1):104–112.

*Turton, E. R. 1972. "Somali Resistance to Colonial Rule and the Development of Somali Political Activity in Kenya, 1893–1960." *The Journal of African History* 13(1):119–143.

*Vincent, Louise. 1999. "A Cake of Soap: The Volksmoeder Ideology and Afrikaner Women's Campaign for the Vote." *The International Journal of African Historical Studies* 32(1):1–17.

*Welch, Cliff. 1995. "Rivalry and Unification: Mobilising Rural Workers in Sao Paulo on the Eve of the Brazilian Golpe of 1964." *Journal of Latin American Studies* 27(1):161–187.

*Whittaker, Cynthia H. 1976. "The Women's Movement during the Reign of Alexander II: A Case Study in Russian Liberalism." *The Journal of Modern History* 48(2):35–69.

Wilkinson, J. Harvie. 1979. *From Brown to Bakke: The Supreme Court and School Integration: 1954–1978*. New York: Oxford University Press.

Zald, Meyer. 1992. "Looking Backward to Look Forward: Reflections on the Past and Future of the Resource Mobilization Research Program." Pp. 326–348 in *Frontiers in Social Movement Theory*, edited by Aldon D. Morris and Carol McClurg Mueller. New Haven, CT: Yale University Press.

*Zieger, Robert H. 1976. "The Limits of Militancy: Organizing Paper Workers, 1933–1935." *The Journal of American History* 63(3):638–657.

Zinn, Howard. 1964. *SNCC: The New Abolitionists*. Boston: Beacon Press.

---

*Articles sampled for this chapter.

Index